A+® Certification Study Guide, Fifth Edition

McGraw-Hill/Osborne is an independent entity from CompTIA. This publication and CD-ROM may be used in assisting students to prepare for the A+ exam. Neither CompTIA nor McGraw-Hill/Osborne warrants that use of this publication and CD-ROM will ensure passing any exam.

CompTIA is a registered trademark of CompTIA in the United States and/or other countries. The logo of the CompTIA Authorized Quality Curriculum Program and the status of this or other training material as "Authorized" under the CompTIA Authorized Curriculum Program signifies that, in CompTIA's opinion, such training material covers the content of the CompTIA's related certification exam. CompTIA has not reviewed or approved the accuracy of the contents of this training material and specifically disclaims any warranties of merchantability or fitness for a particular purpose. CompTIA makes no guarantee concerning the success of persons using any such "Authorized" or other training material in order to prepare for any CompTIA certification exam.

Michael Pastore

McGraw-Hill/Osborne

New York Chicago San Francisco Lisbon London Madrid
Mexico City Milan New Delhi San Juan Seoul Singapore Sydney Toronto

The McGraw·Hill Companies

McGraw-Hill/Osborne
2100 Powell Street, 10th Floor
Emeryville, California 94608
U.S.A.

To arrange bulk purchase discounts for sales promotions, premiums, or fund-raisers, please contact **McGraw-Hill/**Osborne at the above address. For information on translations or book distributors outside the U.S.A., please see the International Contact Information page immediately following the index of this book.

A+® Certification Study Guide, Fifth Edition

67890 CUS CUS 0198765

Book p/n 0-07-222767-2 and CD p/n 0-07-222768-0
parts of ISBN 0-07-222776-4

Publisher
Brandon A. Nordin

**Vice President &
Associate Publisher**
Scott Rogers

Editorial Director
Gareth Hancock

Associate Acquisitions Editor
Timothy Green

Project Editors
Jenn Tust, Lisa Wolters-Broder

Acquisitions Coordinator
Jessica Wilson

Technical Editors
Jane Holcombe, Jarret Buse

Copy Editors
Sally Engelfried, Marcia Baker,
Betsy Manini

Proofreader
Robin Small

Indexer
Irv Hershman

Composition
George T. Charbak, Peter Hancik

Illustrators
Kathleen Edwards,
Michael Mueller,
Melinda Lytle, Lyssa Wald

Series Design
Roberta Steele

Cover Series Design
Peter Grame

This book was composed with Corel VENTURA™ Publisher.

ABOUT THE AUTHOR

Michael Pastore, MA (A+, Net, Security+, MCP) is a 30-year veteran of the IT field. During his career he has been involved in support, programming, and administration of medium- and large-scale networks. Michael has been involved in CompTia certification since 1996 and has published several titles on Microsoft and CompTIA certifications. He has worked in several certification committees and projects in the industry. Michael teaches business and technology related courses at the University of Phoenix and DeVry University. Michael is currently pursuing his Ph.D. in psychology.

About the Technical Editors

Jane Holcombe (A+, Network+, MCSE, MCT, CTT+, and CNA) is a pioneer in the field of PC support training. In 1983, she installed a LAN for her employer, a financial planning company. Since 1984, she has been an independent trainer, consultant, and course content author, creating and presenting courses on PC operating systems. Through the late 1980s and early 1990s, these courses were taught nationwide. She also co-authored a set of networking courses for the consulting staff of a large network vendor. In the early 1990s, she worked with both Novell and Microsoft server operating systems, finally focusing on the Microsoft operating system and achieving her MCSE certification for Windows NT 3.*x*, Windows NT 4.0, and Windows 2000.

Jarret W. Buse (Network+, A+, MCSE+I, CCNA, CNA) is a technical trainer and consultant specializing in Microsoft products. Jarret has worked in the computer industry for almost 10 years and is currently pursuing his Microsoft Certified Solution Developer certification (MCSD) and writing full time. Jarret has trained students to prepare for Microsoft certification exams as well as hardware certifications and has a degree in Computer Programming from Vincennes University. A list of Jarret's work can be found at **www.psci.net/jarretbuse**.

About LearnKey

LearnKey provides self-paced learning content and multimedia delivery solutions to enhance personal skills and business productivity. LearnKey claims the largest library of rich streaming-media training content that engages learners in dynamic media-rich instruction complete with video clips, audio, full motion graphics, and animated illustrations. LearnKey can be found on the Web at **www.LearnKey.com**.

ACKNOWLEDGMENTS

I would like to thank all the incredibly hard-working folks at **McGraw-Hill**/Osborne: Brandon Nordin, Scott Rogers, Timothy Green, Gareth Hancock, Jenn Tust, and Jessica Wilson. I especially wish to express my gratitude to my wife Sheryl for her support and patience through the writing of this book.

CONTENTS AT A GLANCE

v

CONTENTS

This book's primary objective is to help you prepare for and pass the required A+ exam so you can begin to reap the career benefits of certification. We believe that the only way to do this is to help you increase your knowledge and build your skills. After completing this book, you should feel confident that you have thoroughly reviewed all of the objectives that CompTIA has established for the exam.

In This Book

This book is organized around the actual structure of the Microsoft exam administered at Sylvan Testing Centers. Most of the MCSE exams have six parts to them: Planning, Installation and Configuration, Managing Resources, Connectivity, Monitoring and Optimization, and Troubleshooting. Microsoft has let us know all the topics we need to cover for the exam. We've followed their list carefully, so you can be assured you're not missing anything.

In Every Chapter

We've created a set of chapter components that call your attention to important items, reinforce important points, and provide helpful exam-taking hints. Take a look at what you'll find in every chapter:

- Every chapter begins with the **Certification Objectives**—what you need to know in order to pass the section on the exam dealing with the chapter topic. The Certification Objective headings identify the objectives within the chapter, so you'll always know an objective when you see it!

- **Exam Watch** notes call attention to information about, and potential pitfalls in, the exam. These helpful hints are written by MCSEs who have taken the exams and received their certification—who better to tell you what to worry about? They know what you're about to go through!

- **Certification Exercises** are interspersed throughout the chapters. These are step-by-step exercises that mirror vendor-recommended labs. They help you master skills that are likely to be an area of focus on the exam. Don't just read through the exercises; they are hands-on practice that you should be comfortable completing. Learning by doing is an effective way to increase your competency with a product.

- **On the Job** notes describe the issues that come up most often in real-world settings. They provide a valuable perspective on certification- and product-related topics. They point out common mistakes and address questions that have arisen from on-the-job discussions and experience.

- **Scenario & Solution** sections lay out problems and solutions in a quick-read format.

- The **Certification Summary** is a succinct review of the chapter and a re-statement of salient points regarding the exam.

- The **Two-Minute Drill** at the end of every chapter is a checklist of the main points of the chapter. It can be used for last-minute review.

- The **Self Test** offers questions similar to those found on the certification exams, including multiple choice, true/false questions, and fill-in-the-blank. The answers to these questions, as well as explanations of the answers, can be found in Appendix A. By taking the Self Test after completing each chapter, you'll reinforce what you've learned from that chapter, while becoming familiar with the structure of the exam questions.

- The **Lab Question** at the end of the Self-Test section offers a unique and challenging question format that requires the reader to understand multiple chapter concepts to answer correctly. These questions are more complex and more comprehensive than the other questions, as they test your ability to take all the knowledge you have gained from reading the chapter and apply it to complicated, real-world situations. These questions are aimed to be more difficult than what you will find on the exam. If you can answer these questions, you have proven that you know the subject!

Some Pointers

Once you've finished reading this book, set aside some time to do a thorough review. You might want to return to the book several times and make use of all the methods it offers for reviewing the material:

1. *Re-read all the Two-Minute Drills*, or have someone quiz you. You also can use the drills as a way to do a quick cram before the exam.

2. *Review all the Scenario and Solutions* for quick problem solving.

3. *Retake the Self Tests.* Taking the tests right after you've read the chapter is a good idea, because it helps reinforce what you've just learned. However, it's an even better idea to go back later and do all the questions in the book in one sitting. Pretend you're taking the exam.

You should mark your answers to questions on a separate piece of paper when you go through this book for the first time so that you may go back and retake the Self Tests as you review for the exam.

4. *Complete the exercises*. Did you do the exercises when you read through each chapter? If not, do them! These exercises are designed to cover exam topics, and there's no better way to get to know this material than by practicing.

5. *Check out the website*. Global Knowledge invites you to become an active member of the Access Global website. This site is an online mall and an information repository that you'll find invaluable. You can access many types of products to assist you in your preparation for the exams, and you'll be able to participate in forums, online discussions, and threaded discussions. No other book brings you unlimited access to such a resource. Visit this site at **http://access.globalknowledge.com**.

A+ Certification

This book is designed to help you pass the A+ Certification exam. At the time this book was written, the exam objectives for the exam were posted on the CompTIA website, **www.comptia.org**. We wrote this book to give you a complete and incisive review of all the important topics that are targeted for the exam. The information contained here will provide you with the required foundation of knowledge that will not only allow you to succeed in passing the A+ certification exam, but will also make you a better A+ Certified Technician.

How to Take an A+ Certification Exam

This chapter discusses the importance of your A+ certification and prepares you for taking the actual examinations. It gives you a few pointers on methods of preparing for the exam, including how to study and register, what to expect, and what to do on exam day.

Importance of A+ Certification

The Computing Technology Industry Association (CompTIA) created the A+ certification to provide technicians with an industry-recognized and valued credential. Due to its acceptance as an industry-wide credential, it offers technicians an edge in a highly competitive computer job market. Additionally, it lets others know your achievement level and that you have the ability to do the job right. Prospective employers may use the A+ certification as a condition of employment or as a means of a bonus or job promotion.

Earning A+ certification means that you have the knowledge and the technical skills necessary to be a successful computer service technician. Computer experts in the industry establish the standards of certification. Although the test covers a broad range of computer software and hardware, it is not vendor specific. In fact, more than 45 organizations contributed and budgeted the resources to develop the A+ examinations.

To become A+ certified you must pass two examinations—the Core Hardware exam and an OS Technologies exam. The Core exam measures essential competencies for a break/fix microcomputer hardware service technician with six months of experience. The exam covers basic knowledge of desktop and portable systems, basic networking concepts, and printers. Also included on the exam are questions about safety and common preventive maintenance procedures.

The newest revision of the A+ certification (Fall 2003) includes the OS Technologies exam, which covers basic knowledge of Windows 9x, Windows NT 4, Windows 2000, and Windows XP Operating Systems for installing, upgrading, troubleshooting, and repairing microcomputer systems.

Computerized Testing

As with Microsoft, Novell, Lotus, and various other companies, the most practical way to administer tests on a global level is through Prometric or VUE testing centers, who provide proctored testing services for Microsoft, Oracle, Novell, Lotus, and the A+ computer technician certification. In addition to administering the tests, Prometric and VUE also score the exam and provide statistical feedback on each section of the exam to the companies and organizations that use their services.

Typically, several hundred questions are developed for a new exam. The questions are reviewed for technical accuracy by subject matter experts and are then presented in the form of a beta test. The beta test consists of many more questions than the actual test and helps provide statistical feedback to CompTIA to check the performance of each question.

Based on the beta examination, questions are discarded according to how good or bad the examinees performed on them. If a question is answered correctly by most of the test-takers, it is discarded as too easy. Likewise, questions that are too difficult are also discarded. After analyzing the data from the beta test, CompTIA has a good idea of which questions to include in the question pool to be used on the actual exam.

Test Structure

CompTIA announced that the new test will be a standard, single choice/multiple choice exam. They have indicated that the test may go adaptive at a later date but that there were no immediate plans to do that. You should visit the CompTIA web site to check on the status of the exam before you take it. The CompTIA website is **www.comptia.org**.

The exam questions for the A+ exams are all equally weighted. This means that they all count the same when the test is scored.

exam
ⓦatch
An interesting and useful characteristic of the standard test is that questions may be marked and returned to later. This helps you manage your time while taking the test so that you don't spend too much time on any one question.

Remember, unanswered questions are counted against you. Assuming you have time left when you finish the questions, you can return to the marked questions for further evaluation.

Previous versions of the A+ exams have been adaptive. Adaptive tests weights all of the questions based on their level of difficulty. For example, the questions might be divided into levels one through five, with level one questions being the easiest and level five being the hardest. Every time you answer a question correctly you are asked a question of a higher level of difficulty, and vice versa when you answer incorrectly. After answering about 15–20 questions in this manner, the scoring algorithm determines whether or not you would pass or fail the exam if all the questions were answered. The scoring method is pass or fail.

The form test also marks the questions that are incomplete with a letter "I" once you've finished all the questions. You'll see the whole list of questions after you finish the last question. The screen allows you to go back and finish incomplete items, finish unmarked items, and go to particular question numbers that you may want to look at again.

Question Types

The A+ exams are comprised entirely of one-answer multiple choice questions, but the computerized test questions you will see on the examination can be presented in a number of ways, as discussed here. This information is provided primarily for reference purposes and CompTIA states that the current exam is multiple-choice based.

True/False

You are all familiar with True/False type questions, but due to the inherent 50 percent chance of guessing the right answer, you will not see any of these on the A+ exam. Sample questions on CompTIA's website and on the beta exam did not include any True/False type questions.

Multiple Choice

A+ exam questions are of the multiple-choice variety. Below each question is a list of 4 or 5 possible answers. Use the available radio buttons to select one item from the given choices.

Graphical Questions

There are two types of graphical questions. The first type incorporates a graphical element to the question in the form of an exhibit to provide a visual representation of the problem or present the question itself. These questions are easy to identify because they refer to the exhibit in the question and there is also an Exhibit button on the bottom of the question window. An example of a graphical question might be to identify a component on a drawing of a motherboard.

The second type of graphical question is known as a hotspot, and it actually incorporates graphics as part of the answer. These types of questions ask the examinee to click a location or graphical element to answer the question. Instead of selecting A, B, C, or D as your answer, you simply click the portion of the motherboard drawing where the component exists.

Free Response Questions

Another type of question that can be presented on the form test requires a *free response*, or type-in, answer. This is a fill-in-the-blank type question where a list of possible choices is not given. You will not see this type of question on the A+ exam.

Study Strategies

There are appropriate ways to study for the different types of questions you will see on an A+ certification exam. The amount of study time needed to pass the exam will vary with the candidate's level of experience as a computer technician. Someone with several years experience might only need a quick review of materials and terms when preparing for the exam.

For others, several hours may be needed to identify weaknesses in knowledge and skill level and working on those areas to bring them up to par. If you know that you are weak in an area, work on it until you feel comfortable talking about it. You don't want to be surprised with a question knowing it was your weak area.

Knowledge-Based Questions

Knowledge-based questions require that you memorize facts. The questions may not cover knowledge material that you use on a daily basis, but they do cover material that CompTIA thinks a computer technician should be able to answer. Here are some keys to memorizing facts:

- **Repetition** The more times you expose your brain to a fact, the more it sinks in and increases your ability to remember it.
- **Association** Connecting facts within a logical framework makes them easier to remember.
- **Motor Association** It is easier to remember something if you write it down or perform another physical act, like clicking the practice test answer.

Performance-Based Questions

Although the majority of the questions on the A+ exam are knowledge-based, some questions are performance-based scenario questions. In other words, they actually measure the candidate's ability to apply one's knowledge in a given scenario.

The first step in preparing for these scenario-type questions is to absorb as many facts relating to the exam content areas as you can. Of course, actual hands-on experience will greatly help you in this area. For example, knowing how to install a video adapter is greatly enhanced by having actually done the procedure at least once. Some of the questions will place you in a scenario and ask for the best solution to the problem at hand. It is in these scenarios that having a good knowledge level and some experience will help you.

The second step is to familiarize yourself with the format of the questions you are likely to see on the exam. The questions in this study guide are a good step in that direction. The more you're familiar with the types of questions that can be asked, the better prepared you will be on the day of the test.

The Exam Makeup

To receive the A+ certification, you must pass both the Core and the OS Technologies exams. For up-to-date information about the number of questions on each exam and the passing scores, check the CompTIA site at **www.comptia.org**, or call the CompTIA Certification office nearest you.

The Core Hardware Exam

The Core Hardware exam is comprised of six domains (categories). CompTIA lists the percentages as follows:

Installation, configuration, upgrading	35%
Diagnosing and troubleshooting	21%
Preventive maintenance	5%

Motherboard, processors, memory	11%
Printers	9%
Basic networking	19%

The OS Technologies Exam

The OS Technologies exam is comprised of four domains (categories). CompTIA lists the percentages as follows:

OS fundamentals	28%
Installation, configuration, and upgrading	31%
Diagnosing and troubleshooting	25%
Networks	16%

Signing Up

After all your hard work preparing for the exam, signing up will be a very easy process. Prometric or Vue operators in each country can schedule tests at authorized test centers. You can register for an exam online at **www.2test.com** or **www.vue.com/comptia** or by calling the Prometric or Vue Test Center nearest you. There are a few things to keep in mind when you call:

1. If you call during a busy period, you might be in for a bit of a wait. Their busiest days tend to be Mondays, so avoid scheduling a test on Monday if at all possible.

2. Make sure that you have your social security number handy. The test center needs this number as a unique identifier for their records.

3. Payment can be made by credit card, which is usually the easiest payment method. If your employer is a member of CompTIA, you may be able to get a discount, or even obtain a voucher from your employer that will pay for the exam. Check with your employer before you dish out the money.

4. You may take one or both of the exams on the same day. However, if you take just one exam, you have only 90 calendar days to complete the second exam. If more than 90 days elapse between tests, you must retake the first exam.

Taking the Test

The best method of preparing for the exam is to create a study schedule and stick to it. Although teachers have probably told you time and time again not to cram for tests, there just may be some information that just doesn't quite stick in your memory. It's this type of information that you want to look at right before you take the exam so that it remains fresh in your mind. Most testing centers provide you with a writing utensil and some scratch paper that you can utilize after the exam starts. You can brush up on good study techniques from any quality study book from the library, but some things to keep in mind when preparing and taking the test are

1. Get a good night's sleep. Don't stay up all night cramming for this one. If you don't know the material by the time you go to sleep, your head won't be clear enough to remember it in the morning.

2. The test center needs two forms of identification, one of which must have your picture on it (for example, your driver's license). Social security cards and credit cards are also acceptable forms of identification.

3. Arrive at the test center a few minutes early. There's no reason to feel rushed right before taking an exam.

4. Don't spend too much time on one question. If you think you're spending too much time on it, just mark it and go back to it later if you have time.

5. If you don't know the answer to a question, think about it logically. Look at the answers and eliminate the ones that you know can't possibly be the answer. This may leave with you with only two possible answers. Give it your best guess if you have to, but most of the answers to the questions can be resolved by process of elimination. Remember, unanswered questions are counted wrong whether you knew the answer to them or not.

6. Books, calculators, laptop computers, or any other reference materials are not allowed inside the testing center. The tests are computer based and do not require pens, pencils, or paper, although as mentioned above, some test centers provide scratch paper to aid you while taking the exam.

After the Test

As soon as you complete the test, your results will show up in the form of a bar graph on the screen. As long as your score is greater than the required score, you pass! A hard copy of the report will be printed and embossed by the testing center to indicate that it's an official report. Don't lose this copy; it's the only hard copy of the report that is made. The results are sent electronically to CompTIA.

The printed report will also indicate how well you did in each section. You will be able to see the percentage of questions you got right in each section, but you will not be able to tell which questions you got wrong.

After you pass the Core and OS Technologies exams, an A+ certificate will be mailed to you within a few weeks. You'll also receive a lapel pin and a credit card-sized credential that shows your new status: A+ Certified Technician. You'll be authorized to use the A+ logo on your business cards, as long as you stay within the guidelines specified by CompTIA.

If you don't pass the exam, don't fret. Take a look at the areas where you didn't do so well and work on those areas for the next time you register.

Once you pass the exam and earn the title of A+ Certified Technician, your value and status in the IT industry increases. A+ certification carries along an important proof of skills and knowledge level that is valued by customers, employers, and professionals in the computer industry.

The contents of this training material were created for the CompTIA A+ exam covering CompTIA certification exam objectives that were current as of September 2003.

How to Become CompTIA Certified

This training material can help you prepare for and pass a related CompTIA certification exam or exams. In order to achieve CompTIA certification, you must register for and pass a CompTIA certification exam or exams.

In order to become CompTIA certified, you must:

1. Select a certification exam provider. For more information please visit **www.comptia.org/certification/test_locations.htm**.

2. Register for and schedule a time to take the CompTIA certification exam(s) at a convenient location.

3. Read and sign the Candidate Agreement, which will be presented at the time of the exam(s). The text of the Candidate Agreement can be found at **www.comptia.org/certification**.

4. Take and pass the CompTIA certification exam(s).

For more information about CompTIA's certifications, such as their industry acceptance, benefits, or program news, please visit **www.comptia.org/certification**. CompTIA is a non-profit information technology (IT) trade association. CompTIA's certifications are designed by subject matter experts from across the IT industry. Each CompTIA certification is vendor-neutral, covers multiple technologies, and requires demonstration of skills and knowledge widely sought after by the IT industry.

To contact CompTIA with any questions or comments, please call (630) 268 1818 or e-mail: **questions@comptia.org**.

This book requires two tables. One for the Core exam, one for the operating systems exam. This table below is for the Core hardware exam.

Core Hardware Exam

Exam Readiness Checklist

Official Objective	Study Guide Coverage	Ch #	Pg #	Beginner	Intermediate	Expert
Installation, Configuration, and Upgrading (1)						
Identify the names, purpose, and characteristics, of system modules (1.1)	Identifying, Adding, and Removing Systems Components	1	8			
Identify basic procedures for adding and removing field replaceable modules for desktop systems (1.2)	Identifying, Adding, and Removing Systems Components	1	26			
Identify basic procedures for adding and removing field replaceable modules for portable systems (1.3)	Identifying, Adding, and Removing Systems Components	1	34			
Identify typical IRQs, DMAs, and I/O addresses, and procedures for altering these settings (1.4)	Identifying, Adding, and Removing Systems Components	1	36			
Identify the names, purposes, and performance characteristics, of standards/common peripheral ports, cabling and their connectors (1.5)	Identifying, Adding, and Removing Systems Components	1	44			
Identify proper procedures for installing and configuring common IDE devices (1.6)	Installation, Configuration, and Systems Optimization	2	70			
Identify proper procedures for installing and configuring common SCSI devices (1.7)	Installation, Configuration, and Systems Optimization	2	74			
Identify proper procedures for installing and configuring common peripheral devices (1.8)	Installation, Configuration, and Systems Optimization	2	84			
Identify procedures to optimize PC operations in specific situations (1.9)	Installation, Configuration, and Systems Optimization	2	89			
Determine the issues that must be considered when upgrading a PC (1.10)	Installation, Configuration, and Systems Optimization	2	93			
Diagnosing and Troubleshooting (2)						
Recognize common problems associated with modules. Identify and isolate the problems (2.1)	Diagnosing and Troubleshooting Problems	3	118			
Identify basic troubleshooting procedures and tools. Elicit problem symptoms from customers (2.2)	Diagnosing and Troubleshooting Problems	3	140			
PC Preventative Maintenance, Safety, and Environmental Issues (3)						
Identify the various types of preventative maintenance products and procedures (3.1)	Power Protection and Safety Procedures	4	166			
Identify various safety measures and procedures (3.2)	Power Protection and Safety Procedures	4	170			

Exam Readiness Checklist

Official Objective	Study Guide Coverage	Ch #	Pg #	Beginner	Intermediate	Expert
Identify environmental protection measures and procedures (3.3)	Power Protection and Safety Procedures	4	174			
Motherboards/Processors/Memory (4)						
Distinguish between the popular CPU chips in terms of their basic characteristics (4.1)	Motherboards, Processors, and Memory	5	194			
Identify types of RAM, form factors, and operational characteristics (4.2)	Motherboards, Processors, and Memory	5	200			
Identify the most popular types of motherboards, their components, and their architecture (4.3)	Motherboards, Processors, and Memory	5	206			
Identify the purpose of CMOS memory. What it contains, and how to change its parameters (4.4)	Motherboards, Processors, and Memory	5	213			
Printers (5)						
Identify printer technologies, interfaces, and options/upgrades (5.1)	Printers	6	232			
Recognize common printer problems and techniques used to resolve them (5.2)	Printers	6	240			
Basic Networks (6)						
Identify the common types of network cables (6.1)	Basic Networking	7	264			
Identify basic networking concepts (6.2)	Basic Networking	7	283			
Identify common technologies available for establishing Internet connectivity (6.3)	Basic Networking	7				

Operating System Exam

Exam Readiness Checklist

Official Objective	Study Guide Coverage	Ch #	Pg #	Beginner	Intermediate	Expert
Operating Systems Fundamentals						
Identify the major desktop components and interfaces, and their functions (1.1)	Operating Systems Fundamentals	8	306			
Identify the names, locations, purposes, and contents of major system files (1.2)	Operating Systems Fundamentals	8	323			

Exam Readiness Checklist

Official Objective	Study Guide Coverage	Ch #	Pg #	Beginner	Intermediate	Expert
Demonstrate the ability to use command-line functions and utilities to manage the operating system (1.3)	Operating Systems Fundamentals	8	331			
Demonstrate the basic concepts and procedures for creating, viewing, and managing disks (1.4)	Operating Systems Fundamentals	8	338			
Identify the major operating systems utilities, their purpose, location and available switches (1.5)	Operating Systems Fundamentals	8	350			
Installation, Configuration and Upgrading						
Identify the procedures for installing the operating systems (2.1)	Installation, Configuration, and Upgrade	9	375			
Identify the steps to perform an operating systems upgrade (2.2)	Installation, Configuration, and Upgrade	9	396			
Identify the basic system boot sequences and boot methods, including emergency boot disks and utilities (2.3)	Installation, Configuration, and Upgrade	9	401			
Identify procedures for installing/adding a device, including loading, adding, and configuring device drivers (2.4)	Installation, Configuration, and Upgrade	9	415			
Identify procedures necessary to optimize the operating system (2.5)	Installation, Configuration, and Upgrade	9				
Diagnosing and Troubleshooting (3)						
Recognize and interpret the meaning of common error codes and startup messages from the boot sequence (3.1)	Diagnosing and Troubleshooting	10	446			
Recognize when to use common diagnostic tools and utilities (3.2)	Diagnosing and Troubleshooting	10	455			
Recognize common operational and usability problems (3.3)	Diagnosing and Troubleshooting	10	467			
Network (4)						
Identify the networking capabilities of Windows (4.1)	Networks	11	500			
Identify the basic Internet protocols and technologies (4.2)	Networks	11	516			

CORE HARDWARE/OPERATING SYSTEM EXAMS

Part 1

A+ Core Hardware

CORE HARDWARE/OPERATING SYSTEM EXAMS

1
Identifying, Adding, and Removing System Components

T his chapter introduces you to basic computer concepts, including how to identify and replace common components. Familiarity with the components, as well as a good working knowledge of their function, will allow you to work comfortably with most types of computers, in spite of different layouts or new component designs.

You will also be introduced to installation procedures for some common devices. The installations discussed in this chapter are limited to those components that require very little other than physical attachment to the computer to function properly. More complex installations are discussed in Chapter 2.

This chapter also discusses the system resources that allow components to operate within the computer without conflicting with one another. Finally, this chapter describes the physical cables and connections used by devices to communicate with one another, as well as various methods of communication.

on the job

Safety first: Before you begin, you must thoroughly understand two areas before opening the cover of a computer: electrostatic discharge (ESD) can kill your computer, and high voltage (inside the power supply and monitor) can kill you. Following are some basics you should know to avoid these situations.

Electrostatic discharge, or static electricity, can cause irreparable damage to the devices inside your computer. Although your body can withstand 25,000 volts, damage to computer components can occur with as few as 30 volts. Typical ESD discharges range from 600 to 25,000 volts.

To prevent damage to the system, you must equalize the electrical charge between your body and the components inside your computer. Touching a grounded portion of your computer's chassis will work to some extent, but for complete safety, use an antistatic wristband with a ground wire attached to the computer frame.

Leave servicing high-voltage peripherals such as monitors and power supplies to technicians trained in that area. Even when left unplugged for an extended period, enough voltage can be stored to cause severe injury, or even death. Do not use an antistatic wristband when working with high-voltage devices.

For complete power protection and safety procedures, I suggest you read Chapter 4 first; then read it again after you've read Chapters 1 through 3.

Introduction to Computer Systems

This section will provide you a brief overview of computer systems. If you have a good feeling for how the parts of a computer system work together, it is easier to identify, troubleshoot, and replace a component when a malfunction occurs. This coverage is not intended to be comprehensive, merely a place to start.

Computer System Concepts

The basic computer system that sits on your desktop is an extremely complicated piece of equipment. Literally thousands of different simultaneous operations are occurring in the process of doing even one seemingly simple piece of work. As a computer technician, you do not really need to be overly concerned about the actual inner workings of these components, but it will be helpful to understand what they do. The following sections will briefly outline how the CPU, memory, controllers, and programs work together to provide the end user a system that they can accomplish their work on.

on the
O o b

Throughout this book you will be asked to install and remove components on a PC system. Make sure that you always unplug any power cords and turn power supplies off before you do this.

CPU

In a PC, the central processing unit (CPU) is the primary control device for the entire computer system. The CPU is technically a set of components that manages all the activities and does much of the "heavy lifting" in a computer system. The CPU interfaces, or is connected, to all of the components such as memory, storage, and input/output (I/O) through communications channels called *busses*. The CPU performs a number of individual or discrete functions that must work in harmony in order for the system to function. Additionally, the CPU is responsible for managing the activities of the entire system. The CPU takes direction from internal commands that are stored in the CPU as well as external commands that come from the operating system and other programs. Figure 1-1 shows a very simplified view of the functions internal to the CPU. It is important to note that these functions occur in all CPUs regardless of manufacturer.

Notice in Figure 1-1 that there are several paths between components in the CPU. Some of these busses used are used for very special purposes, such as moving data from internal memory to the control unit. Other busses connect the CPU to the

FIGURE 1-1 Simple example of a CPU

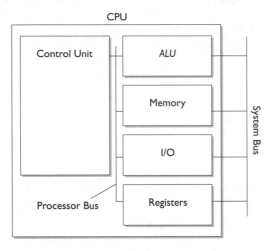

external devices from the CPU. The internal bus of the CPU is usually much faster than the external busses used on the system. These busses are not usually connected directly to external busses such as PCI except through a device called a controller.

Control Unit   The control unit shown in Figure 1-1 is primarily responsible for directing all the activities of the computer. It also manages interactions between the other components in the computer system. In addition, the control unit contains both hardwired instructions and programmed instructions (called *microcode* or *microprograms*) to perform operations. An example of an instruction might be the command to fetch information from memory. In older systems, the control unit would be a large number of integrated circuits on a circuit card. On a microprocessor-based system, the control unit is part of the microprocessor.

ALU   The arithmetic logic unit (ALU) is responsible for all logical and mathematical operations in the system. The ALU receives instructions from the control unit. The ALU can take information from memory, perform computations and comparisons, and then store the results in memory locations as directed by the control unit. An additional type of ALU, called a floating point unit (FPU) or coprocessor, which performs specialized functions such as division and large decimal number operations, is frequently used. Most modern microprocessors include an FPU processor as part of the microprocessor.

The ALU and control unit communicate with each other and perform operations in memory locations called *registers*. A register is a location that is internal to the microprocessor that can be used as a scratch pad for calculations. There are two types of registers used in modern systems: dedicated registers and general purpose registers. Dedicated registers are usually used for specific functions such as maintaining status or system controlled counting operations. General purpose registers are used for multiple purposes, typically when mathematical and comparison operations occur.

on the Job *When a system malfunctions, as in the case of a Blue Screen of Death, the monitor will usually display a message and multiple numbers. These numbers are the contents of the registers and other key memory locations. This information is usually not overly useful to a computer technician, but it can provide a great deal of information to developers and technical support professionals as to the nature of the failure. It is a good idea to capture that information before you contact customer support.*

Memory

Computer memory provides the primary storage for a computer system. The CPU will typically have internal memory (embedded in the CPU) that is used for operations and external memory located on the system or motherboard. The most common general types are Random Access Memory (RAM) and Read-Only Memory (ROM). The important consideration about memory is that the control unit is responsible for controlling usage of all memory. A more detailed discussion about memory occurs in the section on CPUs.

Controllers

The CPU also contains a number of interfaces or controllers to access devices and busses. One of the primary functions of a controller is to free up the time of the control unit by performing routine or clearly identified tasks. A typical microprocessor will have controllers interface to slow-speed devices such as serial data connections, high-speed interfaces connect to a computer bus, and connections to dedicated registers contain and report status. These controllers will also typically interface to other controllers on a bus for specific types of operations. The details of this are not important except that they have a huge impact on system performance. The more work that the CPU can give to a controller, the less work the control unit will have to be concerned with.

These controllers may also be referred to as a *bridge* or *hub*. They are contained in support chips for the CPU and allow access between the internal busses of the CPU and an external bus such as the Peripheral Component Interconnect (PCI) bus.

Programs

The rubber hits the road with programs. The microprocessor has a large number of coded instructions and programs that are used to provide instructions on how to handle specific requests. Some of these programs are hardwired into the processor, while others can be configured as the need arises. Hardwired programs may include the specific method with which data is moved from a memory location to a register, how status of the processor is stored, what specific steps need to occur when an error happens, and hundreds of other activities. Without these programs, the processor will not know how to respond when it is turned on. These programs are very complicated and form the basis for characteristics of the operation of the microprocessor. Additionally, most microprocessors allow for the capability to accept changes to these microprograms by the manufacturer or operating system provider. This allows for program errors and upgrades to occur without replacing the processor.

CERTIFICATION OBJECTIVE 1.01

System Modules

This section describes common devices called *field-replaceable modules*, as well as their role in the computer system as a whole. This information will form the foundation of your ability to discover and resolve computer problems. If you know the functions of each component, you will more easily be able to determine which component is at fault when something goes wrong.

System Board

Each internal and external component is connected to the *system board*. The system board, also referred to as the *main board*, the *motherboard*, or the *planar board*, is made of fiberglass and is typically brown or green, with a meshwork of copper lines, as shown next. These "lines" are the electronic circuits through which signals travel from one component to another and are collectively called the *bus*.

The Processor or CPU

Most computer components are designed to perform only one or a limited number of functions, and they only do so when it is specifically requested of them. The device responsible for organizing the actions of these components is the *processor*, also referred to as the *central processing unit*, or *CPU*. As the "brain" of the computer, the processor receives requests from you, the user; determines the tasks needed to fulfill the request; and translates the tasks into signals that the required component(s) can understand. The processor also does math and logic calculations. For more information about this see the section Chapter 5.

The processor or microprocessor has to be installed on the motherboard of the system. This is accomplished using one of several different methods. Early processors such as the 80286, 80386, and 80486 used a method called a pin grid array (PGA).

The PGA was usually inserted into a socket called a zero insertion force (ZIF) socket or could be soldered directly to the motherboard.

Processors can come in several physical forms. Older processors, such as the Intel 80286, 80386, 80486, and early Pentium processors used pin grid array (PGA) forms. Intel switched back to an updated form called the PGA2 for the Pentium 4. The PGA2 form is shown in Figure 1-2. PGA2 processors are square, with several rows of pins on the bottom. These pins are used to attach the processor to the motherboard using a ZIF socket.

A processor form used in Pentium II, Pentium III, and Celeron processors is the single-edge contact (SEC) cartridge (SECC), which has an upright design and attaches to the motherboard using a slot-1 connector. Slot-1 was a proprietary standard implemented by Intel when these processors were introduced. An SEC processor is shown in Figure 1-3. Processor designs, models, and speeds are discussed in more detail in Chapter 5.

The Pentium 4 and the newest Celeron processors use a form similar to the PGA socket called a PGA2. This new form is called the Socket 478, PGA 478, or PGA2. The 478 refers to the number of pins that the processor uses to connect to the motherboard. The Pentium 4 also has a 423-pin version available for systems integrators. Older PGA configurations did not typically require additional cooling, while all new processors require extensive heat sinks and fans. These new processors will only operate for a few minutes before they malfunction if the cooling system is not installed and working.

The Power Supply

The *power supply* (shown in Figure 1-4), typically located at the back of the computer's interior, has several very important functions. It is responsible for converting the alternating current (AC) voltage from wall outlets into the direct current (DC) voltage that the computer requires. The power supply accomplishes this task through a series of switching transistors, which gives rise to the term *switching mode* power supply.

FIGURE 1-2

The PGA2 processor form or package used in Pentium 4 and other processors

FIGURE 1-3

SEC processors are upright by design and usually include extensive cooling systems

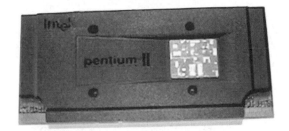

Another function of the power supply is to ensure that the computer receives the proper amount of voltage. Typical North American wall outlets generate about 110–120 vAC (volts AC). However, computers require comparatively smaller voltages: ±12, ±5, or ±3.3 vDC (volts DC). The computer's power supply converts voltages and dissipates heat that is generated in the process.

The buildup of heat can cause computer components (including the power supply) to fail. Therefore, the power supply has a built-in fan that draws air in from outside the computer case and cools off the components inside.

exam

ⓦatch *Make sure you are familiar with the voltages required by computer components: ±12, ±5, and 3.3 vDC.*

Memory

Memory is one of the most important but perhaps most misunderstood computer components. Its function is often mistaken for that of hard drive space. Furthermore,

FIGURE 1-4

A typical computer power supply

computers use several types of memory, each with a different function and different physical form. Typically, when people discuss memory, they are referring to *random access memory*, or *RAM*.

RAM

Recall that when a user makes a request, it is intercepted by the processor, which then organizes the request into component-specific tasks. Many of these tasks must occur in a specific order, with each component reporting its results back to the processor before the next task can be completed. The processor uses RAM to store these results until they can be compiled into the final result(s).

RAM is also used to store instructions about currently running applications. For example, when you start a computer game, a large set of the game's instructions (for example, how it works, how the screen should look, which sounds must be generated) is loaded into memory. The processor can retrieve these instructions much faster from RAM than it can from the hard drive, where the game normally resides until you start it. Within certain limits, the more information that's stored in memory, the faster the computer will run. In fact, one of the most common computer upgrades is to increase the amount of RAM.

The information in RAM is continually being read, changed, and removed. It is also *volatile*, meaning that it cannot work without a steady power supply. When a computer is turned off, the information in RAM is lost.

Cache

Cache memory is a very fast type of memory that is used for storing frequently accessed instructions or data. Cache is a form of RAM, but it is typically faster than normal RAM. Cache memory that is located internally in the processor is called Level 1 cache. Level 2 cache is cache that is external to the microprocessor but is on a very fast bus close to the CPU. A relatively new type of cache has also been defined, Level 3 cache, which may be implemented in systems in the very near future. Level 3 cache is a larger memory area to assist in improving the speed of systems. This approach seems to be a result of the design limits of current processors. It is hoped that Level 3

TABLE 1-1	Caching Sizes and Usage in Typical Systems

Cache	Typical Size	Location	Typical Usage
Level 1	16KB data 16KB instruction	Onboard CPU	Instructions and data
Level 2	256KB	Motherboard or onboard CPU	Data caching
Level 3	1.5-3MB	Motherboard	Applications and data

cache will be able to beef up the performance of existing system architectures. Table 1-1 shows some of the more common cache sizes for Level 1, 2 and 3 caches.

on the **Job**

Many newer processors implement Level 1 and Level 2 cache internally to the processor. The external cache is called Level 3 cache and is much larger than the Level 2 cache provided on older system boards.

Cache memory runs faster than typical RAM and is able to "guess" which instructions the processor is likely to need, then retrieve those instructions from RAM or the hard drive in advance. Cache memory can also hold preprocessed data, such as that used by a game or an applications program. Newer processors can create a decision "tree" of instructions and store these in the cache. This allows for rapid access to information or instructions by the CPU.

The cache also holds data that has been preprocessed, such as out of order processing. Typical applications may require the same instructions to be processed. For example, a game may have similar video instructions that are commonly called over and over. Newer processors create a tree of possible future instructions and store this in cache as well. Even when the tree is generated, some instructions are preprocessed and stored in case the specific branch of logic is followed, and those instructions do not have to be processed again. Intel has this down to an art and the processors are generally correct in the tree they create.

ROM

Although *read-only memory*, or *ROM*, has an important function, it is rarely changed or upgraded, so it typically warrants less attention by most computer users. Unlike RAM, ROM is read-only, meaning its instructions can be read by the processor, but ROM cannot be used to store new information.

SCENARIO & SOLUTION

Which type of memory is responsible for...	Solution
Maintaining a device's basic operating instructions?	ROM
Anticipating processor requests and making the proper data available?	Cache
Providing temporary storage for application files?	RAM

ROM is *nonvolatile*, so it does not lose its contents when the computer's power is turned off. This makes ROM ideal for storing a device's most basic operation and communication instructions. A number of computer components include ROM chips, which contain device-specific basic instructions. Information on these ROM chips is said to be *hardwired* or *hard coded* because it cannot be changed. These types of devices are termed *firmware*, to indicate that they are a mixture of hardware and software.

Storage Devices

The function of all storage devices is to hold, or store, information, even when the computer's power is turned off. Unlike information in RAM, files that are kept on a storage device remain there unless they are manually removed or altered by the user or the computer's operating system.

A great variety of storage devices are available, including floppy drives, hard drives, and Zip drives. However, the A+ tests focus only on the "standard" storage devices explained in the following sections.

Floppy Drives

A 3.5-inch *floppy drive* reads data from removable floppy disks and provides a good method for transferring data from one machine to another. *Floppy disks* contain a thin internal plastic disk, capable of holding magnetic charges. The disk is coated with a thin layer of magnetic materials. The disk is surrounded by a hard plastic protective casing, part of which can be retracted to reveal the storage medium inside (see Figure 1-5). The back of the disk has a coin-sized metal circle that is used by the drive to grasp the disk and spin it. When a floppy disk is inserted in a computer's drive, the drive spins the internal disk and retracts the protective cover. The drive's *read/write head* moves back and forth along the exposed area, reading data from and writing data to the disk.

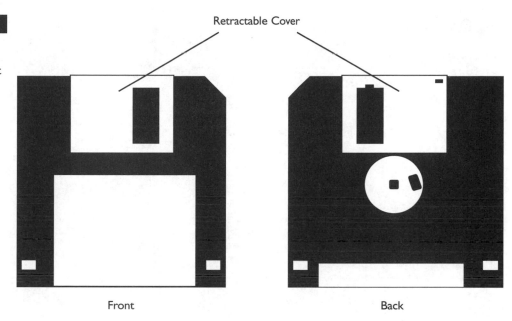

FIGURE 1-5

Typical 3.5-inch floppy disk, front and back

Retractable Cover

Front

Back

Floppy disks themselves are available in several different forms and capacities. The first floppy disks used in PCs were 5.25 inches square and could hold either 360KB or 1.2MB of information. However, these are no longer considered standard computer equipment, so you shouldn't expect to see questions about them on the A+ tests.

The newer 3.5-inch disk can hold 720KB (double density), 1.44MB (high density), or 2.88MB (extra high density) of information. The most commonly used such disk is the 1.44MB. Floppy drives are limited in the types of disks they can access. The obvious size difference precludes a 5.25-inch drive from using a 3.5-inch disk, and vice versa. A 720KB drive can read only 720KB disks. However, a 1.44MB drive can access either a 1.44MB or a 720KB disk, and the 2.88MB drive can read all three 3.5-inch disk densities.

Hard Drives

Hard drives store data in a similar fashion to floppy drives, but they typically are not removable and have a different physical structure (see Figure 1-6). A hard drive, also referred to as a *fixed drive*, consists of one or more hard platters, stacked on top of but not touching one another. The stack of platters is attached through its center to a rotating pole, called a *spindle*. Each side of each platter can hold data and has its own

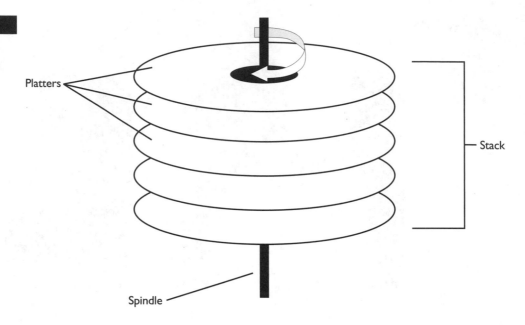

The internal structure of a hard disk

Platters

Stack

Spindle

read/write head. The read/write heads all move as a single unit back and forth along the stack.

Hard drives are available in a wide range of capacities and can hold much more data than a floppy disk. Most new hard drives have a capacity between 30GB and 120GB. The disk must be divided into smaller units, called *clusters*, before it can store data. This division is accomplished through formatting. Depending on the capacity and file system used, each cluster can hold between 512B to 32KB of data. Data storage and file systems are discussed in more detail in Chapters 8 and 9.

CD-ROMs

Compact disc–Read-Only Memory (CD-ROM) offers a balance between the portability of a floppy disk and the capacity of a hard drive. CD-ROMs are composed of a hard medium that contains very small depressed and raised areas, called *pits* and *lands*, respectively. CD-ROM drives read data from the CD using a laser instead of a read/write head.

CD-ROMs can hold roughly 650MB of data and generally cannot be written to, except in the case of CD-Rs (recordable) or CD-RWs (rewritable). Data can be accessed faster from a CD than a floppy disk but much more slowly than from a hard drive.

DVD

Digital versatile discs (DVDs) are similar in technology to CD-ROMs but have a higher storage density. DVDs are used extensively for video storage as well as large amounts of data storage. DVD-recordable (DVD-R) can be recorded on only once. Unlike a CD-RW, which can have multiple recording sessions, a DVD-R can have only one session. DVDs can typically store on the order of 5 to 8GB of data. There are new types of DVD devices coming on the market every day.

on the Job

Because CDs and DVDs have no protective covering, it's important to handle them with care. Scratches, dust, or other material on the CD surface can prevent data from being read correctly. Because data is located on the bottom side of the CD, always lay the CD label side down.

The Monitor

The function of a *monitor* is to produce visual responses to user requests. Most desktop computers use cathode ray tube (CRT) monitors or flat panel displays (FPD). CRTs use an electron gun to activate phosphors behind the screen. Each dot on the monitor, called a *pixel*, has the ability to generate red, green, or blue, depending on the signals it receives. This combination of colors results in the total display you see on the monitor.

Monitors are available in a wide array of colors and resolutions. The word *resolution* refers to the size and number of pixels that a monitor can display. Higher resolutions display more pixels and have better visual output. Lower resolutions result in grainy displays.

Color graphics adapter (CGA) monitors are an older type and can display combinations of red, green, and blue at different intensities, resulting in 16 different colors. The maximum resolution of a CGA monitor is 640×200 pixels in monochrome mode and 160×100 pixels in 16-color mode.

Enhanced graphics adapter (EGA) monitors are capable of generating up to 64 colors, 16 of which can be displayed at any one time. EGA monitors have a maximum resolution of 720×350 when displaying text only and 640×350 in graphics mode.

Virtual graphics array (VGA) monitors were the first to use analog rather than digital output. Instead of creating displays based on the absence or presence of a color (as in digital CGA and EGA monitors), VGA monitors can display a wide range of colors and intensities. They can produce around 16 million different colors but can display only up to 256 different colors at a time. This color setting is often called *16-bit high color*. VGA monitors have a maximum resolution of 720×400 in text mode and 640×480 in graphics mode.

Super VGA (SVGA) monitors introduce yet another improvement: they also use analog input and can provide resolutions as high as 1280×1024. Some SVGA monitors can provide even higher resolutions. SVGA monitors can display up to 16 million colors at once, referred to as *32-bit true color*. Because the human eye can distinguish only approximately 10 million different colors, it is likely that monitor technology will now focus on improving resolution only.

Monitors receive their signals from video cards or adapters attached to the motherboard. The monitor technology must match the technology of the video card to which it is attached. That is, an EGA monitor will work only with an EGA video card, and an SVGA monitor must be attached to an SVGA video card. Table 1-2 presents a summary of monitor types and characteristics.

Modems

A *modulator/demodulator (modem)* allows computers to communicate with one another over existing phone or cable lines. Internal modems attach directly to a computer's motherboard and connect to a regular phone jack using the same connector as a phone. External modems also connect to the phone jack but are attached to the computer via an external port. External modems are typically easier to configure and troubleshoot than internal modems and have the benefit of being easily transported to another computer.

TABLE 1-2   Monitor Capability Types and Their Characteristics

Monitor	Total Number of Colors	Number of Colors That Can Be Simultaneously Displayed	Maximum Resolution	Input
CGA	16	16	Monochrome: 640×200 Color: 160×100	Digital
EGA	64	16	Text mode: 720×350 Graphics mode: 640×350	Digital
VGA	More than 16 million	256	Text mode: 720×400 Graphics mode: 640×480	Analog
SVGA	More than 16 million	More than 16 million	1280×1024	Analog

Analog Modems

Traditional modems, also called *analog modems*, convert the computer's digital signals into analog signals so they can be sent out over phone lines. This process is called *modulation*. The modem is also responsible for converting incoming analog signals from the phone line into digital signals that the computer can use. This is called *demodulation*.

When one computer tries to connect to another via its modem, it must first dial the receiving computer's phone number. This process is known as the *dial-up*. The receiving computer answers, and the two modems engage in a process known as a *handshake*, in which the speed, encryption, and other rules of communication are established. Analog modems tie up the phone line, just as a regular phone call would. That is, you cannot use your analog modem and your phone at the same time if they share a line.

Digital Subscriber Line (DSL)

Digital technology has extended the capabilities of the telecommunications industry and allows for a new type of service, DSL. *Digital subscriber line (DSL)* uses the existing phone lines already brought into the premise and adds data capabilities to existing analog phone lines, which allows bandwidths far exceeding the capabilities of analog modems. The device used to connect a computer to a DSL provider is a modem and shares the 4-wire connection with the analog telephone service.

Cable Modems

Cable modems use the same cable that cable televisions use. Because television cables can transmit digital signals, cable modems are not really modems at all; that is, they do not modulate or demodulate signals. They act more as a router.

Unlike analog modems, cable modems do not need to perform a dial-up or handshake. To understand this concept, compare your phone to your television. When you phone a friend, you can't simply pick up the phone and speak to him; you must first dial his number and wait for him to answer. The same is true for analog modems. Television channels, however, are always there. You don't need to dial up the cable company through your television to request a channel; all you need to do is switch to that channel, which was there all along. This is the case with cable modems. As long as there is a physical connection between cable modems, they can communicate.

Peripherals

The term *peripheral* is typically used to refer to external and internal computer components that are not essential for system operation. On a PC, virtually any device that is not memory or CPU can be considered a peripheral. Interestingly enough, monitors are external devices and are not considered a peripheral. Keyboards, mice, and external devices such as a scanner or Zip drive are considered peripherals. Disk drives, floppy drives, network cards, and other devices that are installed internally to the PC are considered internal peripherals. Many peripheral devices use a proprietary interface or connection to the system, though the trend is to use standardized interfaces as much as possible.

Keyboards

There are several types of keyboards, including 84- and 101-key designs. Newer keyboards might include a variety of additional keys for accessing the Internet, using Microsoft Windows, and other common functions. Some keyboards even include a pointing device, such as a mouse or touch pad.

There are also several keyboard layouts. The keyset on an *ergonomic keyboard* (see Figure 1-7) is split in half and slants outward to provide a more relaxed, natural hand position. The placement of the keys themselves can also vary. Typical keyboards have a QWERTY layout, the name of which is taken from the first six letters on the second row of the keyboard. The Dvorak keyboard has an entirely different key layout (shown in Figure 1-8) and is designed to allow faster typing speeds.

FIGURE 1-7

Ergonomic keyboard with a different structure from a regular keyboard

FIGURE 1-8

QWERTY and
Dvorak keyboard
layouts

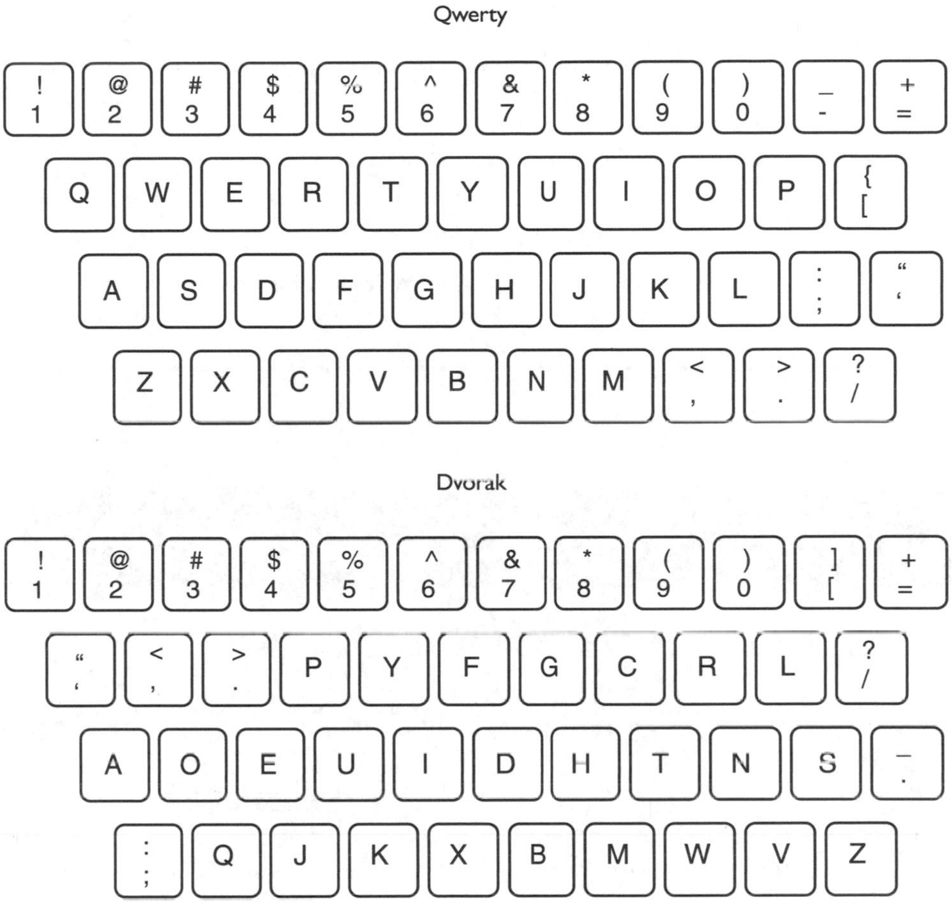

Qwerty

Dvorak

You don't have to actually *buy* a Dvorak keyboard; you can set the layout of your existing keyboard to either Dvorak or QWERTY using your operating system. If you are using Microsoft Windows, follow the steps in Exercise 1-1 to configure your keyboard to use the Dvorak layout.

EXERCISE 1-1

Switching to the Dvorak Keyboard Layout

1. Double-click the My Computer icon.
2. Double-click the Control Panel icon.

3. Double-click the Keyboard icon.

4. Select the Language tab in Windows 9x or the Input Locales tab in Windows NT.

5. Click the Properties button.

6. Select U.S.-Dvorak from the Keyboard Layout drop-down list.

7. Click OK, then click OK again.

8. If you want, you can physically change the keycaps on the keyboard to correspond to their new settings.

FROM THE CLASSROOM

What Happened to the Alphabet?

Ever wonder why the QWERTY keyboard is laid out the way it is, and why it's not laid out in alphabetical order? When the keyboard was invented (by Christopher Sholes, in the late 1800s), the keys were arranged in alphabetical order. However, due to their primitive nature, early typewriters were prone to jam keys. To remedy this problem, Sholes created the QWERTY layout. This layout was designed to slow typists down so that they couldn't type fast enough to jam the keys!

Today, computer keyboards are practically impossible to jam, so there is little benefit to using the QWERTY layout. In the 1930s, August Dvorak redesigned the keyboard layout so that the most commonly used characters are in or closest to the home row and are accessed by the strongest fingers. This layout allows for faster typing speeds, less hand strain, fewer typing mistakes, and less overall "finger travel." Although most people cannot exceed about 60 words per minute on a QWERTY keyboard, speeds on a Dvorak keyboard can reach about 100–120 words per minute— double the rate. Furthermore, the same passage that requires fingers to travel a total of 12 miles on a QWERTY keyboard requires only about 1 mile of travel on a Dvorak keyboard.

Unfortunately, the Dvorak keyboard has been slow to catch on. Most people learn to type on the QWERTY layout because that is the layout they are most likely to encounter. It is exceptionally difficult to learn and accurately use both layouts, so most people stick to the old QWERTY standby.

Firmware

Firmware refers to hardware components that include hardwired and software instructions, usually stored on ROM chips. These instructions are always available, so they do not have to be reprogrammed every time the computer is started. The firmware in a computer keeps settings such as the time, security passwords, screen colors, and component resources. Without firmware, you would have to do things such as setting the time yourself and informing the computer about which types of devices are present each time you turned the computer on.

The concept of firmware can be difficult to understand, but it can be explained using the example of a standard calculator. Any calculations you make on a calculator are "erased" once you turn the calculator off. However, the calculator retains the basic rules for adding, subtracting, multiplying, and the like, even when it is turned off. That is, you don't have to tell the calculator how to add or subtract every time you use it. Each time you turn the calculator back on, the calculator knows which buttons perform which functions.

BIOS

One type of computer firmware is the *basic input/output system (BIOS)*. The BIOS is responsible for informing the processor which devices are present and how to communicate with them. Whenever the processor makes a request from a component, the BIOS steps in and translates the request into instructions that the required component can understand.

Older computers contained true read-only BIOS that could not be altered. This meant that new components could not be added to the computer because the BIOS would not know how to communicate with them. This seriously limited users' ability to upgrade their computers, so *flash BIOS* was introduced. Now when a new component is installed in the computer, the flash BIOS can be electronically upgraded (or *flashed*) so that it can recognize and communicate with the new device.

Usually you can obtain the flash program from the website of the manufacturer of the motherboard. The upgrade process typically requires the flash program be copied to a floppy disk and the system started in DOS mode for the upgrade to work properly.

on the
job

It is very important that you follow the directions given by the manufacturer when performing a flash upgrade. If done incorrectly, the system can become inoperable and need a replacement BIOS chip from the manufacturer.

CMOS

Another important type of firmware is *complementary metal-oxide semiconductor (CMOS)*. The CMOS chip retains settings such as the time, keyboard settings, and boot sequence. (These settings are described in more detail in Chapter 5.) The CMOS also stores interrupt request line (IRQ) and input/output (I/O) resources that the BIOS uses when communicating with the computer's devices. The CMOS chip is able to keep these settings in the absence of computer power because it is attached to a small CMOS battery. This battery is usually good for 2 to 10 years.

on the Job

If the system repeatedly loses track of time when turned off, the battery is probably worn out and will need to be replaced. This is usually a fairly simple process and requires the removal of the outer system covers.

exam

watch   *As complicated as it might seem, make sure you that have an iron-clad understanding of the relationship between the computer's BIOS and CMOS as well as the differences in their functions. The BIOS is a set of instructions, and the CMOS is used to store configuration settings for the BIOS.*

You can view and modify the computer's CMOS settings by entering the computer's Setup program during bootup. Watch the screen for instructions such as "Press CTRL-S to access Startup Configuration" or "Press DELETE to enter Setup." From the time such a message is first displayed, you will have about 3 seconds to enter the appropriate key combination. (The length of this delay can be configured in the CMOS settings. Configuration of the CMOS settings is discussed in more detail in Chapter 5.)

on the Job

Interestingly, the term "CMOS settings" is a bit of a misnomer. When people talk about the computer's CMOS or its settings, they are referring to the items described in the preceding discussion. However, a CMOS is really just a type of physical chip. CMOS chips are used for a variety of things other than retaining CMOS settings. In fact, many processors are actually CMOS chips.

Boot Process

When the computer is started (booted), the BIOS runs a *power-on self-test (POST)*. During the POST, the BIOS checks for the presence and function of each component it has been programmed to manage. It first checks the processor, then the RAM, and then system-critical devices such as the floppy drive, hard drive, keyboard, and monitor. It then tests noncritical components such as the CD-ROM drive and sound card.

Next, the BIOS retrieves the resource (IRQ and I/O address) settings from the CMOS and assigns them to the appropriate devices. The BIOS then processes the remaining CMOS settings, such as the time or keyboard status (for example, whether the number lock should be on or off). Finally, the BIOS searches for an operating system and hands to it control of the system. The CMOS settings are no longer required at this point, but the BIOS continues to work, translating communications between the processor and other components.

on the
Oob

The BIOS contains basic drivers (16-bit) for accessing the needed hardware during bootup, such as the keyboard, floppy disk, and hard disk or any other device needed during a boot.

LCD Portable Systems

Portable systems are small, easily transported computers. They generally weigh less than 6 pounds, can fit easily in a large bag or briefcase, and have roughly the same dimensions as a 2- or 3-inch stack of magazines.

As well as the size difference, portables and desktops (also called *PCs* or *personal computers*) differ in their physical layout. Portable computers have an all-in-one layout in which the keyboard, pointing device, and display are integrated with the computer chassis. Typically, portable computers open in the same manner as a briefcase. The top half contains the display, and the bottom half contains the keyboard and the rest of the computer's components.

Finally, although portable computers are functionally similar to desktop computers, they are primarily proprietary and tend to use components other than the ones described thus far. For example, portables use liquid crystal display (LCD) monitors rather than CRT monitors, and they can use docking stations and PC Cards. Repairing portable systems usually requires a skill set beyond what is necessary to service desktop PCs. Therefore, many of the chapters in this book are divided into "desktop" and "portable" sections.

The term *portable* is often confused with the terms *laptop* and *notebook*. Portable computers are any type of computer that can be easily transported and that contain an all-in-one component layout. A few years ago, most portable computers were called *laptops* because they could fit comfortably on the user's lap. As technology improved, portable computers became smaller and smaller. The newer term, *notebook*, is often used now to refer to portable computers to reflect their smaller size. Within most of the computer industry and throughout the remainder of this book, the terms *notebook*, *portable* and *laptop* are used interchangeably.

Personal Digital Assistants

Personal Digital Assistants, known as PDAs, are even smaller than laptop computers. Typically, PDAs are small enough to fit in your hand, and they are often referred to as "palmtop" or "handheld" computers. Because they are so small, PDAs do not have the functionality of a laptop or desktop computer. In other words, most PDAs allow you to perform only a small number of functions.

on the **Job** *There are two primary types of operating systems used in PDAs today. The Windows CE operating system, and the Palm operating system. In general these two operating systems do not support interchangeable applications, though most PDA software manufacturers now support both platforms.*

One of the most common uses for a PDA is as an organizer—that is, to keep track of appointments, record addresses, and phone numbers, and small notes. Many PDAs also allow you to plug into a fax machine to send faxes or to plug into a network to send e-mail or access the Internet. PDAs are too small to include a regular keyboard layout, so the primary input device is a small stylus, which is shaped like a pen. The stylus can be used to press small keys on a keypad, select items that are displayed on the screen, or write data on the screen. PDAs are entirely proprietary, nonservicable by regular technicians, and different from one another in their technology and functions. Therefore, although you should be aware of their existence, you shouldn't expect to see many questions about PDAs on the A+ exam.

CERTIFICATION OBJECTIVE 1.02

Adding and Removing Field-Replaceable Modules

Most hardware failures are resolved by replacing a "bad," or nonworking, component with a "good," or working, one. This section discusses basic techniques for replacing and installing common computer components. Desktop and portable systems are discussed separately because different skills are required for each.

Whenever you install or replace a computer component, you must turn the computer's power off and ensure that you follow the electrostatic discharge (ESD) procedures discussed in Chapter 4. The exception to this rule are *hot-swappable devices*, which can be added or removed while the computer is operating. Proper removal of the computer's cover will vary, depending on the cover style and attaching mechanisms. In all cases, unfasten all the screws or clips, then *gently* slide or lift the cover away from the chassis. Computer covers are designed to move smoothly, so you should never need to use force. All the exercises described in this section assume that your computer's power has been turned off and that the cover has been removed.

Desktop System Components

Many desktop components, such as the processor, power supply, and RAM, are installed through simple physical attachment to the computer. That is, physical installation is all that is required to make the component functional. Other devices, such as hard drives and keyboards, require the additional assignment of system resources. This section focuses on the physical installation of common components; resource assignment is discussed in the next section, "IRQs, DMAs, and I/O Addresses." Special hardware configurations are discussed in Chapter 2.

Many of the components discussed here conform to some type of standard. This means that you can replace a component with one that was made by a different manufacturer. The skills discussed here can be used on practically any desktop PC. Whenever you install or replace a PC component, it is recommended that you start the PC to ensure that the component works before you replace the cover.

System Board

Because most components are physically attached to the system board, this can be one of the most time-consuming replacements. If you are replacing one system board with another *of exactly the same brand and version*, you should make notes about the jumper and BIOS settings in case they need to be changed on the new board. Most likely, however, you will replace a system board with a newer version, and you should follow the new board's manual rather than the original setup.

All the expansion cards and cables must be removed from the system board. You might also need to remove hard drive and floppy drive bays to get them out of the way. Next, remove any screws or fasteners attaching the system board to the chassis, and lift the board out.

To place the new (or replacement) board in the computer, line it up properly on the chassis screw holes, and fix it into place. Although the BIOS, CMOS, and CMOS battery are included with the system board, you will need to install the processor, memory, and expansion cards separately. Finally, attach the power and drive connectors.

Storage Devices

Replacing storage devices is a common task because they are one of the most common causes of computer failure. They are also often the source of common computer upgrades. Fortunately, since most drives are standardized, they can be recognized by any PC and don't need special configuration.

Hard Drives   Follow the procedure in Exercise 1-2 to remove a hard drive.

EXERCISE 1-2

Removing a Hard Drive

1. Remove the power supply and ribbon cables from the back of the hard drive. Ensure that you grasp the plastic connector, not the wires themselves. If the connector doesn't come out easily, try gently rocking it lengthwise from side to side (never front to back) while you pull it out.
2. Remove the restraining screws that attach the hard drive to the drive bay (these are usually located on the sides of the drive).
3. Slide the drive out of the computer.

To install a hard drive, the procedure is reversed, with a few important notes. The top of the drive is typically smooth and includes a manufacturer's label. The circuit board is on the bottom of the drive. Never install a hard drive upside down.

o n   t h e
()o b

Hard drives and other devices can usually be installed sideways with no impact on operation or performance.

Some ribbon cables have connectors for two hard drives. If the system has only one hard drive, attach it to the end of the ribbon cable. Special configuration procedures are necessary for installing more than one hard drive. These procedures are discussed in Chapter 2.

Some ribbon connectors can physically fit either way in the drive's socket. The red stripe along the length of the cable represents pin 1. Make sure that this stripe is aligned with pin 1, as indicated on the hard drive.

ex**a**m

wa t c h *The primary hard drive is usually attached to the end connector on the ribbon cable.*

Floppy Drives   Floppy drives are installed and removed in a fashion similar to hard drives. To remove the floppy drive, disconnect the power and ribbon cables, unfasten the retaining screws, and then slide the drive out of the bay.

Like a hard drive ribbon, a floppy drive ribbon works only one way. Attach the first floppy drive to the end of the ribbon, and, if necessary, attach the second floppy drive to the middle of the ribbon. Also, ensure that the red stripe on the ribbon cable is lined up with pin 1 on the floppy drive.

ex**a**m

wa t c h *The red stripe on a drive cable indicates pin 1.*

CD-ROM and DVD Drives   The physical removal and installation of a CD-ROM or DVD drive is the same as that for hard and floppy drives. However, the CD drive could require the connection of a sound cable to the sound card. Additionally DVD players will usually be connected using separate cables to a decoder card. The BIOS of the computer needs to be configured to allow the operation of the CD-ROM or DVD. Normally this will happen automatically, but it may be necessary to enable the device in the BIOS settings.

If the computer doesn't recognize or can't communicate with the new drive, you need to load a driver for it. Insert the floppy disk that came with the CD and run the Setup or Install program. This will load the CD driver and allow the computer to recognize the drive.

Power Supplies

Power supplies usually come with the chassis of the computer. However, they do fail from time to time and can be replaced using the procedure outlined in Exercise 1-3.

EXERCISE 1-3

Removing a Power Supply

1. Turn off the power and remove the power connector from the wall socket.

2. Remove the power connector(s) (P1 on an ATX system or P8 and P9 on an AT) from the system board, using the plastic connector, not the wires.

3. Remove the power connectors from all other components, including the hard, floppy, and CD-ROM drives.

4. Remove the screws that hold the power supply to the chassis. Do *not* remove the screws from the power supply case!

5. Slide the power supply away from the computer.

Reverse this procedure to install a power supply. It is important to note that the P8 and P9 (AT system) connectors look almost identical. Although each will attach to the system board only one way, it is possible to place them beside each other the wrong way. When attaching them to the system board, make sure the *black* wires of the connectors are together.

The ATX (P1) power supply connector for the ATX system board offers more safety—it is a 1-piece, 20-pin keyed connector.

e x a m
w a t c h

The P8 and P9 connectors are attached to the system board with the black wires together. Newer ATX style motherboards have a single power connector that prevents incorrect installation.

Processor/CPU

When you install a CPU, it is important to make sure that it is compatible with the type and speed of the system board. System boards can typically use only one processor model and can usually handle only two or three different speeds of that particular model.

PGA/ZIF   Older processors, such as the Intel 80486 and Pentium, are PGA processors and fit into square sockets on the system board. If the socket is of the low insertion force type, simply remove the processor using a special PGA chip puller, then push the new processor into the socket. However, if the system board has a zero insertion force (ZIF) socket, follow the instructions in Exercise 1-4.

EXERCISE 1-4

Removing a PGA Processor

1. Lift the socket lever. You might have to move it slightly to the side to clear it of a retaining tab.
2. Pull out the processor. Because this is a ZIF socket, there should be no resistance when you remove the CPU.

on the **job**

The processor will be very hot when you first turn off a PC. You will lose skin if you touch a hot CPU chip. Always allow at least 5 minutes for the chip to cool off before you remove it.

To install a processor in a ZIF socket, ensure that the lever is raised, line up the pins, and place the processor in the socket, but do not push. Lower the lever to grip the CPU pins.

SEC/Slot I Processors such as Intel's Pentium II, early Celeron, and AMD's Athlon are in the SEC form. To remove an SEC processor from its slot, locate the retaining clips on each side. Push the clips out, away from the processor. You might first need to slide a locking tab out of place. Pull the CPU out of the slot.

PGA2 and OOI The Pentium 4 is available in two different configurations. The standard Pentium 4 uses the pin grid array 2 (PGA2) also referred to as a Socket 478 configuration. This socket resembles the PGA/ZIF connection used in earlier processors. Some Pentium III and Celeron processors are also able to use this 478-pin connection. Intel also introduced the OLGA (organic land grid array) configuration. The OLGA abbreviation has been shortened to OOI according to Intel. The OOI configuration uses 423 pins instead of the 478 used by the PGA2 configuration. OOI is less common in current usage than the socket 478 processor.

Memory

The first RAM chips were dual inline packages (DIP) that attached directly into sockets on the system board. However, their design made them prone to loosening due to the alternating heating and cooling of the system board. Newer memory modules are actually small cards with DIP chips on one or both sides. These cards fit upright into slots on the system board and are held in place by clips that prevent "chip creep" (loosening).

RAM is automatically detected and counted on startup, so its installation is limited to physical placement in the computer. That is, once RAM is physically installed, no additional configuration is required. When installing memory in a motherboard, verify the types and amounts of memory that the motherboard can accept.

SIMM Memory   Single inline memory module (SIMM) memory is available in 30- and 72-connector configurations. Most 80386, 80486, and Pentium computers include slots for both SIMM types. Follow the steps in Exercise 1-5 to install SIMM.

EXERCISE 1-5

Installing a SIMM

1. Line up the SIMM's connector edge with the appropriate-sized slot on the system board, keeping the SIMM at a 45-degree angle to the slot.

2. Gently rotate the SIMM upright until it clicks into place. Note that SIMMs will fit in a slot only one way. If you have trouble installing the SIMM, reverse its orientation in the slot.

To remove a SIMM, pull outward on the slot's retaining clips. The SIMM should fall to a 45-degree angle. Remove the SIMM.

DIMM Memory   The dual inline memory module (DIMM) memory design is newer than the SIMM and is typically used in Pentium, Pentium II, and Pentium III computers. A common misconception is that DIMMs have DIP chips on both sides, and SIMMs have DIP chips on only one side. This is incorrect: DIMMs are so named because they have two rows of connectors, whereas SIMMs have only one row of connectors. DIMM packages, which have 168 connectors, are slightly longer than SIMMs. The technique for installing a DIMM (as shown in Exercise 1-6) is slightly different than for a SIMM.

EXERCISE 1-6

Installing a DIMM

1. Place the DIMM upright in the slot, so that the notches in the DIMM are lined up with the tabs in the slot.
2. Gently press down on the DIMM. The retention clips on the side should rotate into the locked position. You might need to guide them into place with your fingers.

To remove a DIMM, press the retention clips outward, as shown in Figure 1-9. The DIMM should pop out of the slot. Once it is free of the slot, remove it from the computer.

exam
ⓦatch
The word "single" in SIMM and the word "dual" in DIMM refer to the rows of connectors on each side rather than the number of sides that contain memory chips. For example, each side of each pin (connector) on a DIMM (dual inline memory module) has a separate function; however, each side of the pin is the same on a SIMM (single inline memory module). This allows for only one DIMM instead of two SIMMs to make up the 64-bit data path.

Input Devices

Most input devices, such as keyboards and mice, are installed by simply plugging them into the appropriate port on the back of the computer. Keyboards can have either DIN-5 or mini-DIN-6 connectors. Mice typically use either an existing 9-pin serial (COM) port, a mini-DIN-6 port. Although it will physically fit, a mini-DIN-6 keyboard will not work in a mini-DIN-6 mouse port, or vice versa. Newer keyboards and mice can also be configured to use the USB port.

Another type of mouse, the *bus mouse*, requires a more complicated physical installation. A bus mouse expansion card must be installed on the system board and the mouse must then be connected to the port at the back.

FIGURE 1-9

Removing a
DIMM

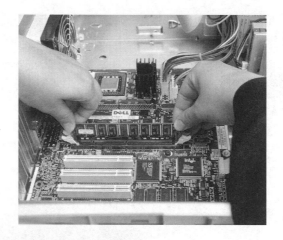

CERTIFICATION OBJECTIVE 1.03

Portable System Components

Because portable systems are largely proprietary, components cannot be mixed among them. Most portables must be returned to the manufacturer to be repaired or upgraded. This section introduces you to some laptop-specific components and describes installation procedures, where applicable.

Portable computers are much more difficult and costly to repair than desktop PCs. To make matters worse, they are also much more likely to need repairs. Because portable are "portable," it's easy to drop them, bang them into things, and so on, all of which can cause damage. Always use a proper carrying case or bag for your portable to avoid the lengthy and costly process of having it repaired.

AC Adapter

The AC adapter's function is to convert AC power to DC power, in the same way that the power supply does in a desktop. The AC adapter is also responsible for recharging the battery. If an external adapter must be replaced, simply unplug it and attach a new one. Because laptops have proprietary designs, check with the manufacturer for instructions on replacing an internal adapter. Furthermore, since AC adapters have varying output voltages, never use an AC adapter with any laptop other than the one for which it was made.

Hard Drive

Laptop hard drives vary in physical size and interface and are typically either 2.5-inch Ultra Direct Memory Access (UDMA) or 2.5-inch Enhanced Integrated Drive Electronics (EIDE). Replace a hard drive only with another of the same type from the same manufacturer. Usually, you can remove a small plastic cover on the bottom of the laptop to access the hard drive. Slide the drive out (see Figure 1-10), then replace it with a new drive and replace the cover. There are also hard drives that can be installed into the PC Card expansion bays.

Keyboard

Most laptops come with small, integrated keyboards. Some laptop keyboards include a pointing device such as a pointing stick or touch pad. Unfortunately, because keyboards are integrated into laptops, they are not easily replaced, and the entire computer must usually be sent back to the manufacturer when there is a problem.

Processor Board

The laptop version of a system board is called a *processor board*. It typically contains both the processor and RAM and in most cases can be repaired or upgraded only by the manufacturer.

Video Board

A portable computer's video output is controlled by a *video board*, in much the same way that a PC's video is controlled by a video expansion card. Video boards are typically

FIGURE 1-10

Removing a hard drive from a portable system

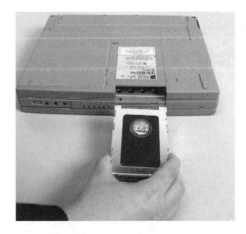

integrated with the system and are difficult to upgrade. In most cases, a faulty video board needs to be replaced by the manufacturer.

DC Controllers

Most portable computers include a *DC controller*, which is designed to monitor and regulate power usage. The function of DC controllers can vary with the manufacturer, but typically, they provide short-circuit protection, give "low battery" warnings, and can be configured to automatically shut down the portable when the power is low.

LCD Panel

To add to their portability, portable computers use thin LCDs. Although their display abilities are typically not as good as those of CRTs, LCDs are much thinner (1 to 2 inches thick) and require much less power. The first LCD panels were called *passive matrix displays*. A passive matrix display is made up of a grid of horizontal and vertical wires. At one end of each wire is a transistor, which receives display signals from the computer. When two transistors (one at the *x* axis and one at the *y* axis) send voltage along their wires, the pixel at the intersection of the two wires is lit.

Active matrix displays are newer and use different technology, called *thin-film transistor (TFT)* technology. Active matrix displays contain transistors at each pixel, resulting in more colors, better resolution, a better ability to display moving objects, and the ability to be viewed at greater angles. However, active matrix displays use more power than passive matrix displays.

LCD displays cannot be repaired. That means a faulty display in a portable will need to be replaced by the manufacturer of the portable.

CERTIFICATION OBJECTIVE 1.04

IRQs, DMAs, and I/O Addresses

You should now be familiar with the physical installation procedures for common computer components. As discussed, physical installation is all that is required to make some components functional. However, some components also require system resources, such as processor time and memory space.

One type of computer resource is called an *input/output (I/O) address*. When the computer is started, the BIOS loads into RAM device-specific information about the existing devices, including their drivers and other rules of communication. Whenever the processor needs to communicate with a device in the computer, it first checks RAM for the entries pertaining to that device. Without an I/O address, components would appear nonexistent to the processor.

Once the processor has finished communicating with or requesting a task from a device, it continues with other functions, rather than waiting for the device to finish its task. When the device has a result to report to the processor, it places the result in RAM. Next, the device "interrupts" the processor's function to indicate that the task is completed. Devices accomplish this through *interrupt request (IRQ) lines*. When the processor receives an interrupt, it can identify the initiating device by its IRQ, and it then turns to that device's I/O (RAM) address to retrieve the information.

In some cases, devices require data from other components in order to complete their tasks. In these cases, it is more efficient to allow the two devices to communicate directly with each other than to communicate via the processor. Devices communicate with one another using *direct memory access (DMA)* channels. DMA channels allow devices to read or write data directly into or from memory without first being asked by the processor. Other devices can read this data directly from memory without asking the processor for it. DMA usage was implemented to overcome the relative slow bus speeds of older PC systems. They are primarily used today for sound cards, floppy disks, printers, and ISA bus functions.

A newer technology was introduced into PC systems called *bus mastering*. A bus master is a DMA-like activity that occurs between two or more devices that are controlled by higher performance controllers. The controller on the bus that wants to transfer a large block of data can actually take control of the bus and make a direct connection between the two devices. The data can be transferred quickly and without CPU intervention. When the data transfer is accomplished, the bus is released and normal functioning is returned. This allows the CPU to continue operation on other tasks without servicing the bus. The PCI bus uses bus mastering as opposed to DMA transfers.

In some cases, IRQs, DMAs, and I/O addresses are automatically assigned to devices by the BIOS. Plug-and-Play operating systems, such as Microsoft Windows 95 and 98, can also automatically assign resources. However, in older machines, you might need to allocate resources manually. For this reason, and because they will appear on the A+ exams, you should become very familiar with the concepts presented in this section.

If you are using Microsoft Windows 9x you can view your computer's resource settings in the Device Manager window. Follow the steps in Exercise 1-7 to view your computer's resource allocations. In Windows 2000 and XP you access this using the Properties button on My Computer | Hardware, and then click the Device Manager button.

EXERCISE 1-7

Viewing the Computer's Resource Assignments

1. Right-click the My Computer icon on the desktop.

2. Select Properties from the shortcut menu.

3. Click the Device Manager tab.

4. Select the Computer icon, and click the Properties button.

Hexadecimal Addresses

When you view a device's I/O address setting, you will probably notice that it contains letters and numbers. This is the device's memory address; in other words, it's the location in memory where the processor must go to find a particular piece of data. This type of numbering is called *hexadecimal*, and it is based on multiples of 16 rather than 10.

The hexadecimal system is mainly used because it is easier to understand than binary. The binary number 0001, for example, is 1 in our decimal system, as well as in the hexadecimal system. 1111 in binary is 15 in our decimal system and F in hexadecimal. The hexadecimal memory address 3D9A is much easier to understand than the equivalent binary representation 11110110011010. See Table 1-3 for related binary, decimal, and hexadecimal number conversions.

Standard IRQ Settings

When the first PCs were designed, eight IRQs were available. However, as more devices were introduced, more IRQs had to be made available so that devices would not be in competition for them (each device must have a unique IRQ address). Eight more IRQs were added, for a total of 16 (numbered 0–15). Although some devices can use one of several IRQs, other devices (typically internal components) are hardwired to use a specific IRQ and cannot be configured otherwise. Although most devices adhere to industry-set standards, some have manufacturer-specific IRQ settings. A device's preferred IRQ setting can usually be found in the manufacturer's documentation that came with the device.

IRQ 0 is set aside for the computer's *system timer*. The system timer is responsible for synchronizing the speed of the computer's activities. Computer systems contain a small quartz crystal that vibrates when exposed to electricity. Each vibration represents

TABLE 1-3	Decimal Numbers and Their Corresponding Hexadecimal and Binary Numbers

Decimal	Hexadecimal	Binary	Decimal	Hexadecimal	Binary
0	0	0000	8	8	1000
1	1	0001	9	9	1001
2	2	0010	10	A	1010
3	3	0011	11	B	1011
4	4	0100	12	C	1100
5	5	0101	13	D	1101
6	6	0110	14	E	1110
7	7	0111	15	F	1111

a cycle. A computer whose quartz vibrates 100 million times a second runs at a speed of 100 megahertz (MHz). Because the system timer is such an important component, it is given the IRQ with the highest priority.

IRQ 1 is assigned to the computer's keyboard. IRQ 1 has the second-highest priority, so keyboard commands take precedence over many other computer functions (as evidenced by the ability to halt some computer operations using special key combinations).

IRQ 2 is typically listed as "cascade" or "redirect to IRQ 9." Recall that the earliest computers had only eight IRQs (0–7) and that IRQs 8–15 were introduced later. The interrupt controller for the new IRQs uses IRQ 2 to access IRQs 8–15. Additionally, some devices at the time were hardwired to use IRQ 2 only. The "redirect" is used to trick these devices into using IRQ 9 instead of IRQ 2.

IRQ 3 is assigned to COM2 and COM4. However, as you already know, devices cannot share an IRQ. Fortunately, most computers include only two COM ports: COM1 and COM2. If COM2 and COM4 both have devices attached, only one can be used at a time. For example, if a modem uses COM2 and a scanner is attached to COM4, you can use one device or the other but not both at the same time. The same principle is true for IRQ 4, which is assigned to COM1 and COM3.

The standard assignment for IRQ 5 is the secondary parallel port (LPT2). However, because most computers include only one LPT port, IRQ 5 is typically available for other devices. IRQ 6 is assigned to the floppy drive, and IRQ 7 is assigned to the primary parallel port (LPT1). Neither of these devices can be reconfigured to use other IRQs.

IRQ 8 is assigned to the computer's real-time clock. This is the clock responsible for keeping the actual time and date. IRQ 9, which was discussed previously, is available for assignment but typically is reserved for devices that are hardwired to use IRQ 2.

IRQ 10 and IRQ 11 are "available." This means that they are not in use by a critical component and are available to be assigned to peripheral devices, or noncritical components, such as Small Computer Systems Interface (SCSI, pronounced "scuzzy") controllers or network cards. IRQ 12 is set aside for the PS/2 mouse. If the computer uses a bus or serial mouse instead, IRQ 12 is available for another device.

IRQ 13 is reserved for the math coprocessor, found in Intel 80486DX and newer processors. If the processor is older and doesn't use a math coprocessor, IRQ 13 is available. IRQ 14 is assigned to the primary hard drive controller, and IRQ 15 is reserved for the secondary hard drive controller, if one exists. Table 1-4 presents a summary of standard IRQ assignments.

All of the above IRQs are *maskable interrupts*, meaning that the processor can ignore them in order to complete a current task. However, in the presence of certain memory errors, the processor must be halted to prevent corruption or loss of data. *Nonmaskable interrupts* are used by memory to indicate a possibly fatal condition, and the processor is stopped mid-task.

e x a m

ⓦatch

You need to memorize these IRQ assignments for the A+ exam and to be able to properly diagnose and resolve IRQ-related computer problems. There is no apparent order or intuitive structure to these assignments, so it might be helpful to write them out on paper, over and over, recalling more of them from memory each time. After enough exposure to them, you will be able to mentally associate an IRA address with its component, rather than merely calling them up by reciting the whole table of addresses.

SCENARIO & SOLUTION

Which interrupts are maskable?	0–15
Which IRQ address has the highest priority?	0
I'm attaching a device that can use either IRQ 11 or 15. Which should I use?	If the computer uses the secondary hard drive controller, you must use 11 for the new device. If there is no secondary hard drive, you can use either 11 or 15, with no noticeable performance difference.

TABLE 1-4	IRQ	Device
	0	System timer
Standard IRQ Assignments	1	Keyboard
	2	Cascade, redirect to IRQ 9
	3	Serial ports (COM2 and COM4)
	4	Serial ports (COM1 and COM3)
	5	Parallel port (LPT2) Primary for ISA sound cards
	6	Floppy drive controller
	7	Parallel port (LPT1)
	8	Real-time clock
	9	Redirected from IRQ 2
	10	Available
	11	Available
	12	PS/2 mouse
	13	Math coprocessor
	14	Hard disk controller
	15	Secondary hard disk controller

I/O Addresses

Input/output (I/O) addresses are simple in concept. Each device in a computer system needs a way to communicate. The early standard was to assign an area in memory designated for a particular device. This allowed for a simple method of communicating between devices. For example, the default I/O address for a joystick is 200h to 20Fh. This address range is used for communications between a joystick and the computer. Generally, no other device uses those addresses. Notice the h on the end of the address. The h signifies that this address is a hexadecimal address (base 16). Table 1-5 gives you the most commonly asked I/O addresses in the A+ exam. Make sure you memorize these addresses, as you can expect to be asked about one or more of them.

TABLE 1-5	170h-17Fh	Secondary IDE controller, master drive
	1F0h-1FFh	Primary IDE controller, master drive
Common I/O addresses needed for the A+ exam	278h-27Fh	LPT 2
	2F8h-2FFh	COM 2
	378h-37Fh	LPT 1
	3F8h-3FFh	COM 1

Common Devices

Most devices require both an I/O address and an IRQ to work properly. This section briefly presents the more common IRQ and I/O addresses used in PC systems.

Modems

Modems require an IRQ and I/O address to function properly. If the modem is external, it attaches to one of the computer's serial ports, typically COM2. Because the modem is attached to COM2, it uses the COM2 resources, namely IRQ 3 and I/O 2F8–2FF.

Internal modems require a different procedure. Even though the internal modem occupies a regular expansion slot inside the computer, it is still assigned the resources of one of the computer's serial ports. This means that the internal modem uses a COM port's resources, even though it is not physically attached to that port. Furthermore, no device should be physically attached to the COM port that the internal modem is associated with. If this situation occurs, it is highly likely that the device connected to the external COM port will not function properly. Internal modems are usually configured to use either COM3's resources (IRQ 4 and I/O address 3E8–3EF) or COM4's resources (IRQ 3 and I/O address 2E8–2EF). The COM port can also be disabled in the BIOS settings, though this is not usually necessary.

Floppy Drive

Floppy drive controllers are assigned to IRQ 6 and assigned I/O address 3F0–3F7. Floppy drives also require the use of a DMA channel and are typically assigned DMA 2.

Hard Drive

The primary hard drive controller is assigned IRQ 14 and I/O address 1F0–1FF. The secondary hard drive controller uses IRQ 15 and I/O address 170–17F. Older hard drive controllers use DMA channel 3. However, newer drives are able to access RAM directly using a protocol called Ultra DMA (UDMA). UDMA is a protocol used only by hard drives and is not functionally associated with a computer's standard DMA channels.

USB Port

The *Universal Serial Bus (USB)* port has become the expansion port of choice for PCs. It is a physical port located at the back of the computer that can be used to connect up to 127 external devices to the computer. Low-speed USB transmits data up to 1.5MBps and high-speed USB supports speeds up to 12MBps.

USB ports can be used only with specially designed USB-compatible components. One benefit of USB ports is that they support Plug and Play, meaning that devices attached to the port are automatically recognized by the computer and are automatically assigned computer resources, such as IRQs and I/O addresses. The USB port's controller typically uses IRQ 9.

In traditional device installation, the computer must be turned off before a component can be installed. When the computer is restarted, it can recognize and use the component. Even devices that can be physically connected while the computer is running (e.g., a printer or scanner) will not usually be recognized until the computer is restarted. USB ports, however, support *hot swapping*, which means that devices can be attached while the computer is running and can be recognized and used immediately.

Infrared and Wireless Ports

Infrared and wireless computer devices use infrared light waves or radio frequency, rather than physical connections, to communicate with each other. Most computers support either the Bluetooth or Infrared Data Association's (IrDA's) data transmission standards. Any two wireless devices can communicate with each other, as long as they adhere to the same standards. The Bluetooth infrared standard is not supported on older Microsoft Windows operating systems but is supported on Windows XP.

IrDA infrared devices support a maximum transmission speed of 4Mbps. Connections can be *point to point*, as in a computer and printer, or *multipoint*, as in computers on a network. One limitation of infrared devices is that they use "line-of-sight" transmission, so the ports on the communicating devices must be directly facing one another. Infrared communications are limited to approximately 1 meter.

Microsoft Windows (9*x*, Me, and 2000, as well as XP) supports Plug and Play for IrDA infrared devices. Again, this means that devices are automatically recognized and assigned system resources. Many new computers come with an infrared port already installed. You can also add IrDA to older systems by installing an infrared adapter. External adapters are attached to the computer via a serial port, so they use that port's system resources. Like most other expansion cards, internal adapters can be installed in an available expansion slot and assigned an available IRQ and I/O address.

CERTIFICATION OBJECTIVE 1.05

Peripheral Ports, Cabling, and Connectors

Earlier in this chapter, we discussed procedures for installing various internal components. As a technician, you will also be expected to install and replace external components, such as mice, scanners, and printers. Many external components are installed by simply plugging them into a port at the back of the computer. However, some components can be attached to a computer in more than one way. How do you decide which way is the best?

This section introduces you to a number of basic peripheral installation concepts, such as cable and connector types, as well as methods of communication. This information will allow you to determine the pros and cons of various connection methods and figure out when a peripheral's connection to the computer is the cause of a problem.

Cable Types

Cables are used to physically connect components and are responsible for transmitting signals between them. Cables transmit electronic signals and can come in a wide variety of physical forms. *Straight-pair cables* consist of one or more metal wires surrounded by a plastic insulating sheath. *Twisted-pair cables* consist of two or more metal wires that are twisted around each other along the entire length of the cable. These wires are also surrounded by a plastic sheath. *Coaxial cables* contain a single copper wire surrounded by several layers of insulating plastic. Figure 1-11 illustrates some common cable types.

Another distinction between cable types is the presence or absence of an interference shield. Cables that transmit electronic signals are susceptible to interference from

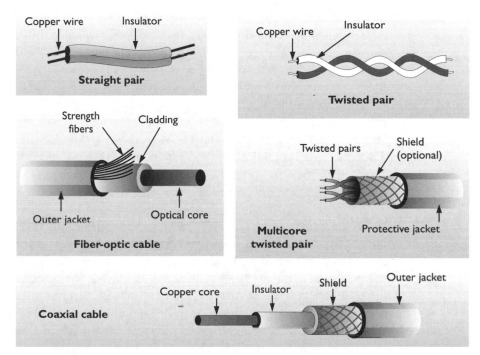

FIGURE 1-11

Common cable types used in computer installations

surrounding objects and the atmosphere. This interference is technically referred to as *electromagnetic interference (EMI)* and is commonly known as "noise." *Shielded cables* have an extra wire or Mylar covering that can help protect signals from EMI. Cables without this type of protection are called *unshielded*. Both straight-pair and twisted-pair cables are available in shielded and unshielded form. Coaxial cables are shielded. *Fiber-optic cables*, which transmit light signals, are unaffected by EMI, so they do not have noise shields. However, a fiber cable does have a physical covering or sheath to protect it from physical damage.

The specific names of peripheral cables are almost as varied as the types of peripherals themselves. Some devices use nonstandardized cables that cannot be used by other devices. The cable types just discussed are examined in more detail in Chapter 7. Other features of cables, such as their use of duplex mode and maximum effective length, are discussed throughout the book as they pertain to different components and hardware configurations.

Cable Orientation

Many computer cables are *bidirectional*, meaning that signals can travel in either direction along the cable. In these cases, the orientation of the cable between devices may not be a limiting factor. For example, when you plug a modem into a phone jack, there is no wrong way to orient the cable; either connector can plug into either the modem or the jack. This is also true for network cables. You can try this by following the steps in Exercise 1-8. Most bidirectional cables will provide different types of connectors on the two ends if they must be oriented a certain way.

Other cables, however, are strictly *unidirectional*, such as the cable that attaches a monitor to the computer. This type of cable transmits signals in one direction only (for example, from the computer to the monitor) and not in the opposite direction. The function of a unidirectional component is entirely dependent on the proper cable orientation. Fortunately, most, if not all, of the unidirectional cables you will use as a technician will have a different type of connector on each end. This makes it physically more difficult to connect a cable backward.

The orientation of the cable connector in the device's port is another important factor. In most cases, the wires in a cable must be lined up properly with the pins in a device's port. For example, if you were to attach a modem's cable upside-down in the phone jack, the modem would not work. Again, almost all cables for which port orientation is a factor are designed so that they can be physically connected only one way. Some cables, however, are not limited by port orientation. Coaxial cables, for example, have only one internal wire that is "twisted" into place. In this case, there is no way to attach the cable upside-down.

EXERCISE 1-8

Experimenting with Cable Orientation

1. On the modem, locate the port that attaches to the wall outlet (not the port that attaches to a phone).

2. Plug one end of the modem cable into this port, and plug the other end of the cable into the phone jack in the wall.

3. Test the modem to verify that it works.

4. Unplug the cable from both the modem and the wall.

5. Reverse the cable: plug the end that was originally plugged into the modem into the phone jack, and vice versa.

Pin Connections

There is a great variety of connector and port types among peripheral devices, and different devices use different cable/connector combinations. For example, the straight-pair cable for a printer has a different connector than the straight-pair cable for a monitor. It is important to make the distinction between a connector and a port. Typically, the term *connector* refers to the end of a cable, and *port* refers to its place of attachment on a device. Even though we refer to connectors and ports bear in mind that the port is also a connector. Additionally, the distinction between male and female should be made here. A *male* port or connector has pins, and a *female* port or connector has holes. Some common connector types are described in the following sections.

DB-9

DB-type connectors can be identified by their trapezoidal shape (see Figure 1-12). In fact, the *D* in *DB* stands for *D-shell*, a reference to the connector's shape. A DB-9 connector has 9 connections in 2 rows (5 in one row and 4 in the other row). DB-9 ports on the computer are typically used for either video or serial communications. Almost all computers include at least one and usually two or more male DB-9 ports at the back. These ports are most commonly used for serial devices such as mice and external modems.

DB-25

DB-25 connectors are D-shell connectors with 25 pins or holes, with 13 in one row and 12 in the other. Most computers include one or two DB-25 connectors for devices such as printers and scanners. Female DB-25 connectors are typically used for parallel communications; the male ports are used for serial communications. An example of a DB-25 connector is shown in Figure 1-12.

FIGURE 1-13

RJ connectors
and cable shown
on a modem card
(left side)

RJ-11

Registered jack (RJ) connectors are rectangular shaped and have a locking clip on one side (see Figure 1-13). The number designation of an RJ connector refers to its size rather than to the number of wire connections within it. RJ-11 connectors contain either two or four wires and are used to attach phone cables to modems and to phone jacks in the wall.

RJ-45

RJ-45 connectors are larger than RJ-11 connectors and contain eight wires. RJ-45 connectors are most commonly used to attach twisted-pair cables to network cards. The RJ-45 connection looks similar to the example of an RJ-11 in Figure 1-13 only wider.

BNC

The acronym BNC is the subject of some debate. Depending on the source you use, you will find that it possibly stands for broadband network connector, Bayonet Neill-Concelman, Bayonet Neill connector, British Naval Connector, Bayonet Navy Connector, Bayonet Nut Connection. There seems to be no real consensus as to the origin of its name. What matters is that you can recognize one when you see it.

BNC connectors are used to attach coaxial cables to BNC ports. As you can see in Figure 1-14, the cable connector is round and has a twist-lock mechanism to keep the cable in place. BNC connectors have a protruding pin that corresponds to a hole in the port. BNC connectors are commonly used in computer networks but cannot connect your television to the cable outlet in the wall.

A BNC
connector
and port

PS/2 and Mini-DIN

DIN connectors get their name from *Deutsche Industrinorm*, which is Germany's standards organization. Most (but not all) DIN connectors are round with a circle or semicircle of pins (see Figure 1-15). The mini-DIN connector, or more accurately, the mini-DIN-6 connector, gets its name from the fact that it is smaller than a customary DIN-6 keyboard connector. Mini-DIN connectors are most commonly used for PS/2 style (Personal System/2) mice and keyboards. For this reason, mini-DIN connectors are often referred to as PS/2 connectors.

IEEE-1394

IEEE (Institute of Electrical and Electronics Engineers) is a standards organization. IEEE-1394 is a computer bus standard that supports very high speeds for external devices. IEEE-1394 (also called FireWire) supports many of the same features as USB (described earlier).

Two mini-DIN
connectors used
for mice and
keyboards

FIGURE 1-16

An IEEE 1394 or
FireWire cable
and connector

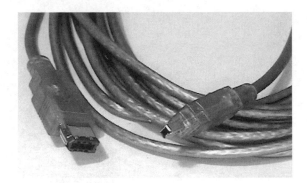

IEEE-1394 connectors are slightly smaller than DB-15 monitor connectors and
contain two sockets. Each socket is round and contains 6 wires. The connector is
roughly rectangular, with one rounded side to ensure proper orientation in the port
(see Figure 1-16).

USB

Because there are two types of USB (slow and fast), there are two types of USB cable.
Each of these has a unique connector to ensure that only the proper cable type is
attached to a slow or fast USB port. A typical USB connector is shown in Figure 1-17.

Serial vs. Parallel

Another important characteristic of an external peripheral is its method of
communication. Serial and parallel communications differ in their speed, transfer
modes, and control signals.

FIGURE 1-17

A USB connector

Serial Communications

Serial communications are most notably distinguished by the fact that they transfer data one bit at a time (in series). Serial communications implement Recommended Standard-232 (RS-232), which defines the connection methods for serial devices. For this reason, serial ports are sometimes referred to as *RS-232 ports*.

Serial communications can be either *synchronous*, in which data is sent in a continuous stream, or *asynchronous*, in which data is sent in intermittent bursts. In synchronous serial communications, the stream of data never stops. When there is no "real" data to send, the devices send "dummy" bits to remain synchronized with one another. This constant activity keeps the devices ready to receive real data.

Asynchronous data is intermittent, so it is accompanied by start and stop bits that indicate the beginning and end of a data stream. This system helps the receiving device distinguish real data from line noise. Most serial devices, such as serial mice and modems, use asynchronous communications.

Synchronous communications are usually driven by a clock or other timing signal that controls communications. The PCI computer bus is an example of a synchronous environment. Each of the controllers that are attached to the bus synchronizes to the other device on the bus. Even though the controller may communicate or control an external device such as a mouse, network, or asynchronous bus, the controllers communicate with each other using the clock speed of the bus. A clearly defined protocol and communications method is established to allow high-speed communications to occur in an orderly manner.

Parallel Communications

Parallel communications are defined by the fact that they can transmit more than one data bit at a time. This results in faster data transfers for large packets. Imagine an elevator that could carry only one person at a time. It would take eight trips to get eight people from one floor to another using this elevator. An elevator that could carry eight people at once could do the same thing in only one trip. The same principle is true for parallel communication. A comparison between a serial connection and a parallel connection is shown in Figure 1-18. In the serial connection, there is more than wire being used to carry signals. The important thing to remember is that each wire functions separately from the others in the serial connection, where the data connection in the parallel occurs simultaneously on each data wire.

Most data inside the computer is transmitted in parallel—one bit on each of several physical wires. Many external devices—including printers and scanners, which typically receive or send large amounts of data—also use parallel

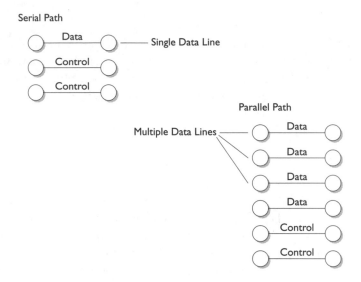

FIGURE 1-18

A comparison of
the wiring of a
serial DB-9
connection and a
parallel DB-25
connection

communications. The term #-bit (8-bit, 16-bit, 32-bit, and 64-bit) is used
commonly in the computer industry to refer to the number of data bits that
can be sent at once (in parallel) between two devices.

SCENARIO & SOLUTION

Why do mice use serial communications?	Because they tend to send intermittent, small bursts of data.
Why do printers tend to use parallel communications?	Because parallel communications are faster at transmitting the large data packets typically sent to printers.
How can I tell a serial port from a parallel port at the back of the computer?	Serial ports tend to be male and parallel ports tend to be female.

Parallel devices must be synchronized with each other to properly send or receive data. To achieve synchronization, the devices carry out a *handshake routine*, in which the speed and rules of communication are agreed on before any data is transmitted.

CERTIFICATION SUMMARY

Common computer components include the processor, memory, storage devices, and input and output devices. All of these devices have specific functions, and your familiarity with them will help you to quickly determine when a component must be upgraded or replaced. Your knowledge of proper installation procedures will allow you to install or replace devices without causing physical damage or interfering with the proper function of other devices.

In addition to physical installation, many devices require system resources, such as IRQ and I/O addresses, to function properly. Because no two devices can share a resource, you must be very familiar with their standard assignments so that you do not cause resource conflicts and so you can resolve them when they occur.

Another important factor in device operation and installation is the way that the device is attached to the computer. There are many types of computer cables, including straight-pair, twisted-pair, and coaxial. Cables can be attached to devices using a variety of connectors. Fortunately, most devices come with the proper cable or connector and fit only one way on the device. A good knowledge of connectors will help you quickly distinguish one cable from another and determine which devices can use it.

TWO-MINUTE DRILL

Here are some of the key points from each certification objective in Chapter 1.

System Modules

❑ All components, including external peripherals, are connected to each other via the system board.

❑ The computer's processor uses RAM as a temporary storage space for its processes and uses the system BIOS to communicate with other devices in the system.

❑ Data is stored permanently on storage devices such as hard disks, floppy disks, and CD-ROMs, each of which offer different capacities and portability.

❑ Portable systems tend to use nonstandardized components or modules. Portable and many desktop systems use LCD or FPD displays.

Adding and Removing Field-Replaceable Modules

❑ Always turn the computer off and follow ESD procedures before installing or removing a computer component.

❑ The red stripe on a drive ribbon must be aligned with pin 1 on the port.

❑ When installing the P8 and P9 power connectors, place the two black wires together.

IRQs, DMAs, and I/O Addresses

❑ The processor uses I/O addresses to locate and communicate with devices, and devices use IRQs to get the attention of the processor.

❑ Some devices use DMA channels to directly read from or write to RAM.

❑ No two devices can share an IRQ or I/O address.

Peripheral Ports, Cabling, and Connectors

❑ Common electronic cables include straight-pair, twisted-pair, and coaxial.

❑ Most cables are physically configured to fit only one way in a port or device.

❑ Common connectors include DB-9, DB-25, RJ-11, RJ-45, BNC, DIN-5and mini-DIN-6.

❑ Serial devices transmit one bit at a time; parallel devices transmit more than one bit at a time.

SELF TEST

The following questions will help you measure your understanding of the material presented in this chapter. Read all of the choices carefully because there might be more than one correct answer. Choose all correct answers for each question.

System Modules

1. Which of the following connections can be used to attach a Pentium 4 processor to the motherboard?

   A. PGA

   B. Slot 1

   C. PGA2

   D. SEC

2. Which of the following most accurately describes a function of the computer's cache memory?

   A. To store instructions used by currently running applications

   B. To provide temporary storage of data that is required to complete a task

   C. To anticipate the processor's data requests and make that data available for fast retrieval

   D. To store a device's most basic operating instructions

3. You are planning to upgrade your computer's display to one that can use 256-color mode and has a resolution of at least 1024×768. Which type(s) of display can fulfill these requirements?

   A. Any type of CRT

   B. Any analog CRT

   C. VGA and SVGA

   D. SVGA

4. Each time you start your computer, it asks you for the proper time. Which component will you most likely need to replace?

   A. The BIOS

   B. The system timer

   C. The CMOS battery

   D. The processor

5. Which statement most accurately describes the relationship between the computer's BIOS and CMOS?

   A. The CMOS uses information stored in the BIOS to set computer configurations, such as the boot sequence, keyboard status, and hard drive settings.

B. The BIOS configuration settings are stored on the CMOS chip so that they are not lost when the computer is turned off.

C. The CMOS uses information stored in the BIOS to communicate with the computer's components.

D. They perform the same functions, but the BIOS is found only in newer computers.

Adding and Removing Field-Replaceable Modules

6. Which procedures should you follow to properly install a single hard drive in a computer system?

A. Install the hard drive in the bay closest to the motherboard and align the cable's red stripe with pin 1.

B. Use the manufacturer's label to identify the top side of the drive and attach the drive to the ribbon connector closest to the motherboard.

C. Align the cable's red stripe with pin 1 and attach the hard drive to the end of the cable.

D. Use the manufacturer's label to identify pin 1 and install the drive in the bay furthest from the motherboard.

7. You have just installed a new power supply, but the computer doesn't seem to be getting any power. Which of the following should you do?

A. Ensure that the P8 and P9 connectors are attached to the motherboard with the black wires together.

B. Ensure that the P8 and P9 connectors are attached to each other with the black wires at opposite ends.

C. Ensure that the red stripe on the cable is aligned with pin 1 on the motherboard.

D. Ensure that the P8 and P9 connectors are properly attached to the hard drive.

8. You are instructing a computer user in the proper removal of a PGA processor, and you tell her to raise the lever on the side of the socket. What should she expect the processor to do when the lever is raised?

A. The processor will slowly rise out of the socket in correspondence with the raising of the lever.

B. The processor will "pop" upward, out of the socket.

C. The processor will fall to a 45-degree angle with the motherboard.

D. Nothing or very little movement in the processor should be noted.

9. The "D" in the acronym DIMM refers to:

A. "Direct," the type of communication between the DIMM and the processor

B. "Dual," the number of connector rows on the DIMM

    C. "Double," the number of sides on the DIMM that contain memory chips

    D. "DIP," the type of memory chips embedded on the DIMM

10. Which of the following statements about a portable's display panel is true?

    A. Most passive matrix displays use TFT technology.

    B. Matrix displays use CRT technology.

    C. Active matrix displays have better resolution than passive matrix displays.

    D. Older display panels use CRT technology, and newer display panels use LCD technology.

IRQs, DMAs, and I/O Addresses

11. Which of the following most accurately describes the function of I/O addresses?

    A. They are used by the processor to identify and communicate with components.

    B. They are used by components to identify themselves when they communicate with the processor.

    C. They are used by components to interrupt the processor.

    D. They are used by components for direct access to the information in RAM.

12. Which term refers to an IRQ that cannot be ignored by the processor?

    A. Maskable

    B. Nonmaskable

    C. Cascaded

    D. Noncascaded

13. You are planning to install a sound card on a Pentium computer that uses both hard drive controllers and whose only noncritical peripheral is a serial mouse. According to the standard assignments, which IRQ(s) is (are) available to be assigned to the sound card?

    A. IRQs 3 and 4

    B. IRQs 4 and 15

    C. IRQs 7 and 13

    D. IRQs 10 and 12

14. A Pentium computer uses a serial mouse and one hard drive controller. From this information only, what can you tell about this computer?

    A. IRQs 12 and 13 are both in use.

    B. IRQ 13 is in use.

    C. IRQs 12, 13, and 15 are all available.

    D. IRQs 12 and 15 are both in use.

15. A Pentium 4 computer has a printer connected to the parallel (LPT) port, a serial mouse, and an external modem. All of these devices use standard IRQ settings. The only other noncritical peripheral in the system is a sound card that works intermittently. Which is a likely problem with this system?

    A. You should verify and change the IRQ assignment of the sound card to IRQ 5.
    B. Sound cards are incompatible with Pentium 4–based systems.
    C. You should unplug the modem, as it is conflicting with the sound card.
    D. The sound card problem is unrelated to IRQ assignment.

Peripheral Ports, Cabling, and Connectors

16. In telling a customer how to properly attach a cable modem to a wall outlet, which of the following are you most likely to mention?

    A. The larger cable connection goes in the outlet and the smaller connection attaches to the modem.
    B. The cable is attached to the modem with the retention tab at the bottom.
    C. The connector will fit only one way into the wall outlet.
    D. The modem uses a coaxial cable that is bi-directional.

17. What differentiates a male connector from a female connector?

    A. Male connectors have pins; female connectors have holes.
    B. A female connector has a shape similar to the universal symbol for "female."
    C. Female connectors are attached to the computer; male connectors are attached to peripheral devices.
    D. Male connectors have an uneven number of wires; female connectors have an even number.

18. Which type of connector can be identified by its rectangular shape, retaining tab, and flat copper connections?

    A. DB
    B. RJ
    C. BNC
    D. Mini-DIN

19. Which of the following ports are *not* used by mice?

    A. DB
    B. Mini-DIN
    C. PS/2
    D. BNC

20. You are planning to buy a printer for your computer. Which of the following factors should you consider when making your choice?

    A. Parallel communications are faster than serial communications.

    B. Serial communications result in fewer errors than parallel communications.

    C. Parallel communications are compatible with more computer types than serial communications.

    D. Serial communications devices are easier to configure than parallel communications devices.

LAB QUESTION

You turned on the computer, used the mouse to open a word processing program, then used the keyboard to create a document. Next, you saved and printed the document. Using the information in Chapter 1, provide as much detail as you can about the resulting processes that took place in the computer.

SELF TEST ANSWERS

System Modules

1. ☑ **C.** A Pentium 4 processor can be attached to the motherboard using a PGA2 pin grid array. PGA2 uses a ZIF (zero insertion force) type socket. ZIF is a socket design used for PGA-form processors. A ZIF socket includes a lever that grips and releases the processor so that it can be easily inserted or removed.

   ☒ **A.** PGA, is incorrect because it refers to a type of processor chip design, a pin grid array. In fact, the 80486 processor *is* a PGA chip. PGA chips are attached to ZIF or LIF sockets on the motherboard. **B,** Slot-1, and **D,** SEC, are incorrect because they refer to chip/connection forms for Pentium II and similar processors. Pentium II and Pentium III processors are SEC cartridges and are attached to the motherboard using a connector called Slot-1.

2. ☑ **C.** A function of the computer's cache is to anticipate the processor's data requests and make that data available for fast retrieval. Cache memory can be accessed faster than regular RAM, so the more data that can be stored there, the faster the computer will run overall. The computer's cache includes a cache controller that is able to anticipate the processor's data needs, retrieve them from regular RAM, and store them in the faster cache memory chips.

   ☒ **A,** to store instructions used by currently running applications, and **B,** to provide temporary storage of data that is required to complete a task, are incorrect because these are both functions of RAM memory. **D,** to store a device's most basic operating instructions, is incorrect because this is a function of a device's ROM memory.

3. ☑ **D.** You can use an SVGA display to use 256-color mode with a 1024×768 resolution. SVGA monitors can display around 16 million colors at once (32-bit true color) and have a maximum resolution of 1280×024.

   ☒ **A,** any type of CRT, is incorrect because this would include CGA, EGA, and VGA monitors. CGA and EGA monitors can display only 16 colors at once, at resolutions of 160×100 and 640×350, respectively. VGA monitors have a maximum resolution of 640×480. **B,** any analog CRT, and **C,** VGA or SVGA, are both incorrect because they refer to VGA technology (VGA is a type of analog monitor).

4. ☑ **C.** The CMOS battery is most likely not working properly. The computer's CMOS is responsible for retaining computer settings, such as the time, BIOS settings, and boot sequence. The CMOS can retain these settings when the computer is turned off because it is attached to a CMOS battery. When this battery starts to get low, the CMOS is no longer able to keep its settings.

☒   **A,** the BIOS, is incorrect because its function is to translate communications between the processor and other computer components. The CMOS battery ensures the BIOS settings are not lost when the power is turned off. The BIOS settings and the time are both retained because of the CMOS battery but otherwise are not related to one another. **B,** the system timer, is incorrect because its function is to synchronize the timing of processes in the computer. It works like a metronome, setting the speed of the computer, and is unrelated to the "real" time. **D,** the processor, is also incorrect. The processor is the brain of the computer, and although it might be responsible for incorporating the time information into other tasks, it does not keep track of the time, even while the computer is turned on.

5.   ☑   **B.** The BIOS configuration settings are stored on the CMOS chips so that they are not lost when the computer is turned off. The CMOS is attached to a small battery, which allows it to retain information when there is no power. When the computer is turned on, the BIOS retrieves its settings from the CMOS. **A,** the CMOS uses information stored in the BIOS to set computer configurations, is incorrect because it is the CMOS, not the BIOS, that stores computer configurations.
☒   **C,** the CMOS communicates with computer components based on the information stored in the BIOS, is incorrect because this is the opposite of the actual relationship between the BIOS and CMOS. It is the BIOS that communicates with components, based on information stored in the CMOS. **D,** the BIOS is a newer version of the CMOS, is incorrect because the functions of the BIOS and CMOS are different, and both are found in all computers, old and new.

Adding and Removing Field-Replaceable Modules

6.   ☑   **C.** When installing a hard drive, align the cable's red stripe with pin 1 and attach the hard drive to the end of the cable. The red stripe on any ribbon cable exists solely to identify the pin 1 connection. Use it to ensure that the cable is properly oriented. Because you are installing a single drive, it must be attached to the connector at the end of the ribbon cable.
☒   **A,** install the hard drive in the bay closest to the motherboard and align the cable's red stripe with pin 1, is incorrect. The drive's bay is simply a compartment in the chassis used to hold the hard drive in place. If there is more than one drive bay, the hard drive can be attached to either one. **B,** use the manufacturer's label to identify the top side of the drive and attach the drive to the ribbon connector closest to the motherboard, is also incorrect. It is good practice to use the label to identify the top of the drive, but the drive itself must be attached to the cable connector that is furthest from, not closest to, the motherboard. **D,** use the label to identify pin 1 and install the drive in the bay furthest from the motherboard, is incorrect. Although the manufacturer's label on the top of the drive can sometimes be used to indicate pin 1, this is rarely the case. Furthermore, as discussed, the drive's installation in one bay or another is not a factor in the drive's operation.

7. ☑ **A.** When installing a power supply, ensure that the P8 and P9 connectors are attached to the motherboard with the black wires together. Although each (P8 or P9) connector can fit only one way onto the motherboard, it is physically possible to connect them in the wrong ports. That is, the P8 connector will fit in the P9 port, and vice versa. When this is the case, the computer will not work. To ensure that the connectors are in the proper ports, place them beside each other so that the black wires of the P8 connector are beside the black wires of the P9 connector.

☒ **B,** ensure that the P8 and P9 connectors are attached to each other with the black wires at opposite ends, and **D,** ensure that the P8 and P9 connectors are properly attached to the hard drive, are both incorrect. The P8 and P9 connectors are attached to the motherboard, not to each other or to the hard drive. **C** is incorrect because it states that you should ensure that the red stripe is aligned with pin 1 on the motherboard. This procedure applies to the installation of hard, floppy, and CD-ROM drives, not power supplies.

8. ☑ **D.** When the user raises the lever on the side of the processor's socket, the processor should either not move or only slightly move. If the processor's socket has a lever, it must be a ZIF socket. The function of the lever is to grip and release the processor's pins. When the lever is raised, the grip on the pins will be released, but the processor itself should not move. **A,** the processor will slowly rise out of the socket in correspondence with the raising of the lever is incorrect because the lever's position, not the insertion of the processor in the socket, determines the grip on the processor's pins.

☒ **B,** the processor will "pop" upward out of the socket, is incorrect because this refers to the action of a memory DIMM when the retaining tabs are released. **C,** the processor will fall to a 45-degree angle with the motherboard, is incorrect because this refers to the action of a memory SIMM when the retaining tabs are released.

9. ☑ **B.** The "D" in DIMM refers to "dual"—the number of connector rows on the DIMM. That is, a dual inline memory module has two rows of connectors on the bottom.

☒ **A,** "direct" is incorrect, and in fact, there is no communication type known as "direct." **C,** "double," the number of sides on the DIMM that contain memory chips, is incorrect because DIMMs can have memory chips on both sides or on only one side. **D,** "DIP," is incorrect because, although it's true that DIP chips are embedded on the DIMM, the "D" stands for "dual," not "DIP."

10. ☑ **C.** Active displays have better resolution than passive displays. Most portables use LCD displays, which can be either passive or active matrix. Active matrix displays are newer and incorporate a technology that allows them to provide more colors, better resolution, and a smoother display of moving objects.

☒ **A,** most passive matrix displays use TFT technology is incorrect because TFT technology is used in active, not passive matrix displays. **B,** they use CRT technology, is incorrect.

Although portables can be connected to CRT monitors, the portable's display panel, which is integrated with the portable, is an LCD display. **D,** older display panels use CRT technology and newer display panels use LCD technology is incorrect, and in fact, most display panels use LCD technology and none of them uses CRT technology.

IRQs, DMAs, and I/O Addresses

11. ☑ **A.** I/O addresses are used by the processor to identify and communicate with components. When the computer is started, information about each device is placed in a specified range in RAM memory. When the processor needs to communicate with a device, it uses that device's I/O address in RAM to retrieve instructions on how to communicate with it.

    ☒ **B and C** are incorrect because they both suggest that I/O addresses are used by components to either identify themselves during communication or to interrupt the processor. These are, in fact, functions of IRQs, not I/O addresses. **D,** they are used by components for direct access to the information in RAM, is incorrect because this is the function of DMA channels.

12. ☑ **B.** The term "nonmaskable" refers to an IRQ that cannot be ignored by the processor. Most IRQs can be temporarily ignored, but some are used to halt the processor during certain error conditions, to prevent loss or corruption of data. Nonmaskable IRQs are typically used to warn the processor of a parity (data transfer) error. The processor must stop and deal with the error before it can continue with other processes.

    ☒ **A,** maskable, is incorrect because this term is used to refer to IRQs that can be ignored (masked) by the processor. IRQs 0–15 are all maskable. **C,** cascaded, is incorrect because this term refers to the secondary IRQ controller's use of IRQ 2 to provide access to IRQs 8–15. **D,** noncascaded, is incorrect because this is not a valid term.

13. ☑ **D.** IRQs 10 and IRQ 12 are available. One key to this answer is the fact that the computer's only noncritical peripheral is a serial mouse. Because the computer uses a serial mouse, IRQ 12 (which is typically reserved for a PS/2 mouse) is not in use, so it is available. Furthermore, IRQ 10 is typically available for assignment to noncritical peripherals. Because there are no other noncritical peripherals in the system, IRQ 10 is available for use.

    ☒ **A,** IRQs 3 and 4, is incorrect because the serial mouse must use the resources of the COM port to which it is attached. If the serial mouse is attached to COM1 or COM3, it will use IRQ 4. If it is attached to COM2 or COM4, it will use IRQ 3. This means that IRQ 3 *and* IRQ 4 cannot both be available. **B,** IRQs 4 and 15, is incorrect because this system uses its secondary hard drive controller. When in use, this controller is assigned IRQ 15. **C,** IRQs 7 and 13, is incorrect because IRQ 7 is assigned to the primary parallel port (LPT1) and IRQ 13 is assigned to the math coprocessor.

14. ☑ **B.** IRQ 13 is in use. This computer is a Pentium, which means it has a math coprocessor. The math coprocessor uses IRQ 13.

☒ **A,** IRQs 12 and 13 are both in use, and **D,** IRQs 12 and 15 are both in use, are incorrect. IRQ 13 is, in fact, in use by the math coprocessor. However, recall that this computer uses a serial mouse. Because there is no PS/2 mouse in this system, IRQ 12 is available. In addition, because the computer uses only one hard drive controller, IRQ 15 is available. (As an aside, although IRQs 12 and 15 might be assigned to peripheral devices, you cannot determine that from the information given in the question.) **C,** IRQs 12, 13, and 15 are all available, is incorrect because IRQ 13 is being used by the math coprocessor.

15. ☑ **A.** The sound card may have an IRQ conflict with another device on the system. Resetting it to the original or default settings may fix this problem. If that does not fix the problem, a defective sound card is highly likely.

☒ **B** is incorrect as the math coprocessor is an integral part of the Pentium 4 processor and would not work if an IRQ conflict existed with another device. **C,** you should unplug the modem, is incorrect because the modem is external and is using the COM port for the IRQ. The modem was not reported as a problem and is such is probably working correctly. **D,** the sound card problem is unrelated to IRQ assignment, is incorrect because the intermittent sound card problem is usually indicative of an IRQ problem.

Peripheral Ports, Cabling and Connectors

16. ☑ **D.** You are most likely to mention that the modem uses a coaxial cable because all the other statements are incorrect. Cable modems use the same cable that your television does, and they plug into the same type of wall outlet and are bidirectional.

☒ **A, B,** and **C** are all incorrect because these are not properties of a coaxial cable. Coaxial cables have the same type of connector on both ends, either of which can be attached to the modem or wall outlet. The connector is round and contains only one wire. The connector is twisted into place, so there is no wrong orientation of the connector in the port. Finally, the locking mechanism on a coaxial cable is an outer ring that is twisted into place, not a tab on one side (as in an RJ connector).

17. ☑ **A.** Male connectors have pins; female connectors have sockets. Pins usually stick out from the interior of the connector and are mated with the receiver or socket in the connector.

☒ **B, C,** and **D,** which make reference to the connector's shape, location of attachment, and number of wires, are all incorrect. Connector shapes, attachment locales, and number of wires are all unrelated to the characteristic of having either pins or holes.

18. ☑ **B.** The RJ connector can be identified by its rectangular shape, retaining tab, and flat copper connections. RJ connectors are often used in network and analog modem connections.

☒ **A,** DB, is incorrect because this type of connector is trapezoidal and has no copper connectors or retaining tab. **C,** BNC, and **D,** mini-DIN, are incorrect because they are both round.

19. ☑ **D.** Mice do not use BNC connectors. BNC connectors are used by coaxial cables and are designed for network or modem connections.

☒ **A,** DB, is incorrect because this type of connector is used by serial mice. **B,** Mini-DIN, and **C,** PS/2, are incorrect because PS/2 mice use a mini-DIN connector, which is often referred to as a PS/2 connector.

20. ☑ **A.** Parallel communications are faster than serial communications. This is because parallel communications support the transfer of multiple bits at a time, whereas serial communications are marked by the transfer of one bit at a time. Most printers are parallel due to the large amounts of data that they are sent by the computer.

☒ **B,** serial communications result in fewer errors than parallel communications, is incorrect because parallel and serial communications differ in their methods of data transfer, not in their reliability or error rates. **C,** parallel communications are compatible with more computer types than serial communications, is incorrect because all computers use both serial and parallel communications. **D,** serial communications devices are easier to configure than parallel communications devices, is also incorrect. These communications types refer to *data* transfer methods, not different device types or configurations. In fact, some devices, such as printers and scanners, are available in either parallel or serial versions.

LAB ANSWER

When you turned on the computer, the processor initiated the BIOS. The BIOS retrieved settings about the computer's components from the CMOS, where they were stored when the power was turned off last. The BIOS used these settings to perform a POST, which checked for the presence and function of critical system components. The BIOS then searched the hard drive for an operating system and handed it control of the computer. Throughout this entire operation, the BIOS was responsible for intercepting and translating communications between the processor and the other devices, and the processor used the video adapter's I/O address to send it data about what to display on the monitor.

When you opened the word processor, your mouse used serial communication to send an IRQ signal to gain the attention of the processor (IRQ 3 or 4 if it was a serial mouse; IRQ 12 if it was a PS/2 mouse). The processor used the I/O address of the display adapter to display the movement of the mouse across the screen and sent a message to the hard drive to retrieve the selected application.

When the hard drive found the appropriate information, it gave the data to the processor using either IRQ 14 or 15, depending on whether it was a primary or secondary hard drive. Many of the files necessary to run the application were stored in RAM for faster access by the processor. The cache controller, judging by the application, was able to predict which information the processor was likely to need and placed that information into the cache memory, from which the processor could retrieve it even more quickly.

When you typed the document, the keyboard used IRQ 1 to send the data to the processor. When you saved the document, the processor used the hard drive's I/O address to instruct it to store the file. When you printed the document, the processor sent the request to the printer, most likely using parallel communication.

2

Installation, Configuration, and System Optimization

I n the previous chapter, you were introduced to common components and installation and configuration procedures. This chapter focuses on devices and configurations that are more specialized and slightly more complex.

First, the chapter discusses alternative hardware configurations, including how to use more than one hard drive in the system and how to set up a SCSI system. You will also learn about peripheral devices that require more complex installation and configuration procedures, including portable-specific components. Finally, you will learn about configurations that you can perform to optimize the performance of your desktop or portable system and keep it running smoothly.

CERTIFICATION OBJECTIVE 2.01

Installing and Configuring IDE Devices

Most computers use Integrated Drive Electronics (IDE) or AT Attachment (ATA) hard and CD-ROM drive systems. The relationship between IDE and ATA is that IDE drives are built using the ATA body of standards. The terms are therefore used interchangeably. The IDE family includes IDE and Enhanced IDE (EIDE) drives. Other drives based on the ATA standards include ATAPI (typically associated with CD-ROM drives), Fast-ATA, and Ultra-ATA. Because IDE drives are built on ATA technology, the term *IDE* is often used to refer to any non-SCSI drive type. (SCSI systems are discussed in Installing and Configuring SCSI later in the chapter.)

Because IDE drives are standardized, they can usually be recognized by the computer's BIOS. In the simplest cases, all that is needed to make a hard drive or a CD-ROM drive functional is to physically install it in the computer. However, some configurations are more complex. The following sections describe alternative drive installations, including how to configure and install multiple drives in a single system.

Master/Slave Configurations

The hard drive or CD-ROM drive controller's function is to receive commands to the drive and control the action of the drive itself. The technology incorporated in IDE and ATA devices allows one controller to take over the function of more than one drive. This means that you can install up to two drives on a single ribbon cable. This setup is called a *master/slave configuration* because one drive's controller directs the activities of both drives. It is important to note here that most computer systems can support a mixture of IDE and ATA drives.

To create a master/slave configuration, follow the steps in Exercise 2-1.

EXERCISE 2-1

Installing Master and Slave Hard Drives

1. Determine which drive will be the master (see the "Choosing a Master" From the Classroom for more information).

2. Locate the master/slave jumpers, which can be found on the bottom of the drive or, more commonly, on the end by the power and ribbon cable connectors. In Figure 2-1, the jumpers are located to the left of the power connector and the jumper settings are indicated by the standard settings information on the label.

3. Use the drive label information to determine which jumper settings to use for a master or a slave configuration.

4. Set this drive as a master using the jumper(s).

5. Using the procedure explained in Chapter 1, Exercise 1-2, physically install this drive on the end of the ribbon cable and secure it to an available drive bay.

6. Using the proper jumper setting, configure the second drive as a slave.

7. Install the second drive in the middle of the ribbon cable. Your hard drive setup should look similar to the one shown in Figure 2-2. Note the position of the hard drives on the ribbon cable.

FIGURE 2-1

The master/slave jumper set on a typical hard drive

FIGURE 2-2

The finished
installation of a
master/slave
configuration

It is important to note that, in most cases, a slave drive will work only if a master drive is present. That is, masters can function without slaves, but slaves cannot function without masters.

Most newer computers will detect the presence of a master/slave configuration

e x a m
w a t c h

The master drive must be set to the master jumper setting and be installed on the end of the ribbon cable.

The slave drive must be set to the slave jumper setting and be installed in the middle of the ribbon cable.

and name the drives appropriately: Typically, the master will be drive C, and the slave will be drive D. However, some older computers require you to perform a drive detection. In this case, when you start the computer, enter the CMOS settings program, as discussed in Chapter 1. Select the Auto-Detect or Detect Hard Drive option (these options might have slightly different names on different computers). This choice forces the BIOS to search all drive controller connections for the presence and configuration of hard or CD-ROM drives.

FROM THE CLASSROOM

Choosing a Master

How do you determine which drive should be the master and which should be the slave? In many cases, it doesn't matter which is which. That is, there is no real performance difference between master and slave drives. However, as with most computer configurations, there are some exceptions.

Some operating systems require that the hard drive containing the OS be configured as a master. This is important to note only if you are installing drives that already contain data. If you are installing new hard drives, you don't have to worry about this; simply load the OS on the master drive after the drives are installed.

When using a mixture of old and new hard drives within the same system, set the newer

drive as the master and the older drive as the slave. This setting is a good idea because newer drives can recognize and communicate with older drives, but the reverse isn't true. An older drive's controller will typically be unable to control the newer drive.

When using a hard drive and CD-ROM drive together in a master/slave configuration, always set the hard drive as the master and the CD-ROM as the slave because the CD-ROM's controller is unable to take control of the hard drive. Additionally, some (but not most) CD-ROM drives are designed to work as slaves, even when there is no master present, and they simply cannot be configured as master drives.

Devices per Channel

Most newer computers have two hard drive controllers. That is, the motherboard has connectors for two ribbon cables (see Figure 2-3). These controllers are termed *primary* and *secondary*. If there is only one drive present, it must be attached to the primary controller. An additional drive can be added as either a primary slave or a secondary master. It is important to note that although they are often referred to as *hard drive controllers*, these devices are not limited to controlling hard drives; they are also used to control CD-ROM drives.

To add a drive to the secondary controller, simply connect the drive to a ribbon cable and attach the ribbon cable to the secondary

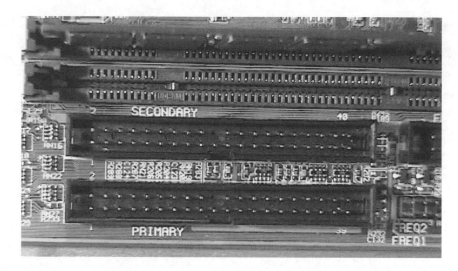

FIGURE 2-3

The primary and secondary controller ports on the system board

controller port on the motherboard, ensuring that the red stripe is aligned with pin 1. You will also of course need to connect a power cable to the drive. There is usually no noticeable performance advantage to configuring a second drive as a secondary master rather than as a primary slave. (See the "Choosing a Master" From the Classroom for a discussion on choosing the master or slave designation.)

As before, the primary master receives the first available drive letter, typically C. The remaining drives are lettered according to this order of priority: primary slave, secondary master, primary master.

on the
job

When you add or remove a drive to or from a multidrive system, the drives are automatically relettered so that no letters are skipped. For example, suppose a system includes drives C:, D:, and E:. If drive D: is removed, the E: drive will be relabeled D: the next time the computer is started. Windows operating systems also allow for a drive to be configured to hold a certain drive letter.

CERTIFICATION OBJECTIVE 2.02

Installing and Configuring SCSI Devices

Another technology standard is *Small Computer Systems Interface (SCSI)*, developed by the American National Standards Institute (ANSI). The SCSI standard applies to external devices such as printers, modems, scanners, and most other types of peripherals, and it supports internal devices such as hard and floppy drives.

SCSI systems differ from non-SCSI systems in several ways. To begin with, SCSI devices are all attached to and controlled by a SCSI controller. That is, all SCSI devices in the system are attached to the computer through the controller. The controller is actually an internal card that is installed on the motherboard. Complete the steps in Exercise 2-2 to install a SCSI controller card.

EXERCISE 2-2

Installing a SCSI Controller Card

1. Turn the computer off, remove the cover, and carry out proper ESD procedures as discussed in Chapter 4, Exercise 4-2.
2. Position the controller card upright over the appropriate expansion slot.
3. Place your thumbs along the top edge of the card and push straight down. If necessary, rock the card along its length (never side to side).
4. Secure the card to the chassis using the existing screw holes.

SCSI systems allow you to attach more devices to the computer than regular IDE systems do. IDE systems are limited to 4 drives, and the number of other devices you can attach is physically limited by the number of available expansions slots and external ports in the computer. By installing a SCSI system, you can attach 7, 15, or 31 additional devices in the computer, depending on the type of SCSI system you are using.

SCSI systems are typically much faster than non-SCSI (IDE) systems. However, SCSI systems have the disadvantage of being more expensive than IDE systems and more difficult to configure. In most cases, SCSI systems are used when speed or the ability to support a large number of devices is a priority. When cost and ease of use are factors, IDE systems are generally preferred. Currently, IDE systems are more prevalent than SCSI systems.

In all SCSI systems, the controller (sometimes called the SCSI host adapter) must be installed in the computer and assigned an IRQ and I/O address, just like any other expansion card. Other devices are attached to the controller in a *daisy-chain configuration*, in which each device attaches to the next in a long chain. Each external SCSI device has two ports: one port is used to receive the cable from the device before it in the chain, and one port is used to attach to the next device in the chain. Many internal SCSI devices will only have one port that requires a special cable for daisy chaining internal devices. Each SCSI device is allocated a special

SCSI ID rather than its own IRQ and I/O address. All communication between the computer and a SCSI device go through and are managed by the SCSI controller.

Types of SCSI Systems

Like many other computer standards, SCSI systems have evolved and improved over time. Newer SCSI standards are backward compatible with older standards, so older devices can typically be installed in newer systems. SCSI standards and their characteristics are described in the subsections that follow. Table 2-1 provides a quick reference to SCSI types and characteristics.

SCSI-1

The first SCSI standard, released in 1986, was simply named *SCSI*. It became known as *SCSI-1* only when the SCSI-2 standard was released. The SCSI-1 system has an 8-bit bus, meaning it can support up to eight devices (including the controller), and it supports speeds up to 5MBps. Unfortunately, SCSI-1 did not include standardized device commands, so many early SCSI devices were not compatible with each other.

The maximum cable length in a SCSI-1 system is 6 meters. This length refers to the entire length of the SCSI chain, not the distance between each device. The use of longer cables in the system can lead to device malfunctions due to signal interference.

TABLE 2-1	SCSI Types and Their Characteristics

Type	Bus Width	Max Throughput	Data Transfer
SCSI-1	8-bit	5MBps	SE
SCSI-2	8-bit	5MBps	SE or HVD
Fast SCSI-2	8-bit	10MBps	SE or HVD
Wide SCSI-2	16-bit	10MBps	SE or HVD
Fast Wide SCSI-2	16-bit	20MBps	SE or HVD
Double Wide SCSI-2	32-bit	40MBps	SE or HVD
Ultra SCSI-3 (Fast-20)	8-bit	20MBps	SE or HVD
Wide Ultra SCSI-3	16-bit	40MBps	SE or HVD
Ultra-2 SCSI (Fast-40)	8-bit	40MBps	HVD or LVD
Wide Ultra-2 SCSI	16-bit	80MBps	HVD or LVD
Ultra-3 (Fast-80 or Ultra 160)	16-bit	160MBps	LVD

SCSI-2

The *SCSI-2* standard, released in 1994, includes a standardized device command set and support for more devices. It also uses more sophisticated device termination (discussed later in the chapter) and supports *command queuing*, which is the ability to send more than one command to a single device at once.

The SCSI-2 standard also introduced the implementation of *differential* (specifically, *high-voltage differential*, or *HVD*) technology. This term refers to the method of data transfer. Regular SCSI data transfer, called *single-ended (SE) transfer*, uses one wire to transmit each data signal. Differential SCSI sends each data signal over a pair of wires in a manner that resists interference. Because differential SCSI is more resistant to interference, it can support much greater cable lengths than SE systems. SCSI-2 systems can use either regular or differential devices, but the two cannot exist on the same system.

The SCSI-2 standard includes several variants, so it can be the subject of some confusion. Simply put, there are five variants: SCSI-2, Fast SCSI-2, Wide SCSI-2, Fast Wide SCSI-2, and Double Wide SCSI-2. The main differences between these types are their bus widths and transmission speeds.

SCSI-2, like SCSI-1, supports an 8-bit bus and transmission speeds up to 5MBps and can support cable lengths up to 6 meters. *Fast SCSI-2* also has an 8-bit bus, but it supports double the speed (up to 10MBps) and has a maximum cable length of 3 meters for SE and 25 meters for HVD. *Wide SCSI-2* supports the traditional 5MBps, but because it has double the bus width (16 bits), its overall data transmission rate is 10MBps. *Fast Wide SCSI-2* combines the Fast and Wide technologies to yield a 16-bit bus and total transfer speed of 20MBps. Both Wide and Fast Wide SCSI-2 systems can support up to 16 devices, including the controller, and have a maximum cable length of 3 meters for SE and 25 meters for HVD.

The final variant, *Double Wide SCSI-2*, is essentially two Fast Wide systems in one. It supports a 32-bit bus and speeds up to 40MBps. However, this variant is rarely used and has been excluded from subsequent SCSI standards.

SCSI-3

The status of *SCSI-3* is a bit of a gray area. SCSCI-3 was approved as a standard in 1996 and has undergone many revisions and changes. The SCSI-3 standard is not really a single cohesive standard but a series of smaller standards rolled up into a single set of standards. The standard is being upgraded quarterly by the T10 committee. You can get information on the current standards and revisions of SCSI at www.t10.org. Therefore, SCSI-3 is not really a single cohesive standard. When people use the term *SCSI-3* or *SCSI-3 system*, they are referring to a system that incorporates the specifications that will be included in the final SCSI-3 standard.

A number of variants use the existing SCSI-3 specifications. *Ultra SCSI*, also called *Fast-20*, is an 8-bit system that can support speeds up to 20MBps. The Ultra

SCSI system's bus width can be doubled to 16 bits (Wide Ultra SCSI), resulting in a total throughput of 40MBps. Like SCSI-2, Ultra SCSI can use either SE or HVD technology. Ultra SCSI supports a maximum cable length of 3 meters if four or fewer devices are attached and 1.5 meters if more than four devices are attached.

Ultra-2 SCSI, also called *Fast-40*, provides a 40MBps data throughput on an 8-bit system and 80MBps on a 16-bit system (Wide Ultra-2 SCSI). Ultra-2 marks the first use of the *low-voltage differential (LVD)* specification and the removal of support for the SE specification. Components that use LVD technology require less power to operate and can operate at higher speeds. LVD also allows Ultra-2 SCSI systems to support cable lengths up to 12 meters.

Ultra-3 SCSI, also referred to as *Fast-80* or *Ultra160*, is the latest implementation of the SCSI-3 specifications. It is available only as a 16-bit system and supports a data throughput of 160MBps. Ultra-3 SCSI systems support LVD technology only and are the first to support up to 32 devices. Its maximum cable length is 12 meters.

Address/Termination Conflicts

Each device in a SCSI system must be correctly configured so that it can communicate with the controller but will not interfere with other SCSI devices in the system. If two devices share an ID, an address conflict will occur. The controller will not be able to distinguish the conflicting devices, and it is likely that *neither* device will work. Equally important is the proper termination of the SCSI system. Improper termination can result in the total or intermittent failure of *all* devices in the SCSI chain.

The following subsections describe the proper procedures for addressing and terminating SCSI devices so that conflicts do not occur.

Addressing SCSI Devices

Although computers can support more than one SCSI system, no two devices in a *single* SCSI chain can have the same SCSI ID address. Some SCSI devices are hard-wired to use one of two or three IDs only; others might be designed to use any available ID. If the device supports Plug and Play, the system will automatically assign it an available ID address. Other devices require manual address configuration. On some devices, this configuration is accomplished via jumpers on the device. Other devices can be assigned an ID address electronically using the device's ROM chip.

Some SCSI devices that require address assignment through jumpers will indicate, by label, which setting to use. However, in some cases, you will need to use the jumpers to emulate the binary equivalent of the device's ID. You must therefore be familiar with binary addressing. In short, binary uses a series of 0s and 1s to indicate the absence or presence of a value, respectively. These values double in number, starting with 1, at the rightmost digit. That is, the rightmost digit of a binary number is used to indicate the presence of a value of 1. The next digit to that is used to indicate a value of 2, the next to indicate 4, and so on.

Using this concept, the binary digit 101 indicates that the "4" value is present, the "2" value is absent and the "1" value is present. This binary's value is therefore 5 (4+1). The binary digit 1110 indicates 8 + 4 + 2. This equals 14.

Proper addressing can prove challenging, so it is best to work out an addressing "plan of action" before implementing addresses. For example, suppose a SCSI system will include a printer that *must* use ID 2, a scanner that can use either ID 2 or 4, and a modem that can use ID 4 or 5. Without knowing the address requirement of the printer, the scanner could be configured to use ID 2 and the modem to use ID 4. When it comes time to install the printer, you'll have to reconfigure the ID addresses of all other components.

The priority of ID addresses is also important. In 8-bit SCSI systems, addresses range from 0 to 7. Higher ID addresses indicate a higher priority. Because the SCSI controller is such an important part of the system, it is usually assigned ID 7.

on the

job

This section talks a lot about the priorities given to various SCSI IDs. If two devices try to send data at the same time, the device with the highest-priority ID will be allowed to transmit, and the other device will be made to wait. Incidentally, "at the same time" means within 0.24 microseconds!

For 16-bit and 32-bit systems, the priority of ID addresses is a bit more complex. In short, addresses increase in priority within each octet, and each successive octet has a lower overall priority than the one before it (see Figure 2-4). That is, IDs 8–15 have a lower priority than 0–7. In a 16-bit system, the order of priority, from lowest to highest, is 8, 9, 10…15, 0, 1, 2…7. Using the same principles for a 32-bit system, 7 has the highest priority, and 24 has the lowest.

exam

watch
Although you can expect some questions about SCSI IDs on the A+ exam, you don't have to memorize the priority of each address. Instead, make sure that you understand the concept behind the priority/address relationship, as explained. When you understand the reasons behind the numbering scheme, you will be able to figure out the priority of any SCSI ID address.

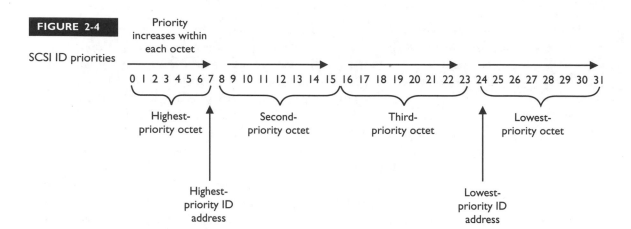

FIGURE 2-4

SCSI ID priorities

SCSI System Termination

Recall that devices in a SCSI system are chained together in a "one after the other" fashion. Signals to a device at the end of the chain must pass through all the devices in between. Because of this unique setup, special terminators, or *terminating resistors*, must be present to ensure signals at the end of the chain are absorbed rather than bounced back along the chain. In some cases, the resistor is shaped to fit into the unused second port on the last SCSI device in the chain. In other cases, the SCSI device will include an on-board terminator that is made active by using the appropriate jumper setting.

Essentially, any SCSI device that is not connected to two other devices must be at one end of the chain. If the SCSI chain is external, the last external device and the controller must be terminated. If the SCSI chain is internal only, the last internal device and the controller must be terminated. Finally, if the SCSI chain is a mixture of both internal and external devices, the last external and last internal devices on the chain are terminated.

on the Job

Many SCSI controllers include internal and external connectors for devices. It is recommended that a single SCSI controller not use both the internal and external connections. This may allow for more devices to be connected but may cause performance issues with the controller. SCSI controllers seem to work most efficiently when 7 or less devices are connected.

Cabling

SCSI systems employ a variety of cable types, depending on the SCSI type, device type, and whether the device is internal or external. Furthermore, each cable type might have a different connector.

8-Bit Systems

All 8-bit SCSI systems use 50-pin cables, called *A-cables*. Internal A-cables are 50-pin ribbon cables, which resemble IDE hard drive ribbon cables (Figure 2-5). External A-cables have either 50-pin Centronics connectors (for 5MBps systems) or 50-pin high-density connectors (for greater-than-10MBps systems). Figure 2-6 shows three different A-cable connector types.

16-Bit Systems

All 16-bit systems use 68-pin cables, also known as *P-cables*. Before the introduction of the P-cable, 16-bit systems used an A-cable/B-cable combination. Internal P-cables are ribbon cables with 68-pin connections, and external P-cables have a 68-pin high-density connector.

32-Bit Systems

Although 32-bit systems are no longer supported by new SCSI specifications, you might be required to work on an older one. All 32-bit systems use a 68-pin P-cable and a 68-pin Q-cable or one 110-pin L-cable.

The information in the "Installing and Configuring SCSI Devices" section has been compiled into Exercise 2-3. These are basic steps that you must perform whenever you install an external SCSI device. Read the steps carefully when performing them because some are performed differently or skipped altogether for some devices.

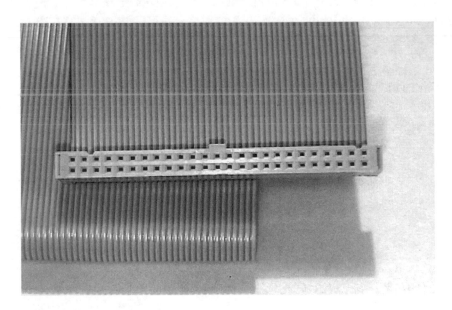

FIGURE 2-5

An internal SCSI A-cable connector

FIGURE 2-6

Internal and external A-cable connectors

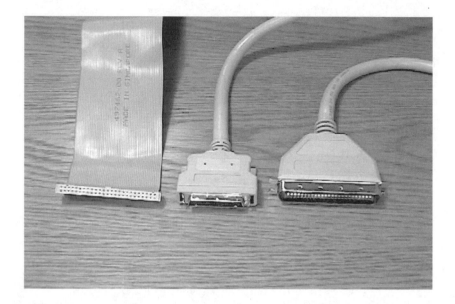

exam
watch

An even larger variety of SCSI cable and connector types are available than are discussed here. The list of possible combinations is beyond the scope of this book. The information that you will be expected to know for the A+ exam is the following: 8-bit systems use 50-pin cables, 16-bit systems use 68-pin cables, and 32-bit systems use 110-pin cables. Internal cables (for any pin size) have the same type of connector as hard drive ribbon cables. External cables (for any pin size) are typically Centronics connectors in older systems and high-density connectors in newer systems.

EXERCISE 2-3

Installing External SCSI Devices

1. **Attach the device to the chain.** If the new device will be the last in the chain, use its cable to attach it to the device that is currently last in the chain. If the device will be between two existing devices, disconnect them from each other and attach them both to the new device.

2. **Terminate the SCSI chain.** Perform this step only if the new device is at the end of the chain. If the device has an on-board terminator, select the proper jumper setting to enable it. If not, place a terminator plug in the unused port on the device.

3. **Set the SCSI ID.** If this is a Plug-and-Play device, the ID will be assigned automatically. Simply restart the computer and skip the remaining steps. If the ID must be configured manually and electronically, restart the computer and run the device's Setup program (this will also load the driver, so you can skip the next step). To set the ID manually using a jumper, consult the manufacturer's documentation and make the proper jumper setting.

4. **Load the device's driver.** Restart the computer and insert the floppy disk or CD that came with the device. Run the Setup or Install program.

SCENARIO & SOLUTION

I want to attach 10 SCSI devices to my computer. Which type of SCSI should I use?	You need to use a type that supports at least a 16-bit bus. These include any of the Wide SCSI types or the Ultra-3 SCSI-3 type. From a performance perspective, you may want to add a second SCSI controller.
I added a SCSI scanner to the middle of my SCSI chain. How do I terminate it?	You don't. Only devices at each end of the chain need to be terminated.
Which ID should I assign to the SCSI controller?	The SCSI controller should be assigned the ID with the highest priority. This is ID 7, regardless of how many IDs your SCSI system supports.
I added another device to the end of the SCSI chain, and now none of the devices works. What's wrong?	The new device might have an ID conflict with another device. However, because *none* of the other devices is working, it is more likely that the new device is not terminated properly or causes the chain to exceed the maximum cable length.

Installing and Configuring Peripheral Devices

The peripherals described in this section have more complex installation and configuration requirements than the peripherals described in Chapter 1. That is, their installation and configuration go beyond simple attachment to the computer or system board. Desktop system components are discussed first, followed by portable devices.

Desktop System Components

Some of the devices described here are considered "common" because they are found in many computers. Other components, such as those described in the USB and IEEE-1394 sections, are commonplace because of their improved speed and performance. Before carrying out the installation procedures described here, turn the computer off, remove the cover, and carry out proper ESD procedures as described in Chapter 4, Exercise 4-2. The installation procedures for internal components assume that you have already removed the computer case.

Display Systems

Monitors must be connected to internal video cards, and the video system relies on the proper function of both components. The video card's function is to create the images that will result in the picture you see. The monitor simply displays the images sent to it by the video card.

Monitors   Monitors and FPDs are not usually field serviceable. That means that they are replaced rather than repaired when they stop functioning correctly. One reason for this is that it would typically cost more in labor and parts to fix a monitor than it would to simply buy a new one. Another reason, and probably the most important one, is that monitors can hold enough electrical charge to cause serious personal injury, even when they have been left unplugged for an extended time. When a monitor needs replacing or upgrading, turn off the computer, unplug the monitor, and replace it with the new one.

Video Cards   If the video card must be replaced or upgraded, follow the steps in Exercise 2-4. Video cards currently come in two styles: PCI and AGP. If the system board has an AGP slot, it is preferable to use an AGP video card because of advanced speed and performance.

e x a m

ⓦ a t c h

Monitors can hold enough charge to seriously injure you, even if they have been left unplugged. Never wear an ESD strap when working with a monitor, *and never open the monitor's case. You can expect to be asked about the dangers of high voltage and ESD straps on the exam.*

EXERCISE 2-4

Installing a Video Card

1. Position the video adapter card over the appropriate expansion slot on the system board (see Figure 2-7).
2. Place your thumbs along the top edge of the card and push straight down. If necessary, rock the card along its length (never side to side) while you apply downward pressure.
3. When the card is fully seated in the expansion slot, secure it to the computer chassis using the existing screw holes.
4. Plug the monitor into the port at the back of the video adapter card and turn it on.

FIGURE 2-7

The installation of a PCI video card

5. Turn the computer on. If the video card is Plug and Play (sometimes the video card will be too new to be recognized by the OS, for example, if you install a 2001 version of a video card into a computer with a Windows 95 OS), it should be automatically detected and assigned resources, and the proper device driver should be loaded. If this is the case, skip the next step.

6. If the computer is not Plug and Play, insert the floppy disk or CD that came with the video adapter and run the Setup or Install program to load the proper device drivers and assign the appropriate system resources.

7. In Windows, right-click the desktop and select Properties and then the Settings tab.

---

e x a m

ⓦatch　　*Most newer computer systems use an AGP controller rather than a PCI controller. A PC system can have multiple controllers to allow more* *than one monitor to be used. The configuration of these multi-monitor systems is usually handled by the operating system.*

Modems

If you are installing an external analog modem, simply plug it into a COM port at the back of the computer. If the modem is Plug and Play, it will be automatically detected and configured when you turn the computer on. If it is not Plug and Play, you will have to run its Setup or Install program to load its device driver. Remember, since the modem is attached to a COM port, it will use that port's system resources (IRQ and I/O).

The installation of an internal modem is a bit more complex. Install the modem as you would any other expansion card. (You may refer to Steps 1 through 3 in Exercise 2-4.) Again, if the modem is Plug and Play, the OS will automatically configure it. However, if the modem does not support Plug and Play, you will have to configure it manually.

To do this, you will first need to assign the modem to an available COM port, even though it is not actually physically attached to that port. Depending on the modem, this can be done using a jumper setting or, more commonly, electronically using a Setup program or the computer's OS. You may also need to enable the COM port (depending on the BIOS). Take care not to choose a COM port whose resources are already being used by another device. For example, if COM1 is already in use, you cannot assign COM3 to the modem (COM1 and 3 share an IRQ, and COM2 and 4 share an IRQ).

Once the internal or external analog modem is properly installed and has the proper resource and device driver, it must be connected to a phone jack. Attach one end of a regular phone cable to the modem, and attach the other end to a phone jack in the wall. Before your modem can communicate with another modem, it must be configured within the OS to establish a dial-up connection. The dial-up settings include the phone number to dial and other dialing properties, such as how to get an external line or disable call waiting. This procedure is described in detail in Chapter 11.

USB Peripherals and Hubs

USB devices were described in Chapter 1 as being Plug and Play and hot swappable. This means that a USB device can be attached to the computer while the computer is in operation. The device will be immediately and automatically recognized and configured. The USB system will even provide power to most devices, such as mice, keyboards, and network adapters. However, devices such as scanners and printers must have their own power supply. To install a USB device, simply attach its USB connector into an available USB port. The maximum cable length between any two devices in a USB system is 5 meters.

e**x**a**m**
watch
USB is supported on all Microsoft operating systems from Windows 95 on. The only exceptions are Windows NT 3.5 and Windows NT 4; these operating systems do not provide USB support.

USB-compliant computers include two or more ports on the back and front of the computer case. USB adapter cards can be added to older computer systems or can be used to expand newer systems. The current standard for USB is 2.0 and it operates at speeds up to 480Mbps. USB 1.1 operated at speeds up to 12Mbps. How then can USB claim to support up to 127 devices? To create more USB ports, you can use an external *USB hub*. An external USB hub contains one cable and several (up to seven) additional ports (see Figure 2-8) and serves to increase the number of ports available for other devices. A USB hub that has its own power supply is preferable to one that doesn't. To attach a USB hub, connect its cable to an available USB port at the back of the computer (called the *root hub*) and plug it in. No additional configuration is required.

To add more USB devices, simply attach them to the USB hub. If you require even more ports, add another tier by attaching another hub to the existing one (see Figure 2-9). However, you should avoid connecting more than five hubs together, because to do so could affect device performance.

FIGURE 2-8

A USB hub that
provides 4
additional USB
connections

FIGURE 2-9   USB hubs can be added to make more ports available

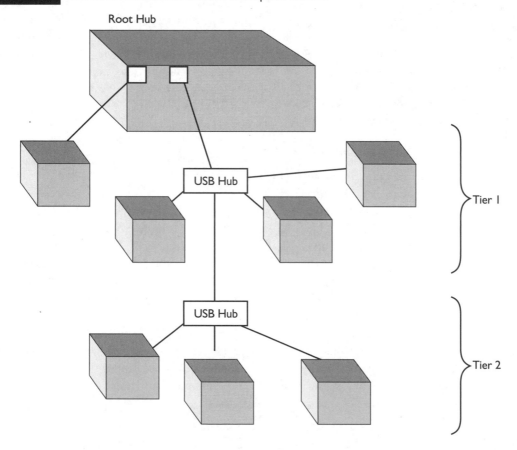

IEEE-1394 or FireWire

IEEE-1394 systems support Plug and Play and hot swapping. However, IEEE-1394 is more expensive than USB. IEEE-1394 runs at speeds to 400Mbps. IEEE-1394 is typically used for devices that require fast transmission of large amounts of data, such as video cameras and digital versatile disc (DVD) players. IEEE-1394 is often referred to as *FireWire*, the trademarked name given to Apple Computer's IEEE-1394 systems. IEEE-1394 is also referred to by other manufacturer-specific names, such as *i.link* or *Lynx*.

FireWire systems can support up to 63 external devices from a single port. Like SCSI, FireWire devices are attached in a daisy chain (peer-to-peer) topology. No single cable in the system can exceed 4 meters. To attach an IEEE-1394 device, simply plug it into the port of the last device in the chain. The FireWire system will provide the device with power and will automatically detect and configure it.

USB systems support most kinds of peripherals. IEEE-1394 (FireWire) systems support specialized high-data/ high-speed devices such as video cameras, hard drives and DVD players.

To use FireWire, your computer must be running Windows 98 or higher, and you must have an IEEE-1394 controller. If the computer didn't come with a controller preinstalled, you can add one yourself. The controller is installed using the same procedures for installing other expansion cards. FireWire controllers are Plug and Play, so there is no need to load device drivers or configure system resources.

CERTIFICATION OBJECTIVE 2.04

Portable System Components

Portable computers tend to be "what you see is what you get" (WYSIWYG) systems. In other words, because they are proprietary, they are very difficult to upgrade, and you are pretty much limited to using the components that came with the system. However, because of their compact size, many portable components, such as the keyboard and pointing device, can be difficult to use. For this reason, most portables allow you to temporarily attach easier-to-use desktop devices, for times when you are not in transit.

Keyboards

Most portable computers include a regular keyboard port in the back. To attach a regular keyboard, turn the portable off, plug in the desktop keyboard, and turn the portable back on. When the portable detects the external keyboard, it will disable the on-board keyboard.

Mouse

Most portables do not come with a mouse. Instead, they use pointing devices such as pointing sticks or touch pads. Because these devices are small and can be difficult to use, many portable computers allow you to attach a full-sized desktop mouse. Simply turn off the portable, attach the mouse to the port in the back, then restart the system.

Some portables, however, do come with a mouse. Typically, the mouse is permanently connected to the portable and can be stored in a compartment within the portable's chassis. Remove the mouse compartment's cover, and take the mouse out in order to use it.

on the job

With the availability of USB devices, it may also be convenient to add a USB mouse and keyboard to your system. These can be added or removed as needed. This allows the use of a full-sized keyboard when you are not traveling.

Docking Stations

Most portable system owners use their computer while in transit but have a "base of operation," such as an office. This is typically where the user will use external devices such as keyboards, printers, monitors, and mice. The user must connect and disconnect these components every time he or she returns to or leaves the office with the portable. *Port replicators* can make this task less time consuming by providing a permanent connection to these external devices. That is, the keyboard, monitor, and mouse (or whichever external devices the laptop is designed to access) are connected to the port replicator and left there. The user can then access them by making one connection to the port replicator rather than connecting to each device separately. Because port replicators are designed to simply replicate a portable computer's existing ports, the devices they allow you to access differ from system to system.

An *enhanced port replicator* provides the same function as a regular port replicator but also includes access to some devices that the portable would not otherwise be able to use. Typical enhanced port replicators provide access to an enhanced sound system and more PC Card slots (discussed later in the chapter).

Portable system *docking stations* go even further than port replicators to allow access to *any* type of desktop component, such as printers, monitors, hard drives, and expansion slots. Simply attach the peripherals to the docking station and leave them there. When you want to access these devices, connect the portable computer to the docking station (see Figure 2-10).

Port replicators and docking stations are proprietary and can be used only with the portable for which they were designed. The method of connection and the devices supported will vary among manufacturers.

FIGURE 2-10

A portable
computer and a
docking station

Answer the following Scenario and Solution questions to evaluate your
understanding of portable system docking stations.

Network Interface Cards

Many computers have network interface cards (NICs), which allow them to
communicate with other computers in a network (discussed in detail in Chapter 7).
When they are not in transit portable computers can also be used on a network.

SCENARIO & SOLUTION

I plug my laptop into a CRT, printer, and keyboard every time I return to the office. Is there an easier way to do this?	Yes. Plug each of these devices into a port replicator and leave them there. To access the devices, simply plug your laptop into the port replicator.
When I'm in the office, I'd rather use my laptop than my desktop because it is faster. What can I do to access the better peripherals that my desktop has from my laptop?	Your laptop might be able to use a full docking station. This device will allow your laptop to access most devices that a desktop can access.
I want to access a USB scanner with my laptop. My docking station doesn't have a USB port, but my colleague's does. How do I use my colleague's docking station?	You can't. Docking stations are designed to work with specific laptops only. You are limited to using the docking station the manufacturer has designed for your system, and you cannot access the USB scanner.

To attach a portable computer to a network, either the portable must have an internal network card or you must first install a NIC. Portables allow for the easy addition and removal of expansion cards using special PC Cards (the name "PC Card" is actually a shortened version of "PCMCIA card," which is named after the association that introduced them). PC Cards are about the size of a credit card but are slightly thicker. To use a PC Card, simply insert it into the appropriate slot. To remove the card, press the ejector button. PC Cards are hot swappable, so they can be added or removed while the portable is in operation.

Once the NIC has been inserted, you must attach it to a network cable. However, the connector on a network cable is much thicker than the NIC. For this reason, some NIC PC Cards have a "flip-up" connector (see Figure 2-11). Open the connector and then attach the network cable to it.

Integrated connectors are included on newer NICs only and are not available on most NIC PC Cards. NICs without an integrated port require a network cable adapter, commonly called a *dongle*. One end of the dongle has a very small connector that is attached to the NIC. The other end contains a regular network (BNC or RJ-45) port, which is attached to the network cable (see Figure 2-12).

FIGURE 2-11

A PC Card
network adapter

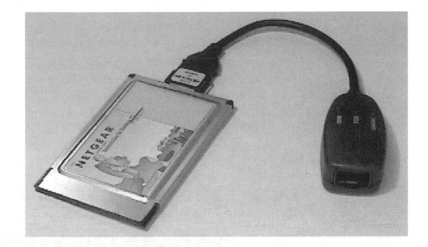

FIGURE 2-12

A PC Card
adapter with a
cable to attach
to a network

CERTIFICATION OBJECTIVE 2.05

Upgrading, Extending, and Optimizing System Performance

Most of this chapter has focused on the installation and performance of *specific* computer components. This section focuses on the performance of the computer system as a whole. In this section, you will learn how to upgrade your computer by replacing special subsystem components, such as the BIOS. You will also learn about procedures that can improve your computer's performance, such as replacing batteries, installing cache memory, and running hard drive utilities. Additionally, you will learn how to extend the abilities of your computer by installing specially designed components, such as portable system PC Cards.

Desktop Computers

The procedures described here can be performed on almost all desktops. However, their relevance to portable systems is limited to the information in the "Memory," "Hard Drives," and "BIOS" sections.

Memory

As you know, one function of RAM is to provide the processor with faster access to the information it needs. Within limits, the more memory a computer has, the faster it will run. One of the most common computer upgrades is the installation of more RAM.

Recall that most computers can use another type of RAM, called *cache memory*. Cache memory chips can be accessed even faster than regular RAM, so their presence can help speed up the computer. Generally, the more cache a computer has, the faster it will run. The type of cache that can be added to the computer is called Level 2 (L2) cache, and it can be installed in available slots on the motherboard.

e x a m

watch

Cache that can be installed on the system board used to be called L2, Level 2, or external cache. Cache located within the processor itself is called L1, Level 1, internal, or on-board cache and cannot be added or upgraded (unless you replace the processor). Newer processors such as the Pentium 4 include L2 cache in the microprocessor and allow for L3 cache to be added on the system board. Make sure your read the exam question carefully about the type of cache the exam is referring to.

Hard Drives

Throughout the operation of the computer, the hard drive will be accessed over and over again. Information will be read from, saved to, and moved from one place to another on the drive. Its operation is critical to the perceived efficiency of the computer. However, the more the hard drive is used, the less efficient it tends to become. The next two subsections describe common hard drive problems and how to resolve them.

Using Scandisk   The indexing of data on a disk is very important when that data is being saved and retrieved. Each file on the disk occupies one or more clusters, and no two files can exist on a single cluster. The first cluster on the disk contains an index of filenames and locations. This index is called a *file allocation table (FAT)*. Whenever you access a file, the OS first looks it up in the FAT to determine its location on the disk, then retrieves it. Without a FAT, the hard or floppy drive would have to search every cluster until it found the requested file.

However, it is possible for the FAT to develop errors over time. *Cross-linked clusters* occur when the FAT records a single cluster as belonging to two different files. *Lost clusters* occur when a cluster containing data is not referenced in the FAT at all. Either of these errors can cause the file to be reported as missing. You can resolve these errors by running Microsoft's Scandisk utility. Scandisk searches the entire disk and compares the contents of each cluster to the information in the FAT. Scandisk then updates the FAT with the proper information about the disk's contents and file locations. Another function of Scandisk is to locate physical "bad spots" on the disk that cannot store data. Any existing data on these spots is moved, and the clusters are marked as "bad" so that no new data is stored there.

Defragmenting the Hard Drive   When files are saved to the hard or floppy drive, they are written to the first available cluster(s). Ideally, subsequent files are all saved in consecutive clusters on the disk. However, suppose a file resided on cluster 4, and another file resided on clusters 5–8. If you increased the size of the first file so that it no longer fit on one cluster, it would occupy clusters 4 *and* 9. Next, suppose you deleted the file on clusters 5–8 and replaced it with a larger file. That file would now reside on clusters 5–8 and perhaps 10 and 11. These files no longer reside on consecutive clusters and are said to be *fragmented*. Fragmentation can cause the hard or floppy drive to retrieve files more slowly and can actually cause undue wear and tear on the drive's read/write heads.

To defragment a hard or floppy disk, you can run Microsoft's Disk Defragmenter in Windows 9x, Windows 2000, and XP. This utility rewrites the data on the disk so that files are placed on contiguous clusters. Follow the steps in Exercise 2-5 to defragment a hard drive.

EXERCISE 2-5

Defragmenting a Hard Drive on Windows 9x, 2000, and XP

1. Exit all running applications, disable the screen saver.

2. From the Start menu, select Programs | Accessories | System Tools | Disk Defragmenter in Windows 9x/2000 or Start | All Programs | Accessories | System | Disk Defragmenter in Windows XP.

3. You will be presented with a Select Drive dialog box. Select the appropriate hard drive from the drop-down menu, then click OK.

4. The Defragmenter utility will begin. You can view the cluster-by-cluster details of the operation by clicking the Show Details button.

5. When the process is complete, you will be informed via a dialog box, the contents of which will vary, depending on the OS you are using. Choose to either exit the utility or defragment another disk.

CPU

Some computers can support more than one type of process. For example, the system board might be able to use a Pentium 4 or a Celeron processor. Most motherboards support more than one speed for a particular type of processor. For example, the computer could support the use of either the Pentium 4 processors with clock speeds from 1.6 -2.4 GHz.

Always consult the manufacturer's documentation for your system board to determine which processors and speeds it supports. In most cases, you will need to configure the board for the new speed or model using a set of jumpers.

CMOS

A computer that consistently asks you for the date and time probably has a low CMOS battery. Because these batteries last only between 2 and 10 years, you are likely to have to replace a computer's battery before the computer becomes obsolete. To properly replace the battery, follow the steps in Exercise 2-6. Note that although this procedure cannot be followed in *all* computers, it applies to most newer computers.

SCENARIO & SOLUTION

The computer reported a corruption error when I tried to access the floppy disk. What should I do?	Run Scandisk.
How can I speed up my hard drive?	Run Disk Defragmenter.
My computer reports that a particular file doesn't exist, but I know I saved it. What happened, and how can I find that file?	It is possible that the file exists but it has lost a cluster. Run Scandisk. If the file exists, the FAT will be updated and you will be able to access it.

EXERCISE 2-6

Replacing the CMOS Battery

1. Enter the computer's Setup program (described in Chapter 1) and write down all CMOS settings.

2. Turn off the computer and remove the cover, ensuring that you carry out proper ESD procedures.

3. Locate the CMOS battery on the motherboard.

4. Slide the battery out from under the retaining clip. The clip uses slight tension to hold the battery in place, so there is no need to remove the clip or bend it outward.

5. Note the characteristics on this battery that distinguish the bottom from the top. Install the new battery so that the bottom is in contact with the motherboard.

6. Restart the computer. Enter the system's Setup program and reset the CMOS settings you recorded in Step 1.

BIOS

Recall that the BIOS is used to translate communications between devices in the computer. The BIOS is able to do this because it contains the basic instruction set for those devices. However, if you install a device with which the computer seems unable to communicate, you might need to upgrade or replace the existing BIOS.

When to Upgrade the BIOS   One way to inform the BIOS of a new device is to access the computer's CMOS settings and select the new device in the BIOS options. For example, if you upgrade the hard drive, you might need to inform the BIOS of its new type and capacity. CMOS settings are described in more detail in Chapter 5. You will also want to upgrade to a BIOS version that is appropriate to the operating system that is being installed.

In some cases, however, the device might be so much newer than the BIOS that it cannot be selected from the CMOS settings. For example, if you are using an old BIOS, you can't inform it of a new 10GB hard drive, because the BIOS won't allow you to enter or select that size. When this is the case, the BIOS itself (not just its options) must be upgraded.

Methods for Upgrading the BIOS   Flash BIOS chips can be electronically upgraded using a disk from the BIOS manufacturer. Turn the computer off, insert the manufacturer's floppy disk, and restart the computer. The disk contains a program that automatically "flashes" (updates) the BIOS so that it can recognize different hardware types or perform different functions than it could before. The BIOS retains the new information, so it has to be flashed only once.

Another way to upgrade the BIOS is to physically replace it with another. You will need to do this if the BIOS manufacturer has stopped supporting that particular BIOS model or if the manufacturer hasn't released a flash program with the options you need your BIOS to support. To physically replace the BIOS, locate the old BIOS chip and remove it with a chip puller. Orient the new BIOS in the same position that the old one used, then push it gently into the socket.

on the
job

The approach of 2000 was a busy time for replacing and upgrading BIOS chips. Many BIOSes were not designed to recognize any year later than 1999 and would have interpreted 2000 as 1900. This problem was called the Y2K bug. These BIOSes had to be flashed so that their basic instruction set included recognition of the year 2000 and later. In some computers, the BIOS was no longer supported by the manufacturer, so it couldn't be flashed. Instead, these chips had to be physically replaced.

Portable Computers

Portable computers contain several components that are not used by desktop computers. This section discusses some portable-specific devices and their functions.

Batteries

When they are not plugged into a wall outlet, portable computers get their power from special batteries. Most portable batteries are either nickel and metal hydride (NiMH) or lithium ion (LiIon). LiIon batteries use newer technology than NiMH and are smaller and lighter and produce more power. LiIon batteries are, however, more expensive.

Portable system batteries must be recharged from time to time, and this is the job of the AC adapter, which plugs into a regular electrical outlet. The adapter recharges the battery while the portable is operating. However, if you are not near a wall outlet when the battery's power fades, you need to replace the battery with a fully charged one.

Due to the necessity for changing the battery frequently, most portables allow easy access to it. In many cases, the battery fits into a compartment on the bottom or in the side of the computer. If this is the case, remove the battery compartment's cover, slide the old battery out, and slide the new one in (see Figure 2-13). If the

A battery located on the underside of a portable system

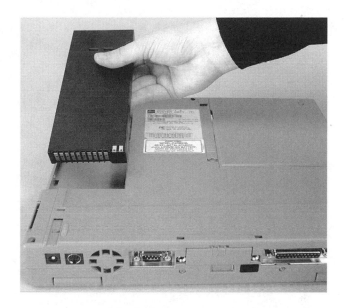

battery's compartment is on the bottom, there might be a release mechanism that allows you to remove the battery. Remove the old one and insert the new one. Many newer systems allow for multiple batteries to be contained in the system. While this adds battery usage time, it also increases the weight of the system.

Fortunately, most portable systems give you plenty of notice before the battery is completely drained. Many systems include a power-level meter that allows you to see the battery's charge level at all times. Other systems give you a visual warning when the battery's power dips below a certain level.

Memory

Additional RAM can be added to a portable system in a number of ways. Some systems include extra RAM slots within the chassis. This type requires you to open the computer's case and place the RAM module in an available slot (see Figure 2-14). Because RAM modules for portables are proprietary, you cannot use them in desktop computers or in other portables.

An easier way to add more RAM to your portable is to use a memory PC Card. PC Cards were described earlier as being small cards that can be easily inserted in a portable to enhance or expand its abilities. In fact, PC Cards originated as PCMCIA cards specifically for the purpose of adding more memory. PCMCIA stands for *Personal Computer Memory Card International Association,* a bit of a misnomer because these cards are usually used in laptops, not in PCs (desktops).

FIGURE 2-14

Installing a RAM
module in a
portable system

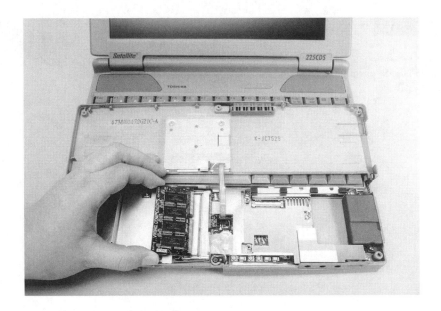

To use a memory PC Card, simply insert it into the appropriate PC slot on the
portable, usually located on the side (see Figure 2-15). Because memory cards are used
so often, they tend to be more standardized than other portable system components.
This means that you can use a generic memory PC Card in your portable system.

Types I, II, and III Cards

Type I PC Cards are roughly the size of a credit card (85.6mm x 54mm x 3.3mm).

Due to the popularity of these cards, the PCMCIA went on to develop another
standard: PCMCIA 2. This standard includes the use of *Type II* cards. These cards
have the same physical dimensions as Type I cards except that they are 5mm thick
instead of 3.3mm. Type II PCMCIA cards are typically used for I/O devices,
including network cards, modems, and sound cards.

In 1994, the PCMCIA released yet another standard, PCMCIA 2.01. This
standard includes the *Type III* card, and the name was officially changed from
PCMCIA card (a real mouthful) to the shortened *PC Card*. Type III cards have the
same length and width measurements as Type I and Type II cards but are 10.5mm
thick. They are usually used for hard drive storage. The 2.01 standard also supports a
wider data bus (the 32-bit Cardbus).

All PC Card standards support hot swapping. A service called *socket services* runs
inside the portable and detects when a PC Card has been inserted or removed.
When a card is inserted, another service, called *card services*, assigns the card the

FIGURE 2-15

A Type I PC Card
being installed in
a portable

proper resources, such as an IRQ and I/O address. A Type III card can be used only
in a Type III slot, but Type II cards can be used in Type II or Type III slots, and Type
I cards can be used in all three.

CERTIFICATION SUMMARY

Some system setups require configurations beyond what is required of most common
systems. Using the proper master/slave configuration techniques, you can install up to
four drives in a single system. Alternatively, you can set up a SCSI system, which,
although more difficult to configure, allows you to install many more devices in the
computer.

Furthermore, some individual devices require special installation or configuration
or are simply too new to be considered "common." Devices such as network cards,
modems, and video cards all require additional, component-specific configuration
in order to work properly. However, some systems, such as USB and FireWire, have
emerged that allow you to install a great number of devices with little or no
configuration at all.

Most computers can be optimized or enhanced by installing special components,
such as cache memory or PC Cards. Other optimization procedures include using
disk utilities such as Disk Defragmenter or Scandisk or upgrading the system's BIOS.

TWO-MINUTE DRILL

Here are some of the key points from each certification objective in Chapter 2.

Installing and Configuring IDE/EIDE Devices

❑ Most computers support the installation of up to four hard and/or CD drives.

❑ Master drives must be configured with the proper jumper setting and are installed at the end of the drive's ribbon cable.

❑ To install a slave drive, set the jumper to the "slave" position and attach the drive to the middle ribbon cable connector.

❑ Another master/slave configuration can be added by using the system's secondary drive controller.

Installing and Configuring SCSI Devices

❑ A SCSI system is controlled by a SCSI controller card, also called a *SCSI host adapter*.

❑ SCSI-1, SCSI-2, and SCSI-3 systems support different speeds, bus widths, and maximum cable lengths.

❑ Each device in a SCSI chain must be assigned a unique SCSI ID address.

❑ Each end of the SCSI chain must be properly terminated.

Installing and Configuring Peripheral Devices

❑ Video cards and modems require additional configuration, such as their display settings and dial-up properties, to work properly.

❑ USB systems require the use of USB hubs, a USB header cable, or USB cards to attach more than one or two devices.

❑ IEEE-1394 (FireWire) systems are similar to USB but support faster devices, such as DVD drives and video cameras.

❑ Most portables can use desktop components through the use of port replicators or docking stations.

Upgrading, Extending, and Optimizing System Performance

❑ A computer system's hard drive access speed can be increased by defragmenting the hard drive or installing cache memory.

❑ The computer's BIOS can be upgraded (flashed or replaced) to recognize new types of devices.

❑ Portable computers can use Type I, Type II, or Type III PC Cards to access additional RAM, I/O devices, or storage, respectively.

SELF TEST

The following questions will help you measure your understanding of the material presented in this chapter. Read all the choices carefully because there might be more than one correct answer. Choose all correct answers for each question.

Installing and Configuring IDE/EIDE Devices

1. Which of the following statements about hard drive configurations is true?

   A. To function properly, a master drive must be accompanied by a secondary drive.

   B. The master drive must be attached to the ribbon cable using the connector that is closest to the system board.

   C. The term for a hard drive on the secondary controller is *slave*.

   D. A slave drive cannot work in the absence of a master drive.

2. You are planning to install a hard drive and a CD-ROM drive in a new system. Which of the following is typically a valid drive configuration for you to use?

   A. Install the hard drive as a primary master and install the CD-ROM as a secondary master.

   B. Install the CD-ROM as a primary master and the hard drive as a primary slave.

   C. Install the CD-ROM as either a primary master or a secondary slave.

   D. Install the CD-ROM anywhere, as long as the hard drive is a secondary master.

3. Your computer has three hard drives installed—two on the primary controller and one on the secondary controller. You are planning to install a fourth drive without changing the designations of the existing drives. Which of the following accurately describes the procedure you should follow?

   A. Enter the new drive's type and capacity in the CMOS settings, set the drive's jumper to the slave position, and install it on the available connector on the drive ribbon.

   B. Set the drive's jumper to the slave position and attach it to the ribbon cable. Restart the computer and enter the new drive's drive letter in the CMOS settings.

   C. Enter the new drive's drive letter in the CMOS settings. Set the drive's jumper to the secondary position and attach it to the ribbon cable.

   D. Set the drive's jumper to the slave position and attach it to the ribbon cable.

4. A computer has an E drive. Assuming that all physical drives in the system have only one partition, what can you tell *for certain* about the computer?

   A. The computer has four drives installed.

   B. The C drive is on the primary controller.

C. The E drive is on the primary controller.

D. The E drive is on the secondary controller.

5. Which of the following is true of master/slave hard drive configurations?

A. Do not mix ATA and IDE drives on a single controller.

B. The primary controller must contain drives that are technologically similar to or newer than drives on the secondary controller.

C. Do not configure a hard drive to be CD-ROM drive's slave.

D. Do not install drives on the secondary controller without a primary slave present.

Installing and Configuring SCSI Devices

6. You are planning to install a non-Plug-and-Play SCSI system controller card. Which of the following most accurately represents the proper steps in the proper order?

A. Add the controller to the end of the existing SCSI chain and assign it an available ID address.

B. Install the controller in an available expansion slot and assign it an IRQ and ID address.

C. Add the controller to the end of the existing SCSI chain and assign it an available IRQ and ID address.

D. Install the controller in an available expansion slot and assign it an ID address.

7. A customer had a properly functioning SCSI system with two internal hard drives and five external peripherals. He tells you that he added another external peripheral to the end of the chain, and now none of the SCSI devices will work. Which of the following cannot be considered a possible cause of this problem?

A. The new device has an IRQ conflict with another peripheral device.

B. There might be too many devices in the SCSI system.

C. The system might not be properly terminated.

D. The SCSI chain might be too long.

8. Refer to Figure 2-16. The maximum supported length of a mixed internal/external SCSI system cable is

A. The length of cable between the two ports of attached devices

B. The length between the far ports of attached devices

C. The length of the SCSI chain from the controller to the last device on either end of the chain

D. The length of the SCSI chain from the last device on the internal chain to the last device on the external chain

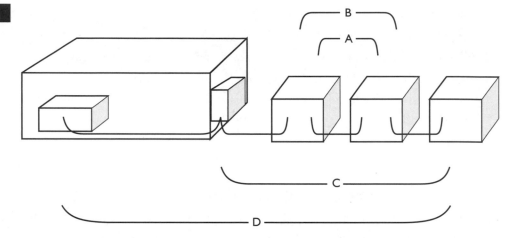

FIGURE 2-16

Select the distance that constitutes the maximum cable length

9. Which type of SCSI system has an 8-bit bus and throughput of 40MBps and can support a maximum cable length of 12 meters?

   A. Ultra SCSI-3

   B. Wide Ultra SCSI-3

   C. Ultra-2 SCSI

   D. Ultra-3 SCSI

10. You are planning to set up a SCSI system in your computer. You want to be able to attach at least 11 devices, and you want to make the SCSI chain about 2 meters long. Which of the following SCSI types can you use?

    A. Fast SCSI-2

    B. Wide SCSI-2

    C. Wide Ultra SCSI-3

    D. Ultra-2 SCSI

Installing and Configuring Peripheral Devices

11. As well as physical installation and resource assignment, which of the following should you configure when installing an analog modem?

    A. A dial-up connection

    B. A handshake routine

    C. An IP address

    D. Resolution settings

12. Which of the following most accurately describes the function of a USB hub?

    A. To increase the speed of the USB system

    B. To increase the number of available USB ports

    C. To allow you to use more than 127 USB devices

    D. To control the assignment of resources to USB devices

13. You are planning to add another USB device your system. What is usually the proper installation procedure?

    A. Turn the computer off, plug in the device, terminate the device, turn the device on, restart the computer, load the proper device driver

    B. Turn the computer off, plug in the device, turn the device on, restart the computer

    C. Plug in the device, turn the device on, load the proper device driver

    D. Plug in the device and turn it on, if necessary (not all USB devices have an on/off switch)

14. A customer is planning to buy a new computer system and has asked your advice. The customer wants to use high-speed video devices but does not want a system that requires a lot of device configuration. The system should be able to handle up to 10 external devices and support hot swapping. Which type of system should you recommend?

    A. IDE/ATA

    B. SCSI

    C. USB

    D. IEEE-1394

15. Which of the following allows you to attach nearly any type of desktop component to a portable computer?

    A. Port replicator

    B. Enhanced port replicator

    C. Extended port replicator

    D. Docking station

Upgrading, Extending, and Optimizing System Performance

16. Which of the following is *not* a function of Microsoft's Scandisk utility?

    A. To restore corrupted files

    B. To resolve FAT/cluster information

    C. To fix bad sectors on the disk

    D. To remove information from bad sectors on the disk

17. Under which circumstance would you run Microsoft's Disk Defragmenter?

    A. On a set schedule

    B. When the disk reports corrupted files

    C. When the computer cannot recognize the hard drive

    D. When you accidentally delete a file

18. Your computer consistently loses its date/time setting, and you suspect the CMOS battery is at fault. Which procedure will you use to solve the problem?

    A. Replace the battery.

    B. Flash the battery using a manufacturer-provided disk.

    C. Use the computer's AC adapter to recharge the battery.

    D. Access the CMOS setting programs at startup and select the low-power option.

19. You want to upgrade your BIOS by "flashing" it. Which procedure should you follow?

    A. Replace the BIOS chip with a newer model from the manufacturer of the original.

    B. Turn on the computer, and when you see the option to enter the system setup, press the given key combination.

    C. Insert the manufacturer's floppy disk and turn the computer on.

    D. Replace the BIOS chip with a newer model that is compatible with the system board and processor.

20. Which of the following represents a typical function of a Type II PC Card?

    A. To add more memory to the computer

    B. To access a computer network

    C. To provide additional power to a portable

    D. To increase storage capacity

LAB QUESTION

This chapter discussed three alternative component systems: SCSI, USB, and IEEE-1394. Use the information you have learned to create a table that compares and contrasts these systems. Be sure to include information about device number, transmission speed, and installation information. You might also want to include information such as ease of use, relative expense, and other system-specific information. Use the template in Table 2-2 to complete your table.

TABLE 2-2   Lab Questions Sample Table

	SCSI	USB	IEEE-1394
Maximum number of devices			
Types			
Speed			
Resources			
Additional required hardware			
Relative cost			
Device power source			
Common devices			
Communication method			
Topology (device connection method)			
Maximum cable length			
Resource configuration			
Supports hot swapping?			
Operating system			

SELF TEST ANSWERS

Installing and Configuring IDE/EIDE Devices

1. ☑ **D.** A slave drive cannot work in the absence of a master drive. In a master/slave configuration, two drives are installed on a single ribbon cable, and the master drive's on-board controller controls the function of the slave drive. If a drive is configured as a slave and there is no master present, the slave drive will not be able to communicate with the computer. **A,** to function properly a master drive must be accompanied by a secondary drive, is incorrect. Master drives can be configured on either the primary or secondary controllers. Both controllers can be set up with a master/slave configuration, and the presence of a master does not necessitate the installation of a drive on the secondary controller. However, to install a drive on the secondary controller, a drive must be present on the primary controller, and to install a slave drive, a master drive must be present on the same controller.

   ☒ **B** is incorrect because it states that the master drive must be attached to the ribbon cable using the connector that is closest to the system board. In fact, the opposite is true. The master drive must be installed at the end of the ribbon cable, and the slave is installed in the middle (closest to the system board). **C,** the term for a hard drive on the secondary controller is *slave*, is also incorrect. The term for a hard drive on the secondary controller is *secondary*. The term *slave* is reserved for a drive that is controlled by a master drive.

2. ☑ **A.** Install the hard drive as a primary master and install the CD-ROM as a secondary master. This is the most common hard drive/CD-ROM setup. You could also install the hard drive as a primary master and the CD-ROM as a primary slave.

   ☒ **B** and **C** are incorrect because they suggest installing the CD-ROM as a primary master. Most OSes will work only if they are installed on a drive that is on the primary controller. Furthermore, hard drives cannot be slaves to CD-ROM drives. You can deduce from this that a hard drive must occupy the primary master position. Finally, **C** also suggests installing the CD-ROM as the secondary slave. However, slave drives must be accompanied by a master drive on the same controller. You have already determined that the hard drive cannot be on the secondary controller (**D** is incorrect for this reason). Therefore, without a master to control the secondary slave position, the CD-ROM cannot be installed there.

3. ☑ **D.** Set the drive's jumper to the slave position and attach it to the ribbon cable. Restart the computer and enter the new drive's type and capacity in the CMOS settings. In the given system, the only available position is secondary slave. Therefore, the drive must first be configured as a slave by setting the jumpers to the slave position. When this is finished, the drive is attached to the ribbon cable at the only remaining place: the middle connector on the secondary cable. Although some computers will automatically detect the new drive on startup, others require you to enter the drive's specifications manually. When the drive is installed,

restart the computer and access the CMOS settings. Enter the drive's specifications.

☒ **A** is incorrect because it suggests setting the new drive's capacity and type before it is physically installed in the computer. This should be the last, not the first, step in a hard drive installation. In fact, the BIOS won't allow you to set characteristics of a drive that doesn't physically exist in the system. **B** and **C** are both incorrect because they suggest manually entering the drive letter of the new drive. This is unnecessary because the computer will automatically letter the drives in the following order every time it is started: primary master, secondary master, primary slave, secondary slave.

4. ☑ **B.** The C drive is on the primary controller. Recall that drives are lettered in this order: primary master, primary slave, secondary master, secondary slave. The primary master is given the C drive, no matter how many other drives are installed. **A** is incorrect because it states that the computer has four drives installed. Although it might indeed have four drives, you can't tell this for certain from the information given. It is also possible for this computer to have only three drives, as explained previously.

☒ **C** and **D** are both incorrect because they suggest that you can tell for certain that the drive is on one controller or another. You can tell for certain that this system has a primary master (the C drive). However, the other two drives might be a primary slave (D) and a secondary master (E) or a secondary master (D) and a secondary slave (E).

5. ☑ **C.** Do not configure a hard drive as a CD-ROM drive's slave. CD-ROM drives cannot control a hard drive, so they cannot be set as a hard drive's master. You can, however, set a hard drive to be a CD-ROM drive's master. **A** is incorrect because it suggests that you shouldn't install a mixture of ATA and IDE drives on a single controller. Both of these drive types are standardized and compatible with each other, so they can be installed together in a variety of configurations in a single computer.

☒ **B** is incorrect because it states that the primary controller must contain drives that are technologically similar to or newer than drives on the secondary controller. Although this is true for the master/slave relationship, it is not true for different controllers. **D** is incorrect because it states that you should not install drives on the secondary controller unless a primary slave is present. Secondary drives can be installed, regardless of the presence of a slave, as long as a primary *master* is installed. In fact, many 2-disk configurations include a primary master, secondary master, and no slaves.

Installing and Configuring SCSI Devices

6. ☑ **B.** Install the controller in an available expansion slot and assign it an IRQ and ID address. SCSI controller cards are installed like any other expansion card inside the computer. Once installed, the card must be assigned system resources, such as an IRQ address, so that the computer can communicate with it. Finally, because the controller is part of a SCSI system, it must be assigned a SCSI ID address so that it can be identified among other devices in the SCSI chain.

☒ **A** and **C** are incorrect because they both suggest that the controller is attached to the end of the existing chain. The controller is the central element in the SCSI system, so it is installed on the system board. Although the controller might represent one end of the chain, it is not attached to end of an existing chain, as a peripheral SCSI device would be. **D** is incorrect because although it suggests assigning an ID address, it doesn't specify the assignment of an IRQ address. In this case, the steps given in **D** are correct but are not as complete or accurate as the steps in **B.**

7. ☑ **A.** The possibility that the new device has an IRQ address conflict with another peripheral device cannot be considered a possible cause for the SCSI system problem. SCSI devices are assigned ID addresses, not IRQ addresses. In any case, although it is true that devices cannot share a SCSI ID, this would most likely affect only the conflicting devices, not the whole chain. Furthermore, if one of the conflicting devices is the controller, it might affect the whole chain, but a peripheral device has been specified here.

☒ **B,** there are too many devices in the SCSI system, is incorrect because this might be the source of the problem. If this is a 16-bit SCSI system, it will support up to 16 devices, including the controller. However, there will be a problem if this is an 8-bit system, because 8-bit SCSI systems can support only eight devices, including the controller. Two hard drives plus the controller plus the five peripherals equals eight devices—the system's maximum. A ninth device would have to share an ID address with a device, causing that device to function improperly. If that device happens to be the controller, the entire system might not work. **C,** the system might not be properly terminated, is incorrect. The system was working properly before the addition of the new device, so you can assume that the problem lies with that device's configuration. Because the new device was installed at the end of the chain, the system's termination will have to be changed. That is, the device that used to be last in the chain will have to have its terminator disabled or removed, and the new device at the end will have to be terminated instead. **D,** the SCSI chain might be too long, is also incorrect because this might be the source of the problem. SCSI systems are limited in terms of the total length they can support from one end to the other. The addition of the new device might have caused the system to be longer than the maximum supported length.

8. ☑ **D.** The maximum cable length refers to the length of the chain from the last device on the internal chain to the last device on the external chain—that is, the total cable length in the entire SCSI system. Signals that must travel further than the recommended maximum might become so degraded by interference that they cannot be received by the intended device.

☒ **A** and **B** are incorrect because they both refer to the length between two devices, not the entire SCSI system. **C** is incorrect because it suggests that the maximum length refers to the total length on *either* side of the controller. As discussed, this length refers to the total length, including devices on *both* sides of the controller.

9. ☑ **C.** Ultra-2 SCSI has an 8-bit bus and a throughput of 40MBps and can support a maximum cable length of 12 meters. It is considered "narrow" because of the 8-bit bus limitation, but it uses SCSI-3 technology to bring the speed up to 40MBps. Because Ultra-2 SCSI can use LVD data transfer, it can support cable lengths up to 12 meters.

    ☒ **A,** Ultra SCSI-3, is incorrect because, although this type has an 8-bit bus, it is limited to a 20MBps throughput and 1.5 meter cable length. **B,** Wide Ultra SCSI-3, is incorrect. This type has a 40MBps throughput but a 16-bit bus and maximum length of 1.5 meters. **D,** Ultra-3 SCSI, is incorrect because it has a 16-bit bus and throughput of 160MBps.

10. ☑ **B.** You can use a Wide SCSI-2 system. It is a 16-bit system and supports up to 16 devices. It also supports cable lengths up to 3 meters. Incidentally, a Fast Wide SCSI-2, Double Wide SCSI-2, or Ultra-3 SCSI system could also be used.

    ☒ **A,** Fast SCSI-2, is incorrect because this type of SCSI has an 8-bit bus and can support a maximum of eight devices. **C,** Wide Ultra SCSI-3, is incorrect because it is limited to a 1.5 meter cable length. **D,** Ultra-2 SCSI, is also incorrect because it can support only eight devices.

Installing and Configuring Peripheral Devices

11. ☑ **A.** When installing a modem, you should configure a dial-up connection. This will instruct the modem about connection procedures, such as which phone number to dial and how to disable call waiting. **B,** a handshake routine, is incorrect. Although modems use handshake routines when making a connection, this is a property of the modem itself, not a configurable setting that you can alter.

    ☒ **C,** an IP address, is incorrect because these are used for network cards, not analog modems. **D,** resolution settings, is incorrect because this type of configuration applies to video cards, not modems.

12. ☑ **B.** The function of a USB hub is to increase the number of available USB ports. Most computers that support USB include only one or two ports. To make more ports available, attach a USB hub. The hub attaches to an existing port and contains up to seven additional ports, to which you can attach USB devices or even more USB ports. **A,** to increase the speed of the USB system, is incorrect. USB systems are limited to about 12Mbps and cannot exceed this limit.

    ☒ **C,** to allow you to use more than 127 USB devices, is incorrect. Although you could physically connect more than 127 devices using a USB port, the USB system itself can use only up to 127 of them. No device will increase this limit. **D,** to control the assignment of resources to USB devices, is incorrect because this is the job of the USB controller.

13. ☑ **D.** To install a USB device, plug in the device and turn it on. The computer automatically detects the device, assigns it any resources it needs, and installs the appropriate device driver.

    ☒ **A, B,** and **C** are incorrect because they refer to turning the computer off, terminating the device, and/or loading a device driver. USB devices are hot swappable, meaning that they can be added to or removed from the system while the computer is operating. USB devices also support Plug and Play, so you do not need to install a device driver for them. Finally, USB devices do not need to be terminated, as SCSI devices do.

14. ☑ **D.** You should recommend an IEEE-1394 system. These systems (also known as FireWire) allow you to attach up to 63 external devices (64,449 if extra-port hubs are used) and support Plug and Play and hot swapping. FireWire supports speeds up to 400Mbps, so it is suited for use with high-speed devices, such as video cameras or other video equipment.

    ☒ **A,** IDE/ATA, is incorrect because it does not meet the customer's requirements. These systems are limited in the number of devices they can support. Although some IDE/ATA devices support Plug and Play, they do not support hot swapping. **B,** SCSI, is also incorrect. Some SCSI systems can support more than 10 devices and speeds up to 160MBps, but they typically require a lot of configuration. **C,** USB, is incorrect. USB systems meet all the customer's requests except the ability to support high-speed devices. USB systems are limited to 12Mbps.

15. ☑ **D.** A docking station allows you to attach nearly any type of desktop component to a portable computer. This is, of course, within the limits set by the manufacturer of the portable and docking station. Most docking stations remain stationary and can be connected to desktop components such as CRT monitors, printers, scanners, sound systems, and extra hard drives. When you want to access these devices with your portable computer, simply plug the portable into the docking station.

    ☒ **A,** port replicator, and **B,** enhanced port replicator, are incorrect because they do not allow access to the number of devices that a docking station does. Although both are used to provide quick access to some desktop components, they are limited in the devices they support. **C,** extended port replicator, is incorrect because this is not a real type of portable system component.

Upgrading, Extending, and Optimizing System Performance

16. ☑ **C.** Microsoft's Scandisk utility does not fix bad sectors on the disk. A bad sector is a "spot" on the disk that physically cannot hold data. Scandisk is simply a software utility and cannot change the physical structure of the disk.

    ☒ **A,** to restore corrupted files, is incorrect because this is a function of Scandisk. If part of a file resides on a bad cluster, Scandisk will attempt to remove the data from the cluster (therefore **D** is incorrect) so that the file can be accessed. If all or part of the file is unreferenced in the FAT, it might also be considered "corrupted." Scandisk will read the data on the disk and ensure that references to it in the FAT are accurate (therefore **B** is incorrect).

17. ☑ **A.** You should run Disk Defragmenter on a set schedule. As files are saved, moved, and deleted, the disk can become more and more fragmented. Fragmented files take longer to retrieve than files located in contiguous clusters. Disk Defragmenter relocates cluster data so that all the clusters belonging to any one file are located close to each other.

    ☒ **B,** when the disk reports corrupted files, is incorrect because in this situation, you should use Scandisk. Disk Defragmenter cannot retrieve bad or lost data. **C,** when the computer cannot recognize the hard drive, is also incorrect. When this is the case, check to ensure that the drive is properly installed and that the BIOS is aware of its presence. **D,** when you accidentally delete a file, is incorrect because Disk Defragmenter does not help in "undeleting" files.

18. ☑ **A.** You should replace the battery. When the computer "forgets" the time and date, it is most likely because the CMOS battery, which normally maintains these settings, is getting low. The only solution is to replace it with a fully charged battery.

    ☒ **B** is incorrect because it suggests flashing the battery. This procedure applies to the upgrade of a BIOS chip, not a CMOS battery. **C** is incorrect because it suggests recharging the battery with the computer's AC adapter. Although this procedure will work with a portable system battery, CMOS batteries cannot be recharged with an AC adapter. **D** is incorrect because it suggests selecting a "low-power" option in the CMOS settings program. Any low-power setting in the CMOS settings refers to the function of the computer itself, not the CMOS battery. You cannot adjust the amount of power the CMOS chip draws from its battery.

19. ☑ **C.** To flash the BIOS, insert the manufacturer's floppy disk and turn the computer on. The computer will read the "flash" program on the disk and automatically update the abilities of the BIOS by providing it with a new instruction set.

    ☒ **A** and **D** are both incorrect because they suggest replacing the BIOS chip with another. The purpose of flashing a BIOS is to reprogram the existing BIOS, not to physically replace it with another. **B** is incorrect because it suggests entering the computer's system setup at startup. This procedure can be used to select different options in the existing BIOS, but it is not the procedure used for flashing (upgrading) the BIOS.

20. ☑ **B.** A typical function of a Type II PC Card is to access a computer network. Type II PC Cards are used for I/O operations such as for network cards, modems, and sound cards. The PC Card can be inserted and removed as needed from the portable computer.

    ☒ **A,** to add more memory to the computer, and **D,** to increase storage capacity, are incorrect because these are the typical functions of Type I and Type III PC Cards, respectively. **C,** to provide additional power to a portable, is incorrect because portable system batteries, not PC Cards, provide the portable with power.

LAB ANSWER

Table 2-3 provides the answer to the lab.

TABLE 2-3   Lab Answer Table

	SCSI	USB	IEEE-1394
Maximum number of devices	8, 16, or 32, including controller	127	63
Types	SCSI-1, SCSI-2, SCSI-3, and variants	Low and high speed	N/A
Speed	5, 10, 20, 40, 80, or 160 MBps	12Mbps	500Mbps
Resources	SCSI ID address	N/A	N/A
Additional required hardware	Terminator, SCSI controller	USB hub	none
Relative cost	More $$$ than IDE/ATA	Less money than FireWire, usually more money than IDE/ATA	More $$$ than USB
Device power source	External	Supplied by system	Supplied by system
Common devices	Hard drives, printers, scanners	Any	High-speed video, DVD, digital cameras
Communication method	Parallel	Serial	Serial
Topology (device connection method)	Daisy chain	Tiered (using hubs)	Daisy chain
Maximum cable length	1.5, 3, 6, or 12 meters for the entire chain	5 meters between devices	4 meters between devices
Resource configuration	Manual	Plug and Play	Plug and Play
Supports hot swapping?	No (yes on certain larger SCSI controllers)	Yes	Yes

3

Diagnosing and Troubleshooting Problems

The most common types of procedures you will perform as a computer technician are troubleshooting and resolving computer problems. The more familiar you are with the functions of the computer's components, the easier it will be for you to find the source of the problem and implement a solution. In the simplest cases, a component will simply do nothing and must be replaced. However, not all computer problems are that simple or obvious. For example, what should you do when your computer gives you a "201" error message at startup? Or if the floppy drive light comes on and won't go off?

This chapter covers troubleshooting techniques and where appropriate performance optimization techniques. It also describes the procedures you should follow in trying to determine obvious and less obvious sources of computer problems.

CERTIFICATION OBJECTIVE 3.01

Symptoms and Problems

This section presents the most common problems associated with typical computer devices and how to resolve them. Keep in mind that these are "common" problems of basic components. They do not, by any means, represent an exhaustive description of the great variety of problems you could come across as a technician. When faced with problems that do not have an obvious solution, you should follow the basic "fact-finding" steps discussed in the "Basic Troubleshooting Procedures" section of the chapter.

Many modern expansion cards and motherboards provide specific diagnostic and testing tools that allow for specific diagnosis of problems. Most of the time if a system is able to run the POST tests described in this section, higher level diagnostics are available. Many of these diagnostics are contained on floppy disks or CD-ROMs to facilitate troubleshooting. These tools should be used when possible to further isolate a defective card or subsystem.

The symptoms described here can be caused by a number of different component problems. For example, suppose you turn the computer on, and nothing happens at all. This problem could be caused by a faulty processor or system board, or it could simply be the result of a disconnected power cable. The troubleshooting procedures described here assume that the component in question has already been determined to be the cause of the problem.

on the
!
() o b

A good rule of thumb when troubleshooting a system that is not functioning properly is to always perform a visual inspection of all cables and connectors. Make sure that everything is plugged in properly before you invest any time in troubleshooting a system.

POST Audio and Visual Error Codes

When a computer is started, the BIOS performs a POST (power-on self-test) to check for the presence and status of existing components. Errors found during the POST are typically indicated by a visual error message on the screen or by a series of beeps. These visual and audio error codes can differ from BIOS to BIOS, so it's best to consult the manufacturer's documentation for the meaning of each code. However, some BIOS error codes are considered "common" because they are used in most machines.

For example, most error codes in the 1** series, such as 120 or 162, indicate a problem with the system board or processor. It is rare to see a 1** error code, since most system board and processor errors are serious enough to prevent the computer from issuing the error code at all.

Memory errors detected by the POST are typically indicated by a 2** error, and keyboard errors are indicated by a 3** error. Fortunately, most visual error codes are also accompanied by a brief description of the problem. Again, consult the documentation for your specific BIOS, because these messages can often be cryptic (for example, "213: DMA arbitration time-out").

Some BIOSes use a series of beeps rather than a visual message when there is a POST error. Typically, one beep indicates that all components passed the POST. This doesn't mean that there are no problems in the computer; it simply means that none of the components has a problem that was detected by the BIOS. When the BIOS issues an audio error code, carefully count the beeps and note whether they are long or short. Again, consult the BIOS documentation for the proper meaning of each code, because these differ from system to system. For example, one BIOS might indicate a video problem by issuing eight short beeps, while another might use one short and two long beeps.

on the
!
() o b

The manufacturer's website is a terrific place to get specific information on the diagnostics and BIOS messages that a motherboard uses. While there is a high level of standardization in codes, it is not unusual for manufacturers to implement codes of their own.

Processor and Memory Symptoms

In most cases, processor and memory problems are fatal, meaning that when there is such a problem, the computer will not boot at all. However, you should be aware of some nonfatal error indicators. As described, 1** error codes are typical of processor problems, and 2** error codes are typical of memory problems.

If you turn on the computer and it does not even complete the POST or it does nothing at all, and you have eliminated power problems, there might be a problem with the processor or memory. The solution to a processor or memory problem is to remove the offending component and replace it with a new one. If the error persists, there might be a problem with the slot or socket that the memory or processor uses to connect to the motherboard. In this case, the motherboard needs to be replaced.

On a final note: Some RAM errors are not reported by the computer at all. That is, if an entire memory module does not work, the computer might just ignore it and continue to function normally without it. Watch as the RAM is counted on the screen at startup to ensure that the total amount matches the capacity installed in the machine. If this amount comes up significantly short, you probably have to replace the memory module.

on the

Memory failures may not cause a system to appear to malfunction at all. Most modern systems will simply ignore a memory card that has malfunctioned and normal operations will continue. The user may note performance loss, which is a key symptom of a memory card failure.

Mouse

A number of different symptoms are associated with mice, and they provide a common source of computer problems. Fortunately, most procedures to resolve a mouse problem are quite simple. Let's look at two common mouse-related problems.

The Mouse Pointer Doesn't Move Smoothly on the Screen

A common mechanical mouse problem is irregular movement of the mouse pointer across the screen. Some mice even appear to hit an "invisible wall" on the screen. These symptoms indicate dirty mouse rollers. This problem is very common because, as the mouse is rolled across a desk or table, it can pick up debris, which is then deposited on the internal rollers. Many of the newer mice have eliminated the mechanical ball and roller system in favor of an optical or electronic motion sensing process. These types of mice may need to be cleaned, but they are proving to be much more reliable than the older mechanical mouse. To clean the mouse rollers, follow the steps in Exercise 3-1.

e**x**a m
watch

The most common problem with mechanical mice is irregular movement due to dust buildup on the rollers. In some situations the ball may be dirty. You can usually clean the ball with alcohol to remove dirt.

EXERCISE 3-1

Cleaning a Mouse

1. Unplug the Mouse, turn it upside-down and remove the retaining ring (usually by twisting it counter-clockwise).

2. Slowly invert the mouse so that the ball drops into your hand.

3. If the ball is dirty or sticky, you can clean it with soapy water.

4. Locate the rollers inside the mouse (see Figure 3-1). There are typically two long black rollers and one small metallic roller.

5. Use your fingers to remove the "ring" of dust from each roller, taking care not to let any material fall even further into the mouse.

6. If the rollers are sticky or if Step 5 is insufficient to clean the rollers, use a cotton swab dipped in isopropyl alcohol to clean them.

7. When you are finished, replace the mouse ball and retaining ring, ensuring that they are secured in place.

FIGURE 3-1

The internal rollers in a typical mouse

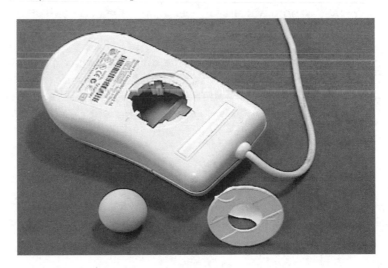

The Mouse Pointer Doesn't Move on the Screen

The mouse pointer's failure to move across the screen indicates that the computer cannot communicate properly with the mouse, so it is not receiving the appropriate signals to move the mouse pointer. One reason for this problem could be an IRQ conflict with another device. Because a serial mouse must use a COM port, it also uses that port's IRQ and I/O address. However, recall that some COM ports can share IRQ addresses. If another device attached to a COM port shares an IRQ with the mouse COM port, the mouse will probably not work at all. If you are running Microsoft Windows 9X you would use the Device Manager which is located under the Control Panel to determine if there is a resource conflict. If there is, move the offending device to a different COM port. Windows 2000 and Windows XP use Device Manager which resides in Computer Management, which is accessible under the Control Panel.

If the problem is not IRQ related, it might be driver related. That is, the mouse driver might be either corrupted or missing altogether. If you suspect a missing driver, you need to manually load the driver from the Setup disk that came with the mouse. If there is no driver disk, try simply restarting the computer. Most mice are Plug and Play, so the OS might automatically detect your mouse and load the appropriate driver for it at startup. If you suspect that a mouse driver exists but has become corrupted, use the Device Manager or the Mouse icon in the Control Panel to remove the existing driver and reload the driver.

Finally, an unresponsive mouse might be a symptom of a malfunctioning adapter card if it is a bus mouse. A bus mouse adapter card must be installed and configured in the same manner as other expansion cards. Ensure that it has the proper resources and that there are no conflicts. Next, ensure that the adapter card's device driver is loaded. You can also try opening the computer to ensure that the card is properly seated in the expansion slot or try replacing the card.

on the
ⓘob

Most newer systems provide a dedicated connection for the mouse and generally do not use a COM port for mouse connections. A USB mouse would be a better choice than a serial mouse if the mouse port physically failed for some reason. You would want to attempt to verify that the port has in fact failed by trying another mouse and reinstalling the driver.

Floppy Drive Failures

There are a number of ways a floppy drive can fail, so there are a number of different symptoms you must be aware of. Fortunately, most floppy failures stem from the disk, not the drive itself. Whenever you encounter a floppy drive failure, the first thing you should do is determine whether or not the disk is at fault. The easiest way to do this is

to eject the disk and insert another. If the problem goes away, the disk, not the drive, is the source of the problem. If you *must* have the information on a particular disk that's giving you trouble, try gently pulling the metal cover back and letting it snap back into place a few times, then reinserting the disk in the drive and trying to access the data again. You can also try to use the disk in a different drive.

An "A: is not accessible" Error Message

If you put a disk in the A drive and receive an "A: is not accessible" message, the drive cannot detect a floppy disk. The most common reason for this error is simply that no disk has been inserted in the drive or was not inserted all the way. Check to make sure that there is a disk inserted. If there is, remove the disk and try pulling the metal cover back a few times to loosen it; if the drive cannot pull the cover back, it cannot access the data on the disk.

An "Error writing to disk" Message

One of the most common symptoms of a floppy drive problem is a message stating that there is an error reading from or writing to the disk. This type of message typically indicates that the floppy drive controller is communicating properly with the computer but simply cannot access disk information. First, try to access a different disk, to rule out the original disk as the cause of the problem. If you determine that the problem is drive rather than disk related, try cleaning the drive's read/write heads.

Floppy drive cleaning kits can be purchased at many computer retail or parts stores. Typically, the kit includes a cleaning solution and what looks like a regular floppy disk. In most cases, the cleaning solution is applied to the disk, and the disk is inserted in the drive. The read/write heads are cleaned as they try to access the disk.

If the drive still cannot access a disk after cleaning, and you can read the floppy in another system, the problem lies within the drive itself, and it must be replaced.

A Floppy Drive Light That Won't Go Off

A floppy drive light that won't go off indicates that the drive's ribbon cable is attached incorrectly. Turn the computer off, remove the computer's cover, and reattach the cable the right way. Remember, the red stripe on the cable must be aligned with pin 1 on the system board and on the drive.

An "Invalid Drive" Error When Accessing the Floppy Drive

When you see this error—and any time the computer doesn't recognize the presence of the floppy drive—it means that the drive is not communicating properly with the computer. Turn the computer off and remove the cover. Make sure that the ribbon cable is present and properly and firmly attached. Next, make sure that the drive is receiving adequate power from the power supply. When you are satisfied that the drive is connected properly, restart the computer and access the CMOS settings program. Ensure that the correct floppy drive configuration is present in the BIOS settings. If the computer still does not recognize the floppy drive, try replacing the cable. If that doesn't fix the problem, the drive must be replaced with a working drive.

Hard Drives

Many things can go wrong with a hard drive, each of which can result in a number of different symptoms, so it can be difficult to determine the cause of the problem. The most common symptoms are discussed here.

The Computer Will Not Boot Properly

When you start the computer, you might receive a 16** POST error message. You could also get a message stating that there is no hard drive present. Typically, these errors are not fatal, and you can boot the computer using a special boot (floppy) disk.

When you receive this error, it means that the computer doesn't recognize or cannot communicate with the hard drive. First, restart the computer and enter the CMOS settings. Ensure that the proper hard drive type is listed in the BIOS drive configuration. If it is not, enter the appropriate settings, or use the system's hard drive detection option.

SCENARIO & SOLUTION

What Should You Do If...	Answer
You receive an "A: is not accessible" error?	Check for the presence of a floppy disk in the drive.
You receive an "Invalid drive" error?	Make sure that the drive works and is properly attached. Check to ensure that the BIOS settings match the drive type.
The floppy drive light comes on and won't go off?	Reverse the orientation of the ribbon cable in the floppy drive port.

If the BIOS settings are correct and the drive still won't work, or if the BIOS cannot detect the hard drive, there could be a cabling problem. Open the computer and ensure that the drive has the proper master or slave driver setting and that the ribbon and power cables are attached properly and securely. You should verify that the ribbon cable is not the problem by replacing it with a known good one. If the cables, jumpers, and BIOS settings have been ruled out, the problem is with the drive itself, and it must be replaced.

on the job

If you are troubleshooting a disk boot problem, it may be helpful to unplug all IDE devices that are not needed for the boot process. If the system boots with these devices disconnected it may help you isolate the problem. You can reconnect them one at a time until you find the problem device.

Nothing Happens When the Computer Is Turned On

Many things can cause the computer not to turn on, including a bad power supply or system board. It can also be a result of the system not being plugged in or an improperly connected hard drive. Check the hard drive ribbon cable to ensure that the red stripe is aligned with pin 1.

on the job

Sometimes your friends may play practical jokes on you. Many power supplies are now configured to support 120 or 220 volts (European standard). Verify that someone did not change the setting to the wrong voltage setting to see if your troubleshooting skills are up to snuff.

The Computer Reports That There Is No Operating System

Once the BIOS has finished the POST, it looks for the presence of an OS on the hard drive. If the BIOS does not find a special OS pointer in the drive's master boot record, it assumes that no OS exists. If you haven't yet installed an OS, you must do so at that point. If an OS exists but cannot be accessed, try using the SYS command at a DOS prompt to make the drive bootable. That is, reboot the computer from the floppy drive. (This command is described in more detail in Chapter 10.) Use the command SYS C:. This command replaces the pointer in the master boot record, and the computer might be able to boot properly.

Unfortunately, most cases of a missing OS stem from the corruption or loss of essential OS files. If this is the case, you need to reload the OS. When data becomes corrupted, it might be a sign that the disk is about to fail. You should consider running Scandisk to resolve these problems. You might also want to consider replacing the hard disk before it fails completely. Before you do this, boot from a floppy disk, then try to access and save any salvageable information from the hard drive.

If Scandisk reports finding corrupted data, consider replacing the hard drive. Data becomes corrupted when it resides on a "bad" spot on the disk. It is common for a hard drive to develop a few bad clusters before it fails completely. This can also occur when a system is powered down by pulling the plug. Usually the operating system will be able to deal with power down problems, but it can occur occasionally.

CD-ROM and DVD Drives

CD-ROM and DVD drives are functionally similar, so you can install or troubleshoot them using similar methods. A common problem with either of these devices is that the computer will report it can't read the disc. First, check to ensure the disc is inserted the right way. The label must be facing up so the drive can access the data from the underside of the disc. Next, visually inspect the disc. Scratches or smudges may prevent the computer from reading the disc. Try another disc in the drive to rule out the media as the cause. Cleaning the laser lens may also help solve the problem.

Commercially available CD-ROM cleaning and repair kits are readily available to restore CDs or clean the laser. Make sure you follow the directions in these kits, as improper use may cause more problems than they solve.

If the drive is the problem, check the Device Manager to ensure it has been recognized. Reload the device's driver if necessary, and check its system resources. If the problem persists, check the ribbon cable connection and jumper setting. Try the drive in another computer to pinpoint it or rule it out as the cause of the problem.

Parallel Ports

Typically, the only symptom of a failed parallel port is that the device attached to it will not work or not be detected by the computer. First, turn the device off, then back on again. Next, try restarting the computer. If there is still no response from the device, try the device in another parallel port or another computer. If the device functions properly, chances are that the original parallel port is at fault. You will also want to verify that the BIOS on the system has the malfunctioning port enabled.

Check the port's resource settings in the Windows Device Manager to ensure that it is not conflicting with another devices IRQ settings. If this is not the cause of the problem, test the function of the port using a *loopback adapter*, which, when connected to the port, can diagnose the port's ability to transmit and receive signals.

If the parallel port is faulty, it should be replaced. In older systems, the parallel port is not integrated with the system board and can be removed. If the parallel port is built into the system board, as in newer computers, you must replace the system board.

on the **Job**

From a practical perspective, it may not be cost effective to replace a motherboard if a parallel or serial port fails. You can purchase expansion cards that will provide additional ports if you need them. These expansion cards are usually very inexpensive and provide higher performance than the integrated ports on the motherboard.

The Sound Card and Audio

The components that make up a computer audio system are the sound card, the speakers, and the supporting software. All sound system problems can be narrowed down to one or more of these components.

The Speakers Produce No Sound

The problem of speakers failing to produce sound can be caused by a number of things. First, start with the speakers. Check to make sure that the volume is turned up to a sufficient level. In addition, check to make sure that they are plugged into the sound card and the proper port.

There are three ports on the sound card: microphone, sound out, and sound in. Although current sound cards and speakers come with color-coded connectors and connections, they didn't always. It is possible that the speaker is plugged into the wrong port.

If the speakers use an external power source, ensure that the power cable is properly attached and that the speakers are turned on. Try the speakers in another system to pinpoint them or rule them out as the cause of the problem.

If the speakers and the cables are not at fault, turn your attention to the audio software in the computer. Make sure that the Mute option has not been enabled and that the software-controlled volume is adjusted to a sufficient level. Try to produce sound in a number of different applications or reinstall the audio software.

If the sound card is at fault, check to make sure that it has the proper resources and device driver. If it does not, reassign an available IRQ, I/O address, and DMA channel, and reload the card's device driver. If the problem is still not resolved, open the computer and make sure that the sound card is properly and securely seated in the expansion slot. If the sound card is no longer working, replace it.

on the **!** **()** o b

Some of the newer sound systems provide advanced speaker output capabilities, which allows for multichannel hi-fi to be played by your computer. Hooking these systems up can sometimes require external connectors, splitters, and other devices. Make sure they are all functioning and connected properly before diving into the audio card.

A Lot of Static Is Coming from the Speakers

The symptom of speaker static might be the result of a number of problems, but it is very unlikely to be caused by the sound card. First, check the volume on the speakers and the software. If the speakers are turned way up but the computer's software-controlled volume is turned down or off, the speakers transmit the only signals they are receiving—static.

The static could also be the result of a failing cable. Replace the cables with known good ones. If the static persists, it could be due to EMI (electromagnetic interference). Move the speakers as far away from desktop lights, the monitor, and other interference-causing devices as you can. To rule out the speakers and cables, replace them with known working ones. The static could also be the result of bad data in the sound file. Try to play a different sound file to see if the static continues. Similarly, if you are listening to a CD, try another CD.

The Computer Is Not Producing the Right Sounds

Sometimes when you play a sound file, it is played incorrectly or just makes "noise." Because the speakers only amplify and cannot alter sound signals, you can rule them out as the cause of the problem. Occasionally a user may be attempting to listen to more than one type of sound file at a time (such as a CD and streaming audio); this may cause the sound card to garble the sounds as a result of the mixing process. Make sure you are only attempting to solve the problem using one audio source.

The problem could be in the sound file itself. Try another sound file or, if you're using a CD, replace the CD with another and try to play a sound file. If the problem is not limited to a specific sound file, try reinstalling the sound application or player software.

on the **!** **()** o b

Most CD-ROMS provide an external audio cable on the back of the CD-ROM drive. This cable must be connected to the sound card if you want your CD-ROM to be able to play music. The most common symptom of this cable being missing is that the CD-ROM and software function properly and no music comes out of the speakers. This cable is frequently not connected when an inexperienced person installs a CD-ROM drive or replaces a sound card.

The Monitor and Video

Like the sound system, a computer's video system contains a number of components, so it can be a bit tricky to diagnose and resolve problems. Another difficulty in resolving display problems is that you often don't see any display, so you can't see the OS or BIOS settings in order to remedy the problem.

The Computer Continues to Beep at Startup and Won't Boot Properly

This is an indication of a missing monitor or a missing or faulty video card. First, check to ensure that the monitor is properly attached to the video card. Don't worry about the monitor's power or settings, because these won't affect the computer's ability to boot. Next, check the function of the video card. Because there is no display, you can't check the resource or driver settings. You can, however, install the card in another computer to determine if it is functioning. If it is not, it must be replaced.

Complete Lack of Picture

If your monitor displays nothing at all and does not issue a beep code, the first thing you should do is move the mouse or press a key on the keyboard. Many computers use screen savers or power modes that cause the screen to go blank after a specified period of time. Using the mouse or the keyboard should return the computer to its normal state.

If this action doesn't solve the problem, begin by checking the video system components. Start with the easiest component first—the monitor. Make sure that the monitor is plugged into a power outlet and is turned on. Also ensure that the brightness is set at an adequate level. Next, check the cable that attaches the monitor to the computer. Verify that none of the pins are bent in on the video connector, straighten them out if necessary. In most cases, a missing or unattached cable will result in a POST error, but it is possible for this cable to come loose during operation. You can determine if the monitor is at fault by swapping it with a known good one. If the new monitor works in the system, you can assume that the original monitor is the problem. Before replacing an expensive monitor or FPD, you should have it checked by a trained technician. Since monitors and FPDs can be very expensive, it would not be prudent to throw one of these out if it is possible to have it replaced at a reasonable cost.

If the monitor is not the cause, check that the video card is seated properly in the expansion slot. AGP cards, especially earlier ones, are not easily seated. Press the card firmly (not too hard) and listen for an audible click to tell you the card is seated.

Later models don't seem to have this quirk. Because you cannot see the card's resources, you will not be able to determine if a configuration error is the problem. You can, however, try to install a different video card in this computer. Doing so might allow you to view the OS so that you can remove a faulty video card configuration, if it exists.

Some newer motherboards include an integrated video adapter. If this is one, look for a jumper setting to disable the on-board video and use an adapter card. If this option is not available, you need to replace the motherboard.

Flickering Monitor

Flickering may be a symptom of a faulty monitor. Replace the monitor with another to see if the problem still exists. Flickering can also be caused by an inappropriate *refresh rate* setting. The refresh rate configures how often the display gets "repainted." If the rate is too low for the video system you are using, it can cause the display to flicker. On a Windows-based system you can access the Control Panel's Display icon, and choose a different refresh rate.

on the **job**

The standard refresh rate for monitors is 75Hz. Older monitors may not work at this rate and may require a refresh rate of 60Hz. An older monitor will usually blank out if run at faster speeds.

Screen Elements Are Repeated Over and Over Again, All Over the Screen

Repeated screen elements are more common in older video systems. This problem is due to the use of an improper resolution setting for your video system. This setting results in multiple copies of the same image, including the mouse pointer, all over the screen. To solve this problem, enter the Display settings and reduce the resolution setting. This task can be cumbersome because more than one mouse pointer appears on the screen, making it nearly impossible to tell which is the real one. To navigate through the appropriate screens, I suggest you use the keyboard.

Modems

External modems are much easier to diagnose than internal modems because they typically have indicator lights that can inform you of their status, and it is easier to see if they are plugged in properly. However, other than internal adapter problems, both types of modems can display a number of symptoms.

A "No Modem Is Present" Message

The display of a message indicating that no modem is present means that the computer doesn't recognize the modem or can't communicate with it. If the modem is external, make sure that it is properly plugged into a serial port. You can test the cable by swapping it with a known good one, and you can test the serial port by attaching and configuring a known working device. Most external modems have an external source of power. Make sure that the power cable is properly attached and that the power switch is turned on. The modem should display a "power on" light.

on the
Job

Before you go diving into your computer to reinstall modem drivers or replace the modem, restart the system and test it again. Some modems are notorious for locking up if an unusual system event occurs. This may be caused by a modem being hung up on the other end. Most newer modems are very capable of dealing with these situations; some older modems are less reliable.

You should also make sure that the modem has been assigned the appropriate resources. If the modem is external, make sure that the COM port to which it is attached doesn't have a resource conflict. If the modem is internal, make sure that it has been assigned to a COM port that is both available (doesn't have a device attached) and has resources that are not in conflict with another device, such as a mouse. If this is not the source of the problem, check for the presence of the modem's device driver. If it hasn't been properly loaded, run the modem's Setup program or install the driver using the Windows Device Manager. If the driver is installed, it may be corrupt and can usually be reinstalled from either the Windows disk or the manufacturers installation media.

This problem can also be caused by incorrect dial-up properties. That is, your dial-up software might be configured to use an incorrect or nonexistent modem. Check the dial-up settings and ensure that the proper modem and modem type are selected.

Finally, if the modem is internal, open the computer and ensure that the modem is properly seated in the expansion slot. If the modem (internal or external) is found to be at fault, replace it.

on the
Job

You can usually test your connection to a modem using one of the communications programs available for your system. Most modems use the Hayes-compatible command set, and you can troubleshoot some functions of a modem using these commands.

A "No Dial Tone" Message

If your screen displays a message saying that your modem does not detect a dial tone, you should first ensure that the cable is properly attached to both the modem and the jack. Try unplugging the cable from the jack, then plugging it in again. Next, you can test the cable by swapping it with a known good one. This problem might also be the cause of a bad phone line. Plug a phone into the suspect jack and pick up the handset, as normal. If there is no dial tone, the problem is with the phone line. If there is a dial tone, the problem is most likely the modem cable.

on the **Job**

Try reversing the modem cable to the telco jack before you replace the cable. This may fix the problem in some modems.

The Modem Dials But Cannot Make a Connection

A modem's failure to connect is usually caused by problems incurred during the handshake phase of the communication process. The first step in a modem handshake is that the receiving (answering) device sends a guard tone to indicate that it is indeed a modem (and not a person or a fax machine). If the dialing modem doesn't receive a guard tone, the connection will be dropped. Check the phone number you are dialing; you might mistakenly be dialing a regular household or fax number.

Another step in the handshake process is for both modems to agree on a transmission speed. If the two modems don't have a single compatible speed, the connection will be dropped. For instance, suppose your modem is able to operate 28.8Kbps or lower, and the modem at the other end is able to operate only at 36.6Kbps. The modems do not have a common transmission speed, so the connection will not continue.

The inability to make a connection can also indicate that there is a lot of interference on the line. You can test for this by listening for line "static" using a regular phone. If static is present, the problem must be resolved by the phone company.

Most modems support multiple protocols; however, it is possible that the remote modem you are attempting to connect with is using an incompatible protocol. If you are having problems connecting to a single modem, it may be that the system requires a password and username early in the handshake process. You may need to provide this in the setup of the communications program that you are using.

The Modem Drops the Connection During Operation, Usually at Random

The main reason for an otherwise functioning modem to suddenly drop the connection is that it has been interrupted by another call. If your phone line has call waiting, ensure that it has been disabled in the modem's dial-up configuration. This problem can also occur if the modem shares a phone line with a regular phone or fax machine. If the phone is picked up during a modem session, the modem connection will be dropped.

The Modem Appears to Receive "Garbage"

Random "garbage," or invalid characters, are typically the sign of a noisy line. That is, static (EMI) on the line is being interpreted by the modem as valid data. Try using another line, moving EMI-causing devices out of the way, or contacting the phone company.

In more serious cases, all the data received by the modem can appear garbled. This means that the modem is interpreting every bit of data incorrectly and is probably using different communication standards than the modem at the other end. Disconnect, then try again; the handshake might be successful a second time. If it is not, ensure that dial-up settings, such as baud rate and parity, match those of the other modem. Systems that use serial mice may have a conflict between the modem and the mouse. Make sure that these resources do not conflict.

Modems attempt to connect at the highest speed that the telephone line supports. In some cases, this may vary from call to call depending on the quality of the phone line. If the line becomes too noisy, one end or other of the connection may drop the call. You can try setting a slower maximum speed on the modem to verify if the line is the problem.

BIOS

If the BIOS has a nonfatal error, you will be notified at startup by a series of beeps or a visual message indicating that there is a BIOS checksum failure. This means that the BIOS chip did not pass the POST. If this is the case, replace the BIOS. This is a very common occurrence if an upgrade is performed on the BIOS and for some reason the upgrade did not complete properly.

If the BIOS fails during the computer's operation, you will notice immediately because the computer will no longer be able to communicate with its peripherals. Most notably, the video system will shut down and the screen will go blank. However, because the BIOS is responsible for the proper function of every other component, it might not be obvious as the cause of the problem. In the case described here, you would most likely attempt to troubleshoot the video system before you came to the conclusion that the BIOS was at fault.

If you are upgrading to a newer operating system, the BIOS will mostly likely need to be upgraded as well. If you do not upgrade the BIOS, devices may not function properly, the system may lock up for no apparent reason, or the system may not recognize devices that are installed on the system.

Motherboards

In many cases, when a motherboard fails, it causes a fatal error that prevents the computer from booting properly. However, if the BIOS is able to run a POST, it might report a problem with the motherboard as a 1** error. Unfortunately, as with a BIOS failure, no one symptom or set of symptoms can immediately be used to pinpoint the motherboard as the point of failure.

A faulty motherboard can cause a great number of different symptoms to occur and can even cause it to appear that a different component is at fault. This is because a problem on the motherboard could be localized in one particular area, such as a single circuit or port, causing a failure of a single device only. For example, if the video card's expansion slot on the motherboard stops working, it will appear that there is a problem with the display system. In this case, you are likely to discover the motherboard as the point of failure only after checking all other components in the video system.

When there is a problem with the motherboard, the only solution is to replace it. However, because of the difficulty and expense of replacing the motherboard, this should be done only when every other possibility, including the BIOS chip, has been examined.

on the **job**

Due to the difficulty and expense involved in replacing a motherboard, it (and the processor) should be the last components that you suspect. Test all other affected components before determining that the motherboard is at fault.

Universal Serial Bus

Recall that USB devices are hot swappable and support Plug and Play. Because so much of a USB device's operation depends on the function of the USB controller, this is where a majority of USB-related problems lie. USB 1.1 is upward compatible with USB 2.0. Some of the most common USB problems are discussed here.

The USB Device Doesn't Seem to Get Power

Most devices get their power from the USB system or, more specifically, from the root or external hubs. First, if the device has a power switch or button, make sure it's turned to the on position. Next, make sure that the cable is securely connected. If this is a new installation, check the documentation and packaging to be sure an external power cord hasn't been overlooked. You should also check to make sure that the device is plugged into the proper type of hub. "Low-powered" USB devices can be plugged into any type of USB hub, but "high-powered" devices (which use over 100 milliamps) must be plugged into self-powered USB hubs only.

The USB Keyboard Won't Work

The keyboard's drivers and resources are typically controlled by the BIOS. When you install a USB keyboard, the BIOS must be informed so that it will hand control of the keyboard to the USB system. Enter the CMOS settings at startup and ensure that the USB keyboard option is turned on. If this option doesn't exist and you still want to use the USB keyboard, you might need to upgrade the BIOS or the computer. The BIOS usually provides a generic drive for USB keyboards. If the system you are using has an older BIOS, the driver may not be included.

"USB Device Is Unknown" Message, or the Device Won't Work

A message stating that the USB device is unknown or the device simply won't work means the computer cannot communicate with the device. First, make sure that the device is properly attached and is receiving power, and try switching it to another port. Make sure that the device's cable is not longer than 5 meters. Although most USB devices are Plug and Play, a few require proprietary drivers. Make sure that a driver is loaded for this device.

Check to make sure that the device is using the proper communications mode. On startup, the USB controller assigns an ID to all devices and asks them which type of data transfer (interrupt, bulk, or continuous) they will use. If a device is set to use the wrong type of transfer mode, it will not work. Finally, check the device by swapping it with a known good one.

None of the USB Devices Will Work

If none of the USB devices work, you could have a problem with the entire system or the USB controller. First, make sure that your OS is USB compliant, such as Windows 98, Windows Me, Windows 2000, or Windows XP. Next, make sure that the number of devices does not exceed 127 and that no single cable length exceeds 5 meters. The USB system is also limited to five tiers or five hubs in a single chain. Check the cable length and cable connections, especially from the root hub to the first external hubs. A loose connection will prevent all devices on the external hub from functioning.

If the problem isn't in the USB physical setup, turn your attention to the USB controller. Make sure that a proper driver has been loaded for it and that it does not have an IRQ or I/O conflict with another device. You should also check the BIOS for USB support, to determine if you can use USB in this system. You may also want to uninstall the driver for the USB hub or controller. When you restart the system, the operating system will notify you to reinstall these drivers. This may fix the problem.

CMOS

Problems stemming from the CMOS include lost or incorrect settings. Lost settings occur when the CMOS battery begins to lose power. You will generally be informed of this problem by a 1** error message at startup or by a prompt to enter the correct time and date. When this is the case, replace the battery.

Incorrect CMOS settings can have many incarnations because there are CMOS settings for a great variety of system elements, including hard drives, floppy drives, the boot sequence, keyboard status, and parallel port settings. The incorrect setting will be manifested as an error relating to that particular device or function, so it can be difficult to pinpoint the CMOS as the source of the problem. However, when you need to change or update the CMOS, enter the CMOS settings at startup, make the appropriate change(s), save the new setting(s), and restart the computer.

Power Supplies, Fans, and Airflow

Power supplies can experience total or partial failures, resulting in inconsistent or displaced symptoms. However, you can identify a few "common" symptoms of power supply failure to pinpoint the problem; those symptoms are discussed here. When the power supply fails, it must be replaced. Never try to open or repair a power supply, because it can hold enough charge to seriously injure you.

on the
Job

Like monitors, power supplies can cause serious personal injury. Never open the case of a power supply!

Nothing Happens When the Computer Is Turned On

There are a few things that can cause lack of any activity at system startup, such as a bad processor or memory, but the most likely suspect is the power supply. When the power supply stops working, so does the computer's fan, which is typically the first thing you hear when you turn the computer on. Check to make sure that the power supply is properly connected to an electrical outlet. In addition, check the power selector (on the back of the computer between the power cord connection and the on/off switch) to ensure that it has the right setting for your geographic region (North American [115] or European [230] voltage).

You should also check to ensure the P8, P9, and other power cables are properly attached to necessary devices, including the computer's power button. If the power supply doesn't work, replace it. If this still does not solve the problem, try removing all power connections to the power supply and turning the PC back on. The fan on the power supply should start. If it doesn't, this is a clear indication that the power supply has malfunctioned.

The Computer Turns On But There's No Fan

If your computer turns on but you don't hear the sound of the computer's fan, save your work and turn the computer off immediately. The power supply's built-in fan draws air into the computer to keep the components from overheating. If the fan isn't working, you can cause serious damage by running the computer.

atch

If the power supply's fan stops working, you must replace the entire power supply, not just the fan.

Once the computer is off, you should try cleaning the fan, using the procedures described in Chapter 4. Because the fan draws air, it can also draw dust, lint, or hair that can cause the fan to stop rotating. If cleaning doesn't resolve the problem, you must replace the entire power supply.

The Computer Behaves Sporadically or Reboots Itself

Sporadic behavior or self-booting is typical behavior from a computer with a bad power supply. If the power supply is providing power to only some devices, the computer will behave irregularly; some devices will seem to work, while others will work only part of the time or not at all. Check to make sure that the P8, P9, and all other power connectors are properly attached.

If the power supply's fan is broken, the computer's components will also behave strangely. Overheated components might work sometimes but not others, and very commonly, an overheated computer will simply shut itself off or spontaneously reboot. Try cleaning the power supply fan. If this doesn't solve the problem, replace the power supply.

Slot Covers

Believe it or not, the removable slot covers at the back of the computer are not there solely to tidy up the appearance of the computer. They serve to keep dust and other foreign objects out of the computer. If you leave the slot covers off, you run the risk of allowing dust to settle on the internal components, especially the empty expansion slots (which are notoriously difficult to clean). Removal of the slot covers can also cause the computer to overheat. The computer is designed so that the devices expected to generate the most heat are in the fan's "line of fire." If the slot covers are left off, the air's path through the computer could be changed or impeded, resulting in improper cooling of the components inside.

The Fan Is Noisy

There are more cooling fans inside a computer than the one on the power supply. Today's computers have one (slot) or two (SEC) cooling fans on the CPU. There can also be one or more strategically placed cooling fans inside the case.

When a fan begins to wear out, it makes a whining or grinding noise. When this happens, replace the fan, unless it is inside the power supply. In that instance, replace the entire power supply. Opening the power supply is dangerous, and the time you'd spend on such a repair is more valuable than the replacement cost of a power supply.

Hard Drive Address Translation

Address translation involves translating the actual addresses on a hard drive into addresses that the BIOS can use. Address translation typically occurs on older systems that cannot access over 528MB of hard drive space. One type of address translation is called *logical block addressing (LBA)*. Here's how it works: in older hard drives, each sector is identified by its *cylinder, head, and sector (CHS)* address (a sort of 3-D grid), and there is no support for addresses over 528MB. Using LBA, each sector is identified by a linear numerical value from 0 to 8.4GB (or the hard drive's total capacity, whichever is lower). When the BIOS asks for a CHS address, it is translated into the actual hard drive sector's number.

To use drive translation, both the BIOS and the hard drive must support its use. BIOS chips that support translation are called *enhanced*. Next, the proper translation mode must be selected in the BIOS options. *Normal* mode is the nontranslation mode. *LBA mode* and *large mode* (also called *enhanced mode*) both provide address translation, but they use different addressing methods. LBA mode is typically faster, but large mode has the advantage of being supported by all EIDE hard drives.

You should never enable or disable address translation on a drive that already contains data, because the data could be lost. If you cannot enable translation, check

SCENARIO & SOLUTION

How do I replace a bad integrated parallel port?	If the parallel port is integrated with the motherboard, you must replace the motherboard.
The computer continually asks me for the time at startup. What should I do?	Replace the CMOS battery.
What should I do with a computer that keeps rebooting itself?	Replace the power supply.
What should I do when the mouse pointer doesn't move smoothly on the screen?	Clean the mouse.

to see if your BIOS supports this feature. Most systems that have been manufactured in the last few years can communicate with drives of nearly any capacity and do not need large or LBA mode to do so.

Troubleshooting Tools

In order to be completely prepared for any onsite computer problem, you would have to equip yourself with every type of cable, connector, battery, or driver that any component might need. Since you can't do this, you should stick to the basic troubleshooting tools, utilities, and devices described here.

Toolkits

Most computer toolkits include an array of Phillips, flathead, and Torx screwdrivers of varying sizes. You should keep the most popular sizes of each. It might also be helpful to include an extended extractor, also called a *parts grabber*. These are useful for retrieving dropped objects, such as jumpers or screws, from inside the computer. Your toolkit should also include a flashlight for peering into dark places and a small container for holding extra screws and jumpers (a film case should work).

Multimeters

Some toolkits come with a multimeter. If not, you should get one separately. *Multimeters* are used to measure the resistance, voltage, and/or current within computer components. They are most commonly used to determine connectivity between two components. For example, if a circuit or cable is measured as having infinite resistance, it means that there is a break somewhere in the line. A multimeter can also be used to ensure that the power supply is generating the appropriate voltage or that a motherboard component is receiving the proper current.

Software Tools

One of the most useful tools you can bring with you to a customer's site is a startup (boot) disk. A boot disk will allow you start the computer in a state of minimal devices and files, so that you can locate an offending device or file before it is loaded and causes the computer to halt or crash. (See Chapter 9 for details on creating a startup disk.) Other software tools that you should have include antivirus software, diagnostic utilities, installation software, and data recovery utilities.

FROM THE CLASSROOM

Tools You Can Do Without

You might come across some tools on the market or that are included in a toolkit that you really should avoid. To begin with, you should never use a magnetized screwdriver when repairing a computer. Remember, lots of computer components rely on magnetic storage. If you use a magnetized screwdriver around the hard drive, for example, you could inadvertently wipe it clean of its data. Many technicians use magnetized screwdrivers to retrieve small parts that get dropped inside the computer. Instead, you should use what is commonly (and not very poetically) referred to as a parts grabber. This is a pen-sized tool with a plunger at one end. When you press the plunger, small, hooked prongs are extended at the other end.

If you absolutely have to magnetize your screwdriver, rub it against the computer's internal speaker. The screwdriver will be magnetized for only a short time, thus reducing the risk of accidentally erasing magnetically stored data.

Another tool to avoid is the two-pronged IC extractor, also known as a chip mangler. These are shaped like tweezers and are designed for pulling chips off the motherboard. However, with the force of your hand localized to only two points on the chip, it is easy to cause damage to the chip. For this reason, you should also avoid using pliers to extract chips. The only chip pullers you should use have one prong that fits between row of the chip's pins, evenly distributing the pressure applied by your hand.

Another chip-mangling device is the chip inserter. This device is placed on top of a chip on the motherboard. By pressing the plunger at the other end of the device, you can insert the chip into its sockets. However, because you can't feel how much pressure you are exerting or whether the chip is lined up properly, it is easy to break or bend the pins. Instead, you should use your fingers or thumb to gently push the chip into its socket.

CERTIFICATION OBJECTIVE 3.02

Basic Troubleshooting Procedures

As you know, to resolve any computer problem, you must first determine its source. However, in many cases, the computer can behave in a way that does not easily lead you to the device that is causing the trouble. In these cases, you need to analyze a combination of the computer's symptoms and its history as well as information from the computer's user.

All computer problems can be resolved. Sometimes this resolution includes adjusting configurations or replacing a component. It can even include replacing the computer altogether. However, before you can make this determination, you must be able to locate the source of the problem. The following discussions describe where to look for the information you need before you can begin troubleshooting.

Information Gathering

In many cases, as a technician, you will be expected to troubleshoot computers that you do not regularly use or know about. You might be called into a client's office or have an unfamiliar computer brought to you for repairs. The first step is to gather as much information as you can about the computer and its peripherals, applications, and history.

on the **job**

Sometimes customers fib. In some situations a customer may be unwilling to tell you that they attempted to install a device or hardware. They may neglect to tell you this to avoid embarrassment. Make sure you treat the customer in a manner that encourages them to be open with you about what they may have done to the system before you became involved.

Customer Environment

If you are performing onsite troubleshooting, notice your surroundings. They might give you a clue as to a problem's cause, and if you notice potential trouble, you can help to prevent future problems.

Take notice of the room's environment, such as the temperature. Most computer components do not work well in the presence of heat. Furthermore, very high or low humidity can cause condensation or electrostatic discharge, respectively, both of which can lead to problems. A safe humidity level is between 50 and 80 percent. You should also be aware of nearby devices that could cause electromagnetic interference (EMI).

Look at the way components are plugged into wall outlets and determine if the outlets are overburdened by too many plugs. Take note of the way cables are arranged. For example, do people have to step over the cable to the printer? Such a setup can lead to a loose cable connection.

Finally, you should notice the way that people use the computer. Although you are not onsite to tutor people in application or shortcut use, it might help you to notice rough handling of the equipment. If the user "bangs" on the keys, you will have a good clue as to the cause of a faulty keyboard. In addition, some users tend to triple- and quadruple-click icons on the screen in an attempt to hurry things along. This practice can lead to computer lock-ups.

Symptoms and Error Codes

One of the best guides in determining the cause of a problem is the user who was working on the computer when the failure occurred. After taking note of the environment, your first question to the user should be, "What happened?" This question will prompt the user to tell you about the problem—for example, "The printer won't work." Ask about other problems: Do other devices work? The answers you receive can tell you a great deal. If no other devices work, you know you are dealing with a more serious, device-independent problem. Ask about the device's history. Did this device ever work? If the user tells you that the device was just installed, you have a very different task ahead of you than if the user tells you it worked fine all day until now.

If the user complains of an error code, ask for as much detail about the error as possible. If the user can't remember, try to recreate the problem. Again, ask if this is a new or old error message, and ask if the computer's behavior changed after the error. For example, the computer might issue a warning that simply informs the user of some condition. These types of messages might not affect performance. If the error code points to a device, ask the device-related questions we've already mentioned. For example, the error message might have stated that the floppy disk couldn't be accessed.

on the Job

A customer called in to the service center to report her computer was not working. The customer was asked what the model number of the computer was. The customer explained that they could not do that. When asked why, the customer explained that the building was in a blackout and that his office was dark. You do the math!

Problem Situation

When you have determined what the problem is (its symptoms, not its cause), you need to get some basic history from the user. Ask if the problem occurred at random or in response to a user action. An error that occurs "out of the blue" is a different matter from an error that occurs every time the user tries to use the scanner, for example.

Try to replicate the problem. That is, if the user says the printer won't work, ask the user to send another print job. Watch closely as the user performs the task. Take note of any error messages or unusual computer activity that the user might not have noticed. Your observation will also give you a chance to see the process from beginning to end. For example, if the user is trying to print an image, watching the task performed might allow you to see a problem such as an incorrect printer selection or the absence of an entry in the Number of Pages field. You should also note the way the user performs the task to determine if it is being performed properly. For example, a CD-ROM drive error could be the result of the user trying to copy a file onto a nonwritable CD.

When the user tries to replicate the problem, the original problem might not recur. In this case, it is likely that there was another process preventing the action from taking place. For instance, if the user tries to access a newly inserted CD before the CD-ROM drive has had a chance to spin up, an error will occur. The next time the user tries to access the CD, there will be no problem.

on the **job**

Be very aware of your personal interactions with the user at this point. These problems are a common occurrence, and a user's initial reaction is often embarrassment.

You should also find out about any recent changes to the computer or the surroundings. For example, ask if a new component or application has recently been installed. If one has, ask if the feature or device has worked at all since the new installation. The answer to this question could lead you to important information about application or device conflicts. For example, if the user tells you that the sound hasn't worked ever since a particular game was loaded, you can suspect that the two events—the loading of the new game and the sound failure—are related.

Pinpointing the Hardware or Software

The information that you gather from the user might be enough to pinpoint the cause of the problem. If it's not, you need to narrow down the search even further by determining if the problem is hardware or software related. In the remaining sections, a hardware problem is considered to include the device as well as its resources, configuration files, and device drivers. Software problems include applications, OSes, and utilities.

One of the quickest ways to determine if the hardware or the software is at fault is to use the Windows Device Manager. Any conflicting or "unknown" devices will be indicated here. If the Device Manager offers no information about problems, it doesn't mean that there isn't a hardware problem; it means only that Windows hasn't recognized one. The Device Manager and its equivalents are discussed in Chapters 9 and 10.

on the **job**

Make sure you work to establish a good rapport with the user. You want to make sure that you know about any expansion or upgrades the customer has tried to make. When troubleshooting, remove these upgrades first.

Most hardware devices can be used by a number of applications, and vice versa. Therefore, you can narrow the search by trying to access more than one type of device from the suspect application or using more than one application to access the suspect device. Suppose, for example, that a user was unable to scan an image into a particular word processor. Use a different application to access the scanner. If it works, you can conclude that the scanner is physically sound and turn your attention to the configuration or reinstallation of the original application. If, however, the scanner does not work in another program, use the original program to access another device, such as the printer.

Continue combining applications with hardware devices to try to rule out one or the other. Keep in mind that this method will not always lead you to a definitive conclusion. For example, suppose a printer can't be accessed by any application. Although it would appear that the printer is at fault, it might be that it is simply not set as the default printer. This is a software, not a hardware, problem.

Troubleshooting, Isolating, and Problem Determination Procedures

Once you have followed these procedures and determined the device or subsystem at fault, you should restart the device or computer. In many cases, restarting the computer releases resources that a device or application needs to use but that are being tied up by another device or application. Restarting the computer also forces the computer to reestablish the presence of existing devices and clear information out of its memory.

Hardware Problems

If restarting the computer doesn't solve the problem, determine if this symptom is familiar to you. For example, if you know the mouse connection often comes loose from a particular computer, you should look there first when the mouse stops working. If the problem is unfamiliar to you, use the information in this section to help you further narrow your search.

Always check the connection of a device to the computer, and make sure that the device is properly configured to use system resources and a driver. If the answer is not apparent, you need to focus your search on the components of the failed system or subsystem. For example, if there is no computer display, there is no need to check the components of the sound system.

When examining a subsystem, always start with the parts that are easiest to access or to see. In the example of a nonfunctioning display, check the monitor before you take the computer apart to check the adapter card. For any subsystem, start with the most accessible part and work your way into the computer. A good knowledge of the system's components, as described in Chapters 1 and 2, will help you determine which devices belong to which subsystems. It is especially important to note whether the device is local or accessed through the network. A problem using a printer, for example, could actually be caused by the computer's inability to make a network connection.

If everything in the current system *appears* to be okay (in other words, everything is powered on and properly attached and there are no resource conflicts), suspect the devices themselves. To identify or rule out a device as the cause of the problem, swap it with another. Take a spare component (one that you know functions correctly) and use it in place of the suspect component. If the new component works, you have discovered the problem.

If the new component doesn't work, there must be a problem elsewhere. In this case, don't assume the original component works; it, plus another component, could have failed at the same time. You can install the original component in another system to determine its functionality. For example, assume that a video system has a bad adapter card *and* a bad monitor. You swap the monitor with another and get no response, so you assume that the monitor is not the cause of the problem and reattach it. When you get the adapter working, there is still no video, because you are using the original bad monitor. Always swap one component at a time. For another example, suppose that a computer can't use a particular scanner. You switch ports, swap the cable, and swap the scanner, all at the same time. If the computer is then able to scan correctly, you will not be able to determine whether it was the port, the cable, or the scanner that caused the problem in the first place.

on the job *It is not unusual for a system to have multiple problems. Do not make the assumption that only one thing is wrong with the system. Be prepared to accept that you may be fighting more than one problem. Don't be afraid to take most of the expansion cards out of the system to establish if you have one or more problems. You can reinstall them one at a time until the problem reoccurs.*

Again, working your way into the computer, swap out each component with a working one. This includes the problematic device and any cables attached to it. If the device is external, try plugging it into another port or try attaching a different device to the suspect port. If the device is internal, switch it to another expansion slot.

If you have tested the attachment and configuration of each device and still have not solved the problem, look at the underlying hardware within the computer. That is, test components that are responsible for the computer's performance as a whole, including the BIOS, the CMOS battery, the processor, RAM, and the system board.

Software Problems

If you have determined that the problem is software related, and rebooting the computer didn't solve the problem, you should turn your attention to the configuration of the application. Most applications or utilities include a Preferences, Tools, or Options feature, through which you can configure its operation and the devices it can access.

You can also try uninstalling the application, then reloading it. Some application installations contain errors that affect only one or a small number of its functions. Use the Uninstall utility that came with the application, or use the Windows Add/ Remove Programs utility.

Check to make sure that the computer meets the application's minimum requirements. It is possible that the computer simply will not support the application. Check the application manufacturer's website for patches and updates. Perhaps this user is experiencing a problem caused by a flaw in the application. Most manufacturers release patches that can remedy discovered problems.

You may also find that a software product works on an older operating system but not in a newer system. Verify that the software that is causing the problem will run on the version of the operating system you are running. This is especially common with older computer games.

The information in this section has been compiled into Exercise 3-2. Follow these steps when troubleshooting a hardware problem.

EXERCISE 3-2

Troubleshooting a Hardware Problem

1. Gather as much information from the customer as you can, including symptoms, error messages, computer history, and the user's actions at the time of the failure.

2. Try to reproduce the problem, taking note of any error messages or unusual system activity.

SCENARIO & SOLUTION

How can I determine if a monitor has gone bad?	Try it in a working system.
What should I do if an application has been incorrectly installed?	Uninstall then reinstall it.
My sound system is bad. Where should I start to look for the problem?	Start with the speakers, and work your way into the computer.

3. Determine whether the problem is hardware or software related. Do this by watching error messages, using the Device Manager, and accessing the hardware using a variety of applications. The remainder of this exercise assumes that the problem is hardware related.

4. Start with the most accessible component in the affected subsystem, making sure that it has power and is properly connected.

5. Check the resources of the device and ensure that a device driver has been loaded for it.

6. Test the device by using it in another computer or by using a known working device in its place.

7. Continue testing and checking all components in the subsystem, working your way into the computer.

8. Finally, test the computer's most basic components, such as the BIOS, system board, memory, and processor.

CERTIFICATION SUMMARY

As a computer technician, you will be required to locate and resolve the source of computer problems. If you have a good knowledge of the functions of the computer's components, you will be able to more quickly troubleshoot problems that occur. However, there are other telltale signs of failed components. For example, you can use POST error codes to determine the cause of a problem. Although the troubleshooting procedures differ from component to component and even for different problems within the same component, a majority of the procedures involve cleaning the component, ensuring that it is properly attached to the computer, and finally, replacing the component.

Unfortunately, not all computer problems are easy to diagnose, and it could take some time for you to find the offending device or application. When trying to determine a problem's source, gather as much information about the problem as you can, and try to reproduce the problem. Next, determine if this is a hardware or a software problem. If it is a software problem, check the application's configuration or try uninstalling and then reinstalling it. If the problem is hardware related, identify the components that make up the failing subsystem. Starting with the most accessible component, check for power and proper attachment to the computer. Check the device's configuration and presence of a device driver. Finally, swap suspected bad components with known good ones.

Remember that every problem has a resolution, whether it is simply reattaching a loose cable, changing an application's settings, or replacing entire subsystems. As a computer technician, you have the responsibility for determining which course of action is the most appropriate for each computer problem you face.

TWO-MINUTE DRILL

Here are some of the key points from each certification objective in Chapter 3.

Symptoms and Problems

❑ POST error codes, such as 1**, 2**, and 3** can indicate system board, memory, or keyboard failures, respectively.

❑ Most system board, processor, and memory errors are fatal, meaning that the computer cannot properly boot up.

❑ The most common mouse problem is irregular movement, which can be resolved by cleaning the internal rollers in the mouse.

❑ A hard drive that begins to develop corrupted data should be replaced before all the information stored on it is lost.

❑ When troubleshooting a video or audio problem, start with the most accessible component and check to ensure that it is getting power and is properly connected to the computer.

❑ When resolving modem errors, make sure that the modem is properly attached and configured and that there is a connection to the phone jack and a good dial tone.

❑ Motherboard errors can be the most difficult to pinpoint and, due to the cost and effort involved in replacement, should be the last device you suspect when a subsystem or the entire computer fails.

❑ Never open the power supply or try to replace the fan; rather, replace the entire power supply when the fan stops working.

Basic Troubleshooting Procedures

❑ When faced with a computer problem, gather information from the customer, such as what the problem is, what happened before the problem occurred, and what, if anything, has changed recently in the computer.

❑ Determine whether the problem is hardware or software related by accessing suspect devices with more than one type of application, and vice versa.

❑ To resolve software problems, check the software's configuration and its minimum requirements, then try to reinstall it.

❑ To resolve a hardware problem, first identify and test the components that belong to the affected subsystem.

❑ Always check to ensure that a failed device has power and is connected to the computer.

❑ Verify a suspect component's status by trying to use it in another computer or by replacing it with a known working component.

❑ Check the configuration of a failed device to ensure that it does not have a resource conflict with another device.

SELF TEST

The following questions will help you measure your understanding of the material presented in this chapter. Read all of the choices carefully because there might be more than one correct answer. Choose all correct answers for each question.

Symptoms and Problems

1. Which component is typically associated with a 3** BIOS error code?
   A. The motherboard
   B. The keyboard
   C. The processor
   D. RAM

2. Which of the following symptoms is not a typical symptom of a RAM error?
   A. The POST cannot be conducted.
   B. When you turn the computer on, nothing happens.
   C. The system reports that there is no operating system.
   D. The BIOS reports a 2** error.

3. A user complains that the mouse pointer does not move smoothly across the screen. Which of the following is most likely to remedy the problem?
   A. Reinstalling the mouse driver
   B. Ensuring that the mouse cable is connected securely to the computer
   C. Ensuring that there are no IRQ conflicts between the mouse and another device
   D. Cleaning the mouse

4. Which of the following should you do first when you receive the error shown in Figure 3-2?
   A. Make sure that there is a floppy disk in the drive.
   B. Ensure that the floppy ribbon cable is attached properly.
   C. Make sure that the floppy drive is properly configured in the BIOS settings.
   D. Clean the floppy disk.

FIGURE 3-2

A typical error message

5. You have just finished building a computer. You notice that when you turn the computer on, the floppy drive light comes on and won't go off. What should you do?

   A. Insert a different disk into the drive.

   B. Reverse the ribbon cable on the drive.

   C. Swap the drive with another one.

   D. Nothing.

6. When you tried to access a hard drive, you received an "Invalid Drive" error. Which of the following can you rule out as the cause of this error?

   A. The hard drive

   B. The BIOS

   C. The ribbon cable

   D. Corrupted files

7. When the Win9x computer is started, it displays a "Missing Operating System" error. Which command can you use to make the drive bootable?

   A. BOOT

   B. BOOT OS

   C. SYS

   D. SYSTEM

8. A user complains that when he plays a CD in the computer, the music is accompanied by a lot of static. All of the following are possible causes of this problem *except*:

   A. The speaker cables

   B. The speaker volume

   C. The CD

   D. The monitor

9. Which of the following might be responsible for your modem producing random "garbage" or meaningless characters?

   A. A missing device driver

   B. An improper resource (IRQ or I/O) configuration

   C. A failed or improper modem handshake

   D. Static on the phone line

10. A customer complains that the computer spontaneously reboots and sometimes will not start at all. Furthermore, even when the computer does start, there's not as much noise as usual. Which device is most likely causing these problems?

A. The power supply
B. The system board
C. The processor
D. The RAM

Basic Troubleshooting Procedures

11. You have just arrived at a customer's office to perform onsite troubleshooting for a faulty sound system. Which of these environmental indicators could be the cause of the problem?

A. The room is humid.
B. The room is cool.
C. Only 3 out of 15 people are using the network.
D. The lights are off in the room.

12. You are trying to resolve a video problem. The screen is blank, and you are fairly certain that the monitor is bad. Which of the following should you do first to verify your suspicion?

A. Make sure that the monitor's driver is properly installed.
B. Ensure that the video adapter is properly configured.
C. Ensure that the monitor does not have an IRQ conflict with another device.
D. Swap the monitor with a known working one.

13. A document was created in a word processing application but will not print properly. After ensuring that the printer has power and a proper connection to the computer, what is the next thing you should do?

A. Use the same application to access the scanner.
B. Reload the printer's device driver.
C. Try to print from another application.
D. Reinstall the word processor.

14. In troubleshooting a display problem, you swapped the monitor with a known good one, but this did not resolve the problem. What should you do next?

A. Reattach the original monitor to the computer.
B. Make sure that the cable from the monitor to the video card is connected tightly.
C. Ensure that the adapter card is properly seated in the expansion slot.
D. Swap the adapter card.

15. A user has complained that she can't print from a particular word processor application or a certain graphics program. However, the spreadsheet program prints fine. Assume that this is a network printer. Which of the following is the likely cause of this problem?

    A. The configuration of the word processor and graphics programs
    B. The printer's device driver
    C. The printer itself
    D. An improper network configuration

16. When your computer's sound system was first installed, it worked fine. Now it produces no sounds at all. Which of the following should you check first?

    A. The sound card's configuration
    B. The speaker's configuration
    C. The sound card
    D. The speaker

17. Assume that a computer has a functioning display system. Which of the following represents the proper order of steps you should perform to most efficiently determine the source of a hardware problem on the computer?

    A. Try to reproduce the error, gather information about the problem, swap the device with a known good one, and check the device's configuration.
    B. Gather information about the problem, try to reproduce the error, swap the device with a known good one, and check the device's configuration.
    C. Gather information about the problem, try to reproduce the error, check the device's configuration, and swap the device with a known good one.
    D. Check the device's configuration, gather information about the problem, try to reproduce the error, and swap the device with a known good one.

18. When a user tries to save to the hard drive in a particular application, the computer locks up. Otherwise, the application works normally. Assume that the computer has only one hard drive installed. Which of the following can you rule out as the cause of the problem?

    A. The hard drive's configuration
    B. An improper installation of the application
    C. An improperly written application
    D. Insufficient system requirements

19. You played a game on the computer about an hour ago and closed the game when you were finished. In the meantime, you opened a word processor, sent a print job to the printer, and

then closed the application. When you tried to restart the game, nothing happened. Which of the following should you do first?

- A. Obtain a manufacturer's patch for the game
- B. Troubleshoot the printer
- C. Restart the computer
- D. Reinstall the game

20. A customer has complained of an error message regarding the scanner but cannot remember the wording of the error message that appeared. Which of the following should you do next?

- A. Restart the computer.
- B. Have the user try to replicate the problem.
- C. Check the scanner's configuration.
- D. Swap the scanner with a known good one.

LAB QUESTION

A customer has complained about a problem in playing a music file. He tells you that the computer seemed to run the file, but no sound was produced, even though it worked properly yesterday. Although you don't know it at first, the problem is that the sound card's expansion slot has failed because of a broken circuit. Describe the steps you will perform, in the proper order, to determine that this is the cause of the problem. Also discuss how you will resolve the problem.

SELF TEST ANSWERS

Symptoms and Problems

1. ☑ **B.** The keyboard is typically associated with a 3** BIOS error code. When the computer is started, the BIOS performs a POST, which checks for the presence and function of certain components. If a keyboard error, such as a missing cable or stuck key, is detected, the BIOS typically reports a 3** error code.

☒ **A,** motherboard, and **C,** the processor, are incorrect because these errors, if detected by the BIOS, are typically indicated by a 1** error code. **D,** RAM, is incorrect because memory errors are typically associated with a 2** error code.

2. ☑ **C.** The system reports that there is no operating system. The OS resides on the hard drive and, following the POST, the BIOS looks for the OS and gives it control. If the computer reports a missing OS, it means that one doesn't exist on the hard drive, it cannot be read from the hard drive, or that the computer cannot communicate with the hard drive. It is very unlikely that you would receive this particular message if there were a memory error.

☒ **A, B,** and **D** are incorrect because these are all typical symptoms of bad memory. If the memory has totally failed, the BIOS cannot conduct or complete the POST and might not be able to even initiate the processor. This might make it appear that the computer does absolutely nothing when it is turned on. Noncritical memory errors can be indicated by a 2** error code.

3. ☑ **D.** Cleaning the mouse is most likely to remedy the problem of a mouse pointer that doesn't move smoothly on the screen. As a mouse is moved, its ball can pick up dust and other particles and deposit them on the internal rollers. Buildup on the rollers causes them to move erratically, resulting in a mouse pointer that "jerks" around on the screen. Remove the mouse's retaining ring and ball, then remove the buildup from the rollers.

☒ **A,** reinstalling the mouse driver, is incorrect because if the mouse does not have a proper driver, it won't work at all. Driver problems for any device will cause that device to stop functioning altogether or to work sporadically. In this case, the mouse is not working sporadically (sometimes working and sometimes not), it is just not moving smoothly. **B,** ensuring that the mouse cable is connected securely to the computer, is also incorrect. If the mouse connector is not plugged into the computer, there will be no response from the mouse at all. If the mouse connector is loose, the operation of the mouse could be sporadic. That is, the mouse might work at some times and not at others. However, it would be extremely rare for a loose mouse connection to continuously make and break contact with the computer fast enough for it to appear that the mouse was working but not moving smoothly. **C,** ensuring that there are no IRQ conflicts between the mouse and another device, is also incorrect. If the mouse has a resource conflict with another device, the mouse either will not work at all or will work only when the other device is not being used. Again, the problem in this case is not a mouse that works sporadically but one that does not move smoothly.

4. ☑ **A.** Make sure that there is a floppy disk in the drive. This error indicates that the drive did not detect a disk. The most common reason for receiving this error is simply that a disk hasn't been inserted or was not inserted all the way.

   ☒ **B,** ensure that the floppy ribbon cable is attached properly, and **C,** make sure that the floppy drive is properly configured in the BIOS settings, are both incorrect. You should suspect a ribbon cable or BIOS setting problem only if the computer cannot communicate with the floppy drive. However, the error shown here is used to indicate that the drive searched for but did not detect a disk. If the drive can look for and report the absence of a floppy disk, the drive must be able to communicate with the computer. **D,** clean the floppy disk, is incorrect because although this message is used to indicate a problem accessing the disk, you will not solve the problem by trying to clean the disk. The disk's surface contains very small magnetic charges that would most likely be removed as soon as you touched it. Never touch the surface of a disk. It is floppy *drives*, not disks, that can be cleaned.

5. ☑ **B.** You should reverse the ribbon cable on the drive. A floppy drive light that comes on and won't go out is a sure indicator of a ribbon cable that has been reversed in the drive's port. Make sure that you align the cable's red stripe with pin 1 on the floppy drive's port.

   ☒ **A,** insert a different disk into the drive, is incorrect because this error will occur at startup, with or without a disk present in the drive. It is is totally unrelated to the presence or integrity of a floppy disk. **C,** swap the drive with another one, is incorrect because although the drive won't work properly in this condition, there is nothing wrong with the drive. Simply reverse the ribbon cable, and the drive will work normally. **D** is incorrect because it suggests that you should do nothing in this case. However, when the stated condition occurs, the ribbon is on backward, and the drive will not work. This is a condition that must be remedied in order to use the floppy drive.

6. ☑ **D.** You can rule out corrupted files as the cause of an "Invalid Drive" error. When you access the hard drive, the computer first checks for its existence, then tries to access information on it. If the computer cannot find or communicate with it, you will receive the error message. The computer has not even attempted to read the information on the drive yet, so the integrity of the data cannot be the cause of the problem. In this case, you must focus on reasons that the drive is not being recognized.

   ☒ **A,** the hard drive, **B,** the BIOS, and **C,** the ribbon cable, are all incorrect because these are all possible causes of the error. Again, the error message indicates that the computer doesn't know about the existence of the drive or can't communicate with it. Reasons for this can include a bad drive; a faulty, loose, or disoriented cable; or an improper hard drive configuration in the system BIOS.

7. ☑ **C.** You can use the SYS command to make a drive bootable. The drive's OS could be considered "missing" because it doesn't exist or because one or more critical system files are missing or corrupted. Using the SYS command, you can get the computer to a point at which

you can at least read the files on the drive and determine the cause of the problem or move important data to another place.

☒ **A,** BOOT, **B,** BOOT OS, and **D,** SYSTEM, are all incorrect because they are not real DOS commands.

8. ☑ **B.** The speaker volume is not a possible cause of the static problem. If the user can hear *anything* coming from the speakers, including static, the volume must be at a sufficient level.

☒ **A,** the speaker cables, is incorrect because if they are old, cracked, too long, or not shielded, they might be susceptible to EMI, a major cause of static. **C,** the CD, is incorrect because this too could be the cause of the static. If the CD is dusty, dirty, or contains scratches or flaws, stray or incorrect data can be read from it, sounding like static. **D,** the monitor, is also incorrect. Speakers that are exposed to EMI produce will static. The monitor is one of the greatest sources of EMI in the entire computer system. For this reason, you should keep the speakers as far away from the monitor as possible.

9. ☑ **D.** Static on the phone line can be responsible for causing the modem to produce random garbage characters. The computer tries to interpret the static as real data. The meaningless characters you see are the modem's interpretation of this "data."

☒ **A,** a missing device driver, and **B,** an improper resource configuration, are both incorrect. Both of these cause the modem to not work at all (or to work sporadically, in the case of a resource conflict). **C,** a failed or improper modem handshake, is also incorrect. During the modem handshake, the two modems determine the rules of communication. If this part fails or is misinterpreted by one modem, all the data transmitted, not just a random character here and there, will appear meaningless.

10. ☑ **A.** The power supply is most likely causing the problems. When a power supply begins to fail, it often manifests itself in a number of different, sporadic symptoms. If the power supply's fan stops working, the computer will overheat and spontaneously reboot itself. If the components are still hot when the system is restarted, the computer will likely do nothing. The computer will also do nothing on startup if the power supply is not providing adequate voltage to the motherboard. Finally, the computer normally issues many noises at startup: counting RAM, spinning up and accessing the hard drive, and the like. However, the most prominent sound is the power supply's fan. If this noise is absent, it is likely that the fan is not working and that the power supply must be replaced.

☒ **B,** the system board, **C,** the processor, and **D,** the RAM, are all incorrect. Although failure of each of these components can result in a nonresponsive computer at startup, they cannot cause all the problems mentioned. For example, although the computer makes noise as it counts the RAM, this is usually only a 2- or 3-second operation, and a RAM failure typically will not cause the computer to reboot. Although an overheated processor can cause the computer to spontaneously reboot, it does not make the noise that you hear when you start the computer.

Basic Troubleshooting Procedures

11. ☑ **A.** The room is humid. High humidity can cause condensation to form on computer components, which can lead to their failure. The humidity should be kept below 80 percent.
☒ **B,** the room is cool, is incorrect because it is warm, not cool, air that can lead to component failure. Note that although most components will fail in extreme cold, it is highly unlikely that an office would be kept at such a temperature. In any case, in this situation, the room is cool, not cold. **C,** only 3 out of 15 people are using the network, is also incorrect. Sound systems do not run from the network, so they would be unaffected by the amount of network traffic. Furthermore, 3 out of 15 people accessing the network is a relatively low number, and in this case, you should expect faster, not slower, access to network devices. **D,** the lights are off, is incorrect. In most cases, the status of the room lights will have no effect on the function of a sound system. In some rare cases, however, they could cause EMI, which can alter the computer's behavior. If anything, there should be fewer problems with the computer when the lights are off than when they are on.

12. ☑ **D.** The first thing you should do is swap the monitor with a known working one. If the second monitor works, you will have pinpointed the original monitor as the source of the problem. If the second monitor doesn't work, you can be fairly certain that the monitor isn't causing the problem. (You should test the original nonworking monitor with another machine to make sure.)
☒ **A,** make sure that the monitor's driver is properly installed, is incorrect. Although monitors do require drivers, if the screen is blank, you will not be able to see whether the driver exists or not. **B,** ensure that the video adapter is properly configured, is also incorrect for this reason. Furthermore, although the video adapter can be the cause of a video problem, you have already narrowed down the monitor as the cause. Adjusting the adapter will have no effect on the function of the monitor. **C,** ensure that the monitor does not have an IRQ conflict with another device, is incorrect because monitors do not have IRQ addresses. Even if they did, you cannot see the OS in this case, so you cannot see the monitor's configuration.

13. ☑ **C.** In this case, the first thing you should do is try to print from another application. This is the fastest way to determine if the printer or the application is at fault. If the second application can send a print job, the original application might need to be reconfigured or reinstalled.
☒ **A,** use the same application to access the scanner, is incorrect. Although you might end up performing this procedure, it shouldn't be the first thing you do. Suppose you did, and the application was able to access the scanner; this would tell you nothing about the printer. You would still be left not knowing whether the printer or its configuration in the application was at fault. **B,** reload the printer's device driver, and **D,** reinstall the word processor, are also

incorrect. These steps could eventually be required to resolve the problem, but remember, always start with the easiest and most basic troubleshooting procedures first. Suppose that the original application was at fault in this case. If you went ahead and uninstalled, then reloaded, the printer driver, you would have performed a time-consuming procedure for nothing. Alternatively, if the printer or its configuration were at fault, you would have reinstalled the application with no effect.

14. ☑ **B.** You should make sure the cable connection is tight. Remember, when diagnosing a hardware problem, start with the outermost components and work your way into the computer. After the monitor, the cable is the next component in the video system.
    ☒ **A,** reattach the original monitor to the computer, is incorrect because both the monitor and another component might be at fault. Use the monitor that you know is functioning until you can get the video system working, then reattach the original monitor. **C,** ensure that the adapter card is properly seated in the expansion slot, and **D,** swap the adapter card, are incorrect because they both involve opening the computer and are more time consuming than a simple cable swap. Always rule out easily installed components before you take the computer apart.

15. ☑ **A.** The configuration of the word processor and graphics programs is the most likely cause of the problem. You should check that these programs are configured to print to the correct printer, using appropriate buffer sizes, resolutions, and any other print job–related application settings.
    ☒ **B,** the printer's device driver, **C,** the printer, and **D,** an improper network configuration, are all incorrect because these would all lead to the inability to print from any program. Recall, however, that in this case, the user can print from a spreadsheet program. This situation indicates that the printer is working and that the computer can access it.

16. ☑ **D.** You should check the speaker. Ensure that it is receiving power and that the volume is turned up to a sufficient level. In addition, make sure that the cables are properly attached and that the speaker is not near any EMI-causing devices. These should be the first steps, since the speaker is the easiest component in the sound system to access (and the most likely to fail).
    ☒ **A,** the sound card's configuration, is incorrect. Because the sound system worked at one time, you can assume that the sound card was properly configured. Although the configuration might have become corrupt and caused this problem, it is more time-consuming to reconfigure the sound card than it is to physically check the speaker for power, volume, and connectivity. **B,** the speaker's configuration, is incorrect. Speakers simply amplify signals from the sound card and do not need to communicate with other components in the computer. Therefore, the speakers do not need computer resources or drivers. **C,** the sound card, is incorrect because this is a more time-consuming procedure than testing the speakers. Because the sound card is internal, checking it requires you to shut down the computer and take it apart.

17. ☑ **C.** Gather information about the problem, try to reproduce the error, check the device's configuration, and swap the device with a known good one. Whenever you troubleshoot a hardware problem, first gather as much information as you can: What is the problem, were there any error messages, has anything changed within the computer? This should be the first step because the answers to these questions could tell you enough to pinpoint the problem's source. If they do not, try to reproduce the error. The device might work this time. This step might also give you a chance to note error messages or unusual system activity. Next, check the configuration of the device to ensure that it has the proper system resources and a valid device driver. If these steps don't resolve the problem, suspect the device itself, and try another in its place.

☒ **A, B,** and **D** are all incorrect because they list the troubleshooting steps in the wrong order. Although the steps can physically be performed in any order, it is not efficient to do so. For example, if an error points to a missing floppy disk, you will have wasted a lot of time by replacing the drive first.

18. ☑ **A.** You can rule out the hard drive's configuration as the cause of this problem. If the computer was configured incorrectly, the application would not work at all and the computer might not even boot properly. Therefore, you must turn your attention to the application as the cause of the problem.

☒ **B,** an improper installation of the application, is incorrect because this might be the cause of the problem. If the application was installed with missing, misplaced, or corrupt files, certain functions of the application (including its ability to save files) might be disrupted. If this is the case, uninstall, then reinstall the application. **C,** an improperly written application, is also incorrect. If the application contains flaws (bugs), it might not perform certain actions properly. If this is the case, it means that the problem is in the application's code. Check for manufacturer updates or patches to resolve the problem. **D,** insufficient system requirements, is also incorrect because this might be causing the problem. If the system's processor or memory capacity is insufficient to run the application, the computer might respond by being unable to fulfill a particular request, causing the computer to lock up.

19. ☑ **C.** You should restart the computer. In some cases, applications can use computer resources, such as memory or processor time, and not release them, even when the application is closed. By restarting the computer, you will remove the application from memory and/or cause it to release any system resources.

☒ **A,** obtain a manufacturer's patch for the game, and **D,** reinstall the game, are incorrect because these procedures are typically used when an application contains corrupt or improper instructions. Since the game worked originally, this is not likely the case. Furthermore, it is typically more time consuming to install a patch or reinstall an application than it is to reboot the system. **B,** troubleshoot the printer, is incorrect. The printer is also an unlikely suspect in this case. Again, although it is not impossible for the printer to be the cause of this problem, troubleshooting the printer is more time-consuming and less likely to resolve the problem than simply restarting the computer.

20. ☑ **B.** You should have the user try to replicate the problem. This will allow you to take note of the error message when it is displayed. It will also allow you to ensure that the user is following the proper procedures, check for configuration settings, and note any unusual system activity. These might all quickly and effectively allow you to determine or narrow down the cause of the problem.

☒ **A,** restart the computer, is incorrect. Although you might end up restarting the computer later, this step by will not allow you to see the error message. **C,** check the scanner's configuration, and **D,** swap the scanner with a known good one, are both incorrect. Again, although you could end up performing these procedures at some point, they should not be the first things you do in this case. You will have wasted quite a bit of time if you reconfigure or replace the scanner when the error message clearly stated that the scanner was simply not turned on.

LAB ANSWER

1. On arrival at the customer's site, take note of potential problem-causing factors, such as the temperature and the humidity.

2. Ask the customer about the computer's history. For example, ask whether this has occurred before or if a new device or application has been installed.

3. Have the customer try to play the sound file again. Watch for irregular system activity, the presence of error messages, and other on-screen indicators, such as a visual volume control on the screen.

4. Check that the speakers are receiving power and that the volume is set at a sufficient level. (You might choose to do this before the previous step, since it is so easy and quick to check.)

5. Make sure that the speakers are securely connected to the sound card.

6. Try to play a different sound file to determine if the original sound file is corrupt. In this particular case, the second sound file should cause the same result as the first.

7. Try to play a sound file in a different application. Do not use the original sound file, because both the file and the original application file could be at fault. Again, considering the actual cause of the problem, the result should be the same. This indicates (but does not prove) that the original application and sound file are not at fault.

8. Restart the computer, then try to have the system produce sound again. This might resolve the problem if the sound card's configuration was improperly loaded the first time or if another application is using a resource the sound card or application needs.

9. At this point, you should have determined that this is a hardware, not a software, problem. Swap the speakers with known good ones.

10. Swap the speaker cables with known good ones.

11. Check the configuration of the sound card. Look for a resource conflict or a bad or missing driver. If you are using Windows 9x, 2000, or XP, you can use the Device Manager. Given the actual cause of this problem, you should see nothing to indicate a configuration error. However, you might want to remove the sound card's driver, then reinstall it, just to rule it out as the cause.

12. Turn the computer off, remove the case, and ensure that the sound card is properly seated in the expansion slot.

13. At this point, you can either try to install the card in another expansion slot or swap the sound card with a known working one. If you swap the card first, turn the computer back on, configure it, then try to play a sound file. If you try the card in another slot first, you will have located the source of the problem (the expansion slot).

14. To determine why the slot has failed, you can use a multimeter to test its ability to receive signals. In this case, you would find that the bad circuit offers infinite resistance, indicating a break in the circuit.

15. To resolve this problem, you can continue to use the original sound card in an alternate expansion slot. However, if you need all the other slots for other components, you will probably end up replacing one of the devices with an external one (to free up a slot) or replacing the entire motherboard.

4

Power Protection and Safety Procedures

CERTIFICATION OBJECTIVES

4.01   Identify various safety measures and
        procedures.

4.02   Identify environmental protection
        measures and procedures.

✓   Two-Minute Drill

Q&A   Self Test

Y ou should now be familiar with proper installation and configuration procedures for many computer devices. You should also be familiar with determining when components need to replaced or reconfigured. In this chapter, you will learn about procedures you can perform to prevent problems from occurring in the first place. You will also learn about procedures you should follow so that you do not cause damage to computer components or cause harm to yourself or the environment.

CERTIFICATION OBJECTIVE 4.01

Preventive Maintenance Products and Procedures

Regular cleaning of computer components can extend a computer's life. For example, by regularly cleaning the power supply fan, you can ensure that it is able to properly cool the computer's internal components. Regular cleaning can also help stop problems before they start, as in dust build-up inside a mouse.

Giving a computer a regular cleaning also gives you a good opportunity to inspect the computer's components and determine if the potential for a problem exists. For example, while cleaning the system, take note of loose components or connections and tighten them up. You should also look for frayed or cracked cables and replace them, even if they have not yet caused a problem.

Liquid Cleaning Compounds

Before using a liquid cleaner on any device, make sure that the computer is off and that the component is completely dry before you turn the computer on again. In addition, note that you should stick to the procedures discussed within this section. That is, do not use a type of liquid cleaner on a device other than the ones discussed here. For example, if you were to use water rather than alcohol on the floppy drive, you might cause permanent damage to it.

Some computer components, such as a mouse ball, the mouse casing, and the case on the monitor and computer itself, can be cleaned using *mild*, soapy water or a damp (not wet) cloth. In short, most plastic external coverings in the computer system can be cleaned this way. Make sure that no liquid drips on the components.

If the keyboard is sticky, you can clean it with plain, distilled water. Make sure that you unplug the keyboard from the computer, and make sure that the water contains no impurities such as soap or iron. Ensure that the keyboard is entirely dry before reattaching it to the computer.

Some devices are harmed by water and/or soap and should be cleaned with denatured (isopropyl) alcohol. For example, the cleaning liquid that comes in most floppy drive cleaning kits is alcohol. You can also use alcohol to clean any residue on a mouse roller that you can't remove with your fingers.

Finally, you can use regular glass cleaner to clean the screen on a CRT monitor. Follow the steps in Exercise 4-1 to properly clean a monitor.

on the **Job**

Cleaning an LCD monitor is different from a glass monitor. You can usually clean an LCD monitor with non-abrasive glasses cleaners, such as those from Lenscrafters, or by using a water mist and an eyeglass cloth to dry the monitor. Avoid glass cleaner, alcohol, or other solvent-based cleaners. Follow the manufacturer's cleaning instructions to avoid scratching or damaging the plastic cover of the monitor.

EXERCISE 4-1

Cleaning a CRT Monitor

1. Shut down the computer.
2. Turn the monitor off and unplug it from the electrical outlet.
3. Spray a small amount of glass cleaner on a clean cloth or paper towel.
4. Use the cloth to rub fingerprints or other smudges off the monitor screen. Be careful not to let any cleaner drip.
5. Allow the glass cleaner to completely evaporate (about a minute).
6. Plug the monitor back in and turn it on.

Cleaning Contacts and Connectors

It's a good idea to check your system's contacts to make sure that they are establishing a good connection. Bad connections cause malfunctions. You can clean connectors using contact cleaner. Remember to make sure that your computer is unplugged and turned off before doing any preventative maintenance.

Removing Dust and Debris from the System

One of the most common reasons to clean a computer is to remove dust buildup. Recall that the power supply's fan draws air into the computer and distributes it over the internal components. It can do the same thing with dust. Because dust can cause ESD (electrostatic discharge) and lead to overheated components, it's important to clean the inside of the computer regularly. Pay particular attention to the system board, the bottom of the computer chassis, and all fan inlets and outlets. Make sure you power down the computer before you start cleaning it.

One of the easiest ways to remove dust from the system is to use compressed air to blow the dust out. Compressed air comes in cans that are roughly the size of spray-paint cans. Typically, a liquid at the bottom of the can compresses the air and forces it out when you depress the can's nozzle. If you turn the can upside-down, you can cause the liquid to be released. Avoid doing so; the liquid can cause freeze burns on your skin and damage the computer's components. You should also be aware of where the dust is being blown. That is, make sure that the dust is not being blown from one component only to settle on another. You can also use compressed air to blow dust out of the keyboard, expansion slots, and ports.

Another common method for removing dust is to vacuum it out. This has the advantage of removing dust without allowing the dust to settle elsewhere. It is best to use a special hand-held vacuum that allows you to get into smaller places and clean the computer without accidentally hitting and damaging other internal components. Remove the nozzle from inside, and move the vacuum cleaner away from the computer before turning it off.

Finally, you can use a lint-free cloth to wipe off dusty surfaces. Avoid using the newer dust cloths that work by "statically attracting" dust. Remember, static is harmful to the computer.

SCENARIO & SOLUTION	
What should I use to clean the CRT monitor's screen?	Use glass cleaner. Spray the cleaner on a cloth, not directly on the monitor.
How can I remove dust from the computer?	Vacuum it or use compressed air to blow it out.
What should I use to remove dirt from the computer case?	Use mild, soapy water on a damp (not wet) cloth.

FROM THE CLASSROOM

Cleaning the Keyboard

Many computer users tend to eat while they use the computer. They also tend to drink, use erasers, shuffle papers, or pick lint off themselves while at the computer. The poor keyboard is usually an unfortunate witness to all these activities, and its design allows it to hold more dust, crumbs, hair, and other gunk than any other device. Keyboards, therefore, typically require a lot of cleaning, and because the debris can be hard to get at, you might need to use some creative cleaning techniques.

If the keyboard is sticky, you can clean it with water; it won't harm the keyboard as long as the water doesn't contain impurities and the keyboard is not plugged into the computer while it's still wet. There are also a number of chemical cleaners available to clean keyboard tops and surfaces. Frequently keyboards become cosmetically dirty much sooner than they become sticky.

on the **job**

Keyboards have become extremely inexpensive. They tend to range in price from less than $10 to $80. In many cases, it is not worth the time to do much repair work or anything more than a superficial cleaning. If the keyboard is misbehaving, replace it.

Another good way to clean the keyboard is to simply turn it upside-down and shake it. You'll probably be surprised at the amount of stuff that falls out. If this doesn't do the trick, use a can of compressed air to blow debris out of the keyboard, or use a small hand-held vacuum. Some types of crud can be stubborn, and you could end up having to remove each keycap to properly clean the keyboard. Use a flathead screwdriver to pry the keycap(s) off. (Make sure that the computer is off before you do so.) To replace a keycap, simply orient it the right way and snap it into place. Be careful of the Spacebar; it sometimes contains springs that can fly out and disappear. Taking the keyboard apart like this can be very time-consuming, so it should really be a last resort.

CERTIFICATION OBJECTIVE 4.02

Power Protection and Safety Procedures

The computer's supply of power is an important consideration when performing maintenance or troubleshooting procedures. The safety of the computer's components is important, and you must ensure that the computer is receiving a safe and steady power supply. Failure to do so can result in lost work, corrupted files, and physically damaged components. Your personal safety is also an important issue. Many of the things that make a computer function properly, such as high voltage and lasers, can cause you harm. You must also keep the safety of the environment in mind. Computers contain many components that, if disposed of improperly, can contaminate the ground, water, or other parts of the environment. Finally, you must protect the safety of computer components, whether they are installed in the computer, in transit, or in storage.

Power Protection

Many things can go wrong with the power supply to your home or office. The power could suddenly decrease, increase, or be cut off altogether. The power can also contain noise due to EMI (electromagnetic interference). To keep your computer functioning properly, you need to be able to recognize signs of power problems and make proper use of the devices that can help control the flow of electricity.

Determining the Signs of Power Issues

A common power problem is a temporary reduction in the amount of electricity to your home or office. In these cases, the power is not totally cut off but can sag to levels that will harm your computer's components, especially when the power returns to its normal level. These power reductions are referred to as *brownouts* because they tend to make regular lights go very dim (but not out).

A *blackout* occurs when the power is totally cut off. Blackouts can last from less than a second to several hours, depending on the source of the problem. When a blackout occurs, the computer loses all power, and you will lose any information that you haven't saved. Furthermore, if the computer is in the middle of saving, moving, or deleting a file when the power goes out, it is likely that that file will become corrupted or missing. The sudden loss of power can also result in the accumulation of temporary files that would have been automatically deleted if the computer had been shut down normally.

Another danger with a blackout is what happens to the computer when the power suddenly comes on again. Most newer computers are designed to come back on only if the power button is pushed again. However, older computers might automatically come back on when the power is restored, resulting in a harmful power surge. When the power goes out, you should always turn the computer and monitor off, or better yet, unplug them.

Power surges or *power spikes* don't just occur when the power is restored; even the regular supply of electricity can contain temporary dips and increases. Like brownouts, power surges are temporary and are not typically very extreme. In fact, you might not even notice when a power surge occurs. However, if the lights become brighter or if electrical devices begin to make more noise than usual, these issues could be due to a power surge. Power surges can be very harmful to computer components. Recall that the power supply not only converts electricity from AC to DC, but it also drops the overall voltage from 110–120 to only 3–12 volts. The power supply does this by using resistors to shield a certain amount of excess voltage. If there is a power surge, however, the total voltage could be more than the resistors can shield, resulting in a higher voltage within the computer itself.

A *power spike* is more extreme than a power surge and typically does not last as long. Due to their extreme nature, power spikes are much more likely to damage computer components.

The electrical supply can also contain interference due to the presence of high-voltage equipment in the area or very long cables. (The longer a cable, the more susceptible it is to EMI.) Current that contains EMI is referred to as *noisy* or *dirty* and can cause problems in the computer because the noise can result in dips and increases in the amount of electricity reaching the computer. Noisy power lines can also create magnetic fields, which can be damaging to magnetically stored data.

Preventing Power Problems

An uninterruptible power supply (UPS) can be used to prevent or remedy some or all of these power issues. A typical UPS has a battery that provides temporary backup power in the case of a blackout. This backup gives users enough time to properly save their work and safely shut their computers down in the event of a power loss. One type of UPS is a *standby power system (SPS)*, which is attached to the computer. The SPS switches to battery power when it detects a loss of electricity. Unfortunately, there can be a brief lapse in power during the time it takes for the SPS to detect a power problem and switch to battery power. This lag is usually not noticeable to the computer system.

SCENARIO & SOLUTION

Which device can absorb excess power?	A suppressor.
What can I use to remove EMI from the power source?	A noise filter.
What should I use to provide backup battery power?	A UPS.
How can I prevent problems from blackouts, surges, and EMI all at the same time?	Get a UPS that has an integrated suppressor and noise filter.

A more expensive but more efficient type of UPS is an *online UPS*, which is located between the computer's power supply and power supply (electrical outlet) from the electric company. Incoming power keeps the UPS battery charged, and all power to the computer comes from the battery. When the power goes out, the UPS simply continues to provide the computer with power from the battery's reserve. This means there is no "break" in the power, as there is in an SPS.

To prevent problems resulting from power surges and power spikes, you can use a surge *suppressor*. Suppressors are designed to "smooth out" the flow of electricity by removing excess voltage caused by power surges and spikes. Suppressors are available as individual devices or integrated with a UPS.

To combat noisy or dirty current, you should use a *noise filter*. Noise filters are designed to condition the flow of electricity by removing EMI. Like suppressors, noise filters can be used as individual devices or as part of a UPS.

You should know the differences between the functions of these devices: A UPS provides backup power, suppressors smooth out surges and spikes, *and noise filters remove EMI. A UPS can also come with an integrated suppressor and/or noise filter.*

Personal Safety Procedures

The power used by the computer, especially the power found in the computer's high-voltage devices, is enough to cause injury or death. Some computers also use lasers. You must always be aware of the potential for injury when working with the devices described here.

Lasers

Computers use lasers to read information from CD-ROMs and DVDs, and some printers use lasers to create printout images. The Level 3 lasers used for these purposes aren't enough to burn you, but they can cause eye damage if you look straight at them. Most CD-ROM and DVD drives and laser printers are designed to stop functioning as soon as their cases are opened or removed. However, you should never tamper with the laser device or try to make it work without its case or cover.

High-Voltage Equipment

Most of a computer's components run on very low voltage (±3v to ±12v DC). However, some components require higher voltage to function properly and can store enough voltage to cause personal injury, such as burns. Two common high-voltage devices, the power supply and the monitor, are described in the following sections. However, always be aware of other potentially high-voltage equipment, such as the power supply in a laser printer. High-voltage devices are typically indicated by a high-voltage warning label. When working with these types of devices, unplug them, never open them up, and always remove your ESD strap.

Power Supplies   Always unplug the power supply from the wall outlet when you are working inside the computer. Even when turned off, the power supply can conduct electricity. Some technicians prefer to leave the power supply plugged in while they work on the computer to allow static to bleed away from the computer into the wall outlet's ground wire. However, there are safer methods for removing static (discussed later in this chapter), so there is no need to leave the power supply plugged in.

As discussed previously, the power supply itself is able to store electrical charges for long periods of time, even when it has been unplugged. Never open the power supply's case, and never wear an ESD wrist strap when replacing or handling the power supply. ESD straps are designed to bleed static charges away from the computer, through your body. If worn near a power supply, the strap could conduct high-voltage electricity as well as static charges. These high voltages are enough to harm you.

Cathode Ray Tubes   Like power supplies, CRT monitors are considered high-voltage equipment and can store a harmful electrical charge, even when they are unplugged. Never open a CRT case, and never wear a wrist strap when working with a CRT.

Environmental Safety Procedures

Many of the computer's components—such as monitors, which may contain lead, and system boards, which may contain mercury—are harmful to the environment. These items, as well as the ones discussed in the following sections, must be recycled or disposed of in the proper manner (in other words, not placed in landfills).

Batteries

Many batteries contain environmentally hazardous materials, such as lithium, mercury, or nickel-cadmium. Therefore, they cannot be placed in landfills lest they contaminate the ground or nearby water. Many communities have special recycling depots that accept batteries to be recharged, reused, or properly processed so that they do not introduce harmful elements to the environment. Many communities also conduct hazardous material pickups once a month, in which you can hand over all toxic materials, such as batteries and paint, for proper disposal.

Toner Kits and Cartridges

Printer toner cartridges also provide a potential environmental hazard, simply due to their large numbers and the space they can take up in a landfill. For this reason, they should not simply be thrown away. Fortunately, most toner cartridges are reusable. That is, many companies will buy back used toner cartridges, then refill and resell them.

Chemical Solvents and Cans

Chemical solvents designed for the computer are just as hazardous to the environment as noncomputer-related chemical solvents. They must be disposed of in a similar manner. Look for a hazardous material pickup in your area.

Material Safety Data Sheet

Whenever you are unsure of the proper disposal procedures for a component, look for its *material safety data sheet (MSDS)*. An MSDS is a standardized document that contains general information, ingredients, and fire and explosion warnings as well as health, disposal, and safe transportation information about a particular product. Any manufacturer that sells a potentially hazardous product is required to issue an MSDS for it. If an MSDS didn't come with a particular component, contact the manufacturer or search for it on the Internet. A number of websites, including sites sponsored by

Cornell University (http://msds.pdc.cornell.edu/msdssrch.asp) and Vermont Safety Information Resources Inc. (http://siri.uvm.edu/), contain large lists of MSDSs.

Component Safety Procedures

You should now be familiar with the procedures for preventing harm to the computer's power supply, yourself, and the environment. It is also important to know how to protect the computer's delicate components from harm. This section focuses on some potential dangers to these components and how you can protect them.

Electrostatic Discharge

One of the most prevalent threats to a computer component is ESD, also known as *static*. Static is all around us, especially when the humidity is low. When you put on a jacket that makes the hair on your arm stand up or when you rub a balloon on your hair to make it stick it to the wall, you are encountering static electricity. When you touch a light switch and receive a jolt, you are experiencing a static discharge. ESD is caused when two objects of uneven charge come in contact with one another. Electricity has the property of traveling to areas with lower charges, and the static shock that you feel is the result of electrons jumping from your hand to the metal screw in the light switch plate. The same process can occur within the computer. If your body has a high electric potential, electrons will be transferred to the first computer component that you touch.

What ESD Can Do   If an ESD charge is very low, it might not cause any damage to the computer. However, recall that most computer components are designed to receive voltages of ±12 or less. Most static electricity has a much higher voltage: up to 3000 volts if you can feel the discharge and up to 20,000 volts if you can see it! These voltages are enough to damage the circuits inside the device and render it inoperable.

Because it takes such a small charge to damage a computer component, you might be unaware of its occurrence. This is referred to as *hidden ESD*. Hidden ESD can also come from a dust buildup inside the computer. Dust and other foreign particles can hold an electric charge that slowly bleeds into nearby components. Hidden ESD can cause more serious problems than ESD, which you cannot feel. For example, if hidden ESD has damaged a component, you will be unaware of it until that device begins to malfunction. Because you weren't aware of the ESD damage when it occurred, it could be difficult for you to pinpoint the problem.

When ESD causes the immediate malfunction of a device, it is considered *catastrophic*. When ESD causes a gradually worsening problem in a device, it is referred to as *degradation*. As unlikely as it might seem, catastrophic damage can be less harmful to the system than degradation. When a device suffers catastrophic damage, the result is immediate and typically quite obvious, so the device will most likely be replaced right away. Degradation, on the other hand, can cause a component to malfunction sporadically, sometimes working and sometimes not. This makes it harder to pinpoint the problem, so the problem itself can persist for a longer period of time. Additionally, a total failure of one component will typically not affect the usability of other components. However, degradation can cause a component to fail in ways that also result in the failure of other components.

Common ESD Protection Devices

There are many ways to prevent ESD from damaging the computer. First, ESD is typically caused by low humidity. Always keep the room's humidity between 50 and 80 percent (but no higher than 80 percent or condensation could form).

You should also use special ESD devices, such as ESD wrist or ankle straps. ESD straps have a cuff that fits around your wrist or ankle and are designed to bleed static charges away from the computer via your body. Some ESD straps have an alligator clip that is attached to a grounded, metal object, such as a table leg. Other straps have a single prong that is plugged into the ground wire in a regular wall outlet. Make sure that you read the directions for your particular strap, and make sure that you know which part of the wall outlet contains the ground wire.

e**x**a**m**
watch   *For your own safety as well as your success on the A+ exam, make sure that you know which plug is for the ground wire. It is the round one in the outlet. Never try to plug an ESD strap into either of the two "slots" on the outlet—they contain electricity!*

ESD mats look like vinyl placemats but have a wire lead and an alligator clip. Their function is similar to that of an ESD strap and can be used as a safe place to put expansion cards or other internal components that you have removed from the computer. Before you pick up a loose computer component, discharge any static electricity in yourself by touching something metal, such as a table leg or chair. This will prevent electrons in your body from being passed onto the device.

Another way to combat ESD is to use antistatic spray. ESD spray is commercially available and is typically used to remove static from your clothes. However, you can also use it to remove static from yourself, from the carpet, and from your work area, to protect computer components.

on the
Job

Some employers require technicians to look like office professionals. This may include wearing a tie. If you are required to wear a tie, make sure that you either tuck the tie into your shirt, or use some kind of tie clip or tie tack. You do not want your tie to come into contact with computer components. Many ties, especially silk ones, can build up a static charge. As a practice, it is better to remove your tie than risk ESD damage.

When I worked for Boeing, a field service technician came into our lab to repair a broken minicomputer. When he opened the case and bent down to examine the system, a metallic screwdriver fell out of his pocket and landed across the expansion bus of the system. This caused the system to short out and basically fried all the components in the system. The manufacturer had to replace the entire CPU to bring the system back into operation. Make sure you do not keep pens, tools, or other metallic devices in your shirt pocket when you are examining a system.

SCENARIO & SOLUTION

When should I use an ESD strap?	Use a strap whenever you perform repairs or maintenance on the computer, except on the monitor, power supply, or laser printer.
Which kind of ESD is usually most damaging to the system?	Degradation is most damaging. This type of ESD can cause a device to fail gradually so that it can affect other components and is hard to troubleshoot.
What ESD devices are available?	ESD wrist and ankle straps drain static from the computer, through your body. Antistatic spray inhibits the buildup of static, and ESD mats offer a good place to put components when they are temporarily out of the computer.

The procedure in Exercise 4-2 will lead you through the process of protecting your workspace and the computer from ESD damage.

ESD-Proofing Your Workspace

1. Maintain the room's humidity between 50 percent and 80 percent.

2. Spray your clothing and the work area with antistatic spray. Do not directly spray the computer or its components.

3. Place an ESD mat (for setting components on) on the workspace and attach its alligator clip to something stationary and metal, such as the leg of a table.

4. Remove all jewelry, including rings.

5. Put an ESD strap around your wrist or ankle, and attach the other end to a stationary metal object (if it has an alligator clip) or plug it into the wall outlet's ground wire (if it has an outlet prong).

Proper Storage of Components

Whenever you remove a component from the computer, it becomes susceptible to damage from external sources. Therefore, you must ensure that components are properly protected when they are placed in storage. Always store computer components in a cool, dry place (but not dry enough to harbor static buildup). Heat can damage a component's circuits and cause magnetically stored data to be lost. Furthermore, damp environments can cause condensation to form, leading to corrosion, or they can cause the component to short-circuit when it is reinstalled in the computer.

You should also make sure that components, especially those that use magnetic storage, are kept safely away from high-voltage devices, EMI-causing devices, and other sources of magnetism. Internal components should always be placed in ESD bags before they are stored or transported. ESD bags are designed to move static from the inside of the bag to the outside, keeping the components inside safe.

Many technicians place components on the ESD bag they're removed from. This can cause damage and should not be done unless specifically instructed to do so by the manufacturer. (Some system board manufacturers instruct you to place the motherboard on the ESD bag it came in.) Some ESD bags work by moving static charges from inside the bag to the outside, and placing a component on one of these bags can expose it to harmful static.

On a final note, never store computer batteries for extended periods of time. Battery casings are notorious for corroding, allowing the chemicals inside to leak or explode out. This can cause a large mess, destroy nearby components, and cause skin burns if you touch it.

CERTIFICATION SUMMARY

This chapter focused on ways to prevent computer problems and how to protect the computer, the environment, and yourself from harm. One of the most effective ways to stop problems before they start is to clean the computer often. Cleaning can prevent damage due to overheating, reverse the progression of a problem before it becomes noticeable, and give you a good chance to inspect the computer's internal components for signs of wear and tear.

Some components, such as plastic casings, can be cleaned with mild, soapy water. Others, such as floppy drives or mouse rollers, require the use of isopropyl alcohol. Always check with the manufacturer for proper cleaning instructions, and never use a liquid cleaner on a device for which it was not intended.

You can also help prevent computer problems by conditioning and "smoothing out" the power source. By using a UPS, suppressor, and/or noise filter, you can remove or minimize problems caused by power outages, surges, or EMI.

Always be aware of potential environmental and personal hazards. Always dispose of computer components properly. You can check the component's MSDS for proper disposal instructions. You should also be aware of components that use high voltage or lasers, such as the monitor, power supply, and CD-ROM drive. Finally, handle components carefully when you store them. Keep them out of hot or damp places, and keep magnetic storage devices away from EMI-emitting devices.

TWO-MINUTE DRILL

Here are some of the key points from each certification objective in Chapter 4.

Preventive Maintenance Products and Procedures

❑ Cleaning the computer can help you prevent problems and replace worn-out components before they stop working.

❑ Use mild, soapy water to clean the mouse ball and plastic casings.

❑ Clean a sticky keyboard with distilled water.

❑ Use isopropyl alcohol to clean floppy drives.

❑ Use regular glass cleaner to remove smudges and fingerprints from the glass screen on a CRT monitor (but not on an LCD).

❑ Check all connections to ensure that there is no corrosion or other buildup.

❑ Use contact cleaner to clean contacts.

❑ Use compressed air or a vacuum to remove dust from the fan and the inside of the computer.

Power Protection and Safety Procedures

❑ Use a UPS to provide backup power in the event of a brownout or blackout.

❑ Suppressors can be used to absorb excess voltage.

❑ Noise filters "condition" the electrical supply by removing EMI.

❑ Monitors and power supplies are considered high-voltage equipment and should never be opened.

❑ Many computer components, such as batteries, contain harmful substances and must be disposed of properly.

❑ Clean the computer often and use ESD straps and mats to reduce the possibility of ESD damage.

❑ Always store computer components in ESD bags, and place them in cool, dry places.

SELF TEST

The following questions will help you measure your understanding of the material presented in this chapter. Read all the choices carefully because there might be more than one correct answer. Choose all correct answers for each question.

Preventive Maintenance Products and Procedures

1. Which of the following is the most effective device for cleaning the internal rollers in a mouse?
   A. An eraser
   B. Isopropyl alcohol
   C. Mild, soapy water
   D. Distilled water

2. Which of the following can you clean with mild, soapy water?
   A. The mouse ball
   B. The monitor screen
   C. The keyboard
   D. Connectors

3. A user has complained that the keys are sticking on her keyboard. Which of the following could you do?
   A. Clean the keyboard with compressed air.
   B. Soak the keyboard in mild, soapy water.
   C. Clean the keyboard with isopropyl alcohol.
   D. Clean the keyboard with distilled water.

4. Which of the following should you avoid using to clean a keyboard?
   A. Compressed air
   B. Water
   C. An eraser
   D. A vacuum

5. There are fingerprints all over your CRT monitor, so you have decided to clean it. Which procedure should you follow?
   A. Turn the monitor off and unplug it from the wall outlet. Spray the screen with glass cleaner, then wipe it off. Wait for the screen to dry, then plug the monitor back in and turn it on.

    B. Turn the monitor off and unplug it from the wall outlet. Wipe the screen with mild, soapy water. When the screen is dry, plug the monitor back in and turn it on.

    C. Use a dry, lint-free cloth to wipe the screen clean of fingerprints.

    D. Ensure that no power is going to the monitor. Apply glass cleaner to a paper towel and wipe the screen with it. Wait for the screen to dry, then use it normally.

6. When checking a malfunctioning sound card in an early Pentium system, you find a buildup of corrosion on the contacts. What do you do?

    A. Use contact cleaner to clean the connector.

    B. Soak the connector in distilled water.

    C. Use a cotton swab soaked in mild, soapy water.

    D. Use a can of compressed air to blow the debris out of the connector.

7. When you turn on your computer, you notice that the fan is not spinning as quickly as usual. What is the first thing you should do?

    A. Replace the fan.

    B. Use compressed air to clean the fan.

    C. Replace the power supply.

    D. Use isopropyl alcohol to clean the fan.

8. Which of the following statements is true regarding the use of compressed air or a vacuum to remove dust from a computer?

    A. Vacuuming is generally messier than using compressed air.

    B. Vacuums make it easier to get into smaller places.

    C. Compressed air has the potential to cause personal injury.

    D. You are more likely to damage a component using compressed air.

9. Which of the following is not a benefit of regularly cleaning the computer?

    A. Reducing the probability of ESD

    B. Preventing the overheating of components

    C. Allowing you to determine the voltage output of the power supply

    D. Allowing you to determine the presence of improper connections

10. You are vacuuming the computer and you come across a cable on which the outer shield is cracked, but the internal wires are still intact. Which of the following should you do?

    A. Pay close attention to the behavior of the computer so that you can tell when to replace the cable.

B. Use electrical tape to patch the cable.

C. Replace the cable.

D. Nothing.

Power Protection and Safety Procedures

11. ESD can be harmful to which of the following?

A. People

B. Expansion cards

C. The computer's power supply

D. The environment

12. Which device can be used to protect the computer from electrical power surges?

A. An ESD strap

B. A suppressor

C. A noise filter

D. A standby power UPS

13. A customer is complaining that the power in the office sometimes surges, sometimes causes blackouts, and has EMI. What single device can you recommend to help the most in this situation?

A. A noise filter

B. A suppressor

C. A UPS

D. A backup battery

14. Which type of UPS is most effective?

A. An SPS because it generates battery power longer than an online UPS

B. An online UPS because it prevents lapses in the power supply when a blackout occurs

C. An SPS because it provides battery power more immediately during a blackout

D. An online UPS because it will draw less power from the electrical source than an SPS

15. Which of the following is not considered a high-voltage device?

A. A printer power supply

B. A computer power supply

C. A monitor

D. A CMOS battery

16. You are planning to replace the internal sound card in your computer. Which of the following describes the proper safety precautions you should take?

    A. Unplug the computer, spray your workspace with antistatic spray, put an ESD strap on, open the computer, remove the card, and place it on an antistatic bag.

    B. Unplug the computer, place an ESD mat on your work surface, open the computer, put an ESD strap on, spray the sound card with antistatic spray, and replace the card.

    C. Put an ESD strap on, place an ESD mat on your work surface, unplug the computer, spray the computer with antistatic spray, open the computer, remove the card, and place it on the ESD mat.

    D. Place an ESD mat on your work surface, unplug the computer, put an ESD strap on, open the computer, remove the card, and place it on the ESD mat.

17. Why should you recycle printer toner cartridges?

    A. Because they contain acids that can cause personal injury.

    B. Because they contain chemicals that can contaminate the nearby soil or water supply.

    C. Because they contain hazardous materials that can contribute to the depletion of the ozone layer.

    D. Because they are sold in very large numbers.

18. You just installed a new video card, but it doesn't work. You remember feeling a little shock when you picked the card up. What is the likely cause of the video card problem?

    A. Catastrophic ESD

    B. Degradation

    C. Hidden ESD

    D. Sudden ESD syndrome

19. Computers in a particular office have been experiencing an unusually high occurrence of ESD damage. Which of the following is most likely to reduce the occurrence of ESD?

    A. Raise the temperature of the room.

    B. Lower the temperature of the room.

    C. Raise the humidity of the room.

    D. Keep the lights as dim as possible.

20. In which type of environment should you store a hard drive?

    A. Cool and damp

    B. Cool and dry

    C. Warm and damp

    D. Warm and dry

LAB QUESTION

While at a friend's place, you notice the following things:

- He often eats while using the computer.
- He has a pet cat.
- The lights flicker when he turns the speakers on.
- He has a habit of rubbing his feet on the floor.
- There are floppy disks stacked near the monitor.

From this information, what types of problems might you expect to occur? How can you prevent or resolve these problems?

SELF TEST ANSWERS

Preventive Maintenance Products and Procedures

1. ☑ **B.** You should use isopropyl alcohol to clean the internal rollers in a mouse. First, you can try to remove debris using your fingers. If this doesn't work, apply some alcohol to a cotton swab and rub the debris off. Ensure that none of the debris falls into the mouse.

   ☒ **A,** an eraser, is incorrect because although this could help remove roller buildup, it is not as effective as alcohol, and it is likely that shavings from the eraser will be deposited on the rollers or other internal areas of the mouse. **C,** mild, soapy water and **D,** distilled water, are incorrect. These are not as effective as alcohol in this case and could damage the mouse.

2. ☑ **A.** You can clean the mouse ball with mild, soapy water. Remove the ball from the mouse, clean it, rinse it thoroughly, and make sure it is completely dry before replacing it in the mouse. As long as you follow this procedure, you don't have to worry about water dripping onto other parts of the mouse, as it would if you used water to clean the rollers.

   ☒ **B,** the monitor screen, is incorrect. The screen is made of glass, and soapy water is likely to leave a visible residue. You should use glass cleaner on the monitor screen. **C,** the keyboard, and **D,** connectors, are incorrect. Although mild, soapy water could make them appear clean, there is a chance that a buildup of soap will be left behind when the keyboard or connector dries. This can lead to sticky keys or poor connections.

3. ☑ **D.** Clean the keyboard with distilled water. Some people have even put the keyboard in the dishwasher. As long as the water doesn't have soap or mineral impurities in it, this practice may be safe. If you use the dishwasher, don't leave the keyboard in the machine for the "dry" cycle, this would melt the keyboard.

   ☒ **A,** clean the keyboard with compressed air, is incorrect because, although this will remove dust, it will not remove sticky residue. **B,** soak the keyboard in mild, soapy water, is incorrect because soap residue can be left on the keyboard, causing the keys to remain sticky. **C,** clean the keyboard with isopropyl alcohol, is incorrect because the alcohol could react with the plastic and will likely evaporate before it can rinse away the sticky residue.

4. ☑ **C.** You should avoid using an eraser to clean a keyboard because parts of the eraser tend to come off as small shavings. These can get under the keys, causing more problems.

   ☒ **A,** compressed air, and **D,** a vacuum, are incorrect because these are both good methods to use for removing dust or other loose debris from the keyboard. **B,** water, is incorrect because it can be used to clean the keyboard when there is a sticky residue.

5. ☑ **D.** To clean fingerprints from a monitor, ensure that no power is going to the monitor. Apply glass cleaner to a paper towel and wipe the screen with it. Wait for the screen to dry,

then use it normally. You should always make sure that there is no power by turning the monitor off and unplugging it. The monitor contains high voltage, and you will be applying liquid to it. Always spray the glass cleaner on the paper towel, not on the screen itself. This prevents stray spray from getting into places it shouldn't and prevents drips. When the screen is clean and dry, plug it in and use it as you normally would.

☒   **A** is incorrect because it suggests spraying the glass cleaner directly on the screen. Again, you should avoid this practice because it could allow spray to get into places it shouldn't and can result in dripping. **B** is incorrect because it suggests using mild, soapy water. However, as with regular glass, if soapy water is used on the screen, it could leave streaks and a soap buildup. **C** is incorrect because it suggests using a dry, lint-free cloth to clean the screen. Although safe, this procedure will be ineffective for removing fingerprints.

6.   ☑   **A.** You should use contact cleaner to clean the contacts. This is a relatively effective way to remove corrosion. Ensure that you follow the cleaner's manufacturers instructions to avoid damage to the contacts.

☒   **B,** soak the connector in distilled water, is incorrect. Not only is this an ineffective way of removing corrosion, but it could also lead to more corrosion. **C,** use a cotton swab soaked in mild, soapy water, is incorrect because this can lead to soap residue on the connector. This residue could prevent a good connection and could add to the buildup of corrosion. **D,** use a can of compressed air, is incorrect. Although effective for removing dust, compressed air is not effective in removing corrosion, which is typically caked on.

7.   ☑   **B.** You should use compressed air to clean the fan. The fan could be spinning slowly because a buildup of dust is preventing it from spinning at its regular speed. Turn the computer off, and use the compressed air to blow the dust out of the fan. Make sure that you blow the dust away from, not into, the computer.

☒   **A** and **C** are both incorrect because they suggest replacing parts. Although this might be the solution, you should try cleaning the fan before you replace a component. If cleaning it solves the problem, you will have saved time and money. Note that you should never carry out the procedure in **A** (replace the fan). The fan is part of the power supply, and when it stops working, you must replace the whole power supply. Never open the power supply. **D** is incorrect because it states that you should use isopropyl alcohol to clean the fan. The fan is housed within the power supply, which is a high-voltage device. Always keep all liquids away from it.

8.   ☑   **C.** Compressed air has the potential to cause personal injury. Compressed air cans contain a pressurizing liquid that can cause skin burns if released. Never hold a compressed air can upside-down, and don't shake the can before spraying.

☒   **A,** vacuuming is generally messier than using compressed air, is incorrect. When you vacuum the computer, the dust is deposited in the vacuum, away from the computer. When you use compressed air, the dust can be deposited everywhere. When using compressed air, you must be very careful not to blow dust from one component onto another. **B,** vacuums make it easier to get into smaller places, is also incorrect. The thin nozzle on a compressed air can creates an air stream that can get into every nook and cranny of the computer. Vacuums (even hand-held ones) are much bulkier and might not be able to get into small places. **D,** you are more likely to damage a component using compressed air, is incorrect. Although it is possible to damage a component by applying pressurized air to it, you are more likely to damage a component by accidentally hitting it with the vacuum.

9. ☑ **C.** Cleaning the computer will not allow you to determine the voltage output of the power supply. Cleaning involves removing dust from the computer and visually inspecting connections and cables. Determining the power supply's voltage output requires the use of voltage testing with a voltmeter or multimeter.

☒ **A,** reducing the probability of ESD, is incorrect because this is a good reason to clean the computer. Dust can hold a static charge that can bleed into components over time, resulting in ESD damage. By removing the dust, you can remove this risk. **B** is incorrect because it suggests that cleaning the computer can't help prevent components from overheating. By removing dust from components, you can ensure that they are cooled properly, and by keeping the fan clean of dust, you can ensure that it rotates as fast as is necessary. **D** is incorrect because it suggests that determining the presence of improper connections is not a benefit of cleaning the computer. However, part of cleaning the computer is checking the connections for corrosion and to ensure they are securely attached.

10. ☑ **C.** You should replace the cable. Even though the cable appears to work now, whatever caused the crack to occur could still be at work and cause the cable to fail altogether. Replace the cable as soon as you find the problem, since you already have the computer taken apart.

☒ **A** is incorrect because it states that you should pay close attention to the behavior of the computer so that you can tell when to replace the cable. This is not a good idea because the eventual failure of the cable could cause more serious problems than a lack of signal to the intended device, such as a power arc or improper data, resulting in harmful component behavior or lost data. **B,** use electrical tape to patch the cable, is incorrect because this is an incomplete solution. This could provide only a temporary fix for the problem. Furthermore, corrosion might have already started on the exposed wires. They should be replaced, not patched. **D** is incorrect because it suggests you should do nothing about the cable. However, it is not normal for a cable to have a cracked shield. You should replace it right away to prevent it from causing problems.

Power Protection and Safety Procedures

11. ☑ **B.** ESD is harmful to expansion cards. It is also harmful to other computer components such as the system board, processor, and RAM modules. These devices are used to receiving

between ±3v and ±12v DC. However, the voltage produced by ESD can be tens of thousands of volts.

☒ **A,** people, is incorrect. Although ESD might be enough for you to feel a small shock, it is not harmful. **C,** the computer's power supply, is also incorrect. The power supply is a high-voltage device that is not affected by the relatively low current of a static discharge. **D,** the environment, is also incorrect. ESD occurs when electrons move from an area of high electrical potential to an area of low electrical potential. It has no effect on the air, ground, or water.

12. ☑ **B.** A suppressor can be used to protect the computer from electrical power surges. Power surges can damage the computer's components. Suppressors are able to remove excess voltage from the power during surges.

☒ **A,** an ESD strap, is incorrect because this is used to drain static charges from the computer's components, not to prevent damage due to power surges. **C,** a noise filter, is incorrect because its function is to remove EMI and other "noise" from the incoming power supply to the computer. **D,** a standby power UPS, is incorrect because this device is used to provide temporary battery power to the computer in the event of a power lapse or blackout.

13. ☑ **C.** A UPS can help the most in this situation. A UPS contains a backup battery system; some also have an integrated noise filter and suppressor. One of these all-in-one units can prevent problems stemming from power surges, blackouts, and EMI.

☒ **A,** a noise filter; **B,** a suppressor; and **D** a backup battery, are all incorrect. Each of these devices is available independently of the others, but each remedies only one of the three power issues. All three issues can be resolved by purchasing a UPS that contains battery backup, a suppressor, and a noise filter all in one unit.

14. ☑ **B.** An online UPS is the most effective because it prevents lapses in the power supply when a blackout occurs. Online UPSes are attached between the computer and the wall outlet. All power from the wall outlet is converted by the UPS into battery power. This battery supplies the computer with power. When the power goes out, the battery continues to work normally, drawing power from its reserve. There is no momentary lapse in power while the UPS switches from regular power to the battery, as there is in an SPS.

☒ **A** is incorrect because it suggests that an SPS can provide power for a longer amount of time than an online UPS. In many cases, the performance of an online UPS is superior to that of an SPS. In any case, short- and longer-term battery power is available for both UPS types, depending on the model and how much you are willing to spend. **C,** an SPS because it provides battery power more immediately during a blackout, is incorrect. As explained, an SPS causes a lapse in power during the switch from regular to battery power. An online UPS always supplies the computer with battery power and continues to do so during a power outage. **D** is incorrect because it suggests that an online UPS is most effective because it will draw less power from the electrical source than an SPS. There is no significant difference between an SPS and online UPS in terms of the amount of electricity they draw from the wall outlet. Even if there were, it would have little or no effect on the operation of the computer, as long as the UPS still produced the proper voltage.

15. ☑ **D.** A CMOS battery is not considered a high-voltage device. This means it doesn't contain enough voltage to harm you. It could, however, contain chemicals or other elements that can burn your skin, so you should never open a battery. You must also dispose of batteries properly so that they do not cause environmental damage.
    ☒ **A,** a printer power supply; **B,** a computer power supply; and **C,** a monitor, are all incorrect because they are all considered high-voltage equipment. This means that they hold enough charge to seriously injure you. Never open the case of a high-voltage device, and never wear an ESD strap when working around one.

16. ☑ **D.** When replacing the sound card, you should place an ESD mat on your work surface, unplug the computer, put an ESD strap on, open the computer, remove the card, and place it on the ESD mat. The ESD mat, when properly grounded, provides a good place to put components when you remove them from the system. As with all electrical equipment, you should unplug the computer before you open it. The ESD strap will help prevent you from causing ESD when you touch the components in the computer.
    ☒ **A** is incorrect because it suggests placing the removed component on an antistatic bag. These bags work by removing static buildup from the inside and placing it on the outside of the bag could possibly cause ESD damage by exposing a component to this static buildup. **B** and **C** are incorrect because they suggest spraying the sound card or the computer with the antistatic spray. This liquid can harm computer components and should never be sprayed directly on them. Furthermore, you should never apply liquid of any kind to the computer's high-voltage power supply.

17. ☑ **D.** You should recycle printer toner cartridges because they are sold in very large numbers. Most computer users go through toner cartridges fairly quickly. It is better to recycle them and keep them out of landfills due to the amount of overall space they would take up if they were thrown away every time they were emptied. This is the same principle as that of recycling bottles and cans; they are not harmful to the environment per se, except that they take up space in landfills and can be better used if they are recycled.
    ☒ **A, B,** and **C** are all incorrect because they suggest that toner cartridges contain harmful acids, contaminating chemicals, and materials that can deplete the ozone layer, respectively. Toner cartridges do not contain any of these elements.

18. ☑ **A.** The likely cause is catastrophic ESD. The term *catastrophic ESD* refers to ESD damage that causes immediate and total failure of the affected component. The only solution is to replace the video card.

☒ **B,** degradation, is incorrect because this refers to gradual ESD damage over time. **C,** hidden ESD, is incorrect because this refers to ESD damage that you are unaware of, such as that being caused by a dust buildup. However, the shock you felt was almost certainly ESD. **D,** sudden ESD syndrome, is not a real term.

19. ☑ **C.** Raising the humidity of the room could help reduce the occurrence of ESD. Although many things contribute to ESD, one of the most significant is low humidity. Keep the room's humidity between 50 percent and 80 percent.

☒ **A** and **B** are incorrect because they suggesting altering the temperature of the room. However, humidity is a more likely contributor to ESD than temperature. **D,** keep the lights as dim as possible, is incorrect because although the presence of lights could cause EMI, it will not cause ESD.

20. ☑ **B.** You should store a hard drive in a cool and dry environment. Components must stay cool to work properly, and dry air is less likely to cause corrosion. Note that although dry air can contribute to ESD, a hard drive in storage will not just "develop" ESD. However, if the room is dry, make sure that you discharge static from yourself before touching the drive.

☒ **A,** cool and damp, is incorrect because damp air can lead to corrosion. **C,** warm and damp, and **D,** warm and dry, are both incorrect because a warm environment could cause the hard drive to lose its data.

LAB ANSWER

Obviously, your friend has some unsafe habits and should be warned about the possible results. If your friend eats at the computer, there is a likelihood of crumbs falling into the keyboard. If this happens, some of the keys might not depress all the way when pressed due to crumbs stuck underneath them. This problem can be resolved by turning the keyboard upside-down and shaking it. You could also clean the keyboard by blowing the crumbs out with compressed air or vacuuming them out. You might have to remove some of the keycaps to get at the material underneath them.

It is also possible for drinks to spill into the keyboard. When the liquid dries, it can leave a sticky residue. This can result in keys that stick when they are pressed. You can remedy this problem by soaking or rinsing the keyboard in distilled water.

If there are crumbs and liquid in the keyboard, there could also be some on the work surface on which the computer sits. These crumbs can be picked up and deposited into the mouse. You can remove the mouse's retaining ring and ball to clean it.

Your friend also has a cat, which means there could be loose fur present. As well as getting into the keyboard and mouse, fur can be drawn in by the power supply fan and deposited inside the computer. Using proper safety procedures, open the computer and used compressed air or a vacuum to remove fur and dust.

The fact that the lights flicker whenever your friend turns the speakers on could mean that the two are located too close to one another. If the speakers can affect the lights, there is a good chance that the lights are affecting the speakers with EMI. Move the two as far from each other as possible. Furthermore, flickering lights indicate an unsteady supply of power. Your friend might want to consider using a UPS that will smooth out the dips and increases in the power supply.

If your friend has a habit of rubbing his feet on the floor, he may be generating static. When he touches the computer or a floppy disk, he could cause ESD and damage the component. Antistatic spray on the floor and your friend's clothing could help prevent this problem.

Recall that floppy disks (and all magnetic storage) are susceptible to damage from EMI. Also recall that the monitor can produce EMI. It can therefore be unsafe to place the two near each other, because doing so could erase the data on the floppy disks. The disks should be moved as far away from the monitor and other EMI-causing devices as possible or placed in a shielded case.

5

Motherboards, Processors, and Memory

Y ou should already be familiar with the roles of the processor, RAM, the motherboard, and CMOS in the computer system. This chapter takes an in-depth look at the characteristics and specifications of each of these complex devices. Common processors in the Intel lineup are examined in terms of their abilities and differences. Various types of RAM are discussed, along with rules you must follow regarding which types of RAM you can use in your system. The motherboard, including different form factors and designs, is also discussed. The chapter finishes up with a description of basic CMOS settings and how these settings can alter the performance of the computer.

CERTIFICATION OBJECTIVE 5.01

Popular CPU Chips

There are many CPU manufacturers, including AMD, Cyrix, and Intel. Over time, these manufacturers have released a number of processor models, ranging from the Intel 8086 (released in 1978) to the currently popular Intel Pentium III, Pentium 4, and AMD Athlon. Beginning in 1995, AMD, Cyrix, and Intel began to seriously compete with one another, releasing processors at roughly the same times. The following subsections discuss the common processors, beginning with what are termed *fifth-generation processors*.

Pentium (586)

The Intel Pentium processor was first released in March 1993. It was the first *superscalar* processor, meaning that it was capable of parallel processing and that two sets of instructions could be processed at the same time. Pentium processors support speeds of 60, 66, 75, 90, 100, 120, 133, 150, 166, and 200MHz. Pentiums 60 and 66 have a 273-pin PGA design and fit into Socket 4 on the motherboard. These earlier processors contained about 3.1 million transistors and used 5vDC. Pentiums 75–200 are 296-pin staggered PGAs that use Socket 7. The Pentium 75–133MHz processors have 3.2 million transistors, and Pentium 150–200MHz processors have 3.3 million transistors. All Pentiums over 66MHz use 3.3vDC and can use either a passive heat sink or a fan (an active heat sink).

All Pentium processors have a 64-bit data bus, meaning that the processor can receive or transmit 64 bits at a time. They also have a 64-bit register (internal data bus), which is the on-board storage area in the processor. Pentium processors have a 32-bit address bus, which means that they can address up to 4GB of memory.

Pentium processors include 16KB of on-board, integrated cache memory. This type of memory is often referred to as L1, or Level 1, cache. They are also able to access between 256KB and 512KB of motherboard (L2) cache. See the "From the Classroom" for more information about L1 and L2 cache.

FROM THE CLASSROOM

The size of memory calculations is based on the bus width. If you think about the binary number system, you notice that 32 bits is 2 raised to the 32nd power. This means that the number progression of binary is 1, 2, 4, 8, 16, 32, 64, 128, and so on, or that $2 \times 10^{32} = 4294967296$, or 4GBs.

Pentium Pro

The Pentium Pro processor was released in November 1995 and was designed for use on servers rather than regular desktops. The Pentium Pro supports speeds of 150, 166, 180, and 200MHz. Its form is a 387-pin dual staggered PGA, and it uses Socket 8 on the motherboard.

The Pentium Pro contains approximately 5.5 million transistors and uses 3.3vDC (3.1 for the 150MHz). Due to the increased number of transistors, Pentium Pro chips require an on-board fan—they generate too much heat to use a passive heat sink.

Like the Pentium, the data bus of a Pentium Pro is 64 bits, and the register size is 32 bits. However, the Pentium Pro has a larger address bus, at 36 bits. This allows it to address up to 64GB of RAM. The larger or wider the register size, the higher the possible number values. If you double the size of the 32-bit register we discussed earlier, you'll see that for each additional bit you get the 64GB size. The Pentium Pro also has a 16KB L1 cache, but it has an on-board L2 cache that runs at the same speed as the processor. The Pentium Pro can support between 256KB and 1MB of L2 cache.

AMD K5

Also released in 1995 was the K5 processor, designed by Advanced Micro Devices (AMD). This processor supports speeds of 75, 90, 100, and 116MHz, contains 4.3 million transistors, and uses 3.52vDC. The K5 processor has a 296-pin PGA design and uses Socket 7. It also requires an active heat sink (fan). Like the Pentium, the K5 has a 64-bit data bus, a 32-bit register, and a 32-bit address bus. It is therefore able to address up to 4GB of RAM. The main difference between the Pentium and K5, other than the supported speeds, is the use of L1 cache. The Pentium supports up to 512KB; the K5 supports only 8KB.

The terms Bus, System Bus, and Expansion Bus are often used interchangeably. A bus refers to either a system bus or an expansion bus attached to the CPU. PC expansion busses, such as PCI, attach through a controller that attaches to the system or expansion bus.

Pentium with MMX Technology

In January 1997, Intel released a processor similar to the Pentium but with an improved instruction set called *multimedia extensions* (MMX) for handling graphics and other multimedia. All Pentium family processors released since this Pentium include the MMX instruction set. The Pentium with MMX supports 166, 200, and 233MHz speeds and uses the same 296-pin staggered PGA form as a regular Pentium. It also uses 3.3vDC externally, but because it uses only 2.8vDC internally, it must use a special Socket 7 that supplies the appropriate voltage. This processor contains 4.5 million transistors and can use either a passive heat sink or a fan.

The Pentium with MMX has the same data bus (64 bits), register size (32 bits), and address bus (32 bits) as the Pentium. It is also able to access up to 4GB of RAM, 32KB of L1 cache, and either 256KB or 521KB of motherboard L2 cache.

Pentium II

The Pentium II processor, released in May 1997, marks a radical form change from previous Intel processors. The Pentium II includes 512KB of on-board L2 cache, so the form was changed from the PGA to the much larger single-edge contact (SEC). SEC processors (242 pins) are attached to the motherboard via a Slot 1 connector.

The Pentium II introduced a number of new characteristics, such as its support for speeds of 233, 266, 300, and 333MHz. It contains approximately 7.5 million transistors, so it must use a special cooling fan. It uses 3.3vDC and includes 32KB of L1 cache. Like other processors in the Pentium family, the Pentium II has a 64-bit data bus and a 32-bit register. However, like the Pentium Pro, it has a 36-bit address bus, so it can use up to 64GB of RAM.

AMD K6

Around the time of the Pentium II processor's release, AMD released its own sixth-generation processor, the K6. This processor supports speeds from 166–266MHz. It has around 8.8 million transistors and uses 3.3vDC. Like previous AMD processors, the K6 is a 296-pin PGA and uses Socket 7 to attach to the motherboard. As with most processors, the K6 has a 64-bit data bus, a 32-bit register, and a 32-bit address bus. It also includes between 256KB and 1MB of L1 cache, but it does not include an on-board L2 cache.

Cyrix MII

Also released in 1997 was the Cyrix MII processor, which supports speeds of 150, 166, or 187MHz. It contains 6 million transistors, uses 3.3vDC, and has a 296-pin PGA form. Although its data bus, register, and address bus match that of the K6, the MII contains only 64KB of L1 cache.

Pentium III

The Pentium III (PIII) processor was released in March 1999. It includes advanced multimedia instructions, called *single-instruction multiple data (SIMD)* technology. Its first variant, referred to as simply Pentium III, has 512KB in on-board L2 cache and uses a 100MHz system bus. The second Pentium III variant is the Pentium III B, the main improvement of which is that it uses a 133MHz system bus. The final PIII variant is the Pentium III E. The PIII E processor uses 256KB of on-board *advanced transfer cache (ATC)*. ATC is a new technology that can increase performance by about 25 percent by including L2 cache in the processor. ATC runs at the processor speed and improves overall cache performance. Pentium III processors range in speeds from 450MHz to 1.13GHz and can include either, neither, or both of the E and B technologies. Pentium III processors are available in two forms. The first form was a 242-pin SEC; later, the PIII was released as a 370-pin PGA. The PIII SEC can use a regular Slot 1, as long as the slot supports 2.0vDC, and the PIII PGA uses a PGA370 ZIF (zero insertion force). Pentium III processors contain 9.3 million transistors and have integrated fans. Like most processors in the Pentium family, the PIII has a 64-bit data bus, a 32-bit register, a 36-bit address bus, and support 64GB of memory. The PIII also includes 32KB of L1 cache.

Pentium 4

The Pentium 4 (P4) processor was released in 2000. It includes all of the features of the Pentium III plus a few more. The chip went through a redesign that includes a new architecture called the NetBurst microarchitecture. Where older Pentiums pretty much topped out at 1GHz, the P4 is designed to work at much faster speeds that allow it to exceed speeds of 2GHz on the desktop. Intel states that NetBurst allows for future processor speeds of up to 10GHz. This makes the P4 the fastest chip in the Intel fleet.

The P4 also includes a number of new instructions and, interestingly enough, a smaller L1 cache than a Pentium III (8KB vs. 32KB on the Pentium III). You would think this would make the system slower, in reality system performance improves. The speed increases due to fact that the cache is refreshed or updated more efficiently when smaller sizes of cache are used. The L2 cache on the Pentium 4 is 256KB, like its predecessor but it operates at a faster speed. In short the caching scheme used on the Pentium 4 is much more efficient then earlier processors.

The NetBurst microarchitecture is an extremely rich and powerful microprocessor capability. If you want to learn more about it, visit the Intel website at **www.intel.com**.

Pentium 4 processors are available in two forms. The most common form is the Socket 478; alternatively, Intel makes a Socket 423 version that is used in earlier Pentium 4 processors.

AMD Duron and Athlon

AMD released the Duron processor in 1999. The Athlon was released in 2000. The Duron supports speeds between 700 and 800MHz; the Athlon gives the PIII a run for its money with support for 850MHz–1.2GHz and 128KB of L1 cache.

The preceding subsections contain a good deal of very specific information about popular processors. However, because Intel processors are the most commonly used, you can expect to see more reference to them than the other processor types on the A+ exam. The information that you should concentrate on for the A+ exam is summarized in Table 5-1.

TABLE 5-1   Intel Pentium Processors

	Pentium	Pentium Pro	Pentium MMX	Pentium II	Pentium III	Pentium 4
Form	273- or 296-pin PGA	387-pin PGA	296-pin PGA	242-pin SEC	242-pin SEC or 370-pin PGA	423- or 478-pin PGA
Socket	4, 5, or 7	8	7	Slot 1	Slot 1 or PGA370	Socket 478 or Socket 423
Voltage (vDC)	3.3 or 5	3.1 or 3.3	3.3	3.3	2	1.44 or 1.75
Speeds	60–200MHz	150–200MHz	166–233MHz	233–333MHz	450MHz–1.1 3GHz	1.3GHz–3.2 GHz
L1 cache (KB)	16	16	32	32	32	8

TABLE 5-1	Intel Pentium Processors *(continued)*					
	Pentium	**Pentium Pro**	**Pentium MMX**	**Pentium II**	**Pentium III**	**Pentium 4**
L2 cache	256–512KB on motherboard	256–1MB on-board	256–512KB on motherboard	512KB on-board	256–512KB on-board	256-512KB
Notes	First to use parallel processing	Designed for servers	Enhanced multimedia	First to use SEC form	SIMD instruction set	Hyper-Threading

FROM THE CLASSROOM

Isn't "On-Board L2 Cache" an Oxymoron?

Traditionally, L1 cache is located within the processor, and L2 cache was located on the motherboard. However, even though the L2 cache of some processors (Pentiums Pro, II, III, and 4) is described as being "on-board," it's actually external to the processor and merely housed within the same casing. That is, the processor and external cache have been bundled together in a convenient package. For example, when you pick up a Pentium 4, you are actually holding both the processor, which has L1 cache, and the L2 cache.

The L2 cache is included in the processor package to speed it up. The L2 cache that is located on the motherboard is limited to the system bus speed. By removing the L2 cache from the motherboard and placing it within the processor, it is able to run at the processor's speed. Intel's newest processor, the Itanium, also includes L3 cache in the processor package and offers sizes up to 4MB. Intel has already announced larger L3 cache sizes in this processor.

It is fairly easy to identify an Intel processor by its physical shape and markings. However, you can also identify the processor without opening the computer. If you are using Microsoft Windows, follow the steps in Exercise 5-1 to find out what type of processor your computer is using.

EXERCISE 5-1

Identifying Your Processor

1. Right-click the My Computer icon.
2. Select Properties.
3. Read the information in the General tab. Use the data in Table 5-1 to determine your processor type.

CERTIFICATION OBJECTIVE 5.02

Random Access Memory

The primary function of RAM is to provide a temporary storage place for information about devices and applications. However, there are many types of RAM with which you should be familiar. This section discusses the many incarnations of RAM as it has been developed and refined over time. This section also discusses important factors to consider when installing or upgrading the RAM in a computer system: there are guidelines you must follow about the type of RAM, the type of package, and the amounts of RAM that you install in a particular system.

Types of RAM

RAM is not all the same. Over time, RAM technology has improved, changed form, and been used for specialized components. The most common types of RAM are discussed here.

SRAM

Static RAM (SRAM) was the first type of RAM available. SRAM can be accessed at approximately 10 nanoseconds (ns), meaning that it takes about 10ns for the processor to receive requested information from SRAM. The structure of SRAM chips limits them to a maximum data capacity of 256KB. Although SRAM is very fast compared with DRAM, it is also very expensive. For this reason, SRAM is typically used only for system cache.

DRAM

Dynamic RAM (DRAM) was developed to combat the restrictive expense of using SRAM. DRAM chips provide much slower access than SRAM chips but can store several megabytes of data on a single chip (or hundreds of megabytes if they are packaged together on a module). Every "cell" in a DRAM chip contains one transistor and one capacitor to store a single bit of information. This design makes it necessary for the DRAM chip to receive a constant power refresh from the computer to prevent the capacitors from losing their charge. This constant refresh can make access even slower and causes the DRAM chip to draw more power from the computer than an SRAM chip. Because of its low cost and high capacity, DRAM is used as "main" memory in the computer.

The term *DRAM* is typically used to describe any type of memory that uses the technology just described. However, the first DRAM chips were very slow (~80 90ns), so faster variants have been developed. The list is quite large and includes fast-paged RAM, EDO RAM, SDRAM, RDRAM, SDLRAM, and BEDO RAM. As computer systems improve, the list of DRAM technologies continues to grow. However, EDO, SDRAM, RDRAM, and DDR RAM are currently the most common, so they are described here.

EDO RAM

Extended data out (EDO) RAM improves on traditional DRAM by performing more than one task at a time. When one piece of data is being sent to the processor, another is being retrieved from the RAM module. While that piece of data is being transferred, the EDO RAM is looking for the next piece to retrieve for the processor. This process enables the chip's data to be accessed at about 60ns. EDO RAM chips can be used only in a computer system whose processor and motherboard support its use.

SDRAM

Synchronous dynamic RAM, or *SDRAM*, is about twice as fast as EDO RAM because it is able to run at the speed of the system bus (up to 100–133MHz). However, as faster system bus speeds are developed, EDO and SDRAM are being replaced with other, faster types of DRAM, such as RDRAM and DDR RAM. Like EDO RAM, SDRAM can be used only in systems that support it.

RDRAM

RDRAM (*Rambus Dynamic RAM*) gets its name from the company that developed it, Rambus, Inc. RDRAM uses a special Rambus channel that has a data transfer rate of 800MHz. The channel width can be doubled, resulting in a 1.6GHz data transfer! RDRAM can be used only in computers with special RDRAM channels and slots. RDRAM is fairly new, so don't expect to see it in computers that were manufactured before 1999.

DDR RAM

Double-data rate (DDR) RAM doubles the rate of speed at which standard SDRAM can process data. That means DDR is roughly twice as fast as standard RAM.

The standards available for DDR RAM are PC 1600, PC 2100, and PC2700. This new labeling refers to the total bandwidth of the memory, as opposed to the old standard, which listed the speed rating (in MHz) of the SDRAM memory—in this case, the PC66, PC100, and the PC133. The numeric value in the PC66, PC100, and PC133 refers to the MHz speed that the memory operates at.

VRAM

Video RAM (VRAM) is a specialized type of memory that is used only with video adapters. The video adapter is one of the computer's busiest components, so to keep up with video requirements, many adapters have an on-board micro-microprocessor and special video RAM. The adapter can process requests independently of the CPU, then store its results in the VRAM until the CPU retrieves it. VRAM is much faster than EDO RAM and is capable of being read from and written to at the same time. The result is better and faster video performance. Because VRAM includes more circuitry than regular DRAM, VRAM modules are slightly larger.

The term *Video RAM* refers to both a specific type of memory and a generic term for all RAM used by the video adapter (much like the term *DRAM*, which is often used to denote all types of memory that are dynamic). Faster versions of video memory have been introduced, including WRAM.

WRAM

Window RAM (WRAM) is another type of video RAM but it provides faster access than VRAM. It uses the same dual-ported technology that allows devices to read and write data to the video memory at the same time. The term "window" refers to its ability to retrieve large blocks (windows) of data at one time.

Physical Characteristics

The RAM types discussed so far can have many different physical forms. Your system must support both the technology and form of a memory module. The system must also support the data width of the memory as well as its method of error correction. The following subsections describe some common physical forms of memory modules and other characteristics that distinguish one module from another.

Single Inline Memory Modules

The first memory chips were dual inline package (DIP) chips, which were inserted directly onto the motherboard. However, as discussed in Chapter 1, their structure made them prone to chip creep. Single inline memory modules (SIMMs) were developed to combat this loosening of memory chips and to recover space on the motherboard.

SIMMs are available in 30-pin and 72-pin forms. Thirty-pin SIMMs are 8-bit, meaning that data can be transferred into or out of the module 8 bits at a time. Seventy-two-pin SIMMs are 32-bit. Because SIMMs are older technology, they are typically used for fast-paged and EDO RAM. You are not as likely to find a SIMM with SDRAM, since dual inline memory modules (DIMMs) were the prevalent form when SDRAM was introduced.

Dual Inline Memory Modules

Dual Inline Memory Modules (DIMM) modules look similar to SIMMs but are slightly longer and are installed into a different type of slot. DIMMs have two rows of connectors, 168 connectors in all, and are 64 bits. DIMMs are likely to contain either EDO RAM or SDRAM because those technologies were common when DIMMs were introduced.

Rambus Inline Memory Module

The *Rambus Inline Memory Module (RIMM)* is designed specifically for use with Rambus memory. RIMMs look just like DIMMs but have 184 connectors. They are also more proprietary and less common than SIMMs and DIMMs. RIMMs are 16-bit.

Small Outline DIMM

Small Outline DIMM (SoDIMM) is a memory module frequently used in laptop computers. The physical size is much smaller than DIMM memory. The most common pin configurations are 72- and 144-pin modules.

MicroDIMM

The MicroDIMM is a module designed primarily for subcompact and portable computers. The MicroDIMM is half the size of an SoDIMM and allows for higher density of storage. The MicroDIMM module is not keyed but will only install properly one way.

Memory Banks

The *bit width* of a memory module is very important; the term refers to how much information the processor can access from or write to memory in a single cycle. A *memory bank* represents the number of memory modules required to match the data bus width of the processor.

For example, a Pentium 4 processor has a 64-bit data bus. You have the option of adding up to 4GB of RAM on the newer motherboards. If you wanted to you could add two 2GB memory modules, four 1GB memory modules, or some number smaller. Each memory module would take a single memory bank.

A memory bank refers to a match between the processor's data bus width and RAM's bit width. If you are using a 64-bit processor, one 64-bit DIMM makes a full bank, and four 16-bit RIMMs make a full bank. The term memory bank does not refer to the slots used to attach the RAM modules to the motherboard.

When dealing with processors from the Pentium family, it is not difficult to determine how much memory you need to create a full bank, since they are all 64-bit processors. However, you might have to work with older processors and older types of RAM. Use the formula in Exercise 5-2 to figure out the number of memory modules you need to install in your computer.

EXERCISE 5-2

Calculating the Memory Bank Size

1. Determine the data bus width of the processor in your computer (16 bits for a 386SX, 32 bits for a 386DX or 486, 64 bits for the Pentium family).

2. Determine the bit width of the memory module (30-pin SIMMs are 8-bit, 72-pin SIMMs are 32-bit, DIMMs are 64-bit, and RIMMs are 16-bit).

3. Divide the processor's data bus width (Step 1) by the memory's bit width (Step 2). The number you get is the number of memory modules you must install to create one full bank.

Parity and Nonparity Chips

One type of memory error checking is called *parity*. In parity, every byte of data is accompanied by a ninth bit (the parity bit), which is used by the receiving device to determine the presence of errors in the data. There are two types of parity: odd and even. In *odd parity*, the parity bit is used to ensure the total number of 1s in the data stream is odd. For example, suppose a byte consists of the following data: 11010010. The number of 1s in this data is 4, an even number. The ninth bit will be a 1, to ensure that the total number of 1s is odd: 110100101.

Even parity is the opposite of odd parity; it ensures that the total number of 1s is even. For example, suppose a byte consists of the following data: 11001011 the ninth bit would be a 1 to ensure that the total number of 1s is 6, an even number.

Parity is not failure-proof. Suppose the preceding data stream contained two errors: 101100101. If the computer was using odd parity, the error would slip through (try it; count the 1s). However, parity is a quick routine and does not inhibit the access time of memory the way a more sophisticated error-checking routine would.

Some memory modules also use parity. These modules include an extra bit for parity for every 8 bits of data. Therefore, a 30-pin SIMM without parity is 8 bits; with parity it's 9 bits. A DIMM without parity is 64 bits; with parity, the DIMM has 8 extra bits (1 parity bit for every 8 data bits). Therefore, a DIMM with parity has 64 + 8 = 72 bits. If your system supports parity, you must use parity memory modules. You cannot use memory with parity if your system does not support it.

SCENARIO & SOLUTION

Which types of memory packages are available?	SIMM, DIMM, and RIMM.
How many DIMMs make a full bank in a Pentium-class computer?	The processor's data bus and the DIMM are both 64-bit.
What is the parity bit for the data stream 10110110 if the RAM uses odd parity?	0. The parity bit in this case is a 1 or 0 to ensure that the total number of 1s is odd. There are five 1s in this data stream, so the parity bit is 0.

CERTIFICATION OBJECTIVE 5.03

Motherboards

As you now know, the type and amount of memory you install depends on the type of processor you are using. You must follow specific guidelines or the computer will not work. The same is true for motherboards. That is, you cannot install just any type of processor or memory in the motherboard and make it work. There are several motherboard form factors, each with different layouts, components, and specifications. Most motherboards are restricted to using only a few types of processors and memory.

This section focuses on types of motherboards and their typical integrated components. You will also learn about the differences between the motherboard's communication busses and the types of systems they allow you to use. However, all motherboards are unique in terms of the type of slots, memory, and processor they support. In other words, you cannot tell which components a motherboard supports solely by knowing which type of motherboard it is. Therefore, you must always check the manufacturer's documentation before you upgrade or install a processor or memory.

Types of Motherboards

Although motherboards can vary from computer to computer, there are two common types: the AT and ATX. Their sizes, typical components, and prevalence are discussed here.

Full and Baby AT

Advanced Technology (AT) motherboards were introduced in 1984 (around the time of the Intel 80286 processor). They measure approximately 12 by 13 inches and typically support 80286 or older processors, 5.25 inches floppy drives, and 84-key keyboards. A smaller version of the AT motherboard, typically measuring around 8.5 by 13 inches was later released. This type was called the Baby AT, and the original became known as the Full AT. The two AT motherboards are similar in layout. The Full AT motherboard is now practically obsolete, but the Baby AT motherboard is still being used by some manufacturers. Depending on when it was manufactured, Baby AT motherboards might contain SIMM and/or DIMM memory slots and 80386, 80486, or Pentium processor slots. Baby AT motherboards also use the 3.5-inch floppy drive rather than the older 5.25-inch drive.

AT motherboards can be identified by the fact that the parallel and serial ports are not integrated with the keyboard; rather, they are installed in an empty chassis slot and attached to motherboard ports via small ribbon connectors. Other identifying characteristics of the AT motherboard are the placement of the processor socket near the end of the expansion card slots, the use of a DIN-5 keyboard connector, two power connector ports (for P8 and P9 connectors), and support for ±12 and ±5vDC only.

on the **job**

Some manufacturers are still using the Baby AT motherboard for new computers. Therefore, although it is rare, you might find this form factor with support for newer processors and support for USB and/or IEEE-1394.

ATX

The *ATX motherboard* was released by Intel in 1996 and is the most commonly used form in new PCs. ATX is not an acronym but is the actual trademarked name of the motherboard form. The ATX is the same size as a Baby AT motherboard but has a different orientation and layout (see Figure 5-1). Note that the processor is located further from the expansion slots, and the hard drive and floppy drive connectors are located closer to the bays on the chassis.

e**x**a**m**
ⓦatch   *Although there are many variants, most of today's computers are based on the ATX motherboard.*

The ATX motherboard also includes integrated parallel and serial ports (I/O ports) and a mini-DIN-6, rather than a DIN-5, keyboard connector. The ATX motherboard's power supply uses a single motherboard connector and supplies voltages of ±12, ±5, and +3.3vDC. Again, depending on when it was manufactured, an ATX motherboard can contain SIMM and DIMM memory slots; support for BIOS-controlled power management; 80386, 80486, or Pentium-class processor sockets; and support for USB.

Bus Architecture

The term *bus* is used to refer to pathways that signals use to travel from one component to another in the computer. There are many types of busses, including the processor bus, which is used by data traveling into and out of the processor. This bus type was described

The ATX
motherboard

earlier in the "Popular CPU Chips" section. The address and data buses described there
are both part of the processor bus. Another type of bus is the *memory bus*, which is
located on the motherboard and is used by the processor to access memory.

SCENARIO & SOLUTION

How do ATX motherboards differ from Baby AT motherboards?	Some differences are that ATX motherboards include 3.3vDC, have integrated I/O ports, and include a mini-DIN-6 keyboard connector.
What is the most commonly used motherboard type?	The ATX.
Which motherboard form is typically the largest?	The Full AT, which measures 12 by 13 inches.

The following subsections focus on various types of I/O buses, the paths between the processors, and I/O components such as peripherals and drives. You can access a motherboard's I/O bus by installing expansion cards into the appropriate expansion slots. Common expansion card types are shown in Figure 5-2.

ISA

The first type of I/O bus was the *Industry Standard Architecture (ISA)* bus. This is an 8-bit bus, meaning that data can travel 8 bits at a time between devices. Later, in 1984, a 16-bit ISA bus was developed. Both the 8-bit and 16-bit ISA busses run at 8.3MHz.

Although some expansion cards (such as most sound or modem cards) require only 8 or 16 bits, the ISA bus is becoming obsolete. Current motherboards carry only one ISA slot, and most new motherboards no longer include any ISA slots. For those motherboards that still have them, the 8-bit and 16-bit slots are different sizes, but an 8-bit card can be used in a 16-bit slot; it uses only the first half of the slot's connectors.

on the **()** o b

ISA, EISA, and VESA have largely become obsolete in new computer systems. You will generally find that all new computer systems use only the PCI bus and AGP for the video.

FIGURE 5-2

ISA, PCI, and VESA (bottom) expansion cards

PCI

The most common bus architecture in new computers is *Peripheral Component Interconnect (PCI)*. It was released in 1993 and is typically found in 80486 and newer systems. The PCI bus is either 32 or 64 bits and can run at half the processor's memory bus speed. PCI is considered a local bus. This means that it moves data at speeds nearer the processor speeds.

PCI slots are smaller than ISA slots and are typically white. PCI cards and slots are not compatible with those of other bus architectures. Although PCI was initially developed for video cards, PCI cards are also available for networking and SCSI controllers, among other peripherals.

AGP

Accelerated graphics ports (AGP) are relative newcomers to the computer industry. AGP is a local bus that was designed for video only. This architecture is typically considered a "port" rather than a bus because it consists of a direct link between the processor and the video card only. AGP is 32 bits and can run at the speed of the processor's memory bus.

AGP slots look very similar to PCI slots, but they are not compatible with PCI cards. To use AGP, the system's chipset and motherboard must support it. The AGP architecture also includes an AGP controller, which is typically a small, green chip on the motherboard.

AGP cards typically run four to eight times faster than PCI. They are now rated as 2X, 4X, or 8X. 2X and 4X are very common on consumer systems, while the 8X is frequently referred to as a Pro version. Faster cards can run in slow AGP slots; however, they will only run at the speed of the AGP port.

EISA

Extended ISA (EISA) bus architecture was developed after 16-bit ISA; it offers a 32-bit data width and bus speed of 8.3MHz. EISA slots on the motherboard look just like 16-bit ISA slots, but the difference is that EISA slots have two rows of connectors, one deeper than the other. The EISA expansion card has two corresponding connector lengths. EISA slots are backward compatible with 8-bit and 16-bit ISA expansion cards. That is, you can use an EISA, 8-bit ISA, or 16-bit ISA card in an EISA slot.

Today, EISA slots are not as common as ISA slots, since faster (and wider) 32-bit architectures have been developed. You are unlikely to find an EISA slot on a motherboard designed for an 80486 or newer processor.

VESA Local Bus

The *VESA Local Bus (VL Bus)* was developed in 1992 by the Video Electronics Standards Association (VESA). It was designed specifically to improve video performance in the 80486 processor. Unlike its predecessors, the VESA bus is not limited to using the regular I/O expansion bus. Rather, the VESA bus provides a direct channel between the VESA card and the processor (called a *local bus*). The VESA bus can run at speeds up to 33MHz.

Like EISA, the VL Bus is a 32-bit bus. VESA slots are actually 16-bit ISA slots with an extra brown slot at the end. VESA video cards are therefore very long and, unfortunately, prone to loosening. VESA slots are backward compatible with ISA cards, meaning that you can use a VESA, 8-bit ISA, or 16-bit ISA card in a VESA slot. In addition to being used for video cards, VESA slots are sometimes used for hard drive controllers.

Expansion cards are all installed using the same procedure, regardless of the slot type. Use the installation procedure outlined in Exercise 5-3.

EXERCISE 5-3

Installing an Expansion Card

1. Turn the computer off and ensure that you carry out proper ESD procedures.

2. Position the controller card upright over the appropriate expansion slot.

3. Place your thumbs along the top edge of the card and push straight down. If necessary, rock the card along its length (never side to side).

4. Secure the card to the chassis using the existing screw holes.

USB

As discussed in Chapters 1 and 2, the Universal Serial Bus (USB), offers a bandwidth of 12Mbps for USB 1.1 and a design data rate of 480Mbps for USB 2.0, and it can be used to connect up to 127 external devices. The USB controller (if it is not integrated) is installed in a PCI expansion slot. It supports both Plug and Play and hot swapping.

Audio Modem Riser

The Audio Modem Riser (AMR) is a relatively new technology that allows for the creation of lower-cost sound and modem solutions. The AMR card plugs directly into the motherboard and utilizes the CPU to perform modem functions, using up to 20 percent of the available processor power for this purpose. The advantage of this is the elimination of a separate modem and sound cards without tying up a PCI slot in newer computers. The AMR card connects to a telephone line and audio output devices directly.

Communication Network Riser

The Communication Network Riser (CNR) is similar to the AMR except it is oriented towards audio, modem, LAN, and multimedia systems. The CNR card plugs directly into the motherboard, thus eliminating the need for separate cards for each capability and reducing the cost of expansion cards.

PC Card and PCMCIA

Recall from Chapter 2 that PC Cards, which were designed for use in portable computers, come in several types. Type I and Type II cards (also referred to as *PCMCIA cards*) are 16 bits. Type III cards are 32 bits. Each PC card slot is backward compatible, meaning that you can insert a Type I or II card in a Type II slot, and you can insert all three card types into a Type III slot.

IDE

The preceding I/O bus architectures are used for attaching video or peripheral cards to the computer. IDE devices, such as hard drives and CD-ROM drives, also use the system's I/O bus. However, recall from Chapter 2 that there are several drive interface standards, including the IDE and ATA families (collectively referred to as *IDE*).

Older ATA or IDE hard drives are 16-bit, so whether they require a controller card or have a controller card that is integrated with the motherboard, they use the 16-bit ISA bus. Faster standards, such as Ultra DMA, ATAPI, and EIDE require the use of a local bus, such as the 32-bit VESA or PCI architectures.

SCSI

When installing a SCSI host adapter, you must use an expansion bus that will at least meet the bit width of the SCSI adapter you are installing. For example, a Wide SCSI-2 adapter requires at least a 16-bit ISA bus because it has a 16-bit data width. Additionally, you must consider the speed of the SCSI controller. The ISA bus is limited to 8MBps,

SCENARIO & SOLUTION

What are the most common bus architectures used today?	ISA, PCI, and AGP.
Which slots can you use to install an 8-bit ISA card?	8-bit ISA, 16-bit ISA, EISA, and VESA.
Which bus architecture should you use to connect an IDE drive interface?	The IDE interface is 16-bit, so you should use a bus type that is 16-bit or wider. You should use a local bus to take advantage of the IDE drive's speed.

so it is sufficient for use with SCSI 1 or regular SCSI 2, which run at a maximum of 5MBps. However, if you plan to use any other SCSI host adapters, consider using a SCSI controller designed for a local bus architecture, such as VESA or PCI.

CERTIFICATION OBJECTIVE 5.04

Complementary Metal-Oxide Semiconductor Settings

Most Personal Computer systems allow you to customize the settings of a number of motherboard components. This is done by selecting options within the CMOS settings program. Literally hundreds of CMOS settings are available in different computers; only the most common ones are discussed here.

To access the computer's CMOS settings, watch the computer screen at startup. Following the POST, a message appears, indicating the proper key sequence you should use to enter the CMOS settings program. This key combination varies among computers but is typically F2, DELETE, or CRTL-ALT-ESC. In most systems, the message will appear for only 3 to 5 seconds. You must use the indicated key combination within that allotted time.

Note also that CMOS settings programs are designed differently. Some allow you to use the mouse and some the keyboard only. Furthermore, the names of the settings might be slightly different. Use the program's Help feature for information about how to navigate through the program and save or discard your changes. It's a good idea to make notes about the current CMOS settings before you change them, in case you need to change them back. Although this won't work in all computers, you can try the procedure in Exercise 5-4 to print the CMOS settings.

EXERCISE 5-4

Backing Up the CMOS Settings

1. Restart the computer using the CTRL-ALT-DELETE key combination (do not use the reset or power buttons to do this).

2. Enter the CMOS settings program using the specified key combination.

3. Press the Print Screen key on the keyboard to print the current screen. Although this will not work in all systems, it can provide you with a handy hard copy of the CMOS settings.

4. Use the Print Screen key on each screen of the CMOS settings program. If this procedure doesn't work on your computer, you can purchase a third-party CMOS backup program or resort to using pen and paper to write a copy of the settings. This will not work with a laser printer or USB and network printers because they require a separate form feed to eject the page. If they do not receive one in a certain amount of time, they may cancel the print request.

Printer Parallel Port

You can use the CMOS settings to configure the IRQ and I/O addresses of the system's parallel port(s). In newer computers, however, most parallel ports support the IEEE-1284 standard, meaning the port is bidirectional and can be configured automatically by the OS.

You must change the CMOS settings to set the parallel port mode. For example, many parallel ports run in *unidirectional mode* by default. This means that peripheral devices attached to the port can receive but cannot send data. This mode might be referred to in the CMOS settings as "Transfer only." However, some parallel devices are designed to send communication signals back to the computer. These devices require a *bidirectional mode* (also called Standard mode on some machines).

Newer devices may take advantage of faster IEEE-1284 bidirectional modes, called ECP or EPP modes. *Enhanced capability port (ECP) mode* allows access to DMA channels and is approximately 10 times faster than regular bidirectional mode. ECP mode is used for printers and scanners. *Enhanced parallel port (EPP) mode* offers the same performance as ECP but is designed for use with parallel devices other than printers and scanners.

It was very common to connect Zip removable drives to a printer port for backup and removable storage. This capability has largely been replaced by USB devices, as USB has grown in popularity.

Another CMOS parallel port setting is *enable/disable*. You can use this feature to instruct the computer to use or ignore the parallel port. It can be useful to temporarily disable the port when troubleshooting or if the port is in conflict with another component. You might also need to disable the on-board parallel port if it has stopped working. Disabling it will allow you to install another (nonintegrated) parallel port.

COM/Serial Port

Like the parallel port, you can use the CMOS settings to configure the IRQ and I/O address of the COM port(s). However, in newer systems, this is accomplished by the OS. You can also use the CMOS settings to enable or disable the COM port.

Floppy Drive

The CMOS settings program contains options for the configuration and use of the floppy drive. You can enable or disable the use of the motherboard's integrated floppy disk controller by selecting the appropriate option. You might want to disable the controller so that you can use an expansion controller card instead. You can also configure the floppy drive controller so that it cannot be used to boot the computer. You might want to do so to prevent boot sector viruses from affecting your computer or to speed up the overall boot sequence if you don't plan to boot from a floppy disk. If you later find you need to boot from the floppy drive, simply change the CMOS settings accordingly.

You can also use the CMOS settings to configure individual floppy drives on the controller if the floppy drive type is not automatically selected by the BIOS; just select the proper setting: 360KB, 720KB, 1.2MB, 1.44MB, or 2.88MB, depending on the type of drive you are using.

Hard Drive

You can use the CMOS settings to set the type and capacity of each hard drive installed in the system. You should set the type to Auto, if this option is available. This setting instructs the BIOS to read the type and capacity from the drive. However, older systems might require you to manually enter the type and capacity (tracks, sectors, and cylinders) of each drive. You can also use the Autodetect feature to force the BIOS to search for and identify all hard drives in the system. This option is typically used when a slave or secondary drive has been added to the system or when the hard drive has been upgraded.

Memory

As discussed in previous chapters, RAM capacities do not have to be configured. RAM is simply installed in the computer and automatically counted by the BIOS at startup. However, you can use the CMOS settings to enable or disable the memory's ability to use parity error checking (although you can use this setting only if the RAM supports parity—if you enable the CMOS parity option but are not using memory that supports parity, the computer will not boot properly). You can also use the CMOS settings to turn the memory "tick sound" off. This is the sound you hear when memory is being counted by the BIOS at startup. Some systems even let you manually set the speed and timing of the existing RAM so that all modules match. This option is typically found only in older machines.

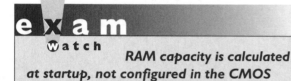

RAM capacity is calculated at startup, not configured in the CMOS settings.

Boot Sequence

The Boot Sequence CMOS setting relates to the order in which the BIOS will search devices for an OS. The default setting on most computers is A:, C:, CD-ROM. You can change this order so that the computer looks first on the hard drive or CD-ROM. This is particularly helpful in keeping boot sector viruses from infecting the computer, when you are troubleshooting, and when you are installing an OS for the first time. For example, many OS CDs contain enough instructions to boot the computer and install the OS, even without a boot (floppy) disk or a minimal OS on the hard drive.

Many computers can also be booted from a network. This usually works using a special boot ROM called a Preboot eXecution Environment (PXE) ROM. The PXE ROM resides on the NIC card and queries the network to get a TCP/IP address and then attempts to connect to a boot server. The boot server provides the operating system for the PC like a disk. The PC then boots from the data provided by the server.

Date and Time

You can use the CMOS settings program to set the computer's real-time clock. The date and time that you set here will be used by the OS, as well as by any applications that are date or time aware. You can also set the date and time using the Windows OS. If you change the date and time in the CMOS, it will automatically be updated in the OS, and vice versa.

Passwords

Most CMOS settings programs allow you to set passwords on the computer. A user password can be set to allow or restrict the booting of the system. A supervisor password can be set to allow or restrict access to the CMOS settings program itself or to change user passwords. Some systems (typically newer ones) include both password options; older systems typically include only supervisor-type passwords, required both to boot the system and enter the CMOS settings program.

You must be especially careful with supervisor passwords. If you forget the CMOS password, you can't even get into the CMOS program to change or disable the password. Fortunately, most systems that have the CMOS password feature include a "clear password" jumper on the motherboard. If you forget the CMOS password, you can open the computer and set the jumper so that the password is removed. If there is no jumper for clearing the password, you can clear the entire contents of the CMOS by temporarily removing the battery. However, this is a last resort because it will cause you to lose all but the default settings.

Plug-and-Play BIOS

If the BIOS is Plug and Play, the CMOS settings program will probably include some options for configuring it. One option is Plug and Play Operating System. When enabled, this setting informs the BIOS that the OS will configure Plug-and-Play devices. If this option is disabled, these devices will be configured by the BIOS. Another Plug-and-Play option allows you to enable or disable the BIOS configuration of Plug-and-Play devices.

CERTIFICATION SUMMARY

This chapter focused on detailed characteristics of CPUs in the Pentium family, motherboard forms, memory types, and CMOS settings. These components are all interrelated, and it is important for you to understand which CPUs can work with which types of memory. You must use a motherboard that supports the CPU and RAM and ensure that the CMOS will support the installed components. A good knowledge of these concepts is especially important when you are repairing or upgrading a computer system.

For example, by knowing the CPU's memory address width, you will know the maximum RAM capacity it can access. In addition, by knowing the CPU's data bus width, you will know how many RAM modules you must install at a time to create a full memory bank. Before purchasing a motherboard, ensure that it has the proper RAM and CPU slots and that the CMOS settings are appropriate for your needs.

✓ TWO-MINUTE DRILL

Here are some of the key points from each certification objective in Chapter 5.

Popular CPU Chips

❏ Processors in the Pentium family include the Pentium, Pentium Pro, Pentium with MMX, Pentium II, Pentium III, and Pentium 4.

❏ Pentium II and Pentium III processors connect to the motherboard using Slot 1, and other Pentium processors use sockets.

❏ Pentium Pro, Pentium II, Pentium III, and Pentium 4 processors include on-board L2 cache.

Random Access Memory

❏ SRAM is very fast and very expensive and used for L2 cache in most systems.

❏ DRAM is slower than SRAM. It is less expensive, has a higher capacity, and is used as main memory in the computer.

❏ You must install SIMMs, DIMMs, and RIMMs in full memory banks so that their total bit width matches the width of the processor's data bus.

❏ Some memory modules use an error-checking method called odd or even parity.

❏ SoDIMM and MicroDIMM are intended for laptop and subcompact computer systems.

Motherboards

❏ The most common type of motherboard in current computers is the ATX form factor, which includes 3.3vDC support, mini-DIN-6 keyboard connectors, and a single P1 power connector.

❏ The most common type of bus architectures are ISA, PCI, and AGP.

❏ VESA, PCI, and AGP bus architectures are considered "local" because they connect more directly with the processor.

❏ When using a drive interface such as IDE or SCSI, use a bus architecture that supports the interface's bit width and use a local bus architecture for faster devices.

Complementary Metal-Oxide Semiconductor Settings

❑ The CMOS settings program allows you to alter the behavior and configuration of many of the system's components.

❑ Parallel ports can be set to unidirectional, bidirectional, ECP, or EPP mode.

❑ You can use the CMOS settings to disable or enable the I/O ports, floppy drive, hard drive, or Plug-and-Play support.

❑ The CMOS settings program allows you to set the time and date, user passwords, and boot sequence.

SELF TEST

The following questions will help you measure your understanding of the material presented in this chapter. Read all of the choices carefully because there might be more than one correct answer. Choose all correct answers for each question.

Popular CPU Chips

1. What is the data bus width of all Pentium-class processors?

    A. 32-bit

    B. 36-bit

    C. 64-bit

    D. Pentium processors have different data bus widths

2. While shopping for computer components, you come across a motherboard that has a Socket 8. Which type of processor can you install on this motherboard?

    A. Pentium

    B. Pentium Pro

    C. Pentium with MMX

    D. Pentium II or III

3. Your computer is a Pentium 4 with 2GB of RAM. You plan to add more memory to the system, but you don't want to add more RAM than the processor can access. How much more memory should you add?

    A. None

    B. 2GB

    C. 30GB

    D. 62GB

4. How does a Pentium II processor attach to the motherboard?

    A. Socket II

    B. Socket 9

    C. Slot 1

    D. The processor is integrated

5. Which of the following processors is available in versions E or B and uses SIMD technology?

    A. Pentium Pro

    B. Pentium with MMX

C. Pentium II

D. Pentium III

Random Access Memory

6. What is the maximum capacity of an SRAM chip?

   A. 256KB

   B. 512KB

   C. 1MB

   D. 64MB

7. Which of the following statements is true regarding DRAM and SRAM?

   A. DRAM is used as main memory because it is cheaper than SRAM.

   B. SRAM is used as main memory because it is faster than DRAM.

   C. DRAM is used as cache memory because it is available in higher capacities than SRAM.

   D. SRAM requires a constant power refresh.

8. A customer is planning to add more RAM to her computer system and has asked your advice. The computer is a Pentium and already has 2GB of memory in DIMM form. She wants to add 4GB of RDRAM but was told that her computer probably wouldn't support it. What do you tell her?

   A. RDRAM is intended for use by video cards, not processors.

   B. She has already reached the RAM capacity for her system.

   C. RDRAM is not supported by the processor in this case.

   D. You'll go ahead and add the RDRAM.

9. You are upgrading a Pentium III computer, and you have installed two RIMMs, totaling 6GB of memory in two of the four slots. However, the computer will not boot. Which of the following could be the problem?

   A. The processor cannot access the memory type.

   B. The memory capacity is too low for the processor.

   C. The memory capacity is too high for the processor.

   D. There are not enough modules installed.

10. A computer uses odd parity. What is the parity bit for the data stream 10110010?

    A. 0

    B. 1

    C. 01

    D. Computers do not use odd parity

Motherboards

11. Which is the most commonly used motherboard type in currently manufactured computers?

    A. Baby AT

    B. AT

    C. Full ATX

    D. ATX

12. You are planning to purchase an internal modem for your Pentium 4 computer. Which type of expansion slot is it most likely to use?

    A. 8-bit ISA

    B. 16-bit ISA

    C. PCI

    D. AGP

13. You are rebuilding a computer that has only VESA slots (a rare case indeed!). Which types of expansion cards can you install in the computer?

    A. VESA only

    B. 8-bit ISA, 16-bit ISA, and VESA

    C. EISA and VESA

    D. 8-bit ISA, 16-bit ISA, EISA, and VESA

14. Which of the following are considered "local" bus architectures?

    A. ISA, VESA, and PCI

    B. EISA, VESA, and PCI

    C. VESA, PCI, and AGP

    D. AGP only

15. Which type of PC Card supports a 32-bit data transfer?

    A. Type III only

    B. Types II and III only

    C. Types I, II, and III

    D. Type II only

Complementary Metal-Oxide Semiconductor Settings

16. You have just installed a *new* printer in your new computer. However, when you try to print, you receive a "Port Mode" error. Which port mode does the printer most likely require?

    A. Output only

    B. Bidirectional

    C. ECP

    D. EPP

17. Which of the following is not a valid CMOS memory setting?

    A. Enable/disable tick sound

    B. Capacity

    C. Enable/disable parity

    D. RAM speed/timing

18. You have just changed the Boot Sequence option in the CMOS settings program. Which of the following will be altered by this change?

    A. The order in which the BIOS searches the drives for an OS.

    B. The location of the BIOS boot instructions.

    C. The order in which the system's bootable drives will be lettered.

    D. The order in which the POST will be conducted.

19. A particular computer's CMOS is set so that a password is required to boot the computer and enter the CMOS settings program. However, the user has forgotten the password. What can you do to remedy the problem?

    A. Use the supervisor password to clear the user password.

    B. Boot from the floppy disk, then look up the user's password in the CMOS.

    C. Remove, then reinstall, the CMOS battery.

    D. Open the computer and use the password jumpers to determine the current password.

20. Which of the following Plug-and-Play options can you use in the CMOS settings program?

    A. Inform the BIOS of Plug-and-Play devices in the system.

    B. Instruct the BIOS to perform an immediate search for all Plug-and-Play devices in the system.

    C. Set the IRQ addresses of Plug-and-Play devices in the system.

    D. Inform the BIOS of a Plug-and-Play OS.

LAB QUESTION

Your current computer has the following specifications:

- Pentium 60
- Baby AT motherboard
- Four 72-pin SIMMs, totaling 4GB of RAM, odd parity

You have decided to upgrade the computer to a Pentium II 300. However, based on your reading of this chapter, you know that you cannot simply buy a new processor and install it in the system. Which other components will you likely have to replace? What new features will the upgraded computer have?

SELF TEST ANSWERS

Popular CPU Chips

1. ☑ **C.** All Pentium-class processors have a 64-bit data bus. This means that 64 bits can enter or leave the processor at a time.

   ☒ **A,** 32-bit, is incorrect. Older processors have 32-bit data buses, but all Pentiums have 64 bits. Pentiums do, however, all have a 32-bit register (internal bus). **B,** 36-bit, is incorrect. No Intel processor has a 36-bit data bus, although some Pentium-class processors have a 36-bit memory address bus. **D** is incorrect because it states that Pentium processors have different data bus widths. Although they do differ in memory address bus width, they *all* have the same data bus width: 64 bits.

2. ☑ **B.** You can install a Pentium Pro on this motherboard. Socket 8 is designed for a 387-pin dual staggered PGA. The Pentium Pro is the only processor that uses this form.

   ☒ **A,** Pentium, is incorrect because this processor uses Socket 4, 5, or 7 but not 8. **C,** Pentium with MMX, is incorrect because this processor also uses Socket 7. **D,** Pentium II or III, is incorrect because these processors do not use sockets at all. Instead, they connect to the motherboard using Slot 1.

3. ☑ **D.** You could add up to 62GB of RAM. The Pentium 4 has a 64-bit address bus and can address up to 64GB of physical RAM. Your motherboard will probably not have enough slots to accomplish this, but it is the limit of addressing for a Pentium 4.

   ☒ **A,** none, is incorrect because the Pentium 4 is not limited to 2GB. **C,** 30GB, is incorrect because this would total 32GB of RAM, 32GB less than the processor can access. **B,** 2GB, is incorrect because it would bring the total RAM capacity to 4GB, which is 58GB less than the processor can access.

4. ☑ **C.** Pentium II processors attach to the motherboard using Slot 1. Pentium II and Pentium III processors have an upright SEC design that requires a different connector than earlier processors.

   ☒ **A,** Socket II, and **B,** Socket 9, are incorrect because no Intel processors use either of these. Furthermore, Pentium II processors use slots, not sockets. **D,** the processor is integrated, is incorrect. None of the Pentium-class processors is integrated with the motherboard.

5. ☑ **D.** The Pentium III is available in versions E or B and uses SIMD technology. The E version includes the use of advanced transfer cache (ATC), and the B version can be used with a 133MHz system bus rather than the traditional 100MHz. The Pentium III's SIMD technology allows it to carry out advanced multimedia instructions.

☒   **A,** Pentium Pro, **B,** Pentium with MMX, and **C,** Pentium II, are incorrect because they were all developed before the creation of the technology used in the E and B variants and SIMD instructions.

Random Access Memory

6.   ☑   **A.** The maximum capacity of an SRAM chip is 256KB. Its technology precludes it from supporting higher capacities in a single chip. DRAM, on the other hand, is able to support much larger capacities.
☒   **B,** 512KB, **C,** 1MB, and **D,** 64MB, are all incorrect. SRAM chips cannot be made to hold more than 256KB.

7.   ☑   **A.** DRAM is used as main memory because it is cheaper than SRAM. It also supports higher capacities than SRAM. However, DRAM draws more power from the computer because it requires a constant refresh, and it is not nearly as fast as SRAM.
☒   **B** is incorrect because it states that SRAM is used as main memory because it is faster than DRAM. Although it is true that SRAM is faster, it is not used as main memory due to its expense and its relatively low capacity per chip (256KB). **C,** which states that DRAM is used as cache memory because it is available in higher capacities than SRAM, is also incorrect. SRAM is used as cache memory because of its speed. Although SRAM is limited in capacity, most systems do not improve when more than 1MB of cache is added. Therefore, the high capacity of DRAM is irrelevant for use as cache memory, and its slow speed makes it a poor cache memory type. **D,** SRAM requires a constant power refresh, is incorrect. It is DRAM that requires a constant refresh.

8.   ☑   **C.** RDRAM is not supported by the processor in this case. RDRAM uses special RIMM slots that weren't yet available when motherboards were being designed for the Pentium processor. Due to the timing of the release of these two technologies, it is very unlikely that a motherboard would have been manufactured that supported a processor that old and a RAM technology that new.
☒   **A** is incorrect because it says that RDRAM is intended for use by video cards, not processors. RDRAM is actually a type of system RAM, not a video RAM technology. **B** is incorrect because it suggests that the computer already has the maximum accessible RAM capacity. However, Pentium processors have a 32-bit memory address bus, so they can access up to 4GB of RAM. **D** is incorrect because it suggests telling her to install the RDRAM. However, as discussed, the motherboard probably doesn't support RDRAM, and it is unlikely that the appropriate RIMM slots are even present.

9.   ☑   **D.** There are not enough modules installed. The Rambus channel requires that all sockets be populated with either a RIMM (at least one) module or a C-RIMM. In this case, you would have to add two C-RIMMS to the empty slots.

☒ **A** is incorrect because it suggests that the processor cannot access the memory type. However, the Pentium III and RIMM memory (RDRAM) were released at roughly the same time and are compatible. The motherboard would not support a processor and memory type that cannot be used together. **B,** the memory capacity is too low for the processor, is incorrect. Although computers must have a certain minimum capacity of RAM to boot properly, it is well below 6GB. **C** is incorrect because it suggests that the memory capacity is too high for the processor. The Pentium III processor can access up to 64GB of memory. Furthermore, if too much memory is installed, the excess will simply be ignored; it will not prevent the computer from booting.

10. ☑ **B.** The parity bit in the data stream 10110010 is 1. In odd parity, the parity bit is used to ensure that the total number of 1s is odd. This data stream contains four 1s. The parity bit is set to 1, bringing the total number of 1s to five (odd parity).

☒ **A,** 0, is incorrect because this would result in an even number of 1s (four). **C,** 01, is incorrect because it suggests that the parity bit is 2 bits long. However, a parity bit is just that—1 bit. **D** is incorrect because it states that computers do not use odd parity. Not all computers use parity, but in those that do, odd parity is the most common type.

Motherboards

11. ☑ **D.** The ATX is the most commonly used motherboard in computers being manufactured today. The ATX motherboard, unlike its predecessors, supports 3.3vDC and mini-DIN-6 keyboard connectors and has integrated parallel and serial ports.

☒ **A,** Baby AT, and **B,** AT, are both incorrect. The term *AT* is typically used to refer to the Full AT or both Full and Baby AT forms. These forms are older and are used much less frequently than the ATX form. AT motherboards typically do not have integrated I/O ports and do not support 3.3vDC. Note that although some manufacturers continue to use upgraded Baby AT motherboard forms, they are not nearly as common as the ATX form. **C,** Full ATX, is incorrect because this is not a real motherboard form. The word *Full* is used to distinguish the original AT form from the newer, smaller Baby AT form.

12. ☑ **C.** You would want to use a PCI slot for the modem. The PCI slot is the current recommended expansion slot for devices in Pentium 4 class computers. This allows for the full plug and play capabilities of the operating system as well as the other features offered by the PCI expansion slots.

☒ **A,** 8-bit ISA, is incorrect because the computer is a Pentium 4. Eight-bit ISA cards can use 16-bit ISA slots, so the 8-bit ISA slot is obsolete in newer computers. **B,** 16-bit ISA is incorrect. 16-bit ISA is obsolete as well. Many newer motherboards no longer include any ISA slots and support PCI expansion slots only. **D,** AGP is incorrect because these slots are designed for video cards only.

13. ☑ **B.** You can install 8-bit ISA, 16-bit ISA, and VESA cards in a VESA slot. The VESA slot is in fact a 16-bit ISA slot with an addition at the end.

    ☒ **A,** VESA only, is incorrect because VESA slots are backward compatible with 8-bit and 16-bit ISA cards. **C** and **D** are incorrect because EISA and VESA are not compatible. EISA cards contain two connector lengths, designed to be inserted into an EISA slot that has two socket depths. However, recall that a VESA slot is simply a 16-bit ISA slot with an addition. Although an EISA slot can hold a 16-bit ISA card, an ISA slot cannot hold an EISA card.

14. ☑ **C.** VESA, PCI, and AGP are all considered "local" bus architectures. This means that they are not limited to the traditional I/O system bus but can access the processor's memory bus or the processor directly. Local buses typically run much faster than the standard I/O system bus.

    ☒ **A,** ISA, VESA, and PCI, and **B,** EISA, VESA, and PCI, are incorrect. The concept of a local bus did not exist until the VESA architecture, which was released *after* the ISA and EISA architectures. **D,** AGP only, is incorrect because the VESA and PCI architectures are also local.

15. ☑ **A.** Type III is the only PC Card that supports a 32-bit data transfer. It is also backward compatible, so some Type III cards are 16-bit, and 16-bit Type I and Type II cards can be used in a Type III socket.

    ☒ **B, C,** and **D** are all incorrect because they suggest that Type I and/or Type II cards support a 32-bit data transfer. They are, in fact, limited to 16 bits.

Complementary Metal-Oxide Semiconductor Settings

16. ☑ **C.** The printer most likely requires ECP mode. ECP mode is newer and faster than output only or bidirectional and is used most commonly for newer printers.

    ☒ **A,** output only, is incorrect because this is an older mode used with printers that can only receive data from the computer. Most newer printers also require the ability to send data to the computer. **B,** bidirectional, is incorrect because this mode uses older technology. Again, since the printer is new, it most likely takes advantage of newer port technology. **D,** EPP, is incorrect. EPP uses technology similar to ECP, but it is used for parallel devices other than printers and scanners.

17. ☑ **B.** The capacity is not a valid CMOS memory setting. RAM is automatically counted on startup, and you cannot configure the system to use more or less RAM than what is actually available.

    ☒ **A,** enable/disable tick sound, is incorrect because this is a common memory setting within the CMOS settings program. This option allows you to turn on or off the sound of the memory count at startup. **C,** enable/disable parity, is also incorrect. In systems that use memory parity, you can choose to disable or enable it. **D,** RAM speed/timing, is incorrect because, although rare, this is a valid CMOS setting on some systems (typically older ones).

18. ☑ **A.** If you change the boot sequence, you alter the order in which the BIOS searches the drives for an OS. On startup, the BIOS performs a POST, then searches for a valid OS. When one is found, the BIOS hands it control of the remainder of the boot process. In many computers, the BIOS will first search the A: drive, then the C: drive, and finally the CD-ROM drive.

☒ **B,** the location of the BIOS's boot instructions, is incorrect. The BIOS's boot instructions are always stored on the CMOS chip, and you cannot alter their location. **C,** the order in which the system's bootable drives will be lettered, is also incorrect. On most systems, the floppy drives will be given A: and B: labels (if a second floppy drive exists), and the hard drives will be given letters starting with C:. Although some utilities and OSes allow you to change these letters, you cannot do so in the system's CMOS settings program. **D,** the order in which the POST will be conducted, is incorrect because you cannot alter this order.

19. ☑ **C.** You can remove, then reinstall, the CMOS battery. This will erase all nondefault settings in the CMOS. However, use this as a last resort because you will then need to reconfigure the CMOS. Incidentally, you could also try looking for a "clear password" jumper on the motherboard.

☒ **A** is incorrect because it suggests using the supervisor password to clear the user password. In this computer, there is one password for both booting the computer and accessing the CMOS program. You cannot even get into the CMOS program without the proper password. Note, however, that some computers have two separate passwords. A user password is required to boot the computer, and a supervisor password is required to enter the CMOS settings. This, unfortunately, is not one of those computers. **B** is incorrect because it suggests that you can look up the password in the CMOS settings if you boot from a floppy disk. Without the proper password, you cannot boot from any device, including a floppy disk. Furthermore, the ability to boot from a floppy disk is completely unrelated to the ability to read CMOS settings. **D,** open the computer and use the password jumpers to determine the current password, is incorrect. Although some systems include a jumper that allows you to erase the password, no system includes a jumper that indicates the password.

20. ☑ **D.** You can use the CMOS Plug-and-Play options to inform the BIOS of a Plug-and-Play OS. If one exists, the BIOS will let it configure Plug-and-Play devices. If not, the BIOS will configure the devices itself.

☒ **A,** inform the BIOS of Plug-and-Play devices in the system, is incorrect. The whole concept of a Plug-and-Play BIOS is that the BIOS will automatically detect those devices. Therefore, they do not have to be manually entered. **B,** instruct the BIOS to perform an immediate search for all Plug-and-Play devices in the system, is also incorrect. The BIOS will automatically search for these devices at startup. The immediate search for devices refers to the Autodetect feature that can be used to force the BIOS to search for all existing hard drives in the system. **C,** set the IRQ addresses of Plug-and-Play devices in the system, is incorrect. Again, a Plug-and-Play BIOS will detect and configure Plug-and-Play devices automatically. This means there is no need to set the IRQs manually. It is however possible to manually set PnP configuration in BIOS. This may be helpful if you have special configuration requirements.

LAB ANSWER

As well as a new processor, you will have to purchase a new motherboard. Although some motherboards will support a range of speeds for a particular processor model, they include only one type of slot or socket, so they only support one model type. Pentium 60 processors use Socket 4, but Pentium II processors require Slot 1. The motherboard you purchase will most likely have to be an ATX form, because Baby AT forms are becoming exceptionally rare. In fact, almost all new computers use ATX rather than Baby AT forms.

If you are buying an ATX motherboard, you will also have to replace the power supply. The Pentium processor uses 5vDC, but the Pentium II requires 3.3vDC. Furthermore, AT motherboards use separate P8 and P9 connectors, whereas ATX motherboards use a single P8/P9 connector. You might also have to replace the keyboard. Baby AT motherboards typically include DIN-5 keyboard connectors, but ATX motherboards have mini-DIN-6 keyboard connectors.

The fact that you are buying a new motherboard could also mean that you cannot use the memory SIMMS that you currently have. Most new computers do not support parity, and due to the age difference between the two technologies, it is unlikely that a motherboard designed for a Pentium II would include SIMM slots. The new motherboard is more likely to include DIMM or RIMM slots. Even if you can use your old SIMMs, they are likely to support older RAM types, such as EDO RAM, whereas the new motherboard is likely to support newer, faster types, such as SDRAM or RDRAM. In any case, you might end up buying more RAM for your computer, since the Pentium II supports up to 64GB of memory.

The new motherboard/processor combination might allow you to use more advanced technologies, such as Plug-and-Play BIOS, AGP bus architecture, or USB. In fact, you might find that some of your older devices, such as your video card, cannot be installed in the new system.

In summary, you can probably keep components such as the monitor, modem, sound card, hard drives, floppy drive, and mouse. Most of the other components will either not physically fit into the computer or will not be recognized by the new BIOS or processor.

6

Printers

CERTIFICATION OBJECTIVES

6.01   Identify printer technologies, interfaces, and options/upgrades.

6.02   Resolve common printer problems and techniques used to resolve them.

✓   Two-Minute Drill

Q&A   Self Test

One of the most commonly used computer peripherals is the printer. Because there are many types of printers, and because they will comprise a large portion of your troubleshooting efforts, this entire chapter is devoted to them. This chapter discusses various printer types as well as how they work. It also introduces you to common printer problems, troubleshooting techniques, and preventive maintenance procedures that can help you keep the printer working properly.

CERTIFICATION OBJECTIVE 6.01

Basic Printer Concepts

The best tool you can have to properly care for and troubleshoot printers is a good understanding of how they work and how to properly set them up. If you know the functions of a printer's components, you will more easily be able to determine the cause of problems when they occur. A good understanding of configuration and setup procedures will allow you to make the printer accessible to the users who need it.

Types of Printers

Over time, printer technology has improved so that they can produce photo-like images. However, a number of printer technologies are still in use, due to cost and quality differences between them. The three most common printer technologies, dot matrix, inkjet or bubblejet, and laser, are discussed here.

Dot Matrix Printers

Dot matrix printers are the "original" type of printer used in PCs; they have been around for a long time. Fortunately, they are no longer used much except for specialized business uses such as printing multiple-page receipts or forms. Dot matrix printers are so named because they use a matrix of pins to create dots on the paper. Each pin is attached to a *solenoid*, which, when activated, forces the pin toward the paper. As the *print head* (which contains the pins) moves across the page, different pins are forced forward to strike a printer *ribbon* against the paper. Because of this action, dot matrix printers fall into the *impact printer* category. This process of the print head or pins physically striking the paper often sounds like a horde of mad hornets, and is often very loud. Furthermore, because their printouts are created line by line, dot matrix printers are also considered *line printers*.

Dot matrix printers use a *continuous form feed* to move special paper through the printer. A continuous form feed (also called a *tractor feed*) comprises two wheels, one on either side of the paper. Each wheel contains "spokes," or sprockets, that fit into corresponding holes at each edge of the paper. As the wheels turn, the paper is pulled through the printer. The perforated sides of the paper can be removed once the printout is complete, and the pages can be removed from each other or left attached to each other in a continuous string of pages.

Because of the print process they use, dot matrix printers do not provide very good resolution. That is, text and images usually appear grainy, and if you look closely at a dot matrix printout, you will be able to see each individual printed dot. Furthermore, dot matrix printers are limited in their ability to use color. Most of these printers can use one printer ribbon only (typically black, although another color can be substituted). Although some dot matrix printers can use ribbons with more than one (up to four) colors and or more than one (up to four) printer ribbons, dot matrix printers are not capable of producing as many color combinations as other printer types.

One advantage of dot matrix printers is that they are relatively inexpensive. Additionally, because they are impact printers, they can be used for making carbon duplicate or triplicate forms. Because of their simple design, dot matrix printers are also easier to troubleshoot than other printer types.

Inkjet and Bubblejet Printers

Inkjet printers (see Figure 6-1) use ink in cartridges, rather than ribbons, to create text or graphic printouts. The ink cartridge in an inkjet printer contains a small pump, which forces ink out of the reservoir, through a nozzle, and onto the page. Inkjet printers create printouts line by line, so they are considered line printers, but their print mechanisms do not make contact with the page, so they are considered nonimpact printers. Inkjet printers provide much better resolution than dot matrix printers and are capable of using colored ink. Unlike dot matrix printers, inkjets can combine basic colors to produce a wide range of colors. Inkjet printers are not nearly as loud as dot matrix printers and are much faster. As you might expect, inkjet and bubblejet printers, because of their ability to print in color inexpensively, are most popular with consumers and end users. Inkjet and bubblejet printers are considered line printers for the purposes of the exam.

A variant of the inkjet printer is the *bubblejet printer*. Bubblejets resemble inkjets, but their ink cartridges contain heating elements rather than pumps. When the

FIGURE 6-1

An inkjet printer

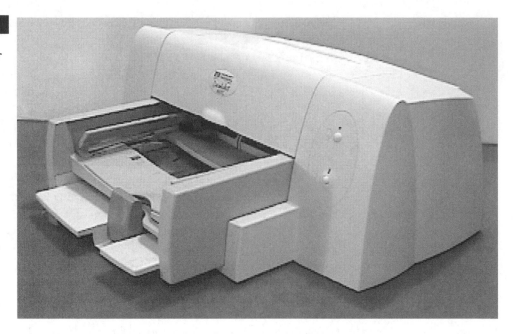

element is heated, the ink expands and forms a bubble of ink on the nozzle. When the bubble becomes large enough, it "bursts" onto the paper and creates a dot of color. Although this process sounds messy, bubblejets provide better printouts than the original inkjets. Today, generally, the term *inkjet* is used to refer to all printers that use ink, including inkjets, and bubblejets.

on the **job**

Inkjet and bubblejet printers are usually inexpensive. The significant costs of these printers are the cartridges: it is not unusual for it to cost between 12 and 25 cents per printed page. So, while inkjet and bubblejets may be inexpensive, often they are not a bargain.

Inkjet printers use *friction-feed* rollers to move the paper through the printer. In friction feed, a stack of pages is kept in a feeder tray. A rubber or plastic roller uses friction to grab the top page and pull it into the printer. Some advantages to this type of feed are that you don't have to worry about lining up the page perforations or the holes and sprockets, and you don't have to separate pages from one another when the printout is finished. Unlike tractor-feed printers, friction-feed printers can be used to print on paper that has an irregular shape or size. You can even print on envelopes and cards.

DeskJet is the proprietary name used for printers made by HP and the term DeskJet has become synonymous with inkjet printer technologies.

Laser Printers

Laser printers are perhaps the most commonly used printers in office environments. They also provide the best quality and have the most complex structure and process. A laser printer is shown in Figure 6-2. Because there are many components in a laser printer, many things can go wrong. This section provides a description of the laser print process. The more familiar you are with it, the easier it will be for you to discover and troubleshoot problems.

The Laser Print Process   Although some laser printers use slightly different processes, the one described here is the generally accepted order of events. Note that these events occur in cycles, so it is not as important to know which step is first or last; rather, it is *order* of events that is important. For example, some sources list charging as the first step, while others list cleaning as the first step. It doesn't really

FIGURE 6-2

A typical laser printer

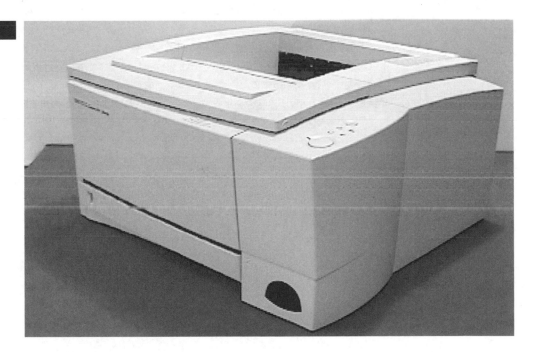

matter which occurs first, but for the purposes of this discussion, we'll consider the charging step first.

1. **Charging** In the charging step, the printer's *high-voltage power supply (HVPS)* conducts electricity to the *primary corona wire*, which in turn passes the voltage on to the printer's *drum*. This voltage is around –5000vDC.

on the **job**

Some newer laser printers use charged rollers instead of corona wires to pass voltage to the drum.

2. **Writing** The photosensitive drum now contains a very high negative charge. In the writing step, the printer's *laser* begins to move along the drum, creating a negative of the image that will eventually appear on the printout. Because the drum is *photosensitive*, each place that the laser touches loses most of its charge. By the end of the writing step, the image exists at around –100vDC, while the rest of the drum remains charged to –5000vDC.

3. **Developing** In this stage, the cover on the printer's *toner cartridge* is opened. The toner itself contains small particles that are attracted to the less negatively charged (–100vDC) areas of the drum. By the end of this stage, the drum contains a toner-covered image (in the shape of the final printout), and the remainder of the drum remains at –5000vDC.

4. **Transferring** At this point, the paper begins to move through the printer, past the drum. The *transfer corona wire* is responsible for applying a small positive charge to the paper as it passes through. This positive charge "pulls" the negatively charged toner from the drum onto the paper.

5. **Fusing** The only thing holding the toner to the paper at this point is electrical charges. The toner itself contains resin, which melts when heated. As the paper leaves the printer, it passes through a set of *fusing rollers*, which have been heated by a *fusing lamp*. The rollers press the toner onto the paper and the heat on the rollers causes the toner to melt, or *fuse*, to the paper.

6. **Cleaning** When the printout is complete, the drum move across a rubber *cleaning blade* to remove residual toner. The toner is then deposited into a small reservoir or returned to the toner cartridge. Next, one or more *erasure lamps* expose the drum to high intensity light. The drum is photosensitive and any remaining charge is eliminated by the light. The printer is now ready to create another image.

SCENARIO & SOLUTION

What is the function of the laser in a laser printer?	To reduce the drum's charge in areas that will later hold toner.
How does the image get from the drum to the paper?	The transfer corona wire applies a positive charge to the paper. As the paper passes the drum, the negatively charged toner is attracted to the page.
How is the drum cleaned?	A cleaning blade removes residual toner from the drum, and an erasure lamp removes any remaining charge from the drum.
What makes the toner stick to the paper?	The toner contains resin, which is melted onto the paper when it passes through the heated fusing rollers.

The laser printer is considered a nonimpact printer, and because it creates printouts one page at a time (rather than one line at a time), it is also considered a *page printer*. Laser printers use very small dots, so they are able to provide excellent resolution. They are also able to blend colors into practically any shade. In a color printer, the writing and developing stages take place four times (once for each basic color—red, green, blue, and yellow) before the image is transferred to the paper. Like inkjet printers, laser printers use friction feed to move the paper through the printer. However, there is more than one set of rollers within the laser printer, to keep the page moving smoothly until it is ejected. Laser printers are the quietest and fastest printers, but they are also the most expensive to purchase.

Make sure that you are familiar with the laser print process. Knowing this process will help you *determine which component is at fault when there is a problem.*

SCENARIO & SOLUTION

What type of medium does each printer type use to create images?	Dot matrix printers use ink ribbons, inkjet printers use ink, and laser printers use toner.
What is an impact printer?	An impact printer is one that uses physical impact to create images, such as the pins on a dot matrix printer.
What are two types of nonimpact printers?	Inkjet and laser printers do not "strike" the print medium onto the page, so they are considered nonimpact printers.
What is a line printer?	A line printer is one that creates an image one line at a time. Dot matrix and inkjet printers are line printers.
Is the laser printer a line printer?	No. The image is created one page at a time, not one line at a time. The laser printer is therefore considered a page printer.
What is the difference between a true inkjet printer and a bubblejet printer?	An inkjet printer uses a small pump to spray ink on the paper. A bubblejet printer uses heat to cause ink bubbles to burst onto the paper.

on the job

Laser printers are usually very inexpensive from a cost per page perspective. The initial investment is usually higher than an inkjet or bubblejet printer, but the cost per page is usually between 2 and 5 cents.

Types of Printer Connections and Configurations

There are a number of different ways to access a printer. For example, you can configure a printer so that it is attached directly to the computer or attached indirectly through a network. You can also configure the printer so that it is accessible to only one person or to an entire network of people. Many printers include multiple interfaces, and common printer setups are described in this section.

Parallel Printers

The most common way to attach a printer to a computer is through the computer's parallel (LPT) port. In fact, most parallel ports can be set to transmission modes designed specifically for use with printers (for instance, ECP mode). To connect a printer in this way, attach the parallel cable to the printer and the computer. The end that attaches to the printer is a 36-pin Centronics connector; the end that attaches to the computer is a DB-25 connector. It is suggested that you do not use a parallel cable longer than 6 feet, because longer cables are more susceptible to errors caused by EMI.

You must also attach the printer's power cable to a wall outlet or other source of power. If the printer is Plug and Play, the OS will detect it on startup and load a device driver for it. If the printer is not Plug and Play, you will need to manually load a driver for it. To do this, insert the disk that came with the printer and run the Setup or Install program. Because the printer is attached to the parallel port, it will use that port's IRQ and I/O address assignments.

USB Printers

More and more printers are being manufactured to support USB connections. To attach a USB printer, simply plug it into a USB external or root hub. There is no need to even turn the computer off. If the printer requires an external power supply, plug the printer into a power source. Most USB devices support Plug and Play. If the USB printer does not, load its driver using the Setup or Install program that came with the printer.

Network Printers

There are two ways to access a printer on a network. The first is to use a true network printer that contains a network interface card (NIC) and is configured in the same manner as other computers on the network. (You'll find more on this topic in Chapter 7.) The printer itself contains a user interface, a small keypad, for configuration.

 on the **Job**

Printers are one of the most commonly accessed network resources and are the cause for a majority of network-related trouble calls.

Another way to network a printer is to configure it as a *shared resource*. Shared printers are attached to a computer's parallel, USB, or IR port, as described in the preceding subsections. The printer is then shared with other users, in the same manner that files and other resources can be shared on the network. In this type of setup, the printer can be accessed only via the network if the computer to which it is attached is turned on and has network access. This computer, incidentally, is called the *print server*. Follow the steps in Exercise 6-1 to make a local printer accessible on a Windows network.

EXERCISE 6-1

Configuring a Printer as a Shared Resource

1. Determine which computer on the network will act as the print server (the computer that the printer will be attached to).

2. Turn the computer off and attach the printer to it with a printer cable. If the printer is USB it is not necessary to turn the computer off unless directed by the installation procedure.

3. Connect the printer to a power source.

4. Turn the computer on and load a device driver for the printer, if required.

5. Double-click the My Computer icon.

6. Double-click Printers.

7. Right-click the printer you want to share, then select Properties.

8. Select the Sharing tab (the default setting should be Not Shared).

9. Select the Shared option and enter the share name (the name that will identify this printer to other users).

10. Click OK. Other users should now be able to access this printer through the Network Neighborhood. See Chapter 7 for more information on how to access a shared printer.

e x a m
ⓦatch

A network printer is different from a printer that is shared on a network. A true network printer has a NIC and is configured as a separate node on the network. A shared printer is attached to a computer on the network and can be accessed only if that computer is turned on and is attached to the network.

CERTIFICATION OBJECTIVE 6.02

Care, Service, and Troubleshooting

There are a great number of moving parts in printers and, because of the frequency at which they are used, moved, and reloaded with paper, ink, or toner, they are prone to developing problems. The following subsections are designed to introduce you to common problems and their resolutions as well as procedures you can use to care for the computer and prevent the occurrence of problems.

Feed and Output

A common printer problem is related to the mechanics of the paper-feed process. If there is too much paper in a friction-feed paper tray, more than one page can feed through the printer at a time. The extra page can cause problems with the print process itself and can cause jams within the printer. The same can happen if there is static within the pages, which can cause the pages to stick together. Moisture in paper can also cause pages to stick together or not feed properly. To avoid multiple-page feeding problems, reduce the amount of paper you place in the tray and use your thumb to "riffle," or quickly separate, the pages before you load them into the paper tray. Another friction-feed printer problem occurs when no pages are fed into the printer. This is more common in inkjet printers that have an upright paper tray. If the stack of paper is too small, the friction rollers might not be able to make contact with the top page.

Tractor-feed printers are notorious for feeding paper incorrectly through the printer. The problem is not usually getting the paper through but lining the paper up properly. Recall that these feed mechanisms require special paper, in which each piece of paper is attached to the page before it, much like a roll of paper towels. If the roll of paper is not lined up properly, the text that is supposed to be on one page could split over two pages. When this is the case, continue advancing the roll of paper until it is properly aligned.

Paper Jams

Many things can cause a paper jam, such as improperly fed pages, pages that are too thin, static, dust build-up, or worn printer components. Paper jams usually stop the current print job. You might also see an error message on the printer itself or on your computer screen. Most printers will not resume operation until the jam is completely cleared. Many printers also require that the reset or clear button be pressed to restart the printer.

When paper jams in a printer, the first thing you should do is lift the cover. Look for the paper, and if it is visible, gently try to remove it. Don't pull too hard because you could end up ripping the page, and the smaller pieces left inside the printer will be even harder to get out. Some printers, typically laser printers, include levers that you can release to more easily remove jammed paper. When removing jammed paper, always pull in the direction that the paper normally travels through the printer. Pulling the other way could damage rollers and other internal components.

If the printer continues to jam often, try using a different paper weight. Printers work best with a particular weight of paper, and if you use paper that is too thin or too thick, jams can occur more frequently. If the paper itself is not the problem, try cleaning the printer of dust and other build-up (techniques are discussed at the end of the chapter). If the printer continues to experience paper jams, you might need to replace the feed rollers.

Print Quality

Any time a printer starts producing poor-quality images, you have a problem. Most quality-related problems are easily resolved by replacing ink, toner, or laser printer drums. However, quality problems can also be caused by failures within the device's print process. This is where your knowledge of the inkjet and laser print processes will come in handy. Let's look at some common problems related to quality.

The Printer Produces Blank Pages

If a dot matrix printer produces blank pages, pay attention to the sound coming from the printer itself. If you cannot hear the pins striking the page, try replacing the print head. If the pins are striking the page but there is a blank printout, there is a ribbon problem. First, check to ensure that the ribbon is lined up with the print head. If the ribbon gets accidentally pulled above or below the print head, no image will be created on the page. If the ribbon is already lined up properly, the ribbon is probably worn out, and you can resolve the problem by replacing the ribbon.

The distance between the print head and the paper can be adjusted in most dot matrix printers. This is especially useful for printing multipart forms. Experimenting with the head settings may also reestablish normal printing.

If an inkjet printer produces blank pages, the likely suspect is the ink cartridge. Use the printer's software utility to determine the amount of ink left in the cartridge. If no such utility came with the printer, remove the cartridge and gently rock it back and forth to determine if there is ink present. If there is not, replace the cartridge. If there is ink, the problem could be a clogged nozzle. Follow the printer manufacturer's instructions for cleaning the print head/printer cartridge(s) with the provided software.

To clean manually, use a clean foam-rubber swab or lint-free cloth slightly dampened with distilled water, again following manufacturer's instructions.

on the **!**
()ob

Most laser cartridges use tape on the cartridge to prevent movement and leakage. Make sure all packing tape is removed from a new print cartridge before installing it.

There are several possible causes of blank pages produced by a laser printer. To begin with, check the toner. If the cartridge is empty, replace it. If it is not empty, try replacing the drum. Sometimes drums become unable to hold a charge after time (in some laser printer models, the toner and drum come as an integrated unit). If this does not resolve the problem, use your knowledge of the print process itself. A blank page means a failure of the toner to be attracted to the paper. Perhaps the laser did not discharge areas of the drum. It could also be that the transfer corona wire (or underlying HVPS) did not apply a positive charge to the paper. Unfortunately, these components are difficult to replace, and you could end up sending the printer to a repair shop that specializes in laser printers. Fortunately, almost all laser print problems can be resolved by changing the toner and/or drum.

FROM THE CLASSROOM

Patience, Patience, Patience

Some users tend to "pull" paper through as it is exiting the printer. However, the paper is ejected at precisely the rate at which the image is created, so pulling the paper can cause gaps in the printed text or image.

Pulling the paper through can also cause small tears in the paper, resulting in small particles or larger pieces of the page being left behind in the printer. If they are left in the paper path, they can impede the passage of subsequent pages, resulting in a paper jam. Even worse, they can build up near moving components,

limiting their range of motion and causing premature wear and tear.

Finally, by pulling the paper, you can end up forcing the printer's rollers to rotate more than they should. This is typically accompanied by a grinding noise akin to nails on a chalkboard. The result can be stripped components, burnt-out motors, and undue wear and tear. Be patient. Pulling paper through the printer to speed up image creation isn't any more effective than pressing an elevator button over and over again to make the elevator arrive more quickly, and it may damage the printer.

Random Speckles on the Page

If any type of printer produces a page with speckles or blotches on it, try cleaning the printer. Ribbon ink, cartridge ink, and toner can be deposited within the printer itself and transferred onto the paper as it passes through the printer. Cleaning procedures are discussed later in the chapter.

Repeated Speckles or Blotches

Repeated speckles are those that appear at regular intervals on each page or down the entire length of a page. Again, for any printer type, try cleaning the printer first, paying particular attention to the feed rollers.

If there are repeated speckles in a laser printout, suspect the drum. If there is a small nick in the drum, toner will collect there and be transferred onto each page. In addition, during the cleaning step, some drums lose their ability to drop their charge. In either case, replacing the drum may solve the problem.

Printout Contains a Faint Image of the Last Printout

A *ghosted image* occurs when an image from a previous printout appears on subsequent printouts. This phenomenon occurs only in laser printers and indicates a cleaning process failure. The drum, as explained, might have lost the ability to drop its charge in the presence of light. Replace the drum to try to resolve the problem. If the drum is not the cause, it could be either the cleaning blade or the erasure lamps. The erasure lamps are not usually easy to replace; you will probably have to send the printer back to the manufacturer or to a specialized printer repair shop.

The Printout Uses the Wrong Colors

Assuming this is not an application-related setting, a problem with incorrect colors is almost exclusively limited to inkjet printers. If the nozzle on one or more of the colors on a color ink cartridge gets clogged, the colors may come out "dirty" or might not be produced at all. Use isopropyl alcohol on a cotton swab to remove dried ink and unclog the nozzles. Another possible cause of this problem is the level of ink. If one color in the color cartridge gets low, the proper shades will not be produced. To resolve this problem, check the cartridge, cleaning the print head and if that doesn't work replace the cartridge.

The Printout Is Smudged

If a dot matrix printer produces a smudged printout, check the pins on the print head. Stuck pins can cause printouts to have a smudged appearance as they drag across the page. If this is the case, replace the print head.

on the job

If you notice that the printer ribbon is shedding fabric you most likely have a stuck printer pin. This almost always requires print head replacement.

If the printer is an inkjet, the smudges are most likely the result of something or someone touching the printout before the ink has had a chance to dry. However, if the problem persists, try cleaning the printer. If this doesn't resolve the problem, it could indicate worn-out cartridge nozzles. Simply replace the ink cartridge.

Smudged laser printouts are usually the result of a failed fusing process. You might need to replace either of the fusing rollers or the halogen lamp.

The Printer Is Producing "Garbage"

Garbage characters in the printout usually indicate a communications problem between the computer and printer. First, make sure to select the right printer in the Print dialog box. If more than one printer driver is installed, it is possible another printer has inadvertently been selected, which will produce garbage. Next, make sure that the cable is firmly and properly attached. Try turning the printer off and then back on. Restarting the computer may also solve the problem. Check the printer port's resources. Make sure that a proper driver has been loaded. If you suspect the driver is corrupt, remove it and reload it. Ensure that the printer port has been assigned the proper IRQ and I/O addresses. If this is a parallel port, you will need to check the resources of the port itself.

If there is more than one printer port on the computer (LPT1 & 2 or multiple USB ports), try the printer in another port or with another computer. Look at the printer settings in the OS to ensure that the attached printer matches the type selected in the printer settings area. Finally, this problem could be the result of insufficient printer memory. You can test this hypothesis by trying to print a very small document. If it works, there is a good chance that the original document was too large for the printer's memory. You can add more RAM to the printer using the same modules that the computer uses (SIMMs or DIMMs).

exam
ⓦatch

Whenever you are faced with an unfamiliar print-quality problem in a laser printer, suspect the drum. If this does not solve the problem, use your knowledge of the laser print process to determine which step (and therefore, which component) has failed.

Errors

Printers are associated with a great variety of error messages. Furthermore, printers often come with their own configuration and monitoring utilities, each with proprietary error messages. Some of the more common errors are described here. Note that these messages could appear on the computer screen or, the printer's console. Some of these messages are generated by the OS. Any time you receive a printer error message that you do not understand, check the message or error code number in the manufacturer's documentation.

on the **job**

If your printer is reporting an error that is not documented by the manufacturer, check the Internet. Most printer manufacturers have websites with frequently asked questions (FAQs), troubleshooting forums, or lists of error codes and their meanings.

Paper Out

This message indicates that there is no paper in the printer. If the printer uses a tractor feed, you will need to lift the printer lid, feed the first sheet of the new stack through the paper path, and line up the holes with the feed wheels. As this procedure differs among systems, consult the manufacturer's documentation.

If you are using a tray-style friction-feed printer such as that used by laser printers and some inkjet printers, simply pull out the appropriate paper tray. Insert a stack of paper, then close the tray all the way. The error message should go away on its own. If you do not close the tray all the way, a "Tray open" or "Close tray" message might appear. If the printer uses an upright friction feed, such as those used in some inkjet printers, follow the steps in Exercise 6-2 to add more paper.

EXERCISE 6-2

Adding Paper to an Upright Friction-Feed Printer

1. Release the tray lever at the back of the printer (if so equipped). This will cause the paper tray to drop slightly away from the friction rollers.

2. Place a small stack of paper in the tray, using the paper guides.

3. Engage the tray lever. This will bring the paper closer to the feed rollers.

4. The printer might automatically detect the paper and continue the print job. If not, look for and press the Paper Advance button on the printer. This instructs the printer to detect and try to feed the paper.

The "Paper out" message could appear even if there is paper in the tray. Again, if the paper gets too low to be grabbed by the feed rollers, the printer will behave as though there is no paper there. If this is the case, remove the paper, then reinsert it in the tray or add more paper to the current stack.

I/O Error

This error can take many forms, including "Cannot communicate with printer" or "There was an error writing to LPT#." This message is typically reported by the OS and indicates that the computer cannot properly communicate with the printer. Start by ensuring that the printer is turned on. If it is not, turn it on, then try to print. You might need to restart the computer to ensure that it redetects the presence of the printer.

Next, make sure that the printer cable is firmly and properly attached to both the printer and the computer and that a proper driver has been loaded. If you suspect that the driver is corrupt, remove it, then reload it. Ensure that the printer port has been assigned the proper IRQ and I/O addresses. If this is a parallel port, you will need to check the resources of the port itself.

Try the printer in another port or with another computer. Furthermore, look at the printer settings in the OS to ensure that the attached printer matches the type selected in the printer settings area.

Incorrect Port Mode

Again, this error message may be worded differently, but it indicates that the parallel port to which the printer is attached is using the wrong mode. This message usually appears on the computer rather than on the printer. Enter the computer's CMOS settings and change the printer to the proper mode (unidirectional, bidirectional, ECP, or EPP). Consult the manufacturer's documentation for the correct mode (the error message itself might indicate the proper mode).

No Default Printer Selected

This is a Windows-generated error, indicating that no printer has been installed or that Windows has not been informed of a default printer to use. As well as running the printer's Setup program, some printers require that you set the printer up in the Windows Printers folder. Double-click My Computer, then double-click Printers. Right-click the icon of the printer you want to set as the default, then select Set as Default. If no printers are listed in the Printers folder, double-click Add Printer, then follow the on-screen installation steps.

Alternatively, you can click My Computer, then click Control Panel, and then click Printers and then follow the installation instructions.

Toner Low

The "Low toner" message applies to laser printers only. It appears well before the toner is completely gone, as an early warning. The computer should continue to print normally. You can make the error message go away by removing the toner cartridge and *gently and slowly* rocking the cartridge back and forth. This will resettle the toner. Note, however, that this is not a solution to the problem. The reason for the error is to warn you to replace the toner cartridge soon. Most laser printers will not work at all if the toner cartridge is empty.

If the printer is an inkjet, an "Ink low" message could appear or an ink level bar be displayed. Replace the cartridge.

on the job

When ink cartridges get low, you should replace rather than refill them. When you buy an ink cartridge, it comes with a new pump/heating element and new nozzles. By refilling an old cartridge, you will be reusing old, possibly worn-out components.

SCENARIO & SOLUTION	
My laser printer produces the same blotch over and over again. What should I do?	Clean the printer, especially the rollers. If this doesn't work, replace the drum.
My inkjet printer is producing smudged printouts. Why?	There is probably something coming in contact with the page before the ink has had a chance to dry.
What is a "ghosted" image?	It is an image from a previous printout that appears on subsequent printouts. This appears in laser printers only. Replace the drum. If this doesn't work, replace the cleaning components.
Why does my printout contain the wrong colors?	You are probably using an inkjet printer that is low in a particular color or has a clogged cartridge nozzle.

Safety Precautions

Printers have lots of moving parts, so there are several safety procedures you should follow whenever you work with or around a printer. Don't let long hair, clothing, jewelry, or other objects near the feed or exit rollers. Furthermore, don't try to operate a printer with the cover off. The cartridge in an inkjet printer and the print head in a dot matrix printer move back and forth quickly across the page, and it is possible to get your hands or other objects in the way. This can harm you and the printer's components.

You must be especially careful when working around laser printers because they contain lasers that can cause eye damage. Fortunately, most printers do not work once their covers are raised. A more common printer-related injury is caused by the fusing equipment. The fusing lamp can generate around 200°F! Any time you open the laser printer to replace the drum or cartridge or to clear a paper jam, give the printer ample time to cool down before you touch any of its parts.

Laser printers also use high voltage and low voltage high-current power supplies. Make sure the laser printer is powered off and unplugged.

Preventive Maintenance

Because of the frequency with which printers are used, they require constant maintenance. Fortunately, the maintenance procedures are usually easy. The best thing you can do to prolong the life of a printer and prevent problems from occurring is to clean it regularly. In all printers, small particles of paper can get left behind and cause a potentially harmful build-up. This build-up can hold static, which can in turn damage components through ESD or cause pages to stick together. Removing build-up

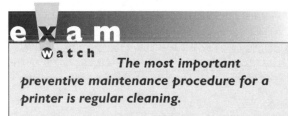

w a t c h *The most important preventive maintenance procedure for a printer is regular cleaning.*

will also keep the paper path clear, thus reducing paper jams and ensuring that the motion of moving parts is not inhibited. You can remove dust and particle build-up using compressed air or a vacuum. As you clean the printer, be on the lookout for small corners of paper that might have been left behind during the print process or when a paper jam was cleared.

If the printer is an inkjet, you should look for and remove ink from the inside of the printer. Ink can leak or get smudged off the paper. As the ink dries, it can cause moving components or paper to stick. Laser printers can accumulate toner. Empty the toner reservoir regularly, and remove other excess toner using a paper towel or cotton swab.

You can also help prevent paper jams and component wear and tear using the proper paper for your printer. If you place typewriter paper and printer paper side by side, you will notice weight and thickness differences. Using the wrong paper can lead to paper jams and cause undue wear on the printer's components.

CERTIFICATION SUMMARY

The focus of this chapter was the components, procedures, troubleshooting, and maintenance procedures for common printer types. The type of printer that a user chooses to work with depends on the printer's cost, resolution, speed, and ability to produce colors. Dot matrix printers are the least expensive, but they also provide the lowest quality. Laser printers, the most expensive, can provide excellent printouts and are the most common type used in offices. For this reason, you are likely to deal with laser printers more frequently than with other printer types.

By understanding a laser printer's print process, you will more easily be able to pinpoint and resolve problems. For example, if you know the components involved in the fusing process, you will be able to determine which components need replacing when the fusing process fails. Furthermore, by regularly cleaning the printer, regardless of its type, you can extend the life of the printer and prevent potential problems from occurring.

TWO-MINUTE DRILL

Here are some of the key points from each certification objective in Chapter 6.

Basic Printer Concepts

❑ Dot matrix printers are impact printers because they create images by striking an array of pins against the page.

❑ Inkjet printers use a small pump to spray ink on the page, and bubblejet printers use heat to place bubbles of ink on the page.

❑ Laser printers use a drum to transfer toner to the page.

❑ Dot matrix and inkjet printers are line printers; laser printers are page printers.

❑ The six steps in the laser print process are charging, writing, developing, transferring, fusing, and cleaning.

❑ Printers can be attached locally to a computer using a parallel or USB connection.

❑ True network printers contain a NIC and are stand-alone network devices.

❑ Regular local printers can be shared on the network as long as the print server is turned on and has network access.

Care, Service, and Troubleshooting

❑ Tractor feeds use sprocketed wheels to pull a continuous roll of paper through the printer, while friction feeds use rubber or plastic rollers to pull single pages through.

❑ Paper jams can be caused by pages sticking (due to static or moisture), worn-out feed mechanisms, particle build-up, or using the wrong paper weight.

❑ Blank pages are usually resolved by replacing the printer's ribbon, ink cartridge, toner cartridge, or drum.

❑ If a printer produces a repeated blotch, clean the printer; if it is a laser printer, replace the drum.

❑ Ghosted images are caused by a failure of the laser printer's cleaning step and can usually be resolved by replacing the drum.

❑ If the printer produces garbled text or cannot be found by the computer, the computer is not communicating properly with the printer.

❑ The most important preventive maintenance procedure you can carry out on a printer is regular cleaning.

SELF TEST

The following questions will help you measure your understanding of the material presented in this chapter. Read all of the choices carefully because there might be more than one correct answer. Choose all correct answers for each question.

Basic Printer Concepts

1. Which type of paper feed uses a continuous roll of paper?
   A. Tractor feed
   B. Friction feed
   C. Roller feed
   D. Dot matrix feed

2. Which of the following printer types contains a heating element within the cartridge?
   A. Dot matrix
   B. Inkjet
   C. Bubblejet
   D. Laser

3. Which of the following does a dot matrix printer use to create printouts?
   A. Ink cartridge
   B. Ribbon
   C. Paint
   D. Toner

4. Which of the following statements about bubblejet and inkjet printers is accurate?
   A. Inkjet printers produce better-quality printouts than bubblejets.
   B. Both are the least expensive types of printer.
   C. Inkjet printers are line printers, and bubblejets are page printers.
   D. Bubblejet printers create images by allowing bubbles of ink to burst onto the paper.

5. A user has removed the primary corona wire from a laser printer. Assuming the printer will still work, which step will fail?
   A. Transferring
   B. Fusing
   C. Charging
   D. Cleaning

6. During which step of the laser print process is the laser used?

    A. Charging

    B. Writing

    C. Developing

    D. Fusing

7. You suspect that a laser printer is not properly performing the cleaning step. Which component might be responsible?

    A. Primary corona wire

    B. Erasure lamp

    C. Laser

    D. Fusing lamp

8. What is the purpose of a laser printer's transfer corona wire?

    A. To apply toner to the drum

    B. To apply toner to the paper

    C. To apply a charge to the drum

    D. To apply a charge to the paper

9. A user is planning to connect a parallel printer to the computer and wants your advice on cable length. What do you tell the user?

    A. Cable length doesn't matter.

    B. Keep the cable under 6 feet to avoid EMI.

    C. Keep the cable over 6 feet to ensure proper communication timing.

    D. Keep the cable under 25 feet to speed communication.

10. A company has one laser printer, which is attached to the secretary's parallel port. However, other users would like to access the printer. Which is the most efficient and cost-effective solution?

    A. Have users e-mail their documents to the secretary for printing.

    B. Have users physically move the printer to their computers when they want to print.

    C. Share the printer as a network resource.

    D. Have the company buy a network printer.

Care, Service, and Troubleshooting

11. You are troubleshooting a printer for which the paper-feed mechanism is experiencing problems. Which of the following can you rule out as the cause?

  A. Improper communication between the computer and printer

  B. Static

  C. Not enough paper in the tray

  D. Wrong paper weight

12. The printer at your office has recently started experiencing paper jams. They seem to be occurring quite frequently. Which of the following should you do first?

  A. Try a different type of paper.

  B. Replace the printer.

  C. Replace the feed rollers.

  D. Replace the transfer corona wire.

13. A bubblejet printer is producing blank pages. Which of the following is *least* likely to be the cause of the problem?

  A. The cartridge nozzles are dirty.

  B. The printer is dirty.

  C. The cartridge is empty.

  D. The heating element is not working.

14. What is the first thing you should do when a printer produces random blotches on the page?

  A. Replace the ribbon, ink, or toner cartridge.

  B. Replace the drum.

  C. Clean the printer.

  D. Check the communication between the computer and printer.

15. A customer tells you that the printer is creating printouts that contain images left over from previous printouts. From this information, you can verify all but which of the following?

  A. This is a laser printer.

  B. There has been a failure in the cleaning step.

  C. This problem can be resolved by replacing the drum.

  D. This is a "ghosted" image.

16. A printer is producing garbled printouts with characters that don't make any sense. Which of the following is true?

  A. There was a failure during the writing step.

B. The printer should be cleaned.

C. There is a communication problem between the computer and the printer.

D. The printer cable should be replaced.

17. Which component are you most likely to replace in a laser printer?

A. The toner/drum assembly

B. The feed rollers

C. The parallel cable

D. The paper tray

18. Which type of printer is most likely to produce a printout with the wrong or "dirty" colors?

A. Dot matrix

B. Inkjet

C. Laser

D. A parallel printer with a cable over 6 feet

19. A color laser printer recently displayed a "Yellow toner low" error message. However, you do not have a replacement toner cartridge at the moment. What should you do?

A. Stop using the printer until you can replace the cartridge.

B. Refill the cartridge with the toner in the reservoir used to store excess toner from the cleaning step.

C. Continue using the printer, but don't print documents or images that contain yellow.

D. Remove the yellow toner cartridge, gently rock it back and forth, then place it back in the printer.

20. Which of the following is most likely to prevent printer problems?

A. Regularly recharging the power supply

B. Regularly replacing the feed rollers

C. Regularly cleaning the printer

D. Giving the printer a two-day rest

LAB QUESTION

Use the information within this chapter to describe the laser print process. Discuss how this information can be used to troubleshoot printer problems. For example, make correlations between particular problems and the likely component or process at fault.

SELF TEST ANSWERS

Basic Printer Concepts

1. ☑ **A.** A tractor feed uses a continuous roll of paper. The roll of paper resembles a roll of paper towel, with a perforated line between each sheet. A row of holes runs down each side of the entire roll. These holes are lined up with sprocketed wheels, which pull the paper through the printer.

   ☒ **B,** friction feed, is incorrect because this type of feed uses rubber or plastic rollers to grab individual sheets of paper. **C,** roller feed, and **D,** dot matrix feed, are both incorrect because they are not real paper-feed types.

2. ☑ **C.** Bubblejet printers contain a heating element within the cartridge. When this element is heated, it causes the ink in the cartridge to expand and form a small bubble on the cartridge's nozzle. When the bubble gets big enough, it bursts onto the paper.

   ☒ **A,** dot matrix, is incorrect because this type of printer uses pins to strike a ribbon against the paper. Dot matrix printers do not use cartridges or heating elements. **B,** inkjet, is incorrect because this printer uses a pump within the ink cartridge to spray ink onto the page. **D,** laser, is incorrect because although this type of printer does have a heating component that is used during the fusing process, it is a fusing lamp, not a heating element, and it is not contained within the printer's toner cartridge.

3. ☑ **B.** Dot matrix printers use a ribbon to create printouts. The ribbon contains ink, which is transferred to the page when the pins strike the ribbon against the paper.

   ☒ **A,** ink cartridge, is incorrect because this is used by inkjet and bubblejet printers, not dot matrix printers. **C,** paint, is incorrect because no mainstream printers use paint. **D,** toner, is incorrect because this is used by laser printers (and photocopiers).

4. ☑ **D.** Bubblejet printers create images by allowing bubbles of ink to burst onto the paper. When the ink inside the cartridge is heated, it expands, forcing a bubble of ink onto the cartridge nozzle. The bubble continues to expand until it bursts onto the page.

   ☒ **A,** inkjet printers produce better-quality printouts than bubblejets, is incorrect. Although bubblejet technology sounds messier than inkjet technology, bubblejets typically produce better images than inkjets. **B** is incorrect because it suggests that inkjet and bubblejet printers are the least expensive types. Of the printers discussed in this chapter, dot matrix printers are the least expensive, laser printers are the most expensive, and inkjet and bubblejet printers are between the two in terms of cost. **C,** inkjet printers are line printers, and bubblejets are page printers, is also incorrect because both types create images line by line, so they are line printers. Laser printers are page printers.

5. ☑ **C.** The charging step will fail. The purpose of the primary corona wire is to apply a very high negative charge to the printer's drum. Without the primary corona wire, the drum will not be charged.

    ☒ **A,** transferring, is incorrect because the transfer corona wire, not the primary corona wire, is used in this step. **B,** fusing, is also incorrect because the fusing step uses a very hot fusing lamp to heat the fusing rollers. The heat causes the toner to fuse to the page as it passes through the rollers. **D,** cleaning, is incorrect because this step uses a cleaning blade and erasure lamps, not the primary corona wire.

6. ☑ **B.** The laser is used in the writing step. Prior to this step, the printer's drum has been given a very high negative charge. In the writing step, the laser draws the image that will be printed. The areas that the laser touches lose most of their charge, and these represent the areas to which toner will be attracted in the developing stage.

    ☒ **A,** charging, is incorrect because the primary corona wire is used in this step. **C,** developing, is incorrect because in this step the toner is released from the cartridge and attracted to the drum. The laser is not used in this step. **D,** fusing, is also incorrect because in this step the fusing rollers are heated so that the toner will fuse to the page as it exits the printer.

7. ☑ **B.** If the cleaning step is not being performed properly, the erasure lamp could be responsible. The cleaning step occurs in two stages. First, a cleaning blade removes excess toner from the drum, then an erasure lamp comes on and removes any residual charge from the drum.

    ☒ **A,** primary corona wire, is incorrect because this component is used in the charging step to apply a high negative charge to the drum. **C,** laser, is incorrect because this is used in the writing step to discharge areas of the drum that will later hold toner. **D,** fusing lamp, is incorrect because this is used to heat the fusing rollers so that the toner is fused (melted) to the page during the fusing step.

8. ☑ **D.** The purpose of a laser printer's transfer corona wire is to apply a charge to the paper. During the transferring step, the transfer corona wire applies a positive charge to the paper so that the negatively charged toner will be attracted to it as the paper moves past the drum.

    ☒ **A,** to apply toner to the drum, and **B,** to apply toner to the paper, are incorrect. Toner is not *applied* during the laser print process; rather, toner is electrostatically attracted to either the drum or the paper. **C,** to apply a charge to the drum, is incorrect because this is the function of the primary corona wire.

9. ☑ **B.** Tell the user to keep the cable under 6 feet to avoid EMI. Parallel cables longer than 6 feet are susceptible to interference and data corruption and loss.

    ☒ **A,** cable length doesn't matter, is incorrect because parallel cables over 6 feet (and serial cables over 25 feet) can experience EMI-related problems. **C,** keep the cable over 6 feet to ensure proper communication timing, is incorrect because the cable should be kept *under* 6 feet. Furthermore, the length of the cable is unrelated to the timing of the communication.

D, keep the cable under 25 feet to speed communication, is incorrect because although it takes data longer to travel long cables than short ones, there is no noticeable difference to the user. Furthermore, the cable should be kept under 6 feet, not 25.

10. ☑ **C.** The most efficient and cost-effective solution listed is to share the printer as a network resource. The printer can remain attached to the secretary's desktop PC, and others will be able to send print jobs to it.

☒ **A** is incorrect because it suggests getting users to e-mail their documents to the secretary and having the secretary open and print the files. This is not an efficient solution; printing other people's documents will most likely interrupt the secretary's work and take up unnecessary time. **B,** have users physically move the printer to their computers when they want to print, is also incorrect because although this solution will work, it is not very efficient. It is time-consuming to reattach a printer over and over again each time someone wants to print. Furthermore, the excess transportation of the printer could cause it premature wear and failure. **D,** have the company buy a network printer, is incorrect because it is not a cost-effective solution. The company already has a printer that can be accessed through the network, even though it is not a true network printer (one with a NIC). In this case, there is no benefit associated with buying and networking another printer.

Care, Service, and Troubleshooting

11. ☑ **A.** You can rule out improper communication between the computer and printer as the cause of this problem. The paper-feed mechanism is under the direction of the printer itself, not the computer. Poor communication between the two will not result in improper paper feeding.

☒ **B,** static, is incorrect because this can cause pages to stick together so that they are fed into the printer two or more at a time. **C,** not enough paper in the tray, is also incorrect because if there is not enough paper in the tray, the friction rollers might not be able to grab the top sheet. **D,** wrong paper weight, is incorrect because this might be the cause of the feeding problem. If the paper is too thick for the printer, it might not fit into the paper path. If it is too thin, more than one page can be fed at a time, or the page might not be fed at all.

12. ☑ **A.** You should try a different type of paper. If the printer has just recently started experiencing paper jams, it indicates that something has recently changed within the printer. The paper you are using might be the wrong weight. Using a different paper weight could solve the problem. Incidentally, cleaning the printer could also resolve the problem.

☒ **B,** replace the printer, is incorrect because, in this case, there is probably nothing wrong with the printer that can't be replaced or otherwise resolved. Replacing the printer as a first measure is wrong. **C,** replace the feed rollers, is incorrect because although this might be the

1. DIMM memory sockets
2. Secondary EIDE channel connector
3. Microprocessor
4. Power supply
5. Power input connector
6. Battery socket
7. 3.3-V power input connector
8. Diskette drive interface connector
9. Primary EIDE channel connector
10. Control panel connector
11. System board jumpers
12. ISA expansion-card connectors
13. PCI expansion-card connectors

The inside of the typical IBM personal computer, showing the most vital system components such as the microprocessor, power supply, expansion cards, drive controllers, and memory sockets. Expansion cards, floppy and hard drive cables, as well as the drives themselves have been omitted for a clear view of the motherboard. Every component seen here will be tested on the exam, in addition to other components that are not shown here: hard drives, CD-ROM drives, and tape drives. For the exam, you will be expected to know the characteristics of each component of a standard computer system, and how to diagnose and resolve problems related to each.

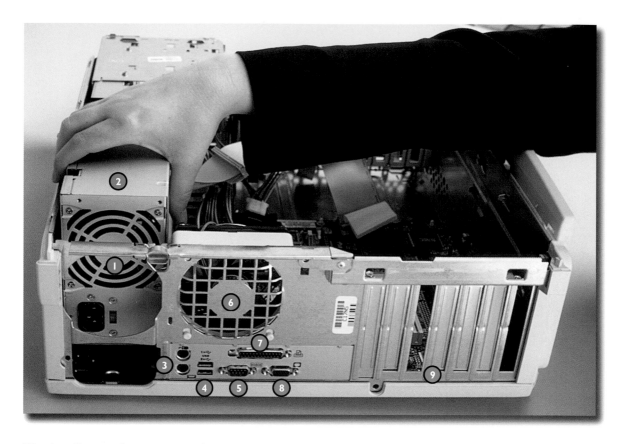

The installation of a power supply in an IBM compatible computer. Most power supplies are removed with four screws on the rear of the power supply. Repair of a power supply should be performed by a skilled technician with the necessary training and equipment to work on power supplies. The replacement of a power supply should occur immediately if the fan stops functioning because the power supply can overheat and destroy the entire computer. For the exam, you will need to understand the symptoms of a failing power supply.

1. Power supply cooling fan
2. Power supply
3. Keyboard and PS/2 mouse connectors
4. USB ports
5. Serial port
6. Cooling fan
7. Parallel port
8. Monitor port
9. Slot covers

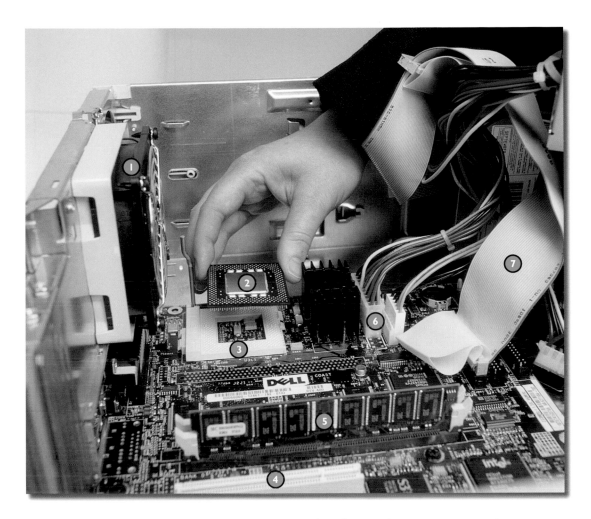

1. Cooling fan
2. CPU (processor) central processing unit
3. Processor socket
4. PCI expansion slot
5. 168-Pin DIMM memory
6. Power supply connectors
7. IDE flat data ribbon cable

Installation of a microprocessor in a computer. Notice how the lever in the processor socket is in the raised position. Once the processor is placed in the socket, you then lower the lever to lock the processor in place. To free the processor, you simply raise the lever. This is known as a Zero Insertion Force (ZIF) socket, and not all motherboards are equipped with this type of socket. For the exam, you most likely will not have to worry about the ZIF socket, but you will need to know about the various types of processors on the market. You will need to know the characteristics of each processor, such as the width of the data bus and address bus, and the register size.

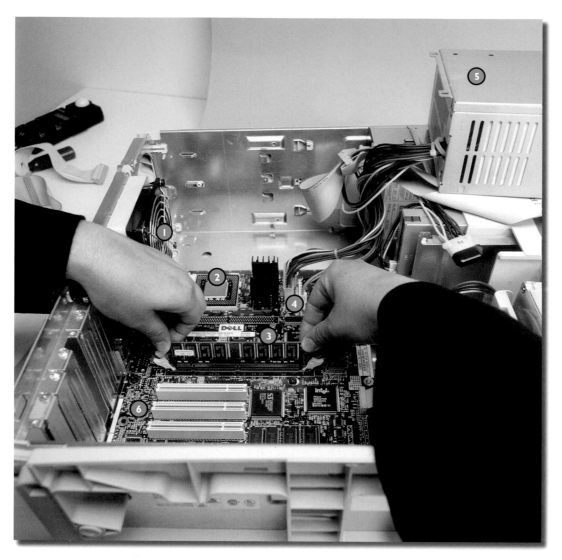

Installation of 168-pin DIMM memory in a computer. With DIMM memory, the module is inserted straight up and down, unlike the insertion method of SIMM memory, which is inserted at a 45 degree angle and then clicked into place when the memory is in the upright position. The notches on the DIMM memory module will lock into place with the keys located on the socket. For the exam, you will need to know the various types of memory available, including ROM, RAM, DRAM, and SRAM, and the characteristics of each.

1. Cooling fan
2. Central processing unit
3. 168-Pin DIMM memory
4. Power supply connectors
5. Power supply
6. PCI expansion slots

Installation of a floppy disk drive in the front bay of an IBM compatible computer. The floppy drive is 3.5 inches in size. Most computers have bays for two 3.5 floppy drives located on the front of the computer. The 5.25-inch bays are used for CD-ROM drives and tape drives. For the exam, you will need to know how to troubleshoot the floppy disk drive subsystem, which includes the media, floppy drive, cable, and the controller.

1. CD-ROM drive
2. Additional CD-ROM or tape drive bay (5.25-inch size)
3. Floppy disk drive bays (3.5-inch size)
4. Floppy disk drive

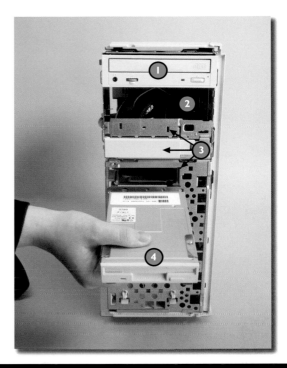

A printer motor used to move the paper through the printer. There are a few motors located in a printer—the main drive, paper feed, and transport motor. Every manufacturer uses different types of motors in varying places throughout the printer, so you must consult your vendor's documentation when replacing or servicing a printer motor. For the exam, you do not need to know about the motor specifically, but you should know what the effect will be on the print quality when a printer motor has failed.

1. Printer motor
2. Paper feed frame

The installation of a CD-ROM drive in an IBM compatible computer. The illustration shows the back of the CD-ROM drive which contains the connector for the 40-pin IDE cable, the power connector, sound card connector, and the master/slave jumpers. You can look down the length of the IDE cable and see another 40-pin connector for attaching another CD-ROM drive or hard drive in a master/slave configuration. For the exam, you should know the connectors and cables used in IDE devices such as hard drives and CD-ROM drives.

1. CMOS battery
2. Master/slave jumpers
3. Sound card connector
4. IDE cable
5. Power cable
6. CD-ROM drive
7. Power supply connectors
8. Additional connector for another IDE device
9. Additional CD-ROM or tape drive bays (5.25-inch size)

An example of replacing an ISA sound card in an IBM compatible computer. Expansion cards are installed with a slight rocking motion with a firm grip on both ends of the card. You can see it is standard for motherboard vendors to color the ISA slots black and the PCI slots white. For the exam, you will need to know the differences between ISA, EISA, MCA, and PCI, and the characteristics of each.

1. Floppy disk drive cable
2. ISA sound card
3. ISA expansion slots
4. PCI expansion slots
5. 168-Pin DIMM memory
6. Additional 168-pin DIMM memory socket

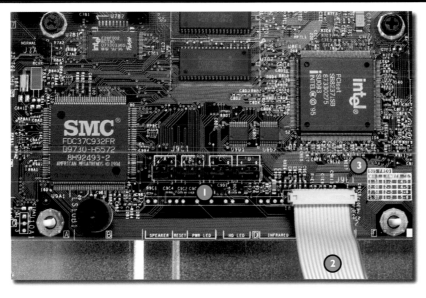

1. Configuration jumpers
2. Floppy disk drive cable
3. Jumper configuration settings

A view of configuration jumpers on a motherboard. Most motherboards have jumpers to configure internal processor speed and external bus speed. These settings are usually stamped on the motherboard in white, as seen in the illustration. If you do not configure these jumpers correctly, you could overclock your processor causing it to burn up; if you underclock the processor, you might not be utilizing the processor to its full potential. For the exam, you probably won't be asked about jumpers on the motherboard, but you will be asked about the data bus, address bus, and register size of the various processors on the market.

Installing an IDE hard drive in an IBM personal computer. From the illustration, you can see the 40-pin IDE connector on the hard drive and the 40-pin ribbon cable. When you are installing a hard drive in a system, you have the ability to make the hard drive the master of its own controller, or to configure the hard drive in a master/slave relationship with another device, such as another hard drive or CD-ROM drive. The exam will test your knowledge of configuring a hard drive using the CMOS SETUP program.

1. ISA expansion slots
2. PCI expansion slots
3. 168-Pin DIMM memory
4. Cooling fan
5. 40-Pin IDE cable
6. 3.5-Inch floppy disk drive
7. 40-Pin IDE connector
8. Power cable
9. Hard disk drive

An internal modem, which has visible jumpers in red for configuring COM port assignments. The illustration also shows a sticker on a chip, which details the various jumper settings to configure the COM port settings. The modem also includes RJ-11 connectors for connecting to the phone line and to the telephone. The exam will test your knowledge of the standard COM ports and IRQs for configuring modems.

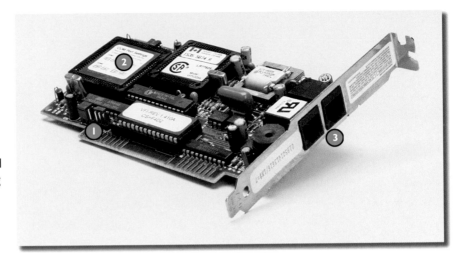

1. Com port setting jumpers
2. Jumper diagram
3. Telephone and phone line connectors

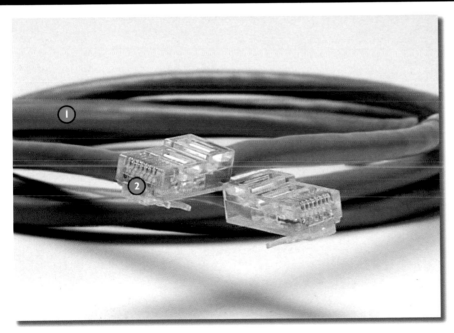

Twisted-pair coaxial cabling with an RJ-45 connector. Coaxial cable is resistant to the interference and signal weakening that other cabling, such as unshielded twisted-pair (UTP) cable, can experience. In general, coax is better than UTP for connecting longer distances and for reliably supporting higher data rates with less sophisticated equipment. For the exam, you should know the type of connector used with UTP cabling.

1. Twisted-Pair cabling
2. RJ-45 connector

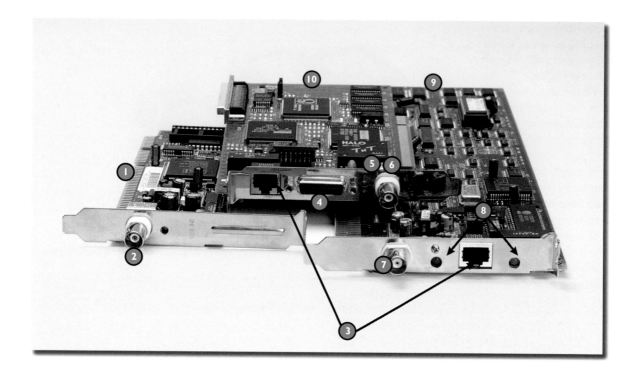

Various network interface cards with support for coax, twisted-pair, and AUI. The network interface card on the left has only one interface for a coax BNC connector. The network interface card on top has an interface for a coax BNC connector, an AUI connector, and a UTP RJ-45 connector. The network interface card on the right has an interface for a coax BNC connector and a UTP RJ-45 connector. Both the top and right network interface cards have power and link lights also. For the exam, you should know what interfaces are available on network interface cards, and the common resources, such as IRQ and I/O address, used for network cards.

1. Coaxial network interface card
2. Coaxial connector
3. Twisted-Pair connectors
4. AUI connector
5. Link and power lights
6. Coaxial connector
7. Coaxial connector
8. Link and power lights
9. Combo network card with twisted-pair and coaxial support
10. Combo network card with twisted-pair, coaxial, and AUI support

A typical printer's system board that consists of the logic required to operate the printer. Every manufacturer uses different types of logic boards in varying places throughout the printer, so you must consult your vendor's documentation when replacing or servicing the logic board. For the exam, you do not need to know about the logic board specifically, but you should know what the affect will be on a printer if the logic board is faulty and needs to be replaced.

1. Power input
2. Centronics port

A printer's sublogic board which works in conjunction with the primary printer system board that enables you to replace or upgrade the capability of the sublogic board. Most printer sublogic boards allow you to change the port, such as replacing the Centronics port. For the exam, you should be able to identify the characteristics of parallel ports on a computer, such as ECP, EPP, and Bi Directional printer ports.

1. Power input
2. Centronics port
3. Add-on adapter card with parallel (Centronics) port

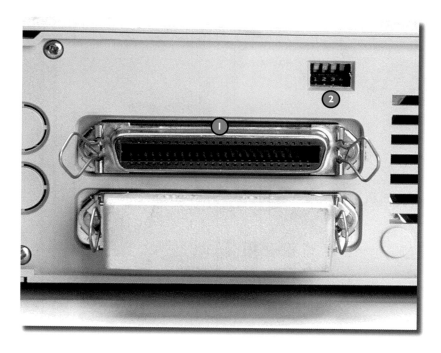

A device with external SCSI interfaces. This particular device uses a 50-pin Centronics SCSI connector, which is nearly identical to the Centronics printer cable connector. Also visible is the SCSI address ID jumper, which enables you to configure a SCSI device for a particular SCSI ID from 1–4. There are eight available addresses for SCSI IDs, with seven usually being reserved for the SCSI adapter itself. The exam will test your knowledge of the various SCSI connectors that are available.

1. Centronics 50-pin
   SCSI connector
2. SCSI address ID jumpers

The types of Small Computer Systems Interface (SCSI) connectors available. The top SCSI connector is a 50-pin high-density connector. The middle SCSI connector is a 68-pin high-density connector. The bottom connector is a Centronics 50-pin connector, not to be confused with a Centronics printer connector, which looks almost identical. For the exam, you need to know the types of SCSI connectors presented here.

1. 50-Pin high-density SCSI
2. 68-Pin high-density SCSI
3. Centronics 50-pin SCSI

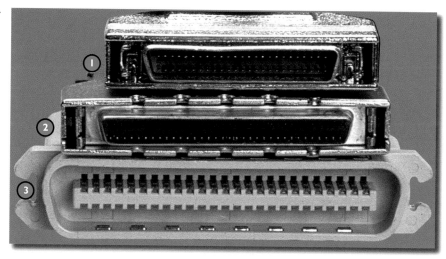

A notebook computer combination cable with support for twisted-pair and coaxial cable. This unit plugs into the PCMCIA network interface card located inside the PC card bay of the notebook computer (not shown). As a travelling network technician, it's a good idea to have a combination cable like the one shown so you can connect to both a coaxial or twisted-pair network with the same PCMCIA network card. For the exam, you should know what interfaces are available in a network adapter such as this.

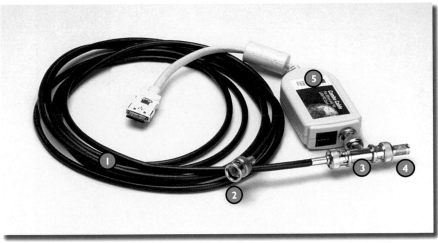

1. Thinwire 10Base2 coaxial cable
2. BNC connector
3. BNC connector
4. Terminator
5. Combination twisted-pair/ coaxial dongle

PCMCIA Ethernet Combo Network Interface Card, with Twisted-Pair and Coax Support

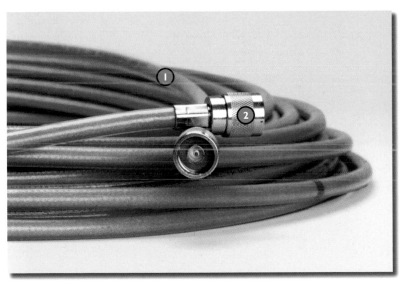

A thickwire (10Base5) cable with a BNC connector. Thicknet is extremely bulky and difficult to work with, therefore it is rarely used. Thickwire cabling is used as a network backbone or a connection between two different hubs or routers. For the exam, you should know the type of connector used with UTP cabling.

1. Thickwire (10Base5) coaxial cable
2. BNC connector

Thickwire Coaxial Cable and the Corresponding BNC Connector

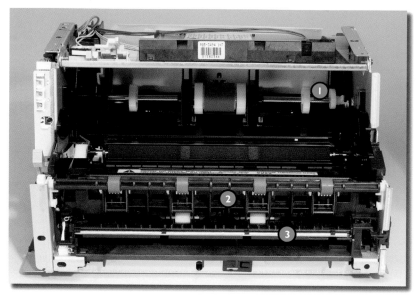

The front view of a printer roller assembly showing the numerous rollers and gears associated with a modern printer. The only internal components of a printer that you will have to be familiar with for the exam is the laser printer and the laser printing process. These components include the primary corona wire, cleaning blade, transfer corona, and the photosensitive drum. Each laser printer component is responsible for a phase during the printing process.

1. Pickup roller assembly
2. Delivery assembly
3. Separation assembly

A side view of the printer roller assembly with a view of the numerous gears involved in the printing process. From the illustration, you can see how the pickup roller assembly is removable and can be replaced in the event it becomes defective. For the exam, the only components of the printing process you should be familiar with are those of the laser printer. In addition, you should know the various phases of the laser printing process, such as the cleaning, charging, writing, developing, transferring, and fusing phase, and what occurs during each of the phases.

1. Pickup roller assembly

1. Power supply cooling fan
2. Cooling fan
3. Power input
4. PS/2 mouse connector
5. Keyboard connector
6. USB ports
7. Serial port
8. Parallel port
9. Monitor port

The back of a computer, illustrating the power supply and common connectors found on a personal computer. You can see the cooling fan for the power supply in addition to the CPU's cooling fan. The illustration also shows a PS/2 mouse connector, Mini-DIN keyboard connector, two USB ports, and a parallel, serial, and monitor port. For the exam, you should be able identify the physical characteristics of a serial or parallel port.

Installing memory modules in a portable notebook computer. Although most notebook computers are different, the illustration shows one method of upgrading the memory in a notebook computer. For the exam, you will not need to know anything memory-related on a notebook computer. You will need to know about memory in general, including the types of memory chips available, such as the difference between SIMMs and DIMMs.

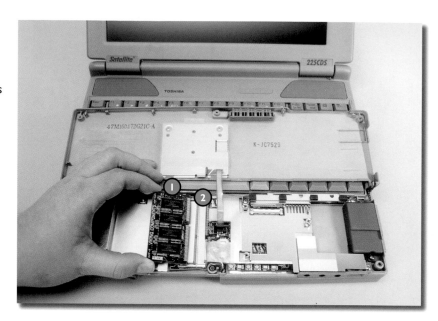

1. Memory module
2. Contacts

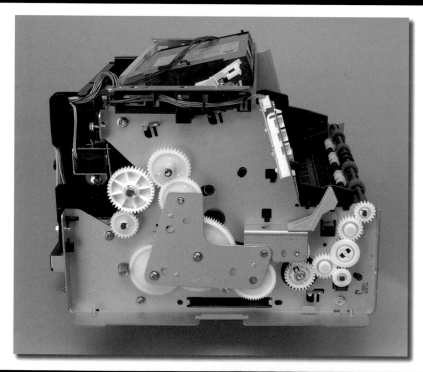

A side view of a printer's rollers and gears. You can see the complex innerworkings of a printer and how you need to provide continual routine preventative maintenance on the printer to keep the rollers and various mechanical devices working correctly. For the exam, you should know how to clean and maintain a dot matrix, ink jet, and laser printer.

ultimate resolution to the problem, it shouldn't be your first step in this case. Changing the paper type is much simpler and faster and more likely to resolve the problem than taking the printer apart to change the feed rollers. **D,** replace the transfer corona wire, is incorrect because this component is used to charge the paper as it passes through the printer. It is unrelated to the mechanism used to move the paper through the paper path.

13. ☑ **B.** The least likely cause of blank inkjet printouts is that the printer is dirty. Dust or ink build-up in the printer can cause paper jams and smudged printouts, but it will not cause blank printouts.

☒ **A,** the cartridge nozzles are dirty, is incorrect because that might be the cause of the problem. If the nozzles get dirty, they can become clogged so that no ink can get from the cartridge onto the page. **C,** the cartridge is empty, is incorrect because this might be the cause of the problem. If there is no ink in the cartridge, there is no medium with which to create the printout. **D,** the heating element is not working, is incorrect because if the heating element in a bubblejet ink cartridge stops working, the ink cannot expand and form the bubbles that will eventually create the image on the page. To replace the heating element, simply replace the ink cartridge.

14. ☑ **C.** When a printer produces random blotches, the first thing you should do is clean the printer. In any printer type, these blotches or speckles are most likely caused by excess ink or toner deposits inside the printer.

☒ **A,** replace the ribbon, ink, or toner cartridge, is incorrect because the problem in this case is not a lack of toner or ink but the presence of excess toner or ink. **B,** replace the drum, is incorrect because this might resolve the problem of repeated speckles in a laser printer, but it is not typically the cause of random blotches. **D,** check the communication between the computer and printer, is incorrect. Communication problems result in garbled printouts or no printouts but are not responsible for causing blotches on a printout.

15. ☑ **C.** You cannot verify that the problem can be resolved by replacing the drum. Although that might be a solution to the problem, it is not the only possibility. In this case, the cleaning blade or erasure lamps might need to be replaced.

☒ **A,** this is a laser printer, is incorrect because laser printers are the only type that experience the stated problem. **B,** there has been a failure in the cleaning step, is incorrect because this problem is caused when toner or a residual charge is left on the drum during subsequent printouts. It is the job of the cleaning step to remove the toner and charge. **D,** this is a ghosted image, is incorrect because that is the proper name for this type of printout.

16. ☑ **C.** There is a communication problem between the computer and the printer. Whenever the printer produces garbled or nonsensical printouts, it received the wrong or incomplete instructions from the computer or it interpreted those instructions incorrectly. All of these are communication problems.

☒ **A,** there was a failure during the writing step, is incorrect because a failure during the laser printer's writing step is likely to result in a blank or incomplete printout. The writing step simply draws the printed image that it is instructed by the printer to draw. The writing step is not responsible for interpreting signals from the computer. **B,** the printer should be cleaned, is incorrect because a dirty printer can cause paper jams or blotches, but it will not cause the wrong characters to be printed. **D,** the printer cable should be replaced, is incorrect because this is just one of many issues that could be responsible for the communication problem. For example, the printer might have a corrupted driver, have a resource conflict, or be different from the printer that Windows has been configured to use.

17. ☑ **A.** You are most likely to replace a laser printer's toner/drum assembly. The toner cartridge will eventually run out of toner and need to be replaced. In many printers, the toner and drum are an integrated unit.

    ☒ **B,** the feed rollers, **C,** the parallel cable, and **D,** the paper tray, are all incorrect because although these components do require replacing in some printers, it is rare for them to fail. Therefore, they are not replaced nearly as often as toner/drum assemblies.

18. ☑ **B.** An inkjet printer is the most likely to produce a printout with the wrong or dirty colors. This is caused by low levels of one of the basic ink colors or by dirty, semiclogged cartridge nozzles. The solution is usually to clean the nozzles or replace the cartridge.

    ☒ **A,** dot matrix, and **C,** laser, are incorrect because although they can produce the wrong colors, they are less likely to do so than an inkjet printer. Furthermore, dot matrix and laser printers are not likely to produce "dirty" colors. **D,** a parallel printer with a cable over 6 feet, is incorrect because a parallel cable over 6 feet can cause EMI-related problems, but these will tend to be in the form of garbled printouts or other communication problems. It would be very rare for a cable to cause a printout that had the proper content but the wrong colors.

19. ☑ **D,** you should remove the yellow toner cartridge, gently rock it back and forth, then place it back in the printer. This action could settle the toner so that the error message temporarily goes away. Incidentally, most printers allow you to keep printing, even with this error displayed. That is because the "Toner low" message is a warning, designed to inform you to replace the cartridge before it is completely empty.

    ☒ **A,** stop using the printer until you replace the cartridge, is incorrect because again, this message is a warning, not a fatal error. Continue using the printer, but be aware that some of the colors might not appear in the proper shade. **B,** refill the cartridge with the toner in the reservoir used to store excess toner from the cleaning step, is incorrect because although this might work in a black laser printer, it will not work in a color printer. Recall that the drum in a laser printer contains all four toner colors for each color printout. When the excess toner is cleaned from the drum, the colors are not separated. Therefore, in this printer, the toner reservoir contains toner for all four colors. **C,** continue using the printer, but don't print documents or images that contain yellow, is incorrect because this message is a warning, given before the toner drops below levels that would affect the printer's performance. Go ahead and use yellow, but replace the cartridge as soon as colors start to come out incorrectly. Incidentally, it would be nearly impossible to avoid printing images that contain yellow. Laser printers use nearly infinite combinations of colors, and it is extremely difficult to tell if yellow has been used in some color combinations.

20. ☑ **C.** Regularly cleaning the printer is most likely to prevent printer problems. Build-up inside the printer can cause ESD, block the paper path, and cause moving components to wear out. By cleaning the printer, you can also remove excess ink or toner that can produce stray marks on printouts.

☒ **A,** recharging the power supply, is incorrect because printer power supplies do not need to be recharged. **B,** regularly replacing the feed rollers, is incorrect because it is rare for these rollers to fail, so replacing them on a regular basis is unlikely to prevent future problems. **D,** giving the printer a two-day rest, is incorrect because printers do not need to "rest" and do not perform better after being left idle for a period of time.

LAB ANSWER

In the charging step of the laser print process, the HVPS charges the primary corona wire to approximately –5000vDC. This charge is passed on from the primary corona wire to the photosensitive drum. This high charge represents areas of the drum that will not contain toner. A totally black printout can result from an HVPS or primary corona wire failure.

In the next step, writing, the laser draws (writes) the document or image to be printed on the surface of the drum. All areas that are touched by the laser are reduced in voltage to about –100vDC. These areas attract toner. If the laser does not perform its function or if the drum does not hold the proper –100vDC charge, the entire drum will remain at –5000vDC. If this is the case, the drum will not attract toner to the proper areas, and the result will most likely be a blank printout.

In the developing step, the toner cartridge is opened, and toner is attracted to the –100vDC areas of the drum. Again, if the charging step has failed, toner could be attracted to the entire drum, resulting in a black printout. If the writing step has failed, the drum might not attract any toner. The result would be a blank printout. If, in the developing step, there is no toner in the cartridge or if the cartridge fails to open, no toner will be attracted to the drum. Again, the result would be a blank printout.

Next, the paper begins to move through the printer. This is the beginning of the transferring step. The HVPS applies a positive charge to the transfer corona wire, which in turn applies a positive charge to the paper. As the paper passes the drum, the negatively charged toner is attracted from the drum onto the paper. If the HVPS or transfer corona wire fails during this step, the toner will remain on the drum, rather than being attracted to the paper. The result will be a blank page.

In the fusing process, a fusing lamp applies very high heat to the fusing rollers. As the page passes through the rollers, the toner is melted (fused) onto the paper. If the fusing procedure fails, the printout will contain loose toner powder and will most likely be smudged.

Finally, during the cleaning process, a cleaning blade removes the excess toner from the drum and deposits it into a toner reservoir. A series of erasure lamps are then activated, removing any excess charge from the drum. If the cleaning blade does not work, leftover toner will remain on the drum and be transferred to the next printout. This results in a ghosted image. If the erasure lamps do not properly discharge the drum, toner can be attracted to the wrong areas during subsequent developing steps. Again, the result is a ghosted image.

7

Basic Networking

7.01   Identify basic network concepts and how a network works. Identify the common types of network cables, their characteristics, and connectors.

7.02   Identify network setup procedures and troubleshooting networks.

✓   Two-Minute Drill

Q&A   Self Test

Networks provide users with the ability to share files, printers, resources, and mail, as though they resided locally on the user's computer. Computer networks have become so important in some settings that they provide the basis for nearly all business transactions. Networks make it possible to share documents and images with people all around the world, literally at the click of a mouse.

Computer networking is a very broad topic. There are many types of networks, from simple peer-to-peer ones to huge intranets and even the Internet itself. Each type of network can employ a different combination of network OS, cabling, protocols, and security measures. These combinations are known as the network's *architecture*. In fact, CompTIA's Network+ certification is based entirely on networking concepts and network architectures. Obviously, a discussion of the full spectrum of network details and specifications is too broad in scope to be contained in this chapter. However, as a computer technician, you should be aware of basic networking concepts so that you can troubleshoot minor problems on networks that have already been established. This chapter focuses on basic concepts of physical networks; Chapter 11 focuses on network protocols and how to configure Windows for network access.

CERTIFICATION OBJECTIVE 7.01

Networking Concepts

To properly maintain and troubleshoot a network, you must first be familiar with basic network concepts such as physical layout, cable types, and protocols. The combinations of these factors can be implemented in hundreds of different arrangements. The most common types of each are discussed in this section.

Local Area Network

A *local area network* (LAN) is a network that covers a relatively small area, such as a building, home, or an office. LANs are defined by three primary characteristics: topology, protocol, and media. A typical LAN may share resources such as printers, files, or other resources on the LAN. LANs are typically very fast and have become extremely cost effective in most situations. An office or home can share a single high-speed laser printer using a LAN and each user would have the perception that they are directly connected to the printer. There are two primary types of LAN models used to describe networks: peer-to-peer, and client/server-based.

Peer-to-Peer Networks

In a *peer-to-peer* network all computer systems in the network have equal capabilities and responsibilities; each computer user is responsible for controlling access, sharing resources, and storing data on their computer. All of the systems essentially operate both as servers and work systems as shown in Figure 7-1. Security in a peer-to-peer environment is established by the respective computer user. There are no central administrative functions or capabilities in this type of network. Peer-to-peer networks are usually very effective in environments that are small. Microsoft recommends that peer-to-peer networks not exceed ten or so systems in the network. This is primarily for administrative convenience because an office with ten systems in a peer-to-peer environment will have ten separate security policies, file sharing, and access permissions. This can cause the network management issues to become extremely cumbersome because each machine must be individually configured and managed.

Many homes with multiple computers are being connected to each other using either wired or wireless LAN technologies. These technologies have become very cost effective over the last few years.

Client/Server-Based Networks

A client/server-based environment uses dedicated computers called servers to store data, provide print services, or other capabilities. Servers are generally more powerful computer systems with more capacity than a typical workstation. Client/server-based models also allow for centralized administration and security. These types of networks are also considerably more scalable in that they can grow very large without adding additional administrative complexity to the network. A single model for security, access, and file sharing can be established by the network administrator when the network is configured. This configuration may remain unchanged as the network grows.

Client/server environments are also extensively useful in situations where a centralized communications system is needed. Servers can be multipurpose, performing a number of functions, or dedicated, as in the case of a web or mail server. Figure 7-2 shows a network with servers being used for e-mail, web services, and communications. Notice in this situation that each of the servers is dedicated to the task that they are assigned.

FIGURE 7-1   A peer-to-peer network in a home

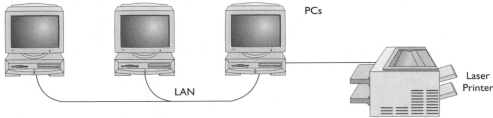

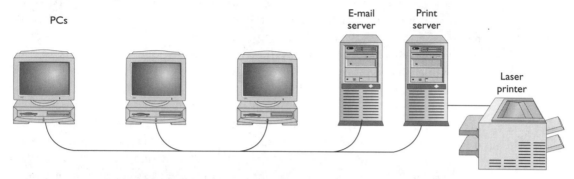

FIGURE 7-2   A client/server environment where dedicated or special purpose servers perform assigned functions

Topologies

The term *network topology* refers to the physical layout of computers and other equipment in the network. The most commonly used topologies are star, bus, and ring. The characteristics, special equipment, and advantages and disadvantages of each are discussed here.

Star Topology

Star networks consist of computers that are all attached to a network device called a *hub* (see Figure 7-3). The hub's job is to receive signals from one computer and relay them to all other attached computers. The computer to which a packet is addressed opens and reads the data. All other computers attached to the hub ignore the packet.

Star networks do not always appear like the one in Figure 7-3 when they are implemented. It might be inconvenient to place a hub and cables in the middle of an office. In most implementations, the hub will be placed on one side of the room, with the cables running under tables or desks to the hub. In these cases, the topology doesn't physically resemble a star but is still considered a star topology.

FIGURE 7-3   In a star network, computers are attached to a central hub

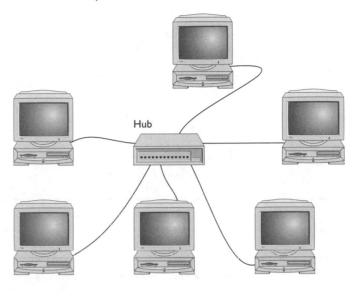

One advantage to implementing a star network is that if a single computer goes down, the rest of the network is not affected. The same is true for the cables. No single cable in a star network can cause the downfall of the entire network. This type of arrangement also makes it easy to add new computers to the network (this is called *scalability*). The new computer can be set up in any free space and its cable attached to any available hub port.

One disadvantage of this type of network is the extra expense of the hub itself. Furthermore, the hub can provide a single point of failure for the entire network. That is, if the hub goes down, the entire network will fail. Another disadvantage is the method of data relay. Recall that when the hub receives data from any computer, it sends it to all other computers. This is called a *network broadcast*, and it can cause enough unnecessary network traffic to result in slow data transmission, especially in networks with a large number of computers. Finally, star networks allow only one computer to transmit at a time.

Bus Topology

In a *bus topology*, each computer is connected to a cable backbone (see Figure 7-4). In most cases, the backbone itself is a series of connected cable segments. At each junction in the backbone is a three-way T-connector that also attaches to a computer in the network. When one computer sends data, the packet travels along the backbone. Each computer examines the packet, but only the computer to which the packet is addressed

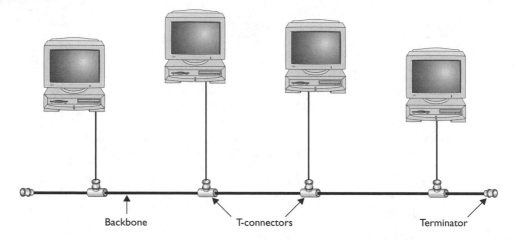

| FIGURE 7-4 | In a bus topology, each computer is attached to a cable backbone |

Backbone   T-connectors   Terminator

will accept it. To prevent data from "bouncing" back and forth from one end to the other, a 50-ohm terminator must be attached to each end of the backbone.

Another method of creating a bus network is to use a single length of cable for the entire backbone and to attach each computer using a vampire tap. A *vampire tap* contains prongs that are used to pierce the backbone cable and make contact with the wires inside. However, these devices are more difficult to use than T-connectors and are more prone to failure, and the single length of backbone is more difficult and costly to replace than a single backbone segment. A bus network that uses vampire taps must still be terminated at both ends.

The bus network is by far the simplest topology to implement; it requires no special additional network equipment and uses less cable than a star topology. However, bus networks allow only one computer to send data at a time across the network. Bus networks are not easily scaled, meaning that it is more difficult to add another computer to the network than with other topologies. The failure of a computer on a bus network may affect the other computers, and if there is a break in the backbone, the entire network will fail. The entire network will also fail if all cable ends are not properly terminated.

Ring Topology

In a *ring network*, each computer is attached to the next in a circle formation (see Figure 7-5). Each computer therefore has two network ports—one for the incoming cable and one for the outgoing cable. Data always travels in one direction in a ring network. When one computer sends data, that data is received by the next computer in line. That computer reads the packet address and passes the packet on. This process continues until the packet reaches its destination.

FIGURE 7-5 In a ring network, each computer is attached to the next in a circular formation

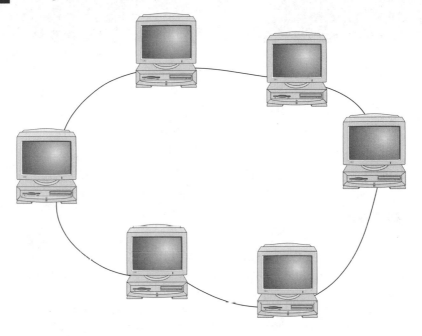

One advantage of a ring network is that more than one computer can send data at a time. Furthermore, as a packet travels around the ring, it is examined and regenerated to full signal strength by each computer until it reaches its destination. This means that ring networks experience very little signal loss (called *attenuation*).

Disadvantages of a ring topology are its expense and the relative difficulty of setting them up. Ring networks also have many points of failure. If any computer in the ring goes down, or if there is a break in any of the cables, the entire network will fail.

exam
ⓦⓐⓣⓒⓗ
Understanding how data is passed on a particular topology is essential to your understanding the effect if a single computer or cable on the network fails.

Protocols

A network's protocol is the "language" it uses for data transmission. The protocol includes the rules for communication, packet size, addressing, and ability to be routed. Computers on a network cannot communicate with other computers unless they are using the same protocol. The three most common protocols on Windows-based systems are TCP/IP, NetBEUI, and IPX/SPX.

SCENARIO & SOLUTION

How is a star network arranged?	Each computer is attached to a single hub using a separate cable.
What are the advantages of a bus network?	It is simple to implement and uses less cable.
Which topology has the highest number of potential failure points?	A ring. If any cable or computer fails, the entire network will go down.
How many computers can transmit on each type of topology?	Star and bus topologies are limited to one transmission at a time; ring topologies are not.

TCP/IP

Transmission Control Protocol/Internet Protocol (TCP/IP) is by far the most common protocol on internal networks and is the protocol of the Internet. TCP/IP requires more configuration than other protocols but is the most robust, can be used on very large networks, and is routable. The term *routable* refers to the ability to send data to other subnetworks, typically connected by a bridge or router. TCP/IP allows for cross-platform communication. That means that computers using different OSes (such as Windows and Unix) can send data back and forth, as long as they are both

exam

ⓦatch   *TCP/IP is the most common protocol and is the only one that allows networks to access the Internet.*

using TCP/IP. Each computer in a Windows TCP/IP network must be configured with a computer name and workgroup (or domain) and a unique IP address. An *IP address* is a 32-bit address that is indicated by four numbers from 0–255, each separated by a period. An example IP address is 238.14.82.31.

NetBEUI

NetBEUI stands for *NetBIOS Extended User Interface* and can be used only in small networks. It requires no address configuration and provides faster data transfer than TCP/IP. Each Windows computer in a NetBEUI network is configured only with a computer and workgroup name. However, NetBEUI's cross-platform support is limited to Windows and other Microsoft OSes. Furthermore, NetBEUI is not routable and not robust in unstable networks.

The NetBEUI protocol is useful if you are creating a very small internal network at the office or at home. NetBEUI is included with Windows, so all that is required is that you connect the computers, elect to use the protocol, and assign a computer name to each computer. It's free and it's extremely easy to implement.

IPX/SPX

IPX/SPX stands for *Internetwork Packet Exchange/Sequenced Packet Exchange*. It is designed specifically for use with the Novell NetWare OS. It is routable and otherwise similar to TCP/IP, except that it has limited cross-platform support and cannot be used on the Internet.

AppleTalk

Apple Computer was an early player in networks. AppleTalk allows for connection between Apple Macintosh and other systems. AppleTalk can work through a variety of network topologies and is included with Mac computers.

Cabling

There are many types of network cables, but the most common fall into one of three categories: twisted-pair, coaxial, and fiber-optic. Their characteristics, advantages, and common implementations are discussed here.

Twisted-Pair Cable

Twisted-pair cable is the most popular cable type for internal networks. These cables are so named because the cable contains pairs of wires that are twisted around each other. These twists help "boost" each wire's signals and make them less susceptible to EMI. Additionally, twisted-pair cables may be shielded. *Shielded twisted-pair (STP) cables* contain an extra insulating layer that helps prevent data loss and block EMI. However, due to the expense of STP cables, *unshielded twisted-pair (UTP) cables* are used more often.

There are several standards for twisted-pair cables, each with a different number of wires, speed, and implementation. These standards are often referred to as *CAT#*— for example, CAT3 or CAT4 (*CAT* is short for *category*). CAT5, a type of UTP, is the most common twisted-pair cable. Table 7-1 presents a summary of twisted-pair cable

TABLE 7-1	Type	Speed	Common Use
Twisted-Pair Cable Standards	CAT1	1Mbps	Phone lines
	CAT2	4Mbps	Token Ring networks
	CAT3	16Mbps	Ethernet networks
	CAT4	20Mbps	Token Ring networks
	CAT5	100Mbps	Ethernet networks
	CAT5/e	100Mbps Usually tested to 350Mbps	Ethernet networks
	CAT 6	200Mbps Preliminary standard	Ethernet networks

offerings. CAT 5/E is an enhanced version of CAT5 that is more stringently tested and offers better transmission characteristics than CAT5. CAT6 is the newest twisted pair standard and offers higher bandwidth and improved signal handling characteristics.

CAT6 is still a tentative specification and may go as high as 550MHz testing as opposed to the proposed 200MHz rating.

Twisted-pair cables can be identified by their use of RJ-45 connectors, which look like regular phone connectors but are slightly larger. This type of cable is most commonly implemented in star networks.

Coaxial Cable

Coaxial cables (*coax* for short), which are used to connect televisions to cable outlets, are also used in bus networks and, to a lesser degree, in star networks. Coax cables contain a single copper wire surrounded by an insulating layer and have BNC connectors. Coax cables are less susceptible to interference than STP or UTP cables, so they can typically be used in longer lengths.

Most coaxial connections in the networking environment use the BNC connector. There are four primary types of connectors used. These are the end connector, the terminator, the inline connector, and the *T-connector*. Figure 7-6 shows these standard connectors. T-connectors are used to connect computers to the network, while inline connectors are used to connect two cables together.

Coaxial cable is often categorized as either thinnet or thicknet. *Thinnet cable* is physically thinner and has a lower throughput rate. *Thicknet* is a thicker coaxial cable, and because it is better shielded, can be used for longer distances. Thicknet cable is usually connected to a device using an *Attachment Unit Interface* (*AUI*) connector. The AUI connector is a 15-pin connector.

BNC end, terminator, inline, and T-Connectors

BNC connector   BNC T-connector   Inline connector   50Ω

Thicknet is physically harder to work with than thinnet because the coax is thicker and less pliable than thinnet. This makes it difficult to bend the cable to go around corners or tuck behind desks.

The most common coaxial cables in communications are RG6, RG8, RG58, and RG59. The RG stands for registered gauge. RG6 is most frequently used for television and cable modem applications. RG8 is used for thicknet networks. RG58 is used for thinnet cabling. RG59 is used for primarily for an older network called ArcNet and is not used in modern data communications networks.

Plenum/PVC cable

Most commonly used coaxial cables use a PVC outer sheath to protect the cable. PVC is not fire resistant and cannot, by code, be used in overhead or plenum areas in offices. Plenum cable uses a special fire-resistant outer sheath that will not burn as quickly as PVC. Plenum cable frequently costs more but is required in most areas. Most of the standard cables discussed in this chapter are available with plenum-grade ratings.

Fiber-Optic Cable

Fiber-optic cable, or *fiber* for short, is not commonly used within local area networks (LANs) but is often used to join separate networks over long distances. Fiber transmits light rather than electrical signals, so it is not susceptible to EMI. It is capable of faster transmission than other types of cable, but it is also the most expensive cable. Fiber-optic cable is most commonly implemented in ring networks but can also be used in ring and bus topologies.

A single light wave passing down a cable is a mode. Fiber optic cables are either single-mode or multimode. A single-mode cable allows only a single wave to pass down the cable. Multimode fiber allows for multiple modes or waves to be passed simultaneously. Multimodes are usually accomplished using a larger diameter fiber, and each wave uses a certain portion of the fiber cable for transmission.

The standard connectors used with fiber cable are ST and SC connectors (see Figure 7-7). The *straight tip (ST)* connector is a straight round connector used to connect fiber to a network device. The *subscriber connector (SC)* is square and is used to connect network devices or other cables.

FIGURE 7-7   ST and SC connectors used in a fiber network

In most new network implementations, twisted-pair is used in star networks, coax is used in bus networks, and fiber-optic is used in rings.

IDC/UDC Connectors

The *IBM-type Data Connector* (*IDC*) and the Universal Data Connector (UDC) are two types of cable connectors used by IBM computer systems. These connectors were designed to be universal data connectors for IBM communications networks. Neither of these types of connectors is commonly found in PC systems.

Network Access

Network access refers to the method that computers use to determine when they can communicate, how messages are transferred, and what to do in the case of a data collision. The two most commonly implemented access methods are CSMA/CD and token passing.

CSMA/CD

CSMA/CD stands for *carrier sense multiple access/collision detection*. In this access method, when a computer wants to send a data packet, it first "listens" to the network to determine if another transmission is already in progress. If there is another transmission, the computer waits, then listens again. When there is no other network activity, the computer sends its data packet. However, if another computer has sent a packet at the same time, a collision will occur.

When the collision is detected, both computers stop transmitting, wait a random amount of time, then begin the listening/transmitting process again. This procedure is carried out until the data is properly transmitted. On large networks, the number of collisions can be quite high, so it can take a number of tries until a computer can send its packet. CSMA/CD is the most common LAN access method.

Token Passing

Token passing is less common but much more orderly than CSMA/CD. In this access method, one computer in the network generates an electronic signal, called a *token*. The token is passed from computer to computer on the network. If a computer receives the token but has no data to transmit, it simply passes the token along. If the computer does have data to transmit, it places the data behind the token, then sends them both to the next computer in line. A computer cannot transmit data until it receives an "empty" token (one with no data packet attached).

When a token is accompanied by data, its address is examined by each computer, then sent along again until it reaches its destination. The destination computer examines the token, removes the data packet, and then sends the empty token around again. Unfortunately, if there is a lot of network traffic, it could take a very long time for a computer to get an empty token so that it can transmit its data. For this reason, token passing is typically used only on smaller networks.

Because computers can transmit only if they have the token and because there is only one token per network, there is no chance of a data collision. However, the token itself can get lost in the network, or a computer could hang on to the token without resending it. In either case, network traffic is halted until the token is regenerated.

Full- and Half-Duplex Transmission

In computer terms, data can be unidirectional or bidirectional. In unidirectional communications, data can travel in one direction only. This type of communication is used in ring networks. In bidirectional communications, data can travel in either direction. The term *half-duplex* indicates that data can travel in either direction but only in one direction at a time. In *full-duplex* communications, data can travel in both directions at the same time.

Ways to Network PCs

By combining topologies, cable types, protocols, access methods, and other network variables, it is possible to come up with hundreds of different network architectures. There are, however, a few standardized combinations, as described in this section.

802.3 (Ethernet)

The Ethernet standard, developed by IEEE, is by far the most common. Also known as IEEE 802.3, this type of network combines CSMA/CD access with half-duplex communication and supports transmission speeds of either 10Mbps or 100Mbps. Ethernet networks can use twisted-pair, coax, or fiber-optic cable and can use bus or star topologies. You must use a special Ethernet NIC to access an Ethernet network.

Ethernet networks are often referred to by their speed, channel type, and cable type. For example, the term *10BaseF* indicates a 10Mbps network that uses one (base) channel and fiber-optic (F) cable. 100BaseT is a 100Mbps Ethernet network that uses twisted-pair. Table 7-2 contains Ethernet types and their characteristics.

e x a m
ⓦatch
Ethernet networks are identified by this configuration: speedBasecable. *The 10 or 100 at the start of the configuration signifies the* *speed in Mbps, and the letter or number at the end indicates the cable type (T = twisted-pair, 2 = thinnet, 5 = thicknet, and F = fiber).*

Token-Passing Networks

Token-passing networks are those that use the token-passing access method. There are several IEEE-defined standards for token passing, including Token Ring, Token Bus, and Fiber Distributed Data Interface (FDDI). Token-passing networks can use star, ring, or bus topologies and coax, twisted-pair, or fiber-optic cabling. For each token-passing network type, you must install the proper type of NIC.

Token Ring networks are based on the IEEE 802.5 standard and have transmission rates of either 4Mbps or 16Mbps. They use twisted-pair cable and half-duplex communication. Although Token Ring networks may actually have a physical ring topology, it is more common for them to have a star topology. In either case, the

TABLE 7-2   Ethernet Types and Characteristics

Type	Speed	Cable	Maximum Cable Length	Topology
10BaseT	10Mbps	Twisted-pair	100 meters	Star
10Base2	10Mbps	Coax (thinnet)	185 meters	Bus
10Base5	10Mbps	Coax (thicknet)	500 meters	Bus
10BaseF	10Mbps	Fiber-optic	2000 meters	Star
100BaseTX 100BaseT4	100Mbps	Twisted-pair	100 meters	Star
100BaseFX	100Mbps	Fiber-optic	412 meters	Star

token travels from one computer to the next, in order, in a conceptual ring. This type of network uses a multiple access unit (MAU) instead of a hub. See Figure 7-8 for an illustration of a conceptual ring on a physical star topology.

Token Ring networks with a star topology use a MAU, not a hub.

Another type of token-passing network is Token Bus. This network, based on IEEE standard 802.4, is similar to Token Ring but uses a coax bus topology rather than a twisted-pair ring or star. A Token Bus network can transmit at 4Mbps only.

FDDI networks use the FDDI standard, which was developed by ANSI and based on the IEEE 802.5 Token Ring standard. FDDI networks use a fiber-optic dual-ring structure and are capable of transmitting up to 100Mbps.

Dial-Up Networks

A *dial-up network* connection uses a modem rather than a network card and uses regular phone cables instead of network cables. In a dial-up connection, one computer must be configured to dial the host computer, and the host computer must be configured to permit dial-up access. Once a dial-up connection has been established, the two computers can communicate as though they were part of a LAN. If the host computer is already part of a LAN, the dial-up connection can be used to allow remote access to it.

Direct Connection

It is possible to network two PCs simply by connecting them via their network adapter, parallel, or serial ports. Direct connections require special cables with different pinouts so that the send wires on one computer match the receive wires on the other computer. This is called a *crossover cable*. Although this type of connection provides

FIGURE 7-8   A conceptual ring on a physical star network

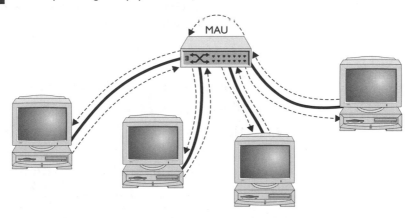

relatively fast data transmission, it is limited to two computers only. Distances are limited by the cable characteristics of the connection used. To configure a direct cable connection in Windows 9x and Me, follow the procedure in Exercise 7-1. This exercise describes how to first configure the host, then the guest machine.

In the case of a serial connection the connection is usually accomplished using the RS 232 serial standard. Parallel connections typically use the IEEE 1284 standard for communications.

EXERCISE 7-1

Configuring Windows 98 Computers for a Direct Connection

1. Click Start, then select Programs | Accessories | Communications | Direct Cable Connection. If you do not see Direct Cable Connection in the Communications menu, use the Add/Remove Programs utility to install it.

2. The Direct Cable Connection Wizard will open. Select Host, then select Next.

3. You will be prompted to select a computer port to use for the connection. Select the appropriate port. Plug the cable in, and click Next.

4. You will be prompted to configure the computer to use File and Printer Sharing, if it has not already been set up. Click File and Printer Sharing.

5. The Network dialog box will open. Click File and Print Sharing, then elect to allow access to both files and printers. Click OK, then click OK again. If you have made a change in the network dialog box, you will need to restart your computer.

6. Click Next in the Direct Cable Connection Wizard.

7. In the final screen, you can choose to force guests to use a password to access the host computer. To do so, enable the Use Password Protection option, then click Set Password. Enter the password, and click OK.

8. Click Finish.

9. To configure the guest computer, start the Direct Cable Connection Wizard and select Guest rather than Host.

10. Select the port, then click Next.

11. Click Finish.

12. The two devices should be able to "see" each other in Network Neighborhood.

FIGURE 7-9   An ISDN network connection between two computer systems

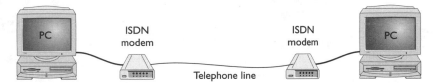

ISDN Connections

Integrated Service Digital Network (ISDN) was an early international standard for sending voice and data over digital or normal telephone wire; these days it is being largely replaced by newer technologies such as DSL and cable. ISDN uses existing telephone circuits or higher speed conditioned lines to get speeds of either 64K or 128K. This considerably beats the maximum speed of 56K that you can get from a dial-up modem. ISDN lines also have the ability to simultaneously carry voice and data over the circuit. ISDN connections are made using an ISDN modem on both ends of the circuit. Figure 7-9 shows a typical ISDN connection between two networks. This connection uses a conditioned phone line provided by the phone company.

DSL Connections

Digital subscriber line (DSL) is a relatively new entry into the data market. DSL uses existing copper telephone wire for the communications circuit. The existing phone line is split into two bands to accomplish this, and the frequency below 4,000Hz is reserved for voice transmission while everything else is used for data transmission. This is accomplished through a DSL modem. Figure 7-10 shows the total bandwidth being separated into two channels; one is used for voice, the other for data. Voice communications operate normally, and the data connection is always on and available. DSL is up to 140 times faster than available analog dial-up connections.

Cable Connections

Cable communications or cable modems use existing cable TV connections for data transmission. The cable provider uses an existing channel in the cable network for data communications, which are connected via a cable modem. The cable modem provides a network connection for a local computer or is installed directly in a PC system. This allows for very high-speed, always-on networking for clients that have cable TV installed. Figure 7-11 shows the cable connection in a household. Interestingly enough, if you have digital cable service into a house, you have been using cable modem technology for some time, whether you were using it with your computer or not. The cable box actually contains a cable modem to use advanced services of digital cable.

DSL connection showing both data and voice over a single phone line

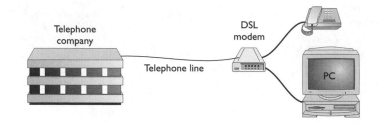

Satellite Connections

Satellite communications systems have come a long way over the last few years. Satellite communication systems were initially used extensively to allow communications with remote locations and for military purposes. These systems usually work off of Microwave radio frequencies and require an antenna, receiver, and transmitter. Early satellite communications systems were very expensive to maintain and operate.

There are a number of companies that offer relatively high bandwidth at affordable prices for Internet connection and other applications. The bandwidth capabilities of these systems rival those of cable or DSL networks and offer speeds for downloading of up to 1.2MBps (uploading speeds typically range from 40 to 90Kbps). Satellite connections are now available for both fixed and mobile applications.

Infrared Networks

Computers can also be networked using *infrared communications*. There are several ways to do this, including direct cable connection, in which two computers can be networked as long as their IrDA (Infrared Data Association) ports are properly configured and are facing each other (see Chapter 1 for more information about IrDA devices). Most PDAs and handheld computers can communicate with each other using IR technologies. IR networks are most commonly used to connect slow speed devices such as printers to a computer. IR networks tend to be slower than other networks, though higher speed alternatives are becoming available.

Cable modem configuration in a house

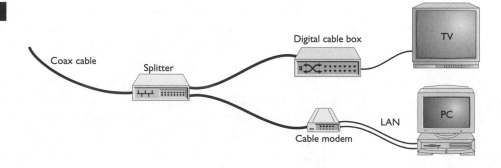

Wireless Connections

Wireless communication is becoming very popular. The most common wireless standard is 802.11 or Wireless Fidelity (Wi Fi). There are several standards within the 802.11 protocol and more are being proposed all the time. These systems use either 2.4GHz or 5GHz frequencies to communicate between systems. The range on these systems is relatively short but it offers the advantage of not having to install cable to have network services. Figure 7-12 shows a typical wireless network in a home. Notice that in this installation, all of the users in the network have access to the Internet using a single cable modem. The wireless communications network uses a wireless router to connect to the Internet. Each workstation in the network has a wireless adapter to connect to the router.

Many devices including video gaming systems have either wireless or wired network connections for integration into home networks. These systems can connect to WANs, such as the Internet, for use in multi-player gaming. Retail stores, libraries, and many coffee shops are also implementing *hot spots*—network access points (or wireless access points) that allow customers to connect their PCs using existing Wi FI controllers in their laptops to gain network access.

In this example, the teenage son even has his Sony Playstation connected to the Internet using a wireless bridge. The Playstation provides a LAN connection option using the 802.3 Ethernet standard. This requires a device called a wireless bridge to translate the wired LAN to the 802.11 wireless network. To configure this device, each side of the bridge must have a separate TCP/IP address. The bridge converts signals from the Playstation to 802.11 and converts signals from the wireless network to an 802.11 standard.

FIGURE 7-12   Typical home network environment using a wireless router

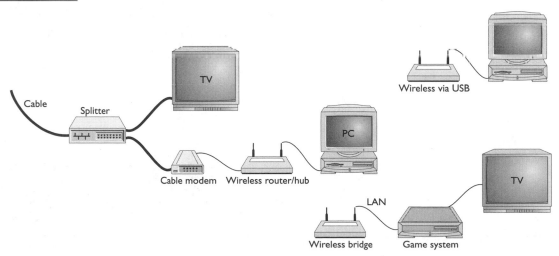

SCENARIO & SOLUTION

What is a 10BaseT network?	This nomenclature indicates an Ethernet network. The *10* signifies the speed in Mbps, and the *T* means the network uses twisted-pair cabling.
Which types of networks use token passing?	Token Ring, Token Bus, and FDDI.
Which type of cable is the most common?	Twisted-pair.
What is the most popular network protocol?	TCP/IP.

Connecting LANs

Most computer LANs are now connected to other LANs or wide area networks (WAN) such as the Internet. These connections usually require some form of translation and routing capability. In the case of the Internet, each computer in the network requires a TCP/IP address. In order to reach another network, the originating computer must know how to reach the other computer. To accomplish this, routes are established and a router–a device that connects networks–is used to store information about destinations. A router knows the addresses of the networks to which it is connected and the addresses of other routers on those networks and it knows at least the next destination that information can be transferred to. The Internet has thousands of routers managing the connections between the millions of computers connected to it. Figure 7-13 shows a router between a LAN and a WAN. Many routers include bridging circuitry, a hub, and the necessary CSU to connect multiple network technologies together, such as a LAN and a T-1 network. This technology is very complicated but is needed to manage the millions of connections that exist in the Internet.

The second commonly used technology is called a *bridge*. As you saw earlier in the discussion about wireless LANs, a bridge was needed to provide a translation of protocols from 802.11 to 802.5. There are numerous types of bridges that allow connections between the various protocols, network topologies, and media. If you wanted to connect a 100BaseT network to a ring network, a device would be needed to bridge these two topologies. This bridge device would be used to tie the two network

FIGURE 7-13   A router connecting a LAN to an T-1 network

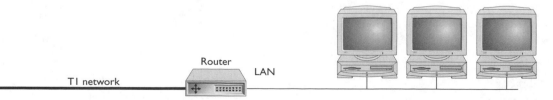

FIGURE 7-14   Network bridge used to connect an 802.11 network to an 802.5 network

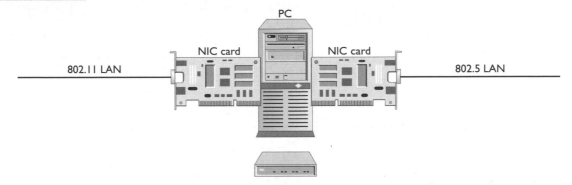

topologies together, as shown in Figure 7-14. PC systems can also be used to bridge networks if they have multiple network interface cards in them. This might be the case if you were working with a communication server to bridge an IBM proprietary communications standard to the Internet.

CERTIFICATION OBJECTIVE 7.02

Network Setup and Troubleshooting

The actual implementation of a network is a very large and complex task. It requires intensive preplanning in terms of design, access, security, fault tolerance, and scalability issues, on top of the physical implementation of the protocols, topologies, and access methods described already in this chapter. This job is typically the domain of computer network specialists. However, there are some relatively common and simple network problems that you will be able to resolve without complete training as a network specialist. These troubleshooting issues, as well as procedures for configuring a computer to join a network, are described in this section.

Installing and Configuring Network Cards

A connection to a LAN requires a NIC or similar network device for each computer. The purpose of the NIC is to translate the computer's data into signals that can travel on the network and to take care of actually sending and receiving network traffic. As well as configuring the computer's NIC with the proper driver and system resources, you must also configure the computer with the settings it will need to join the intended network. The physical installation of a NIC is a relatively simple matter that includes physically attaching it to the motherboard, then loading its Setup or Install program (unless it is Plug and Play).

The next step is to configure the NIC to use the proper protocol. In Windows, these protocols include TCP/IP, NetBEUI, and IPX/SPX. The computer must be given a unique address and/or name, and it might need to be configured to join a particular workgroup or domain. The process for configuring an Ethernet card to use TCP/IP in Windows 9x is described in Exercise 7-2. This exercise assumes that the Ethernet card has already been installed and configured to use the proper system resources.

EXERCISE 7-2

Configuring an Ethernet Card for TCP/IP

1. Open the Windows Control Panel and double-click Networks. Ensure the Configuration tab is displayed.

2. Select the TCP/IP protocol from the list, then click Properties. If TCP/IP does not appear in the list, proceed with steps 2a through 2c to add it.

   A. If TCP/IP is not in the list, click Add.

   B. Select Protocol and click Add.

   C. Select Microsoft from the Manufacturers list and select TCP/IP from the Protocols list. Click OK.

3. Select the Specify an IP Address Option.

4. Enter the IP address and subnet mask for the network adapter (you can obtain these from the network's administrator).

5. Click OK.

6. Click the File and Print Sharing button. If desired, select the options to give others access to your files and/or printer, then click OK.

7. Select the Identification tab.

8. Enter a unique computer name and the name of the workgroup that this computer will join on the network.

9. Click OK. You will be prompted to restart your computer. None of the new network settings will take effect until the computer is restarted.

Increasing Bandwidth

A network's *bandwidth* is the amount of data that can transmitted on the network at one time. For example, a 10Base2 network has a bandwidth of 10Mbps. If a network is perceived to be slow, increasing the bandwidth can improve its speed. That is, the more data that can be sent at once, the faster transmissions will be delivered from beginning to end and the faster the network will run overall.

In many cases, you can increase the bandwidth by upgrading the network's components. For example, you can replace 10Mbps cards with 100Mbps cards. You might also need to upgrade the cable types—for example, from CAT3 to CAT5/E—to support the new speed. The entire network will run at the speed of the hub or MAU (if one exists) or the speed of the cable, whichever is slower. If a single NIC supports a lower speed than all other network components, the network will be unaffected except in communications with that NIC. For example, suppose that an entire network supports 100Mbps, except for a NIC that supports only 10Mbps. All communications to or from that NIC will run at 10Mbps. All other communications will run at 100Mbps.

Most networks are *baseband*, meaning they use the entire bandwidth of the cable to transmit data on a single channel. Network technologies, such as 1000BaseT, break the cables bandwidth into multiple channels. This is called *broadband* technology and is commonly used in cable TV and other high-speed networks.

Loss of Network Connectivity

When you suspect that a computer is not on the network, first check the Windows Network Neighborhood. Under normal conditions, all other computers that can be accessed in the current workgroup will be listed. If a computer cannot access the network, the Network Neighborhood window will open and a message will appear, stating "Unable to browse network." If this is the case, check the NIC itself. Most NICs indicate network connectivity with an indicator light. Check the cable by swapping it with a known good one. Try to restart the computer, and ensure that the proper network name and password are entered, if necessary.

If these procedures don't work, check the configuration of the NIC in Network Settings. Make sure that it is configured with the proper workgroup, and ensure that it is not using a conflicting IP address. You should also check the NIC's driver and use of system resources. As a last resort, replace the NIC.

on the

!

j o b

As with other hardware troubleshooting methods, start by trying to replicate the problem, then restart the computer. Pinpoint a hardware-related network problem by checking the outermost, most accessible components first, then work your way in.

Data Loss

Because NICs use error checking, it is rare for data to get lost en route. However, many networks use servers that store users' data. A *server* is a computer that controls network access or provides resources to a network, such as a printer, application, or storage space. It is very important in these cases to ensure that data is available if the server temporarily goes down or to ensure that data is not permanently lost if the server is not recoverable. There are several techniques for preventing loss of data in the event of a server failure. Data-loss prevention techniques provide *fault tolerance* to the network, meaning that the network can tolerate a failure and continue to function even if there is a failure.

Tape Backups

Servers can be configured to automatically and regularly back up their entire contents to tape. For example, if a server performs a nightly backup, it makes a copy of all data that was saved on the server earlier that day. Then if the server fails, the current day's data will be lost, but all previously created files can be recovered from the tape.

Mirroring

Many networks employ backup servers that take over the function of the primary server if it fails. This is called server *mirroring*, and it involves saving all data to both the primary and backup servers. If the main server fails, the backup server can take over its function, and users might never even know the problem occurred. Unfortunately, the process of saving all data twice can be time consuming and might make the network appear slow.

Clustering

Another way to prevent data loss is to spread data over more than one server so that data and services can be accessed even if the original server loses its data. This type of strategy is called server *clustering*. As well as providing fault tolerance, clustering also provides *load balancing*, which means that the workload is divided (balanced) between two or more servers.

Network Slowdown

Many things, including reduced bandwidth or excessive traffic, can result in network slowdowns. The very nature of some networks makes them prone to slow data transmission. For example, recall that in a token-passing network, a computer cannot

SCENARIO & SOLUTION

What is fault tolerance?	Fault tolerance is the ability of a network to continue functioning, even when there is a failure among one of its components.
What are common data-loss prevention techniques?	Server mirroring, server clustering, and tape backups.
Which fault-tolerance method provides load balancing?	Clustering, which divides work between two or more servers, provides load balancing.

transmit until it has an empty token. If there is a lot of traffic on the network, it could take a long time before the computer gets the empty token. The reason for this delay will not be apparent to the user, however. To the user, it will simply appear that the data is taking a long time to get to its destination.

Recall the function of a hub. When a computer sends data, the hub receives it and retransmits it to all other computers. On a 16-port hub, this means that 14 packets were sent out unnecessarily. Switching hubs eliminate this by creating a virtual circuit between the two computers. This keeps unnecessary network traffic down and improves network performance.

If the network experiences a single busy period, there is little you can do to resolve the problem. However, if a network gradually gets slower and slower over time, it could be that there is too much traffic for the network's capabilities, and the network will have to be split up or upgraded. Furthermore, if there is a lot of interference, there could be many data errors, which result in the resending of entire data packets. Again, this situation raises the total amount of traffic on the network and slows down its overall performance.

CERTIFICATION SUMMARY

The field of networking is very large and diverse. However, as a computer technician, you should be familiar with basic network terminology and network arrangements. For example, you should be able to recognize a star, bus, or ring topology and be familiar with the cable types they employ, as well as the advantages and disadvantages of each. You should also understand the differences between common network protocols, from the very simple NetBEUI to the more complex protocol of the Internet, TCP/IP.

The combination of these factors makes up the network's architecture. The 10BaseT Ethernet standard, for example, employs CSMA/CD 10Mbps access on a star network and typically uses CAT5 twisted-pair cabling. A Token Bus network uses 4Mbps token passing on a coaxial cable bus network. Knowing the characteristics of each network component or factor will help you make decisions about the type of network to deploy and will also help you pinpoint and resolve networking problems.

TWO-MINUTE DRILL

Here are some of the key points from each certification objective in Chapter 7.

Networking Concepts

❑ Computers are connected to a hub in a star topology, to a main backbone in a bus topology, and to each other in a ring topology.

❑ The TCP/IP protocol is the standard protocol of the Internet. TCP/IP requires some technical expertise to configure.

❑ The NetBEUI protocol is simple to implement but is not routable.

❑ The most common twisted-pair cable is CAT5, which can transmit up to 100Mbps. CAT6 cable is not yet standardized but is expected to support speeds of 10 times that of CAT5.

❑ Twisted-pair cable can be shielded or unshielded and uses an RJ-45 connector. The maximum length of twisted pair is 185 meters per run of wire.

❑ Coaxial cable is more shielded than STP, contains a single copper wire, and uses a BNC connector.

❑ Fiber-optic cable transmits light signals, and although it can transmit faster and at longer distances, it is not popular due to its expense.

❑ In CSMA/CD access, each computer is free to transmit as long as no other computer is also transmitting.

❑ Ethernet networks, such as 10BaseT or 100BaseFX, use CSMA/CD and can transmit data at either 10Mbps or 100Mbps.

❑ Token-passing networks support 4Mbps or 16Mbps, and computers can communicate only if they have the network's empty token.

Network Setup and Troubleshooting

❑ A computer's NIC (for example, Ethernet or Token Ring) must support the type of network it is joining.

❑ The NIC must be configured for use by the computer and is also configured to communicate on the network.

❑ Network communications can occur only as fast as the slowest involved element, such as the NIC, hub, or cable.

❑ Some network servers use mirroring or clustering to prevent or reduce data loss in the event of a server failure.

❑ Network slowdowns can be caused by interference, heavy traffic, or insufficient equipment.

SELF TEST

The following questions will help you measure your understanding of the material presented in this chapter. Read all of the choices carefully because there might be more than one correct answer. Choose all correct answers for each question.

Networking Concepts

1. A network consists of five computers attached to a hub. There is a break in one computer's network cable. How will this break affect the network?

    A. The entire network will fail.

    B. Only the computer attached to the faulty cable will be unable to access the network.

    C. Only computers that were booted before the computer with the faulty cable will be able to access the network.

    D. Only computers that were booted after the computer with the faulty cable will be able to access the network.

2. Which of the following points of failure will affect the connectivity of an entire star network?

    A. A single computer

    B. A single cable

    C. The backbone

    D. The hub

3. Which type of network uses terminators and T-connectors?

    A. Bus

    B. Star

    C. Ring

    D. FDDI

4. A computer in a ring network won't boot properly. What effect will this have on the network?

    A. The entire network will fail.

    B. Only the failed computer will be unable to access the network.

    C. All computers located after the failed computer will be unable to access the network.

    D. All computers located before the failed computer will be unable to access the network.

5. Which protocol requires that each computer have a unique 32-bit address?

    A. TCP/IP

    B. NetBEUI

C. IPX/SPX

D. All of the above

6. Your company has a large network, and due to increased traffic, you have decided to split the network into two connected subnetworks. Which of the following protocols must you avoid using?

A. TCP/IP

B. NetBEUI

C. IPX/SPX

D. You can use any of the above.

7. Which network cable type has a maximum speed of 16Mbps?

A. CAT2

B. CAT3

C. CAT4

D. CAT5

8. Which of the following is the most common type of cable used in bus networks?

A. CAT5

B. STP

C. Coaxial

D. Fiber-optic

9. Which of the following most accurately describes the CSMA/CD network access method?

A. An electronic signal is constantly passed around the network, and no computer can transmit until it receives the signal.

B. A central device polls each computer in order, asking if the computer has any data to transmit.

C. When a computer wants to transmit, it interrupts the network's central device and is given a transmission priority.

D. When a computer wants to transmit, it first listens for traffic. If a data collision occurs, each transmitting computer waits a random amount of time, then retransmits.

10. A customer has set up a twisted-pair star topology and wants to implement a Token Ring standard. What do you tell the customer?

A. They must first change the topology to a ring.

B. They must first change the cable type to fiber-optic.

    C. They must change the topology to a ring and change the cable type to fiber-optic.

    D. The Token Ring standard can be implemented on the current topology.

11. A customer has called about a network problem. When asked, the customer tells you that it is a 10Base5 network. What can you tell about this network without even seeing it?

    A. It supports a maximum cable length of 185 meters.

    B. It uses token passing.

    C. It has a bus topology.

    D. It uses twisted-pair cabling.

12. A customer works at an office that uses an Ethernet network, but she cannot remember the network's supported maximum speed. What do you tell the customer?

    A. The network's speed is 4Mbps.

    B. The network runs at 4Mbps, 10Mbps, or 16Mbps.

    C. The network runs at either 10Mbps or 100Mbps.

    D. The network runs at 4Mbps, 10Mbps, 16Mbps, or 100Mbps.

13. Which of the following network connections requires a crossover cable?

    A. Ethernet

    B. FDDI

    C. Dial-up

    D. Direct cable connection

Network Setup and Troubleshooting

14. When configuring a computer for network access, the computer name must:

    A. Be unique

    B. Match the names of the other computers on the network

    C. Match the computer's IP address

    D. Be entered only if you are using the NetBEUI protocol

15. Which of the following are required to properly configure a computer to use the NetBEUI protocol?

    A. Computer name

    B. Workgroup name and IP address

    C. Subnet mask and computer name

    D. Subnet mask and IP address

16. One computer on a Token Ring network has a 4Mbps NIC. All other network components, including NICs, MAUs, and cables, support 16Mbps. What effect will the slower NIC have on the network?

    A. The entire network will run at 4Mbps.

    B. All devices will be able to communicate except the 4Mbps NIC.

    C. When communicating with the 4Mbps NIC, communications will run at 4Mbps; otherwise, the network will run at 16Mbps.

    D. No computer will be able to access the network.

17. A user calls you and complains that he cannot get his computer on the network. You tell him to open the Windows Network Neighborhood. Which of the following will occur in support of the user's claim?

    A. All computers within the user's workgroup will be displayed.

    B. The Network Neighborhood window will not open.

    C. A message stating "Unable to browse network" will be displayed.

    D. The Network Neighborhood window will contain the text "Network Access Not Configured."

18. What is the purpose of mirroring a network server?

    A. To speed up network activity

    B. To provide fault tolerance

    C. To provide load balancing

    D. To increase bandwidth

19. Which type of fault tolerance method provides load balancing?

    A. Mirroring

    B. Tape backups

    C. Clustering

    D. All of the above

20. Your company is growing and your 100BaseTX network has been getting consistently slower over the past month. A coworker has stated that the problem is being caused by the hub. How might the hub be responsible?

    A. The hub might not support 100Mbps.

    B. The hub might be causing excess network traffic.

    C. The hub might be unable to find all the computers on the network.

    D. The hub cannot be responsible.

LAB QUESTION

One of your clients owns a company that currently uses a 4Mbps Token Ring network. The network uses a star topology and CAT3 cabling. The company has been growing, and its owner would like to upgrade the network to the Ethernet standard. Your client has asked what the options are. In a few paragraphs, discuss Ethernet options as well as the network components that must be added, replaced, or upgraded. Discuss the advantages, disadvantages, and performance of each option. Supply as much information as you can so that the customer can make an informed decision.

SELF TEST ANSWERS

Networking Concepts

1. ☑ **B.** Only the computer attached to the faulty cable will be unable to access the network. In a star network, each computer has its own cable, which is attached to the hub. One computer's cable will not affect the performance of other computers.

   ☒ **A,** the entire network will fail, is incorrect. The only single point of total network failure on a star network is the hub. That is, if the hub stops functioning, no computer will be able to access the network. **C** and **D** are incorrect because they suggest that only computers booted before or after the computer with the bad cable will be affected. First, only the computer attached to the bad cable will be affected. Furthermore, in networks in which one computer's failure results in the failure of other systems, the order in which the computers booted is irrelevant.

2. ☑ **D.** The hub is a point of failure that will affect an entire star network. All computers in a star network are attached to the hub. If the hub stops functioning, the computers will have no method of communication. Therefore, if the hub fails, the entire network will fail.

   ☒ **A,** a single computer, and **B,** a single cable, are incorrect. In a star network, each computer has its own cable and is connected to the hub independently of the other computers. The failure of a single computer or cable does not affect other machines on a star network. **C,** the backbone, is incorrect because star networks do not have backbones. Backbones are implemented in bus networks.

3. ☑ **A.** A bus network uses terminators and T-connectors. Bus networks consist of a coaxial cable backbone, which must be terminated with a 50-ohm terminator at each end, to prevent signal "bouncing." Each computer in a bus network is attached to the backbone via a T-connector or, in some cases, a vampire tap.

   ☒ **B,** star, is incorrect because it does not use terminators or T-connectors. Instead, each computer is attached to a hub. **C,** ring, is also incorrect. In a ring network, each computer is attached to the next in a circular daisy-chain fashion. **D,** FDDI, is incorrect because this is a network standard that uses token passing on a fiber-optic double-ring topology.

4. ☑ **A.** The entire network will fail. In a ring network, each computer is connected to the next. All network traffic must go through each computer and be retransmitted until it reaches its destination. If one computer cannot access the network, is turned off, or will not boot properly, the network will not function.

   ☒ **B** is incorrect because it states that only the failed computer will be unable to access the network. Although this is true in a star or bus network, the structure of a ring network is such that a single point of failure anywhere in the network will result in a total network failure. **C** and **D** are incorrect because they suggest that only certain computers, located before or after the failed computer, will not be able to access the network. Again, because of the ring's structure, all computers will fail. Furthermore, because of its ring topology, all computers could be said to be before or after the failed computer.

5. ☑ **A.** TCP/IP requires that each computer have a unique address. This is the computer's Internet Protocol (IP) address, and it identifies the computer on the network, between connected networks, or on the Internet.

   ☒ **B,** NetBEUI, is incorrect because it requires a unique computer name and common domain or workgroup name only. **C,** IPX/SPX, is incorrect because this protocol requires a simple network address, not a 128-bit address. For this reason, **D,** all of the above, is also incorrect.

6. ☑ **B.** You must avoid using the NetBEUI protocol. NetBEUI is effective only on small networks and is not routable. That means that computers using NetBEUI cannot communicate with computers on other subnetworks, even if they are physically connected.

   ☒ **A,** TCP/IP, and **C,** IPX/SPX, are incorrect because, depending on the network's needs, you could potentially use either of these protocols. They are both routable, meaning that they can both be used to access computers on connected subnetworks. **D** is incorrect because it states that you can use NetBEUI, TCP/IP, or IPX/SPX. Again, this is incorrect because you cannot use NetBEUI.

7. ☑ **B.** CAT3 has a maximum speed of 16Mbps. It is frequently used in 10Mbps Ethernet networks.

   ☒ **A,** CAT2, is incorrect because this cable type supports a maximum of 4Mbps. It is typically used only in token-passing networks such as the Token Bus or 4Mbps Token Ring. **C,** CAT4, is incorrect because it supports a maximum speed of 20Mbps. It is typically used in 16Mbps Token Ring networks. **D,** CAT5, is incorrect because its maximum speed is 100Mbps. It is typically used in 100Mbps Ethernet networks.

8. ☑ **C.** Coaxial cable is the most common type of cable used in bus networks. It is typically used to create the bus network's backbone. In most bus networks, small segments of coax cable are attached using T-connectors, which also connect to individual computers.

   ☒ **A,** CAT5, is incorrect because this is a type of UTP that is not commonly found in bus networks. Rather, CAT5 is usually implemented in star networks. **B,** STP, is also incorrect for this reason. STP is a type of twisted-pair cable that is typically used in star topologies. **D,** fiber-optic, is incorrect because this type of cable is not used as commonly in bus networks as coax cable. Fiber is more often found in ring networks.

9. ☑ **D.** In CSMA/CD, when a computer wants to transmit, it first listens for traffic. If a data collision occurs, each transmitting computer waits a random amount of time, then retransmits. In other words, when the computer detects that the line is clear, it will transmit its data, listening all the time for collisions. If another device transmits at the same time, both devices will stop transmitting, then try to resend the data after a random period of time.

☒ **A** is incorrect because it suggests that computers will not transmit until they have received a special network signal. This is a description of token passing. The electronic token continues to move from one computer to another, and no computer can transmit without first having the token. **B** is incorrect because it suggests that a network device checks each computer to determine if it has data to send. This is a description of polling. **C** is incorrect because it suggests that networked computers use interrupts to receive a transmission priority. Although this is true of the relationship between computer components and the processor, it does not apply to network access.

10. ☑ **D.** Tell the customer the Token Ring standard can be implemented on the current topology. Although Token Ring networks use a conceptual ring, in which each device passes an electronic token from one computer to another, this standard can be implemented on a star network. In fact, due to its relatively low occurrence of single-point failure, the star is the most common topology for Token Ring networks. In this setup, a computer will receive the token, then pass it on to the hub, where it is sent to the next computer.

☒ **A,** which suggests that the network must have a ring topology, is incorrect. As explained, a conceptual ring network does not have to exist on a physical ring. **B** is incorrect because it suggests that the cable must be changed to fiber-optic. Although fiber-optic cable can be used in FDDI token-passing networks, it is not required for Token Ring networks. In fact, the Token Ring standard specifies the use of twisted-pair only. **C** is incorrect because it suggests changing both the topology and the cable type. Again, in this case, the customer can use the existing cable and topology.

11. ☑ **C.** This network is a bus topology. The first thing step you would take to troubleshoot this network would be to check that all network connections and terminators are working.

☒ **A** is incorrect because it states that the network supports a maximum cable length of 185 meters. Because the 10Base5 standard uses thicknet coax, it actually supports up to 500-meter cable lengths. **B,** it uses token passing, is incorrect because as an Ethernet standard, it uses CSMA/CD. **D,** it uses twisted-pair cabling, is incorrect. Again, the 5 in 10Base5 indicates thicknet coaxial cable.

12. ☑ **C.** You should tell the customer that the network runs at either 10Mbps or 100Mbps. These are the two standard speeds for Ethernet networks. As an aside, newer Ethernet standards support 1Gbps, but these are rare. You are probably safe in guessing that this network runs at either 10Mbps or 100Mbps.

☒ **A, B,** and **D** are all incorrect because they suggest that the network can run at a maximum speed of 4Mbps and/or 16Mbps. However, these are the maximum supported speeds for Token Ring networks, not Ethernet networks.

13. ☑ **D.** Direct cable connections require special cables called *crossover cables*. Crossover cables cross transmit and receive lines so that they can be connected without an additional device such as a hub. Many network devices, such as hubs, provide a normal and a reverse connection to allow connection between devices. This allows for maximum configuration flexibility.

☒ **A,** Ethernet, is incorrect because this type of network requires regular twisted-pair, coax, or fiber cabling. **B,** FDDI, is incorrect because this requires regular fiber-optic cables. **C,** dial-up, is incorrect because this type of connection requires a modem and a phone line.

Network Setup and Troubleshooting

14. ☑ **A.** The computer name must be unique. The computer name is the name that identifies your computer to other users on the network.

☒ **B** is incorrect because it states that the computer name must match the names of the other computers on the network. This is true of domain or workgroup names, but not computer names. **C,** match the computer's IP address, is also incorrect. IP addresses are required only for computers that use TCP/IP. If the computer does require an IP address, it does not have to match the computer name, and in fact, the computer name should be easy to recognize and be different from the IP address. **D** is incorrect because it states that the computer name is entered only if you are using the NetBEUI protocol. The TCP/IP, IPX/SPX, and NetBEUI protocols all require the entry of a computer name.

15. ☑ **A.** All that is required to properly configure a computer to use the NetBEUI protocol is a computer name. The NetBEUI protocol is the simplest to configure, and since it is not routable, there is no need (and no way) to enter complex configuration information.

☒ **B, C,** and **D** are all incorrect because they contain elements that are required to configure TCP/IP only. NetBEUI does not require a workgroup name or IP address, because the protocol allows the computer to communicate with only one workgroup (it is not routable). Subnet masks are required only when an IP address is being configured, so they are not entered in a NetBEUI configuration.

16. ☑ **C.** In this case, when communicating with the 4Mbps NIC, communications will run at 4Mbps; otherwise, the network will run at 16Mbps. In other words, the network will support 16Mbps. However, all transmissions sent by the 4Mbps NIC will be sent at 4Mbps only. Furthermore, data can be received by this NIC at 4Mbps only. When a faster NIC tries to communicate with it, the 4Mbps NIC will "miss" most of the data and have to continually ask the faster NIC to resend it.

☒ **A,** the entire network will run at 4Mbps, is incorrect. This is not a case of the network being as slow as its slowest component. Although that might be the case if the MAU or cables supported only 4Mbps, the slower NIC will not affect transmissions in which it is not involved. **B** is incorrect because it suggests that the slower NIC will not be able to access the network. As long as it supports the proper protocol, it will be able to communicate with other devices. **D** is incorrect because it suggests that the network won't work at all. Again, the network will function, and transactions that do not involve the slower NIC will be unaffected by its speed.

17. ☑ **C.** A message stating "Unable to browse network" will be displayed. This error message indicates that the current computer does not have network access.

    ☒ **A** is incorrect because it states that all computers within the user's workgroup will be displayed. Such a list, however, will be displayed only if the user's computer *does* have network access. **B,** the Network Neighborhood window will not open, is incorrect because the computer will open the window and attempt to locate another computer on the network before the error message appears. **D** is incorrect because it suggests a "Network Access Not Configured" message will appear in the Network Neighborhood window. This is not a valid Windows message.

18. ☑ **B.** The purpose of mirroring a network server is to provide fault tolerance. A mirrored server is a type of backup server that contains the same data as the primary, or main, server. All data that is stored on the main server is also stored on the mirrored server. If the primary server fails, the mirrored server will simply take over, and no data will be lost.

    ☒ **A,** to speed up network activity, is incorrect because the time it takes to write all data twice can actually result in a slower network. **C,** to provide load balancing, is also incorrect. *Load balancing* refers to dividing tasks up equally among servers so that one server is not doing all the work. However, in a mirrored server, all work is being done twice. The mirrored server doesn't take any of the workload off the primary server. **D,** to increase bandwidth, is incorrect because keeping a duplicate copy of server data is unrelated to the speed at which computers can communicate with one another.

19. ☑ **C.** Clustering provides load balancing. In clustering, data is split up and saved on two or more servers so that if one server fails, the other(s) can continue to provide files and services. Because the workload is divided among servers, clustering also provides load balancing.

    ☒ **A,** mirroring, is incorrect. Although mirroring does provide fault tolerance, it works by writing all data twice—once to the primary server and once to the backup, or mirrored, server. Each server must therefore do a full share of work. **B,** tape backup, is also incorrect. Creating scheduled tape backups of server data provides fault tolerance but does not take any of the server's regular workload. Therefore, this method does not provide load balancing. For these reasons, **D,** which suggests that all methods provide load balancing, is incorrect.

20. ☑ **B.** The hub might be causing excess network traffic. When a computer on a hub transmits data, the data is received by the hub, then retransmitted to all other computers on the network. This is called *broadcasting*, and it can result in excessive network traffic. Since your company is growing, it is likely that there are more computers on the network, so the hub is generating even more unnecessary traffic than before.

    ☒ **A,** the hub might not support 100Mbps, is incorrect. If the hub supports a slower speed, it will result in slower network activity. However, the problem has been worsening gradually over time. If the hub did not support 100Mbps, it would have caused slow network traffic from the beginning, not gradually over the period of a month. **C** is incorrect because it states that the hub might be unable to find all the computers on the network. The hub does not "look" for computers; it simply retransmits data to all network cables that are attached to a hub port. The hub itself does not read the destination address on data packets, so it does not need to find the network's computers. **D** is incorrect because it suggests that the hub cannot be responsible for the network slowdown. While the hub *might* not be the cause, it is certainly a likely candidate.

LAB ANSWER

The simplest option to implement in this case is 10BaseT. The existing topology can be used, and because CAT3 cables support up to 16Mbps, the existing cables can be used as well. However, the NICs will have to be replaced, and the network's MAU will have to be replaced with a hub. This network will run at 10Mbps, and cable lengths will be limited to 100 meters.

The network could also be converted to 10Base2 or 10Base5. The advantage to this conversion is longer cable lengths (185 meters and 500 meters, respectively). However, to implement either of these options, the NICs must be replaced, and the cable must be changed from CAT5 to coaxial. Furthermore, these networks will require 50-ohm terminators, and the topology must be changed from star to bus. This option is not recommended because it requires much more work and expense than 10BaseT but will provide the same speed (10Mbps).

If the network is converted to 10BaseF, the network will run at 10Mbps and support cable lengths up to 2000 meters. The existing topology (star) can be used, but the cables will have to be replaced with fiber-optic, and the MAU will have to be replaced with a hub. Again, this option is not recommended, because it requires more effort than 10BaseT but will still provide only 10Mbps access.

If the customer wants an even faster network, the 100BaseTX or 100BaseT4 standards can be implemented. Like 10BaseT, this requires the replacement of the Token Ring NICs with Ethernet NICs, and the MAU must be replaced with a hub. Although the existing topology (star) can be used, the CAT3 cables will not support the new speed. In this case, they should be upgraded from CAT3 to CAT5.

Another 100Mbps option is the 100BaseFX standard. The existing topology can be used, but again, the MAU and NICs must be replaced. Like the 100BaseTX or 100BaseT4, the 100BaseFX requires the replacement of the network cables—in this case, to fiber-optic. This type of network requires no more effort than the 100BaseTX or 100BaseT4 but is likely to cost more, since fiber-optic cabling is significantly more expensive than twisted-pair. However, the network will be less susceptible to interference and will support cable lengths over 400 meters.

CORE HARDWARE/OPERATING SYSTEM EXAMS

Part II

A+ Operating Systems Technologies

8

Operating System Fundamentals

The remainder of this book is focused on the A+ Operating System Technologies exam. This exam tests your knowledge of Windows 9*x*, Windows NT 4, Windows 2000, and Windows XP as they relate to installation, configuration, troubleshooting, and networking procedures. This chapter describes the basics of these OSes, including their functions, main characteristics, system files, and file, disk management, and utilities.

CERTIFICATION OBJECTIVE 8.01

Operating System Functions and the Windows Family

This section will focus on a brief history of the Windows environment and describe the major differences between the Windows 9*x* family and the Windows NT/2000/XP family of operating systems.

A Brief History of Windows

Microsoft introduced its first Windows-based operating system in the early 1980s. The operating concept was to free users from having to memorize increasingly complicated commands and to provide a graphical interface to systems that had been text oriented. An additional objective was to continue to support text-based programs until users had made the shift to the new *graphical user interface* (GUI). The early releases of Windows, while moderately successful, were not widely accepted until Microsoft introduced Windows for Workgroups (WFWG) in the early 1990s. WFWG offered the advantages of a windows-based environment and added networking as a core component of the operating system. Sales of WFWG were high, but the GUI, while usable, left much to be desired.

Microsoft introduced Windows 95 in August 1995. This product was released with such a fanfare that people were standing in line at computer stores to buy it. Windows 95 included a new and more modern interface, improved stability, and added enhanced functionality to desktops. Windows 95 was soon upgraded to Windows 98, and finally Windows Me. These three products are known collectively as Windows 9*x*; they were desktop operating systems that worked well for most home users and many business users.

Microsoft recognized that business, corporate, and government users had a different set of needs than home users, so they created an operating system designed for higher-power computers that provided increased security and better networking than the previous Windows operating systems. Windows NT Server was born because Microsoft also recognized that the server market was growing and needed an operating system that would support large and busy servers. The first release of Windows NT occurred in 1993 with Windows NT 3.1.

Market acceptance of Windows NT 3.1 was not as high as Microsoft anticipated, but it did offer many technological advantages over Windows 3.1 because Windows NT could take advantage of the higher-speed microprocessors and larger disk storage capabilities that were becoming available.

In 1994, Microsoft simultaneously released Windows NT 3.5 Workstation and Server to improve the performance and add features to the operating system. In 1995, Microsoft released Windows 3.51, an update of Windows 3.5, for both workstations and servers, which was considered by many the first stable version of Windows NT. It offered enhanced networking and improved security, and it seemed able to run with a minimum of administrative intervention. Windows NT 4 Workstation and Server products were released in 1996, and Windows 2000 Workstation and Server were released in April of 2000 and get their origins from Windows NT.

As you can see from this brief history lesson, Windows had two significant operating systems that were independently evolving, which created problems for customers and businesses. Microsoft recognized this problem and decided to roll all of its desktop operating systems into one. In 2001, Microsoft consolidated the two disparate desktop environments into Windows XP: Windows XP Home Edition replaces the Windows 9x family, and Windows XP Professional Edition replaces the Windows NT family. This allows for a single development group to take responsibility for the entire operating systems line for desktop systems. Microsoft also recently announced and started shipping Windows Server 2003, which is intended to replace the Windows 2000 Server product line.

Microsoft once again appears to be diverging desktop and server products with the release of Windows Server 2003. Windows 2003, while still built around the Windows 2000/XP kernel is optimized for server applications more than earlier server products.

Major Operating System Components

The purpose of an operating system (OS) is to control all of the interactions between the various systems components, human interactions with the computer, and network operations for the computer system. This is accomplished by building an increasingly complicated set of layers between the lowest level of a computer system (the hardware) and the highest levels (user interaction). From a user perspective, this means that the user either points, types, or displays data using a device under the control of the operating system.

The OS is also responsible for managing the computer's files in an organized manner. The OS keeps track of the functions of particular files and calls or runs those files when they are needed. Furthermore, the OS is responsible for maintaining file associations so that files are launched in the proper applications.

Additionally, the OS is responsible for managing the computer's disks. That is, the OS keeps track of which disk is associated with a particular drive letter. The OS is also responsible for creating and using the disk's cluster, file structures, and file system.

Common Windows Components

This section discusses the primary components of the operating system that you will need for the A+ exam. This includes the graphical user interface (GUI), the Registry, virtual memory, and file systems.

Graphical User Interface

Windows 9*x*, NT 4, 2000, and XP provide a graphical user interface (GUI) that the user can navigate using either a mouse or keyboard. These operating systems have more or less adopted a common interface that uses the concept of a desktop on the computer system. This allows for easy access to the commonly used files and programs using a mouse for point and click operations. The main Windows screen is called the *desktop* because it is intended to resemble an actual desk. The Windows 9*x* GUI is shown in Figure 8-1.

FIGURE 8-1

The Windows 9*x* desktop

As you read through this chapter, notice how similar the user interface is between the operating systems we will be discussing. Most of the user interface has remained largely unchanged for desktop users since Windows 95. The locations of key utilities, how they function, and the underlying approach to the operating system has changed dramatically, but the GUI has largely only been enhanced.

The desktop contains several graphics, called *icons*. These icons represent applications, folders, or navigation tools. Applications and folders can be launched or opened by double-clicking the appropriate icon.

The *taskbar*, typically located at the bottom of the desktop, contains the Start menu, a button for each running application, and the time of day. You can switch between open applications by clicking the appropriate taskbar button. Depending on its configuration, the taskbar can also contain device status meters and buttons for launching applications. The Start menu, shown in Figure 8-2, provides access to Windows Help, configuration options, and most of the computer's applications.

The Windows environment also provides *shortcut menus* that, when enabled, provide you with quick access to task-specific features. For example, the desktop's shortcut menu includes options for arranging icons, creating new files and folders,

FIGURE 8-2

The Windows XP Start menu and taskbar

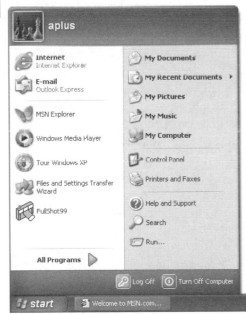

and configuring the appearance of the desktop itself. The taskbar's shortcut menu provides you with a list of tasks and configuration options related to the taskbar.

You can also create shortcuts on the desktop by right-clicking the program, file, or icon and choosing Create Shortcut. You can then either move or copy and paste the shortcut on your desktop or Start menu.

The Registry

The Registry is a database-oriented environment that Microsoft introduced in Windows 95 to make the task of tracking configuration, applications settings, and other system information easier to maintain. The Registry is a large database that exists on all Windows 9x systems and Windows NT systems since Windows NT 4. The Registry keeps track of all settings, user and applications configurations, and other information necessary for the system to function effectively.

The Registry interfaces with setup, hardware-oriented programs, administrative tools, device drivers, and the operating system itself. In a nutshell, the Registry is the central repository for all information about the system, as detailed in Figure 8-3. The Registry is read from and written to when the system starts up, when devices are installed, when applications are installed, and when programs are executed. Information such as your desktop preferences, browser configuration, and almost everything else relevant to your system is stored in the Registry.

Windows 9x stores Registry information in the system.dat and user.dat files. In Windows 2000 and XP, the Registry is a set of files that typically exist in the system32/config directory of the Windows directory.

To make the Registry easier to navigate, it is broken into subsets of data called keys. The Registry keys are accessed either by the program Regedit in Windows 9x or Regedt32 in Windows NT and 2000.

The Windows XP Registry editor is Regedit. Regedit appears is similar in function to earlier Registry editors but is a more comprehensive tool. Figure 8-4 shows the five main keys of the Registry in a Windows 2000 system. The Registry editor is not a program listed on the applications shortcuts in a Windows system and must be run

FIGURE 8-3

The Registry and its interfaces to the system

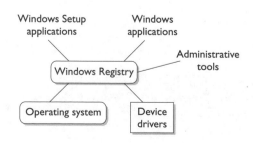

FIGURE 8-4

The Registry keys
in a Windows
2000 system

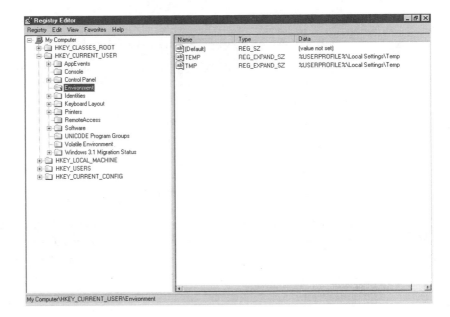

separately using the Run command. In Windows XP Regedt32 is a small program
that runs the Regedit program and all registry changes are made with Regedit.

There are thousands of key entries contained in the Registry, and each one is
significant to some aspect of the system or an application. You should not edit the
Registry unless you are certain of the consequences of the change. Numerous books,
websites, and technical articles are published on the Registry, and it is without a
doubt the most complicated areas of configuration for Windows systems. Most of the
changes that occur in the Registry are done using the Control Panel. The Registry
editor should only be used when you have no other option available.

The Registry is broken into five keys. These keys are collectively called the root
key and the five areas listed next:

```
HKEY_LOCAL_MACHINE
HKEY_CURRENT_USER
HKEY_USERS
HKEY_CLASSES_ROOT
HKEY_CURRENT_CONFIG
```

- **HKEY_CURRENT_USER**   Contains the configuration information for the
  currently logged on user. This key contains information about user's folders,
  Control Panel settings, and screen colors and wallpaper settings. This is also
  referred to as a user's profile.

- HKEY_USERS   Contains all of the user profiles on the computer. The HKEY_CURRENT_USER key is a subset of the HKEY_USERS key.
- HKEY_LOCAL_MACHINE   Contains all of the configuration information that is unique or particular to the computer.
- HKEY_CLASSES_ROOT   Is a subset of HKEY_LOCAL_MACHINE and stores information related to applications, Windows Explorer, and settings.
- HKEY_CURRENT_CONFIG   Contains information that is used for startup.

Each of these keys can contain thousands of values that can be individually altered to troubleshoot or configure settings on your computer.

on the

job

Great places to get additional information on the Registry are the Microsoft website (www.microsoft.com) *and the WinGuides site* (www.winguides.com). *Do not use the Registry editor unless absolutely no alternative exists. Improperly altering Registry keys can render your system inoperable. Virtually all administrative applications handle Registry key management for you.*

Virtual Memory

Larger operating systems such as the Windows family usually require more memory than is physically installed on the computer. *Virtual memory* implementations allow for a portion of the disk to be accessed as memory. This allows extremely large files and applications to be loaded into memory and pulled in from virtual memory when needed, which improves system performance by not requiring large programs to be broken down into smaller sections and individually loaded. When needed information is *swapped* in and out of disk in pages or blocks of memory. From the disk drive.

Virtual memory makes it possible for Windows OSes to support *multitasking* applications, which means the operating system can run more than one application or utility at once. This feature is very handy if you are using information from one application to create a file in another. As you can see in Figure 8-5, the taskbar shows that the computer is running Microsoft Notepad and Internet Explorer. Users can switch back and forth between these applications and work on more than one file at a time, improving productivity. This has become the standard way of operation for most computer users.

Virtual memory environments run slower than purely real memory environments, but it does allow multitasking to be viable. Almost all modern operating systems extensively use virtual memory to enhance usability of the system. In most cases, the operating system will calculate and allocate the optimal amount of disk used for virtual memory.

FullShot99

Windows XP
desktop showing
Microsoft
Notepad and
Internet Explorer
loaded

Recycle Bin

Windows Media
Player

Internet
Explorer

File Systems

Windows operating systems use a hierarchical storage method based on folders and files. Files are individual programs or data that is stored on disk. Folders are an organizational tool that groups files together based on criteria established by the user or the operating system. Figure 8-6 uses Windows Explorer to show a sample of a Windows XP file system.

The file system can be accessed either on the desktop or by using file management tools provided by the operating systems. These are covered in more detail in the Disk Management section of this chapter. File systems are established when the operating system or a new disk is installed on a computer system. There are a number of different file system implementations that are described in the "Disk Management" section of this chapter.

Windows OSes use My Computer and Windows Explorer as the preferred method by Microsoft to view, move, rename, copy, or delete files and folders. When files are deleted, they are placed in the Recycle Bin by default. Files are not actually deleted from the system, however; they can be recovered from the Recycle Bin until you

Windows XP
Explorer viewing
the system disk

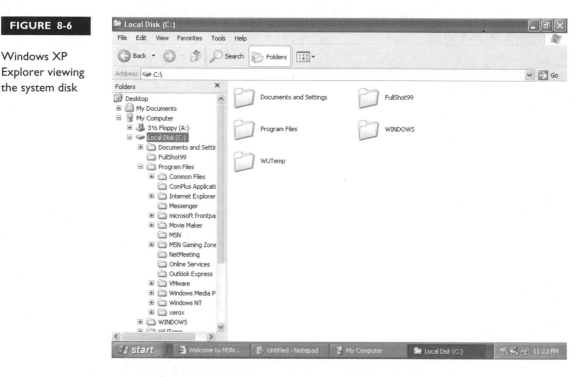

empty it. The Recycle Bin configuration can be altered by the Properties tab, where you can specify the percentage of the disk to be allocated to the Recycle Bin; the default is 10 percent. If this quota is exceeded, old files in the Recycle Bin will be overwritten to keep the Recycle Bin from growing too large. You can bypass the Recycle Bin by pressing the Shift key when you delete a file; this permanently removes the file without placing it in the Recycle Bin first. If you delete a file from removable media, it will be deleted; it will not be moved to the Recycle Bin.

Contrasts Between Windows 9x, Windows NT, 2000, and Windows XP

The main difference between the Windows 9x and Windows NT/2000/XP OSes is in their configuration and internal operation. Windows 9x was designed for smaller computers and networks and does not support the large-scale security models used in many large businesses. Windows XP Home Edition does not support large security models either and replaces the Windows 9x family of products. Windows NT, 2000 and Windows XP Professional do support larger security models, improved security and improved technologies first introduced in Windows NT. In fact, this is the major difference between Windows XP Home and Professional, as Windows XP Professional includes all of the features of Windows XP Home.

Windows 2000 Professional was intended for business use, not for home use. It supports business hardware, uses a great amount of computer resources, and is quite expensive. Microsoft released a 2000 version of the Windows 9x line for home users called Windows Millennium (Windows Me); Windows Me was replaced by Windows XP Home, while Windows 2000 Professional and Windows NT 4 Professional were replaced by Windows XP Professional. The 2003 CompTIA test standard introduced Windows XP to the exam.

Windows 9x

Windows 9x systems are smaller desktop systems that are still a viable choice for many home and small office users, despite Microsoft's attempt at making it obsolete. This is primarily because it is simple, well understood, and for the most, part reliable. Windows 9x does not provide much security, use large memory well, or manage large disks as effectively as Windows NT, 2000, or XP, but it does include some features that have been adopted by the newer operating systems such as Plug and Play, USB support, enhanced multimedia, and video gaming. Until the release of Windows XP Home edition, virtually all home users used Windows 9x computer systems. These systems will probably be around for many years to come.

The last version of Windows 9x to be released was Windows Me, which included enhanced multimedia and attempted to make configuration, installation, and support easier for technical professionals. Some people raved about Windows Me, while some ranted; Windows Me did not receive particularly positive reviews in the market and was viewed as a stopgap effort by Microsoft until Windows XP was released.

Windows NT 4

Windows NT 4 provides a Windows GUI similar to Windows 9x systems, but is much more reliable and robust. The Windows NT 4 operating system supports full network capabilities, high security, and efficient memory and disk management tools. However, Windows NT 4 does not support USB or Plug-and-Play capabilities. Windows NT 4 Server and Workstation is most commonly used for business systems, software development, and server products. Windows NT 4 is the forerunner of Windows 2000 and was built on the strong capabilities developed in earlier Windows NT environments.

Windows 2000

The Windows 2000 Professional and Server operating systems were built on the stable environment that existed with Windows NT and they are a significant enhancement to Windows NT 4. In addition to supporting USB and Plug-and-Play capabilities, Windows 2000 addressed many of the concerns that users of Windows NT 4 had about graphical devices, gaming, and multimedia. Windows 2000 also introduced a new storage structure that allowed for large disks to be installed and used effectively. Windows 2000 systems generally run faster than Windows NT 4 systems and take fuller advantage of the newer high-speed processors. Multimedia support is better than Windows NT 4, but it still not as good as Windows 9x systems.

Windows XP

Windows XP is now the standard operating system shipped on PC systems. It supports the best features of Windows 2000/NT 4 and Windows 9x and is intended to be the single replacement for all those systems. Windows XP added enhanced multimedia, large networking support, security, and all of the features used by home users on Windows 9x systems. In Exercise 8-1, you can verify the type of operating system installed on your computer system.

EXERCISE 8-1

Determining the Operating System Type

1. Right-click the My Computer icon.

2. Select Properties from the shortcut menu that appears. The System Properties dialog box will appear.

3. Ensure that the General tab is displayed. The OS version and edition are listed under System.

CERTIFICATION OBJECTIVE 8.02

Major Operating Systems Interfaces

This section discusses the interfaces used by the operating systems you will encounter on the A+ exam. While they are similar between systems, there are some differences in appearance and function that you will need to explore before you take the test.

Navigating Through Windows

Windows 9*x*, 2000, and XP allow you to navigate through files and folders using either Windows Explorer or My Computer. Each provides the same management tools; the only difference is their display methods. These two methods are provided to accommodate user preferences.

The term *navigation* refers to your ability to find files and ensure that they are saved in the proper locations, which will determine your ability to find them later.

Windows Explorer

Windows Explorer displays the drive and folder structure in the left pane and the selected folder's (or drive's) contents on the right; you can display the contents of a folder by clicking the folder's icon. As you can see in Figure 8-7, the Mike's Document folder contains two subfolders and two files.

To view the contents of a subfolder, click the + sign to the left of the main folder. The subfolders will be displayed in the folder structure on the left. You can now view the contents of these subfolders by clicking them.

FIGURE 8-7

Explorer on a Windows XP system

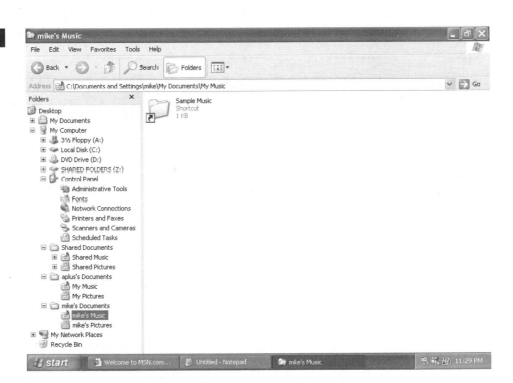

My Computer

When you navigate using My Computer, a folder's contents are displayed in a window by themselves. To start using My Computer, double-click the My Computer icon on the desktop. A window similar to the one shown in Figure 8-8 will appear. This window lists the system's drives as well as commonly used utilities such as the Control Panel.

To view a drive's contents, double-click its icon. To access the My Documents folder, you must first double-click the C: drive icon. The contents of the C: drive will be displayed, as shown in Figure 8-9. Your computer might be configured to either open a new window to display these contents or replace the previous My Computer window with the new contents.

From here, you can open the My Documents folder by double-clicking it. Within that window, double-click the My Pictures folder, and the contents of My Pictures will be displayed. To return to a previous window or folder, click the Back button. In this case, the contents of the My Documents folder will be redisplayed. If you click the Back button again, the contents of the C: drive will be redisplayed.

Management Tools

Whether you use Windows Explorer or My Computer, you can manage files and folders using the same procedures. As you already know, when you double-click a folder, it opens.

FIGURE 8-8

My Computer showing drives and Control Panel on a Windows 2000 system

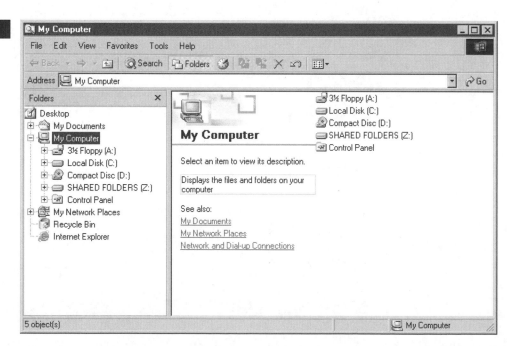

FIGURE 8-9

The Explorer showing the system disk on a Windows 9x system

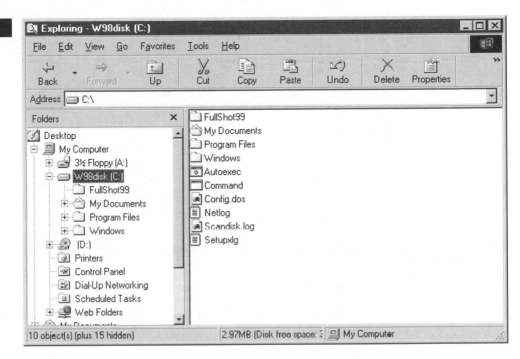

When you double-click a file, it is activated. If it is an executable file, that program will be launched. If you double-click an application's file, the file will be opened within the host application. For example, if you double-click a Microsoft Word document icon, Microsoft Word will be launched and it will open the selected document.

To delete a file, select it by clicking it, and press the DELETE key on the keyboard. Because this is easy to do by accident, Windows will ask you to confirm the deletion. You can also delete a file by right-clicking it, then selecting Delete from the shortcut menu that appears. Files and folders that are deleted from the hard drive will be placed in the Recycle Bin. They will stay there until they are either restored to their original locations or removed permanently when you empty the Recycle Bin. If you delete a hidden, read-only, or system file, Windows will ask you to confirm again. Note that you cannot delete a file that is currently in use or that you do not have proper permissions to access.

on the **Job**

If you press the SHIFT key while pressing the DELETE key, the file will be permanently deleted from the system.

You can rename a file or folder by clicking its icon, then clicking its name. This is two separate clicks, not a double-click. Next, type the new name and either click in a neutral area on the screen or press the ENTER key on the keyboard. You can also rename a file or folder by right-clicking and selecting Rename from the file's shortcut menu. You cannot rename a file that is currently in use. Furthermore, Windows will warn you if you are about to give the file an improper name (naming conventions are described later in the chapter). Note that you cannot give a file a blank name (one with no characters), and you can't give a file the same name as another file in the same location.

Windows also lets you move and copy files from one location to another. To move a file, you must be able to see both the file itself and the destination folder or drive. Use your mouse to click and drag the file to the new location. Hold the CTRL key on the keyboard while you do this to copy the file. Again, as with other commands, you cannot move or copy a file that is in use.

on the
Job

Because it is so easy to rename, delete, or move files and folders, Windows contains lots of safeguards, such as confirmation screens and an Undo feature on the desktop shortcut menu.

You can view the details of any file or folder by selecting Properties from its shortcut menu. As shown in Figure 8-10, a file's Properties window displays the type,

FIGURE 8-10

File properties being displayed on a Windows XP system

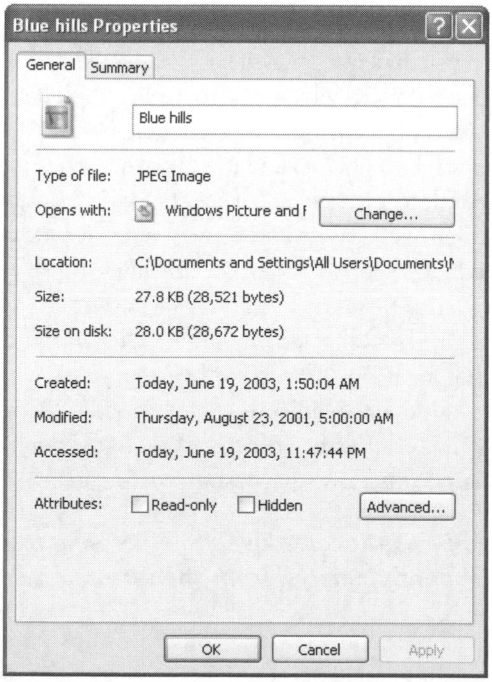

Blue hills Properties

General | Summary

Blue hills

Type of file: JPEG Image
Opens with: Windows Picture and F   [Change...]

Location: C:\Documents and Settings\All Users\Documents\N
Size: 27.8 KB (28,521 bytes)
Size on disk: 28.0 KB (28,672 bytes)

Created: Today, June 19, 2003, 1:50:04 AM
Modified: Thursday, August 23, 2001, 5:00:00 AM
Accessed: Today, June 19, 2003, 11:47:44 PM

Attributes: ☐ Read-only ☐ Hidden   [Advanced...]

[OK] [Cancel] [Apply]

full name, location, and size of the file, as well as the creation, last modification, and last access dates. You can also use this window to view or apply file attributes. File attributes are discussed in more detail in the next section.

Control Panel

The Windows 9x Control Panel provides you with a safe way to configure many of the system's configuration settings. To access the Control Panel, double-click My Computer, then double-click Control Panel, or select Start | Settings | Control Panel. A typical Control Panel includes applets for configuring the keyboard, the mouse, and network and date/time settings, among other things. To open an applet, double-click its icon, make the necessary changes, then click OK. The Registry will be automatically and safely updated with your changes.

on the **ⓘ o b**

To edit the Registry directly, use the Registry Editor. To edit the Registry safely, use the Control Panel.

Network Neighborhood/My Network Places

Network Neighborhood and My Network Places are ways to connect, explore, or manage network connections in Windows systems. This allows for easy visual management of the various network connections that are common in network pc systems. Figure 8-11 displays the My Network Places on a Windows XP system.

Device Manager

The Windows 9x Device Manager provides you with a single location to view and modify hardware configurations. To access the Windows 9x Device Manager, right-click My Computer, then select Properties, and the System Properties dialog box will open.

Windows XP offers the same functionality as Windows 9x with a slightly different look. Figure 8-12 shows the System Properties dialog box for a Windows XP system. You can select any of the tabs to get to the various configuration options available in this dialog box.

All hardware devices attached to the system are categorized and listed on the Device Manager tab. To view a device, double-click its device category. You can view a device's system resource configuration by selecting it, then clicking Properties. The device's IRQ, I/O address, and/or DMA allocation will be displayed. You can also view, remove, or reload the device's driver.

If you suspect a hardware configuration problem, you can use the Device Manager to determine its cause. Devices that are not recognized by Windows or that are improperly configured will be marked with a warning symbol (a yellow question

FIGURE 8-11

FIGURE 8-11

My Network
Places on a
Windows XP
system

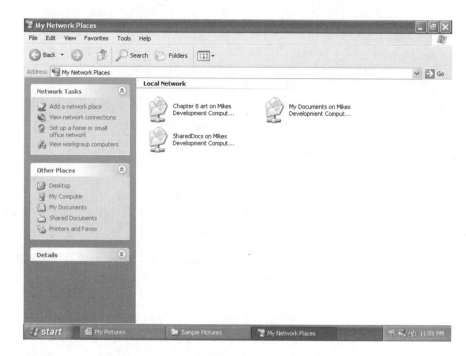

mark and/or a yellow exclamation point). For example, you can see this warning
symbol next to a malfunctioning device on a Windows 98 system in Figure 8-13.

FIGURE 8-12

Systems
Properties dialog
box on a
Windows XP
system

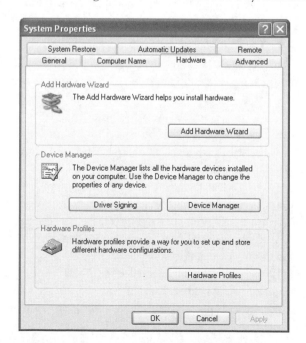

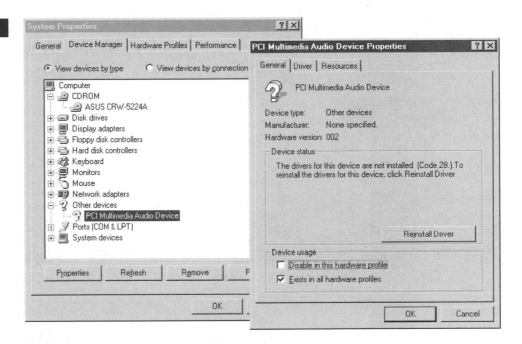

FIGURE 8-13

Device Manager
showing a
warning symbol
next to the
sound card on
this system

CERTIFICATION OBJECTIVE 8.03

System Files

System files are files that the OS requires in order to function properly. Each system file
has a function that alters, manages, or runs part of the OS or other system files. Contrast
this with a data or *application file,* such as a saved game, document, or image file. The
existence of an application file will not alter the behavior of the OS. You can change,
create, or delete a nonsystem file without affecting the performance of the computer.

In most cases, a deleted, missing, or corrupt system file will result in an improperly
functioning OS feature or an OS that will not function at all. A thorough knowledge of
the Windows OS system files and their functions will allow you to pinpoint and resolve
OS problems based on the behavior of the computer or on the error messages you receive.

Several types of system files are discussed in the following subsections. First, the
system files specific to Windows 9*x* are discussed, followed by system files specific to
Windows NT, 2000, and XP. Memory management files are described, as are command-
line interface files.

Many of the OS system files are location-dependent. That is, they will not be
loaded and properly executed if they are not in a specific location. For this reason,
and to keep them from being accidentally deleted, most system files are *hidden.* This

means that they will not be displayed in the My Computer or Windows Explorer navigation windows. To view system files in 9x, follow the steps in Exercise 8-2; to view them in XP, follow the steps in Exercise 8-3.

EXERCISE 8-2

Viewing System Files in Windows 9x

1. Double-click the My Computer icon.
2. Click the View menu and select Folder Options.
3. Select the View tab.
4. Under Hidden Files, select the Show All Files option.
5. Click OK. All files that are listed as system and/or hidden files will now appear, but hidden files will be grayed out to indicate their status.

EXERCISE 8-3

Viewing System Files in Windows XP

1. Double-click the My Computer icon.
2. Click the Tools menu and select Folder Options.
3. Select the View tab.
4. Under Hidden Files, select the Show All Files option.
5. Unclick the Hide Protected Operating Systems box.
6. Click OK. All files that are listed as system and/or hidden files will now appear, but hidden files will be grayed out to indicate their status.

Windows 9x Specific Files

Some of the Windows 9x system files discussed here are required to properly boot the computer and run the OS. Others exist as *legacy files*, to provide backward compatibility

e**x**a**m**

watch

Make sure that you are familiar with the role of all these files as well as whether they are required and where they are located.

with older applications. There are hundreds of system files in the Windows 9*x* OS, but you don't need to be familiar with all of them. The ones that tend to crop up in installation and troubleshooting procedures are the boot files and configuration files, explained in the following sections. Also discussed here are Windows 9*x* utilities for configuring or managing system files.

IO.SYS

The IO.SYS file is responsible for organizing and conducting the early stages of the Windows 9*x* boot process. It is responsible for finding and loading other system files and checking to ensure that those files contain the proper settings. IO.SYS also provides the OS with details about the hardware installed in the computer. IO.SYS is a required system file; its role in the boot process is described in more detail in Chapter 9. To function properly, IO.SYS must be located on the root directory (for example, C:).

FROM THE CLASSROOM

A Legacy of Problems

Windows 9*x* and NT are both 32-bit OSes, meaning that the OS code can be accessed 32 bits at a time. Applications written for these OSes are also 32-bit, which means they use memory better, access the hardware differently, and cause fewer lock-ups than older, 16-bit applications.

However, many users want to be able to run 16-bit applications with newer OSes. For this reason, Windows 9*x* includes legacy configuration files so that these older applications can be used. For example, an application written for Windows 3.1 was probably designed to access the SYSTEM.INI

configuration file and knows nothing about the Windows Registry. Without the SYSTEM.INI file, the application could not run in Windows 9*x*.

Unfortunately, these older programs can still cause problems in newer OSes, such as device hogging and computer lockups. However, Windows 9*x* is the home user's OS, and most home users cannot afford to upgrade their software every time they upgrade the OS. The NT lineup, on the other hand, is designed for business use. Windows 2000 provides much less support for legacy applications, and it does not use the older configuration files found in Windows 9*x*.

MSDOS.SYS

In Windows 9*x*, the MSDOS.SYS file contains startup configuration parameters, such as which OS to use by default if more than one OS is installed on the system (a multiboot configuration). This file must be located in the root directory. MSDOS.SYS also contains the location of required boot files, the default boot mode, and the presence and display time for the Windows startup screen (the one that says "Starting Windows"). The MSDOS.SYS file's role in system startup is explained in more detail in Chapter 9.

AUTOEXEC.BAT

The AUTOEXEC.BAT file, found in the root directory, is used in conjunction with the CONFIG.SYS file and contains application or environment settings, such as color settings or the command to automatically launch a particular application. This file is included in Windows 9*x* for backward compatibility.

COMMAND.COM

COMMAND.COM is the DOS command processor. When DOS is started or the DOS emulator in a Windows system is launched, the COMMAND.COM file runs and allows you access to all command-line programs and settings.

CONFIG.SYS

The CONFIG.SYS file, originally used in MS-DOS, is even older than the WIN.INI and SYSTEM.INI files. It loads device drivers and configure memory usage. CONFIG.SYS is included in Windows 9*x* to retain backward compatibility with devices and applications that can run properly only if they are installed using the CONFIG.SYS file. CONFIG.SYS must be located in the root directory to be properly processed.

Memory Management Files

The first PCs could access only 1MB of memory, which was sufficient for most of the applications of that time. However, technology improved and the 1MB limit became a hindrance as applications were developed that required more than the allotted memory space. Several memory management utilities were developed to allow these older computers to access more memory, and some of these utilities are still used today. These files, as well as their common implementations, are described here.

Conventional Memory   The first 640KB of RAM have traditionally been used for running applications and the OS itself (DOS). This memory area was originally called *system memory*. The term system memory now refers to all the memory available in the system.

Upper Memory   The remaining 384KB of memory were set aside (reserved) for ROM BIOS, and the RAM and ROM that was installed on devices. Applications could not access this memory space even if it wasn't being entirely used by the system. This memory space was initially termed *reserved memory*. It was very common for devices such as video adapters to use a portion of this memory for its purposes.

Extended and High Memory   When the Lotus 1-2-3 spreadsheet application was released, users often found that it required more than 640KB of memory. To resolve the 1MB memory barrier problem, Lotus, Intel, and Microsoft joined forces and developed the LIM memory specification. In this specification, system memory was renamed *conventional memory* and reserved memory was renamed *upper memory*.

More important, however, was the development of a memory manager that allowed applications to use memory over 1MB (called *extended memory*). This manager, a file called HIMEM.SYS, could also load the OS into the first 64KB of extended memory, an area called the *high memory area (HMA)*.

To use the extended memory specification (XMS), HIMEM.SYS must be referenced in the CONFIG.SYS file, as shown here:

```
DEVICE=C:\DOS\HIMEM.SYS
DOS=HIGH
```

The first line instructs the computer to locate and initialize the HIMEM.SYS file, thus enabling the extended memory area. The second line loads DOS into the high memory area (HMA).

Expanded Memory   At the time of the LIM specification release, many users still had older Intel 8088 and 80286 computers, which, because of the small memory address bus, could not be made to access memory over 1MB. For these individuals, the LIM specification included an expanded memory manager that could "trick" the processor into using extended memory. In the 80386 processor, a file called EMM386 .EXE is able to swap pages of memory between extended memory and upper memory.

In other words, when the processor requests data that is located in extended memory, EMM386.EXE retrieves the information and then places it in upper memory, which is accessible to the processor. This process is also known as *paging*.

The EMM386 file will not work unless the HIMEM.SYS file is loaded.

EMM386.EXE also enables programs to use upper memory as system memory. In other words, upper memory is no longer reserved for device drivers; it can be accessed by regular applications. To enable the expanded memory specification (EMS), the EMM386.EXE file must be referenced in CONFIG.SYS, as shown here:

```
DEVICE=C:\DOS\HIMEM.SYS
DEVICE=C:\DOS\EMM386.EXE
DOS=HIGH,UMB
```

The last line instructs the computer to load as much DOS into high memory as it can and to load whatever is left over into upper memory blocks (UMB). The EMM386.EXE reference in the CONFIG.SYS file must come *after* the reference to HIMEM.SYS because expanded memory relies on the existence of the extended memory area.

Fortunately, Windows 9x, 2000, and XP are able to manage memory without the use of the memory managers described previously. That is, these Windows OSes can load any type of data (application, system, drivers) into any available memory blocks. However, Windows 9x retains the ability to use these files for backward compatibility with older applications and requires HIMEM.SYS during startup. Windows 2000 and XP has removed virtually all of backward compatibility for memory management and does not use these memory management files at all.

SCENARIO & SOLUTION

What is extended memory?	All memory above 1MB.
What is expanded memory?	A routine that swaps memory between extended and upper memory so that it may be accessed by the processor.
What is the function of HIMEM.SYS?	To enable access to extended memory and load DOS into high memory.
What is the function of EMM386.EXE?	To enable expanded memory and to use upper memory as though it were conventional memory.

WIN.COM

The last operation of the Windows 9x IO.SYS file is to locate and run WIN.COM. This file is responsible for conducting the remainder of the Windows 9x OS startup. WIN.COM is located in the WINDOWS folder, and its role in system startup is explained in more detail in Chapter 9.

WIN.INI

In older OSes, the WIN.INI file, rather than the USER.DAT file, stores application settings. Some older applications are designed to use the WIN.INI file and cannot even recognize the newer USER.DAT file. Without access to the WIN.INI file, these applications will not function properly, so Windows 9x includes WIN.INI for backward compatibility. Typical settings in the WIN.INI file include the registered fonts, icons, and display settings, such as colors and window border thickness. WIN.INI is located in the WINDOWS folder.

SYSTEM.INI

Like WIN.INI, SYSTEM.INI is located in the WINDOWS folder and is typically used in older (pre-Windows 95) OSes. It stores data about the system's hardware, such as device drivers and configuration settings. It is included in Windows 9x to allow older 16-bit applications to access the system's hardware.

SYSTEM.DAT

Most Windows 9x application, user, and hardware settings are stored in a large database called the Windows Registry. The Registry is composed of two files: USER.DAT and SYSTEM .DAT, which contains settings about the computer's hardware, such as drivers, resources, and configuration data. SYSTEM.DAT is so important to the function of Windows 9x that every time you shut down the computer, a backup copy of the file is made. This backup copy, called SYSTEM.DA0 (that's a zero, not the letter "O") will be used at startup if the original SYSTEM.DAT file is missing or corrupted. SYSTEM.DAT must be located in the WINDOWS folder.

SYSTEM.DAT and USER.DAT are Windows 9x Registry files and are the heart of the OS. The Registry for Windows 2000 and XP are a set of files, and each file is a hive of keys.

USER.DAT

The other half of the Windows Registry, USER.DAT, contains user-specific information such as installed applications, file associations, color settings, and passwords. Every user profile on the computer is represented individually in the USER.DAT file. Like the SYSTEM.DAT file, USER.DAT is located in the WINDOWS folder and is backed up each time the computer is properly shut down. The backup USER.DAT file is used if there is something wrong with the USER.DAT file.

Windows NT-Based Specific Files

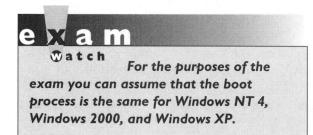

For the purposes of the exam you can assume that the boot process is the same for Windows NT 4, Windows 2000, and Windows XP.

Windows NT uses none of the same system files as Windows 9x; it does not support the same level of backward compatibility as Windows 9x. While it does use a Registry, it is completely different in function and layout, and SYSTEM.INI and WIN.INI are not present in Windows 2000. Windows 2000 has some utilities that were introduced in Windows 9x, such as the Control Panel and Windows Scripting Host. Other system files unique to Windows 2000 are described in the following subsections.

NTLDR

The function of the NTLDR file is similar to that of IO.SYS in Windows 9x: it coordinates the system's startup procedure and is responsible for locating and initializing other required startup files. NTLDR's role in the Windows 2000 startup process is explained in more detail in Chapter 9.

BOOT.INI

The BOOT.INI file is used by Windows NT if the computer contains more than one OS. This is referred to as a *dual-boot configuration*. When a dual-boot machine is started, you must select which OS to use. The BOOT.INI file is responsible for displaying the OS choices at startup. It also contains the location of each OS so that the computer knows where to look for the selected one. Once an OS has been selected and found, the function of BOOT.INI is complete.

NTDETECT.COM

NTDETECT.COM is also part of the Windows NT boot process. Once NTLDR is initialized, it finds and initializes the NTDETECT.COM file, which is responsible for gathering information about the hardware that currently exists in the system. This information is reported back to NTLDR, which writes the information in the Windows Registry.

NTBOOTDD.SYS

This file's only purpose is to allow Windows NT to boot from some SCSI devices if needed. If required, it is located and initialized by NTLDR.

NTUSER.DAT

The NTUSER.DAT file contains profile information about users in a Windows system. A profile is simply the settings that are used by Windows NT, 2000, and XP to load configuration settings when a user logs on. When the user successfully logs on, these become the settings in the HKEY_CURRENT_USER Registry key.

CERTIFICATION OBJECTIVE 8.03

Command-Line Functions and Utilities

Windows 9x includes a DOS command shell, which enables you to run commands from a DOS prompt. Additionally, Windows 9x includes a DOS mode, in which the computer can be restarted with DOS-only components.

To open a DOS shell, enter **COMMAND** on the Windows Run line. You can also run any of the DOS commands described in this section by entering them on the Windows Run line. A DOS shell will open automatically and run the command. To run in DOS mode, from the Windows 95 and 98 Start menu, select Shut Down, then Restart in MS-DOS Mode. Windows ME does not support this mode.

Windows NT, 2000, and XP call up a virtual DOS machine that runs under the operating system. These systems also have a 32-bit command-line interpreter that can be accessed using the CMD.EXE program. You can run this using the RUN command in the Start menu and entering **CMD**. However, Microsoft discourages the use of the DOS interpreter and prefers everything be done through graphical interfaces because the CMD.EXE and programs that run under it bypass many of the safeguards that are built into the Windows interface.

As a technician, you might be required to use DOS commands when troubleshooting a computer that won't load Windows properly, getting a hard drive ready for an OS, or loading an OS from a CD-ROM drive that isn't recognized by the BIOS. For this reason, we discuss common DOS commands and their uses here.

Command Syntax

To enter a DOS command, type the command and press ENTER. For example, to clear the screen, enter **CLS**. To view the OS version, type **VER**. Other commands require certain parameters. For example, when run by itself, the DIR command displays the contents of the *current* directory. By adding a parameter to the DIR command, you can display the contents of a different directory. The command that follows displays the contents of the GAMES directory:

```
DIR GAMES
```

The number of required parameters depends on the command itself. The COPY command, for instance, requires that you enter the command, the name of the file to copy, and the destination. The following command copies the RESUME document into the LETTERS directory, as long as the RESUME file and LETTERS directory are within your current location in the directory structure:

```
COPY RESUME LETTERS
```

Some commands have options that can be enabled by using switches. For example, when the DIR command is used, the /p switch can pause the listing after every full screen, and the /w switch can display the listing in wide format.

These commands are all case-insensitive, meaning that they can be entered in lowercase, uppercase, or a combination of the two. However, you must be careful to enter the appropriate spaces to differentiate between elements of the command: the only case in which the presence of a space doesn't matter is when you're entering a switch. For example, the DIR command can be entered to use the /p switch with or without a space:

```
DIR/p
DIR /p
```

When you enter a command improperly, you will receive a syntax error or an "Invalid switch" error. You can get help on the purpose, syntax, and available switches for any command by entering the command, followed by /?, as shown here:

```
C:\DOCUMENT\test>dir/?
Displays a list of files and subdirectories in a directory.
DIR [drive:][path][filename] [/A[[:]attributes]] [/B] [/C] [/D] [/L] [/N]
  [/O[[:]sortorder]] [/P] [/Q] [/S] [/T[[:]timefield]] [/W] [/X] [/4]
  [drive:][path][filename]            Specifies drive, directory, and/or files
to list.
  /A          Displays files with specified attributes.
  attributes  D  Directories                R  Read-only files
              H  Hidden files               A  Files ready for archiving
              S  System files              -  Prefix meaning not
  /B          Uses bare format (no heading information or summary).
```

```
/C          Display the thousand separator in file sizes.  This is the
            default.  Use /-C to disable display of separator.
/D          Same as wide but files are list sorted by column.
/L          Uses lowercase.
/N          New long list format where filenames are on the far right.
/O          List by files in sorted order.
sortorder   N  By name (alphabetic)      S  By size (smallest first)
            E  By extension (alphabetic)  D  By date/time (oldest first)
            G  Group directories first    -  Prefix to reverse order
/P          Pauses after each screenful of information.
/Q          Display the owner of the file.
/S          Displays files in specified directory and all subdirectories.
/T          Controls which time field displayed or used for sorting
timefield   C  Creation
            A  Last Access
            W  Last Written
/W          Uses wide list format.
/X          This displays the short names generated for non-8dot3 file
            names.  The format is that of /N with the short name inserted
            before the long name. If no short name is present, blanks are
            displayed in its place.
/4          Displays four digit years
Switches may be preset in the DIRCMD environment variable.  Override
preset switches by prefixing any switch with - (hyphen)--for example, /-W.
```

Internal and External Commands

DOS commands are all either internal or external. *Internal commands* are included in the COMMAND.COM file. This means that if you can access a DOS prompt, you are able to use these commands. CLS, DIR, COPY, and DELETE/DEL are all internal commands. *External commands* are not part of COMMAND.COM and are contained in separate files. For example, to execute the XCOPY command, you must have the file XCOPY.EXE.

DIR The DIR command displays a directory of a disk or directory. Examples of the DIR commands were given previously.

```
C:\WINDOWS\Desktop\mike>dir/w
 Volume in drive C is HP_PAVILION
 Volume Serial Number is 1A67-12E6
 Directory of C:\WINDOWS\Desktop\mike
[.]               [..]              MIKE1.TXT        [TEST1]          MIKE2.TXT
          2 file(s)            62 bytes
         '3 dir(s)       29,223.94 MB free
```

ATTRIB   With the ATTRIB command, which uses the file ATTRIB.EXE, you can view or modify a file's attributes. File attributes include hidden (h), archive (a), system (s), and read-only (r). These attributes affect your ability to modify or view the files. Attributes are explained in more detail in the "File Attributes" section later in the chapter.

To view a file's attributes, enter the ATTRIB command, followed by the filename. To add or remove a file's attribute, enter **ATTRIB**, a + or a – sign (which mean add or remove, respectively), the letter representing the appropriate attribute (*h, a, s,* or *r*), then the filename. In the following command, the read-only and hidden attributes are applied to a file called RECIPE:

```
ATTRIB +H +R RECIPE.DOC
```

VER   VER displays the current version of Windows:

```
C:\WINDOWS\Desktop\mike>ver/?
Displays the Windows version.
VER
C:\WINDOWS\Desktop\mike>ver
Windows 98 [Version 4.10.2222]
```

MEM   The MEM command displays memory allocation information. To view the used and available amounts of conventional, expanded, and extended memory, simply enter **MEM** at the command prompt.

You can use the /c (classify) switch to display memory use by application. That is, the switch will generate a report that lists each active application or driver and how much memory it is using. The /d (debug) switch is the most detailed and displays a block-by-block report of memory usage.

```
C:\WINDOWS\Desktop\mike>mem
Memory Type          Total        Used         Free
---------------    --------    --------     --------
Conventional          640K         68K         572K
Upper                 127K        127K          0K
Reserved               0K          0K           0K
Extended (XMS)     65,345K           ?      129,712K
---------------    --------    --------     --------
Total memory       66,112K           ?      130,284K
Total under 1 MB      767K        194K         572K
Largest executable program size         572K (586,064 bytes)
Largest free upper memory block          0K        (0 bytes)
MS-DOS is resident in the high memory area.
```

EDIT   DOS includes a text editor that allows you to create batch files or small documents. The editor is available in a file called EDIT.COM. When you enter the EDIT command, the text editor will open, allowing you to create, open, save, print, or search text files. This is a menu-driven application that is accessed using the keyboard in DOS mode or using the mouse in a DOS shell.

XCOPY   XCOPY is similar to the COPY command but allows you to copy entire directories and their files and subdirectories. The XCOPY command requires the presence of the XCOPY.EXE file. To use the XCOPY command, enter **XCOPY**, followed by the directory you want to copy, then the destination. There are several options for the XCOPY command, including /s, which copies all directories and subdirectories within the current directory, and /y, which overwrites existing files without prompting you for confirmation.

COPY   The COPY command makes copies of files. The format is fairly simple: copy *source destination*, where *source* is the location and name of the file to be copied, and *destination* is the new file name. The COPY command will return either a success or failure message. The following example illustrates a success:

```
C:\WINDOWS\Desktop\mike>copy mike1.txt mike2.txt
          1 file(s) copied
```

FORMAT   Recall that disks must be formatted before data can be stored on them. The DOS format command uses the FORMAT.COM file and is executed by entering **FORMAT**, followed by the appropriate drive letter. The FORMAT command is discussed in more detail later in this chapter, in the section entitled "Disk Management."

FDISK   Before a disk can be formatted, it must first be partitioned. The DOS tool for partitioning hard drives is the FDISK.EXE file. FDISK has been replaced in Windows by the disk administration tools located in the Control Panel. You should use these newer tools because they provide better interfaces, simplify the process, and have more safeguards, which are needed because a disk once partitioned loses all of its data.

SETVER   The SETVER command, supplied by the SETVER.EXE file, allows you to manually set the DOS version reported to a particular application. That is, older applications might not be able to recognize newer versions of DOS, but you can use the SETVER command to set the DOS to an older version. To use the command, enter **SETVER** followed by the application filename, followed by the DOS version number. For example, to inform the application Game that the DOS version is 6.22, use this command:

```
SETVER GAME.EXE 6.22
```

SCANREG   Windows 98 includes the utility SCANREG.EXE, which is a Registry backup utility. This utility runs in the Windows background and backs up the Registry each time the computer is started. To manually back up the Registry, run SCANREG /BACKUP from the Windows Run line. The Registry files will be saved in the Windows\Sysbckup folder by default. To use the Run command line, click the Start menu, then select Run. Enter the appropriate command (in this case, SCANREG) in the Open text field, then click OK.

To use a backed-up copy of the Registry, you must be running in MS-DOS mode. That is, start the computer from a DOS boot disk or select Shutdown and Restart in MS-DOS mode. At the DOS command prompt, enter the command **SCANREG/ RESTORE**. The last five backup copies of the Registry will be displayed. Select the appropriate copy.

MD/CD/RD   MD (for make directory) is the command-line command that makes a new directory anywhere on the disk. CD changes to a different directory than the one you're in. RD removes a directory if the directory is empty and contains no subdirectories. The formats for these commands are briefly shown.

The following command creates a subdirectory in the current directory called test:

```
C:\files> MD test
```

The following command changes your location or working directory to the subdirectory called test:

```
C:\files> CD test
C:\files\test>
```

The test subdirectory, if created as shown, would be a subdirectory of the current directory. CD allows you to quickly navigate from wherever you are to other locations on a disk. Two types of movement occur with CD, relative and absolute: relative movement is relative to where you currently are; Absolute moves you to a specified directory.

The following command moves you one directory up:

```
C:\files\documents> CD ..
C:\files>
```

This is an example of relative movement. For example, if you were in the directory c:\aplus\test, this command would move you to the c:\aplus directory.

The following command moves you to the root directory of the drive you are looking at:

```
C:\files> CD \
C:\>
```

This is an example of absolute movement. For example, if you were in the c:\files directory, this command would move you to the c:\ root directory.

Delete/Rename   The DEL or DELETE command deletes a file or set of files based upon criteria specified. To delete a file called aplus.doc, you would type in the following command:

```
C:\files> Del aplus.doc
C:\files>
```

This would remove the file aplus.doc from your current directory. If there is no file by that name in this directory, you will receive a message indicating the file has not been successfully removed. A new command prompt indicates the file was successfully deleted.

Deltree   The DELTREE command deletes an entire subdirectory and all of its files, as shown here:

```
C:\files\> deltree test
Delete directory "test" and all its subdirectories [yn] y
Deleting test ...
C:\files>
```

DELTREE requires a directory name to operate. In the example, if the test directory had multiple subdirectories, only the test directory would be deleted; the others would be left untouched.

Echo   The ECHO command allows the user to send messages to the screen when running a batch program, as shown here:

```
C:\files> echo hello there
Hello there
C:\files>
```

Set   The SET command allows for the display or modification of system variables. The following example lists the entire environment that DOS uses for operation:

```
C:\WINDOWS\Desktop\mike>set
TMP=c:\windows\TEMP
PROMPT=$p$g
winbootdir=C:\WINDOWS
PATH=C:\WINDOWS;C:\WINDOWS\COMMAND;
```

The TMP variable tells DOS where to put temporary files. The PROMPT command pg tells the command processor to how display the directory location on the command prompt: the $p tells it to display the directory information, and the $g tells it to display a > sign after the directory information.

Ping   The Ping program allows a user to verify the connectivity and existence of another system in a network. Ping is a great troubleshooting tool. To verify the existence of **www.google.com**, for example, you could type the following command and receive the following results:

```
c:\mike\test> ping www.google.com
Pinging www.google.com [216.239.51.99] with 32 bytes of data:
Reply from 216.239.51.99: bytes=32 time=84ms TTL=45
Reply from 216.239.51.99: bytes=32 time=84ms TTL=45
Reply from 216.239.51.99: bytes=32 time=91ms TTL=45
Reply from 216.239.51.99: bytes=32 time=79ms TTL=45
Ping statistics for 216.239.51.99:
    Packets: Sent = 4, Received = 4, Lost = 0 (0% loss),
Approximate round trip times in milli-seconds:
    Minimum = 79ms, Maximum =  91ms, Average =  84ms
```

Notice that you get the TCP/IP address of **www.google.com** as well as the time it took for the connection to respond back to you.

CERTIFICATION OBJECTIVE 8.04

Disk Management

Disk Management is the set of activities necessary to create, manage, and maintain disk drives. Using Disk Management you can rearrange drive letters, change partitions, convert disk systems, and other functions provided by the operating system.

In older systems such as Windows 3.1 and DOS the primary disk management tools were FDISK and FORMAT. With newer systems such as Windows NT, 2000, and XP you have a whole suite of tools available to help you manage your disk resources. A key component of disk management is deciding which file systems to use on the operating system. This section provides you with an overview of disk management and some of the considerations you will need to make as an A+ technician.

Disk Partitions

Before a new disk drive can be used to save data, it must first be partitioned and formatted. Partitioning a disk means you divide the disk into several *volumes*. Each volume can have a different file system, as explained in the following discussion. If you plan to install more than one OS on the computer, each should be loaded on its own partition. Each partition will be treated by Windows as a separate drive and will therefore get its own individual drive letter. If you don't want to divide the hard drive into several volumes, you must create a single partition that uses the entire drive. Windows 9*x* operating systems allows a maximum of 1 primary and 1 extended partition on a single physical drive. Windows NT allows for a maximum of 4 partitions per disk. Windows 2000 and XP allow up to 4 partitions during installation, but after installation, you can use Disk Management to create additional partitions.

e x a m

w a t c h *Windows 9x systems can only have two partitions created using FDISK. Windows NT allows up to 4, and Windows 2000 and XP allow beyond 4 once installation is completed. It is recommended that you use the Disk Management utilities to configure disk partitions rather than other tools such as FDISK.*

Active Partition

The active partition is the partition that is set as the bootable partition. The operating system is typically installed on this drive. Only one drive can be set as the active partition on a computer system. Active partitions are flagged as available and can be accessed by the operating system. If a partition is not active, it will not be bootable by the operating system.

Primary Partition

The primary partition that is marked as active contains the operating system. The partition that contains the operating system files is also referred to as a system partition. If the primary partition also contains all the operating systems files it will also be referred to as a system partition.

Extended Partition

An extended partition is a special type of partition that can be broken down into smaller drives that are accessible to the operating system. These drives are referred to as logical partitions or logical drives and are explained briefly in the next section. Once the system boots, the logical drives that exist in the extended partition will be assigned drive numbers.

Logical Partition

A logical partition or logical drive exists in an extended partition. Logical partitions are portions of the extended partition that can be established and accessed by the operating system as separate drives. The term logical partition and logical drive are used interchangeably.

When you format a drive, it is divided into usable areas, called *clusters*, and you must configure the disk to use a specific file system. The file system will determine the type of OS it can support and how much data the disk can hold. Some common file systems are described in the following sections. Partitioning and formatting procedures are described in detail in Chapter 9.

on the

job

Most preconfigured systems will usually allocate the entire disk as a primary drive, which creates a single large drive. To change this configuration, you will need to entirely repartition the disk. This will cause a loss of all existing data, and the operating system will need to be reinstalled from scratch.

File Systems

This section explores the more common file systems used in Windows environments. The file systems have evolved from relatively simple file systems to extremely robust and complex file systems such as those used in Windows 2000 and XP. What is important to remember is that there are primarily two types of file systems in use on Windows systems: FAT (used in Windows 9x) and NTFS (used in Windows NT, 2000, and XP). In most cases, newer operating systems can read earlier operating systems' file systems, but it is less common that older operating systems can read newer file systems.

FAT and FAT16

The original file system was called FAT, short for *file allocation table*. The file system's name is a reference to the use of the FAT, which behaves as a type of disk index. FAT is a 16-bit file system, meaning that it is capable of 16-bit addressing. The FAT file system can address up to 2GB of data. To use FAT on a larger hard drive, you must create separate partitions of no more than 2GB each. FAT is a sort of "universal" file system, in that it can be used by DOS, Windows 9x, Windows NT, Windows 2000, and Windows XP.

on the **job**

The term FAT actually has two meanings. First, it describes a drive's "index" (its file allocation table). The second and the one we refer to is the storage technology used in Microsoft operating systems. The FAT file system was later renamed FAT16 to distinguish it from its successor, FAT32. The file system used on floppy disks is a carryover from early MS-DOS file systems, which were called FAT 12. FAT 12 used a 12-bit addressing scheme, FAT16 uses a 16-bit scheme, and FAT32 uses a 32-bit scheme. The second and less commonly used convention involves referring to the creation of a hierarchical file system.

Due to its addressing and capacity limitations, FAT is not a particularly efficient file system. Here's why: The maximum number of addressable clusters in a FAT system is 65526, regardless of the drive's capacity. In a 500MB system with 65526 clusters, each cluster is roughly 8KB. Howevr, in a 2GB system with 65526 clusters, each cluster is 32KB.

Now consider that when a file is saved, the entire cluster, even the leftover part of the cluster that the file is not using, becomes dedicated to that file. This leftover space is, in essence, wasted. This waste is called *slack*. The larger a drive's clusters, the greater the overall drive slack.

Suppose, for example, that a drive uses 32KB clusters. A 1KB file will reserve the entire cluster, resulting in 31KB of unusable "slack" space. However, if the clusters were 8KB, the same 1KB file would result in only 7KB of slack. Because of this characteristic, as well as its capacity limitations, the FAT file system has been largely replaced by newer file systems.

FAT32

FAT32 is an improvement of the FAT16 file system because it supports up to 2 terabytes (TB) of drive capacity. Furthermore, its 32-bit addressing allows it to recognize a greater number of clusters (over 250 million), so its cluster sizes are typically much smaller (around 4KB), resulting in less drive slack.

on the
Job

A terabyte is 1024 gigabytes. A gigabyte is 1024 megabytes. So a terabyte is over a million megabytes!

The FAT32 file system can be used by Windows 95 OSR2 and later, as well as by Windows 98 and 2000. If you boot using one of these OSes, you will be able to view the contents of a FAT16 drive. However, if you boot using an older OS, you will not be able to view the FAT32 drive.

NTFS 4

NTFS 4, originally called *new technology file system (NTFS)*, was introduced with the Windows NT OS. NTFS 4 is a 32-bit file system, which means it supports large capacities and small cluster sizes. NTFS 4 also includes native file compression, so files and folders can be compressed individually without using a third-party utility.

NTFS 4 allows you to set access permissions on individual files and folders and supports a *spanned disk* (known as a *volume set* in Windows NT), a partition that is made up of space on more than one physical disk. This allows you to create partitions that exceed the size of a single hard drive and to create a partition out of the extra space on multiple drives.

on the
Job

Windows 9x can use and access FAT16 or FAT32 partitions. Windows NT can access FAT16 or NTFS 4 partitions, and Windows 2000 and XP can access FAT16, FAT32, NTFS 4, and NTFS 5 partitions. When you mount an NTFS 4 drive in Windows 2000 or XP it will automatically be upgraded to NTFS 5.

NTFS 5

NTFS 5 is a new file system, released in Windows 2000. It has the same features as NTFS 4 but includes several improvements, such as native encryption. NTFS 5 also allows administrators to set disk quotas for network users. NTFS 5 can be used by Windows 2000 and XP only.

HPFS

HPFS, for *high-performance file system*, is traditionally used in OS/2 systems. OS/2 stands for Operating System/2 and is IBM's native OS. HPFS cannot be used with Windows 9x or 2000. HPFS can support volumes up to 64GB and results in less slack space than FAT due to its use of much smaller storage units (single sectors rather than larger clusters).

on the job   *It's very unlikely that you will encounter HPFS either on the exam or in the field. However, there are still some very large companies that use HPFS and OS/2 out there.*

HPFS uses a different disk structure from FAT file systems. While FAT systems use a single file allocation table in the first cluster of the volume to keep an index of the volume's contents, HPFS volumes are divided into 16 "bands." Each band includes its own index, meaning that the drive's read/write head travels less when accessing files, and file access is much faster. It also means that volumes become less fragmented. That is, fragmentation can occur within a single band, but it is unlikely to occur across the entire volume.

Drive Converter

Windows 9x includes a converter utility, CVT.EXE, that allows you to convert existing FAT16 volumes to FAT32 without loss of information. This is an important utility, because the conversion of a file system type typically requires repartitioning and reformatting of the volume. When you partition and/or format a volume, all of that volume's data is lost.

To use the Windows 98 drive converter utility, click Start, then select Programs | Accessories | System Tools | Drive Converter. It's important to note that, although this utility will convert from FAT16 to FAT32 without data loss, the opposite is not true; this is a one-way conversion utility. To revert back from FAT32 to FAT16, the volume must be repartitioned and reformatted. Windows NT, 2000, and XP do not provide a separate conversion utility.

CERTIFICATION OBJECTIVE 8.05

File and Folder Management

Recall that one function of any operating system is to manage files and folders, and Windows is no exception. To properly manage the files and folders on your system, such as creating, renaming, moving, and deleting them, you must be familiar with the folder structure, navigation techniques, and management procedures.

Creating Folders and Files

A folder is simply a container that holds files and other folders. By organizing items into folders, it is easier for you and the OS to find the files you need. As an analogy, think of a dresser that holds your clothing. By placing different types of items into different drawers, you can find them more easily than you could if the items were simply piled on the floor. When you need a pair of socks, you open the sock drawer, and you can ignore other items that are in the shirts and belts drawers.

The same idea can be applied to OSes. If you place all your pictures, for example, in a different folder from your documents, you will be able to more quickly retrieve the pictures. However, just like a dresser, the ability of the OS to maintain an organized structure depends on your ability to keep items in the proper places. This means consistently saving files to the proper folders and not moving files into places where they don't belong.

To create a folder in Windows 9x system, you must first open the drive or folder in which you want to create the new folder. Once the folder is created, give it a name that will help you easily identify its contents. Folders can be created using either Windows Explorer or My Computer. Exercise 8-4 lists the steps required to create a folder in Windows Explorer. Files can be created either by an application such as Word, or by the same process that you used to create a folder.

on the **Job** *The process of creating a folder in Windows XP is similar to that in Windows 9x and is found at Start | All Programs |Accessories.*

EXERCISE 8-4

Creating a Folder in Windows 9x in Windows Explorer

1. Click Start, point to Programs, and click Windows Explorer. A window similar to the one in Figure 8-14 will open. The folder structure is displayed on the left, and the selected drive or folder contents are displayed on the right.

2. Click the drive or folder in which you want to create the new folder.

3. Select File | New | Folder.

4. A new folder icon will appear within the selected drive or folder. Enter a name using the keyboard, then press the ENTER key.

FIGURE 8-14	

Windows Explorer on a Windows 98 system

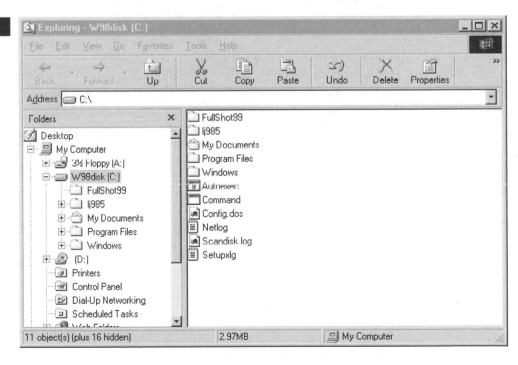

File Attributes

As mentioned earlier, a file or folder can have any or all of the read-only, hidden, system, and archive attributes. The read-only and hidden attributes can be viewed or altered using either a command prompt or the file's or folder's Properties dialog box. To apply an attribute in Windows, in Windows Explorer, right-click the file and choose Properties, then, in the Properties dialog box, place a check in the appropriate attribute's check box. You can apply more than one attribute to a file or folder. To remove an attribute, remove the check from the appropriate check box. Note that some attributes are applied automatically by the OS or other applications. In all cases, when an attribute is applied to a folder, it will not be applied to the files within that folder. That is, attributes must be applied to files independently of their folders. The system attribute can only be altered at the command prompt with the ATTRIB program.

Windows 2000 and XP have additional attributes, including compressed and encrypted. These attributes can be set with Windows Explorer or Control Panel options. The compressed and encrypted options are mutually exclusive, that is, only one of these properties can be set on a file at a time. You can view these attributes by right-clicking a folder or file and viewing its properties.

The Read-Only Attribute

The read-only attribute ensures that the file or folder won't be modified, renamed, or deleted accidentally. In Windows, if you try to delete a read-only file, you will receive the following message: In the example below we are using the DOS ATTRIB command to show the files attributes.

```
C:\WINDOWS\Desktop\test>attrib
  A    R    TEST.DOC       C:\WINDOWS\Desktop\test\test.doc
C:\WINDOWS\Desktop\test>del test.doc
Access denied
```

The Windows Explorer message for this presents the same message under the Windows GUI.

When you open a read-only file such as a document, you can view the file and make changes. However, to save the changes you have made, you must save the document as a new file; the original file will be left intact, and a second file that contains the modifications will be created.

The Hidden Attribute

Under normal circumstances, hidden files and folders will not be displayed in Windows Explorer or My Computer and will not be listed by the Windows Find feature. The idea is that if a user can't see a file, the user won't accidentally change or delete it.

However, by changing the Windows View options, as explained in Exercise 8-2, you can display all files and folders, even if they are marked as hidden. These files and folders will appear grayed out to indicate their status. It is recommended that you select either the Do Not Show Hidden Files or Do Not Show Hidden or System Files option so that hidden files remain truly hidden.

If a folder is hidden, the files in the folder cannot be viewed using My Computer or Windows Explorer, even if those files are not marked hidden because if you cannot view a folder, you cannot open it to view the files inside. These files will be found by the Find command, however.

The Archive Attribute

The archive attribute selects particular files or folders to back up. System backups are explained in the "Backup and Restore" section in the chapter. Briefly, many backup utilities include the option to back up only files marked with the archive attribute. By default, Windows applies the archive attribute to all files but not to folders. You can, of course, manually add or remove the archive attribute.

The System Attribute

The Windows GUI does not allow you to apply or remove the system attribute from files or folders. Rather, files are given the system attribute automatically by the OS or the application, depending on their function. Most system files are also given the hidden attribute to keep users from accidentally modifying or deleting them. In DOS, you can apply or remove the system attribute, but in Windows, you can only view the presence or absence of the attribute.

File-Naming Conventions

In Windows, filenames (and folder names) can be up to 255 characters, including the full path name. A full path name includes the drive, folder, and subfolders in which a particular file is located. For example, suppose a file called JACKET is located in the WINTER subfolder, which is located in the CLOTHES folder on the C: drive. This file's full path name is C:\CLOTHES\WINTER\JACKET. The file's name can include letters and numbers, spaces, and several other characters. Its name cannot include the following characters: \ / ? * : " |

Most files include a filename extension, which is separated from the remainder of the name by a period, that signifies the file's type. For example, a file with the .SYS extension is a system file. The extension is very important because it indicates to Windows which application will open a particular file. For example, when you double-click a file with the .XLS extension, Windows will launch the Microsoft

TABLE 8-1	Extension	Function or Application
	EXE	An executable file (a program)
Commonly Used Windows file Extensions	BAT	A batch file (a program)
	COM	A command file (a program)
	DOC	A document, typically associated with Microsoft Word or WordPad
	BMP	A bitmap (graphic)
	SYS	A system file
	TXT	A text file
	CFG	A configuration file

Excel application to open the file. Table 8-1 contains some common extensions and their functions or associated applications.

Each extension is associated with a particular icon, which allows you to quickly determine the type of a particular file. This is especially handy if the Windows View settings have been configured to hide file extensions.

If you rename or remove a file's extension when you rename the file itself, a warning message will appear stating that if you change the extension, the file could become unusable. You must then confirm or cancel the operation because without an extension Windows might be unable to determine with which application a file is associated. Furthermore, some applications simply won't open a file without the proper extension. For example, suppose the file POEM.DOC was created in WordPad. If you change the file's name to POEM.ODE, WordPad will not automatically open the file.

File and folder names in Windows 9x are case-sensitive when they are displayed, but no two items with the same name can exist in the same location, regardless of their use of uppercase or lowercase characters. That is, if you name a file POTATO, it will be displayed as POTATO. If you name a file Potato, it will be displayed as Potato (note the use of lowercase letters).

SCENARIO & SOLUTION

What is the purpose of a file's extension?	To identify the file type or the application with which it is associated.
What is an .EXE file?	An executable file—a program or small application. When you double-click its icon, the application will be launched.

SCENARIO & SOLUTION

What is a hidden file?	A file that has the hidden attribute set and will not be displayed by default.
How can I view a system or hidden file?	Use the Windows View options to select Show All Files.

Windows 2000/XP Compression and Encryption

Windows 2000 and XP include native file and folder compression and encryption, which means that files and folders can be compressed or encrypted without the use of a third-party utility. When you work with a compressed or encrypted file or folder, Windows 2000 and XP must continually work in the background to uncompress or recompress or decrypt or re-encrypt it. These processes can make the computer seem to perform more slowly than normal. Windows NT 4 did not support encryption but did support compression. You cannot have a file that is both compressed and encrypted; these options are mutually exclusive meaning you can only have one of them at a time.

Compression

Compressed files and folders are saved in a manner that allows them to take up less space than normal. Windows 2000 compression can be applied only to hard drives that use the NTFS file system. All files that are saved in or copied into a compressed folder will also be compressed. You can compress a folder in Windows 2000 by following the steps in Exercise 8-5.

EXERCISE 8-5

Compressing a Folder in Windows 2000 and XP

1. In My Computer or Windows Explorer, right-click the folder you want to compress.

2. Select Properties from the shortcut menu, then click Advanced.

3. Enable the Compress Contents to Save Disk Space option, then click OK.

4. Click the OK button in the Properties dialog box.

5. A confirmation window will appear, prompting you to apply compression to the current folder only or the current folder and its subfolders and files. Select the appropriate option, then click OK.

Encryption   Windows 2000 and XP native encryption can prevent users from accessing files to which they have otherwise been given permission to access on NTFS 5 volumes. Normally, Windows NT, 2000, and XP is configured to either permit or restrict access to files based on a user's profile or group profile. Suppose, however, that a sensitive file has been placed in an otherwise accessible folder. Encryption can be placed on that single file to restrict access to it, without affecting access to the rest of the folder.

Encrypted files and folders are "encoded." Authorized users' computers are given the "decoder" (decryption) key so that they can access the encrypted files or folders. It is important to note that compressed files and folders cannot be encrypted. You can encrypt a file or folder by accessing its Advanced Properties dialog box (as explained in Exercise 8-6) and enabling the Encrypt Contents to Secure Data option.

CERTIFICATION OBJECTIVE 8.07

Major Operating System Utilities

This section covers the operating systems utilities you need to know for the A+ exam. In general, these utilities are available on all systems, though there are some exceptions. Utilities help keep your system running, configure options, and perform systems maintenance. It is important that you understand how and when to use them when you are supporting computers in the field.

Disk Management Tools

This section discusses the various disk management tools and utilities available for Windows 9x, NT, 2000, and XP systems. These tools are useful in configuring, installing, and maintaining your disk systems. Make sure you understand how these utilities work and what they do before you use them. Some of these utilities can irrevocably change the contents of a drive and cause the data to be lost.

DEFRAG

The DEFRAG program, or Disk Defragmenter, is a utility that improves disk drive performance. Over time, disk files tend to get spread over the disk, which causes file access to take longer. The DEFRAG program moves files around and sets them up so that they are no longer fragmented. DEFRAG is available for Windows 9x and Windows 2000 and XP. DEFRAG was not shipped with Windows NT 4 but you could acquire third party deframentation programs.

on the **Job**

It is a good idea to run DEFRAG on a regular basis. Typically, you should defrag a drive once a month or so. On an extremely busy system once every other week is probably more than enough. DEFRAG can take several hours to complete on a large system. It is a good idea to dedicate the system to this process until the defragmentation is completed.

FDISK

FDISK is the primary tool for creating disk partitions on Windows 9x systems. FDISK is not a supported utility under Windows 2000 and XP. To partition a disk under XP or 2000, use Disk Administration under Computer Management. On Windows NT 4, the Disk Administrator utility accomplishes this.

Backup and Restore

Windows 2000 and Windows XP Professional include a native backup utility called Backup. This utility allows you to save large amounts of data on floppy disk or other storage media. One benefit of using the Backup utility is that it can compress data so that it takes up less storage space than it would otherwise.

Another benefit to Backup is that it allows you to save a single large file over more than one floppy disk. In most other cases, you cannot split a file over two disks: the file must fit entirely on one floppy disk, or it cannot be saved at all. However, for files over 1.44MB (the capacity of most floppies), Backup will catalog and convert the file so that it can span two or more disks. Windows 9x systems do not include a backup program, though there is a version available that is included with most backup devices such as magnetic tape.

To access Backup in Windows 2000 or XP, click Start, then select Programs | Accessories | System Tools | Backup. Although the screens might differ between products, the procedure is similar for both OSes. Exercise 8-6 lists the steps necessary to back up select files to floppy disk in Windows XP.

EXERCISE 8-6

Using the Windows XP Backup Utility

1. When you launch the Backup utility, a welcome screen will appear. Click the Advanced Mode text in the middle of the screen.

2. The Backup Wizard (Advanced) screen will appear. You can use this wizard to get step-by-step instructions. Click the Backup Wizard button and the Next button.

3. This brings up the backup options screen as shown in Figure 8-15.

4. In the What to Back Up section, select the Backup Selected Files option.

5. Navigate through the file structure as you would in Windows Explorer to find the appropriate files. Click the check box for each file you want to back up. When you are finished, click the Next button.

6. In the Backup Type, Destination, and Name section, click the folder icon and select the floppy disk (A:).

7. From the Job menu, select Save.

8. Enter a name for the backup job, then click Save Selections.

9. From the Job menu, select Start. This will start the backup job.

To restore a backup job's files, open the Backup utility and select the Restore tab. Select the backup job to restore, then click Start.

FIGURE 8-15

Backup wizard on a Windows XP system

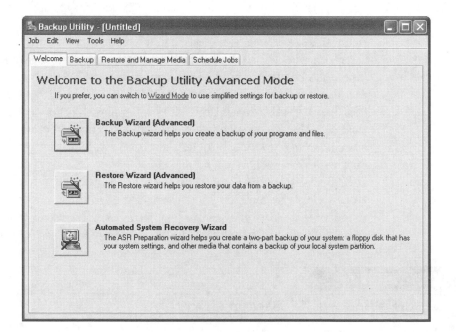

MSBACKUP   MSBACKUP is the program name of the Windows 9x backup program. MSBACKUP can be started either as a DOS command or by using the Backup icon in the Systems Tools folder.

NTBACKUP   NTBACKUP is the Windows NT, 2000, and XP command line backup utility. It can be called either as a command-line program or by using the Windows interface. You can use batch commands with Windows NT/2000/XP to automate the backup process using NTBACKUP. This differs from the GUI program BACKUP which only runs in immediate mode.

SCANDISK

SCANDISK is a disk utility that can check the integrity of a FAT disk on a Windows 9x or DOS system. SCANDISK is not shipped with Windows NT, 2000, or XP, but there are third-party vendors that sell SCANDISK utilities for these operating systems.

CHKDSK

CHKDSK is an older utility originally released with DOS. CHKDSK can fix some errors on a hard drive or floppy, but SCANDISK should be used for most disk maintenance utilities. CHKDSK has been periodically updated and is included with Windows NT, Windows 2000, and Windows XP; it is still a command-line tool.

Windows 2000 and XP include an Error Checking Option on the Tools menu of the properties of a drive. This is often referred to as Scandisk but it is a different program.

Disk Cleanup

Disk Cleanup is a program that ships with Windows 9x and Windows 2000 and XP to help identify and remove temporary files from a system. With the advent of the Internet, the number of temporary or Internet files on many systems has grown astronomically. Disk Cleanup can help you recover this space for other uses (such as browsing the Internet and collecting more temporary files).

When you browse the Internet, every site you ever visit gets stored in a file on your computer. This provides faster response times to highly used websites, but it can consume an enormous amount of data over time.

FORMAT

The FORMAT program initializes media such as hard disks and floppy discs. The syntax for FORMAT is very simple. To format the A: floppy disk you type:

```
Format a:
```

This creates a FAT structure on the disc. However, it is generally recommended according to Microsoft that you use the utilities provided under either Explorer or Administrator as opposed to the FORMAT program. The FORMAT program is less reliable and provides less safety than the Explorer or Administrator tools.

System Management Tools

This section discusses the various system management tools you'll need as an A+ technician. These tools configure, install, and troubleshoot systems problems on Windows computer systems. Many of these tools are available in all of the platforms, and all them are generally available through the Control Panel.

Device Manager

Access the Device Manager by clicking the System icon and then choosing the Device Manager Tab in the Control Panel on Windows 9x systems. Windows 2000/XP systems use the Computer Management icon and then selecting the Device Manager.

The Device Manager allows you to manage devices on your computer by disabling devices, refreshing drivers, or reallocating resources on your system. Device Manager is one of the primary methods of troubleshooting problems involving hardware.

System Manager

Access the System Manager is available under the Control Panel as the System icon. This allows for configuration of environment parameters as well as performance settings on the computer system. You can change or modify settings such as the file performance, video acceleration, and virtual memory. This icon also gives you the version of the operating system and other general information about your system.

Computer Manager

The Computer Manager function as described by CompTIA is the Computer Management option available from the Control Panel on Windows 2000 and XP systems. The closest function to the Computer Manger on Windows 9x systems is the System Icon available through the Control Panel. Computer Management provides access to all of the commonly used systems management tools. This includes the Device Manager, Disk management, and Systems settings that have been previously described. These are listed separately because they are able to run as separate utilities or accessed using Computer Management. The Easiest way to keep this straight is to consider that the Computer Management Icon accesses them from a single icon and then runs them separately.

MSCONFIG

Windows 98 and Windows XP includes a System Configuration utility that allows you to modify legacy configuration files without having to alter the files directly, as you do in the Sysedit utility. To launch the System Configuration Utility, enter **MSCONFIG** in the Windows Run line.

REGEDIT.EXE

During normal operation, the Registry is automatically updated when you install or delete an application or when you change the computer's configuration using Windows configuration utilities (usually using the Control Panel). However, it is possible to open and manually edit the Registry using the *Registry editor*. The Registry editor is a file called REGEDIT.EXE, and it can be launched by entering **REGEDIT** in the Windows 9*x* Run line.

The Registry editor organizes the Registry database into 5 root keys, also known as *Hkeys*, but it does not identify to which Registry file each entry belongs. Entries are displayed in a tree structure on the left, and the selected entry's values are displayed on the right. When you double-click an Hkey, its subkeys are displayed. There can be several levels and sublevels within a single Hkey, so it can be difficult to find the proper entry. Furthermore, many subkeys throughout the Registry can have the same name. This makes it even more difficult to navigate the database. Fortunately, the Registry editor includes a Find feature that can locate entries for you.

REGEDT32.EXE

REGEDT32.EXE is the XP version of the Registry editor that was available on Windows NT and 2000. It is recommended that you use REGEDIT.EXE for all Registry editing on Windows XP. REGEDT32 actually calls the REGEDIT program when REGEDT32 is run.

When you modify, create, or remove an entry in the Registry, it is saved automatically and immediately. A single change to the Registry can cause fatal OS errors, so you should never use it unless you are absolutely sure about what you are doing. It is best to stick to the Windows configuration utilities when you make a change.

SYSEDIT

The legacy configuration files discussed here can be opened and modified in any Windows text editor, such as Notepad. However, Windows 9*x* includes a utility called the System Configuration Editor that allows you to view and modify all these files at once. To launch the System Configuration Editor, type **SYSEDIT** in the Windows Run line. The WIN.INI, SYSTEM.INI, AUTOEXEC.BAT, CONFIG.SYS, and

PROTOCOL.INI files will be displayed. You can modify each of these files as though it had been opened individually.

Using this utility, you can elect to process all, none, or some of the system's legacy configuration files. By selecting a specific file's tab, you can also elect to process or ignore individual command lines. Using the MSCONFIG utility is much safer than using SYSEDIT because it does not allow you to edit the configuration files directly. This means that you cannot accidentally cause a fatal error by modifying or deleting the wrong entry.

HWiNFO

HWiNFO32 is a hardware detection utility for Windows 9*x*, 2000, and XP. It is similar to the Device Manager but provides more detail about components, such as the capacity, speed, and manufacturer of RAM, hard drives, printers, and ports. HWiNFO is not included with Windows but can be downloaded from REALiX at **www.hwinfo.com**. The HWiNFO utility can be run any time during the operation of the computer. First, the utility completes a hardware detection phase, then it displays the results in a window.

This utility includes a *log file*, which allows you to log the current system settings and track them over time. HWiNFO also performs benchmark tests on the processor and memory. This means that the utility tests their speed and capacity, then compares the results with those of components built by other manufacturers. HWiNFO also allows you to monitor the temperature of the CPU and motherboard. Although HWiNFO can be used in either Windows 9*x* and NT environments, it is really designed for the NT, 2000, and XP platform, so some features might not be available in Windows 9*x*.

Automatic Skip Driver

When the computer starts up, the Windows 9*x* device drivers are loaded with the OS. However, if a driver is missing, corrupt, or incompatible with the OS, it could prevent the OS from loading, even if the driver is not for a critical device (such as the video card). To help prevent drivers from halting the system, Windows 98 and ME includes a utility called Automatic Skip Driver (ASD). This utility automatically detects potential driver problems and configures the computer to skip over them at startup. When this is the case, the driver will not be loaded, but the OS will otherwise start up normally, allowing you to troubleshoot the problem.

The ASD utility runs automatically in the Windows background. To view ASD results, you must run ASD.EXE. Enter **ASD** at the Windows 98/ME Run line or select Start | Programs | Accessories | System Tools | System Information. Then access ASD from the Tools menu of the System Information window. ASD will report all drivers that it has disabled and give you an opportunity to re-enable them.

WSCRIPT

Windows includes a Windows Scripting Host, which allows you to create and use non-native (non-DOS) scripts such as Visual Basic, Java, and Perl. The WSCRIPT.EXE utility runs in the background and allows you to view, run, or modify non-Windows scripts using Windows tools such as Notepad.

Most of the time, you will be totally unaware of the Scripting Host because it simply runs in the background. However, you can use the WSCRIPT command to modify the behavior of scripts by entering **WSCRIPT** at the Windows Run line. Here, you configure the scripting host to automatically shut down long or indefinite scripts after a specified period of time.

Event Viewer

The Event Viewer displays all event logs on Windows NT, 2000, and XP systems. Error messages, status reports, and system events, such as startup and shutdown, are displayed in the Event Viewer. The user can set the level of messages recorded, and messages can be broken down by type. The Event Viewer is very helpful for troubleshooting system problems because it keeps an activity trail of all system events. Figure 8-16 shows the Event Viewer and Event Properties on a Windows XP system.

Task Manager

The Task Manager displays information about activities that are currently happening on the system. Task Manager is accessed by pressing CTRL-ALT-DEL on Windows 9x or pressing CTRL-ALT-DEL and then selecting Task Manager on Windows NT-based systems. Windows NT systems can also access the Task Manager by right clicking the

SCENARIO & SOLUTION

Which configuration files are typically associated with Devices?	
Windows 9x Devices?	SYSTEM.DAT
Windows 9x Applications?	USER.DAT
Legacy Devices	SYSTEM.INI
Legacy Applications	WIN.INI
Which tool should you use to modify them safely?	
Windows 9x SYSTEM.DAT and USER.DAT Legacy Applications SYSTEM.INI and WIN.INI	Control Panel MSCONFIG.EXE

FIGURE 8-16

Event Viewer on
a Windows XP
system

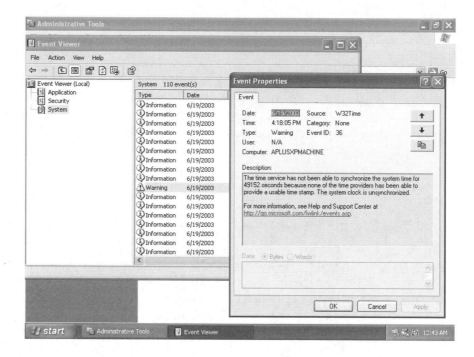

taskbar or running Task Manager from the Systems Utilities. Figure 8-17 shows the
Task Manager running on a Windows 2000 system. If a program freezes or stops
responding to commands you can use Task Manager to end the frozen program. You
can also use Task Manager to display current system usage.

File Management Tools

ATTRIB.EXE

The ATTRIB.EXE program allows for attributes to be set on files and folders on disks.
There are four primary attributes that can set by this program:

- **Read-only** Marks a file that can be opened only for reading. This file
  cannot be edited or deleted unless this attribute is changed.

- **System** Marks a file as an important system file.

- **Hidden** Prevents the file from being displayed with normal directory or file
  management commands. Many systems files are marked as hidden to prevent
  accidental deletion. Hidden files can be viewed by changing view options in
  Explorer or by using the DIR command to display hidden files.

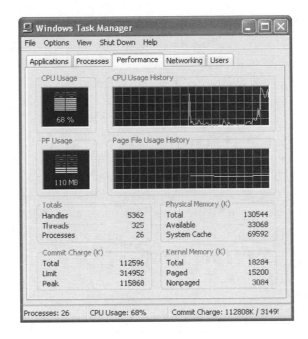

FIGURE 8-17

Task Manager
running on a
Windows XP
system

- **Archive** Tells backup programs to back up the file when a backup occurs.
  The Recovery Console for Windows 2000 and XP have additional options to
  assist in recovering systems files. For additional information on the Recovery
  Console, visit the Microsoft website at **www.microsoft.com** and do a keyword
  search for Recovery Console.

EXTRACT.EXE

The Windows 9x installation disks contain compressed cabinet (.CAB) files. These
files are automatically extracted during the setup process. Windows 9x includes an
extract tool, called EXTRACT.EXE, to allow you to manually extract .CAB files from
the installation media. This is handy when you want to install a single application,
feature, or driver from the installation disk without rerunning the Windows setup.

The EXTRACT.EXE tool must be run from a command prompt. To use this tool,
enter **EXTRACT** followed by the name of the cabinet and the name of the file you
want to extract. Follow this with the destination in which to place the specified file.
For example, suppose the file DRIVER.DRV exists on the Win98_4 cabinet on the
CD-ROM drive (D:); you'd use the following command to extract and place the
driver in the WINDOWS folder:

```
EXTRACT D:\WIN98_4.CAB DRIVER.DLL C:\WINDOWS
```

Edit.com

Edit is a text editor that can edit text and systems files. Edit is most frequently used to edit batch and command files. It is extremely fast and small in memory size. Edit does not provide much in the way of a GUI, but it is helpful for quickly changing configuration files.

Windows Explorer

Windows Explorer is one of the main tools used for file management and was discussed earlier in this chapter in the section "Navigating Through Windows."

A large number of Windows utilities are discussed in this chapter. Use the following questions and answers to refresh your memory on the functions of these utilities.

CERTIFICATION SUMMARY

There are a great many components to the Windows OSes, including their system files, disk management tools, and configuration utilities. This chapter focused on those that are most important to the system and the ones you are most likely to have to deal with as a computer technician. However, even with all the differences between the Windows 9x and Windows NT/2000, and XP platforms, they have a great many file and disk-related components in common.

For example, Windows 9x and Windows NT, 2000, and XP rely on the system Registry for most configuration and other system values. Both environments support Plug and Play (with the exception of Windows NT 4), contain Registry editors, use virtual memory, and can execute DOS prompt commands. The interface of the two platforms is also similar. They use a "desktop" concept that contains icons, a Start menu, a taskbar, and shortcut menus.

There are, however, a great number of differences between Windows 9x and NT/2000/XP. Because Windows 9x is aimed at home users, it supports backward compatibility with older applications and therefore includes many legacy system files, such as SYSTEM.INI, WIN.INI, and memory management files (HIMEM.SYS and EMM386.EXE). Because Windows NT/2000/XP is intended for business networks, it supports more sophisticated file systems, networking components, security, compression, and configuration utilities.

✓ TWO-MINUTE DRILL

Here are some of the key points from each certification objective in Chapter 8.

Operating System Functions and the Windows Family

❏ Some functions of an OS is to provide an interface between the user and the hardware, manage an organized file and folder structure, and provide procedures for preparing and managing disks.

❏ Windows 95, 98 and Me are part of the Windows 9x family, which is aimed at home users, and Windows NT 4, 2000, and XP are part of the Windows NT family, which is aimed at business networks.

❏ Windows XP Home Edition is the XP replacement for the Windows 9x family. Windows XP Professional is intended to replace all desktop versions of Windows NT.

❏ Windows XP Professional includes all of the features of Windows XP Home with the addition of enhanced capabilities for business users.

❏ Windows 9x, 2000 and XP have a similar-looking interface, which includes a desktop, My Computer, Windows Explorer, a Start button, and a taskbar.

❏ Windows 9x supports older applications and has more Plug and Play support for home computer devices; Windows 2000 has more sophisticated security, fault tolerance, and disk management utilities. Windows XP support all of the features of Windows 9x and Windows 2000. Windows XP also includes enhanced multimedia and other capabilities.

System Files and Utilities

❏ The majority of configuration information for the Windows 9x and NT OSes is located in the system Registry.

❏ You can safely edit the Registry using the Control Panel in 9x, 2000, and XP, or the Computer Management utility in Windows 2000 and XP. When possible, the Registry should only be updated using these provided administrative utilities, not by using the Registry editors.

❏ You can directly edit the Registry using the Registry Editor. The Registry editor should not be used except as a last resort. Always back up your Registry before making Registry changes.

❑ Because Windows 9*x* supports older applications, it includes older system configuration files such as SYSTEM.INI, WIN.INI, CONFIG.SYS, and AUTOEXEC.BAT.

❑ Windows 9*x* uses memory managers such as HIMEM.SYS and EMM386.EXE to maintain backward compatibility with older applications.

❑ Windows 9*x*, 2000, and XP include the Device Manager, which allows you to view and modify hardware configurations.

❑ The Windows 98 Automatic Skip Driver detects and disables potentially problematic drivers.

❑ Windows 9*x*, NT, 2000, and XP use virtual memory, which is space on the hard drive that is used temporarily as though it were RAM.

❑ Windows allows you to run DOS commands such as EDIT, DIR, MEM, and ATTRIB from a DOS command prompt.

File and Folder Management

❑ Windows allows you to view, create, rename, delete, move, or open files and folders using either My Computer or Windows Explorer.

❑ Windows 2000 and XP Professional include a Backup utility for storing and compressing files, and Windows 2000 and XP include native file encryption and compression. Third-party backup programs are available for Windows 9*x* system.

Disk Management

❑ Before a disk can store data, it must be partitioned using DOS FDISK and formatting using the FORMAT command.

❑ Windows 9*x* supports the FAT16 and FAT32 file systems.

❑ Windows 2000 and XP supports the FAT16, FAT32, and NTFS file systems.

SELF TEST

The following questions will help you measure your understanding of the material presented in this chapter. Read all of the choices carefully because there might be more than one correct answer. Choose all correct answers for each question.

Operating System Functions and the Windows Family

1. Which of the following procedures should you use to activate a shortcut menu in Windows?

    A. Click Start, then select Programs | Accessories | Shortcuts.

    B. Double-click the component for which you want to access the shortcut.

    C. Right-click the component for which you want to access the shortcut menu.

    D. Double-click My Computer, then select Menu | Shortcut.

2. Which of the choices below will show the system's active (running) applications?

    A. The taskbar

    B. Each running application's desktop icon will turn blue

    C. The Start menu

    D. The desktop's shortcut menu

3. Which of the following statements about Windows 9x and Windows 2000 is the most accurate?

    A. Windows 2000 can be networked and Windows 9x cannot.

    B. Windows 9x is aimed at home users and Windows 2000 is not.

    C. Windows 9x supports Plug and Play and Windows 2000 does not.

    D. Windows 2000 is the successor to the Windows 9x line of operating systems.

System Files and Utilities

4. Which Windows OS(es) require(s) IO.SYS?

    A. Windows 9x

    B. Windows 98 only

    C. Windows 2000 only

    D. Windows 9x and 2000

5. When you started your Windows 9*x* computer, you received a message stating that the Registry was corrupt. Which of the following files might be corrupt?

   A. WIN.DAT

   B. SYSTEM.INI

   C. WIN.INI

   D. USER.DAT

6. A user is nervous about losing data in the Windows 98 Registry. Which utility should you advise the user to use?

   A. REGEDIT

   B. REGEDT32

   C. SCANREG

   D. MSCONFIG

7. Which of the following is required by both the Windows 9*x* and Windows XP OSes?

   A. CONFIG.SYS

   B. IO.SYS

   C. BOOT.INI

   D. The Registry

8. What does Windows XP use the SYSTEM.INI file for?

   A. To store required hardware settings for the system.

   B. To store application settings for legacy programs.

   C. To store hardware settings for older applications.

   D. Windows XP does not use SYSTEM.INI.

9. What is the function of the NTLDR file?

   A. To initialize and organize the Windows 2000 boot process

   B. To initialize and organize the Windows 9*x* boot process

   C. To allow users to select the OS in a multiboot configuration

   D. To boot Windows 2000 from a SCSI drive

10. Which of the following can you use to *safely* make changes to the Windows 9*x* Registry?

   A. Computer Management utility

   B. Control Panel

   C. Registry Editor

   D. System Configuration utility

11. Which of the following most accurately describes the function of the HIMEM.SYS file?

    A. To initialize the Windows 9*x* boot process

    B. To enable access to extended memory

    C. To enable memory paging between extended and upper memory

    D. To store hardware configuration settings in Windows 9*x*

File and Folder Management

12. You double-click a Windows file icon on the desktop. Which of the following is most likely to happen?

    A. The file's Properties dialog box will open.

    B. You will be given an opportunity to rename the file.

    C. The file will open.

    D. Nothing will happen.

13. Which of the following file attributes are you unable to change in Windows?

    A. Archive

    B. Read-only

    C. System

    D. Hidden

14. A user calls you with a question about Windows. Several files that she knows should be hidden are showing up on the desktop. What do you tell her?

    A. The hidden files will be listed but cannot be opened or modified.

    B. The hidden files can be truly hidden by selecting the appropriate option in the My Computer | View menu.

    C. The hidden files should be moved to the Recycle Bin.

    D. The user is incorrect because hidden files cannot be shown on the desktop.

15. Which of the following statements is inaccurate?

    A. The file's extension determines the type of icon used for that file.

    B. The file's extension indicates the file's type.

    C. You cannot change a file's extension.

    D. You can make a file unusable by changing its extension.

16. Which of the following procedures should you use to compress a directory on your Windows XP Home Edition computer?

    A. Use the Backup utility and select the option to compress the files.

    B. Right-click the directory, select Properties | Advanced, and select the Compression option.

    C. Open the Disk Management utility and select the Compress Selected Files option.

    D. Use My Computer to move the appropriate files into the COMPRESSED folder.

Disk Management

17. An OS uses the NTFS 5 file system. When you boot the computer with this OS, which other types of volumes will you be able to access?

    A. FAT16 only

    B. FAT16 and FAT32

    C. FAT16 and HPFS

    D. None

18. Which of the following statements about the FAT16 and FAT32 file systems is true?

    A. FAT16 supports volumes up to 16MB, and FAT32 supports volumes up to 32MB.

    B. FAT16 volumes typically have about half the amount of slack as FAT32 volumes.

    C. Some versions of Windows 9x cannot access FAT16.

    D. FAT16 can be used by more versions of Windows than FAT32.

19. Which of the following file systems support native file compression and encryption?

    A. FAT32, NTFS 4, and NTFS 5

    B. NTFS 4 and NTFS 5

    C. FAT32 and NTFS 5

    D. NTFS 5

20. You want to upgrade a FAT32 disk to NTFS on a Windows XP Home system. Which process should you use?

    A. Run the Drive Convert utility prior to the upgrade.

    B. Use the Windows 9x FDISK program to partition the drive to NTFS.

    C. Use the Disk Management tools to convert the drive.

    D. Use the CVT program to upgrade the drive.

LAB QUESTION

In this chapter, you were introduced to a great number of Windows 9x, 2000, and XP utilities. As a technician and in preparation for the A+ exam, it is important for you to know which utilities are included with each OS and to understand their functions. Fill in Table 8-2 with information about the function of each utility as well as how you can access the utility and which OSes include the utility.

TABLE 8-2   Lab Worksheet

Utility	Purpose	Access	Operating System(s)
Scanreg			
Registry Editor (REGEDIT.EXE)			
Registry Editor (REGEDT32.EXE)			
System Configuration Editor (SYSEDIT)			
System Configuration utility (MSCONFIG)			
Control Panel			
Device Manager			
Automatic Skip Driver			
Computer Management utility			
Backup			
EXTRACT.EXE			
Drive Converter (CVT1.EXE)			

SELF TEST ANSWERS

Operating System Functions and the Windows Family

1. ☑ **C.** To access a Windows shortcut menu, right-click the component for which you want to access the shortcut menu. A menu with items pertaining to that component will appear.

   ☒ **A,** click Start, then select Programs | Accessories | Shortcuts, is incorrect. The only way to access a shortcut menu is to right-click the component. Furthermore, there is no Shortcuts option in the Accessories menu. **B,** double-click the component for which you want to access the shortcut menu, is also incorrect. When you double-click certain components, such as an empty area of the desktop or taskbar, there will be no result. Other components, such as folders or icons, will be opened or activated when you double-click them. **D,** double-click My Computer, then select Menu | Shortcut, is also incorrect. Again, the only way to access a shortcut menu is to right-click. Furthermore, there is no Menu or Shortcut option in the My Computer window.

2. ☑ **A.** You can use the taskbar to view the system's active applications. All applications, utilities, and folders that you open will appear in the taskbar until you close or end them. You can switch between open applications by clicking the appropriate application button on the taskbar.

   ☒ **B** is incorrect because it states that the icon of each running application will appear blue on the desktop. In fact, many applications do not have icons on the desktop. Icons on the desktop typically turn blue when they are selected, but will not turn blue to indicate the application is running. **C,** the Start menu, is incorrect because this provides access to programs, help, and utilities but does not list active applications. **D,** the desktop's shortcut menu, is incorrect because this displays configuration options for the desktop, not a list of running applications.

3. ☑ **B.** Windows 9x is aimed at home users, and Windows 2000 is not. Windows 2000 is designed for use by businesses, especially those with sophisticated networking needs. The required hardware, cost, and lack of backward compatibility makes Windows 2000 a poor choice for home use.

   ☒ **A** is incorrect because it states that Windows 2000 can be networked, and Windows 9x cannot. It is true that Windows 2000 is dedicated to networking and has more sophisticated network features, but Windows 9x can also be networked. Although networking is not the strength of Windows 9x, it can be set up in a peer-to-peer configuration and can even be configured to join a Windows 2000 network. **C,** Windows 9x supports Plug and Play and Windows 2000 does not, is incorrect. Both OSes support Plug and Play. However, whereas Windows 9x supports home user-type devices, such as specialized video or sound cards, Windows 2000 supports a more limited set of devices. **D** is incorrect because it states that Windows 2000 is the successor to the Windows 9x line of OSes. In fact, these represent two different OS lines. Windows 2000 is the successor in the Windows NT line.

System Files and Utilities

4. ☑ **A.** Windows 9*x* requires IO.SYS. This file is responsible for initializing and organizing the OS's boot process, and it is required for the OS to load properly.

   ☒ **B,** Windows 98 only, is incorrect because IO.SYS is also required by Windows 95. **C,** Windows 2000 only, is incorrect because Windows 2000 does not use IO.SYS. Instead, it uses NTLDR to initialize and organize the boot process. For this reason, **D,** Windows 9*x* and 2000, is also incorrect.

5. ☑ **D.** USER.DAT might be corrupt. This file, along with SYSTEM.DAT, makes up the Windows 9*x* Registry. These files contain the bulk of the OS's operation and configuration settings.

   ☒ **A,** WIN.DAT, is incorrect because this is not a valid Windows system file. **B,** SYSTEM.INI, and **C,** WIN.INI, are incorrect because they are not part of the Windows Registry. Windows 9*x* uses these files only for backward compatibility with older applications.

6. ☑ **C.** You should advise the user to use the SCANREG utility. Included in Windows 98, this utility will back up the Registry's contents. If the Registry becomes corrupt or otherwise unusable, the Registry backup can be restored.

   ☒ **A,** REGEDIT, and **B,** REGEDT32, are incorrect because these utilities are used for directly editing the Registry files. Editing the files can be dangerous and will not prevent the Registry from losing data. Furthermore, REGEDT32 is available only in Windows NT. **D,** MSCONFIG, is also incorrect. This is a Windows 98 utility that allows you to enable or disable the processing of legacy configuration files during startup. For example, using MSCONFIG, you can opt to skip the AUTOEXEC.BAT file or process only select lines of the SYSTEM.INI file.

7. ☑ **D.** The Registry is required by Windows 9*x*, 2000 and Windows XP OSes. Although the data contained in the Registry is different for Windows 9*x*, Windows 2000, and XP, they both still require the Registry's presence to function properly.

   ☒ **A,** CONFIG.SYS, is incorrect. Windows 9*x* includes this file so that older applications can access the hardware. However, it is not required in Windows 9*x* and is not even present in Windows 2000. **B,** IO.SYS, is incorrect because although this file is required to properly boot a Windows 9*x* system, it is not present in Windows 2000. **C,** BOOT.INI, is also incorrect. This file is required by Windows 2000 and XP only if the OS is not installed in the default WINNT directory or is part of a dual-boot configuration (a system with more than one operating system). BOOT.INI is not present in Windows 9*x*.

8. ☑ **D.** Windows 2000 does not use SYSTEM.INI. This file was required by older 16-bit OSes to store hardware settings. Windows 9*x* includes this file for backward compatibility, but it is not present in Windows 2000 or XP.

   ☒ **A,** to store required hardware settings for the system, is incorrect. Again, SYSTEM.INI is required in older OSes such as Windows 3.1 but not in Windows 2000. **B,** to store application settings for legacy programs, is incorrect. This is the function of the WIN.INI file, which is used in Windows 9*x*, not Windows 2000. **C,** to store hardware settings for older applications, is also incorrect. Although Windows 9*x* uses SYSTEM.INI for this purpose, Windows 2000 does not. Windows 2000 does not support backward compatibility with older applications, so it does not include the SYSTEM.INI file.

9. ☑ **A.** The function of NTLDR is to initialize and organize the Windows 2000 boot process. On startup, NTLDR is responsible for locating and initializing other startup files, including NTDETECT and the Registry.

   ☒ **B,** to initialize and organize the Windows 9*x* boot process, is incorrect because this is the function of the IO.SYS file. NTLDR is not present in Windows 9*x*. **C,** to allow users to select the OS in a multiboot configuration, is incorrect because this is the function of the BOOT.INI file. **D,** to boot Windows 2000 from a SCSI drive, is incorrect because this is the function of the NTBOOTDD.SYS file, which, incidentally, is initialized by NTLDR.

10. ☑ **B.** You can use the Control Panel to safely make changes to the Windows 9*x* Registry. The Control Panel provides you with applets to configure the keyboard, mouse, system colors, printers, and many other features. The Control Panel provides you with configuration options, none of which can damage the Registry. When you make a change in the Control Panel, the Registry is automatically updated with the new settings.

    ☒ **A,** Computer Management utility, is incorrect because this is available only in Windows 2000 and XP. **C,** Registry Editor, is incorrect because this utility allows you to edit the Registry directly. It is therefore possible to delete important settings or to enter incorrect settings that could cause a fatal OS error. **D,** System Configuration utility, is incorrect because this utility, present only in Windows 9*x*, allows you to configure the settings of legacy configuration files such as CONFIG.SYS and WIN.INI.

11. ☑ **B.** The function of HIMEM.SYS is to enable access to extended memory. Many older applications were written when computers were limited to 1MB of memory address. The HIMEM.SYS file allows these applications to use memory over 1MB (the extended memory area).

    ☒ **A,** to initialize the Windows 9*x* boot process, is incorrect because this is the function of the IO.SYS file. **C,** to enable memory paging between extended and upper memory, is incorrect because this is the function of the expanded memory manager, EMM386.EXE. **D,** to store hardware configuration settings in Windows 9*x*, is also incorrect. This is the function of SYSTEM.DAT and, to a lesser degree (for backward compatibility), SYSTEM.INI.

File and Folder Management

12. ☑ **C.** When you double-click a file's icon, the file will open. If this is an application file, such as a document or image, the host application will be launched and the file opened within it. If it is an executable file, the program will run.

☒ **A,** the file's Properties dialog box will open, is incorrect. To open the Properties dialog box, you can right-click the icon, then select Properties. **B,** you will be given an opportunity to rename the file, is also incorrect. To rename a file, click the file's icon once, then click the file's name. This process involves two separate clicks, not a double-click. **D,** nothing will happen, is incorrect. Any icon that is double-clicked will open, whether it is a file icon, folder, or navigation icon, such as My Computer or Network Neighborhood.

13. ☑ **C.** You cannot change the system attribute in Windows. This attribute is assigned automatically by the file's host application or by Windows itself. Although it is possible to view this attribute, you cannot change it.

☒ **A,** archive, **B,** read-only, and **D,** hidden, are all incorrect. You can apply or remove any of these attributes by right-clicking the file's icon, then selecting Properties. You can place a check beside each attribute you want to apply, or remove the check from attributes you want to remove.

14. ☑ **B.** The hidden files can be truly hidden by selecting the appropriate option in the My Computer | View menu. It is possible to view all files, even hidden ones, by selecting View in the My Computer window. The Show All Files option will display hidden files as grayed-out icons. Use either the Do Not Show Hidden Files or Do Not Show Hidden or System Files option to keep hidden files from being displayed.

☒ **A** is incorrect because it states that the hidden files will be listed but cannot be opened or modified. If you can see a hidden file, you can manage it just as you would any other file. This means you can open, modify, move, rename, or delete it. You will, however, receive a confirmation message when renaming or deleting it to prevent accidental actions. **C,** the hidden files should be moved to the Recycle Bin, is incorrect. This action is the same as deleting the files. **D,** the user is incorrect because hidden files cannot be shown on the desktop, is incorrect. Again, even hidden files can be displayed by choosing the appropriate Windows View option.

15. ☑ **C.** The statement that you cannot change a file's extension is inaccurate. You can remove or change the extension along with the rest of the file's name. However, when you change the extension, Windows will issue a warning that this can render the file unusable. By changing a file's extension, you essentially remove the file's association with its host application.

☒ **A,** the file's extension determines the type of icon used for that file, is incorrect because this statement is *true*. Windows automatically associates most extensions with a particular icon type. For example, the .DOC extension is indicated by a Word or WordPad icon, and the .TXT extension is indicated by a Notepad icon. **B,** the file's extension indicates the file's type, is also incorrect because this statement is true. Files will be given an extension according to their role in the system or by the host application. For example, executable files are indicated by the .EXE extension, and bitmaps are indicated by the .BMP extension. **D,** you can make a file unusable by changing its extension, is also incorrect because it is true. As explained, when you change a file's extension, you remove its association with the host application. When you later double-click the file, Windows will either open the wrong application or simply report an error, depending on the new extension.

16. ☑ **B,** right-click each file, select Properties | Advanced, and enable the Compression option.
☒ **A.** To compress files using Backup, is incorrect because the Backup utility is not included in Windows XP Home Edition. **C,** which suggests using the Disk Management utility, is incorrect Disk Management only deals with disks not individual files. **D,** use My Computer to move the appropriate files into the COMPRESSED folder, is also incorrect. There is no native COMPRESSED folder in Windows XP. Although you can create a folder with this name, moving files into it will not compress them.

Disk Management

17. ☑ **B.** You will also be able to access FAT16 and FAT32 volumes. The NTFS 5 file system can be used only by Windows 2000 and XP. Windows 2000 retains backward compatibility with older file systems and is able to access FAT16, FAT32, and NTFS 4 volumes.
☒ **A,** FAT16 only, is incorrect. If the OS uses NTFS 5, it must be Windows 2000 or XP. Again, Windows 2000 can access FAT16, FAT32, and NTFS 4 volumes. **C,** FAT16 and HPFS, is also incorrect. HPFS was developed for OS/2 and is not accessible to Windows 9*x* or Windows 2000. **D,** none, is incorrect because Windows 2000 is not limited to using only NTFS 5.

18. ☑ **D.** FAT16 can be used by more versions of Windows than FAT32. FAT16 can be used by Windows 9*x*, Windows NT, and Windows 2000. FAT32, however, can be used only on later releases of Windows 95 (OSR2 or later), Windows 98/Me, and Windows 2000.
☒ **A** is incorrect because it suggests that FAT16 and FAT32 support 16MB and 32MB of volume capacity, respectively. The numbers 16 and 32 indicate the bit addressing of the file system. Using 16-bit addressing, FAT16 can support up to 2GB of volume space. The FAT32 file system uses 32-bit addressing and can support volumes up to 2TB. **B** is incorrect because it suggests that FAT16 volumes have less slack than FAT32 volumes. In fact, FAT32 volumes have far less slack than FAT16 volumes. FAT16 is limited to 65,526 clusters, which, in a 2GB volume, means clusters are 32KB each. FAT32 volumes use much smaller clusters, meaning that less cluster space is left over when a file is saved, so there is less overall volume slack (leftover, unused space). **C** is incorrect because it states that some versions of Windows 9*x* cannot access FAT16. Although early versions of Windows 95 cannot access FAT32 volumes, all can access FAT16.

19. ☑ **D.** NTFS 5 supports native file compression and encryption. This means that you can compress or encrypt files and folders simply by enabling those options in the file's or folder's Properties dialog box.

☒ **A,** FAT32, NTFS 4, and NTFS 5, is incorrect because FAT32 supports neither compression nor encryption, and NTFS 4 supports native compression only. For this reason, **B,** NTFS 4 and NTFS 5, and **C,** FAT32 and NTFS 5, are incorrect.

20. ☑ **C.** The Disk Management tools provide a safe and reliable mechanism to upgrade from FAT drives to NTFS 5 drives.

☒ **A** is incorrect because there is no Drive Convert utility program for Windows XP. For this reason, **D** is also incorrect, because there is no CVT program on Windows XP. **B** is incorrect because FDISK cannot create NTFS partitions.

LAB ANSWER

Utility	Purpose	Access	Operating System(s)
Scanreg	To back up and restore the Windows Registry files	Runs automatically, can be accessed by entering SCANREG on the Windows Run line	Windows 98/Me
Registry Editor (REGEDIT.EXE)	To directly edit the Registry files	Enter **REGEDIT** on the Windows Run line	Windows 95, Windows 98, Windows NT 4, Windows 2000, and Windows XP
Registry Editor (REGEDT32.EXE)	To directly edit the Registry files	Enter **REGEDT32** on the Windows Run line	Windows NT and Windows 2000
System Configuration Editor (SYSEDIT)	Allows you to directly edit legacy configuration files (e.g., WIN.INI, SYSTEM.INI, AUTOEXEC.BAT, CONFIG.SYS)	Enter **SYSEDIT** on the Windows Run line	Windows 95 and Windows 98
System Configuration utility (MSCONFIG)	Allows you to safely modify legacy configuration files (WIN.INI, SYSTEM.INI, AUTOEXEC.BAT, CONFIG.SYS)	Enter **MSCONFIG** on the Windows Run line	Windows 98

Utility	Purpose	Access	Operating System(s)
Control Panel	Allows you to safely modify hardware, application, or desktop settings	Start | Settings | Control Panel *or* double-click My Computer	Windows 9x, and Windows NT, 2000, and XP
Device Manager	Allows you to view and modify hardware configurations and load device drivers	Right-click My Computer and select Properties	Windows 9x, Windows NT, 2000, and XP
Automatic Skip Driver	Detects and disables potentially problem-causing device drivers	Runs automatically; to view results, enter **ASD** on the Windows Run line *or* select Start | Programs | Accessories | System Tools | System Information	Windows 98/Me
Computer Management utility	Allows you to configure and manage hardware configurations, disks, printers, and security settings	Start | Programs | Administrative Tools | Computer Management	Windows 2000, XP
Backup	Allows you to create backup copies of all or selected files; also enables you to compress backed-up files	Start | Programs | Accessories | System Tools | Backup	Windows 2000 and Windows XP Professional Edition. Available as third-party software on other systems.
EXTRACT.EXE	Allows you to manually extract applications or drivers from the .CAB installation files	Enter **EXTRACT** at a DOS command prompt	Windows 9x, Windows NT, 2000, and XP
Drive Converter (CVT.EXE)	Allows you to convert a volume from FAT16 to FAT32 without loss of existing data	Start | Programs | Accessories | System Tools | Drive Converter	Windows 98

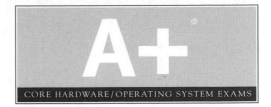

9

Installation, Configuration, and Upgrade

Themaphe focus of this chapter is the proper setup and configuration of Windows 9*x* and Windows NT 4, 2000, and XP. Whether you are installing from scratch, upgrading, or configuring the system, you must follow certain guidelines and procedures. First, we discuss basic preparation and installation procedures, followed by upgrade paths and procedures. Alternative methods of booting Windows are also described. The chapter wraps up with a discussion about installing non-Plug and Play drivers and third-party applications.

CERTIFICATION OBJECTIVE 9.01

Installing Windows

Installing modern Windows operating systems has largely become an automatic process, but there are still many things that can go wrong, so the more familiar you are with the normal process, the easier it will be for you to determine the cause of installation problems. Because the Windows 9*x* and Windows NT/2000/XP installation procedures are quite different, they are discussed individually in the following subsections.

Before starting any OS installation, you must ensure that your computer meets the minimum hardware requirements. The minimum and recommended requirements for Windows 95, 98, NT 4, 2000 and XP are listed in Tables 9-1 and 9-2. Additional required hardware includes a 1.44-inch high-density floppy disk drive and keyboard. A CD-ROM drive and a mouse are also required.

TABLE 9-1   Minimum Configurations for Windows Systems

	Windows 95	Windows 98	Windows NT	Windows 2000	Windows XP
Processor	386DX	486DX 66	Pentium	Pentium 133	Pentium 233
RAM	4MB	16MB	16MB	64MB	64MB
Hard Disk	55MB	165MB FAT16 175MB FAT32	110MB	2GB	1.5GB

TABLE 9-2	Recommended Configurations for Windows Systems				
	Windows 95	**Windows 98**	**Windows NT**	**Windows 2000**	**Windows XP**
Processor	486DX	Pentium	Pentium	Pentium 300	Pentium III
RAM	8MB	24MB	32MB	128MB	128MB
Hard Disk	84MB	355MB	200MB	3GB	3GB
Video	SVGA	SVGA	SVGA	SVGA	SVGA

o n   t h e

Ø o b

Never install a system with its minimum configuration unless absolutely necessary for data recovery or something equivalent. A good rule of thumb is to consider that the system will eventually require an upgrade, and you should install double the memory and disk requirements at the minimum. Disk and memory prices have fallen dramatically over the last few years. Do not be afraid to provide lots of both.

Windows 9x

The Windows 9x installation is almost completely automated; typically, little input is required on your part. However, you must carry out a number of important preparation procedures, and you should be familiar with the installation options and how they will affect the outcome of the installation. It is important to note here that although the Windows 95 and Windows 98 installation procedures are very similar, the exercises contained within this section are specific to Windows 98. You might notice some slight screen differences if you use these procedures to install Windows 95.

Startup

The first challenge when installing an OS from scratch is that computers cannot boot without an OS of some kind. How, then, can you get the computer started to install an OS if an OS doesn't already exist in the computer?

The answer is that you use the boot disk that came with the installation CD. The Windows 9x boot disk contains drivers that will start the system and allow the computer to read from the CD. To use the boot disk, insert the appropriate floppy disk and start the computer.

If you do not have the proper OS's boot disk, your task is a bit more difficult because you must create your own startup disk; this procedure is explained later in the chapter in the section "Creating a Startup Disk." A startup disk contains just enough of an OS's components to allow you to access a DOS command prompt and access the CD-ROM drive. From there, you can initiate the Windows 9x Setup program.

Partitioning

Before you can install an OS, you must prepare the hard drive to store data after the computer has booted properly. If the hard drive has already been prepared, you don't need to perform the procedures described in this section or in the "Format Drive" section later in the chapter.

The first step in preparing the hard drive is creating partitions. Recall that a partition is a division of the hard drive into one or several volumes. Most hard drives come from the manufacturer unpartitioned. To partition the drive, enter **FDISK** at the command prompt, and then press ENTER. FDISK.EXE is included on the Windows 9x boot disk.

If the hard drive is 2GB or less, FDISK will automatically partition the drive using FAT16. If the drive is larger than 2GB, you will be given the option to use FAT16 or FAT32. Recall that you can create more than one partition on a hard drive. Windows 9x must be installed on the first primary partition. Follow the steps in Exercise 9-1 to create a primary partition and an extended partition with one logical drive. This exercise assumes that you are using the Windows 98 boot disk and that the hard drive is larger than 2GB.

EXERCISE 9-1

Using FDISK to Create Hard Drive Partitions

1. Reboot the computer using Windows 98 boot floppy.

2. Enter **FDISK** at the command prompt. The FDISK utility will start, and you will be asked if you want to enable large disk support. If you select Yes, the drive will be partitioned using the FAT32 file system. If you select No, the FAT16 file system will be used.

3. Enter **Y** and press the ENTER key to use FAT32. The FDISK screen shown in Figure 9-1 will appear.

4. Press 1, then press ENTER to create a partition. The screen shown in Figure 9-2 will appear.

FIGURE 9-1   The primary FDISK screen

```
                      Microsoft Windows 98
                     Fixed Disk Setup Program
                 (C)Copyright Microsoft Corp. 1983 - 1998

                         FDISK Options

Current fixed disk drive: 1

Choose one of the following:

1. Create DOS partition or Logical DOS Drive
2. Set active partition
3. Delete partition or Logical DOS Drive
4. Display partition information


Enter choice: [1]




Press Esc to exit FDISK
```

FIGURE 9-2   The Create Partition screen

```
                Create DOS Partition or Logical DOS Drive

Current fixed disk drive: 1

Choose one of the following:

1. Create Primary DOS Partition
2. Create Extended DOS Partition
3. Create Logical DOS Drive(s) in the Extended DOS Partition


Enter choice: [1]




Press Esc to return to FDISK Options
```

5. Select 1, then press ENTER to create the first primary partition. You will see the message Verifying drive integrity.

6. You will be asked if you want to allocate all drive space to this partition. Press N, then press ENTER. You will again see the message Verifying drive integrity.

7. Enter the size of the first partition in megabytes or percentage of total drive space, and then press ENTER.

8. Press ESC to return to the main FDISK menu.

9. Press 2, then press ENTER to set this partition active (bootable). Enter 1 to make the C partition active. (C is always 1).

10. Repeat Steps 3 to 7 to create the extended partition, ensuring that you select the Extended Partition option in Step 4, and use all remaining drive space.

11. At this point, you will be asked to enter the logical drive size in megabytes or percentage. Enter a size or percentage (up to 100 percent) for each additional drive you wish to create. Each time a logical drive is created, FDISK will check its integrity. Press ESC *twice* to exit FDISK, then restart the computer.

FDISK allows you to create only one primary and one extended partition on a physical disk drive, which means you can only have one bootable partition on a disk using FDISK. You can, however, create up to 23 logical disks in the extended partition.

Extended partitions differ from primary partitions in that they are not assigned a drive letter. Rather, you use extended partitions to create logical drives, which are then assigned drive letters. It is important to note that the file system allows for the creation of more than one primary partition but that FDISK allows the creation of only one primary partition per disk.

ex**a**m
ⓦatch   *Primary partitions are*
bootable if they are marked as active, and
logical drives are not. However, you may
create only four primary partitions.

Although you may create up to four
primary partitions, if you want more drive
letters, you must create an extended
partition with logical drives.

Logical drives cannot contain the OS because they are not bootable as initially configured during installation. Furthermore, the system's first partition must be a primary partition. All other partitions, including those on secondary or slave drives, can be either primary or extended.

Primary partitions and logical drives also differ in the way that they are assigned letters. The system assigns drive letters starting with the first hard drive's primary partitions, then the primary partitions on other drives (such as a slave). Next, the logical drives will be lettered, starting with the primary hard drive.

For example, suppose a system has two hard drives with the following volumes:

Primary Hard Drive	Secondary Hard Drive
Primary partition Logical drive Logical drive	Primary partition Logical drive

The system will automatically letter these volumes as follows:

Primary Hard Drive	Secondary Hard Drive
C: E: F:	D: G:

Format Drive

Once the hard disk is partitioned, it is assigned a drive letter for each volume. However, these volumes cannot store data until they are formatted. (FDISK requires that the computer be restarted before formatting can take place.) To format a partition, enter the FORMAT command, followed by the drive letter. For example, to format the C: drive, use the following command:

```
FORMAT C:
```

You will receive a message stating that all data on the specified volume will be lost, even if the drive currently contains no data. Confirm the FORMAT command by entering **Y**, then pressing ENTER. A percentage counter will appear, indicating the progress of the formatting process. When the volume has been completely formatted, a message will appear asking you to enter a name for the volume. Enter a name, or press ENTER to leave the volume unnamed.

Running the Setup Utility

Once the hard drive is partitioned and formatted, you can proceed with the Windows 9x installation. Start the Setup utility by entering **SETUP** at the command prompt. If you are using a homemade boot disk, you might need to access the CD-ROM drive first, and then enter the SETUP command.

on the **!** ob

The Windows 98 Setup disk is different from the Windows 98 startup disk. The SETUP Program on the CD boots and automatically installs the operating system. The startup disk is created using the already-installed operating system. It boots the system but does not begin the SETUP program. The startup disk is a valuable resource for troubleshooting a system that is malfunctioning.

Prefile Copy Phase   The first phase of the Windows 9*x* Setup is called the *prefile copy phase*. In this phase, the installation utility checks the integrity of the hard drive by running Scandisk. Next, the utility automatically selects the installation location and gives you an opportunity to change it.

You are then asked to select an installation type. The Typical option loads drivers and applications that most people tend to use, the Portable option is used for portable systems, the Compact option loads minimal drivers and applications, and the Custom option allows you to hand pick which drivers and/or applications will be installed. Finally, you will be prompted to create a startup disk. Enter a blank floppy disk and follow the on-screen instructions. You can also use the methods described in the Windows 9x Creating A Startup Disk section to create a startup disk after the OS is installed.

File Copy Phase   The *file copy phase* typically takes the longest but requires the least input from you. During this phase, the required files (depending on the selected installation option) are copied from the installation CD into the proper locations on the hard drive.

Detection Phase   When the file copy phase is complete, Windows will begin the *detection phase* by detecting Plug-and-Play hardware in the system and loading the appropriate device drivers. You will most likely be required to restart the computer so that the drivers can be initialized.

Configuring System Settings   *Configuring system settings* is the final phase of the Windows 9*x* installation. You will be asked to verify the Date/Time setting and select the proper time zone. Next, you will be prompted to install a printer (if one exists). Windows 9*x* will then continue to load, and the installation will be complete.

Throughout the entire installation process, Windows 9*x* keeps a log of installation processes. This log is contained in the SETUPLOG.TXT file. If any part of the installation fails, restart the Setup utility, choose Safe Recovery, and Windows will use the SETUPLOG.TXT file to determine where the interruption occurred, skip the failed step, then proceed with the rest of the installation process.

Windows 9x also keeps a log of the hardware detection phase during installation. A log called DETCRASH.LOG is generated and can be used by the Setup utility to determine and avoid failure points during the hardware detection phase of a safe recovery. A text (readable) version of the DETCRASH.LOG file is also produced so that users can view a listing of which hardware was or was not successfully detected. This file is called DETLOG.TXT.

Windows NT, 2000, and XP

The Windows NT, 2000, and XP installation process differs significantly from that of Windows 9x. To begin with, although you can use the Windows 9x methods for partitioning and formatting the hard drive, the Windows 2000 and XP Setup program itself contains a partition and format utility. The order of events is also different for the Windows 2000 and XP installation.

on the **job**

Whether you are performing a clean installation or an upgrade, Windows 2000 and XP have some pretty steep hardware requirements and compatibility specifications. Check the installation package or the Microsoft Web site (www.microsoft.com/windows2000) or (www.microsoft.com/windowsxp) to ensure that your computer meets these requirements and specifications.

Startup

If the computer's BIOS supports booting from the CD-ROM drive, you can boot directly from the Windows NT, 2000, or XP installation CD by inserting the CD and starting the computer. The installation utility (WINNT.EXE) will begin automatically.

If your computer cannot boot from the CD-ROM drive, you must use the Windows 2000 boot disks (there are four). Place the first boot disk in the floppy drive, then start the computer. You will be prompted to insert the remaining disks as they are required.

Once you start the computer using the Windows 2000 installation CD or boot disks, a welcome screen will be displayed. You will be prompted to select one of three setup options: to install Windows 2000, repair a failed installation, or exit the Setup utility. Choose to install Windows 2000.

Windows XP requires more disks than Windows 2000, and the only place to acquire those disks is on the Microsoft website. A setup program creates six disks that are used in the XP setup. You can get more information about this process from the Microsoft Knowledge Base at support.microsoft.com; reference Knowledge Base article 310994 for additional information.

on the !ob

Microsoft recently announced that all new operating systems will require a bootable CD-ROM or network connection to be installed. Most CD-ROMs that have been built in the last several years are bootable. If you have a CD-ROM that does not boot, you may want to verify the BIOS is up to date with the manufacturer of the system board.

Partitioning and Formatting

If you are installing Windows 2000 or XP on an unpartitioned hard disk, you will automatically be prompted by the Setup program to create partitions. Therefore, unlike Windows 9x, partitioning and formatting can be done during the Windows 2000 or XP installation. You can also use FDISK to install Windows NT, 2000, or XP on a disk that has already been partitioned. Disk Management is accomplished in Windows NT, 2000, and XP using a utility called Disk Management. This utility provides the ability to partition, and format drives and partitions.

The Disk Management partitioning and formatting utility is recommended over FDISK for Windows NT, 2000, and XP because it supports the creation of NTFS partitions and is more sophisticated and safer. You can also use the Disk Management utility after the OS is installed. This is completely different from the utility used during setup, so it is discussed separately in the "From the Classroom" sidebar. Follow the instructions in Exercise 9-2 to partition and format the hard drive during the Windows 2000 installation.

exam
watch

The Windows 2000 and XP setup partitioning utility is very different from the FDISK utility. FDISK can create two partitions on a disk, and it creates file systems that can be used by FAT16 or FAT32 file systems. The Windows 2000 partitioning utility can create partitions that can use FAT16, FAT32, or NTFS file systems and can establish a maximum of four partitions on a disk drive.

EXERCISE 9-2

Partitioning and Formatting the Hard Drive During the Windows 2000 Installation

1. To create a new partition, press C when prompted by the installation process to create a new partition.

2. Enter the size of the partition and press ENTER.

3. You will be prompted to install Windows 2000 on this partition. Press ENTER to accept. At this point, you can also elect to continue creating partitions, but Microsoft recommends creating only the boot partition at this step. The remaining partitions should be created using the Disk Management utility after the OS has been installed.

4. Select the file system for this partition. You can select either FAT or NTFS (recommended). The partition will be formatted with the selected file system. Note that if you select FAT on a drive that is less than 2GB, FAT16 will be used. If you select FAT for a drive larger than 2GB, FAT32 will be used.

The Setup utility will automatically copy the required installation files to the new partition, then reboot the computer. When the computer starts up again, the Windows 2000 Setup Wizard will begin automatically.

FROM THE CLASSROOM

Windows NT/2000/XP Disk Management

Partitioning and formatting a disk is pretty serious business; if you use DOS or Windows tools to partition or format a volume that already contains data, that data will be lost. If you partition a volume incorrectly before loading the OS, the only way to change the partition is to remove the OS, repartition the volume, then reload the OS.

Although these rules apply to all Windows OSes, Windows NT/2000/XP's Disk Management partitioning utility makes partitioning much easier. Disk Management can only be used once Windows 2000 is properly installed, which means that you will

have to partition at least one volume—the partition the OS is installed on—using basic methods.

The Disk Management utility isn't limited to creating primary and extended partitions the way FDISK is. Rather, Disk Management lets you create as many partitions as you want, using whichever file system you deem appropriate. You can create, remove, or modify partitions without having to reboot the system (this process is often called "on-the-fly" partitioning). The only partition you cannot modify or remove is the boot partition, which contains the OS itself.

The Setup Utility

At this point, the Setup utility will detect basic hardware components such as the mouse and keyboard. You will also be prompted to enter regional settings such as language and to enter personal and company information. Next, you will be asked to supply the Windows 2000 product key and enter a computer name and administrator password.

Because Windows NT/2000/XP are essentially a network OS, you will be asked to enter network settings, such as sharing options, protocols, services, and a workgroup or domain name. When the appropriate information has been gathered, the Windows 2000 Setup utility will begin copying the required files to the hard drive (depending on the options you selected and the information supplied). The computer will restart, and Windows 2000 will start for the first time.

Windows XP

Windows XP boots and installs similarly to Windows 2000. A significant difference between Windows 2000 and Windows XP is that there are two different versions of Windows XP: Home and Professional. Windows XP Home Edition was intended as a replacement for Windows 9x systems and has less features for corporate network support than Windows XP Professional Edition. The primary difference between Windows XP Home and Professional are shown in Table 9-3 below.

Note that the examples and screen shots presented in this section were performed with Windows XP Home Edition.

Installing Windows XP

Let's look at a clean installation of Windows XP on a PC system. The installation process starts with the booting of the CD-ROM and proceeds through the installation phase. Notice the similarities between this installation and the Windows 2000 installation.

SCENARIO & SOLUTION		
	Windows 9x	Windows NT/2000/XP
How can I start the computer prior to installing the OS?	Use the Setup disk.	Use the Setup disks or boot from the installation CD.
How do I create partitions before installation?	Use FDISK.	Use the Windows installation's partition utility on the installation CD.
How do I start the Setup utility?	Enter the command **SETUP**.	The Setup utility starts automatically when you boot from the setup disks or installation CD.

TABLE 9-3	Windows XP Home Edition	Windows XP Professional Edition
Differences between Windows XP Home and Professional	Peer to peer network support	Windows NT domain support
	No remote desktop support	Remote desktop support
	No encryption of files	Encrypted File System (EFS) support
	$199 for new version, $99 for upgrade version (Microsoft website, July 2003)	$299 for new version, $199 for upgrade version (Microsoft website, July 2003)

The installation process proceeds from the booting steps to the disk initialization phase (see Figure 9-3). Notice that you are initializing a 4GB hard drive. The next step is to determine which type of partition the system should have. If this system is only going to be used for Windows XP, select NTFS, as shown in Figure 9-4.

Windows XP will then proceed to copy all of the files it needs to operate onto the hard drive, as shown in Figure 9-5. At the end of the copy process, Windows XP will reboot from the disk drive.

FIGURE 9-3   Initialization of a 4GB hard drive on Windows XP Home Edition

```
Windows XP Home Edition Setup

  The following list shows the existing partitions and
  unpartitioned space on this computer.

  Use the UP and DOWN ARROW keys to select an item in the list.

    •  To set up Windows XP on the selected item, press ENTER.

    •  To create a partition in the unpartitioned space, press C.

    •  To delete the selected partition, press D.

  4095 MB Disk 0 at Id 0 on bus 0 on atapi [MBR]
        C:  Partition1 [New (Raw)]            4087 MB  ( 4086 MB free)
            Unpartitioned space                 8 MB




  ENTER=Install   D=Delete Partition   F3=Quit
```

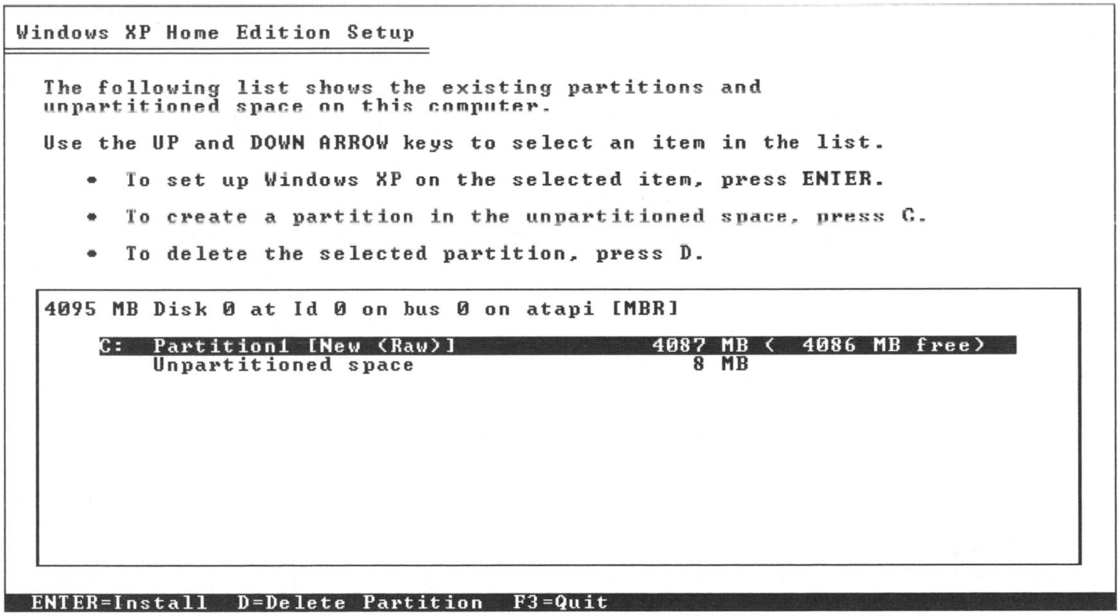

```
Windows XP Home Edition Setup
═══════════════════════════════

   The partition you selected is not formatted. Setup will now
   format the partition.

   Use the UP and DOWN ARROW keys to select the file system
   you want, and then press ENTER.

   If you want to select a different partition for Windows XP,
   press ESC.

     Format the partition using the NTFS file system (Quick)
     Format the partition using the FAT file system (Quick)
     Format the partition using the NTFS file system
     Format the partition using the FAT file system
```

```
  ENTER=Continue   ESC=Cancel
```

```
Windows XP Home Edition Setup
═══════════════════════════════



                    Please wait while Setup copies files
                     to the Windows installation folders.
                 This might take several minutes to complete.




        ┌──────────────────────────────────────────────────┐
        │ Setup is copying files...                        │
        │                          2%                      │
        │ ┌──────────────────────────────────────────────┐ │
        │ │■                                             │ │
        │ └──────────────────────────────────────────────┘ │
        └──────────────────────────────────────────────────┘
```

```
                                          Copying: winrnr.dll
```

FIGURE 9-6   Windows XP installation steps

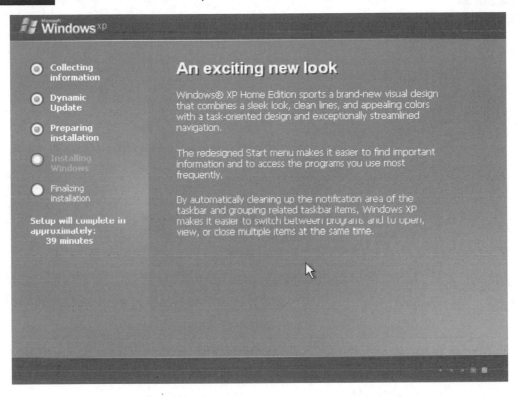

After the system reboots, Windows XP will show you the stage of installation that it is performing, as shown in Figure 9-6. Notice that the installation program states that it is installing Windows. During the installation phase, Windows XP displays the approximate time until completion and provides a dynamic slide show of features of Windows XP.

The next step is the End User License Agreement (EULA) step, as shown in Figure 9-7. Make sure you read and understand the licensing agreement that is provided by Microsoft. The EULA is several pages long and provides for almost any system licensing scenario imaginable.

After the system installs the software from the CD, the configuration phase begins. The system will continue to copy files from the CD and install Windows XP. Notice that so far you have to intervene only to initialize the disk and agree to the EULA. The XP installation process has been greatly streamlined compared to previous Microsoft operating system versions. At the completion of the Windows installation phase, the process moves to the

| FIGURE 9-7 | End User License Agreement screen |

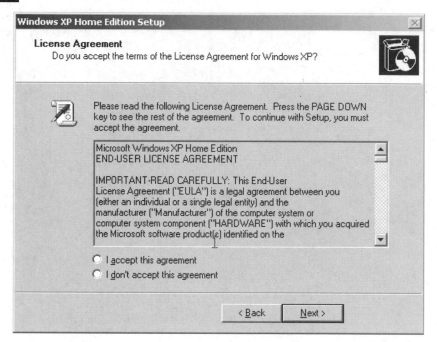

Finalizing Installation phase, as shown in Figure 9-8. Windows XP will save all settings and reboot.

Windows XP will reboot and walk you through the final configuration options. The first step is configuring the network. In this case, you will be connecting to the Internet through a LAN.

Next, you'll be given the option of registering the operating system with Microsoft either now or later. If you select Now, you will be asked for your name and other personal information, which will be sent to Microsoft. If you select later, you will be periodically reminded until you register. Registration allows you to receive product updates and other Microsoft offers and is used for internal marketing purposes at Microsoft.

Now it's time to activate your operating system. Windows XP uses a license manager that requires you to activate your operating system within 30 days, or it

FIGURE 9-8 Finalizing Installation phase of the Windows XP installation process

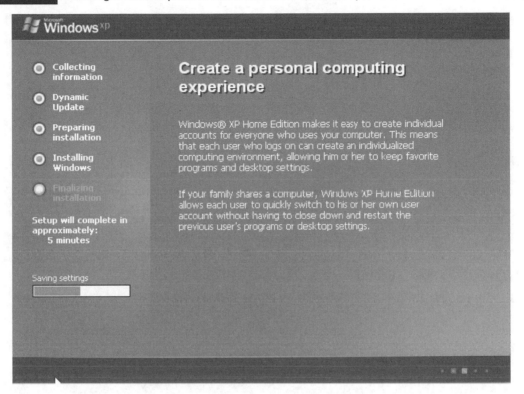

will stop working. The activation process will remind you of this each time the system is rebooted and at other times until you activate it. Figure 9-9 shows the activation process occurring for an XP system. Once an XP system has been activated, additional attempts may inform you that the product has already been registered on another system. This helps prevent copyright infringement of XP software. This is the same process used with Office XP and other Microsoft software.

When you activate a Windows XP system, either by the Internet or telephone, that activation will generally be good as long as the system configuration is unchanged. However, if, for example, you upgrade the processor or change video

FIGURE 9-9   The Activate Windows process on an XP system

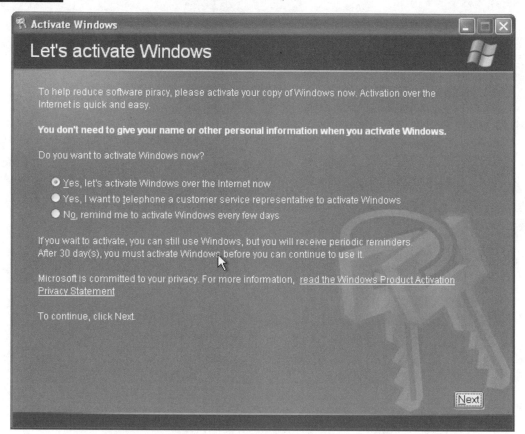

cards, you may get the message shown in Figure 9-10 if you try to reinstall Windows XP for some reason. This may occur if you retire a system and want to use the existing operating system on a newer system. The activation process will consider this operating system to be already activated. You can at this point either buy a new license for Windows XP or you can contact the telephone support people using the phone number provided. The customer support person will provide you with a new

FIGURE 9-10   Windows XP product key screen for a system that has already been activated

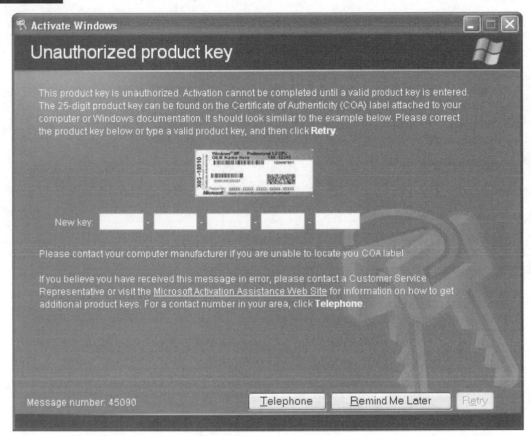

activation number that you can use to activate the license. If you do not do this, you will get the activation messages, and the system will only work for 30 days.

You should run the update program immediately after you install Windows XP so that you have all the latest updates and patches for your operating system— you'll leave your user seriously vulnerable unless you do this. Figure 9-11 shows the

FIGURE 9-11 Windows Update screen

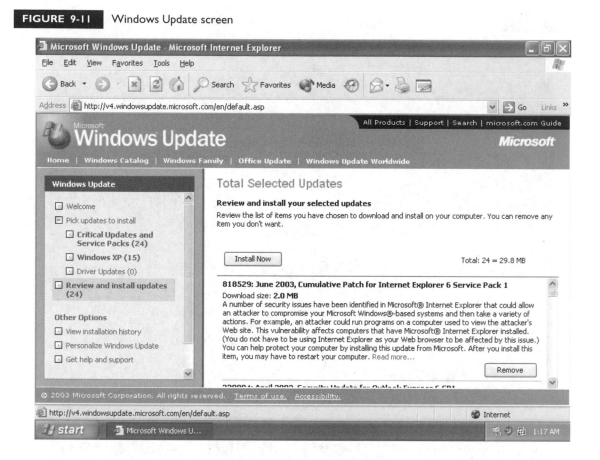

update process for a Windows XP Home Edition system. Many of these updates are very large, and a dial-up update can take several hours to accomplish. You can also view the installed updates by viewing installation history, as shown in Figure 9-12. The history will show you all successful and failed installations. It is a good idea to check this periodically to verify that updates are being made and that they are successful.

FIGURE 9-12   Installation History screen

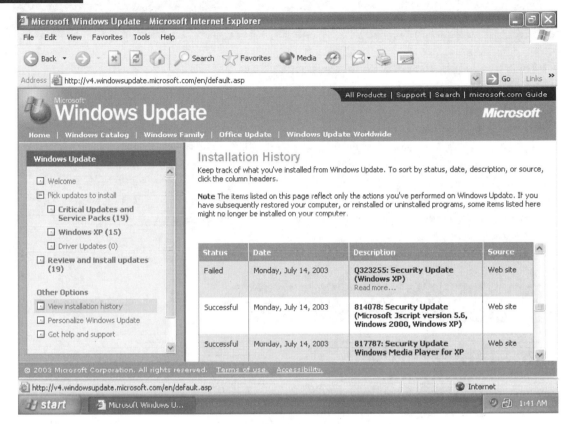

on the
Job   *It is a good idea to disable or remove any antivirus or personal firewall software before you begin any upgrades. This will simplify the installation process and prevent possible installation errors. When you are upgrading a system, it is very possible that the antivirus software will think the computer has become infected with a virus.*

FROM THE CLASSROOM

Practicing with All of These Systems

Practicing installation and configurations of the numerous options available on all of these operating systems requires access to several machines or a single machine on which you can install software over and over again. A company called VMWARE created a software product called VMWARE Workstation that allows for the creation of virtual machines that can run under a single desktop system using Windows NT, 2000, or XP. This software allows for a single machine to simultaneously run operating systems needed to prepare for the A+ exam. The website for VMWARE is *www.vmware.com*. A similar product to VMWARE Workstation is Virtual PC by Connectix. You can visit their website at **www.connectix.com**.

CERTIFICATION OBJECTIVE 9.02

Upgrading Windows

In some cases, you might want to upgrade the Windows OS rather than performing a clean installation. When you upgrade the OS, you replace the old one with a new version. The main advantages to performing an upgrade rather than purchasing a full new version are the lower cost of the installation disk and the fact that most of the existing applications, network settings, and nonsystem files are migrated into the new OS.

However, it is typically recommended that you perform a clean installation whenever possible to eliminate the migration of problems from the old OS to the new. It also ensures that the new OS uses known compatible drivers rather than old ones that might not function properly, even though they worked with the old OS.

Before you perform an upgrade, it's a good idea to back up your computer in case the upgrade fails and you are left without an OS. You must also ensure that your computer has a sufficient OS to upgrade to the new OS. These are called *upgrade paths*: you can upgrade to Windows 98 from Windows 95. You can upgrade to Windows 2000 Professional from Windows 95, Windows 98, and Windows NT 4 Workstation. You can upgrade to Windows XP from Windows 98, Windows NT 4, and Windows 2000.

on the job *If you want to upgrade to Windows XP from Windows 95 you must either perform a new installation or first upgrade Windows 95 to Windows 98. To upgrade from earlier versions of Windows NT (before NT 4), you must first either upgrade to Windows NT 4 or perform a clean install. You should make sure that you then update Windows NT 4 with the latest service pack (currently Service Pack 6A).*

Upgrading from Windows 95 to Windows 98

You can run the Windows 98 Setup utility directly from Windows 95. When you perform the upgrade, Windows 98 will overwrite the Windows 95 system files while leaving applications, nonsystem files, and settings intact. Follow the steps in Exercise 9-3 to perform the upgrade from Windows 95 to 98.

EXERCISE 9-3

Upgrading from Windows 95 to Windows 98

1. Start Windows 95 as you normally do, and close any running applications and utilities.

2. Insert the Windows 98 installation CD. In most cases, the Setup utility will start automatically. If it doesn't, access the CD using My Computer or Windows Explorer, and double-click the Setup icon.

3. The Setup utility will detect the existence of Windows 95 and ask if you want to perform an upgrade. Select Yes.

4. Follow the on-screen instructions to complete the upgrade, ensuring that you select Yes when prompted to save the system files. This will allow you to uninstall Windows 98 and revert to Windows 95 if problems occur. When Windows 98 is removed, the Windows 95 system files will be restored.

The remainder of the installation will proceed as described earlier in the chapter, with the exception of a few steps. To begin with, you will not be asked to select an installation type (compact, typical, and the like). Windows 98 will simply migrate existing features when possible or upgrade existing features that cannot be migrated. The hardware detection and configuration steps will also be skipped. Again, Windows 98 will simply use the existing hardware configurations.

Upgrading from Windows 9x to *Windows 2000*

The upgrade process for Windows 9x to Windows 2000 is relatively simple. From the Windows 9x operating system, launch the Windows 2000 Setup utility. Because you are currently using a 32-bit OS, the 32-bit Setup utility will be used (WINNT32.EXE). The Setup utility will detect the Windows 9x OS and ask if you want to upgrade. Choose Yes.

The setup will proceed as normal, except that all existing compatible applications, OS settings, and network configurations (such as username, password, and IP address) will be migrated into Windows 2000. Some files that will not be upgraded include the Windows 9x System Tools and virtual device drivers. These files will be replaced with Windows 2000 versions.

on the Job

It is recommended that you back up the system before upgrading Windows 9x to Windows 2000. Windows 2000 does not have an uninstall feature, so the only way to revert to Windows 9x is to delete Windows 2000 and reinstall Windows 9x. It is also highly recommended that you disable any memory-resident programs before you begin an upgrade.

Upgrading from Windows NT 4 to Windows 2000

Like Windows 9x, Windows NT 4 provides an easy upgrade to Windows 2000 or XP. From the Windows NT 4 OS, launch the 32-bit Windows 2000 Setup utility (WINNT32.EXE). Choose to perform an upgrade and follow the on-screen instructions.

Like Windows 9x, some Windows NT 4 utilities will be replaced rather than migrated. However, all existing compatible applications and utilities, as well as network and other configuration settings, will be migrated.

Upgrading from Windows XP Home Edition to Windows XP Professional

The upgrade from Home to Professional may be needed if you need to move a Home Edition system to a Windows domain environment, need the additional security of encrypted files, or you need to maintain compatibility with other systems in your network. The installation process is fairly straightforward. When you load the Professional CD, the system will take you to the installation/upgrade screen, as shown in Figure 9-13. You have two options here, to either upgrade or do a new install. In this case, choose upgrade.

FIGURE 9-13 Upgrade process for XP Home to Professional

The upgrade will ask you to agree to the EULA and then take you to the product key screen. Enter the product key provided by Microsoft to continue. From this point, the installation process will be identical to the XP Home Edition installation you performed earlier in this chapter. The upgrade from Home to Professional will keep your existing settings intact and retain your account information.

Dual-Booting Windows

A dual-boot configuration includes two working OSes on a single computer. At startup, a boot menu will be presented from which the user will have to select which OS to use. To create a dual-boot system, the two OSes must be installed separately. When users install applications or configure OS settings in one OS, the other OS will remain unaffected. In other words, if you want to be able to access a particular application from both OSes, you must install the application twice, once from within each OS.

It is recommended that you install each OS in a dual-boot configuration on a separate partition. The OS that you boot with will determine whether you can access files on the other partitions in the system. For example, suppose a computer has Windows 9*x* installed on a FAT32 partition and Windows 2000/XP installed on an NTFS partition. If you boot from Windows 9x, you will be unable to access files on the NTFS partition because Windows 9x cannot recognize this file system. However, because Windows 2000/XP is backward compatible with FAT32 and FAT16, you will be able to access the FAT partition if you boot from Windows 2000 or Windows XP.

Recall that Windows 9x must be installed on the first primary partition. Windows 2000 or XP, on the other hand, can occupy any partition. Therefore, if you plan to create a dual-boot configuration in the future, don't install Windows 2000/XP on the first partition. Although the location of each OS is important, the *order* of installation is usually irrelevant. That is, it makes no difference which OS you install first when creating a dual-boot configuration. The exception is that if you are dual-booting with Windows 95 and Windows 2000, it is recommended that you install Windows 95 first.

Creating a dual-boot configuration is similar to performing an upgrade, except that you select a *different* location in which to install the second OS. Follow the steps in Exercise 9-4 to create a dual-boot configuration with Windows 9x and Windows 2000. Note that this basic procedure (not including network configuration) can also be used to dual-boot Windows NT 4, Windows 2000, and Windows XP. It is highly recommended that you install the oldest operating system first.

EXERCISE 9-4

Creating a Dual-Boot Configuration with Windows 9x and Windows 2000

1. Install Windows 9x using the procedures discussed earlier in the chapter, ensuring that there are at least two partitions on the hard drive.

2. Insert the Windows 2000 installation CD. The Setup utility will run automatically. If not, activate it using the Windows 9x My Computer or Windows Explorer.

3. You will be asked to choose between upgrading or installing a new copy of Windows 2000. Choose to install a new copy.

4. The Windows 2000 installation will proceed, and the computer will be restarted.

5. When the computer restarts, you will be prompted to select the Windows 2000 installation location. Select a different partition from the one Windows 9x is using. (This is not necessary, but it is recommended.)

6. Follow the on-screen directions to complete the Windows 2000 setup. Windows 2000 will automatically detect the presence of Windows 9x and generate and configure the dual-boot menu (BOOT.INI) that will appear at startup.

SCENARIO & SOLUTION

When should I perform an OS upgrade?	When you want to keep existing applications, configurations, and nonsystem files.
How do I perform an upgrade?	Load the original OS normally and run the new OS installation utility. Select the upgrade option.
How do I create a dual-boot configuration?	Install the first OS using basic methods and start the computer normally. Run the Setup utility for the second OS and choose to perform a new installation rather than an upgrade.

By default, the system will display a boot menu for 30 seconds at startup. If no OS is selected, the system will automatically boot into Windows 2000. You can change these options by right-clicking My Computer and selecting Properties. Click the Advanced tab, then click the Startup and Recovery button and alter the options as you wish.

CERTIFICATION OBJECTIVE 9.03

Booting Windows

Under normal conditions, Windows will boot in normal mode, loading all its required device drivers and utilities. However, in some cases, such as when you encounter problems, you can use alternate boot methods to determine or troubleshoot the problem. These boot methods, as well how to manually boot or repair an OS that will not load, are discussed in the following sections.

Windows 9x

Windows 9x retains backward compatibility with older hardware and applications, so its boot files are different from those of Windows 2000/XP. Furthermore, Windows 9x includes a DOS mode that allows you to boot the computer without loading Windows. The normal boot sequence, boot modes, and boot troubleshooting procedures for Windows 9x are described in the following subsections.

Boot Sequence and Required Files

When you first turn on the computer, the BIOS performs a POST, then searches the drives for the *master boot record (MBR)*. This is known as the *BIOS bootstrap phase*. The BIOS then hands control to the OS loader, located in the MBR, which also contains data about the partitions on the drive and which partition has been marked as active. The OS loader uses this information to find and initialize IO.SYS on the boot partition.

The boot process then enters what is called *real-mode boot*, indicating that real-mode files required to boot the system will be processed. See the "From the Classroom" sidebar that follows for more information about real mode and protected mode. First, IO.SYS locates and reads MSDOS.SYS, which contains boot parameters, such as how long to display the "Starting Windows 9*x*" message or which OSes exist if there is a non-Windows 2000 dual-boot configuration. The LOGO.SYS file (the Windows splash screen) is then displayed. Next, IO.SYS searches for the SYSTEM.DAT and USER.DAT files and checks the integrity of their data, then loads SYSTEM.DAT.

The boot process then enters the *real-mode configuration stage*, during which real-mode (legacy) configuration files will be processed, if they exist. CONFIG.SYS is processed first, followed by AUTOEXEC.BAT. Note that these files are not required by Windows 9*x* to boot properly. Values in the CONFIG.SYS file will override values in SYSTEM.DAT, and IO.SYS will then load HIMEM.SYS, if it has not already been referenced in the CONFIG.SYS file.

The next boot stage is called *protected-mode boot* because it includes the initialization of protected-mode (32-bit) system files. First, WIN.COM is executed, and IO.SYS hands it control of the boot process. WIN.COM then locates and loads the virtual memory manager (VMM386.VXD), which is responsible for loading 32-bit device drivers into memory. VMM386.VXD also switches the processor from real mode to protected mode. Next, WIN.COM reads SYSTEM.INI, and its values are implemented. Note that values in the SYSTEM.INI file will be overridden by corresponding parameters in the Registry.

Finally, the Windows 9*x* screen is loaded. The kernel (KRNL32.DLL) contains the actual screen components, and GDI.EXE and USER.EXE enable the graphical interface. Entries in the WIN.INI file are read, and the Windows shell (EXPLORER.EXE) is loaded.

ⓦatch *It is essential that you be familiar with the phases and files of the Windows 9x boot process as well as how they differ from those of Windows 2000/XP.*

Boot Modes

The boot process described previously is known as *normal mode*: it is how Windows 9*x* will boot when things are running normally. However, in some cases, you might want to alter the boot process so that some or most of the normal steps are skipped. For example, if Windows 9*x* will not load properly, you can use an alternate boot method to at least get to a command prompt so that you can determine and troubleshoot the cause of the problem.

There are several boot modes for Windows 9*x*. To select an alternate boot mode, press F8 at startup when you see the message "Starting Windows." On some Windows 98 systems, you might be required to press CTRL rather than F8. The two most commonly used alternate boot modes, Safe mode and MS-DOS mode, are described in the subsections that follow.

FROM THE CLASSROOM

Real Versus Protected Mode

What are real and protected modes? The term *real mode* refers to older systems and applications—or rather, their behavior. Real mode indicates an inability to access extended and virtual memory, and real-mode systems do not support multitasking. Applications that run in real mode typically run by trying to directly access the hardware. Another feature of real mode is that it is possible for an application to take over memory space that is already in use by a utility or driver. Real mode is a processor mode that was used in early microprocessors; it had a limit of 1MB of RAM, which is why the division of memory into conventional and upper, as described in Chapter 8, is so important.

Protected-mode systems, such as the Intel 386 and newer chips, support multitasking and access to extended and virtual memory. While most real-mode applications are 16-bit, protected-mode applications are usually 32-bit. The term *protected mode* refers to the fact that each application's memory space is protected from use by other applications.

DOS cannot run in protected mode, even if it is installed on a computer whose processor can run in protected mode. Windows 95 and higher can run in protected mode, and Windows 9*x* retains the ability to run real-mode applications. In general, however, Windows 9*x* legacy files and drivers work in real mode, and native 32-bit Windows 9*x* files and drivers work in protected mode.

Safe Mode   If Windows 9x contains a bad device driver or a corrupt legacy configuration file, the OS might not be able to load at all. By booting in Safe mode, you can instruct the OS to skip these files on startup, which might allow Windows 9x to load so that you can troubleshoot the problem. For example, suppose the device driver for a NIC is corrupted and preventing the OS from loading. When you start the computer in Safe mode, the NIC device driver is skipped altogether—that is, the driver is not processed, so the error does not occur.

When the OS boots in Safe mode, the real-mode configuration phase is skipped. That is, legacy configuration files such as AUTOEXEC.BAT and CONFIG.SYS are not processed. Furthermore, the only device drivers to be loaded are the standard mouse, keyboard, and VGA display drivers. Again, you will not have the full functionality of Windows 9x when you boot in Safe mode, but enough of the OS will load to allow you to troubleshoot the problem. Troubleshooting is covered in more detail in Chapter 10, including how to use Safe mode to install and remove drivers.

When the OS boots in Safe mode, the text "Safe Mode" will appear in each corner of the monitor to indicate this status. While in Safe mode, you will be unable to access the Network Neighborhood or any mapped network drives.

MS-DOS Mode   In some ways, MS-DOS mode is the opposite of Safe mode. In Safe mode, only the protected-mode configuration files are processed. In MS-DOS mode, only the DOS-based real-mode configuration files, such as AUTOEXEC.BAT and CONFIG.SYS, are processed. You can run Windows 9x in real mode, either by selecting Command Prompt Only from the Startup menu or by selecting Start | Shutdown | Restart in MS-DOS mode.

There are several reasons for starting the computer in real (DOS) mode. For example, some DOS applications, such as games, will not run properly from within a Windows 9x DOS shell. These applications require full control of the hardware, so they cannot be run from Windows. You might also need to start the computer in real mode if the Windows 9x OS is too badly corrupted to start in Safe mode. The DOS mode might allow you to delete problematic utilities or drivers from the hard drive or to reinstall Windows 9I.

There are several other Windows 9x boot modes, as listed in Table 9-4.

Creating a Startup Disk

In some cases, the Windows 9x OS will be too badly damaged to even present the Startup menu, and you must have an alternate method for booting the computer. A startup disk is one of the most useful tools you can have in troubleshooting serious OS problems. As described previously, a startup, or boot, disk contains just enough of an OS to provide you with a DOS command prompt.

TABLE 9-4	Boot Mode	Description
Windows 9x Boot Modes	Normal mode	The OS will load normally, using all drivers and Registry values.
	Logged mode	The OS will load normally and will log boot activities in a text file called BOOTLOG.TXT.
	Safe mode	The OS will load with minimal drivers (mouse, keyboard, and standard VGA).
	Safe mode with network support	Same as Safe mode but with network drivers and configurations to allow network access.
	Step-by-step confirmation	The OS will load normally but will allow you to selectively process or skip individual AUTOEXEC.BAT and CONFIG.SYS lines.
	Command prompt only	Begins the boot process normally but stops before the protected-mode boot phase.
	Safe mode command prompt only	Loads in MS-DOS mode without the real-mode configuration files. The only files loaded are IO.SYS, MSDOS.SYS, and COMMAND.COM.
	Previous version of MS-DOS	Loads an earlier version of DOS than the one that is included with Windows 9x. Can be used only if a previous version of DOS exists on the system.

You can create a startup disk for a Windows 9x system either manually or by using the Windows 9x startup disk utility. These methods are described in the following subsections.

Creating a Startup Disk Manually   The most important feature of a startup disk is that it is configured to be bootable. To make a floppy disk bootable, you can format it using the system switch, as shown in the following command:

```
FORMAT A: /S
```

Startup disks must contain the core DOS files: IO.SYS, MSDOS.SYS, and COMMAND.COM. As long as these files are loaded, the computer will boot and you will be able to carry out internal DOS commands. Transfer these files, as well as any configuration or external command files that you might need, to the system disk. Common startup disk files include FORMAT.COM, FDISK.EXE, MSCDEX.EXE, SCANDISK.EXE, CONFIG.SYS, and AUTOEXEC.BAT.

The MSDOS.SYS file used on a startup disk is different from the MSDOS.SYS file used in the Windows 9x boot process. The startup disk must contain the DOS version, which is responsible for translating commands between COMMAND.COM and IO.SYS. The Windows 9x version of MSDOS.SYS is used only in startup and contains boot parameters, such as how long to display the "Starting Windows" message or which OS to use by default in a dual-boot configuration.

You can also use the SYS command to create a system disk. You can use this command only if the disk is already formatted. When you use the SYS command, the disk is made bootable, and the IO.SYS, MSDOS.SYS, and COMMAND.COM files are copied onto it. You will still be required to manually copy any driver, configuration, or external command files that you want to use.

Finally, you can create a bootable disk using the Windows 9x Format utility. Right-click the floppy drive icon in either My Computer or Windows Explorer, then select Format. A window similar to the one shown in Figure 9-14 will open.

If the disk is already formatted, select the Copy System Files Only option. The disk will be marked as bootable, and IO.SYS, MSDOS.SYS, and COMMAND.COM will be copied to it. If the disk is not formatted, select the appropriate Format type, then enable the Copy System Files option. The result will be the same, but the disk will be formatted first. As before, you will need to manually copy external command and driver files onto the disk.

FIGURE 9-14

The Windows 9x
Format utility
window

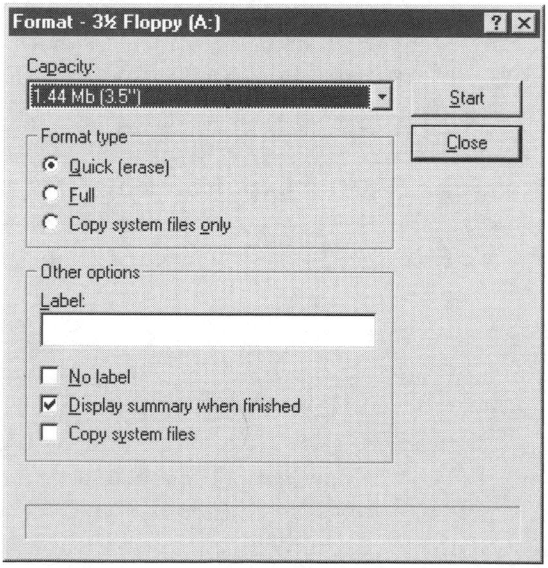

on the Job

When creating a startup disk, it's also a good idea to back up SYSTEM.DAT and USER.DAT. However, as long as you are running Windows 9x, these files are in use, so they cannot be copied. You can copy the Registry files to the startup disk only if you are using the computer in real mode.

Creating a Windows Startup Disk   You can create a Windows 9x startup disk during the OS installation. Simply follow the on-screen procedures when you are prompted to create the disk. Alternatively, you can create a Windows 9x startup disk at any time, once the OS is loaded. To create a startup disk in Windows 9x, follow the steps in Exercise 9-5.

EXERCISE 9-5

Creating a Windows 9x Startup Disk

1. Insert a blank, formatted floppy disk into the floppy drive.

2. Access the Control Panel by choosing Start | Settings | Control Panel or My Computer | Control Panel.

3. Double-click the Add/Remove Programs icon.

4. Click the Startup Disk tab, then click the Create Disk button. You might be required to insert the Windows 9x installation CD at this time. A progress meter will be displayed.

5. When the process is finished, click OK or Cancel to exit the Add/Remove Programs window.

The startup disk will contain IO.SYS, MSDOS.SYS, and COMMAND.COM. It will also allow you to use external commands such as SCANDISK, FDISK, FORMAT, EDIT, and EXTRACT. Note that you will not see a separate file for each of these external commands because they are compiled and contained in the EBD.CAB file. If you created the boot disk using Windows 98, the disk will also contain drivers for standard IDE and SCSI CD-ROM drives as well as the AUTOEXEC.BAT and CONFIG.SYS files. When you use the startup disk, the process will create a virtual disk in RAM that the files contained in EBD.CAB are copied to. This is used until a permanent operating system is installed and allows for maintenance to occur on the system.

on the **Ü o b** *If you look in the Help system for Windows 98 Backup, you will find instructions for creating ERDs (emergency repair disks). However, if you follow the instructions, you will see that the option to create these disks doesn't exist. Microsoft has since released technical documents stating that Windows 98 Backup (created by Seagate Software, Inc.) does not support the creation of ERDs. You can, create Windows 98 ERDs with the full third-party version of Seagate's Backup utility. You can, however make a startup disk using the Add/Remove programs icon in the Control Panel. This does not provide recovery as it does in Windows XP, but it is a good place to start.*

Windows 2000/XP

Windows 2000 and XP do not operate in real mode, so their boot process is quite different from that of Windows 9x. Windows 2000 and XP provide more powerful troubleshooting and diagnostic boot modes then earlier operating systems.

on the **Ü o b** *The boot process for Windows NT 4, 2000, and XP are the same with few exceptions. This boot process was introduced with Windows NT 3.5 and has changed little in process.*

Boot Sequence and Required Files

When a Windows 2000 or XP computer is started, the BIOS bootstrap phase is conducted, just as it is in Windows 9x. Following this phase, the MBR locates the bootstrap loader, NTLDR. NTLDR is responsible for initiating and organizing the boot process, much like IO.SYS in Windows 9x. First, it switches the processor into 32-bit protected mode, then it locates and reads the BOOT.INI file. BOOT.INI is responsible for providing the boot menu in a Windows 2000 or XP dual-boot configuration.

Once Windows 2000 or XP has been selected, or if there are no other OSes in the computer, the message "Starting Windows" will appear on the screen. At this time, NTLDR runs NTDETECT.COM, which detects existing hardware configurations. This is known as the *hardware detection phase*. The information gathered during this phase is placed in the Registry via NTLDR. As this process is being conducted, an on-screen bar indicator is displayed to indicate its progress.

When the hardware detection phase is over, the *kernel load phase* begins. This change is evident to the user because the display mode changes from text to graphics. During this phase, NTLDR locates the Windows kernel (NTOSKRNL.EXE) and loads it into memory. NTLDR then locates the hardware device drivers referenced in the Registry. These files are not yet initialized; rather, they are simply located and prepared for initialization by the kernel. The last function of NTLDR is to initialize

SCENARIO & SOLUTION

What is the function of NTOSKRNL?	NTOSKRNL is the kernel of a Windows 2000/XP system. It loads the core operating system, memory management, and other system functions.
What is the function of NTLDR?	To control the Windows 2000 boot process until the kernel is loaded.
Which Windows OSes load real-mode configuration files at startup?	Windows 95 and Windows 98.

the kernel and hand it control of the rest of the boot process. The kernel will then initialize the device drivers, virtual memory and load the graphical interface.

Boot Modes

As with Windows 9x, you can choose alternate boot modes during the Windows 2000 startup. To do so, press F8 when the boot menu is displayed. You'll see the Windows 2000 Advanced Options menu, from which you can select the appropriate boot mode. There are several choices, including Safe mode, Safe mode with networking, Last Known Good configuration, and Debugging mode. A complete list of Windows 2000/XP boot modes is displayed in Table 9-5. The most commonly used (other than Normal) are Safe mode, Safe mode with command prompt, and Last Known Good configuration.

TABLE 9-5	Mode	Definition
Windows 2000/ XP Boot Modes	Safe mode	Minimal drivers and services to start windows
	Safe mode with networking	Adds network support to Safe mode
	Safe mode with command prompt	Starts the same as Safe mode but with the command prompt instead of GUI loaded
	Enable VGA mode	Starts Windows with 640x480 pixel resolution
	Last Known Good configuration	Starts Windows using previously good configuration
	Directory Service Restore mode	Valid only for Windows domain controllers
	Debug mode	Allows remote diagnostics using the COM2 port
	Enable Boot Logging	Saves boot log of process; works with all boots except Last Known Good

Safe Mode   The Windows 2000 and XP Safe mode is very similar to the Windows 9x Safe mode. That is, the OS will load with minimal drivers and files. Standard drivers will be loaded for the mouse, keyboard, CD, and VGA video drivers. However, unlike Windows 9x, Windows 2000 Safe mode will load Plug-and-Play drivers, so it can isolate problems related to third-party applications and drivers.

Safe Mode with Command Prompt   Because Windows 2000 and XP cannot run in real mode, no MS-DOS mode is available. However, you can elect to load the OS in Safe mode with command prompt. The difference between this mode and regular Safe mode is that a command prompt, rather than the Windows graphical interface, will be displayed. This allows you to use command-line troubleshooting techniques to resolve graphical interface-related problems.

Last Known Good Configuration   The Last Known Good configuration boots from the last time the system was started successfully. This includes Registry and driver information. The Last Known Good configuration option is useful if you installed a driver or other software and the system becomes inoperable as a result; it can allow you to get your system restarted so you can fix the problem.

Creating a Windows 2000 Setup Disk

The Windows 2000 setup disks also serve as startup disks that you can use to boot the computer when Windows 2000 will not load properly. Four startup disks are required to boot a Windows 2000 machine, and you can create them by entering the following command at the Windows Run line:

```
\BOOTDISK\MAKEBOOT32 A:
```

You can also create a startup disk by formatting a floppy disk using the operating system and then copying BOOT.INI, NTLDR, and NTDETECT.COM to the floppy disk. If you need access to SCSI devices, you will also want to copy NTBOOTDD.SYS to the floppy. The startup disk will boot the operating system from the floppy and then load the remainder of the operating system from the hard drive. This procedure is identical in Windows 2000 and XP.

Note that the MAKEBOOT32.EXE command must be executed from the installation CD unless it has been manually copied to the hard disk. When you boot the computer using the Windows 2000 startup (setup) disks, you will be prompted to either install Windows 2000 or repair a failed installation. Press R to select repair. You will then be provided with the option to repair the OS using either the Recovery Console or the emergency repair process.

If you need to make a bootable disk for NT/2000/XP using a Windows 9x system, use the MAKEBOOT.EXE program.

Creating a Windows XP Startup Disk

Windows XP does not include a startup disk with the CD-ROM. If you need startup disks, you must download them from the Microsoft website. The setup disks are extracted and copied to floppy disks on the system that you use to download these files. Microsoft has announced that it is discontinuing floppy disk startup processes. They recommend either obtaining a bootable CD-ROM (almost all are these days), or using a network installation.

The Recovery Console

Windows 2000 and Windows XP provide a utility called the Recovery Console, which allows you to access the system's hard drives using basic DOS-like commands to repair problems. These commands will allow you to move, copy, delete, and expand files. Other commands allow you to format drives, replace the Registry from backup, and repair the boot sector or MBR. The Recovery Console is a special program that must be installed from the installation CD. To install the Recovery Console, execute the following command line. The d in the command line represents the location of the installation CD. While not recommended in an emergency you can run the Recovery Console from the installation CD.

```
d:\i386\winnt32.exe /cmdcons
```

The installation takes a few minutes; when it's completed your startup screen will change, as shown in Figure 9-15. The Recovery Console has a number of options that can be accessed by typing **help**, as shown in Figure 9-16. Individual

```
Please select the operating system to start:

     Microsoft Windows XP Professional
     Microsoft Windows Recovery Console

Use the up and down arrow keys to move the highlight to your choice.
Press ENTER to choose.
Seconds until highlighted choice will be started automatically: 23




For troubleshooting and advanced startup options for Windows, press F8.
```

command help can be gotten for an option by typing **help *command name***, as shown in Figure 9-17.

```
For more information on a specific command, type
command-name /? or HELP command-name.
ATTRIB
BATCH
BOOTCFG
CD
CHDIR
CHKDSK
CLS
COPY
DEL
DELETE
DIR
DISABLE
DISKPART
ENABLE
EXIT
EXPAND
FIXBOOT
FIXMBR
FORMAT
HELP
LISTSVC
LOGON
MAP
MD
MKDIR
MORE
NET
RD
  More:   ENTER=Scroll (Line)    SPACE=Scroll (Page)    ESC=Stop
```

FIGURE 9-17 Command help for chkdsk

```
MAP
MD
MKDIR
MORE
NET
RD
REN
RENAME
RMDIR
SYSTEMROOT
TYPE

C:\WINDOWS>help chkdsk
Checks a disk and displays a status report

CHKDSK [drive:] [/P] [/R]

  [drive:]        Specifies the drive to check
  /P              Check even if the drive is not flagged dirty
  /R              Locates bad sectors and recovers readable information
                  (implies /P)

CHKDSK may be used without any parameters, in which case the
current drive is checked with no switches.  You can specify the listed
switches.

CHKDSK requires the AUTOCHK.EXE file. CHKDSK automatically locates
AUTOCHK.EXE in the startup (boot) directory. If it cannot be found in
the startup directory, CHKDSK will attempt to locate the Windows
installation CD. If the installation CD cannot be found, CHKDSK prompts
for the location of AUTOCHK.EXE.

C:\WINDOWS>_
```

on the **job**

Be very careful with the Recovery Console because you can directly and immediately change the configuration of your system and make it nonusable. Make sure you consult the Microsoft website if you are working on a specific problem with either Windows 2000 or Windows XP.

Creating an Emergency Repair Disk in Windows 2000

An emergency repair differs from the Recovery Console process because it is an automated process. To perform an emergency repair, start the computer using the Windows 2000 setup disks, elect to repair a failed installation, and choose the emergency repair process. You will then be prompted to select Manual Repair or Fast Repair. Fast Repair will automatically perform all repair options; Manual Repair will allow you to select which repair functions to perform.

The repair process includes checking the existence and integrity of boot files, such as NTLDR and BOOT.INI and system files such as NTOSKRNL.EXE. If any of these files are missing or corrupt, they will be replaced by files on the installation CD. The repair utility will also check the integrity of the boot sector and rebuild it if necessary.

To create an ERD, access the Windows 2000 Backup utility and select Emergency Repair Disk from the Welcome tab. It is important to note here that the ERD will contain information about the computer's *current* configuration. If you use an ERD that was created with an older configuration, the repair utility might not function correctly. For this reason, you should create a new ERD each time you change the configuration of the system.

Automated Systems Recovery

Windows XP introduced a new system recovery tool called Automated Systems Recovery that replaced the ERD process used in Windows 9x and Windows 2000. The ASR program is accessed through the Backup wizard. To create an ASR disk, select Advanced, as shown in Figure 9-18, and then select the Automated System Recovery Preparation Wizard, as shown in Figure 9-19.

The process creates a floppy disk that you can use to recover your system in the event of a systems failure. In the event of a failure, boot the system from the floppy disk and you can begin repairing or reinstalling components of the operating system. To use this process, you must also have a backup using the Windows backup program. You can only recover from supported media of the backup program.

System Restore

Windows 2000 and Windows XP provide the ability to set recovery points in the event of a system failure. If you are in the process of reconfiguring a system, you can

---

FIGURE 9-18 Backup Program screen on Windows XP

Backup or Restore Wizard

Welcome to the Backup or Restore Wizard

This wizard helps you back up or restore the files and settings on your computer.

If you prefer, you can switch to Advanced Mode to change the settings used for backup or restore. This option is recommended for advanced users only.

☑ Always start in wizard mode

To continue, click Next.

< Back   Next >   Cancel

FIGURE 9-19 Automated System Recovery Preparation Wizard on Windows XP

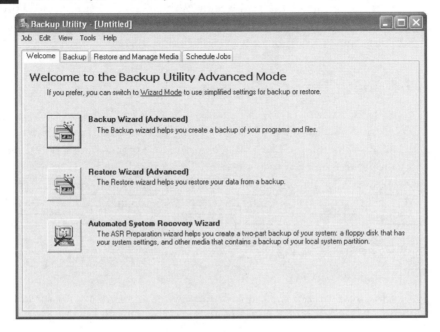

use the System Restore option to set a recovery point that can be used if the upgrade or installation fails. This recovery point can then be accessed with the System Restore program. Each restore point will have a unique, user-assigned name and a date and time the restore point was created. Choose a restore point, and the system will perform the process and then reboot. The System Restore is not supposed to cause the loss of data files and current work. For additional information, check either your system help or visit the Microsoft website.

CERTIFICATION OBJECTIVE 9.04

Installing and Configuring Device Drivers and Applications

Depending on the options you select during the Windows installation, several or all of the native Windows utilities and applications will be installed. Furthermore, because Windows supports Plug and Play, a number of device drivers can be installed automatically. However, in many cases, you might want to install native Windows applications or Plug-and-Play drivers after the OS has been installed. The following subsections describe the procedures you should use, as well as the procedures for installing third-party (nonnative) applications and device drivers.

Loading and Adding Device Drivers

In most cases, when you install or attach a new device, Windows will detect it automatically at startup. If the device is Plug and Play, a driver will automatically be installed, and if it is not Plug and Play, you will be prompted to supply the third-party driver. In other cases, Windows will not detect the device, and you will have to prompt Windows to load the driver. These procedures, as well as the procedure for using Device Manager to reinstall an existing driver, are discussed in the following subsections.

Loading Drivers on Startup

Every time Windows 9x starts, it compares the existing hardware in the system to the hardware values stored in the Registry. In Windows 2000 and XP, information about the existing hardware is gathered and placed in the Registry. All devices that have been previously configured in the system will be allocated system resources, and their device drivers will be initialized.

If Windows detects a new device (one that has not previously been configured), you will receive a message stating that Windows found a new device and is installing a driver for it. Windows then checks its driver library for the appropriate Plug and Play driver. If the appropriate driver exists, it will be initialized and loaded in the Registry. You will then be able to use the new device. However, if an appropriate driver does not exist in the Windows driver library, you will be prompted to supply the proper third-party driver. Insert the manufacturer's driver disk and select the appropriate drive when prompted. Windows will locate and load the driver.

The Add Hardware Wizard

Anytime you install or attach a hardware device that Windows does not recognize at startup, you must prompt Windows to load the driver, or you must load it manually. Many devices come with a manufacturer's setup disk. When you attach the device and restart the computer, run the Setup utility. In most cases, the driver will be installed without the use of the Add Hardware Wizard.

However, some manufacturers' driver disks do not have a Setup program, and sometimes Windows simply doesn't recognize a Plug-and-Play device at startup. In these cases, you will need to use the Add Hardware Wizard. To do this, access the Add New Hardware utility in the Windows 9x Control Panel or the Add/Remove

Hardware utility in the Windows 2000 or XP Control Panel. Follow the instructions in Exercise 9-6 to use the wizard to install a Plug-and-Play driver in Windows 98.

on the Job

Windows 2000 and XP have greatly enhanced the installation process and made it much easier than it was in earlier versions of Windows. Virtually all supported devices will automatically install. It is essential that the system you are configuring contains devices that are approved for either Windows 2000 or XP. Some older devices work fine in Windows 2000 and will not configure in Windows XP.

EXERCISE 9-6

Using the Add New Hardware Utility in Windows 98 to Install Plug-and-Play Drivers

1. Double-click the Add New Hardware icon in the Control Panel. The window shown in Figure 9-20 will be displayed.

2. Click Next. Windows will inform you that it will search for all new Plug-and-Play devices in the system.

3. Click Next to begin the Plug-and-Play hardware search. If the device is found, Windows will automatically install the driver for it, and you can skip the remaining steps.

4. If the device is not detected, Windows will ask you if it should search for all new non-Plug-and-Play devices. For this exercise, select No. A window similar to the one shown in Figure 9-21 will be displayed.

FIGURE 9-20

The Windows 98 Add New Hardware Wizard

FIGURE 9-21

The Add New
Hardware
Device list

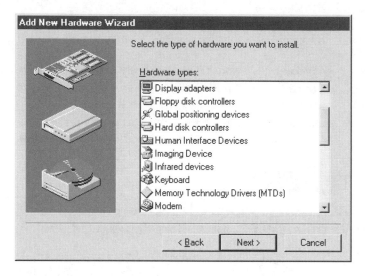

5. Select the device type from the list, then click Next.

6. A list of supported manufacturers and models of the selected device type will
   be displayed (see Figure 9-22). The contents of this window will depend on
   the device type you selected in Step 5. Select the appropriate manufacturer
   and model, then click Next.

7. Click Finish. Windows will load the appropriate driver for the device. You
   might be prompted to insert the Windows installation disk at this point.

FIGURE 9-22

The Add New
Hardware
manufacturer and
model selection
window

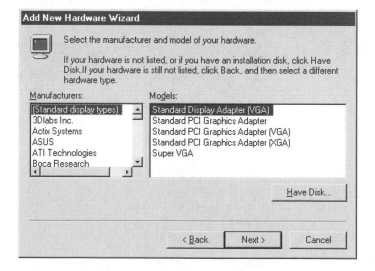

It is only in rare circumstances that you will have to use the Add Hardware Wizard to install drivers for Plug-and-Play devices. This wizard is more commonly used to install device drivers for third-party (non-Plug and Play) devices that did not come with their own Setup utility. It should be noted that some Plug-and-Play devices may be newer than the OS; therefore, the OS won't yet have the necessary drivers. Follow the steps in Exercise 9-7 to install a third-party driver in Windows 98.

EXERCISE 9-7

Using the Add New Hardware Utility in
Windows 98 to Install Third-Party Drivers

1. Double-click the Add New Hardware icon in the Windows 98 Control Panel.

2. Click Next, then click Next again. Windows will search for Plug-and-Play devices that have not been configured yet.

3. You will be asked to choose between letting Windows search for the device or selecting it yourself. For this exercise, choose to select it yourself.

4. Select the proper device type from the Hardware list, and click Next.

5. Click the Have Disk button.

6. Insert the third-party driver disk in the computer and click the Browse button. A window similar to the one shown in Figure 9-23 will be displayed.

7. Select the drive and path location of the driver, then click OK.

8. Click OK again. The driver will be located and loaded by Windows.

FIGURE 9-23

Use this dialog box to indicate the location of the third party device driver

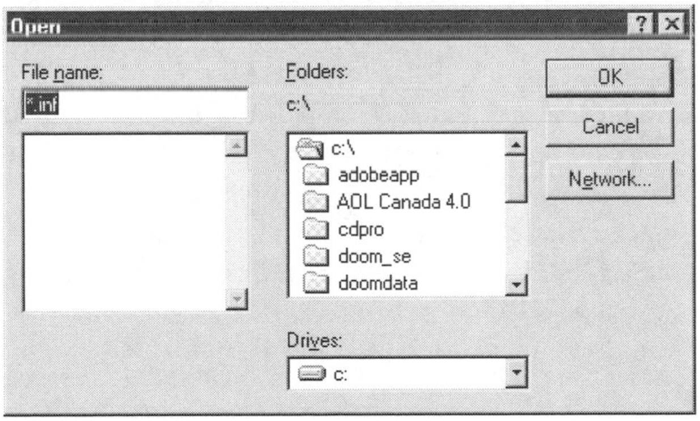

Reinstalling and Replacing Drivers for Windows

If a device's driver becomes corrupted, you will need to reinstall it. In some cases, you might want to replace a working driver with another driver. For example, the manufacturer of a device could release an updated driver that is better than the one you are currently using, or you might decide to replace a generic Windows driver with a more sophisticated third-party driver.

To replace or reinstall an existing device driver, use the Windows Device Manager. In Windows 9*x* and 2000/XP, right-click My Computer, select Properties, click the Hardware tab, and then click the Device Manager button.

View the appropriate device's Properties and elect to update the driver. The Update Driver Wizard will launch. Follow the on-screen instructions to replace a bad driver with a good one or to update the driver with one from another location. You might need to restart the computer for the changes to take effect.

Installing and Launching Applications

The main objective in installing an OS is to be able to run applications such as word processors, games, or multimedia applications. In this section, three types of applications are discussed: native Windows applications and utilities, non-native Windows applications, and non-native, non-Windows (DOS) applications.

Installing Native Windows Applications

A native Windows application is a program or utility that is included on the Windows installation disk. You can install all or most of these applications by selecting them when you install the OS. However, depending on the installation options you selected, you might later find yourself in need of a Windows application that hasn't yet been installed.

To install a Windows application, double-click the Add/Remove Programs icon in the Windows Control Panel and select the Windows Setup tab. In Windows 2000, click the Add/Remove Windows Components button. A window similar to Figure 9-24 will open. You can use this dialog box to add or remove any native Windows application or utility.

Select the appropriate category, and click Details. All applications and utilities within that category will be listed. Add a check mark beside all applications you want to add, and remove the check mark from all applications you want to remove. Windows will make the appropriate changes. You might be required to insert the Windows installation disk at this time.

Installing Non-Native Windows Applications

The majority of applications you use will be designed to run in Windows but will not be part of the Windows OS itself. In these cases, you will need the third-party software

The Windows
Setup dialog box

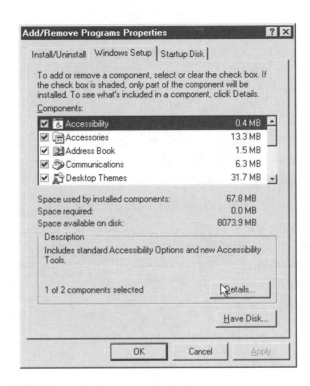

manufacturer's installation disk(s). Most applications require more than simply copying files to the hard drive because many application installation disks do not contain the actual application files. Rather, the application files must be compiled, created, or uncompressed during the application's Setup process. Furthermore, many applications must register themselves in the Windows Registry. This cannot be done by manually copying files from the installation disk to the computer. You can usually tell if an application has registered itself in the Registry, because you will be prompted to restart the computer before the application will run properly.

In most cases, you can install an application by running the Setup or Install program that is included on the installation disk. If the installation disk has an Autorun file and the CD-ROM has Autorun enabled on the computer, the Setup program will be launched as soon as you insert the CD. Otherwise, access the Setup program by double-clicking its icon in My Computer or Windows Explorer. Application Setup programs differ from one manufacturer to another. Simply follow the on-screen instructions.

You can also install an application using the Add/Remove Programs utility. In the Install/Uninstall tab, click Install. You will be prompted to select the location and setup file for the application. The installation will proceed in the same manner as it would if you had run it from My Computer or Windows Explorer.

Non-Native, Non-Windows Applications

Recall that Windows 9x retains the ability to run older DOS applications in real mode. Both Windows 9x and 2000/XP can run some DOS applications like any other third-party Windows application. That is, they will be run within a DOS shell inside Windows. Special procedures relating to the two types are described here.

DOS Shell Applications   You can alter the appearance and behavior of applications that run in a Windows DOS shell. By modifying the application's Program Information File (PIF), you can configure whether the application runs in a regular window or in full-screen mode. You can also select the font and resolution of text and specify memory access limits for the application. To modify a DOS application's PIF, locate the application's executable file icon in My Computer or Windows Explorer. Right-click the icon and select Properties (see Figure 9-25).

e x a m

ⓦ a t c h   *An application's executable file is responsible for starting (launching) the application and initializing or using the application's supporting files.*

DOS Mode Applications   Some DOS applications cannot be run in a DOS shell and must instead be installed and run in DOS mode. To install the application,

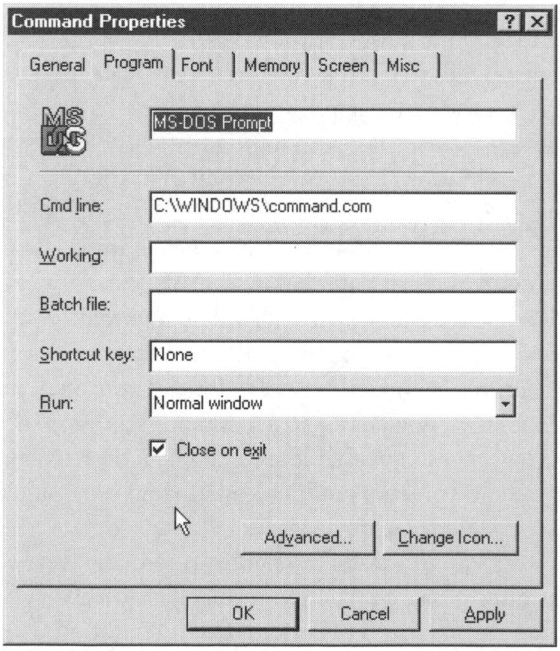

FIGURE 9-25

The DOS application's Properties windows allow you to modify its PIF file use the DIR command to determine the name of the Setup program, then enter the appropriate command to start the installation. For example, if the application's Setup program is SETUP.EXE, enter the command **SETUP** at the command prompt. Note again that Windows 2000 and XP cannot run DOS applications in real mode.

To launch the application, start the computer in MS-DOS mode and enter the command to start the application's executable file. For example, if an application's executable file is GAME.EXE, enter the command **GAME** at the command prompt.

o n t h e
Ø o b

PIF files are used with DOS shell applications only. You can use Windows to alter the behavior or appearance of a real-mode DOS application. The behavior and appearance of real-mode DOS applications are by default configured using CONFIG.SYS.

The Windows Printing Subsystem

One feature of the Windows OSes is that they can control application-generated print jobs. That is, when you print from a third-party application, the print job is handed over to the OS so that the application can continue working on other things. This is an improvement over earlier systems in which each application was in control of its print jobs and could not continue working until the print job was complete. Furthermore, each application had to be configured with the appropriate printer settings.

In Windows, the printing subsystem provides a link between all applications and the printer. Printers are installed and configured in Windows, and every print job is intercepted by the OS and sent to the printer using the defined Windows print settings. Each installed printer will appear in a Printers list in most applications. To use a particular printer, simply select it from within the application.

You can view all the installed printers in the system by double-clicking Printers in My Computer or from Windows Explorer or by selecting Start | Settings | Printers. Any printers that are currently unavailable will appear grayed out. This might occur when the printer is turned off, unplugged, or unavailable (if it is a network printer).

Installing and Configuring Printers

Windows includes extensive Plug-and-Play support for printers. As with other Plug-and-Play devices, most printers are automatically detected and configured by Windows at startup. However, in the event that you attach a non-Plug-and-Play printer, you will have to install and configure it manually. To install a printer, follow the instructions in Exercise 9-8. Note that this procedure is specific to Windows 98. The procedure to install a printer in 2000 and XP is similar but uses different screens.

Installing a Windows Printer

1. Double-click the Printers icon in My Computer or Windows Explorer, or select Start | Settings | Printers. The Printers windows will open (see Figure 9-26).

2. Double-click the Add Printer icon. Click Next to start the Add Printer Wizard.

3. You will be prompted to choose whether this is a local or network printer. Select Local, and click Next (network printers are discussed in the next section).

4. Select the manufacturer and model of the printer you want to install, then click Next. At this point, if you do not see your printer listed, click Have Disk and supply the manufacturer's third-party device driver.

5. Select the port to which the printer is physically attached, and click Next.

6. Enter a name for the printer, and choose whether or not this printer will be the default system printer.

7. Click Next.

FIGURE 9-26

The Windows
Printers window

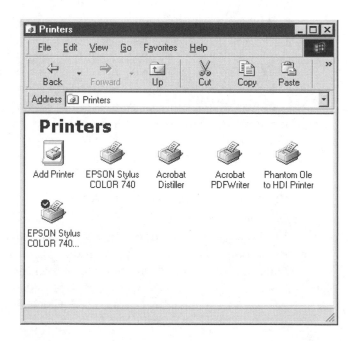

8. Select whether to print a test page or not, then click Finish. Windows will load the printer's driver or ask you to supply a third-party driver.

The default printer is the one to which all print jobs will be sent unless you specify otherwise in the application from which you are printing.

When the printer is successfully installed, the Printers window will be displayed with an icon representing all printers in the system (including the new one). The default printer might be indicated by a check mark. To configure a printer as the default, right-click its icon, then select Set as Default.

You can configure a printer's settings by accessing its properties. Right-click the appropriate printer's icon and select Properties. A window similar to Figure 9-27 will open. Note that this window is the Printer Properties window on a Windows XP system.

Depending on the manufacturer's design, you might be able to use this window to set the resolution, paper type, color use, and density of the printer. Many printers also include test and cleaning modes in this window.

FIGURE 9-27

The Printer Properties window

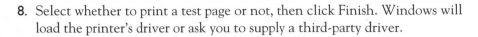

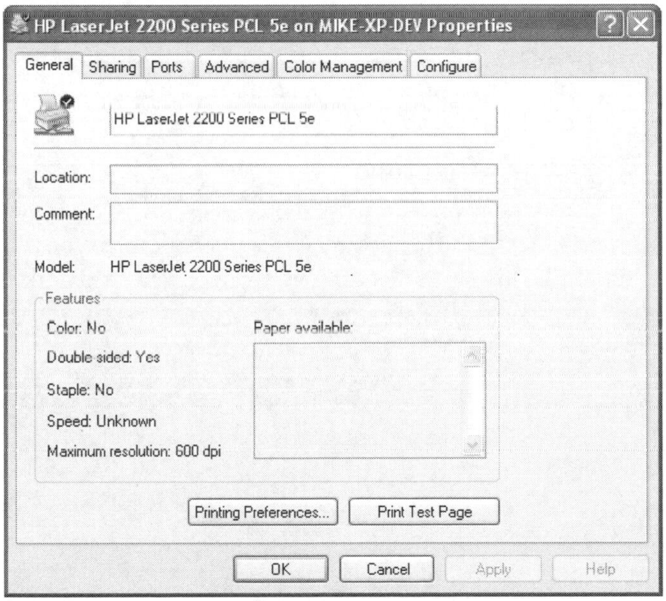

An important printer configuration is its spool settings. If spooling is enabled, applications will write print jobs to the hard disk, where they will be picked up and handled by the OS. Again, this allows the applications to resume work on other things more quickly. To configure the printer's spool settings, select the Details tab in the printer's Properties window. The Details window allows you to configure the printer's port and timeout settings. Click the Spool Settings button. The windows shown in Figure 9-28 will be displayed.

Enable spooling by selecting Spool Print Jobs So Program Finishes Printer Faster. The alternative to spooling is to select the Print Directly to the Printer option. If spooling is enabled, you will be able to select whether the printer begins printing after the first page is spooled or after the last page is spooled.

You will also be able to select the spool data format. Enhanced Metafile Format (EMF) is the default Windows graphic-rendering language. When you use EMF spooling, the printing application builds an EMF file representing the print job. Windows sends this file to the printer, and the RAW option configures Windows to translate each print job into printer-specific code. RAW mode sends data directly to the printer with no processing of file commands done in the printing subsystem. EMF printouts look the same as RAW printouts, but not all printers can print EMF print jobs. When this is the case, you should use the RAW option, although these print jobs will take longer because they must first be translated by the OS into a format the printer can understand.

Network Printing

If Windows is on a network, you can use the OS to access network printers. Recall from Chapter 7 that printers on a network might be true network printers, or they might be local printers that are shared on the network. In either case, their installation and access methods are the same.

FIGURE 9-28

The Windows 98 Spool Settings dialog box

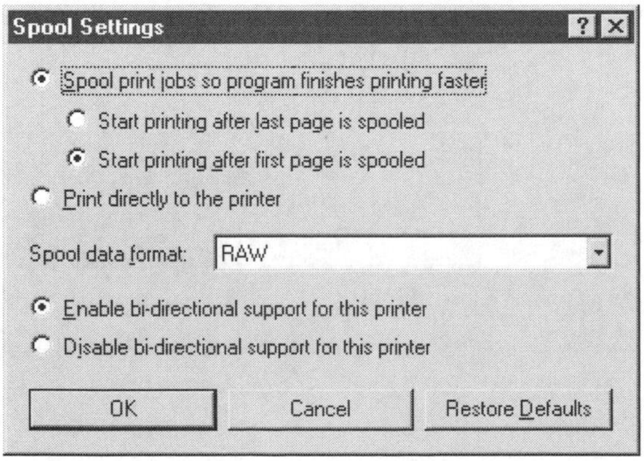

The procedure for installing a network printer is similar to the procedure outlined in Exercise 9-8. Instead of starting the Add Printer Wizard by double-clicking Add Printer in the Printers window however, launch the Add Printer Wizard by using Network Neighborhood and find the printer on the network. Right-click the printer's icon, and select Install.

Within the Add Printer Wizard, you must select Network Printer instead of Local Printer, and you must navigate through the network to locate the proper printer. In some cases, the drivers from that printer or its server will be transferred to your computer. In other cases, you might need to install a third-party driver.

CERTIFICATION SUMMARY

As a computer technician, you will likely be required to set up Windows systems and configure them for use. The Windows installation programs are almost entirely automated, so it is a relatively simple matter to install or upgrade the OS. However, you might need to do some preparation work to partition and format the disks. Furthermore, you must be aware of the procedures for upgrading and dual-booting Windows because these are common OS configurations.

Once Windows is installed, it will be automatically loaded every time you start the computer. You must be familiar with these boot processes so that you can pinpoint and troubleshoot boot problems. For example, if a Windows 9x system is missing the WIN.COM file, you know that the protected-mode boot phase cannot be carried out. If the Windows 2000 BOOT.INI file is corrupted, dual-booting cannot be enabled.

When there is a problem with the boot process, you might be able to start the computer using an alternate boot mode. Safe mode, for example, will boot Windows with minimal drivers in the hopes that the faulty driver will be bypassed so that it cannot halt the boot process. If Windows is too badly damaged to boot in an alternate mode, you can start the computer and try to repair the problem by booting with a boot or startup disk. These disks can be made during the OS installation or within the OS itself.

Equally important to the proper function of Windows is the configuration of device drivers, applications, and printers. Because Windows supports Plug and Play, many devices will be automatically detected and configured at startup. However, you will need to use the Add Hardware utility or a third-party Setup program to install non-Plug-and-Play drivers. The same is true for third-party Windows utilities. These must be installed using either the manufacturer's Setup program or the Add/Remove Programs utility.

TWO-MINUTE DRILL

Here are some of the key points from each certification objective in Chapter 9.

Installing Windows

❑ When performing a clean install of Windows 9x, you must boot the computer using the Windows boot disks.

❑ Use the FDISK and FORMAT commands to prepare hard disks for Windows 9x installation.

❑ The Windows 2000 installation disk includes its own partitioning and formatting utility, and the CD itself can be used to boot the computer.

❑ Once the hard disk is prepared, install Windows by accessing its Setup program.

Upgrading Windows

❑ When you upgrade from one version of Windows to another, nonsystem files, applications, and configurations are migrated from the old OS to the new.

❑ You can revert from Windows 98 to 95 following an upgrade if you choose the Save System Files option during the upgrade.

❑ You cannot revert back to Windows 9x or NT after a Windows 2000 or XP upgrade.

❑ To upgrade Windows, start the computer normally, insert the new OS's installation CD, and run the Setup program, ensuring that you select the Upgrade option.

❑ Windows XP and 2000 can read FAT16, FAT 32, and NTFS formatted drives. Windows 9x cannot read NTFS formatted drives.

❑ To create a Windows 2000 or XP dual-boot system, start the computer normally and run the Setup program, ensuring that you install the new OS in a different location, or select the New Installation option (rather than the Upgrade option).

Booting Windows

❑ The Windows 9x boot process includes the BIOS bootstrap, real-mode boot, real-mode configuration, and protected-mode boot phases.

❑ Windows' Safe mode loads minimal drivers to bypass potential problems and allow you to troubleshoot the OS.

❑ You can create a startup disk by accessing the Windows 9x Add/Remove Programs utility.

❑ You can create a Windows 2000 Setup Boot Disk using the command \BOOTDISK\MAKEBOOT32 A:.

❑ You can create a Windows 2000 or Windows XP Startup Disk by formatting the floppy using the operating system and copying BOOT.INI, NTLDR, and NTDETECT.COM files. If you need access to SCSI drives, you should also copy the NTBOOTDD.SYS file.

❑ The Windows XP and 2000 boot process uses BOOT.INI and NTLDR to boot.

❑ Windows 2000 and XP provide a Recovery Console utility to restore system files and perform other maintenance activities.

❑ You can create a recovery disk using the Automated System Recovery program in Windows 2000 and XP. This requires supported media to be used for the Backup program.

❑ Windows XP provides the ability to establish recovery points that allow you to restore systrem operation to earlier states.

Installing Device Drivers and Applications

❑ Most Plug-and-Play devices are detected by Windows at startup and are automatically configured.

❑ Use the Add New Hardware (Windows 9x) or Add/Remove Hardware (Windows 2000) utilities to install third-party device drivers.

❑ Windows 2000 and XP will attempt to automatically install device drivers when they are detected.

❑ Install third-party applications by running their Setup programs or by using the Windows Add/Remove Programs utility.

❑ Install and configure Windows printers using the Printers utility in the Control Panel.

SELF TEST

The following questions will help you measure your understanding of the material presented in this chapter. Read all of the choices carefully because there might be more than one correct answer. Choose all correct answers for each question.

Installing Windows

1. You are planning to partition a hard drive using FDISK. Which of the following can you do?

A. Create a primary partition and one extended partition with 14 logical drives.

B. Create as many partitions as will fit on the drive.

C. Create NTFS or FAT16 partitions.

D. Create one FAT16 and one FAT32 partition.

2. A computer has two hard drives installed, each of which has been partitioned. The primary hard drive has two primary partitions and one extended partition with two logical drives. The secondary hard drive has one primary partition and two extended partitions, each with one logical drive. Which drive letters will be assigned to the partitions on the secondary hard drive?

A. D:, F:, H:

B. E:, H:, I:

C. G:, H:, I:

D. This cannot be determined without knowing the order in which the partitions were created.

3. Which file does Windows 9x use to determine non hardware-related failure points when performing a safe recovery installation?

A. SETUPLOG.TXT

B. RECOVER.LOG

C. DETCRASH.LOG

D. DETLOG.TXT

4. Which Setup utility does Windows 2000 use when you boot from the Windows 2000 installation CD?

A. SETUP.EXE

B. SETUP32.EXE

C. WINNT.EXE

D. WINNT32.EXE

5. You are planning to install Windows XP on an unpartitioned hard disk, and you have only the Windows 2000 setup disks and the installation CD-ROM. In which order will you perform the necessary installation procedures?

   A. Partition the disk, format the disk, restart the computer, run the Setup utility

   B. Partition the disk, restart the computer, format the disk, run the Setup utility

   C. Run the Setup utility, partition the disk, format the disk, restart the computer

   D. Partition the disk, restart the computer, run the Setup utility, format the disk

Upgrading Windows

6. A customer who currently uses Windows 95 has asked for your advice. He wants better security and networking abilities but is concerned about losing his existing documents and having to reinstall the system's applications. What is your advice?

   A. Back up the applications and files, remove Windows 95, perform a clean install of Windows XP, then restore the applications and files.

   B. Create a Windows 95 and Windows XP dual-boot configuration.

   C. Upgrade Windows 95 to Windows 98, then create a Windows 98 and Windows XP dual-boot configuration.

   D. Upgrade Windows 95 to Windows XP.

7. You are planning to upgrade Windows 95 to Windows 98, but you are concerned that you might need to revert to Windows 95 if problems occur. Which step must you perform to revert from Windows 98 to Windows 95?

   A. Make sure that you elect to save the system files when prompted during the installation.

   B. Start the computer using the Windows 95 setup disk and choose Revert.

   C. Access the Windows 98 Startup menu and choose Previous Version of Windows.

   D. You cannot revert from Windows 98 to Windows 95.

8. A computer has recently been upgraded from Windows 98 to Windows 2000 but is experiencing problems. Which of the following must you do to remove Windows 2000 and use Windows 98?

   A. Uninstall Windows 2000, ensuring that you select the Restore Previous Operating 7System option.

   B. Delete Windows 2000 and reinstall Windows 98.

   C. Run the Windows 98 Setup utility and choose to install the OS in the WINNT folder.

   D. Access the Windows 2000 Startup menu and choose Previous Version of Windows.

9. A computer has a Windows 98 and Windows 2000 dual-boot configuration. Which file must you modify if you want to change the options in the system's boot menu?

   A. NTLDR

   B. MSDOS.SYS

   C. IO.SYS

   D. BOOT.INI

10. A computer has a Windows 2000 and Windows 98 dual-boot configuration. Windows 98 was installed first on a FAT32 volume, then Windows 2000 was installed on an NTFS volume. Which of the following is true?

   A. If you boot the computer using Windows 95, you will not be able to access the NTFS volume.

   B. When Windows 2000 was installed, it converted the Windows 95 volume to NTFS.

   C. The computer will not boot properly in this configuration.

   D. You can run Windows 95 from within Windows 2000, but not vice versa.

Booting Windows

11. What is the function of the IO.SYS file in the Windows 9x boot process?

   A. To store dual-boot configuration settings

   B. To initialize and conduct the real-mode boot and configuration stages

   C. To conduct the protected-mode boot stage

   D. To switch the processor into protected mode

12. Which of the following is true of the Windows 9x VMM386.VXD file?

   A. It is responsible for initiating the protected-mode boot stage.

   B. It contains Windows 9x 32-bit device drivers.

   C. It reads the values in the SYSTEM.INI file during the boot process.

   D. It is included in Windows 98 but not Windows 95.

13. Which of the following occurs when you start a Windows computer in Safe mode?

   A. The boot process ends with the real-mode configuration stage.

   B. The computer will provide a command-line interface rather than a graphical interface.

   C. The Network Neighborhood will be unavailable.

   D. The Device Manager will be unavailable.

14. Which of the following is not a proper method for creating a boot disk in Windows 9*x*?

    A. Use the Backup utility.

    B. Use the Format utility.

    C. Use the Startup Disk tab in the Add/Remove Programs utility.

    D. Use the SYS command in a DOS shell.

15. Which file is responsible for conducting the Windows XP boot process before the kernel is loaded?

    A. IO.SYS

    B. NTLDR

    C. BOOT.INI

    D. NTOSKRNL.EXE

Installing Device Drivers and Applications

16. Which of the following can you use to replace an existing device driver in Windows?

    A. The Install/Uninstall tab of the Add/Remove Programs utility

    B. The Windows Setup tab of the Add/Remove Programs utility

    C. The Device Manager

    D. The Hardware Configuration Manager

17. Which of the following is a function of a Program Information File (PIF)?

    A. To configure the appearance of applications that run in DOS mode

    B. To configure shared files for 32-bit Windows applications

    C. To store information about the creation and modification dates of nonsystem files

    D. To configure the memory usage of applications that run in a DOS shell

18. Which of the following is true of the Windows printers?

    A. The printer that you plan to use as the default must be installed first.

    B. By default, the Printers window in the Control Panel displays only the default printer.

    C. Applications can print only to whichever printer is set as the default.

    D. The default printer will be used by Windows applications unless a different printer is specified within the application.

19. Which of the following will occur when you enable printer spooling in Windows?

    A. Print jobs will be stored on the hard drive by the originating application.

    B. The application, rather than Windows, will send the print job to the printer.

    C. Windows will poll all printers and send the print job to the first available printer.

    D. Print jobs will be processed in the order of the originating application's priority.

20. You have just installed a new printer, but it seems to take a long time for print jobs to start printing once they are sent. Which of the following could help speed up printing?

    A. Disable printer spooling

    B. Set this printer as the default

    C. Set the data format to EMF

    D. Reinstall the printer's device driver

LAB QUESTION

Throughout this chapter, a number of differences between Windows 9*x* and Windows 2000 and XP have been discussed. As a technician, it is very important for you to be familiar with which files, processes, and utilities are associated with which OS. For each of the following items, indicate whether it is specific to Windows 9*x* or Windows 2000/XP or used by both.

1. ___ Supports printer spooling

2. ___ Has an Add Printer Wizard

3. ___ Uses FDISK for partitioning

4. ___ The installation file is SETUP.EXE

5. ___ Requires a minimum of 32MB of RAM

6. ___ Can partition the hard disk during OS installation

7. ___ Allows you to create startup disks

8. ___ Allows you to select Typical or Compact installation

9. ___ Can automatically detect and configure Plug-and-Play devices

10. ___ Can be booted in real mode

11. ___ Can use FAT16 or FAT32 volumes

12. ___ Can be used in a dual-boot configuration

13. ___ Uses four startup disks

14. ___ Can be uninstalled

15. ___ Can be booted in Safe mode

16. ___ Has an Add/Remove Programs utility

17. ___ Uses PIFs to configure DOS applications

18. ___ Allows you to access network printers

19. ___ Uses IO.SYS

20. ___ Loads real-mode configuration files

21. ___ Uses a Windows kernel

22. ___ Allows you to create an ERD

23. ___ Has a Device Manager

SELF TEST ANSWERS

Installing Windows

1. ☑ **A.** When using FDISK, you can create a primary partitions and one extended partition with 14 logical drives. The maximum number of partitions you can create with FDISK is four, and the number of logical drives you create on an extended partition is limited only by the remaining number of letters in the alphabet. In total, you can create four partitions, and if one is an extended partition, you can create up to 21 logical drives.

   ☒ **B,** create as many partitions as will fit on the drive, is incorrect. Although this is true for partitions in Windows 2000, FDISK does not allow you create more than a single primary and a single extended partition. **C,** create NTFS or FAT16 partitions, is incorrect because FDISK can create FAT16 and FAT32 partitions only. **D,** create one FAT16 and one FAT32 partition, is incorrect because FDISK does not allow you to mix file system types on a single drive.

2. ☑ **B.** The partitions on the secondary drive will be given the letters E:, H:, and I:. The system always letters the primary partitions first, starting with the primary drive. Next, the system letters the logical drives, starting with the primary drive. Therefore, the primary drive's primary partitions are given C: and D:. The secondary drive's primary partition is given E:. Next, the primary drive's logical drives are lettered F: and G:. Finally, the secondary drive's logical drives are lettered H: and I:.

   ☒ **A,** D:, F:, and H:, is incorrect because this would be the result of assigning letters equally back and forth from one drive to the next, regardless of partition type. **C,** G:, H:, and I:, is incorrect because this indicates that all partitions on the primary drive are lettered first, followed by the secondary drive. **D** is incorrect because it suggests partitions are lettered according to the order in which they were created. The lettering scheme for primary partitions and logical drives always follows the order described. When you create a new partition, it will be lettered according to this scheme, regardless of current drive-letter assignments.

3. ☑ **A.** Windows 9x uses SETUPLOG.TXT to determine nonhardware-related failure points when performing a safe recovery installation. The SETUPLOG.TXT file is generated at the start of the installation process and documents the success or failure of each step. If the installation process fails, you can choose to reinstall the OS. If you choose the safe recovery method, Windows 9x will use the values in SETUPLOG.TXT to determine where the installation failed, then skip that step in an attempt to complete the installation.

   ☒ **B,** RECOVER.LOG, is incorrect because this file is not generated or used by the Windows 9x installation process. **C,** DETCRASH.LOG, is incorrect because this file is generated during the hardware detection phase of the installation and is used by the OS to determine which, if any, hardware devices failed to be detected. This file relates specifically to the system's hardware. **D,** DETLOG.TXT, is incorrect because this is the text version of the DETCRASH.LOG file. It is not used by Windows; rather, it is generated by Windows to allow you to view the information contained in DETCRASH.LOG.

4. ☑ **C.** Windows 2000 uses WINNT.EXE when you boot from a CD. By default and unless otherwise instructed, the processor runs in real mode. When you boot from the CD, the processor remains in real mode. Therefore, the real-mode installation utility WINNT.EXE is used.

    ☒ **A,** SETUP.EXE, is incorrect because this is the Setup utility used in Windows 9*x*, not Windows 2000. **B,** SETUP32.EXE, is incorrect because this is not a valid Windows Setup file. **D,** WINNT32.EXE, is incorrect because this Setup utility is used only if the computer is already running in protected mode. For example, if you run the Windows 2000 installation from within Windows 9*x*, WINNT32.EXE will be used.

5. ☑ **C.** To install Windows 2000 on an unpartitioned hard disk, run the Setup utility, partition the disk, format the disk, then restart the computer. The Windows 2000 Setup utility will start automatically when you boot the computer using either the Setup disks or the installation CD. You will then be prompted to create and format hard disk partitions. When the disk has been prepared, the computer will be restarted and the Setup process will continue.

    ☒ **A** and **D** are incorrect because they suggest partitioning the disk first. However, in the Windows 2000 installation, disk partitioning and formatting are part of the Setup and can only be conducted once the Setup utility has been started. **B,** partition the disk, restart the computer, format the disk, run the Setup utility, is incorrect. This procedure is used when installing Windows 9*x* on an unpartitioned hard disk. That is, you must first partition the disk using FDISK, then restart the computer for the changes to take effect. When the computer restarts, format the partitions, then start the Setup utility.

Upgrading Windows

6. ☑ **D.** Your advice should be to upgrade Windows 95 to Windows XP. The customer's desire for better security and networking abilities indicates a need for Windows XP. When you upgrade from one Windows OS to another, applications, nonsystem files, and other settings are migrated into the new OS.

    ☒ **A** is incorrect because it suggests backing up the applications and other files, replacing Windows 95 with Windows XP, then restoring the applications and files. Although this procedure might satisfy the need to keep nonsystem files, it will not work for the applications. Most Windows applications must register themselves in the Windows Registry. Simply restoring these applications from backup will not ensure their proper function. Furthermore, many applications place files in more than one folder, and it can be almost impossible to determine which files belong to which applications. **B,** create a Windows 95 and Windows XP dual-boot configuration, is incorrect. If the user boots in Windows XP, he will be able to access the files and applications on the Windows 95 volume. However, these applications might not run correctly, because they will not be registered in the Windows XP Registry. Furthermore, if the user boots to Windows 95, he cannot take advantage of the Windows XP OS features. **C** is incorrect because it suggests creating a dual-boot configuration after upgrading Windows 95 to Windows 98. Again, a dual boot is not the best configuration for this user's needs.

7. ☑ **A.** Make sure that you elect to save the system files when prompted during the installation. The Windows 95 installation files will be saved on the hard drive. When you uninstall Windows 98, the Windows 95 system files will be restored. If you do not opt to save the system files, you will be left without an OS when you uninstall Windows 98.

☒ **B,** start the computer using the Windows 95 setup disk and choose Revert, is incorrect. There is no Revert option on the Windows setup disks. **C,** access the Windows 98 Startup menu and choose Previous Version of Windows, is also incorrect. There is a startup option that allows you to use a previous version of DOS, but there is no option to use a previous version of Windows. **D** is incorrect because it suggests you cannot return to Windows 95 after upgrading to Windows 98. This is true only for Windows 2000, which does not have an Uninstall feature.

8. ☑ **B.** Delete Windows 2000 and reinstall Windows 98. Windows 2000 does not have an Uninstall feature and does not allow you to save and revert to an older OS the way Windows 9*x* does.

☒ **A,** uninstall Windows 2000, ensuring that you select the Restore Previous Operating System option, is incorrect. Again, Windows 2000 cannot be uninstalled or reverted to a previous OS. **C** is incorrect because it suggests installing Windows 98 over Windows 2000. Windows 2000 will not replace itself with an older version of Windows. **D** is incorrect because it suggests selecting the previous version of Windows in the Startup menu. This is not a Windows 2000 Startup menu option. Furthermore, when Windows 98 is upgraded to Windows 2000, none of the Windows 98 OS is saved by Windows 2000.

9. ☑ **D.** To change the boot menu in a computer with a Windows 2000 dual-boot configuration, you must modify the BOOT.INI file. This file is automatically generated by Windows 2000 and contains settings such as the default OS and countdown time until an OS is selected automatically.

☒ **A,** NTLDR, is incorrect because this file is the boot loader and is responsible for organizing and conducting the boot process. However, it does not contain the boot menu parameters. **B,** MSDOS.SYS, is incorrect because this file contains the boot menu in systems that use Windows 9*x* but not Windows 2000. **C,** IO.SYS, is incorrect because this is the boot loader for Windows 9*x*. That is, it organizes and conducts the early boot stages of Windows 9*x*.

10. ☑ **A.** If you boot the computer using Windows 98, you will not be able to access the NTFS volume. Windows cannot recognize NTFS volumes. However, if you boot into Windows 2000, you will be able to see the FAT32 volume because Windows 2000 and XP can recognize FAT16, FAT32, and NTFS volumes.

☒ **B** is incorrect because it suggests that Windows 2000 converted the Windows 95 volume to NTFS. Windows 2000 does not convert volumes unless specifically instructed to do so. If the computer's volumes were converted to NTFS by the Windows 2000 installation, you couldn't create a Windows 9x dual boot because Windows 9x cannot recognize NTFS volumes. **C,** the computer will not boot properly in this configuration, is incorrect. Although you cannot guarantee that no problems will exist, the configuration described here is perfectly legitimate. That is, the configuration itself will not be the cause of boot-related problems. **D,** you can run Windows 95 from within Windows 2000, but not vice versa, is incorrect. You cannot run a Windows OS from within another. You can run one *or* the other.

Booting Windows

11. ☑ **B.** The function of IO.SYS is to initialize and conduct the real-mode boot and configuration stages of the Windows 9x boot process. IO.SYS is responsible for locating MSDOS.SYS, SYSTEM.DAT, and other real-mode boot files. Next, IO.SYS locates and processes real-mode configuration files, such as CONFIG.SYS and AUTOEXEC.BAT. IO.SYS, then locates WIN.COM and gives it control of the rest of the boot process. This marks the beginning of the protected-mode boot stage.

☒ **A,** to store dual-boot configuration settings, is incorrect because this is the function of the Windows 9x MSDOS.SYS file. **C,** to conduct the protected-mode boot stage, is incorrect because this the function of several protected-mode boot files such as WIN.COM and VMM386.VXD. **D,** to switch the processor into protected mode, is incorrect because this function is performed by VMM386.VXD.

12. ☑ **B.** The Windows 9x VMM386.VXD file contains Windows 9x 32-bit device drivers. These drivers are read and loaded into memory during the boot process, and they include devices such as the mouse, the keyboard, and the display adapter.

☒ **A,** it is responsible for initiating the protected-mode boot stage, is incorrect. The protected-mode boot stage begins when IO.SYS locates and runs WIN.COM. From there, WIN.COM is in control of the boot process. **C,** it reads the values in the SYSTEM.INI file during the boot process, is incorrect because this is done by WIN.COM. **D,** it is included in Windows 98 but not Windows 95, is incorrect because both OSes use VMM386.VXD.

13. ☑ **C.** When you start a Windows computer in Safe mode, the Network Neighborhood will be unavailable. Safe mode loads standard mouse, keyboard, and VGA display adapters only. This means the NIC will not be configured, and the computer will not have network access. Safe mode with networking will load the network drivers, but these are two different modes. ☒ **A,** the boot process ends with the real-mode configuration stage, and **B,** the computer will provide a command-line interface rather than a graphical interface, are both incorrect. These describe events that occur when you select the Command Prompt Only or Safe Mode Command Prompt Only startup options. In the case of the latter, the boot process will end before the real-mode configuration stage. **D,** the Device Manager will be unavailable, is incorrect. While in Safe mode, you can still access the Device Manager, and if you are troubleshooting a driver problem, this will most likely be the utility you use to resolve the issue.

14. ☑ **B.** By using the Windows 9*x* Format utility, you can choose to format a disk *and* make it a system disk, or you can choose to configure it as a system disk without formatting it.
☒ **A,** use the Backup utility, is incorrect. Although a boot disk must contain system files, which the Backup will allow you to create, boot disks must also be configured to be bootable, and the Backup utility will not perform this function. **C,** use the Startup Disk tab in the Add/ Remove Programs utility, is also incorrect. When you click Create Disk in the Startup Disk tab, the floppy disk will be made bootable, and several system files, external commands, and utilities will be copied onto the disk. **D,** use the SYS command in a DOS shell, is also incorrect. When you use this command, the disk is marked as bootable, and IO.SYS, MSDOS.SYS, and COMMAND.COM are transferred to it.

15. ☑ **B.** The NTLDR file is responsible for conducting the Windows XP boot process before the kernel is loaded. NTLDR locates and initializes startup files throughout the boot process. Once the kernel is loaded, it takes over control from NTLDR.
☒ **A,** IO.SYS, is incorrect because this file is used in the Windows 9*x* boot process but is not used in Windows XP. **C,** BOOT.INI, is incorrect because this file contains boot menu settings. It is located and initialized by NTLDR. BOOT.INI is not responsible for locating or initializing other startup files. **D,** NTOSDRNL.EXE, is incorrect because this is the file name of the Windows XP kernel itself.

Installing Device Drivers and Applications

16. ☑ **C.** You can use the Device Manager to replace an existing device driver in Windows. View the device's properties, and in the Driver tab, select Update Driver.
☒ **A** and **B** are both incorrect because they suggest using tabs in the Add/Remove Programs utility. This utility is used to install applications or Windows utilities, not device drivers. **D,** the Hardware Configuration Manager, is incorrect because this is not a real Windows utility.

17. ☑ **D.** The primary function of a PIF is to configure the memory usage of applications that run in a DOS shell. By modifying a DOS application's PIF, you can also modify its window size, text font, and text resolution.

    ☒ **A,** to configure the appearance of applications that run in DOS mode, is incorrect. A PIF is used specifically for configuring the appearance and behavior of DOS applications that are run within Windows, not in DOS (real) mode. **B,** to configure shared files for 32-bit Windows applications, is incorrect. PIFs are associated with non-Windows applications that use the DOS shell only. **C,** to store information about the creation and modification dates of a nonsystem file, is incorrect. PIFs are used only with non-Windows executable files.

18. ☑ **D.** The default printer will be used by Windows applications unless a different printer is specified within the application. By setting a printer as the default, you are instructing Windows applications to use that printer unless you specify otherwise.

    ☒ **A,** the printer that you plan to use as the default must be installed first, is incorrect. You can set any printer as the default by right-clicking it and selecting Set as Default. **B,** by default, the Printers window in the Control Panel displays only the default printer, is incorrect. The Printers window displays all printers in the system. **C,** applications can print only to whichever printer is set as the default, is incorrect. Applications can print to any printer in the system, as long as the printer is selected within the application.

19. ☑ **A.** When you enable printer spooling in Windows, print jobs will be passed on to the Windows spooler by the originating application. From there, they will be saved to the hard drive. The application can then resume other functions. Windows will retrieve the print job from the hard drive, process the job, and send it to the printer.

    ☒ **B,** the application, rather than Windows, will send the print job to the printer, is incorrect. In fact, this is the opposite of print spooling. When you elect to have applications send print jobs directly to the printer, you disable printer spooling. **C,** Windows will poll all printers and send the print job to the first available printer, is incorrect. Windows will send print jobs to the printer specified within the originating application. There is no option to configure Windows to send print jobs to the first available printer. **D,** print jobs will be processed in the order of the originating application's priority, is incorrect. Print jobs are processed in the order in which they are received by Windows. Applications cannot be given printing priorities.

20. ☑ **C.** Set the data format the EMF. EMF is the default rendering language of Windows. If the data format is set to RAW, Windows must first translate the print job into the printer's native code. This can take longer than sending EMF print jobs, so the print process might appear slow.

    ☒ **A,** disable printer spooling, is incorrect. If you disable spooling, the application itself, rather than Windows, will control the print job. The print job won't arrive at the printer any faster, and you will lose the ability to work in the application until the print job is finished. **B,** set this printer as the default, is incorrect. The default printer is the one that applications will print to unless otherwise specified. This prevents you from having to select the printer every time you print. The default printer is not given any time priority, so the speed of a print job is unrelated to the printer's status as default. **D,** reinstall the printer's device driver, is incorrect. If the device driver is missing or corrupted, the printer won't work slowly; it will probably not work at all.

LAB ANSWER

For the following items, "9x" indicates the function or feature is specific to Windows 95 and Windows 98; "2000" indicates it is specific to Windows 2000 or XP; and "B" indicates it is common to Windows 95, 98, and 2000.

1. B Supports printer spooling

2. B Has an Add Printer Wizard

3. 9x Uses FDISK for partitioning

4. 9x The installation file is SETUP.EXE

5. B Requires a minimum of 32MB of RAM

6. 2000 Can partition the hard disk during OS installation

7. B Allows you to create startup disks

8. 9x Allows you to select Typical or Compact installation

9. B Can automatically detect and configure Plug-and-Play devices

10. 9x Can be booted in real mode

11. B Can use FAT16 or FAT32 volumes

12. 2000 Can be used in a dual-boot configuration

13. 2000 Uses four startup disks

14. 9x Can be uninstalled

15. B Can be booted in Safe mode

16. B Has an Add/Remove Programs utility

17. B   Uses PIFs to configure DOS applications

18. B   Allows you to access network printers

19. 9*x*   Uses IO.SYS

20. 9*x*   Loads real-mode configuration files

21. B   Uses a Windows kernel

22. 9*x*   Allows you to create an ERD

23. B   Has a Device Manager

10

Diagnosing and Troubleshooting

CERTIFICATION OBJECTIVES

10.01   Recognize and interpret the meaning of common error codes and start messages from the boot sequence and identify how to correct the problems.

10.02   Recognize when to use common diagnostic utilities and tools. Troubleshoot scenarios and select the appropriate steps to resolve the problem.

10.03   Recognize common operational and usability problems and determine how to resolve them.

✓   Two-Minute Drill

Q&A   Self Test

Y ou should now be familiar with the major functions of the Windows operating systems and the procedures they use to boot, run, and maintain computers. However, these procedures can fail, and it is important for you to know how to return the system to a normal functioning state in the event of a failure. A familiarity with the concepts presented in previous chapters is the best tool you can have in diagnosing and resolving OS errors. This chapter will help you use what you already know about Windows to locate and resolve some common OS problems.

Windows OS problems can be related to either boot processes or runtime processes. This chapter presents boot and runtime errors separately, focusing on the most common errors associated with each. As you work through this chapter, note that a majority of the information presented here relates specifically to Windows 9x. Windows NT/ 2000/XP does not support potentially problematic legacy files, and it has been specifically designed to fail less and to automatically recover from many types of errors. For these reasons, Windows 2000 typically requires less troubleshooting than Windows 9x.

CERTIFICATION OBJECTIVE 10.01

Boot Failures and Errors

Boot failures are not all that common of an event and they are usually pretty easy to fix. Fortunately, the error messages for a boot failure are fairly self-explanatory. Remember, each boot file has a specific job, and in most cases, if a required file is missing, in the wrong place, or corrupt, the boot process will not continue. Fortunately, most boot problems can be reliably and easily diagnosed from the behavior of the computer or the error messages you receive. That is, because the Windows boot sequences are so predictable, it is usually quite simple to determine and troubleshoot the problem, as long as you are familiar with the normal boot process. Some common boot problems, along with typical resolution procedures, are discussed here.

Invalid Boot Disk

The "Invalid boot disk" error may occur if the drive that is configured as the system partition no longer contains essential systems files to boot the operating system. This type of message usually occurs after the BIOS has successfully found the Master Boot Record (MBR) and locates the boot sector of the system partition. You will generally only see this message if you are using a DOS-formatted disk, not on an NTFS file system.

To fix this error in Windows 9x, boot from a startup floppy disk and SYS the boot drive. A good copy of the IO.SYS and MSDOS.SYS files on the boot disk will be placed on the boot drive. You will also need to copy over the COMMAND.COM file if it's missing from the drive you want to boot.

The "Bad or missing command interpreter" message occurs after the operating system has been loaded and the command processor is attempting to load. This is the COMMAND.COM program that resides on the system partition in the case of a DOS system. You will not see this type of error message on a Windows NT/ 2000/XP system.

However, if you receive the "BOOT: Couldn't find NTLDR" message on Windows NT, 2000, or XP, use the startup disks or CD with the Recovery Console to boot the computer and select to perform a repair. Use the emergency repair process to replace the NTLDR file on the boot drive.

This error can also occur if a virus attacks the MBR. First, you should run an antivirus application to be sure you don't have a boot sector virus. If you don't, it may be possible to replace the MBR. To do so, boot from the Windows 9x startup disk and execute the following command:

```
FDISK /MBR
```

This command should create a new MBR on the boot drive. Be aware that using it can produce unexpected results and cause unrecoverable damage, and that FDISK/ MBR may not work if you have used the manufacturer's tools to partition the hard drive.

As a last resort, use the drive manufacturer's program to completely initialize the drive. You can usually find this on their website.

If the problem persists, it could be a hardware problem. That is, the BIOS might not be able to communicate with the boot drive itself. If this is the case, use the hardware troubleshooting procedures discussed in Chapter 3.

CONFIG.SYS Errors

Problems with the CONFIG.SYS file are typically displayed as "Error in CONFIG. SYS Line *xx*" or "There is an unrecognized command in CONFIG.SYS on line *xx*." These messages indicate that the specified (*xx*) line in the CONFIG.SYS file contains an invalid command or parameter or that it references a file that doesn't exist. This error is specific to Windows 9x; Windows NT/2000/XP does not use the CONFIG.SYS file.

This is a nonfatal error, meaning that Windows 9x will boot properly, with the exception of the referenced command. When Windows has finished loading, use the System Configuration Editor (SYSEDIT) or Notepad to open and view the CONFIG .SYS file. Count the lines of text to find the line referenced in the error message. If the line contains spelling or syntax errors, make the appropriate changes, save the CONFIG.SYS file, then restart the computer.

If this doesn't solve the problem, look at the command variable itself (usually a filename). Check to ensure that the referenced file exists and is located in the specified path. If the problem persists, enter **REM** at the beginning of the specified line. This instructs the computer to skip over that line, thus avoiding the error message.

AUTOEXEC.BAT Errors

Recall that the AUTOEXEC.BAT file can be used to automatically launch applications or carry out other DOS commands during the Windows 9x startup process. The lines in the AUTOEXEC.BAT file must use the same syntax as commands that you would manually enter at a command prompt. If the AUTOEXEC.BAT file contains an invalid or incorrectly spelled command, an "Invalid Command" message will appear on the screen, just as it would if you manually entered a bad command. If the AUTOEXEC.BAT file references an invalid drive letter, you will receive a "Current drive is no longer valid" error.

These errors are nonfatal, meaning that the OS will continue to load in an otherwise normal manner. When Windows has finished loading, use the System Configuration Editor or Notepad to open the AUTOEXEC.BAT file. Ensure that the existing commands are all valid and spelled correctly. If the problem persists, configure the system to skip over suspect lines by placing the text REM at the beginning of the line.

HIMEM.SYS Not Loaded

The "HIMEM.SYS not loaded" error occurs only during Windows 9x startup. Windows 9x requires the presence of the HIMEM.SYS file in the Windows folder to boot properly. If this file is missing, corrupted, or in the wrong location, Windows will not start properly. However, at this point, the computer can run in real (DOS) mode and you will be presented with a DOS command prompt. Follow the steps in Exercise 10-1 to resolve the HIMEM.SYS file problem.

EXERCISE 10-1

Resolving HIMEM.SYS Boot Errors

1. Type the following commands to check the WINDOWS folder for the presence of the HIMEM.SYS file:

   ```
   CD \WINDOWS
   DIR
   ```

   If HIMEM.SYS is present, proceed to Step 2. If the file is not present, skip to Step 3.

2. The contents of the WINDOWS folder will be listed. If HIMEM.SYS is present, you should assume that it is corrupted (otherwise, the error wouldn't have occurred). To delete the HIMEM.SYS file, enter the following command:

   ```
   DEL HIMEM.SYS
   ```

3. Insert a floppy disk that contains the same version of the HIMEM.SYS file you want to replace and enter the following commands to copy the file from the disk into the hard drive's WINDOWS folder:

   ```
   A: COPY HIMEM.SYS C:\WINDOWS
   ```

4. Restart the computer.

watch   *Although Windows 9x doesn't require the SYSTEM.INI, CONFIG.SYS, and AUTOEXEC.BAT files, it does require HIMEM.SYS. Errors related to this file are fatal, meaning that Windows will not load.*

Missing or Corrupt HIMEM.SYS

The extended memory file HIMEM.SYS is required for DOS and other non-windows programs. If this file is missing or corrupt, it will need to be replaced. Normally, it is either placed in the Windows Directory C:\Windows or in the root directory C:\. In either case, you should verify the location in the CONFIG.SYS file. It is not unusual for multiple copies of HIMEM.SYS to be on a Windows 9x system, and usually one of them can be used. If not, you will need to copy it from either a boot disk or from the distribution media.

Device/Service Fails to Start

Windows NT, 2000, and XP extensively use services to manage system activities. A service is simply a program that starts when the operating system is booted and runs in the background. When a service fails to start it can usually be started manually using the Service icon in the Control Panel. If the service fails to start it may be caused by a configuration error, a malfunction of a particular device (such as a network card), or other problems. Normally you can find the purpose and function of a service at the Microsoft website or in the documentation. If a device fails to start it may be a result of a hardware failure, configuration error, or other problems. Again, Microsoft is a great place to start your investigation of the problem and any known fixes.

A Device Referenced in SYSTEM.INI or Registry Could Not Be Found

During Windows 9x startup, you could receive the message, "A device referenced in SYSTEM.INI or Registry could not be found" or "The Windows Registry or System.INI file refers to this device file, but the device file no longer exists." These messages indicate that a file or device is listed in the SYSTEM.INI file or Registry but Windows could not find it. For example, the SYSTEM.INI file could refer to a driver called DRIVER.DRV. If Windows cannot find DRIVER.DRV, one of these messages will be generated. The most common cause of this problem is that an application or device has been removed from the system and references to it were left in either the SYSTEM.INI file or the Registry.

These errors are typically nonfatal, meaning that the computer will continue to boot after the error. When the error occurs, note the referenced file or device. If this file is required for a device or application in Windows 9x, use SYSEDIT or Notepad to open SYSTEM.INI. Determine where the referenced file should be located. Next, check for the presence of that file in the proper location. If it doesn't exist, reinstall or copy it. If it does exist, it might be corrupted and will have to be replaced. When you are finished, restart the computer.

If the problem persists or if the referenced file is not needed, open the SYSTEM.INI file and place a semicolon (;) in front of the line referencing the problem file. This symbol instructs Windows to skip over that line during startup. If the problem still persists or if you are using Windows NT/2000.XP, you might need to look at Registry entries. Before you open the Registry and remove or change entries, make a backup copy of the Registry that you can restore if more serious problems occur. Use the Registry Editor to search for and remove the referenced entries.

on the !Job *One of the most common causes of this referencing error is deleting an application rather than uninstalling it. When you uninstall an application, its files are removed from the computer, Its references are removed from the Registry and SYSTEM.INI files, and its listing in the Programs menu is removed. If you simply delete an application's files, these references remain in the system. You should always remove applications using the manufacturer's uninstall utility or the Windows Uninstall utility, located in the Add/Remove Programs dialog box. In Windows 2000 and XP, this is the Add or Remove Programs Icon.*

Event Viewer—Event Log Is Full

Event Viewer is the primary tool for investigating error messages on Windows NT 4, 2000, and XP. The Event Viewer accesses log files maintained by the operating system and is accessible through the Control Panel. All critical systems events, as well as user configurable events, can be captured in the event logs. Over time, this log can become full. You should periodically erase the event logs or configure the logs so that they rollover or start writing from the top of the file when full. The rollover causes the Event Viewer to write over existing log entries with new log entries when space is needed. Event Viewer is covered in more detail later in this chapter in the section "Event Viewer."

Failure to Start GUI

In some cases, Windows 9x or NT, 2000, and XP can simply fail to load the graphical user interface (GUI). This problem might occur due to a missing or corrupted display driver. To determine if this is the cause, restart the computer and boot in Safe mode. A standard VGA driver will be loaded, bypassing potentially problematic third-party, 32-bit video drivers. If the system will boot in Safe mode, use the Device Manager to locate and/or reinstall the nonfunctioning video adapter. If the display driver is not the problem, turn your attention to other potentially corrupt drivers. Devices with corrupt drivers will be indicated in the Device Manager by a warning icon. Windows NT 4 does not have a Safe mode, but one of the boot-up options is to start with the standard VGA driver loaded. In most cases, this is functionally equivalent to Safe mode in the other operating systems.

Another, more serious cause of a failure to load the GUI is a missing or corrupted GUI file. That is, during startup, Windows could simply be unable to load a file responsible for producing the interface, such as GDI.EXE or the Windows kernel. If you are using Windows NT, 2000, or XP, boot into the setup program and select the emergency repair process from the setup menu. You will need, at minimum, the software CD-ROM. If your computer will not boot from CD-ROM, you will need the Setup Boot Disks in addition to the CD-ROM.

The Windows NT 4 emergency repair process is similar to that of Windows 2000 and XP: you insert the boot up and operating system installation CD and select Repair when prompted. If you previously created an Emergency Repair Disk (ERD), you will be prompted for it during the repair. You can also elect to repair without the ERD and the system will be configured to the initial configuration. Be aware that if choose to repair without the ERD, you will need to reinstall your applications but you will usually not have any data loss.

If the problem persists or if you are using Windows 9x, reinstall the operating system. To do this, boot from the Windows startup disk(s) and install the OS in the same location as the nonworking OS. Setup will overwrite the Windows system files while leaving other files and applications intact. Note that you will lose all OS-related configurations such as screen colors and Windows network settings.

Windows Protection Errors

Windows protection errors occur during startup before the GUI is loaded, when a 32-bit virtual driver fails to load. The failed driver will typically be indicated along with the error message. Restart the computer in Safe mode. If the OS loads properly, use the Device Manager to reinstall corrupted or missing drivers. If you are using Windows 9x and cannot determine which driver is at fault, restart the computer using step-by-step confirmation. This choice will allow you to select which drivers to process and view the success or failure of each. Once you have determined the source, replace the driver.

If the OS will not load in Safe mode, there could be an error with the standard VGA driver or another Safe mode device driver. You will need to replace the driver by copying it from the installation disk into the WINDOWS\SYSTEM folder. If you are using Windows 9x, you can do this using the EXTRACT command from the boot disk.

User-Modified Settings Causing Improper Operation

Occasionally users like to experiment or change settings of a perfectly working system to see what happens. They may also install new hardware, utility software, and other tools to help them manage their work. If the system refuses to start up, you can usually get the system back up by booting in Safe mode. This allows you to investigate the problem and make corrections as needed.

Safe Mode Recovery

Windows 9*x* and Windows 2000/XP can run in Safe mode. This is an excellent diagnostic tool, and you can use it by selecting Safe Mode from the Windows Startup menu (Windows 9*x*) or advanced startup options (Windows 2000). However, if Windows detects a potentially fatal driver error on startup, it might boot in Safe mode automatically. This action is typically accompanied by a message indicating the source of the problem. Use the Device Manager to find nonfunctioning hardware and replace bad drivers. If you are using Windows 9*x* and suspect a problem with a 16-bit driver, use the System Configuration utility to bypass suspect 16-bit drivers, then restart the computer.

exam

ⓦatch *Registry operations can render a system unusable. The following examples are intended to provide you with a general idea of how to repair a Registry. Do not attempt this on a production system until you investigate the Microsoft Knowledge Base about the operations you intend to try.*

Registry Corruption

Registry corruption is a very serious error if it occurs. As you may recall, the Registry contains references to virtually every aspect of the system. If the Registry becomes corrupt, you may be able to partially recover if you created a Registry backup or recovery disk.

Windows 9*x* users have the ability to back up, restore, and scan the Registry in an attempt to repair Registry entries using the program SCANREG.

The Registry structure for Windows 2000 and XP are considerably different. Both operating systems provide utilities and methods to repair the Registry. The simplest method involves the Last Known Good configuration. The Last Known Good option uses settings that are known to be good by the operating system. If that does not work, you will need to repair the system using the installation CD unless you have made a system restore.

Windows NT 4 uses an Emergency Repair Disk (ERD) process to back up and repair the Registry. When you make changes to the system configuration or applications software, make sure you run the ERD program to back those changes up to the system so you can use the ERD to recover your system to its most recent state. There is also a program in the Windows NT 4 resource kit called REGBACK that can be used to back up and restore Registry hives.

on the
ⓘob *There are many possible ways to work with the Registry that are explained in great detail at the Microsoft Support website at www.support.microsoft.com. If you are having a problem, this is a good place to get information that may help you recover your system more quickly.*

Corrupted Swap File

Recall that Windows 9x and NT/2000/XP can use space on the hard drive to store temporary data that will not fit in regular RAM. This space is the swap file, and it can become corrupted just like any other file on the hard drive. When there is a swap file problem, you will typically be notified by a "Swapfile corrupt" error message. However, swap file problems can also manifest themselves as other problems, such as a system that frequently hangs or locks up.

Fortunately, corrupt swap file problems are easy to resolve. If Windows is configured to use a swap file but one doesn't exist, Windows will automatically generate it at startup. To force Windows 2000 or XP to generate a new swap file, simply reboot the system. In Windows 9x, boot the computer using a boot disk (so that Windows doesn't load), locate the existing swap file, called WIN386.SWP, and delete it. To adjust the swap file, double-click the System Control Panel and select the Performance tab, then Virtual Memory. Once the file is deleted, restart the computer. Note that corrupted files sometimes indicate a failing hard drive. Run Scandisk to locate and eliminate other disk-related problems.

e x a m
ⓦatch
It might seem like a trick, but it really is this simple: All you have to do to resolve a swap file error in Windows 9x is delete the existing swap file and restart the computer. Don't dismiss "Delete the swap file" as the correct answer on the exam simply because it sounds too easy. In Windows NT, 2000, and XP it's not necessary to delete the swap file; rebooting generates a new one.

SCENARIO & SOLUTION

What does the "BOOT: Couldn't find NTLDR" message indicate?	The boot loader file cannot be accessed. Try NTLDR in Windows NT/2000/XP.
The HIMEM.SYS file is missing. What should I do?	Boot from a startup disk and copy a good version of the HIMEM.SYS file from the floppy disk to the C:\Windows folder.
The swap file is corrupted. What should I do?	In Windows 9x, delete the file (WIN386.SWP). When you restart the computer, Windows will automatically rebuild the swap file. In Windows NT/2000/XP, restart the computer.

CERTIFICATION OBJECTIVE 10.02

Runtime Problems

Unlike boot problems, runtime problems can be quite difficult to diagnose. The problem could be inherent in the OS, the result of a recently conducted runtime operation, or the result of a user error. Some runtime problems are quite common and easy to troubleshoot. However, the causes of most runtime problems are not immediately apparent, and you will need to do some detective work to determine the cause. This section begins with basic troubleshooting guidelines and steps you can use to determine a problem's source. It follows up with ways to resolve common problems once you have found their sources. Note that these procedures do not apply to Windows boot problems.

Diagnosing Problems

In some cases, the cause of a runtime error could be apparent from the error message displayed by Windows. In other cases, the error message might simply state that there has been an error without indicating the potential source. A problem could even take the form of a nonfunctioning or locked-up component that is not accompanied by an error message. Whenever you must resolve a problem for which the cause is unfamiliar, you must do everything you can to narrow it down before troubleshooting. This will be easier to do if you establish some basic fact-finding and troubleshooting guidelines and stick to them.

The following subsections provide basic guidelines for you to following in determining the cause of common Windows problems. The procedures for troubleshooting printer problems are quite different from troubleshooting system problems, so they are presented individually later in the chapter.

Gathering Information

The first step in determining the cause of a Windows runtime error involves gathering as much information as you can about the problem. Ask the customer what happened to indicate an error. For example, did an application lock up, or is the system refusing to launch a utility? Ask the customer about the presence and content of error messages. This could be an excellent clue to the cause of the problem. For example, if the user can't save to the floppy drive and Windows produced a "Device is not ready" error, you will have pinpointed the source of the problem. Unfortunately, other messages, such as "Illegal operation," are more vague.

If possible, ask the user to reproduce the problem. That is, have the user perform the procedure that brought on the problem. This will allow you to see error messages that the user might not have noticed or remembered; it will also allow you to watch the sequence of events that caused the problem. As the user reproduces the error, pay attention to the techniques used—they could be the cause of the error. Is the user trying to save a file to the Recycle Bin? Is the user impatient and overloading the OS by clicking and double-clicking items too quickly?

It is also important to determine whether there have been recent changes to the system. For example, an application that worked normally until a virus scan utility was installed is most likely being affected by the virus scan utility.

General Troubleshooting Procedures

Sometimes the information you gather from the customer is sufficient to pinpoint the cause of an error. However, this is not always the case. If the error persists or if you have not yet determined its cause, restart the computer. It is not uncommon for applications to exit improperly, thus tying up resources that other applications are trying to access. By restarting the computer, you will clear the system's RAM and possibly put an end to the problem.

Once the computer has restarted, try again to reproduce the problem. This might help you determine if the problem occurs at random or with regularity. For example, does the screen go blank at random, or does it happen every time a particular application is started? If the problem persists, reboot the computer in Safe mode. If the problem does not occur in Safe mode, you can start looking at 16-bit configuration files as the cause.

Next, determine the components that are involved in the problem. That is, try to determine whether the problem is limited to a single utility or perhaps to a specific function within all applications. For example, if a utility won't start, try to start another utility. If one application won't import images from the scanner, try to access the scanner from another application. If a program won't save to the floppy drive, try to save from another application, or use the original application to save to a different drive.

If the problem seems to stem from a particular device, check its configuration in the Device Manager and ensure that the driver is not corrupted. (Refer to Chapter 3 for more hardware-related troubleshooting procedures.) If the problem seems to occur within a single application, uninstall it, then reinstall the application. If the problem persists, check with the application's manufacturer for bug fixes or patches because the problem could be caused by an error within the application itself. If the problem is more widespread or if the OS will not run at all, try reinstalling the OS itself.

Windows Troubleshooting Utilities and Tools

Windows includes several troubleshooting utilities that can help you quickly and easily pinpoint the causes of some problems. Some of the utilities described here can help you resolve problems.

Startup Disks   Having a boot disk available for use in troubleshooting a system is a great asset. Most technicians carry around a DOS disk that can be used to boot a system if there is a problem ; this can tell a lot about a system. If the system can boot from the DOS disk, you know that the processor, memory, and critical components are probably functioning correctly.

One of the simplest ways to build a startup disk is to make a Startup disk from a Windows 9x system. This disk supports the options for extended memory, CD-ROM support, and other utilities. The contents of the major components of a Windows startup disk are described in Table 10-1.

These files constitute the majority of what needs to be on a bootable floppy disk or CD-ROM. FDISK and FORMAT are also contained in the EDB.CAB file. I prefer to keep them separate, however, because it allows them to be used without extracting them from the compressed file.

TABLE 10-1	File	Description
Files Needed for a Boot/ Recovery Disk	IO.SYS	Input/output code used at booting
	MSDOS.SYS	Core or kernel of operating system
	HIMEM.SYS	Extended memory manager
	COMMAND.COM	Command processor or shell
	AUTOEXEC.BAT	Batch file that loads utility programs
	CONFIG.SYS	System file that loads DOS driver
	ASPI (MULTIPLE FILES).SYS	Device drivers
	OAKCDROM.SYS	CD-ROM driver
	EBD.CAB	Utilities for systems maintenance (compressed file)
	EXTRACT.EXE	Decompression software used with EBD.CAB
	FDISK.EXE	Disk partitioning software
	FORMAT.EXE	Disk formatting software

Startup Modes   There are several modes with which you can start a system to allow for troubleshooting. The most common modes you will use are discussed briefly in this section:

- **Safe mode**   Loads a minimal set of drivers and services and starts Windows.
- **Safe mode with networking load network drivers**   Loads minimal networking on top of Safe mode configuration.
- **Safe mode with command prompt**   Similar to Safe mode in Windows 9*x* except the DOS cmd (COMMAND.COM) file is loaded instead of the Windows GUI. In Windows 2000/XP, this loads the basic GUI drivers but does not execute them when you log on.
- **Step-by-step/single-step mode**   Steps the user through startup and requires a prompt for each step in the process. This is helpful to determine what file is not working correctly during system startup. This option is not available in Windows 2000 and XP.

Automatic Skip Device (ASD)   ASD tracks any failed device driver loads during startup that may be caused by a malfunction of physical device or a corrupt driver. This allows Windows to continue to boot without that device being functional. The driver that is not functioning will be disabled and can either be enabled or reinstalled manually using the Device Manager.

User Installation Manuals   A good place to start when troubleshooting a system problem is the installation manuals. It may sound obvious and it is, but many people do not investigate the installation manuals for troubleshooting tips. Most manufacturers of hardware and software provide either printed manuals or access to Internet resources for configuration and installation. If in doubt, start with the manuals.

Internet/Web Resources   The Internet and Web provide computer support professionals with a rich and robust source of information. It is highly likely that you are not the first person to have encountered the problem you are working on. Students, organizations, and schools provide a wealth of information on almost any computer-related issue. This is a great place to learn the field and learn how to troubleshoot a problem.

Some of the more popular websites that are used for technical support include

- **www.microsoft.com**   Includes a Knowledge Base and extensive how-to articles relating to Microsoft operating systems.

- **www.webopedia.com** A great resource for definitions of terms and a starting point for searching other websites.
- **www.google.com** Enter a keyword or term and you will be returned literally thousands of websites on virtually any number of topics relating to computer technology.

There are thousands of websites available to help computer support technicians; over time, you will collect your favorites.

Training Materials Training materials are a great way to gain insights into the workings of computer systems. Training materials such as this study guide are a terrific way to broaden your knowledge and provide ready access to tips, suggestions, and refresher knowledge.

Task Manager The Task Manager is a program provided on most current Microsoft operating systems that allows you to monitor activities, see what programs are running, end applications and services, and shut down your computer. Figure 10-1 shows the Task Manager's applications panel, which shows what applications are running on the system; Figure 10-2 shows the Task Manager's processes panel, which shows what processes are running on the system. These figures were taken from a Windows XP Home Edition system.

FIGURE 10-1

Applications panel on Task Manager From a Windows XP system

FIGURE 10-2

Processes Panel
on Task Manger
from a Windows
XP System

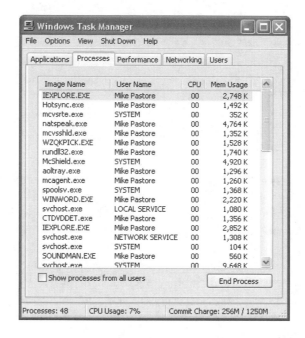

A process is simply a running program. A process that runs in the background and manages system functions is called a service, a process that runs in the foreground or your screen is called an application.

Dr. Watson   Windows 9*x* and Windows 2000/XP include a utility called Dr. Watson, which can help you pinpoint the causes of errors in running applications. When an error occurs or when the program is initiated by the user, Dr. Watson takes a "snapshot" of the system's current configuration (see Figure 10-3). This information includes all currently running applications and tasks as well as currently loaded device and user drivers. Also included is a Diagnosis tab, where Dr. Watson will indicate error information such as which program experienced the error, which program caused the error, and which memory address was the site of the error.

The Dr. Watson snapshot can be saved as a log file so that you can refer to it at a later time. Dr. Watson does not run automatically when you start Windows, so when an error occurs, you must initiate the utility right away to get an accurate record of the system's configuration. Note that some applications start the Dr. Watson utility automatically when you run them. Once Dr. Watson is running, it will continue to monitor application performance and can automatically inform you when an error occurs. Follow the steps in Exercise 10-2 to start Dr. Watson, take a system snapshot, and log the details in Windows 98.

FIGURE 10-3

The Windows 98
Dr. Watson
Utility

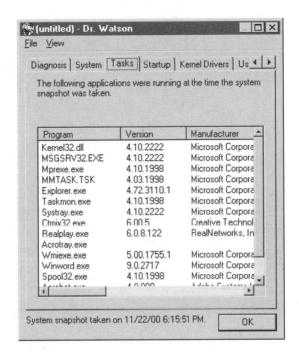

Program	Version	Manufacturer
Kernel32.dll	4.10.2222	Microsoft Corpora
MSGSRV32.EXE	4.10.2222	Microsoft Corpora
Mprexe.exe	4.10.1998	Microsoft Corpora
MMTASK.TSK	4.03.1998	Microsoft Corpora
Explorer.exe	4.72.3110.1	Microsoft Corpora
Taskmon.exe	4.10.1998	Microsoft Corpora
Systray.exe	4.10.2222	Microsoft Corpora
Ctmix32.exe	6.00.5	Creative Technol
Realplay.exe	6.0.8.122	RealNetworks, In
Acrotray.exe		
Wmiexe.exe	5.00.1755.1	Microsoft Corpora
Winword.exe	9.0.2717	Microsoft Corpora
Spool32.exe	4.10.1998	Microsoft Corpora

EXERCISE 10-2

Using Dr. Watson to Log System Details

1. Select Start | Programs | Accessories | System Tools | System Information.

2. In the Tools menu, select Dr. Watson. An icon will appear in the taskbar to indicate that the Dr. Watson utility is running.

3. Double-click the Dr. Watson icon in the taskbar. The utility will create a snapshot of the system's current configuration and running applications and will open a window similar to the one shown in Figure 10-4. Note that in this case, no problems were detected.

4. Click the View menu and select Advanced View. The tabs displayed in Figure 10-5 will become available. You can click each of these tabs to view system details In the File menu, select Save As.

5. Select the path C:\Windows\Drwatson and enter a name for the snapshot.

6. Click Save. You can later open this snapshot by selecting Open Log File from the File menu.

FIGURE 10-4

The Windows 98
Dr. Watson
Diagnosis screen

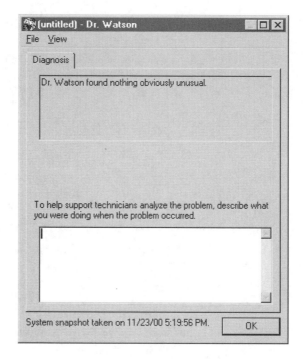

FIGURE 10-5

Windows 98
Dr. Watson
Advanced View

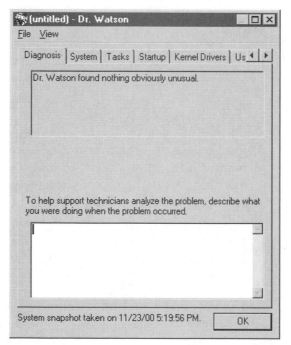

To start Dr. Watson in Windows 2000, select Start | Administrative Tools | Computer Management | Tools | Dr. Watson. The alternative to starting Dr. Watson manually is to place the utility in the Windows Startup folder so that it launches automatically every time you start Windows. The Dr. Watson Utility can use a fair amount of systems resources on a smaller machine which is why you may want to be able to start it manually.

Boot Disk　One of the handy tools to have in your tool box is a boot disk. Minimally, you can use a Windows 98 or ME system to make a recovery floppy disk that will allow you boot the system and perform installations. The boot disk should contain the operating system, HIMEM.SYS, edit.com, smartdrv, and CD-ROM drivers. A minimal boot floppy can be made by inserting a blank disk in a the floppy disk (for example, drive a:) and then loading the operating system as shown next:

```
C:\format a:/s
```

The /s option installs the operating system on the floppy drive once it has been formatted.

Event Viewer　Windows NT, 2000, and XP include a utility called the Event Log service. This service starts automatically when Windows loads, and it keeps three separate activity logs: a system log, an application log, and a security log. The system log records system-related events such as driver loading and display changes. The application log records application-specific activities such as loading, saving, and file access. The security log is available only to system administrators and records events such as logon attempts and failures and network resource access attempts.

Each logged event is accompanied by the date and time as well as the event type (error, warning, information, success or failure notations). In the event of a problem, you can use the Event Viewer to read these logs and see the events and tasks leading up to the problem. To open the Event Viewer, select Start | Programs | Administrative Tools | Event Viewer.

You can also execute Event Viewer using the command prompt by clicking Start | Run and typing **eventvwr**.

In addition to reading the event logs, you can use the Event Viewer to set the log size, save logs, clear current entries in the logs, and select what happens when the log becomes full. In most cases, older events are replaced by newer events as they occur. However, you can configure the log service to display an error message when the log is full. This allows you to save the log before old items are overwritten with new items.

Device Manager   The Device Manager is one of the key programs that you will need to troubleshoot problems on a system. Device Manager allows you to remove, refresh, and install drivers. You can access it by right-clicking My Computer and selecting Properties. Click the Hardware tab to see a window similar to the one in Figure 10-6, which shows you the options on a Windows XP system. Select Device Manager to view all of the devices on the system, as shown in Figure 10-7.

To perform maintenance on a device driver, you can select the options shown in Figure 10-8. You can install a driver, update, or roll back a driver to a previous version. As you can see, Device Manager is a central tool in correcting system problems.

WinMSD   WinMSD is a system information and diagnostic program that can provide you with a wealth of information about your system. You can display and save information for submission to either Microsoft or another vendor for troubleshooting. This program has been around for several years and ships with all Microsoft operating systems. The system information screen of this system shows you the BIOS date and other information that will be helpful in troubleshooting

---

FIGURE 10-6

Systems
Properties on a
Windows XP
system

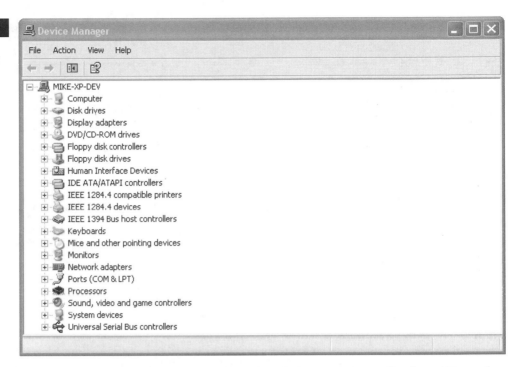

FIGURE 10-7

Device Manager
on a Windows
XP system

systems problems. Figure 10-9 shows the system information on a Windows XP system. Notice on this system that this system has Service Pack 1 installed and runs American Megatrends Version 3.4.11.

FIGURE 10-8

Device Driver
options in
Windows XP

MSD   MSD is an older version of WinMSD that was shipped with DOS and early Windows systems. MSD reports a smaller set of information and is seldom used anymore. However, MSD does have the advantage of being able to run under DOS.

Recovery CD   Many manufacturers of PC systems provide a Recovery CD with the purchase of a system. The Recovery CD is typically a mirrored or copied image of the operating system and all of the base products that came with the system. When you perform a recovery using this CD, be sure to follow directions carefully because these CDs frequently reinitialize the hard drive and set the system to the configuration that it came out of the box with. It is possible that all data will be lost in that situation.

CONFIGSAFE   CONFIGSAFE is a tool that saves a snapshot of your system and can be used to save and restore your system to a configuration at a certain point in time. This program also tracks changes and provides some troubleshooting capabilities. CONFIGSAFE essentially helps make your recovery quicker if a crash occurs. CONFIGSAFE runs on Windows 9x, NT, 2000, and XP. The website for CONFIGSAFE is **www.configsafe.com**.

CERTIFICATION OBJECTIVE 10.03

Common Operational and Usability Problems

This section discusses the major operational and usability problems you will encounter on Windows 9x, NT, 2000, and XP systems. For the most part, the sophistication of newer operating systems greatly reduces the types of problems that you will encounter and makes resolution more standard.

Specifically, this section provides you with the information you will need to identify, troubleshoot, and repair common runtime, application installation, and operating systems problems. You will also learn about printer- and virus-related problems.

Common Runtime Problems

Every OS problem can be resolved. Whether it involves replacing a missing file or reinstalling the entire OS, you *can* get the system up and running again. The more familiar you are with the normal function and processes of the OS, the easier it will be to determine the source of a problem and repair it. You must also be familiar with the procedures described so far in this chapter and the troubleshooting techniques and tools described in this and previous chapters. However, you can save some time troubleshooting Windows OS problems by familiarizing yourself with some of the most common problems and their resolutions.

General Protection Faults

A *general protection fault (GPF)* occurs when an application attempts a procedure that could compromise another application or the OS itself. GPFs can occur in Windows 9x and Windows NT/2000/XP when an application attempts to access a corrupted driver. More often, GPFs occur when an application attempts to directly access the system's hardware or to use memory space that is already being used by another application. These behaviors are typically limited to older 16-bit (real-mode) applications unless the application has internal flaws.

When the computer experiences a GPF, a blue screen with white text that describes the problem will appear. Unfortunately, GPF messages are typically cryptic and offer you no help in pinpointing the cause of the problem. Furthermore, GPF errors are often fatal on a system-wide scale. Under ideal conditions, a GPF error should result in the termination of the offending program only. However, in most cases, GPFs cause fatal OS errors, requiring you to restart the computer. The causes of GPFs can be obscure, and if the error never occurs again, you will probably never know what caused it in the first place.

You should, however, try to restart the offending application. If the GPF occurs again, reinstall the application. Note that the GPF can be localized within a particular application. For example, it might occur only when you try to access a particular printer from a particular program. If reinstalling does not resolve the problem, check with the manufacturer for a patch.

Blue-Screen Error

Windows systems can exhibit what is called the Blue Screen of Death (BSOD) or, more formally, stop errors. When a BSOD occurs, it means that the operating system has been loaded but the process has hung. Usually, the BSOD will provide information about what failed. If it does not, you can start the machine in Safe mode and try reinstalling drivers. If the problem persists, you may need to turn on boot logging to determine which file is not loading properly. As a last resort, you can repair or reinstall the operating system, and that will usually fix the problem. You can get detailed information on stop errors by searching the Microsoft Support website.

Illegal Operation

Illegal operations are caused in Windows 9*x* and NT/2000/XP when an application asks the OS to perform a function that cannot be carried out. This could be due to an error (bug) in the application's code, or it might occur when the application tries to access a corrupted system file. When an illegal operation occurs, a window will appear with an error message, such as "This program has performed an illegal operation and will be shut down." You can click the Details button to view messages about the cause of the error. Like GPF messages, illegal operation details can be cryptic. For example, one illegal operation associated with Microsoft Internet Explorer is "Exception: access violation (0xc0000005), Address: *address*."

The only other option in the Illegal Operation window is Close. When you click this button, the offending application will be shut down. In most cases, the OS and other applications will continue to function normally. Try to reproduce the error.

Some illegal operations result from a very specific set of circumstances and will not be repeated. However, if the error persists, restart the computer. If you continue receiving illegal operation errors, try to resolve the problem by reinstalling the application.

In most cases, illegal operations are application specific, so you might have to check with the manufacturer of the application to solve the problem via a patch or an upgrade. Additionally, the Microsoft website contains an extensive list of known illegal operation causes in a variety of applications. When an illegal operation occurs, note its details, then search for its cause and resolution in Microsoft's Knowledge Base at **http://search.support.microsoft.com/kb/c.asp**.

e x a m
ⓦ a t c h
Don't confuse GPFs with illegal operations. The main difference between the two is that GPFs occur when an application tries to perform a function that can disrupt or damage another application or device, such as taking over its memory space or trying to access the hardware directly. Illegal operations occur when an application tries to perform an operation that simply cannot be carried out due to a corrupted file or an incorrect path. Both error types are often caused by bad code within the application itself.

Invalid Working Directory

When you first launch an application in Windows 9x or NT/ 2000/XP, you might receive an "Invalid working directory" error. The application's working directory is typically the location in which the application itself is located. The application can use the working directory to create and save temporary files, create default backups, and look for other application files it might need to call during normal operation. The "Invalid working directory" error indicates that the working directory does not exist. This problem occurs most often if the working directory is located on a network to which the computer currently has no access. However, this error can also occur if you accidentally move or delete the application's working directory.

If the working directory has been accidentally moved or deleted, simply recreate it or place it in the proper location. If the working directory requires a network connection, wait until the computer can access the network, or change the working directory to a location on the local computer. To view and change an application's working directory in Windows 9x, perform the steps listed in Exercise 10-3. Note that not all applications use a working directory.

EXERCISE 10-3

Changing an Application's Working Directory

1. Right-click the Start button and select Open, or open the C:\Windows\ Start Menu folder.

2. Navigate through the Programs folder until you have located the proper application shortcut.

3. Right-click the shortcut's icon and select Properties.

4. Select the Shortcut tab. A dialog box similar to the one shown in Figure 10-10 will appear. Note that in this example, the WinZip application has been selected.

5. View and modify the entry in the Start In field. This is the application's working directory.

6. Click OK when you are finished. Note that Windows will not allow you to enter a working directory that doesn't exist.

FIGURE 10-10

An application's working directory is displayed in the Start In field

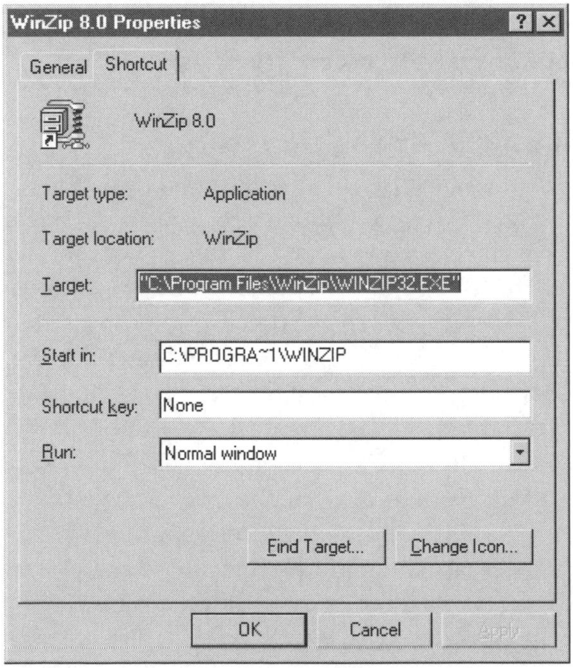

System Lockup

System lockups are one of the most common application/OS errors. They are characterized by an application or an entire system that appears "frozen" or "hung up." In some cases, you might not even be able to move the mouse pointer. System lockups can be caused by a variety of things, including a poorly written application or an application's attempt to access a corrupted or temporarily unavailable file or resource.

If a single application hangs, you can usually close it using the Windows Task Manager. Follow the steps in Exercise 10-4 to close an unresponsive application in Windows 9x.

EXERCISE 10-4

Using the Windows 98 Task Manager to Close an Unresponsive Application

1. Press CTRL-ALT-DEL on the keyboard. A dialog box similar to the one shown in Figure 10-11 will appear. Note that in this case, the hung application (Microsoft Word) is identified by the message "Not responding."

2. Select the application you wa`nt to close, and click End Task. The dialog box shown in Figure 10-12 will appear.

3. Click End Task. The Task Manager and the offending application will close and the computer should return to a normal state.

The Windows 98 Task Manager allows you to close unresponsive applications

Close Program

Snaglt
Microsoft Word [Not responding]
Explorer
Realplay
Acrotray
Systray
Ctmix32

WARNING: Pressing CTRL+ALT+DEL again will restart your computer. You will lose unsaved information in all programs that are running.

End Task   Shut Down   Cancel

This dialog box informs you that the selected application is not responding.

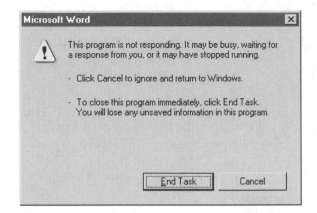

In some cases, a hung application will continue to affect the entire system after you close it. That is, you could notice increased performance degradation. This situation typically occurs if the hung application's resources were not returned to the system once the application was shut down. The Windows NT/ 2000/ XP Task Manager includes a more sophisticated tool for ending not only applications, but any other processes that might have been spawned by the unresponsive application (see Figure 10-13).

If the entire system is locked up, you need to restart the computer. You can do this by selecting Shut Down in the Windows Task Manager. If this doesn't work, or if you cannot open the Task Manager window, restart the computer manually, using the power or restart button.

When the computer has restarted, open the offending application and try to reproduce the error. In many cases, an application lockup stems from a very specific state and order of events, and you might not be able to reproduce it. If the application continues to hang, reinstall the application. Again, some applications simply lock up because they contain bugs. For example, Microsoft Word 2000 sometimes locks up when you close a large document and elect to save the file when prompted. In cases like these, check with the manufacturer for an application patch.

Option Will Not Function

Whenever a computer device doesn't function, examine its configuration in the OS before troubleshooting the hardware itself. First, retry the device, because it might have been busy when you first tried to access it. Next, close and restart the host application and try to access the device again. Try to access the device from another

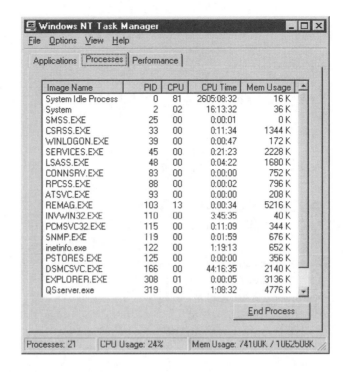

FIGURE 10-13

The Windows
NT/2000/XP
Task Manager
allows you to end
applications and
individual
processes

application. These steps can help you pinpoint whether the problem is caused by the device or the application.

If the application is at fault, restart the computer. If the problem persists, check the application's settings for accessing the device. For example, if you are trying to access a scanner, ensure that the imaging application is configured to access the proper device and that it is using valid scan settings for that device.

If the problem is not limited to a single application, check the device's configuration in Windows. Use the Device Manager to determine if there is a resource or driver problem. If the Device Manager indicates an error, you might need to reinstall the device driver.

If the Device Manager doesn't indicate a driver problem, or if reinstalling the driver doesn't resolve the problem, restart the computer. If the device still doesn't work, use the Device Manager to remove the device's configuration from the system. That is, select the device and click Remove. Restart the computer, then reinstall and reconfigure the device. If you are using Windows 2000, restart the computer using the Last Known Good Configuration option in the Windows 2000 Advanced Options menu. The OS will load with a previous configuration in which the device might have worked.

A new feature in Windows XP is called Device Driver Rollback. This is available from the Device Manager, when you open the properties for a device. If you have upgraded a driver and the system starts to act in unexpected ways, you can roll back to an earlier driver that will still be contained on the system. This simplifies the recovery process in unstable situations in some situations. You can attempt to reinstall the driver to verify if it is interacting improperly with the rest of the system. When you encounter this type of situation you should file a trouble report with the manufacturer of the driver so that they can be made aware of the problem. In all likelihood, other users are having similar problems.

Applications Don't Install

In some cases, an application installation will halt before the installation is complete. You might receive an error message, or the installation could simply stop. The first thing you should do is check the application's minimum computer and OS requirements. For example, if there is not enough memory or if the OS is too old, you will be unable to install or run the application. If the minimum requirements are met, restart the computer. This will free any resources or memory space that the installation utility requires.

Next, ensure that all other applications are shut down because they could interfere with the installation process. You should also check for and shut down applications and utilities that are running in the background. These applications are often referred to as *terminate and stay resident (TSR)* applications because they continue to work even if they do not have an open and active window. TSRs include Windows and third-party monitoring utilities or virus scan programs. You can check for and close any running TSRs using the Windows Task Manager.

If the application still won't install, double-check the manufacturer's recommended installation instructions. Next, check the installation disk itself by using it to install the application on another computer. If the installation works, you can be confident that the problem is caused by the original computer, not the application itself. Finally, check with the manufacturer for known installation problems and obtain a patch or upgrade if necessary.

Application Will Not Start or Load

If an application will not start, you must determine whether the application has worked before or has just been installed. If the application has just been installed, it is likely that the problem lies within the application itself. If the application has worked before, you might need to look at other applications in the system or at the OS itself as the cause of the problem. In either case, watch the screen for error messages; these could provide you with important clues, such as insufficient resources in a Windows 9*x* system, an invalid working directory, a missing .EXE file, or an expired trial period.

The Application Has Worked Before   If the application has worked before, you should first restart the computer. Doing so will release the system's resources and free memory space that the application might need in order to load properly.

If the application still won't start, ensure that all required hardware or network resources are available. Next, determine whether the computer's configuration has been changed recently. If, for example, this problem started only after you installed a new device or another application, you can assume the problem and that installation are related. In this case, check the configuration of the other application or device and focus your attention on troubleshooting it, not the original application, as the cause of the problem.

If the computer's configuration has not changed, uninstall and then reinstall the application. This will cause any corrupted application files to be replaced by working files from the installation media. If the application still won't start properly, check with the manufacturer for known causes of this problem and obtain a patch or application upgrade if necessary.

The Application Has Just Been Installed   If you have just installed an application and can't get it to start, chances are that the problem lies within the application itself. You should first restart the computer. Many applications must make Registry updates to function properly, and restarting the computer will force the OS to initialize those Registry settings.

Next, ensure that the computer and the OS meet the minimum requirements for the application. If so, try reinstalling the application and use the manufacturer's documentation for instructions on specific configuration or installation settings. If the application still won't run, treat this as you would a failed installation, as described previously.

Cannot Log On to Network

Computer networks are complex entities, and a failure to log on properly can be caused by a variety of things. First, however, note any error messages that are displayed. If you are using an incorrect password, for example, try retyping it, and ensure that the Caps Lock feature is not enabled on the keyboard. If you have forgotten your password or if the password is otherwise not working, you will need the system administrator to reset it for you.

You might also be unable to log on to a network if the computer has been configured to use network resources that are already in use by another computer. Check the network configuration settings to ensure that the IP address or network ID (if used) is unique. Also ensure that the computer name is unique and that the proper workgroup or domain name is configured, if required.

If you are still unable to log on to the network, there is a more serious problem, such as an absent network connection or bad Windows network configuration. Refer to Chapters 7 and 11 for more information on troubleshooting network problems.

Windows-Specific Printing Problems

Recall that Windows has a printing subsystem in which all printers are configured, accessed, and monitored by the OS rather than by individual applications. This section focuses on troubleshooting printer problems related to this printing subsystem.

Print Spool Is Stalled

When printer spooling is enabled in Windows, print jobs are sent to a spooler, which in turn saves the print jobs to the hard disk. This method allows the application to return to other functions more quickly and allows Windows to hold print jobs in a

SCENARIO & SOLUTION	
What causes GPFs?	GPFs occur when an application tries to perform an activity that would compromise the data or integrity of another application, such as trying to take over its memory space.
How do illegal operations affect the system?	They are typically limited to a single application. However, they could cause the gradual degradation of the system after the offending program has been closed.
What should I do if an application keeps causing errors even after I have reinstalled it?	There could be a problem (bug) in the application itself. Check with the manufacturer for known errors and patches.

queue until the printer is available. However, the print spool can become stalled so that a print job and all print jobs submitted after it will not print.

Unfortunately, spool errors are not indicated by error messages. Rather, you will probably become aware of a spool problem only if a print job gets sent but is not printed. If the print job is large or contains a lot of high-resolution graphics, simply wait. It could take a long time for the print job to spool. However, if the job is not printed after an excessive amount of time, you should begin troubleshooting. The first thing you should do is access the Printer Properties window. You can do this by double-clicking the printer's icon in the Control Panel. A window similar to the one in Figure 10-14 will appear.

Each pending print job will be listed here, and its status will be indicated in the Status column. If the spool is stalled, right-click the print job marked Spooling, and select Cancel Printing from the shortcut menu. The print job's status will be listed as Deleting and the job will be removed from the queue. This should allow other print jobs to continue normally.

Once you have cleared a print job from a stalled spool, try to print it again. If the spool continues to stall, restart the computer and the printer. If the problem continues, defragment the hard drive and ensure that there is at least 10MB of free hard drive space for spooled files.

If the problem continues, change the spool setting from EMF to RAW. (Refer to Chapter 9 for details about changing the spool settings.) You might also need to disable the spooling option. This action will instruct applications to print directly to the printer, thus bypassing the print spool altogether.

Incorrect or Incompatible Driver

The drivers for printers are configured and managed by Windows. If a printer is configured to use the wrong driver, it will not print. Check the Device Manager for configuration problems. If the driver is corrupted or missing, reinstall it. Third-party manufacturer drivers are recommended over generic Windows drivers for Plug-and-Play printers. If the problem persists, remove the printer from the Device Manager and restart

FIGURE 10-14

A Windows 98
Printer
Properties
window

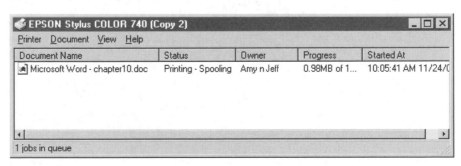

the computer. If the printer is Plug and Play, Windows will reload a driver for it. If the printer is not Plug and Play, you will be prompted to supply the manufacturer's driver.

Incorrect Port

Printers must be configured with the proper port settings as well as driver and spool settings. If a printer is configured to use the wrong port, open the Details tab in the printer's Properties window (see Figure 10-15).

Ensure that the port listed in the Print to the Following Port field is the port to which the printer is actually attached. If it's not, use the drop-down list to select the proper port. If you are printing to a network printer, click the Capture Printer Port button. In the dialog box that appears, you will be able to create an association between a computer port and the actual network printer (see Figure 10-16).

Viruses and Virus Types

A great number of computer problems can be caused by computer viruses. Virus effects could be minor or severe (fatal), and they might be predictable or sporadic. Unfortunately, diagnosing and removing viruses can be difficult, and with the increased information

FIGURE 10-15

The Windows XP printer Properties window displays the port settings

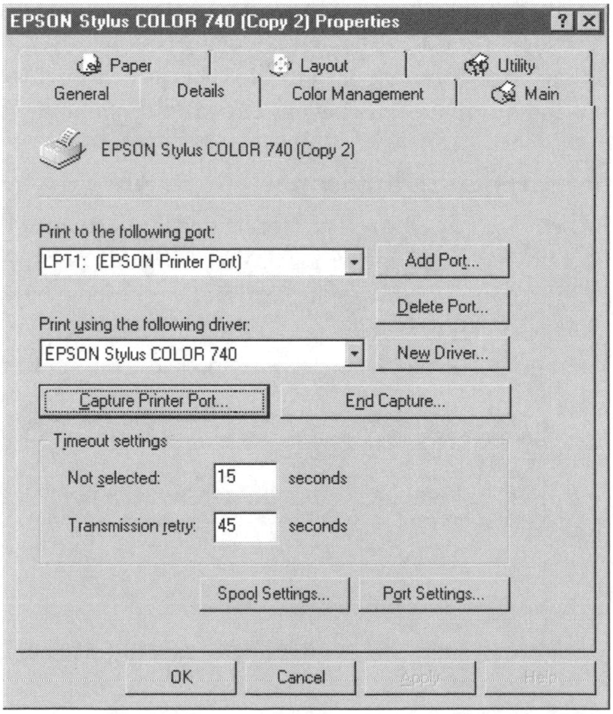

The Capture
Printer Port dialog
box allows you to
associate a port
with a printer

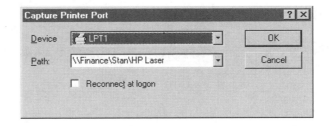

exchange brought on by access to the Internet, viruses are becoming more and more
prevalent.

Computer viruses are not caused by corrupted files or internal OS or application
flaws. Rather, they are intentionally created programs, the purpose of which is to
cause some effect in the computer and replicate themselves to be passed on to other
computers. The effect that a virus has on a computer is called its *payload*. A virus
payload could be nondestructive to the computer, meaning that it could merely
display a particular message, run a video clip, or change the display colors. However,
if a payload is destructive, it can delete files, close running applications, or destroy a
drive's master boot record.

Virus Types

Many types of computer infestations are actually not viruses at all. A true virus is a
piece of code that attaches itself to an executable file and is not activated until the
executable file is launched. A *worm*, on the other hand, is a program in itself and does
not need to attach itself to a legitimate application in order to run. Viruses are
typically more common than worms.

Viruses can be categorized by where they hide themselves. The most common
virus type is the *file virus*. File viruses hide themselves in executable files. When the
executable file is run, the virus is activated.

Another virus type is a *macro virus*. These viruses attach themselves to portions
of applications and disguise themselves as macros. A *macro* is simply an automated
process within an application, such as reading and automatically updating a date
field or searching for and formatting specified text.

Another type of virus is a *boot sector virus*. This type of virus hides itself in the
MBR and is activated during startup when the MBR is located and initialized.

Sources and Spreading of Viruses

When a virus is introduced into a computer system, it typically replicates (copies) itself
into memory. From there, it can copy itself into other files in the system. This is an

FROM THE CLASSROOM

Viruses: Open Up and Say "ARRGGHHH!"

Computer viruses are no fun to deal with and can often be very frustrating. Although some viruses are simply destructive, others are quite creative and, if they didn't result in computer damage and lost files and time, would probably be considered awfully clever. Take, for example, the I Love You virus. This virus is transmitted via a Visual Basic e-mail attachment with the subject line "I Love You." When the attachment is opened, the I Love You virus destroys multimedia files, such as JPG and MP3 files, then sends itself to every user in your e-mail address book.

Virus creators have also come up with a number of interesting activation methods. Some viruses are activated when their host application is activated; others are time sensitive. For example, the Michelangelo virus of 1992 was automatically activated when an invaded computer's date rolled to March 6, Michelangelo's birthday. Other viruses are activated when you use a particular key combination or access a particular feature.

Some viruses require you to play games. For example, one virus turns your mouse pointer into a graphic of a block of cheese. Out of nowhere comes a pack of mice, which follow the cheese wherever you move it. If you click the mouse, the cheese turns into a mousetrap and "squishes" any mice it touches. Once all the mice have been caught with the mousetrap, the computer returns to normal. The Oreo virus displays a message stating "I want a cookie." The user cannot use the computer until the word "Oreo" is entered. The message is repeated 15 minutes later, then repeated 10 minutes later, then 8 minutes later, and so on until it stops altogether.

One of the most clever viruses was the Good Times virus, which was reported to have devastating effects on a computer's system files. A "watchdog" group issued this warning via e-mail: "If you receive an e-mail message with the subject line "Good Times," *do not* read the message but delete it immediately." Being helpful by nature, people circulated this e-mail all over the world until—guess what? It was found that the Good Times virus didn't even exist. The punch line is that this virus hoax caused a tremendous amount of worry, preparation, increased Internet traffic, and wasted time, and the originator didn't have to do an ounce of coding.

intentional behavior, configured by the programmer who created the virus. These copies of the virus can then be spread via floppy disks, downloading files from the Internet, or executing e-mail attachments that launch a host program, such as a word processor.

You can minimize the spread of viruses by using antivirus programs that scan all new files introduced into the computer system. You should scan all files on floppies that have been used in other computers, all e-mail messages with attachments, and all files that you download from the Internet.

on the Job *You can help prevent infection of your computer via a boot sector virus by not leaving floppy disks in the computer at startup. When you receive the "Invalid system disk" error, restart the computer using the Restart or power key rather than pressing the SPACEBAR, as prompted. This practice ensures that the computer's memory is wiped clean of any boot sector viruses that might have copied themselves into RAM.*

Detecting and Removing Viruses

Unfortunately, even if you take all the precautions I've mentioned, you are not immune to computer viruses. New viruses are created all the time and could be too new for your antivirus utility to detect. When the computer starts behaving sporadically or begins to unexpectedly crash, close, or launch applications or lose files, suspect a virus and begin troubleshooting the problem immediately. If you have an antivirus utility, run it and instruct it to perform a virus scan and removal. A variety of antivirus utilities are available from third parties, such as GriSoft, Symantec, and McAfee. Windows 2000 includes a native antivirus utility called AVBoot.

In most cases, antivirus utilities work by recognizing and removing specific viruses. They are typically useless against viruses that have been created since the release of the utility itself. For this reason, most third-party virus utility manufacturers keep an up-to-date list of new virus signatures and offer upgrades via the Internet. It is therefore important that you update your antivirus utility's capabilities often. In fact, you should configure your antivirus utility to automatically check for viruses at regular intervals and to automatically retrieve updates from the Internet.

If an antivirus utility has failed to detect and remove a virus and you suspect the virus is limited to the boot sector, use the FDISK/MBR command. If all goes well, this command will replace the infected MBR with a good copy from a floppy disk.

If you are unable to remove a virus before it has caused fatal damage, you will probably have to reinstall the OS from scratch. It is important in these cases to repartition and reformat the hard drive because viruses could still exist on the drive (especially in the boot sector).

SCENARIO & SOLUTION

Where do viruses come from?	They are created by programmers. They are spread via the Internet, sharing disks, and e-mail.
What is the function of a virus?	To replicate itself and deliver its payload, which is the effect the virus has on the computer, such as deleting files or displaying messages.
How can I prevent viruses from attacking my system?	Keep an antivirus utility running in the background. Do not start the computer with floppies in the drive unless necessary. Scan all incoming files.
How can I eradicate a virus from my system?	Run an antivirus utility. If the virus is not detected and removed, get the latest utility update from the manufacturer.

CERTIFICATION SUMMARY

Because the OS conducts so much activity, a great number of things can go wrong. The more familiar you are with an OS's normal processes, the more easily you will be able to troubleshoot problems when they occur. For example, if you know the steps of the boot process, you will be able to identify which file is at fault when you receive a specific error, such as "HIMEM.SYS not loaded" or a "Swapfile corrupt" error.

When diagnosing runtime errors, keep in mind that a number of diagnostic utilities and boot modes are available to you. There might be no way to prevent system lockups, GPFs, and illegal operations, but you can certainly help resolve them by pinpointing and reinstalling suspect applications or improving the system's resources.

Some OS errors occur due to computer viruses. You can help protect a computer against viruses by using antivirus utilities to scan all incoming files. Viruses can cause unpredictable behavior, so they might be difficult to pinpoint. However, as long as you are aware of their potential and know the proper recovery steps, you can limit the amount of damage viruses do or stop their spread.

TWO-MINUTE DRILL

Here are some of the key points from each certification objective in Chapter 10.

Boot Problems

❑ The "No operating system found" error indicates that the BIOS could not find and initialize the boot loader file (IO.SYS in Windows 9x and NTLDR in Windows NT/2000/XP).

❑ Windows 9x CONFIG.SYS or AUTOEXEC.BAT startup errors can be resolved by booting in Safe mode and removing or modifying the problematic file entry.

❑ If the HIMEM.SYS file is missing or corrupted, Windows 9x will not start and the file will have to be replaced from the installation or boot disk.

❑ Faulty display driver, kernel, or graphical user interface files could cause a failure to load the GUI during startup.

❑ Windows protection errors occur in Windows 9x when a 32-bit driver is corrupted or missing.

❑ Missing application files that are referenced in the Registry or SYSTEM.INI files will result in nonfatal errors during startup.

❑ If the Windows 2000 or XP swap file is corrupted, restart the computer. If the Windows 9x swap file is corrupted, start the computer with a boot disk and delete WIN386.SWP.

Runtime Problems

❑ When diagnosing a runtime error, gather as much information as you can about the nature of the problem, error messages, and recent changes to the computer.

❑ You can use the Dr. Watson utility to take a snapshot of the system's current configuration in either Windows 9x or Windows 2000/XP.

❑ Windows 2000 and XP use an Event Log service that keeps a record of all system activities.

❏ GPFs occur when an application tries to perform an activity that might compromise another running application.

❏ If an application produces an illegal operation error or locks up, try restarting the computer and reinstalling the application. If those actions fail, check with the manufacturer for a resolution or patch.

❏ Use a printer's Properties window to troubleshoot stalled print spools or incorrectly set printer ports.

❏ Viruses are programs that are designed to have an unwanted effect on a computer and to replicate themselves so that they can be spread from one computer to another.

❏ Use an antivirus utility to detect and remove viruses, and update the utility often so that it recognizes new viruses.

SELF TEST

The following questions will help you measure your understanding of the material presented in this chapter. Read all of the choices carefully because there might be more than one correct answer. Choose all correct answers for each question.

Boot Problems

1. You have just installed a new video card on your Windows XP system. You install the drivers and reboot, but the system does not work properly. What should you do to return the system to operation?

    A. Reboot the system in Safe mode and roll back the drivers you just installed

    B. Run the Emergency Repair Disk Process and restore the system

    C. Boot the recovery console and replace NTLDR

    D. Use ASD to bypass this driver

2. A Windows 9x computer is experiencing boot problems because the IO.SYS file is corrupted. Which of the following procedures could help you resolve the problem?

    A. Starting the computer in Safe mode and replacing IO.SYS from the boot or installation disk

    B. Starting the computer with the boot disks and electing to use the emergency repair process

    C. Starting the computer with the boot disk and entering the command **SYS C:**

    D. Starting the computer with the boot disk and entering the command **FDISK/MBR**.

3. During a Windows NT 4 boot process, you receive an error that says, "BOOT: Couldn't find NTLDR." What step should you take first to restore operation?

    A. Reinstall the operating system

    B. Use the Recovery Console to copy the file from the installation CD

    C. Run the Repair process from the installation CD

    D. Run the Repair process from the GUI

4. Which of the following problems might you be able to resolve by using the System Configuration Editor?

    A. The computer generates an "Error in CONFIG.SYS line 42" message.

    B. The swap file is corrupted.

    C. The computer generates a "HIMEM.SYS not loaded" message.

    D. The BOOT.INI file is missing.

5. When starting a computer, you receive an error stating "HIMEM.SYS not loaded." Which of the following is true?

 A. The error is nonfatal and the OS will load.

 B. You should restart the computer in Safe mode.

 C. This is not a Windows 2000 computer.

 D. The error is caused by a faulty CONFIG.SYS file.

6. Why should you restart the computer in Safe mode if the system fails to load the GUI?

 A. Because Safe mode will detect and replace corrupted or missing drivers.

 B. Because Safe mode allows you to edit legacy configuration files.

 C. Because Safe mode loads a standard video driver.

 D. You shouldn't restart the computer in Safe mode.

7. You have a message indicating the log files are full on your XP system. What should you configure to eliminate this problem?

 A. Turn off logging services

 B. Configure Event Viewer to overwrite full log files

 C. Erase all log files

 D. This error will not occur in Windows XP

8. A computer generates an error that states that a device referenced in SYSTEM.INI cannot be found. Which of the following is true?

 A. This error occurs when an application is started.

 B. This error can be resolved using the Dr. Watson utility.

 C. If the device is a video driver, the GUI will not load.

 D. This is a nonfatal error.

9. You are getting a message that the swap file is corrupt on your Windows XP system. What steps should you take to correct this problem?

 A. Shut down and restart the system.

 B. Erase the WIN386.SWP file and create a new one.

 C. Run the recovery process to initialize the swap file.

 D. Extend the size of the swap file.

10. Your Windows 98 computer is reporting that the swap file is corrupted. What should you do to resolve the problem?

 A. Delete the WIN386.SWP file.

B. Replace the PAGEFILE.SYS file from the startup or installation disk.

C. Ensure that the WIN98.SWP is properly referenced in the SYSTEM.INI file.

D. Defragment the hard drive.

Runtime Problems

11. Which of the following is a function of the Windows Dr. Watson utility?

A. To find and reload missing or corrupt device drivers

B. To keep a continuous log of all system events

C. To allow you to access and modify Registry files

D. To record the system's current configuration

12. Which of the following items keeps a running log of runtime activities in Windows XP?

A. The Event Log service

B. The Event Viewer

C. Dr. Watson

D. The Enable Boot Logging boot mode

13. Which of the following error is typically associated with an application that tries to use another application's memory space?

A. Illegal operation

B. Invalid working directory

C. General protection fault

D. Program not responding

14. A computer has generated an Illegal Operation dialog box. Which of the following is true?

A. This is typically not a system-wide fatal error.

B. The error resulted from the application trying to directly access the hardware.

C. You must restart the computer.

D. The application will be shut down automatically.

15. You are using an application and it hangs. Which of the following should you do *first*?

A. Restart the application.

B. Restart the computer.

C. Click the Details button.

D. Press CTRL-ALT-DEL on the keyboard.

16. You are installing an application but the installation process hangs just before finishing. Which of the following is *least* likely to be the cause of the problem?

    A. The system doesn't meet the minimum requirements.

    B. There is bad internal code in the application.

    C. TSRs are running on the system.

    D. The installation utility has tried to use an occupied memory location.

17. When you select a program from the Start menu, nothing happens. After you repeat attempts to start the program, it continues to do nothing. Which of the following should you do first?

    A. Reinstall the application.

    B. Restart the computer.

    C. Check the Device Manager for device configuration errors.

    D. Install the application in another computer.

18. The Windows print spool is stalled and documents aren't being sent to the printer. Which of the following actions is *least* likely to resolve this issue and allow you to print?

    A. Disabling Windows print spooling

    B. Restarting the computer

    C. Defragmenting the hard disk

    D. Replacing the printer's driver

19. You suspected that your computer had a virus, so you ran an antivirus utility. However, the utility reported that no viruses were found. What should you do next?

    A. Reinstall the affected application(s).

    B. Delete the affected file(s).

    C. Download an update for your antivirus utility.

    D. Assume that there is no virus.

20. Which command should you use if you suspect your Windows 9x computer has a boot sector virus?

    A. CLEAR /VIRUS

    B. FDISK /MBR

    C. VIRUS /REMOVE

    D. MBR /CLEAR

LAB QUESTION

Being familiar with common Windows errors is key to your role as a computer technician. So that you can effectively troubleshoot problems, it is important for you to understand why errors occur and where the problems lie. For example, you shouldn't expect to see an "Error in CONFIG.SYS line *xx*" error message when you start an application, and you shouldn't expect to see an "Invalid working directory" error message during Windows startup. This lab has two components; one dealing with Windows 9*x*, and the other dealing with Windows NT/2000/XP.

PART I: WINDOWS 9*x*

This part of the exercise tests your knowledge of Windows 9*x* startup and runtime processes and the errors that can occur along the way. Place the following problems in the order in which they can occur, beginning with the Windows startup. For example, errors relating to IO.SYS must occur before errors relating to the Registry, since IO.SYS is processed before the Registry during startup. Note that some errors, such as GPFs or those caused by viruses, can occur at practically any time, so they are not listed here.

- ■ ___ Windows protection error
- ■ ___ COMMAND FILE not found
- ■ ___ Error in CONFIG.SYS line *xx*
- ■ ___ HIMEM.SYS not loaded
- ■ ___ No operating system found
- ■ ___ Invalid command
- ■ ___ Print spool is stalled
- ■ ___ A device referenced in SYSTEM.INI could not be found

PART II: WINDOWS NT/2000/XP

This part of the exercise deals with Windows NT, 2000, and XP startup, runtime, and related issues. Place the following problems in the order in which they can occur, beginning with the Windows NT/2000/XP startup process.

- ■ ___ Application hangs
- ■ ___ GUI performance slows down or hangs

- ▪ ___ NTLDR not found error
- ▪ ___ GUI does not load
- ▪ ___ Print spool is stalled
- ▪ ___ Windows protection error
- ▪ ___ A device that was previously working no longer functions
- ▪ ___ Blue Screen of Death

SELF TEST ANSWERS

Boot Problems

1. ☑ **A.** You would reboot the system in Safe mode, go to the Device Manager, and roll back the system to the older drivers.

☒ **B,** running the Emergency Repair Process is premature at this point because a driver is malfunctioning, not the operating system. **C.** You would only replace NTLDR if the operating system had become corrupt, making this the incorrect answer. **D.** ASD is used only in Windows 9*x* and would not apply in Windows XP.

2. ☑ **C.** Start the computer using the boot disk and enter the command SYS C:. This command replaces the IO.SYS file on the hard drive with a good copy from the boot disk.

☒ **A,** start the computer in Safe mode and replace IO.SYS from the boot or installation disk, is incorrect. If the IO.SYS file is corrupted, the computer cannot even begin to load the OS, so you will not even reach the point where you can elect to boot in Safe mode. **B,** start the computer using the boot disk and elect to use the emergency repair process, is incorrect. The emergency repair process exists for Windows 2000 only. Windows 2000 does not use the IO.SYS file, so it cannot produce IO.SYS-related errors. **D,** start the computer using the boot disk and enter the command FDISK/MBR, is also incorrect. Although this command could help resolve boot errors caused by a bad MBR, it will not replace or repair a corrupted IO.SYS file.

3. ☑ **C.** Run the Repair process from the installation CD. This will allow you to choose and repair system files. You should install the NTLDR file from the installation CD.

☒ **A,** should not be your first choice because a reinstallation will initialize all your operating system, and it has not been determined if that's needed yet. **B,** Use the Recovery Console is incorrect because the Recovery Console is a Windows 2000 and Windows XP capability and is not available on Windows NT 4. **B,** SYSTEM.INI, is incorrect because errors in this file typically result in the following error message: "A device referenced in SYSTEM.INI could not be found." Furthermore, like CONFIG.SYS, SYSTEM.INI contains parameters and settings, not commands. **D,** Running the Repair process from the GUI is not an option. You need the operating system loaded in order to load the GUI.

4. ☑ **A.** The computer generates an "Error in CONFIG.SYS line 42" message. This message indicates a problem within the CONFIG.SYS file. You can use the System Configuration Editor to open the CONFIG.SYS file and view, correct, or remove line 42.

☒ **B,** the swap file is corrupted, is incorrect because the System Configuration Editor allows you to access legacy configuration files only. These files are AUTOEXEC.BAT, CONFIG.SYS, SYSTEM.INI, WIN.INI, and PROTOCOL.INI. For this reason, **C** and **D** are also incorrect because they suggest using the System Configuration Editor to resolve problems relating to the HIMEM.SYS and BOOT.INI files, respectively.

5. ☑   **C.** This is not a Windows 2000 computer. Windows 2000 does not use the HIMEM.SYS file, so this message cannot be generated on a Windows 2000 computer.

   ☒   **A,** the error is nonfatal and the OS will load, is incorrect. This message indicates a Windows 9*x* computer, and although Windows 9*x* can boot without other legacy configuration files, such as SYSTEM.INI and CONFIG.SYS, the HIMEM.SYS file is required. **B,** you should restart the computer in Safe mode, is incorrect. Booting in Safe mode will not bypass the HIMEM.SYS file, as it does with other legacy configuration files. If you boot in Safe mode, the HIMEM.SYS error will still occur and Windows will not load. **D,** the error is caused by a faulty CONFIG.SYS file, is incorrect. Although the CONFIG.SYS file can be used to load HIMEM.SYS, it is not required. If the CONFIG.SYS file does not reference HIMEM.SYS or does not load it properly, the IO.SYS file will search for it and load it.

6. ☑   **C.** You should restart the computer in Safe mode if the system fails to load the GUI because Safe mode loads a standard video driver. This allows you to determine if a third-party display driver or other device driver is causing the problem.

   ☒   **A,** because Safe mode will detect and replace corrupt or missing drivers, is incorrect because Safe mode is not a diagnostic tool, it is a boot method in which only standard video, mouse, and keyboard drivers are loaded. **B,** because Safe mode allows you to edit legacy configuration files, is incorrect because the System Configuration Editor, not Safe mode, allows you to access these files. Furthermore, the GUI is loaded after the configuration files in the startup process. Problems with these files would have occurred before the system attempted to load the GUI. **D,** is incorrect because it suggests that Safe mode cannot help you resolve this problem. However, as discussed, booting in Safe mode can actually be a helpful troubleshooting procedure in this case.

7. ☑   **B.** Configuring the Event Viewer log files to overwrite will prevent this message from reoccurring: You can specify which log files you want to be overwritten using the Properties button on the logs.

   ☒   **A,** you would not want to disable logging service because this is one of the primary tools for analyzing system problems and tracking system errors. **C,** erasing the log files, is a temporary solution; you will receive the error again sometime in the future, so a better choice is A. **D,** this error will occur regularly unless you regularly erase the log files or set them to be overwritten.

8. ☑   **D.** "A device referenced in SYSTEM.INI could not be found" is a nonfatal error. That is, once this error message is displayed, Windows will continue to boot normally. The SYSTEM.INI file contains legacy configurations to be used by older 16-bit applications. This file is not required by Windows to boot properly.

☒ **A,** this error occurs when an application is started, is incorrect because this error can be generated during startup only, when the SYSTEM.INI file is processed (if it exists). **B,** this error can be resolved using the Dr. Watson utility, is incorrect because that utility can be used only after Windows has loaded. SYSTEM.INI errors occur during startup, before the Dr. Watson utility can be used. **C,** if the device is a video driver, the GUI will not load, is incorrect. Devices in the SYSTEM.INI file are overridden by devices in the Registry. If a 16-bit video driver fails to load from SYSTEM.INI, Windows 9*x* will simply ignore it and load a standard virtual device driver for the video adapter.

9. ☑ **A.** Shut down and restart the system. Windows 2000 and XP automatically reinitialize the swap file during startup.
☒ **B,** WIN386.SWP, is the Windows 9*x* swap file. **C,** is incorrect because using the Recovery Console would not help you correct the swap file. **D,** is incorrect because you would not extend the size of a corrupt swap file. You can extend the size of a swap file manually though this is not recommended.

10. ☑ **A.** You can resolve a corrupted swap file in Windows 98 by deleting the WIN386.SWP file. When Windows is restarted, it will look for the presence of the WIN386.SWP swap file. If it doesn't exist, Windows will regenerate one.
☒ **B,** replace the PAGEFILE.SYS file from the startup or installation disk, is incorrect because this is the name of the swap file in Windows 2000, not Windows 98. **C,** ensure that WIN98.SWP is properly referenced in the SYSTEM.INI file, is incorrect because WIN98.SWP is not a valid Windows 98 file. **D,** defragment the hard drive, is incorrect because although this might speed up access to the swap file, it will not correct or restore a corrupted swap file.

Runtime Problems

11. ☑ **D.** A function of the Windows Dr. Watson utility is to record the system's current configuration. When enabled, Dr. Watson will take a snapshot of current configuration settings as well as all running applications. You can then use this information to pinpoint the cause of a runtime error.
☒ **A,** to find and reload missing or corrupted device drivers, is incorrect. Although this is a function of the Windows 2000 emergency repair process, Dr. Watson is limited to information gathering. **B,** to keep a continuous log of all system events, is incorrect because this is a function of the Windows 2000 Event Log service. Although it is true that Dr. Watson snapshots can be saved as a log, this utility does not keep a running log of all activities. Rather, it gathers system information only when instructed by the user or when an application error occurs. **C,** to allow you to access and modify Registry files, is incorrect because this is the function of the Registry editor. Dr. Watson cannot be used to access the Registry.

12. ☑ **A.** The Event Log service keeps a running log of runtime activities in Windows NT 4, 2000, and XP. This service is started automatically and keeps logs of application, system, and security activities. You can later view these logs to view the events leading up to a runtime problem.

☒ **B,** the Event Viewer, is incorrect because this is used to view the entries generated by the Event Log service. The Event Viewer does not itself log events. **C,** Dr. Watson, is incorrect because this utility can take a snapshot of the system's current configuration but does not maintain a running log. **D,** the Enable Boot Logging boot mode, is incorrect because this will generate a log of boot activities only. It will not log runtime activities.

13. ☑ **C.** The GPF is typically associated with an application that tries to use another application's memory space. GPFs can also occur whenever an application tries to access a resource that is currently in use or to control the hardware directly. Fortunately, GPFs are usually caused by 16-bit applications, so they occur less now than they did when all applications were 16 bits.

☒ **A,** illegal operation, is incorrect because this error usually occurs when an application makes a request that the OS cannot carry out—for example, if an application tries to access a corrupted file or a device that does not exist. **B,** invalid working directory, is incorrect because this error is generated at application startup if the application's working directory no longer exists or has been moved. **D,** program not responding, is incorrect because this error is generated when you use the Task Manager to close an unresponsive (locked up) application.

14. ☑ **A.** This is typically not a system-wide fatal error. Illegal operations usually affect only the application that caused the problem in the first place. Click the Close button in the Illegal Operation dialog box to close the application. The OS and other open applications should continue to work normally.

☒ **B,** the error resulted from the application trying to directly access the hardware, is incorrect because this type of activity results in a GPF, not an illegal operation error. **C,** you must restart the computer, is incorrect because in most cases, once you close the offending application, the computer will continue to work normally. **D,** the application will be shut down automatically, is incorrect because the application won't be shut down until you click the Close button in the Illegal Operation dialog box.

15. ☑ **D.** When an application hangs, you should first press CTRL-ALT-DEL on the keyboard. This will open the Windows 9x Task Manager, and you can close the application from there. On a Windows NT/2000/XP system, CTRL-ALT-DEL brings up the Security dialog box and you can select Task Manager at that point.

☒ **A,** restart the application, is incorrect because you should close the application before trying to start another instance of it. In some cases, you will not be able to open another instance of a hung application. **B,** restart the computer, is incorrect. Although this action might eventually be required, you should first try to shut down the hung application. The computer might continue to operate normally, once the offending application is closed. Furthermore, restarting the computer could cause problems such as corrupted or temporary files, and you will lose any unsaved work you have created in other applications. **C,** click the Details button, is incorrect because applications do not generate Details button when they hang. The Details button is a feature of an Illegal Operation dialog box.

16. ☑ **D.** The least likely cause of this problem is that the installation utility has tried to use an occupied memory location. This type of behavior will result in a GPF and is indicated by a blue screen, not a single hung application.

 ☒ **A,** the system doesn't meet the minimum requirements, is incorrect because this might be the cause of the problem. For example, if the computer doesn't have enough memory or a fast enough processor, the installation could fail. **B,** bad internal code in the application, is incorrect because the application itself could contain a bug or flaw that is preventing it from loading correctly. **C,** TSRs are running on the system, is also incorrect. Any running programs or TSRs could interfere with a Setup utility's ability to access system resources and therefore cause the installation to fail.

17. ☑ **B.** The first thing you should do is restart the computer. Some applications don't release their resources when they are closed. This could be preventing other applications from starting properly. When you restart the computer, you free the computer's resources and memory. If this application has just been installed, restarting the computer might allow Registry entries for that application to be initialized.

 ☒ **A,** reinstall the application, is incorrect because although you could end up performing this step, you shouldn't reinstall until you have verified that the problem is not due to a temporary state of the system. **C,** check the Device Manager for configuration errors, is also incorrect. Applications can be affected by faulty device configurations, but you should examine this possibility after restarting the computer. Restarting the computer takes only a few moments and tends to eradicate a large number of application errors. Reconfiguring a device, on the other hand, can take longer and there is no clear way of telling whether the device is responsible for the failure of the application to start. Furthermore, in most cases, a device reconfiguration requires you to restart the computer anyway. **D,** install the application in another computer, is also incorrect. You could end up performing this step to determine if the application or installation medium itself is at fault. However, this typically takes longer and is less likely to resolve the problem than a system restart.

18. ☑ **D.** Replacing the printer's driver is least likely to resolve this issue. The driver itself is used to allow Windows to communicate with the printer. This is unrelated to the system's use of print spooling, which configures applications to send print jobs to the hard drive rather than to the printer directly.

    ☒   **A,** disable Windows print spooling, is incorrect. When you disable print spooling, you configure the system so that applications send print jobs directly to the printer. Print jobs will therefore bypass the spool service altogether. **B,** restart the computer, is incorrect because this is a common resolution to a stalled printer. The spool service can hang, just as other applications can. By restarting the computer, you also restart the spool service. **C,** defragment the hard disk, is incorrect. The print spooler places print jobs on the hard disk. By defragmenting the hard disk, you make it easier for the Windows printing subsystem to write and retrieve this print job information. This can result in faster print service and fewer stalls.

19.   ☑ **C.** You should download an update for your antivirus utility. Because new viruses are being released all the time, antivirus software manufacturers typically provide regular updates so that your utility can recognize and remove new viruses. Most manufacturers make these updates available on the Internet.

    ☒   **A,** reinstall the affected application(s), and **B,** delete the affected file(s), are incorrect. Viruses are usually designed to remain hidden, so it will be nearly impossible for you to tell which applications and files have been affected. With the virus still in your computer, you could inadvertently help it spread. **D,** assume that there is no virus, is incorrect because antivirus utilities can deal only with viruses that they have been programmed to recognize. They cannot detect viruses that did not exist at the time the utility was released. Therefore, unless you receive regular antivirus utility updates, there is a good chance that the utility will miss a new virus.

20.   ☑ **B.** Use the FDISK /MBR command. Restart the computer using the startup disk(s). At the command prompt, enter **FDISK /MBR** to replace the MBR on the hard drive with uninfected data from the floppy disk.

    ☒   **A,** CLEAR /VIRUS, **C,** VIRUS /REMOVE, and **D,** MBR /CLEAR, are all incorrect because they are not valid commands.

LAB ANSWER

PART I: WINDOWS 9x

The list below puts the Windows 9x answers in order.

1. **No operating system found**   The first system file accessed during startup is IO.SYS. If there are problems accessing this file, the "No operating system found" error could appear.

2. **Error in CONFIG.SYS line _xx_**   IO.SYS then loads MSDOS.SYS and enters the real-mode configuration phase. First, it loads the settings in the CONFIG.SYS file.

3. **Invalid command**   Next, IO.SYS runs the AUTOEXEC.BAT file. If this file contains a bad command, the invalid command error will occur.

4. **HIMEM.SYS not loaded**   If HIMEM.SYS is not referenced in CONFIG.SYS or if it is not referenced correctly, IO.SYS will load it. If HIMEM.SYS is missing or corrupted, the HIMEM.SYS not loaded error could occur.

5. **Windows protection error**   The boot process then enters the protected-mode configuration phase. WIN.COM finds and initializes VMM386.VXD, which in turn loads the system's 32-bit virtual device drivers. If a required driver is missing or corrupted, a Windows protection error will occur.

6. **A device referenced in SYSTEM.INI could not be found**   WIN.COM then reads values in the SYSTEM.INI file. If this file refers to a file or device that does not exist or is in the wrong location, this message will be displayed.

7. **Invalid working directory**   If an application's working directory has been moved or deleted, this error could occur when you launch the application.

8. **Print spool is stalled**   This problem can occur when you try to print from within a running application. This error message means that the print spooler is not writing print jobs to the hard drive properly or is not retrieving them properly to send to the printer.

PART II: WINDOWS NT/2000/XP

The following list shows the NT/2000/XP answers in order.

1. **NTLDR not found error**   The first system file accessed during startup is NTLDR. If there are problems accessing this file, the "NTLDR not found" error could appear.

2. **Blue Screen of Death**   This occurs normally if some key component of the operating system cannot load or has become corrupt. Most commonly this occurs before or during the GUI loading process.

3. **GUI does not load**   The GUI or Windows interface is not loading for some reason. This would occur after the operating system is loaded.

4. **A device that was previously working no longer functions**   This could occur if a device driver is corrupted or is lost from the system. Normally this will occur during or after the GUI is loaded.

5. **GUI performance slows down**   This usually occurs when a program or process becomes hung and starts utilizing all available processor resources.

6. **Application hangs** If an application hangs, it may become non responsive to user input. This usually means that the program has stopped responding to the operating system. Windows NT/ 2000/XP will usually indicate that the program is not responding and give you the option to end the program.

7. **Print spool is stalled** This problem can occur when you try to print from within a running application. This error message means that the print spooler is not writing print jobs to the hard drive properly or is not retrieving them properly to send to the printer.

11

Networks

This chapter builds on the hardware and software concepts introduced in Chapter 7, where you were introduced to networking concepts and the hardware configurations required to set up a physical network. This chapter focuses on the concepts and procedures required to access an existing physical network using Windows OSes. This chapter discusses how to enable resource sharing and introduces some commonly used access protocols. The chapter ends with a discussion of concepts related to the largest network in the world: the Internet.

CERTIFICATION OBJECTIVE 11.01

Networking with Windows

Windows 9*x*, Windows NT, 2000, and XP can join computer networks and access network information and resources. Windows NT, 2000, and XP are designed to support server-based networks, in which network access is controlled (permitted or denied) by a single controlling computer called a *server*. This design is also referred to as *user-level security*. That is, users log on when the OS starts up, and they are given or denied access to network resources based on their identities.

Windows 9*x* is designed for use in peer-to-peer networks, in which all computers can access the network and each computer is configured to manage its own resources. This is called *share-level security*. In this type of security, users can view all shared resources, but they might be asked for a password when they try to access a specific resource.

In share-level security, restrictions are placed on individual resources via access passwords. In user-level security, restrictions are placed on users via profiles.

Windows 9*x* can also perform user-level security in which resources can be assigned by a server. Windows NT and 2000 is designed to accomplish both types of security. Windows XP Home Edition operates similarly to Windows 9*x*, and Windows XP Professional Edition is designed to operate like Windows NT and 2000.

Note that these are simply the *common* implementations of Windows 9*x* and 2000/XP. A Windows 9*x* computer can be configured to authenticate using a Windows 2000 server-based network, and Windows NT, 2000, and XP Home Edition computers can join a peer-to-peer network. Server-based networks can be quite complex, and most organizations with server-based networks employ *systems administrators*, specialists whose job it is to maintain and update network settings, privileges, and connectivity. These concepts are complex enough to warrant their own CompTIA certification exam, the Network + certification. For this reason, the A+ exam focuses mainly on peer-to-peer networks.

Before introducing Windows networking concepts, it is important to note that a Windows computer cannot access a network simply by connecting to it. First, a network card must be properly installed and configured. Next, the OS must be configured for network access.

Activating Network Neighborhood

Network Neighborhood is the network viewing and management tool implemented on the desktop, which allows a user to view and manipulate network resources from the desktop. Network Neighborhood isn't automatically installed with the operating system; it is installed when you install a client network protocol such as Client for Microsoft Networks. If you don't find it on your desktop, it may be because the PC is not configured to join a network.

Windows Me and XP use a new icon for this called My Network Places. This performs the same functions as Network Neighborhood with an upgraded interface and additional options. To configure your computer to support a client network protocol, for the steps in Exercise 11-1 for a Windows 9x system.

EXERCISE 11-1

Setting Up Network Neighborhood

1. Click Start | Settings | Control Panel, then double-click Network to open the Network dialog box.

2. Click Add.

3. Click Client and then click Add.

4. Follow the instructions on the screen to set up Network Neighborhood.

on the **!** **Windows XP uses a shortcut called My Network Places to perform similar** **Ü o b** **functions to Network Neighborhood.**

Enabling Network Sharing

The purpose behind connecting computers together in a network is to allow them to access each other's resources. Using Windows, you can configure which resources other users can and cannot access. However, before you can share your computer's resources, you must enable network sharing in the Network Properties. Follow the steps in Exercise 11-2 to enable sharing in Windows 9x.

EXERCISE 11-2

Enabling Resource Sharing in Windows 9x

1. Right-click the Network Neighborhood icon on the desktop and select Properties. A dialog box similar to the one shown in Figure 11-1 will appear.

2. Click the File and Print Sharing button. The dialog box shown in Figure 11-2 will open.

3. Enable access to your files and/or printer(s) using the available check boxes.

4. Click OK to return to the Properties dialog box.

FIGURE 11-1

The Windows 98
Network
Properties
dialog box

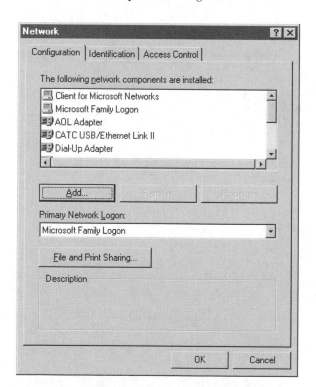

FIGURE 11-2

Use this dialog box to enable or disable access to your computer's resources

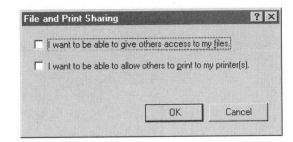

5. Click OK. You will be prompted to restart your computer.

Sharing Disk Drives

One important shared resource on a network is the computer's disk drives. If a hard drive or folder is configured as shared, other users can access its data as though the hard drive or folder resides in their own computers. You can also share floppy drives and CD-ROM drives. This is particularly useful if you want to install applications on several computers at once using a single installation disk. To share a drive in Windows XP Home or Professional, follow the procedure in Exercise 11-3.

EXERCISE 11-3

Sharing a Drive in Windows XP

1. Open My Computer and right-click the drive you want to share.

2. Select Sharing and Security from the shortcut menu. The window shown in Figure 11-3 will open. If this is the first time that a share has been established on a Windows XP system, you will be given the option to configure your system for network. Following those instructions will help you configure your system properly. In this case, the system is already part of a local area network.

3. Select the Share This Folder on the Network option. You will then need to provide a share name for the folder and configure the other options in the window.

4. Enter a name for the drive in the Share Name field. The drive's letter or label will be entered by default, but you can enter a more descriptive name if you like.

5. Check the Allow Network Users to Change My Files box.

6. Check the Users Will Be Able to View and Change Files in the Shared Directory option.

FIGURE 11-3

A hard drive's
sharing window

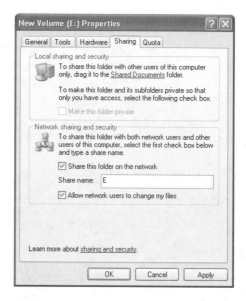

7. Uncheck the Users Will Only Be Able to Download and View Files in the
   Shared Directory option.

To access a shared drive as indicated by the icon shown in Figure 11-4, users must
find it using Windows My Network Places. Double-click the Network Neighborhood
icon on the desktop. All computers in your computer's workgroup or domain will be
listed as in Figure 11-5. To view computers in other workgroups or domains,
double-click the Entire Network icon.

FIGURE 11-4

This icon is used
to indicate the
drive is shared

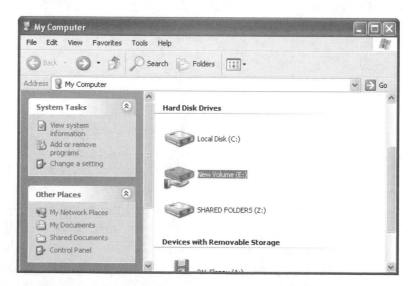

The My Network
Places showing a
LAN with four
computers

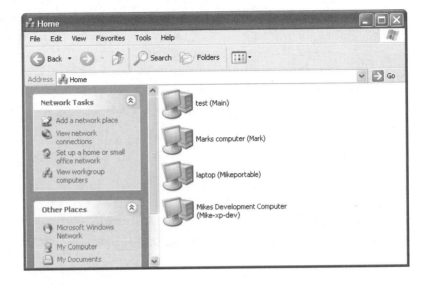

When you double-click a computer's icon in the My Network Places window, its shared
resources are listed, as shown in Figure 11-6. This computer has two shared folders.

This computer
has two shared
folders

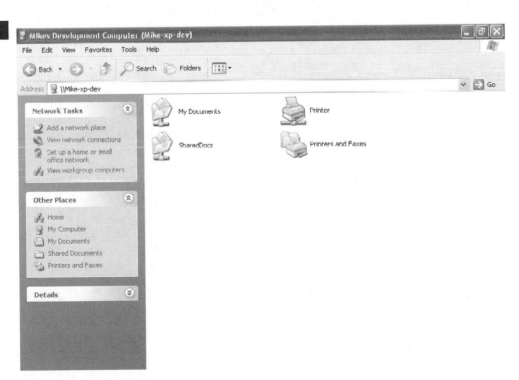

To access data on a shared drive, double-click the drive's folder icon. To enable faster access to shared drives, users can create *mapped drives*. Mapped drives appear as a hard drive that can be connected to your system. A mapped drive appears in the user's My Computer window as though it exists on the local system. This option provides a faster method of accessing system drives than navigating through Network Neighborhood. Follow the steps in Exercise 11-4 to map a network drive in Windows 9x.

It's important to remember that a share is established on the sharing computer, and the mapping is done on the computer that needs access to the shared information.

EXERCISE 11-4

Mapping a Network Drive in Windows 9x

1. Navigate through Network Neighborhood until you locate the network drive you want to map.

2. Right-click the drive's icon and select Map Network Drive. A dialog box similar to the one shown in Figure 11-7 will open. Note that the path to the network drive has been entered automatically.

3. The next available drive letter in your system will be selected by default. However, you can use a different drive letter by selecting it from the Drive drop-down list.

4. Enable the Reconnect at Logon option if you want Windows to automatically map this drive every time you log on.

5. Click OK. You can now access the shared drive by accessing drive E: (or whichever drive letter you assigned) in My Computer.

FIGURE 11-7

The Map
Network Drive
window

Sharing Print and File Services

When you share a drive or folder, all its subfolder and files become accessible to other users on the network. If you prefer to share selected folders only, set the drive to Not Shared. Next, enable sharing on the appropriate folders only, using the steps presented in Exercise 11-3. Each shared folder will appear as a separate icon in Network Neighborhood. Note that when you share a folder, all its files become accessible on the network. You cannot enable or disable sharing for individual files. However, if the sharing system is using the NTFS file system, you can set individual permissions for shared folders.

One of the most commonly shared resources is a printer. You can share printers the same way that you share drives or folders. The difference is that users can access drives and folders simply by opening them. Shared printers, however, can only be used once they are properly configured within the remote user's computer. The simplest way to do this is to locate the printer in Network Neighborhood. Right-click the printer's icon and select Install. Carry out the installation as you would for a local printer (refer to Chapter 9 for printer installation procedures). You can also assign permissions for a user that is sharing a printer. These permissions allow for users to be configured to print jobs, manage the printer, or alter its characteristics.

on the !
Ö o b

When accessing a network printer, you can pause or cancel your own print jobs but not the print jobs of other users. If the printer is attached to a print server, the print server can be used to pause or cancel all print jobs in the queue.

SCENARIO & SOLUTION	
How can I share my hard disk on the network?	Enable File Sharing in the network Properties. Right-click the drive in My Computer, select Sharing, then set the appropriate share options.
How can I view a shared drive on the network?	Double-click Network Neighborhood, locate the appropriate computer, then navigate through the shared drive as you would in My Computer.
Is there a faster way to access a shared resource than using Network Neighborhood?	Yes, you can map the resource so that it appears as a local drive in My Computer. Navigate through Network Neighborhood until you find the resource. Right-click and select Map Network Drive. Assign a drive letter.

CERTIFICATION OBJECTIVE 11.02

Protocols

A *protocol* is a set of rules and procedures that computers use to communicate with one another on a network. You have already been introduced to several access protocols, such as TCP/IP, IPX/SPX, and NetBEUI. You will be expected to answer questions about these protocols on both the Core and OS A+ exams.

TCP/IP is the most common network protocol and is used to access the Internet. It requires configuration of a unique TCP/IP address and allows routing across networks. IPX/SPX is also routable, but it is designed specifically for use with Novell systems and cannot be used to access the Internet. NetBEUI is the simplest of the three protocols. It requires no ID configuration but is not routable.

TCP/IP

The *Transmission Control Protocol/Internet Protocol (TCP/IP)* is the protocol of choice for Internet connections. TCP/IP is actually a series of tools and protocols that are designed to connect disparate or dissimilar systems together for communications. The two primary protocols used in TCP/IP are TCP and IP. TCP primarily focuses on moving data between applications, while IP primarily focuses on moving data between computers (also known as hosts).

While you will not be expected to know much detail about these settings, you should know where they are set, what they mean, and how to configure them in the Windows 9x and Windows 2000/XP environment.

There are several configuration settings that need to be set properly for TCP/IP to work correctly. These include the gateway, subnet mask, IP address, and DNS settings. This section briefly describes these settings.

Gateway

The gateway or default gateway setting tells your network where to look if an address is not contained in the local network. Typically, the default gateway is the address of a router that connects your network to other networks such as the Internet. If you are connecting your network through an Internet Service Provider (ISP), the ISP will typically provide you with the address information for the default gateway. In a corporate network, your systems administrators should have this information.

Subnet Mask

The subnet mask provides a mechanism to break a network into smaller components. TCP/IP addresses represent two distinct types of information. The first part of the

IP address is the network identification. The second part is the host addresses. Your ISP or network administrators will provide you with this information as well.

IP Addresses

IP addresses can be assigned manually to computers using the TCP/IP network protocol. Every time a new computer is added to a network, it must be assigned an IP address and subnet mask. If the network is connected to another network, each computer must also be configured with a gateway address as discussed previously. If a computer is physically moved from one network to another, as in the case of a portable computer, it must be configured with these new addresses and settings. Because these configurations can be time consuming, many networks use automatic IP addressing.

Static Address Assignment

When static addresses are used, each computer must have its IP information manually configured and established. This can become a very time consuming and inconvenient process in a large network. All versions of Windows provide the ability for manual configuration of TCP/IP settings. Figure 11-8 shows the TCP/IP configuration Window on a Windows XP system.

DHCP

A *Dynamic Host Configuration Protocol (DHCP)* server is used to dynamically assign IP addresses to computers as they join the network. The DHCP server is configured to use

FIGURE 11-8

TCP/IP
configuration
window

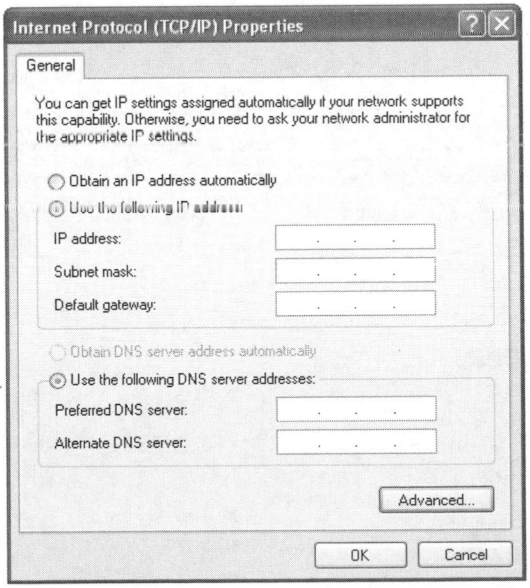

a specified range of IP addresses. When a computer configured as a DHCP client joins the network, it first asks the DHCP server for an IP address. The DHCP server gives the computer an IP address and subnet mask as well as the addresses of the gateway, DNS server, and WINS server, if they exist. The setup and configuration of a DHCP server are beyond the scope of the A+ exam, but you should know how to configure computers to use DHCP services. Follow the steps in Exercise 11-5 to configure a Windows 9x computer as a DHCP client.

EXERCISE II-5

Configuring a Windows 9x Computer to Use DHCP

1. Right-click the Network Neighborhood icon and select Properties.
2. Select the TCP/IP protocol from the list of installed components and click Properties.
3. Select the Obtain an IP Address Automatically option.
4. Click OK to return to the Network Properties dialog box.
5. Click OK and restart the computer when prompted.

APIPA

Automatic Private IP Addressing (APIPA) is a new feature available in Windows 98/ Me, Windows 2000, and Windows XP. APIPA allows a client to self configure IP addresses in a private IP address range if a DHCP server is not available. This will not allow these computers to connect to the Internet without a gateway, but it does allow the network to operate. APIPA, according to Microsoft, checks the network regularly to determine if a DHCP server becomes available, if so, it releases the system to DHCP for configuration.

WINS

Windows Internet Naming Service resolves Microsoft NetBIOS names to IP addresses. This configuration option usually contains the address of a WINS server in your network, if so equipped.

DNS

The Domain Name System (DNS) setting provides the address of a server that translates from the names used in Uniform Resource Locators (URLs) to IP addresses. This setting allows users to access Internet resources by names such as **www.omh.com**. DNS can also perform lookups of IP addresses using a process called a reverse lookup.

IPX/SPX (NWLink)

Internetwork Packet Exchange (IPX) is the protocol used by early Novell networks. (Novell now uses TCP/IP as its primary network protocol.) IPX performs a similar function to IP in the TCP/IP protocol suite. Sequenced Packet Exchange (SPX) provides connection capabilities between systems similar to TCP in the TCP/IP suite. NWLink is the Microsoft implementation of IPX/SPX for Microsoft operating systems, which allows Microsoft clients to be able to connect to Novell Client/Server applications and systems.

Configuration of IPX/SPX on a Microsoft system usually means installing only the protocol to the computer system. There are configuration options if manual configuration is needed, though NWLink will usually be able to configure these options automatically.

exam

ⓌＡｔｃｈ   *Microsoft dropped support of AppleTalk when XP was released. If networking between Apple computers and Microsoft operating systems is required with an XP system, you need to use another protocol, such as TCP/IP.*

AppleTalk

Apple computer was one of the early providers of network products, with its protocol AppleTalk. AppleTalk is a simple network that ships with all Apple computers. Microsoft provides a host for Windows servers to communicate with AppleTalk clients, and Microsoft clients can obtain AppleTalk for Windows 9x and Windows 2000.

NetBEUI/NetBIOS

Configuring NetBEUI/NetBIOS is extremely simple: if you install the protocol on a Windows client, the protocol self configures. This protocol is typically installed on most Windows-based computers.

CERTIFICATION OBJECTIVE 11.03

Network Troubleshooting Tools

There are several tools readily available to help any technician troubleshoot a network configuration problem. This section identifies and describes the tools you will need to know for the A+ exam.

WINIPCFG.EXE

Windows 9x includes an IP Configuration utility, which allows you to view the computer's current IP configuration if the TCP/IP protocol stack is installed on the computer. To run the IP Configuration utility, enter **WINIPCFG** on the Windows Run line. A dialog box similar to the one shown in Figure 11-9 will open.

If there is more than one network adapter in the system, select the appropriate one from the drop-down list. Its details will be listed. The adapter's Media Access Control (MAC) address is listed first. This is a hard-coded ID placed on the adapter by the manufacturer, and the adapter uses it to identify itself to the DHCP server at startup. You cannot change an adapter's MAC address. The computer's current IP address, subnet mask, and default gateway are also listed. You can view more details by clicking the More Info button (see Figure 11-10). Note that the DHCP, DNS, and WINS servers are displayed.

If your computer is configured to be a DHCP client and you want to obtain a new IP address from the DHCP server, click the Release button. This action forces the adapter to stop using its currently assigned IP address and releases the address to the DHCP address pool. Next, click Renew. The adapter will ask the DHCP server for a new IP address from the DHCP address pool.

FIGURE 11-9

The Windows 9x IP Configuration utility

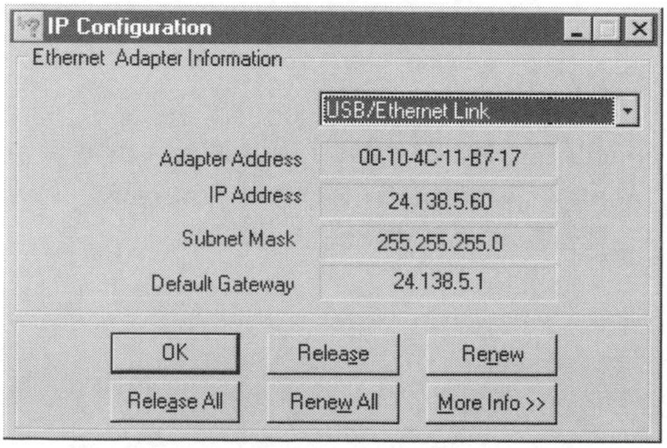

The IP
Configuration
utility's detailed
view

IPCONFIG.EXE

IPCONFIG.EXE is a command-line version of the IP Configuration utility and is used in Windows 9*x* and Windows NT/2000/XP systems. This command only works if the TCP/IP protocol stack is installed. To use IPCONFIG.EXE, enter **IPCONFIG** at a command prompt. The IP address, subnet mask, and default gateway of each network adapter in the system will be listed (see Figure 11-11). To release an IP address, enter the command **IPCONFIG /RELEASE**. To renew an IP address, enter **IPCONFIG / RENEW**

Ping

The Ping utility allows you to bounce a signal off another computer system, similar to Sonar. You can ping another computer system by typing either its IP address or its Internet Name. The following example shows the result of two pings of system in the local network. The first ping shows the results of a successful ping, the second section an

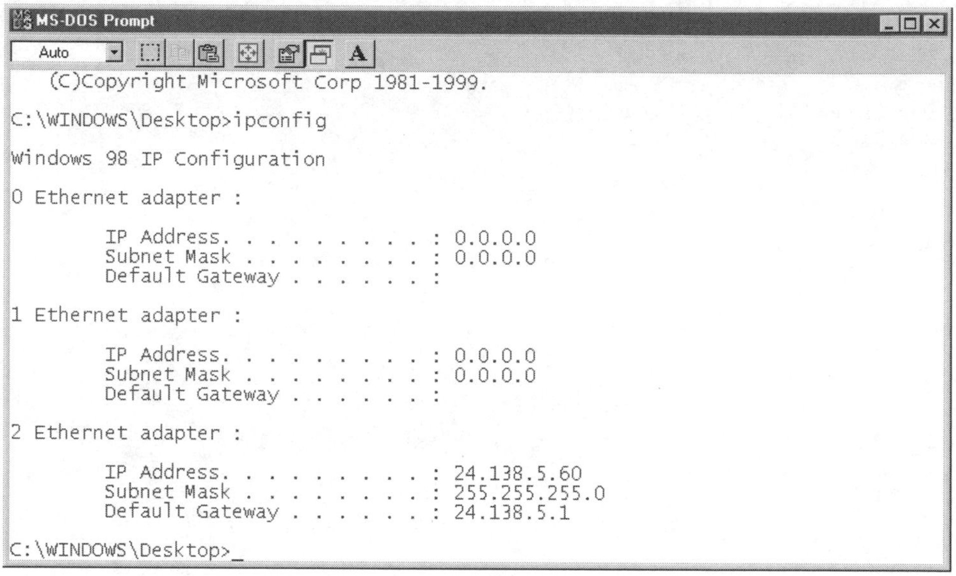

FIGURE 11-11

The IPCONFIG
utility screen

```
MS-DOS Prompt                                                    _ □ ×
Auto      ▼  ⬜  🔳 🔲 🔳 A

     (C)Copyright Microsoft Corp 1981-1999.

C:\WINDOWS\Desktop>ipconfig

Windows 98 IP Configuration

0 Ethernet adapter :

        IP Address. . . . . . . . . : 0.0.0.0
        Subnet Mask . . . . . . . . : 0.0.0.0
        Default Gateway . . . . . . :

1 Ethernet adapter :

        IP Address. . . . . . . . . : 0.0.0.0
        Subnet Mask . . . . . . . . : 0.0.0.0
        Default Gateway . . . . . . :

2 Ethernet adapter :

        IP Address. . . . . . . . . : 24.138.5.60
        Subnet Mask . . . . . . . . : 255.255.255.0
        Default Gateway . . . . . . : 24.138.5.1

C:\WINDOWS\Desktop>_
```

unsuccessful one. Notice that in each case the ping connection tries four times before it finishes. The results tell you about the speed of the connection between the two systems.

```
C:\> ping 192.168.0.1
Pinging 192.168.0.1 with 32 bytes of data:
Reply from 192.168.0.1: bytes=32 time<1ms TTL=250
Reply from 192.168.0.1: bytes=32 time<1ms TTL=250
Reply from 192.168.0.1: bytes=32 time<1ms TTL=250
Reply from 192.168.0.1: bytes=32 time<1ms TTL=250
Ping statistics for 192.168.0.1:
    Packets: Sent = 4, Received = 4, Lost = 0 (0% loss),
Approximate round trip times in milli-seconds:
    Minimum = 0ms, Maximum = 0ms, Average = 0ms
C:\> ping 192.168.0.220
Pinging 192.168.0.220 with 32 bytes of data:
Request timed out.
Request timed out.
Request timed out.
Request timed out.
Ping statistics for 192.168.0.220:
    Packets: Sent = 4, Received = 0, Lost = 4 (100% loss)
```

You can also use Ping to test your IP address and TCP/IP protocol. If you enter your own TCP/IP address, you will get a response if it is configured properly. You can also test your protocol suite by issuing command ping 127.0.0.1, which is the loopback value of your own network card. This is useful to determine if TCP/IP is working properly.

To troubleshoot a TCP/IP problem, first ping 127.0.0.1 to test your protocol suite. Then ping your IP address, your default gateway, and finally a system on the other side of the default gateway. In this manner, you can move from your system to the network to the Internet to verify that configurations are set properly.

Trace Route

Because the Internet contains so many servers worldwide, data that you receive could take a different route each time between the Internet server and your computer. For example, suppose you are accessing data from a server in Europe. The data could be relayed to your computer through routers in England, New York, Iowa, and Colorado. The next time you access that server, the data may be relayed through routers in Minnesota, Wisconsin, Illinois, and Kansas.

Windows' The Trace Route utility allows you to trace the current route to that server. It can be executed from a command prompt, as long as your computer currently has Internet access. You can also use Trace Route within an internal network. To use the Trace Route utility, enter the following command, where *www.website.com* is the host name of the server you want to trace:

```
TRACERT www.website.com
```

The DNS server that is configured in the TCP/IP protocol suite will return the IP address of the host that is used to find the route. Note that the domain name and IP address of each server in the route are displayed. This route may be different each time the system is traced given the dynamic routing capabilities of the Internet.

NSLookup

NSLookup is primarily used to troubleshoot DNS problems; it allows you to query DNS servers and find information contained in a DNS server. There are web-enabled NSLookup programs that can easily return much detail about an Internet site.

CERTIFICATION OBJECTIVE 11.04

Internet Concepts

The largest internetwork in the world is the Internet. All computers that provide a service for or that access the Internet are considered part of the Internet itself. Each server is responsible for one or more services, such as supplying web pages, transferring e-mail, or relaying messages to the next server. The networks are connected using phone lines, cable lines, and fiber optic cabling.

There are many ways to access the Internet, including a single-computer dial-up connection to an Internet Service Provider (ISP), including an entire network that accesses the Internet through a single server, a computer that has dial-up access to a network with Internet access, or two computers that exchange documents using servers already in place on the Internet—the list goes on and on. Because there are so many access methods, and due to the sheer volume of data transfer, a number of concepts, protocols, and procedures are associated with the Internet that are not used on simple internal networks.

Internet Service Providers

An ISP is a company that provides Internet access to home or business users. ISPs have traditionally been phone companies, but now the role of ISP is moving toward cable companies and third-party firms that lease phone or cable time. When you connect to the Internet from home or the office, you first connect to your ISP's server. All your data transfers are relayed to and from the appropriate Internet server via the ISP.

Dial-Up Access

Even with the advent of fast DSL and cable Internet access, dial-up access remains the most popular Internet access method. Dial-up access requires the use of a phone line and a modem that dials up and establishes a connection with the ISP's Internet server. Before you can connect to the ISP's server, however, you must configure Windows to use a dial-up connection, including configuring the modem with the appropriate phone number and communication settings. Follow the steps in Exercise 11-6 to create a dial-up connection to your ISP using Windows 98.

EXERCISE 11-6

Creating a Dial-Up Connection

1. Double-click the Dial-up Networking icon in My Computer.

2. Double-click the Make New Connection icon. The Make New Connection Wizard will open.

3. Enter a name for the connection. Ensure that the name is descriptive because you can create dial-up connections to more than one server.

4. In the Select a Device drop-down list, select the modem you want to use for this connection. (Some computers have more than one modem installed.)

5. Click Next.

6. Enter the area code and phone number of the ISP's Internet server.

7. Click Finish. You can now establish a connection to your ISP. Note that you will be asked to enter a username and password. These must be obtained by the ISP.

on the job

If you are accessing the Internet using a cable modem or DSL modem, you do not need to configure dial-up access. Rather, an internal NIC is installed and communicates with the external cable modem using regular network protocols. The modem itself has a direct connection to the ISP.

Internet Names and Addresses

The access protocol of the Internet is TCP/IP. That is, all computers on the Internet are identified by an IP address and can identify other computers by their IP addresses. However, when accessing a computer on the Internet, users tend to use domain names instead of IP addresses. This section describes these methods of computer identification on the Internet as well as their supporting services.

Domain Names

A *domain name* is a "common" name for a computer or group of computers on the Internet. By combining computers into domains, organizations can allow access to a group of computers without requiring users to enter individual addresses for each computer.

For example, Microsoft makes information available on the Internet through its *Microsoft* domain. This domain contains more than one computer, each with a different IP address. When you access the Microsoft domain on the Internet, you are able to access all the servers in the Microsoft domain without addressing each one separately.

Domain Name Service

The function of Domain Name Service (DNS) is to translate domain names into IP addresses, and vice versa. Recall that all computers are identified on the Internet by their IP addresses. However, remembering these addresses can be very difficult for users, so DNS allows users to identify computers on the Internet by their domain names instead. That is, it is much easier to remember *www.syngress.com* than it is to remember *205.181.158.215*. Note that when accessing Internet sites, you can use either the domain name or the IP address.

exam

ⓦatch   *You might also see DNS described as Domain Name System. Domain Name System and Domain Name Service are the same thing.*

exam

ⓦatch   *DNS and WINS servers are both used to translate host names to IP addresses. DNS translates into domain names, and WINS translates into computer (NetBIOS) names.*

Windows Internet Naming Service

Windows Internet Naming Service (WINS) has a function similar to that of a DNS server but is used to resolve IP addresses to NetBIOS names rather than host names.

Uniform Resource Locator

A Uniform Resource Locator (URL) is the full address of an Internet location. A URL indicates the data transfer protocol and either a domain name or an IP address. For example, the URL *http://www.osborne.com* indicates an HTTP (Web) site that has the domain name *www.osborne.com*. The URL *ftp:// 198.45.24.162* indicates an FTP download site that uses the IP address *128.102.34.2*. If a website or FTP site does not respond to the IP address that was directly entered or located by the DNS service, the browser or client will return an error message indicating that service or protocol is not available at that location.

Ping

Ping stands for Packet InterNetwork Groper. The Ping utility allows you to determine the IP address of a particular Internet domain. You can run ping from a

FROM THE CLASSROOM

The Domain Name Game

When you visit a website by entering *www.website.com*, you are actually entering that site's domain name. The first part of the name (*www*) indicates the type of site. For example, WWW indicates a World Wide Website; OWA stands for Outlook Web Access. The last part of the domain name (*.com*) is used as a website identifier. COM, the most common extension, is typically used for commercial businesses. Some common extensions and their uses are as follows:

AU	Australian
CA	Canadian
COM	Commercial business
EDU	Educational organization
GOV	Government agency
MIL	Military
ORG	Nonprofit organization
US	American

In addition, several new identifiers, such as AERO (aviation), BIZ (business), INFO (Afilias.Ltd.) and NET (Verisign Global), have been added.

Domain names must be unique and must be registered with an Internet Corporation for Assigned Names and Numbers (ICANN)–accredited registrar. Domain names are no longer directly registered with the Internet Network Information Center (InterNIC). That is, you cannot configure a server to use a domain name that you selected out of the blue.

Most large companies have domain names that are very similar or identical to the company name. For example, the Microsoft Internet domain name is *microsoft.com*, and the 3Com domain name is *3com.com*. This makes it easy for users to locate a company's website by guessing the name. Unfortunately, this is not always the case. For example, the website *scsi.com* is owned by Summit Computer Systems, Inc. and has nothing to do the SCSI that stands for Small Computer Systems Interface technology, as you might expect.

command prompt or the Windows Run line. Enter the command using the following syntax:

```
Ping www.domainname.com
```

Here, *www.domainname.com* is the domain name, the IP address you want to find. An output similar to that shown in Figure 11-12 will be generated.

FIGURE 11-12

A ping command output

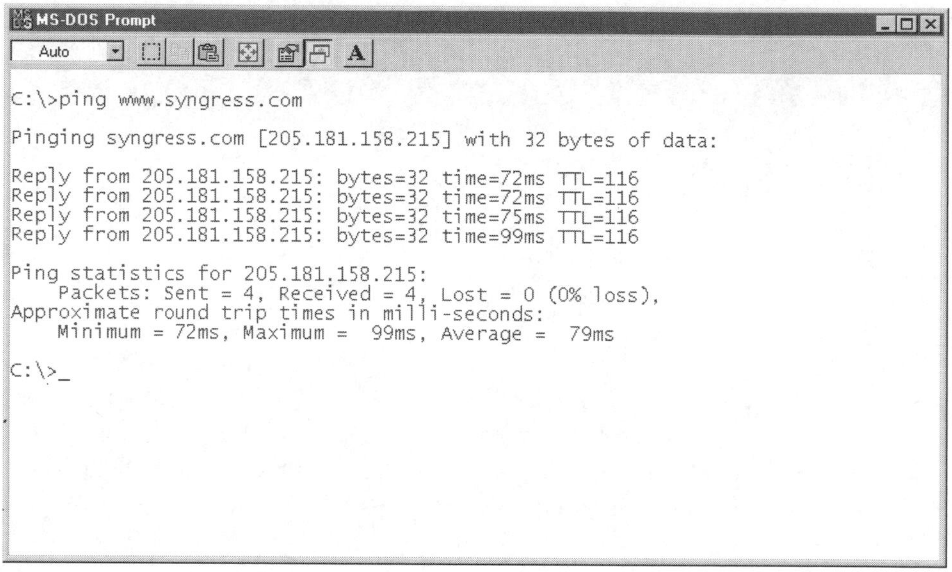

```
C:\>ping www.syngress.com

Pinging syngress.com [205.181.158.215] with 32 bytes of data:

Reply from 205.181.158.215: bytes=32 time=72ms TTL=116
Reply from 205.181.158.215: bytes=32 time=72ms TTL=116
Reply from 205.181.158.215: bytes=32 time=75ms TTL=116
Reply from 205.181.158.215: bytes=32 time=99ms TTL=116

Ping statistics for 205.181.158.215:
    Packets: Sent = 4, Received = 4, Lost = 0 (0% loss),
Approximate round trip times in milli-seconds:
    Minimum = 72ms, Maximum =  99ms, Average =  79ms

C:\>_
```

Note that the IP address is indicated (205.181.158.215). The Ping utility sends a data packet to the specified location, then waiting for a reply. Using the reply data, the ping utility will then report the amount of data loss (if any) and the amount of time it took for packets to be transferred.

E-Mail

One of the most common activities on the Internet is the transmission of e-mail (electronic mail). E-mail is a messaging service in which users can create letters and send them to other users via the Internet. To send or receive e-mail, your computer must be using an e-mail application, have access to the Internet, and be connected to a server that provides e-mail services.

Most e-mail applications use the Simple Mail Transfer Protocol (SMTP) for sending mail and the Post Office Protocol 3 (POP3) for receiving mail. Both protocols are part of the TCP/IP suite. Each user must have an e-mail address, which is typically in the form of *name@domain*, where *name* is a username and *domain* is the domain name of the e-mail server. An example of an e-mail address is *joeb@hotmail.com*.

In most e-mail applications, you can send e-mail by electing to create a new message, entering the recipient's e-mail address, entering the message, then selecting Send. Furthermore, most e-mail applications poll the e-mail server on startup and automatically display all new (received) e-mail messages.

The World Wide Web

The most commonly used Internet service is the World Wide Web. The Web comprises text and graphical web pages that users can browse. Typically, web pages contain links to other web pages so that users can move from one site to another without having to enter new addresses each time.

w a t c h *The World Wide Web is often confused with the Internet itself. However, the Internet is a huge worldwide network that supports many different* *services, including e-mail, FTP sites, bulletin boards, newsgroups, and HTTP sites. The World Wide Web refers to HTTP services on the Internet.*

Web pages come from web servers that organizations set up to make information available. When you access a web page, either by requesting its URL or by clicking a link to that page, the hosting server sends that page to your computer. You can then view the page as though you were using the web server itself. Every time you receive data from the Internet, whether by e-mail, FTP, or the Web, you are *downloading* that information. Every time you send data, such as sending an e-mail or posting a message, you are *uploading* data.

Installing and Configuring Browsers

To access web pages on the Internet, you must be using a web browser. A *web browser* is simply an application that allows you to access and read web pages on the Internet. Common web browsers include Netscape Navigator and Internet Explorer, as shown in Figure 11-13. These two browsers might look different, but they contain similar navigation buttons, such as Back, Stop, Search, and Print. Both have a field in which you can directly enter a URL, and the two display the same Location or Address line for the selected web page (*www.comptia.org*).

Web browsers are installed like any other application, but they require quite a bit of configuration. You might be prompted by a wizard to configure the browser at installation time, or you might need to configure it manually once the installation is complete. You will need to supply the browser with information such as the default page to open at startup, your Internet access setup (such as server names), and e-mail information (most web browsers include a native e-mail service). You might also need to obtain some settings from your ISP or systems administrator, such as the name of the mail server and the manual proxy settings, if required.

FIGURE 11-13

The Internet
Explorer web
browser

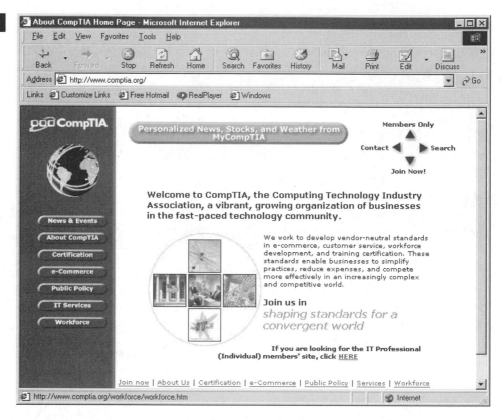

HyperText Markup Language

HyperText Markup Language (HTML) is the language of web pages. The HTML language
is used to create web page code, which is converted by your browser into the web pages
that you see when you browse the Internet. HTML supports text, hyperlinks, graphics, and
streaming media, such as video clips or sound files that play when you view the web page.

HTML has evolved into HTML 4 and continues to evolve, Languages such as
XHTML, and XML while separate can trace their ancestry back to HTML, To learn
more about these, go to http://www.xhtml.org/. HTML pages can be created using
graphics applications that can translate pages into HTML format. You can also create
HTML pages using Notepad or another text editor to manually enter the HTML
code. Follow the steps in Exercise 11-7 to create and view a small HTML web page.

EXERCISE 11-7

Creating an HTML Web Page

1. Start Notepad by selecting Start | Programs | Accessories | Notepad.

2. Enter the following lines:

```
<html>
<title>Osborne A+ Certification Study Guide</title>
<body>
<p><strong>I am "enter your name here" and I am working on my </strong></p>
<p><strong> A+ Certification </strong></p>
<p><strong> I am using </strong></p>
<p align="center"><em> The A+ Certification Study Guide Fifth Edition </p>
<p align="Center"> From Osborne</em></p>
<p>I can get information on Osborne McGraw Hill at <a
href="http://www.osborne.com">Osborne</a></p>
<p>I can get information from CompTIA at <a href="http://
www.comptia.org">CompTIA</a>
</body>
</html>
```

3. Save the file on the desktop and give it the filename testpage.htm.

4. Close Notepad.

5. Double-click the testpage icon on the desktop. Your default browser will open and the web page you created will be displayed (see Figure 11-14). Note that you can visit the CompTIA and Osborne websites by clicking the hyperlinks you created.

HyperText Transfer Protocol

HyperText Transfer Protocol (HTTP) is the protocol used for downloading HTML web pages. HTTP is part of the TCP/IP suite and is responsible for locating and downloading pages in response to user requests. That is, when you request a web page by entering a URL or clicking a hyperlink, the HTTP protocol works in the background to locate and retrieve that page.

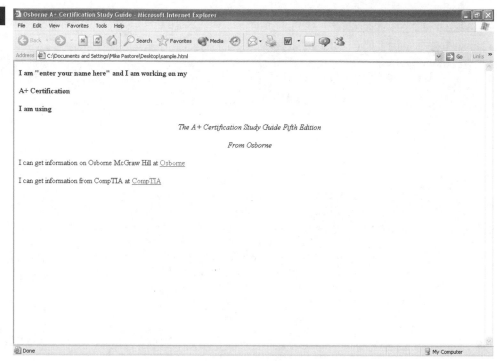

FIGURE II-14

The HTML page as displayed on a browser

Hyper Text Transfer Protocol Secure

Hyper Text Transfer Protocol Secure (HTTPS) is a version of HTTP that uses Secure Socket Layer (SSL) for data security. An HTTPS site is usually indicated by a small lock in the right -bottom corner of Internet Explorer. HTTPS is assumed to be secure because all communications using the browser are encrypted.

Secure Socket Layer

Secure Socket Layer (SSL) is a protocol that uses encryption to guard privacy. SSL is very secure and is the standard protocol used for Internet commerce. SSL uses 128-bit encryption for security. This makes SSL very secure and suitable for all but extremely high security needs.

Telnet

Telnet is used to provide terminal emulation capabilities for computer systems. When most of the Internet was based on Unix systems, Telnet was used to allow interactive sessions with these servers. Telnet has been largely replaced by the World Wide Web.

File Transfer Protocol

File Transfer Protocol (FTP) is a much faster transfer protocol than HTTP. However, it does not support the transfer and display of graphical pages or the use of hyperlinks. FTP sites are therefore typically used for downloadable archives only and typically contain a directory structure of downloadable files, as shown in Figure 11-15. Note that the URL of an FTP site starts with *ftp://* rather than *http://*. Because most browsers assume HTTP, you must manually specify FTP.

exam
watch

Make sure that you understand the differences between HTTP and FTP. HTTP allows you to download and view HTML-based web pages, while *FTP allows you to download files only, much as you would by accessing a shared drive on a network. FTP offers faster file downloading than HTTP.*

FIGURE 11-15

FTP sites contain directory structures of downloadable files

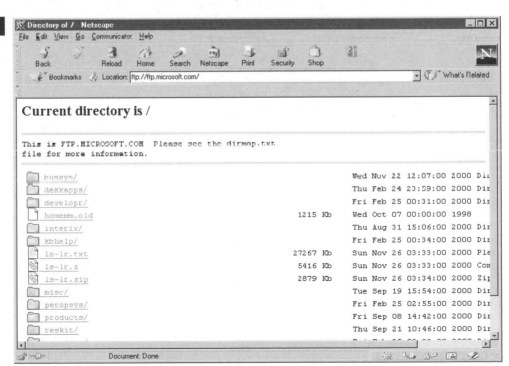

SCENARIO & SOLUTION

What is HTTP used for?	For downloading and viewing HTML web pages.
What is FTP used for?	Downloading non-HTML files.
What are the major differences between HTTP and FTP?	HTTP supports graphics, hyperlinks, and streaming media. FTP supports the simple transfer (copying) of files from one computer to another and is much faster than HTTP.

CERTIFICATION SUMMARY

In this chapter, you were introduced to a number of concepts and procedures associated with sharing and accessing network resources, including those on the Internet. To share a resource on an internal Windows network, you must first enable resource sharing in the Network Properties, then you can selectively share disk drives, individual folders, and/or printers. You can access data on an internal network using Network Neighborhood or by mapping a drive to the appropriate drive or folder.

Most users can only access the Internet via a connection to an ISP. To take advantage of Internet services such as e-mail or the World Wide Web, you must also have an appropriate e-mail or web browser application installed. Most web pages are created using HTML, XHTML, or XML and are transferred using HTTP. FTP is used for simple file transfers such as downloading (copying) a file from an Internet server to your computer.

All computers on the Internet are identified by an IP address. Because these addresses can be difficult for users to remember, a number of supporting utilities and protocols have been developed to simplify access to Internet resources. For example, a DNS server can be used to resolve or translate domain names to IP addressees, which are much easier for users to remember than strings of numbers. The Ping and Trace Route utilities can then be used to determine which IP address is associated with a particular domain name. The Ping utility can also be used to measure packet loss, and the Trace Route utility can be used to show you which servers are being used to relay data between your computer and a destination Internet server.

TWO-MINUTE DRILL

Here are some of the key points from each certification objective in Chapter 11.

Networking with Windows

❑ Share-level security allows users to specify which of their computers' resources will be made accessible on the network, and user-level security allows or denies resource access according to each user's profile and permission settings.

❑ To share resources on a network, you must first enable sharing in the Network Properties dialog box.

❑ To share a resource, right-click it and select Sharing, then set the appropriate share type and passwords.

❑ To access a shared resource, use Windows Network Neighborhood.

❑ You can map a network resource to a mapped drive by right-clicking the resource in Network Neighborhood and selecting Map Network Drive.

❑ The function of a DHCP server is to automatically assign IP addresses to computers as they join the network.

❑ The IP configuration utilities (WINIPCFG and IPCONFIG) can be used to request a new IP address from a DHCP server.

Internet Concepts

❑ The Internet is a huge network of networks that connects computers all over the world.

❑ Most home and business users access the Internet through an Internet Service Provider (ISP).

❑ A DNS server is used to translate easily remembered domain names to IP addresses.

❑ A URL defines the protocol and the transfer method (HTTP, FTP, and so on) and the domain name or IP address of the server to which you want to connect.

❑ You can use the Ping utility to determine packet transfer speed and data loss from a particular Internet server, as well as its IP address.

❑ To use Internet e-mail, you must have an installed e-mail application and access to an Internet mail server.

❑ The World Wide Web is an Internet service that uses HTTP to transfer HTML (web) pages from a web server to your computer.

❑ FTP cannot be used to view web pages, but it offers fast transfer rates for downloadable files.

SELF TEST

The following questions will help you measure your understanding of the material presented in this chapter. Read all of the choices carefully because there might be more than one correct answer. Choose all correct answers for each question.

Symptoms and Problems

1. To share your CD-ROM drive on the network, you right-clicked the CD drive in My Computer, but there was no Sharing option available. Why?

   A. You cannot share CD-ROM drives.

   B. File sharing has not been enabled in the Network Properties.

   C. This machine has no resources to share.

   D. The CD-ROM drive has already been configured as shared.

2. Which statement is true regarding shared resources in Windows?

   A. All files and folders on a drive are made available to other users when you share the drive.

   B. You can configure sharing options on individual files and folders.

   C. To share a folder, you must first share the drive, then configure the folder as shared.

   D. To access a shared folder, users must map a network drive to it.

3. You are planning to share a folder on the network. However, you would like to give some users full access while limiting others to read-only access. Which of the following can you do in Windows 9x to accomplish this goal?

   A. Map a network drive to each user who should have full access.

   B. Select each username from the list of users and apply full or read-only access to each one.

   C. Use the Depends on Password option.

   D. You cannot apply more than one access type to a single shared folder.

4. Your computer is part of a Windows network, and you are planning to share your printer. Which of the following lists the appropriate order of the steps you should follow?

   A. Right-click the printer and select Share.

   B. Enable printer sharing in the Network Properties dialog box, access the printer's sharing dialog box, and select the Shared As option.

   C. Access the printer's sharing dialog box, select the Shared As option, and enable printer sharing in the Network Properties dialog box.

   D. Enable printer sharing in the Network Properties dialog box.

5. What is the purpose of mapping a network drive?

    A. To receive automatic updates whenever data changes on the shared drive

    B. To inform users of a shared drive's name

    C. To access to a shared drive without having to navigate through Network Neighborhood

    D. To specify which users can access a shared drive

6. Which type of server is used to automatically assign IP addresses to computers when they join the network?

    A. DHCP

    B. WINS

    C. DNS

    D. IP addresses cannot be automatically assigned

7. Which of the following cannot be provided to computers by a DHCP server?

    A. Subnet mask

    B. URL

    C. Gateway address

    D. WINS server address

8. Your Windows 2000 computer is part of a network that uses dynamic IP address assignment. Which utility can you use to request a new IP address?

    A. WINIPCFG

    B. IPCONFIG

    C. Ping

    D. Trace Route

Basic Troubleshooting Procedures

9. You are configuring a computer for dial-up access. Which of the following will you need to supply?

    A. The URL of the default web page

    B. The address of the proxy server

    C. A username

    D. The name of the e-mail server

10. *www.website.com* is an example of which of the following?

    A. A URL

    B. An e-mail address

    C. An HTML filename

    D. A domain name

11. Which of the following services is used to translate domain names into IP addresses, and vice versa?

    A. HTTP

    B. DHCP

    C. WINS

    D. DNS

12. Which of the following most accurately describes the function of a WINS server?

    A. To assign IP addresses to computers on a network

    B. To supply and transfer HTML pages

    C. To translate NetBIOS computer names into IP addresses

    D. To establish and maintain a dial-up connection

13. You are accessing data on the Internet, and it seems to be taking a very long time for requested web pages to load. A coworker has suggested that your computer is just being slow. Another coworker states that there is a bad connection between your computer and the Internet server. Which Windows utility can you use to rule out or pinpoint your Internet connection as the source of the problem?

    A. IPCONFIG

    B. WINIPCFG

    C. Ping

    D. Trace Route

14. Which of the following is true of the URL *ftp://ftp.blitz.ca*?

    A. The site is served by the Blitz company.

    B. It is most likely a Canadian website.

    C. The site is a file transfer site and will not support streaming media.

    D. The URL is using an invalid syntax.

15. Which of the following is a function of the Windows Trace Route utility?

    A. To display the routers used to relay data between your computer and a specified Internet location

    B. To establish a connection between your computer and your ISP

    C. To request a new IP address from a DHCP server

    D. To measure packet loss between your computer and a specified Internet server

16. Which of the following must you have in order to send and receive e-mail on the Internet?

    A. A web browser

    B. A connection to a mail server

    C. A dial-up connection

    D. All of the above

17. Complete the sentence: The World Wide Web...

    A. Uses the HTTP protocol

    B. Uses the FTP protocol

    C. Is the largest network in the world

    D. Allows users to send e-mail and view web pages

18. What is HTML?

    A. A protocol used for transferring web pages

    B. A service that resolves IP addresses to domain names

    C. A service that supplies computers with IP addresses

    D. A language used to create web pages

19. Which of the following statements about HTTP is true?

    A. Most web browsers use HTTP by default.

    B. HTTP is faster than FTP.

    C. HTTP and FTP are used to transfer HTML web pages.

    D. HTTP is unable to support streaming media.

20. Which of the following would you expect to see on an FTP site?

    A. A web page with hyperlinks and graphics

    B. A directory structure of downloadable files

    C. A directory structure of websites

    D. A directory structure of the servers used to relay data between your computer and the specified Internet server

LAB QUESTION

TCP/IP is the protocol of the Internet and the most popular protocol on internal networks. TCP/IP is the basis for an entire suite of information exchange protocols, services, and utilities. Match each of the following items on the left with the proper description of its function on the right.

1.	HTML	>___	Reports packet transfer time and loss
2.	DNS	>___	Translates IP addresses into computer names
3.	FTP	>___	Transfers web pages
4.	IPCONFIG	>___	Language used to create web pages
5.	WINS	>___	Reports all servers used between your computer and a specified Internet server
6.	ping	>___	Dynamically assigns IP addresses to computers
7.	DHCP	>___	Requests a new IP address
8.	TRACERT	>___	Resolves IP addresses to domain names
9.	HTTP	>___	Provides fast transfer of non-Web downloadable files

SELF TEST ANSWERS

Symptoms and Problems

1. ☑ **B.** File sharing has not been enabled in the Network Properties. Before you can share any resource in Windows, you must first access the Network Properties dialog box and enable file and/or printer sharing.

    ☒ **A,** you cannot share CD-ROM drives, is incorrect because you can share any type of drive on a Windows network, including a hard drive, a CD-ROM drive, a floppy drive, or a tape drive. **C,** this machine has no resources to share, is incorrect. If a printer or drive or folder exists on the computer, it can be shared. **D,** the CD-ROM drive has already been configured as shared, is incorrect because even devices that are already being shared will allow you to right-click the Sharing option and view and/or modify the Sharing options.

2. ☑ **A.** All files and folders on a drive are made available to other users when you share the drive. That is, when you share a disk drive, all its contents are configured as shared. To share individual folders, configure the drive as not shared, then share each individual folder that you want to make available to other users.

    ☒ **B,** you can configure sharing options on individual files and folders, is incorrect because you can share individual folders but not files. **C,** to share a folder, you must first share the drive, then configure the folder as shared, is incorrect because when you share a drive, its folders and files are also shared. **D,** to access a shared folder, users must map a network drive to it, is incorrect. Users *can* access shared folders by mapping a network drive to it, but they don't have to. They can also access shared folders using Windows Network Neighborhood.

3. ☑ **C.** Use the Depends on Password option. In the folder's Sharing dialog box, select Depends on Password. Enter a password for full access and a different password for read-only access. Give the full-access password to users who should have full access, and give the read-only password to users who should have read-only access.

    ☒ **A,** map a network drive to each user who should have full access, is incorrect. You can map a network drive to a resource that is already shared, not to configure the resource for sharing with others. **B,** select each username from the list of users and apply full or read-only access to each one, is incorrect. There is no option in the Sharing dialog box to apply different access options to individual network users. **D** is incorrect because it suggests that you can only apply either full or read-only access but not both. As described, you can accomplish both using the Depends on Password option.

4. ☑ **B.** Enable printer sharing in the Network Properties dialog box, access the printer's sharing dialog box, and select the Shared As option. Before you can share a printer, sharing

must be enabled in Network Properties. Next, right-click the printer you want to share and select the Sharing option. The printer's Sharing dialog box will open. Select the Share As option.

☒ **A,** right-click the printer and select Share, is incorrect because there is no Share option in the printer's shortcut menu. Rather, you must select Sharing and select the appropriate options in the Sharing dialog box. **C** is incorrect because although it lists the appropriate steps, they appear in the wrong order. Printer sharing must be enabled in Network Properties before you can configure individual printers as shared. **D,** enable printer sharing in the Network Properties dialog box, is incorrect because this alone is not sufficient to share a printer. Once printer sharing is enabled, you must individually configure specific printers as shared.

5. ☑ **C.** The purpose of mapping a network drive is to access a shared drive without having to navigate through Network Neighborhood. When you map a drive, that drive appears in My Computer, just as local drives do. You can then use My Computer rather than the Network Neighborhood to access the drive.

☒ **A,** to receive automatic updates whenever data changes on the shared drive, is incorrect. There is no Windows utility that will update users whenever you change data on a shared drive. **B,** to inform users of a shared drive's name, is incorrect because there is no such utility in Windows. It is therefore important that you give the drive a descriptive name when you share it. **D,** to specify which users can access a shared drive, is incorrect. Although you can create mixed access types to a shared drive, you cannot apply access to individual users.

6. ☑ **A.** A DHCP server can be used to automatically assign IP addresses to computers when they join the network. Rather than manually entering IP addresses on all computers, they can be configured to obtain an IP address from the DHCP server. When the computer joins the network, the DHCP will assign it a dynamic IP address.

☒ **B,** WINS, is incorrect because this type of server is responsible for translating IP addresses into computer names, and vice versa. **C,** DNS, is incorrect because this type of server translates IP addresses into domain names, and vice versa. **D** is incorrect because it suggests that IP addresses cannot be automatically assigned.

7. ☑ **B.** A URL cannot be provided to computers by a DHCP server. The function of a DHCP server is to provide computers with IP addresses. A URL is an address used on the Internet to identify the transfer method and domain name or IP address of an Internet server.

☒ **A,** subnet mask, **C,** default gateway, and **D,** WINS server address, are all incorrect. All computers are assigned a subnet mask by the DHCP server and are supplied with addresses of the gateway and WINS server, if they exist.

8. ☑ **B.** You can use IPCONFIG to request a new IP address. Windows 2000 and Windows 9*x* allow you to run the IP Configuration utility from a DOS prompt, and by using the /release and /renew switches, you can request a new IP address from the DHCP server.

☒   **A,** WINIPCFG, is incorrect because this utility is available in Windows 9*x* only. **C,** Ping, is incorrect because the purpose of this utility is to measure connectivity, view the IP address associated with a particular domain name, and measure packet speed and loss. **D,** Trace Route, is incorrect because this utility is used to report which servers are being used to relay data between your computer and another on the Internet.

Basic Troubleshooting Procedures

9. ☑   **C.** When configuring dial-up access, you need to supply a username. You also need to supply a password. The username must be obtained by the ISP to which you are trying to connect. Furthermore, you have to supply the phone number at which the ISP's server can be reached.

    ☒   **A,** the URL of the default web page, **B,** the address of the proxy server, and **D,** the name of the e-mail server, are all incorrect because these are all settings that are entered when configuring a web browser for Internet access. The dial-up access settings are required to make a dial-up connection to an ISP and are unrelated to the web browser's settings.

10. ☑   **D.** *www.website.com* is an example of a domain name. The *www* indicates that this is a site on the World Wide Web. *website* is the name of the domain, and *com* indicates that this is a commercial site.

    ☒   **A,** a URL, is incorrect because a URL includes the transfer method (HTTP or FTP) and the domain name or IP address. *www.website.com* is not considered a URL because there is no HTTP or FTP reference. *http://www.website.com* is a URL. **B,** an e-mail address, is incorrect because e-mail addresses have the form *name@domain*. For example, *joe@hotmail.com* is an e-mail address. **C,** an HTML filename, is incorrect. HTML files are named in the same way that other files are named and have an HTM or HTML extension. For example, WEBPAGE. HTM is an HTML filename.

11. ☑   **D.** DNS is used to translate domain names into IP addresses, and vice versa. All computers on the Internet are identified by their IP addresses. However, these addresses can be difficult for users to remember, so DNS servers allow users to locate Internet locations using their easy-to-remember domain names. For example, *www.syngress.com* is much easier to remember than *205.181.158.215*.

    ☒   **A,** HTTP, is incorrect because this is the protocol responsible for transferring HTML web pages on the Internet. **B,** DHCP, is incorrect because it is a protocol used to dynamically assign IP addresses on a network. **C,** WINS, is incorrect because this service is used to translate between computer names and IP addresses.

12. ☑ **C.** The function of a WINS server is to translate IP addresses into computer names. This is similar to the function of a DNS server, except that a WINS server is able to keep track of which computers have been assigned which IP addresses in a DHCP environment.

☒ **A,** to assign IP addresses to computers on a network, is incorrect because this is the function of a DHCP server. The WINS server keeps track of which computers have been assigned which IP addresses, but it cannot assign addresses itself. **B,** to supply and transfer HTML pages, is incorrect. HTML pages are supplied by web servers on the Internet and are transferred using HTTP. **D,** to establish and maintain a dial-up connection, is incorrect because this is the function of your computer's analog modem.

13. ☑ **C.** You can use the Ping utility. This will report the transmission times between your computer and the Internet server and will report the amount of packet loss (if any). If the transmission times are low and there is no packet loss, you should assume that the speed problem is originating within your own computer. If transmission times are high and there is significant packet loss, you can assume that your Internet connection is slow because data packets are taking a long time to travel from the server to your computer.

☒ **A,** IPCONFIG, and **B,** WINIPCFG, are incorrect because these utilities are used to view your computer's current IP address and the IP addresses of the gateway, WINS server, and DNS server (if they exist). **D,** Trace Route, is incorrect because this utility reports the servers that are being used to relay data between your computer and a specified Internet server, but it does not report on the fitness of the connection or the amount of packet loss.

14. ☑ **C.** The site will not support streaming media. The URL *ftp://ftp.blitz.ca* indicates an FTP site. FTP supports fast file transfers but cannot support HTML-based components such as graphics, links to other sites, or streaming media.

☒ **A,** the site is served by the Blitz company, is incorrect because there is no way of knowing the relationship between the domain name and the organization until you visit the site. Although this site could be provided by a company called Blitz, it is conceivable that anyone could use this domain name, as long as the name was approved and purchased from InterNIC. **B,** it is most likely a Canadian website, is incorrect. Although the *ca* extension indicates that it is Canadian, the *ftp* identifies this as an FTP site, not a website. **D,** the URL is using an invalid syntax, is incorrect. URLs contain the data transfer method, followed by a colon and two forward slashes, followed by the domain name. The URL given here has a valid syntax.

15. ☑ **A.** The function of the Windows Trace Route utility is to display the servers used to relay data between your computer and a specified Internet server. Depending on where you are located, you will use a number of different servers to access a particular Internet server. These intermediary servers can be identified by the Trace Route utility.

☒ **B,** to establish a connection between your computer and your ISP, is incorrect. You can configure a dial-up connection between your computer and your ISP, then establish the connection by activating the appropriate dial-up icon. **C,** to request a new IP address from a DHCP server, is incorrect because this is the function of the WINIPCFG and IPCONFIG utilities. **D,** to measure packet loss between your computer and a specified Internet server, is incorrect because this is a function of the Ping utility.

16. ☑ **B.** To send and receive e-mail on the Internet, you must have a connection to a mail server. For most users, mail servers are supplied by an ISP. You also need an e-mail application and a username to use e-mail.

☒ **A,** a web browser, is incorrect because although many web browsers include an e-mail application, you can purchase separate applications that provide e-mail only. **C,** a dial-up connection, is incorrect. Many users access the Internet using a cable or DSL connection, which does not require a dial-up connection. For these reasons, **D,** all of the above, is also incorrect.

17. ☑ **A.** The World Wide Web uses the HTTP protocol. The World Wide Web is an Internet service that uses HTTP to transfer HTML web pages.

☒ **B,** uses the FTP protocol, is incorrect because the World Wide Web is composed of HTTP websites only. FTP sites use a different protocol and are not part of the World Wide Web. **C,** is the largest network in the world, is incorrect because the Internet is the largest network in the world. The World Wide Web is simply one of several services available on the Internet. **D** is incorrect because it suggests that the World Wide Web is used for both e-mail and web page viewing. Again, the World Wide Web supports web page access only. E-mail is a separate service that can be used on the Internet.

18. ☑ **D.** HTML is a language used to create web pages. Web browsers can request and download HTML files from web servers. The browser then translates the HTML code into the appropriate text and graphics that we view as web pages.

☒ **A,** a protocol used for transferring web pages, is incorrect. HTTP is used for transferring web pages, and HTML might the format of the web pages themselves. **B,** a service that resolves IP addresses to domain names, is incorrect because this service can be provided by a DNS or WINS server. **C,** a service that supplies computers with IP addresses, is incorrect because this is the function of the DHCP protocol, not the HTML language.

19. ☑ **A.** Most web browsers use HTTP by default. That is, if you enter a domain name, the browser assumes that you are trying to contact an HTTP website. If you are trying to access an FTP site, you must specifically enter *ftp://* in the URL.

☒ **B,** HTTP is faster than FTP, is incorrect. Because FTP does not support the display of graphics or streaming media, it can transfer files much faster than HTTP. **C** is incorrect because it suggests that both HTTP and FTP can transfer web pages. HTTP, not FTP, can be used for web page transfer. **D,** HTTP is unable to support streaming media, is incorrect. HTTP supports graphics, text formatting, streaming media, and hyperlinks.

20. ☑ **B.** You should expect to see a directory structure of downloadable files on an FTP site. FTP does not support the display of web pages; instead, it is used for locating and downloading files, much as you would in Network Neighborhood on an internal Windows network.

    ☒ **A,** a web page with hyperlinks and graphics, is incorrect because this is what you could expect to see on an HTTP (web) site, not an FTP site. **C,** a directory structure of websites, is incorrect because FTP sites contain files and folders, not hyperlinks or lists of websites. **D,** a directory structure of the servers used to relay data between your computer and the specified Internet server, is incorrect. Although the Windows Trace Route utility can be used to list these servers, there is no utility or Internet FTP site for providing them as a directory structure.

LAB ANSWER

1.	HTML	>6	Reports packet transfer time and loss
2.	DNS	>5	Translates computer names into IP addresses
3.	FTP	>9	Transfers web pages
4.	IPCONFIG	>1	Language used to create web pages
5.	WINS	>8	Reports all routers used between your computer and a specified Internet server
6.	Ping	>7	Dynamically assigns IP addresses to computers
7.	DHCP	>4	Requests a new IP address
8.	Trace Route	>2	Resolves domain names to IP addresses
9.	HTTP	>3	Provides fast transfer of non-Web downloadable files

CORE HARDWARE/OPERATING SYSTEM EXAMS

Appendix

About the CD

This CD-ROM contains the CertTrainer software. CertTrainer comes complete with ExamSim, Skill Assessment tests, CertCam movie clips, and the e-book (electronic version of the book). CertTrainer is easy to install on any Windows 98/NT/2000 computer and must be installed to access these features. You may, however, browse the e-book directly from the CD without installation.

Installing CertTrainer

If your computer CD-ROM drive is configured to autorun, the CD-ROM will automatically start up upon inserting the disk. From the opening screen you may either browse the e-book or install CertTrainer by pressing the *Install Now* button. This will begin the installation process and create a program group named "CertTrainer." To run CertTrainer use START | PROGRAMS | CERTTRAINER.

System Requirements

CertTrainer requires Windows 98 or higher and Internet Explorer 4.0 or above and 600 MB of hard disk space for full installation.

CertTrainer

CertTrainer provides a complete review of each exam objective, organized by chapter. You should read each objective summary and make certain that you understand it before proceeding to the SkillAssessor. If you still need more practice on the concepts of any objective, use the "In Depth" button to link to the corresponding section from the Study Guide.

Once you have completed the review(s) and feel comfortable with the material, launch the SkillAssessor quiz to test your grasp of each objective. Once you complete the quiz, you will be presented with your score for that chapter.

ExamSim

As its name implies, ExamSim provides you with a simulation of the actual exam. The number of questions, the type of questions, and the time allowed are intended to be an accurate representation of the exam environment. You will see the screen shown in Figure A-1 when you are ready to begin ExamSim.

When you launch ExamSim, a digital clock display will appear in the upper left-hand corner of your screen. The clock will continue to count down to zero unless you choose to end the exam before the time expires.

FIGURE A-I

Beginning
ExamSim

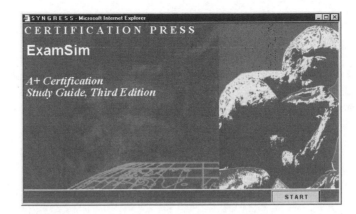

Saving Scores as Cookies

Your ExamSim score is stored as a browser cookie. If you've configured your browser to accept cookies, your score will be stored in a file named *History*. If your browser is not configured to accept cookies, you cannot permanently save your scores. If you delete this History cookie, the scores will be deleted permanently.

E-Book

The entire contents of the Study Guide are provided in HTML form, as shown in Figure A-2. Although the files are optimized for Internet Explorer, they can also be viewed with other browsers including Netscape.

FIGURE A-2

Using the Study
Guide via the
Internet

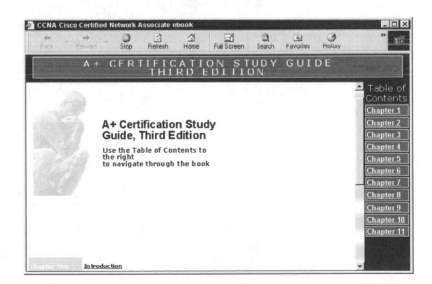

CertCam

CertCam .AVI clips provide detailed examples of key certification objectives. These clips walk you step-by-step through various hardware and operating system configurations. You can access the clips directly from the CertCam table of contents (shown in Figure A-3).

The CertCam .AVI clips are recorded and produced using TechSmith's Camtasia Producer. Since .AVI clips can be very large, ExamSim uses TechSmith's special AVI Codec to compress the clips. The file named **tsccvid.dll** is copied to your Windows\ System folder when you install CertTrainer. If the .AVI clip runs with audio but no video, you may need to re-install the file from the CD-ROM. Browse to the "bin" folder, and run TSCC.EXE.

Help

A help file is provided through a help button on the main CertTrainer screen in the lower right hand corner.

Upgrading

A button is provided on the main ExamSim screen for upgrades. This button will take you to www.syngress.com where you can download any available upgrades.

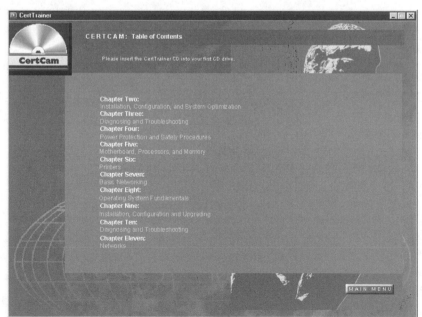

Glossary

AC Adapter   A type of power supply that converts AC power to voltages needed for the PC system. AC adapters are usually used in portable PC systems.

Access Methods   Also known as "network access," these are the methods by which a device communicates on a network. Network access provides a standard that all devices that wish to communicate on a network must abide by in order to eliminate communication conflicts.

Active Matrix Display   Based on thin-film transistor (TFT) technology. Instead of having two rows of transistors, active matrix displays have a transistor at every pixel, which enables much quicker display changes than passive matrix displays and produces display quality comparable to a CRT.

Adapter Card   Refers to any PC that is added to the motherboard to enhance functionality or expansion. Monitor cards and network cards are examples of adapter cards.

AGP   Accelerated graphics port. A monitor interface designed for high-performance graphics processing.

AMR   Audio Modem Riser. A card that allows for connection of multimedia and communications to a PC. AMR technology utilizes excess capacity in the CPU to emulate hardware devices.

ANSI.SYS   A DOS system file that is loaded by CONFIG.SYS if required. This file loads an extended character set for use by DOS and DOS applications that includes basic drawing and color capabilities. Normally used for drawing and filling different boxes for menu systems, it is seldom used today. By default, it carries no attributes and is not required for OS startup.

Antenna   Radiates and receives radio frequency signals. Usually used with wireless technology.

AppleTalk   The network protocol used by Apple Computers for inexpensive networking.

ARCHIVE Attribute   Set automatically when a file is created or modified and automatically removed by backup software when the file is backed up.

AT   Advanced Technology. A type of motherboard used in older PC systems; also refers to a class of processors based on the Intel 80286 architecture.

ATA   Advanced Technology Attachment. The specification used for the IDE connection.

ATAPI   Advanced Technology Attachment Packet Interface. The interface standard for connection CD-ROMs, tape drives, and optical disks to a computer system.

ATTRIB.EXE   A command-line utility that can change the attributes of a file or group of files.

ATX   A type of motherboard most commonly used in modern PC systems.

AUTOEXEC.BAT   A user-editable system file that contains commands to modify the PC environment (PATH, COMSPEC, other SET commands) and to execute applications. It can create a menu system, prompt for user input, or call other batch files to maintain a modular structure. By default, it carries no attributes, and is not required for OS startup.

Basic Input Output System   See BIOS.

Bidirectional Print Mode   Most common in some of the newer and more advanced printers, bidirectional print mode means that the printer is able to talk back to the computer, enabling, for example, the printer to send the user exact error messages that are displayed on the workstation. It also helps the spooler to avoid print spooler stalls.

BIOS   Basic Input Output System. A standard set of instructions or programs that handle boot operations. When an application needs to perform an I/O operation on a computer, the operating system makes the request to the system BIOS, which in turn translates the request into the appropriate instruction set used by the hardware device.

BOOT.INI   The startup file that allows for selection of the operating system to be booted in Windows NT 4 through Windows XP.

Brownout   Momentary lapses in power supply. Brownouts can cause problems with computer components that are not designed to withstand these events.

Bus   The actual pathway that transmits electronic signals from one computer device to another.

Bus Topology   In a local area network, a topology with each device on the network connected to a central cable, or bus. Most common with coaxial cabling.

Cable   A network connection that uses existing cable television connections for data transmission. See DSL.

Cache Memory   Stores frequently used instructions and data so that they can be accessed quickly by the computer.

Carrier Sense Multiple Access/Collision Detection   See CSMA/CD.

Case   The box that houses the system unit, adapter cards, and devices and which usually provides mounting locations for all internal devices in the system.

CD   Compact disc. Stores data or audio files; a read-only device.

CD-RW   Compact disc-rewritable. A type of compact disc that allows information to be written or burned onto it using a CDRW drive.

Central Processing Unit   See CPU.

Centronics   A standard originally developed for connecting printers to computer systems whose connections allow for up to 36 wires to be used for communications.

Chip Creep   A phenomenon where a computer chip becomes loose within its socket.

Cleaning Blade   This rubber blade inside a laser printer that extends the length of the photosensitive drum. It removes excess toner after the print process has completed and deposits it into a reservoir for re-use.

CMOS   Complementary Metal-Oxide Semiconductor. An integrated circuit composed of a metal oxide that is located directly on the system board. The CMOS, which is similar to RAM in that data can be written to the chip, enables a computer to store essential operating parameters after the computer has been turned off, enabling a faster system boot.

CNR   Communications Network Riser. A type of connection used for communications purposes. CNR uses excess processor capabilities to emulate hardware on the system board.

Coaxial Cable   A high-bandwidth network cable that consists of a central wire surrounded by a screen of fine wires.

COMMAND.COM   A DOS system file that is automatically executed in the root directory at startup. This file contains the internal command set and error messages. By default, it carries no attributes, but it is required for OS startup.

Complementary Metal-Oxide Semiconductor   See CMOS.

CONFIG.SYS   A user-editable system file that provides the ability to install device drivers used in DOS. Windows 9x does not require any specific settings to be made in CONFIG.SYS.

Cooperative Multitasking   As opposed to preemptive multitasking, cooperative multitasking forces applications to voluntarily relinquish control of the CPU. When an application relinquishes control of the CPU, Windows then decides which application will execute next. The most common way for an application to relinquish control is by asking Windows if any messages are available.

CPU   Central Processing Unit. The operations center of a computer. Its job is to provide the devices attached to the computer with directives that retrieve, display, manipulate, and store information.

CSMA/CD   Carrier sense multiple access/collision detection. Most common on Ethernet networks, a network communication protocol that operates in much the same way that humans communicate. With CSMA/CD, a device listens to the network for a pause in communication and attempts to transmit data onto the network during the pause. The device then detects if any other devices have transmitted onto the network at the same time. If they have, the device waits an unspecified random amount of time and retransmits its data.

DB-9   A type of connector that uses nine wires for connections. Most commonly used for serial port connections.

DB-25   A type of connector that uses 25 wires for connection. Most commonly used for parallel communications or older serial communications.

DDR   Double Data Rate. A type of memory technology used to effectively double the data rate of SDRAM memory.

Digital Versatile Disc   See DVD.

Defragmentation   A process that reorganizes fragmented files in a proper, contiguous fashion. This is done by moving several of them to an unused portion of the drive, erasing the previous locations in contiguous clusters, then rewriting the files back in proper sequence. Performed periodically, defragmentation is probably the single best operation a user can perform to maintain a high-performance system.

Device Driver   Programs that translate necessary information between the operating system and the specific peripheral device for which they are configured, such as a printer.

Dial-Up Access   Access provided to the Internet, a LAN, or even another computer by using a phone line and a modem.

Dial-Up Networking   The type of network in which a modem connects two or more workstations.

DIMM   Dual In-Line Memory Module. Similar to a SIMM, a DIMM is a small plug-in circuit board that contains the memory chips you need to add certain increments of RAM to your computer. Because the memory chips run along both sides of the chip, DIMM chips can hold twice as much memory as SIMM chips.

DIP Switch   Dual in-line package switch. Very tiny boxes with switches embedded in them. Each switch can set a value of 0 or 1 and provides user-accessible configuration settings for computers and peripheral devices.

Direct Memory Access   See DMA.

Dirty Current   Noise present on a power line caused by electro-magnetic interference (EMI) that can stray or leak from the current into nearby components. EMI that leaks from power current creates a magnetic field that can damage computer components.

Display Device   A device that provides a visual output to the user, typically the CRT or monitor.

DMA   Direct memory access. A facility by which a peripheral can communicate directly with RAM, without intervention by the CPU.

DNS   Domain Name System. The Internet-based system that resolves symbolic names, also called host names, to IP addresses (which are a series of numbers) that the computer is able to understand.

Docking Station   A port that allows users to add desktop-like capabilities, such as a mouse, monitor, or keyboard, to their portable computer. The components and the portable are all plugged into the docking station, rather than the portable connecting to each individual component. Docking stations frequently allow for additional expansion capabilities for disk and other peripherals.

Domain Name System   See DNS.

DOS   Disk Operating System is the earliest operating system used on PC computer systems.

DOS Mode   Commonly called DOS Compatibility Mode. Allows execution of some older MS-DOS applications that are not capable of running in Windows 9x. Applications that require MS-DOS mode are usually blocked from operation within Windows 95.

Download The process of transferring a file or files from one computer to another. Unlike uploading, the transfer is always initiated by the computer that will be receiving the file(s).

Downtime The time wasted as a result of a malfunctioning computer or network.

DRAM Dynamic Random Access Memory. These chips use smaller capacitors, rather than unwieldy transistors and switches, that represent 0s and 1s as an electronic charge. This allows more information to be stored on a single chip, but it also means that the chips need a constant refresh and hence more power.

DSL Digital subscriber line. A network communications method that uses existing telephone lines for network connections.

Dual In-Line Memory Module See DIMM.

Dual In-Line Package Switch See DIP Switch.

DVD Digital versatile disc. A type of disc storage similar to a CD that allows for high density storage of information. DVDs are used for video and large volumes of text/graphics materials.

DVD-RW DVD-rewritable. A type of DVD that allows information to be written onto it using a DVD-RW burner.

Dynamic RAM See DRAM.

EBKAC Error Between Keyboard and Chair. As the name implies, an error that is not technical, but rather occurs on the part of the end user. Common EBKACs include power cords being unplugged, having no paper in the printer, and power switches being turned off.

ECC Error Correcting Code. A type of memory that uses a special code to verify accuracy of data in the memory chip.

ECP   Extended Capability Port. A parallel printer interface designed to speed up data transfer rates by bypassing the processor and writing the data directly to memory.

EDO RAM   Extended Data Output RAM. A type of DRAM chip designed for processor access speeds of approximately 10 to 15 percent above fast-page mode memory.

EIDE   Enhanced Integrated Drive Electronics. An upgraded version of IDE that allows for more devices, higher speed, and improved performance of storage devices. Usually the standard disk interface on PC systems.

EISA   Extended Industry Standard Architecture. An industry standard bus architecture that allows for peripherals to utilize the 32-bit data bus that is available with 386 and 486 processors.

Electrophotographic Printing Process   See EP Process.

EMM386.EXE   A DOS system file that, along with HIMEM.SYS, controls memory management. It is not required for system startup in pre-Windows 95 machines. Basically, this is an expanded memory emulator that performs two major functions: it enables and controls EMS if desired and enables the use of upper memory as system memory.

EMS   Expanded Memory Specification. A standard that allows programs that recognize it to work with more than 640K of RAM.

Enhanced Parallel Port   See EPP.

EP Process   Electrophotographic printing process. The six-step process that a laser printer goes through to put an image on a page: cleaning, charging, writing, developing, transferring, and fusing.

EPP   Enhanced Parallel Port. An expansion bus that offers an extended control code set. With EPP mode, data travels both from the computer to the printer and vice versa.

Error Between Keyboard and Chair   See EBKAC.

Exit Roller   One of four types of printer rollers, exit rollers aid in the transfer and control of the paper as it leaves the printer. Depending on the printer type, they direct the paper to a tray where it can be collated, sorted, or even stapled.

Expanded Memory Specification   See EMS.

Extended Capability Port   See ECP.

Extended Data Output RAM   See EDO RAM.

Extended Industry Standard Architecture   See EISA.

eXtended Memory Specification   See XMS.

Fan   A cooling device that blows air over computer circuitry.

FDD   Floppy disk drive. A type of disk device used for reading and riding floppy disks.

FDISK.EXE   A DOS-based utility program that partitions a hard disk in preparation for installing an operating system.

Feed Roller   One of the four types of printer rollers. Also known as paper pickup roller, the feed roller, when activated, rotates against the top page in the paper tray and rolls it into the printer. The feed roller works together with a special rubber pad to prevent more than one sheet from being fed into the printer at a time.

Fiber Optic Cable   Extremely high-speed network cable that consists of glass fibers that carry light signals instead of electrical signals. Useful for transmission over long distances because it is much less susceptible to environmental difficulties, such as electronic and magnetic interference, than other network cables.

File System   The process or method that an operating system uses to manage files and data on the storage devices.

File Transfer Protocol   See FTP.

FireWire   See IEEE 1394.

Firmware   The software or programs and hardware that are written into Read-Only Memory (ROM) for the computer to operate.

Flash Memory   A faster version of ROM that, while still basically developed as ROM, can be addressed and loaded thousands of times.

Floppy Disk Drive   See FDD.

Fragmentation   Files that are written in noncontiguous clusters scattered all over the disk. This occurs because DOS writes files to the hard disk by breaking the file into cluster-sized pieces and then stores each piece in the next available cluster. See Defragmentation.

FTP   File Transfer Protocol. Much older than HTTP, this protocol is downloads files from an FTP server to a client computer. FTP is much faster than HTTP.

Fully Qualified Path   A fully qualified path is the entire path of a file, from the root of the file system to the file being referenced.

Fusing Rollers   One of four types of laser printer rollers, fusing rollers comprise the final stage of the electrophotographic printing (EP) process, bonding the toner particles to the page to prevent smearing. The roller on the toner side of the page has a nonstick surface that is heated to a high temperature to permanently bond the toner to the paper.

Ghosted Image   Occurs when a portion of an image previously printed to a page is printed again, but not as dark. One cause of this is if the erasure lamp of the laser printer fails to operate correctly and doesn't completely erase the previous image from the EP drum. Another cause can be the cleaning blade not adequately scraping away the residual toner.

Handshaking   The process by which two connecting modems agree on the method of communication to be used.

Hard Disk Drive   See HDD.

HDD   Hard Disk Drive. A mass storage device that allows for rapid random access of data in a computer system.

Heat Sink   A device that is typically attached to an electronic component to remove heat from the component. Used extensively with microprocessors, a heat sink may also include a cooling fan to assist in the cooling process.

Hidden Attribute   Keeps a file from being displayed when a DIR command is issued.

HIMEM.SYS   A DOS system file that, along with EMM386.EXE, controls memory management. It is not required for system startup in pre-Windows 95 machines.

HTML   Hypertext Markup Language. Derived from the Standard General Markup Language (SGML), the markup language that dictates the layout and design of a web page.

HTTP   Hypertext Transfer Protocol. The TCP/IP-based protocol that is most commonly used for client/server communications on the World Wide Web.

Hub   Common connection points for devices in a network that contain multiple ports and commonly connect segments of a LAN.

Hypertext Markup Language   See HTML.

Hypertext Transfer Protocol   See HTTP.

IDE   Integrated Drive Electronics. A standard for connecting hard drives to a computer.

IEEE 1394   A high speed interface that connects video and other devices to a computer system. Also known as FireWire.

Impact Printer   As the name suggests, these printers require impact with an ink ribbon to print characters and images. An example of an impact printer is a daisy wheel.

Industry Standard Architecture   See ISA.

Infrared   See IR.

Input Device   Takes data from a user and converts it into electrical signals used by your computer. Examples of devices that provide input are keyboards, mice, trackballs, pointing devices, digitized tablets, and touch screens.

Internet Service Provider   See ISP.

Internetwork Packet Exchange/Sequenced Packet Exchange
See IPX/SPX.

Interrupt Request Line   See IRQ.

IO.SYS   A DOS system file that defines basic input/output routines for the processor. By default, it carries the hidden, system, and read-only attributes and is required for OS startup.

IPX/SPX   Internetwork Packet Exchange/Sequenced Packet Exchange. A very fast and highly established network protocol most commonly used with Novell Netware.

IR   Infrared. A portion of the nonvisible light spectrum used extensively for communications. Both transmitter and receiver must be in visual proximity of each other for IR to work.

IRQ   Interrupt Request. The physical lines over which system components such as modems or printers communicate directly with the CPU when the device is ready to send or receive data.

ISA   Industry Standard Architecture. An industry standard bus architecture that allows for peripherals to utilize the 16-bit data bus that is available with 286 and 386 processors.

ISDN   Integrated Services Digital Network. A network technology that used existing copper cable for high-speed data networking. ISDN has been largely replaced by DSL and cable applications.

ISP   Internet Service Provider. A company that provides people with access to the Internet, usually for a fee. Conversely, a company that gives their employees Internet access through a private bank of modems is usually not considered an ISP. ISPs typically charge customers for the use of their connection to the Internet.

Jumper   Like DIP switches, jumpers accomplish configuration manually. Jumpers are made of two separate components: a row of metal pins on the hardware and a small plastic cap that has a metal insert inside of it. The two parts together form a circuit that sets the configuration. Jumpers can set only one value for a feature at a time, as opposed to DIP switches, which can handle multiple configurations.

Keyboard   An input device that accepts user input by depressing keys.

LAN   Local area network. A network made up of two or more computers in a limited geographic area (within about a two-mile radius) linked by high-performance cables that allows users to exchange information, share peripheral devices, or access a common server.

LCD Panel   Liquid crystal display panel. A type of display or monitor that is very thin and lightweight. Used extensively in portable systems and thin screen monitors.

Liquid Cooling   A process or method where a special cooling liquid is passed through a device to remove heat from it. Liquid cooling is very common in large-scale computer systems where heat sinks and fans are not adequate for cooling.

Legacy Device   A device that is considered obsolete or out of date and does not utilize the newest capabilities and technologies available to PC users. Manufacturers recommend that legacy devices be replaced by newer devices.

Local Area Network   See LAN.

Material Safety Data Sheets   See MSDS.

MEM.EXE   A simple command-line utility that, using various command switches, can display various reports of memory usage.

MEMMAKER.EXE   A Microsoft utility that automatically determines the best possible configuration and load sequence for a given set of applications and drivers used.

Before using MEMMAKER, the PC should be configured for normal operation (for example, the mouse driver, network operation, sound support, and so forth), including any items that are loaded from the AUTOEXEC.BAT and CONFIG.SYS files.

Memory   The internal storage areas in the computer. Memory is either considered volatile, such as RAM, which loses its contents when the power is turned off, or nonvolatile, such ROM, PROM, or EPROM, which retains its contents during power off states.

Memory Address   Receives commands from the processor that are destined for any device attached to a computer. Each device must have a unique memory address in order for it to function.

Memory Bank   The physical slot that memory goes into.

Memory Effect   When a nickel cadmium (NiCad) battery is recharged before it is fully discharged, the battery loses the ability to fully recharge again; this is the memory effect.

MicroDIMM   A type of DIMM used in subnotebooks and computers that are too small for SoDIMM.

Microprocessor   See CPU.

Modem   Modulator/demodulator. A device that connects the computer system to an analog connection, most typically the phone network, for communication.

Motherboard   The main circuit card of a PC system. The motherboard contains all of the critical circuitry necessary for the computer to operate. The motherboard also contains all of the expansion slots, connections, and circuitry for the system to function properly. Also known as the system board.

Mouse   A device that controls the cursor or pointer by movement on a flat surface. A mouse is typically used as an alternative or augmentation to a keyboard on modern computer systems.

MSD   Microsoft Diagnostics. A DOS-based utility that provides a great deal of information about the system. It is most useful in determining what the system has installed in it, such as memory and hard drives.

MSD.EXE A Microsoft System Diagnostics program that roots out almost every conceivable item about your system that you'd ever want to know (and then some!) and displays it in a menu-driven format for you to browse.

MSDOS.SYS A DOS system file that defines system file locations. By default, it carries the hidden, system, and read-only attributes and is required for OS startup.

MSDS Material Safety Data Sheets. White pages that contain information on any substance that is deemed hazardous, most notably cleaning solvents. The purpose of MSDS is to inform employees about the dangers inherent in hazardous materials and the proper use of these items to prevent potential injuries from occurring.

Multiboot Configuration A system that has been configured to allow a user to select one of multiple installed operating systems at boot time.

Multimeter A device that measures current, resistance, or voltage to determine whether certain computer components are functioning correctly.

NetBEUI NetBios Extended User Interface. An extremely fast network transport protocol that is most common on smaller networks.

NetBios Extended User Interface See NetBEUI.

Network Interface Card See NIC.

Network Topology The arrangement of cable links in a local area network. There are three principal network topologies: bus, ring, and star.

NIC Network interface card. Connects a PC to a network cable.

Noise Filter A special filter in a UPS that reduces the amount of noise present in electrical current and eliminates magnetic fields caused by noise, thus providing some protection to the components that utilize the current or are nearby.

Nonimpact Printer Printers that do not use an ink ribbon and therefore do not require direct contact with the paper for printing. An example of a nonimpact printer is a laser printer.

Normal Mode   The mode in which Windows 9x is started by default, which provides full functionality of the Windows 9x Explorer.

NTLDR   A file that helps Windows NT through XP boot. When first run, it displays the NT startup menu.

Null Modem Cable   A special cable that has the send and receive lines reversed on the connector and enables you to connect two computers directly without using a modem.

Operating System   See OS.

Operator Error   Occurs when the customer inadvertently makes a configuration change.

OS   Operating system. A set of computer instruction codes, usually compiled into executable files, whose purpose is to define input and output devices and connections and provide instructions for the computer's central processor unit (CPU) to operate on to retrieve and display data.

Output Device   A device that takes electronic signals from a computer and converts them into a format that the user can use. Examples of output devices include monitors and printers.

Overlays   Library files that include additional commands and functions. Most developers choose to modularize their applications by creating overlays rather than put all available functions into a single huge executable file.

Page Description Language   See PDL.

Parallel Port   One of two types of communication ports on a motherboard (the other is the serial port), the parallel port connects a peripheral device (most commonly a printer for this type of port) to the computer. A parallel port allows transmission of data over eight conductors at one time. The processor socket is the physical socket that attaches the processor to the motherboard.

Parallel Processing   The ability to execute instructions simultaneously and independently from each other. The Intel 586 (Pentium) chip combined two 486DX chips into one, called the dual independent bus architecture, which made this possible.

Parity   An error-checking mechanism that enables the device to recognize single-bit errors.

Partition   A section of the storage area on a computer's hard disk. A hard disk must be partitioned before an operating system can be installed.

Passive Matrix Display   Most common on portable systems, the passive matrix display is made from a grid of horizontal and vertical wires. At the end of each wire is a transistor. In order to light a pixel at (X, Y), a signal is sent to the X and Y transistors. These transistors then send voltage down the wire, which turns on the LCD at the intersection of the two wires.

PC Card   A bus first created to expand the memory capabilities in small, hand-held computers and now used mostly with laptop computers. These provide a convenient way to interchange PCMCIA-compatible devices, which are only slightly larger than credit cards. Before the name was changed to PC-Card these cards were referred to as PCMCIA cards.

PCI   Peripheral Component Interconnect. A bus that was designed in response to the Pentium-class processor's utilization of a 64-bit bus. PCI buses are designed to be processor-independent.

PCMCIA   See Personal Computer Memory Card International Association.

PDA   Personal Digital Assistant. A small handheld device that stores information such as telephone numbers and appointments. The two most popular PDA systems are based on the Palm OS or Windows CE.

PDL   Page Description Language. A language that laser printers use a to send and receive print job instructions one page at a time, rather than one dot at a time, as with other types of printers.

Peripheral Component Interconnect   See PCI.

Personal Computer Memory Card International Association
International standards organization concerned with promoting interchangeability of computer cards for mobile computers. PCMCIA is promotes a commonly accepted standard called PC Card. See PC Card.

Photosensitive Drum   The core of the electrophotographic process inside the laser printer. This light-sensitive drum is affected by the cleaning, charging, writing, and transferring processes in the six-step laser printing process.

PIO   Programmed Input/Output. Data transfer that occurs through the CPU. PIO speeds are very high and utilize processor resources to be accomplished.

Plug and Play   A software interface that offers automatic driver installation as soon as hardware or software is "plugged in," or installed. Microsoft first offered PnP support on the PC with Windows 95.

Pointing Stick   A small pencil-eraser-size piece of rubber in the center of the keyboard, one of the three most common types of pointing devices on portable systems. The on-screen pointer is controlled by pushing the pointing stick in the desired direction.

Point-To-Point Protocol   See PPP.

POLEDIT.EXE   This Windows 9x System Policy feature builds a Registry template that is later used during logon to set common-denominator defaults for all network users, and add certain restrictions on a global basis if deemed necessary.

POP   Post Office Protocol. A common protocol by which an Internet server lets you receive e-mail and download it from the server to your own machine.

Port   An interface that allows connection to a computer system. Common ports include disk connectors, serial, parallel, and USB ports. A port may be either internal or external depending on the configuration of the system.

Port Replicator   A type of device that contains expansion ports such as serial, parallel, and USB connections for a portable PC. Usually does not contain additional storage expansion capabilities. See also Docking Station.

POST   Power On Self Test. A self-test performed by the computer that occurs during boot time and diagnoses system-related problems.

Post Office Protocol   See POP.

Power On Self Test   See POST.

Power Spike   A sudden, huge increase in power that lasts for a split second. Power spikes can fry computer components.

Power Supply   The component of the computer system that provides power for all components on the motherboard and devices that are internal to the system case.

PPP   Point-To-Point protocol. A serial communications protocol that connects two computers over a phone line via a modem. SLIP is the alternate protocol that is acceptable to most browsers, but it's not as common as PPP.

Preemptive Multitasking   As opposed to cooperative multitasking, preemptive multitasking passes control from one program to another automatically through the Windows process scheduler.

Primary Corona Wire   A highly negatively charged wire inside a laser printer that is responsible for electrically erasing the photosensitive drum, preparing it to be written with a new image in the writing stage of the laser print process.

Processor   See CPU.

Processor Socket   The physical socket that attaches the processor to the motherboard.

Protocol   A set of communication standards between two computers on a network. Common protocols include TCP/IP, NetBEUI, and IPX/SPX.

PS2   Early computer standard introduced by IBM as an update to the AT class computer systems. Now most commonly used when referring to connector types for keyboards and mice.

PS2/MINI-DIN   Connects keyboards and mice to computer systems.

RAID   Redundant Array of Inexpensive Disks. A disk system that utilizes multiple disks to provide enhanced performance and fault tolerance. Used extensively in servers and higher-end PC systems.

Rambus   Rambus is the developer of memory interface technologies that include RDRAM. Systems that use Rambus technology are frequently said to as Rambus systems.

Read-Only Attribute   Prevents a user or application from inadvertently deleting or changing a file.

Refresh   The automatic process of constantly updating memory chips to ensure that their signals are correct. The refresh rate is the frequency by which chips are refreshed, usually about every 60 to 70 thousandths of a second.

Registration Roller   One of four types of laser printer rollers, the registration roller synchronizes the paper movement with the writing process inside the EP cartridge. Registration rollers do not advance the paper until the EP cartridge is ready to process the next line of the image.

Registry   A complex database used by all Windows Operating systems since Windows 95 and NT 4. Contains application settings and hardware configuration information.

Removable Storage   A type of storage device that can be removed from a computer and used in other computers. Removable storage is also extensively used for system backup operations.

RIMM   Rambus Inline Memory Module. A copyright name for memory similar to DIMM.

Riser Card   A type of expansion card that allows connection to external connections. The most common riser cards are used for audio and networking connections.

RJ-11   A type of UTP cable used extensively for telecommunications connections.

RJ-45   A type of UTP cable used extensively for networking connections.

Rollers   A device located inside a printer to aid in the movement of paper through the printer. There are four types of rollers: feed, registration, fuser, and exit.

Safe Mode   A diagnostic mode of Windows that starts the operating system with minimal drivers. This special mode allows you to change an incorrect setting, which will in most cases allow you to return an abnormally functioning system to its correct operation.

Satellite Connection   A type of connection that uses orbiting satellites for network communications.

SCSI   Small Computer Systems Interface. A parallel interface for connecting peripherals such as storage devices to the computer system. SCSI is very fast and efficient when compared to other serial and parallel interfaces. SCSI devices are frequently used in high-volume server and graphics-intensive environments.

SDRAM   Synchronous Dynamic RAM. A type of RAM that can run at much higher clock speeds than conventional ram. SDRAM can operate in burst mode for high speed transfers of data.

Serial Port   One of two types of communication ports on a motherboard (the other is the parallel port), the serial port connects to a serial line that leads to a computer peripheral. Used most commonly with modems and mice. The serial port transmits data sequentially, bit by bit over a single conductor.

SIMD   Single Instruction Multiple Data. Processor architecture introduced with the Pentium III. SIMD allows a single instruction to operate on multiple pieces of data when an application is performing a repetitive loop. This is used extensively with graphics oriented applications.

SIMM   Single In-Line Memory Module. A small plug-in circuit board that contains memory chips that you need to add certain increments of RAM to your computer. The chips are positioned along one side of the board.

Simple Mail Transfer Protocol   See SMTP.

Single In-Line Memory Module   See SIMM.

Single Instruction Multiple Data   See SIMD.

Slack   The space left between the end of a file and the end of the cluster in which the file resides.

SLIP   Serial Line Interface Protocol. A protocol that manages telecommunications between a client and a server over a phone line. PPP is the alternate (and more common) protocol that is acceptable to most browsers.

Small Computer Systems Interface   See SCSI.

SMTP   Simple Mail Transfer Protocol. The underlying protocol for Internet-based e-mail.

Socket Services   A layer of BIOS-level software that isolates PC Card software from the computer hardware and detects the insertion or removal of PC Cards.

SoDIMM   Small Outline DIMM. A type of DIMM typically used in notebook computers.

Solenoid   A resistive coil in dot matrix and daisy wheel printers. When the solenoid is energized, the pin is forced away from the print head and impacts the printer ribbon and ultimately the paper, thus impressing the image on the page.

Sound Card   A type of expansion card that provide multimedia capabilities to a computer system. A sound card will typically have both audio input and output capabilities.

SRAM   Static RAM. Unlike DRAM, SRAM retains its value as long as power is supplied; it is not constantly refreshed. However, SRAM requires a periodic update and tends to use excessive amounts of power when it does so.

Star Topology   In a local area network, a topology with each device on the network connected to a central processor, usually a hub. Most common with twisted-pair cabling.

Static RAM   See SRAM.

Storage Device   Any device that permanently stores large quantities of information. Disk drives, CD-ROM drives, and floppy drives are examples of storage devices.

STP   Shielded Twisted Pair. A type of twisted-pair wiring that includes an electrical shield to reduce interference.

Stylus   Shaped like a pen, a stylus is selects menu options and the like on a monitor screen or draws line art on a graphics tablet.

Sync Frequency   A setting that monitors use to control the refresh rate, which is the rate at which the display device is repainted. If this setting is incorrect, you get symptoms such as a "dead" monitor, lines running through the display, a flickering screen, and a reduced or enlarged image.

System Attribute   The System attribute is usually set by DOS or Windows and cannot be modified using standard DOS or Windows commands, including the ATTRIB command or File Manager.

System Board   See Motherboard.

SYSTEM.DAT   The Registry file that contains hardware or computer specific settings.

SYSTEM.INI   A Windows system file that configures Windows to address specific hardware devices and their associated settings. Errors in this file can and do cause Windows to fail to start or crash unexpectedly.

Tape Drive   A type of mass storage device that uses magnetic tape to record and play back data.

TCP/IP   Transmission Control Protocol/Internet Protocol. The suite of protocols upon which the Internet is based. It refers to the communications standards for data transmission over the Internet, although TCP/IP can also be used on private networks without Internet connectivity. TCP/IP is the most common protocol suite in use today.

Time Slicing   The process of the CPU dividing time up between applications for preemptive multitasking.

Token Passing   A network communications protocol in which a token is passed from device to device around a virtual (and frequently physical) ring on a network. Whenever a device receives the token, it is then allowed to transmit onto the network.

Token Ring   A LAN specification that was developed by IBM in the 1980s for PC-based networks and classified by the IEEE (Institute of Electrical and Electronics Engineers) as 802.5. It specifies a star topology physically and a ring topology logically. It runs at either 4Mbps or 16Mbps, but all nodes on the ring must run at the same speed.

Toner   Finely divided particles of plastic resin and organic compounds bonded to iron particles. Toner is naturally negatively charged, which aids in attracting it to the written areas of the photosensitive drum during the transfer step of the laser printing process.

Touch Pads   A stationary pointing device commonly used on laptop computers in place of a mouse or trackball. They are pads that have either thin wires running through them, or specialized surfaces that can sense the pressure of your finger on them. You slide your finger across the touch pad to control the pointer or cursor on the screen.

Touch Screen   A type of display device that includes a touch-sensitive face to accept input from the user.

Trackball   A device most commonly used in older portable computers in place of a mouse. Trackballs are built the same way as an opto-mechanical mouse, except upside-down with the ball on top.

Transfer Corona   A roller inside a laser printer that contains a positively charged wire designed to pull the toner off of the photosensitive drum and place it on the page.

Transistor   A device that processes information in the form of electronic signals and is the most fundamental component of electronic circuits. A CPU chip, for example, contains thousands to millions of transistors. The more transistors a CPU has, the faster it can process data.

Transmission Control Protocol/Internet Protocol   See TCP/IP.

Twisted Pair   By far the most common type of network cable, twisted pair consists of two insulated wires wrapped around each other to help avoid interference from other wires.

Ultra-DMA   A disk drive data protocol that allows for high-speed data transfer between the disk drive and the motherboard.

Uninterruptible Power Supply   See UPS.

Universal Serial Bus   See USB.

Upload   The process of transferring files from one computer to another. Unlike downloading, uploading is always initiated from the computer that is sending the files.

UPS   Uninterruptible power supply. A device designed to protect your computer and its components from possible injury from the problems that are inherent in today's existing power supply structure.

USB   Universal serial bus. A type of connection used in modern computer systems to connect multiple devices to a computer system. USB eliminates the need for individual adapters for each device.

USER.DAT   The Registry file that stores user specific information.

UTP   Unshielded Twisted Pair. A type of twisted-pair wiring used for network and communications. UTP does not provide any external electrical shielding. See also STP.

VESA Local Bus   See VL-Bus.

Video Card   A type of expansion card that provide connection between the CPU and the display adapter or monitor.

Virtual Memory   Virtual memory is memory that the processor has been "tricked" into using as if it were actual physical memory.

Virus   Any program that is written with the intent of doing harm to a computer. Viruses have the ability to replicate themselves by attaching themselves to programs or documents. They range in activity from extreme data loss to an annoying message that pops up every few minutes.

VL-Bus   Originally created to address performance issues, the VESA (Video Electronics Standards Association) Local Bus (VL-Bus) was meant to enable earlier bus designs to handle a maximum clock speed equivalent to that of processors.

VRAM   Video RAM. A type of high-speed RAM used for video applications.

WAN   Wide area network. A network with two or more computers linked by long-distance communication lines that traverse distances greater than those supported by LANs (or greater than about two miles).

Wide Area Network   See WAN.

WIN.COM   The executable file that is responsible for starting up Windows.

WIN.INI   A dynamic Windows system file that contains configuration information for Windows applications. Errors made in this file seldom have global implications to Window's operation, but they can cripple specific applications or features. Printing is also controlled by settings in this file.

Windows Accelerator Card RAM   See WRAM

WINFILE.INI   The configuration file in pre-Windows 95 systems that stores the names of the directories that File Manager displays when starting.

Wireless   A type of communications technology that uses either radio frequency or infrared to communicate information between systems.

Wireless Access Point   A type of connection point in a building or area that allows for wireless equipped computer systems to connect to a network.

WRAM   Window random access memory. WRAM utilizes memory that resides on the video card to perform Windows-specific functions, and therefore speeds up the OS.

XMS   eXtended Memory Specification. A set of standards that allows applications to access extended memory.

Zoomed Video   See ZV.

ZV   A direct data connection between a PC Card and host system that allows a PC Card to write video data directly to the video controller.

INDEX

C

D

N

O

P

Q

R

S

T

X

Z

INTERNATIONAL CONTACT INFORMATION

AUSTRALIA
McGraw-Hill Book Company
Australia Pty. Ltd.
TEL +61-2-9900-1800
FAX +61-2-9878-8881
http://www.mcgraw-hill.com.au
books-it_sydney@mcgraw-hill.com

CANADA
McGraw-Hill Ryerson Ltd.
TEL +905-430-5000
FAX +905-430-5020
http://www.mcgraw-hill.ca

GREECE, MIDDLE EAST, & AFRICA
(Excluding South Africa)
McGraw-Hill Hellas
TEL +30-210-6560-990
TEL +30-210-6560-993
TEL +30-210-6560-994
FAX +30-210-6545-525

MEXICO (Also serving Latin America)
McGraw-Hill Interamericana Editores
S.A. de C.V.
TEL +525-1500-5108
FAX +525-117-1589
http://www.mcgraw-hill.com.mx
carlos_ruiz@mcgraw-hill.com

SINGAPORE (Serving Asia)
McGraw-Hill Book Company
TEL +65-6863-1580
FAX +65-6862-3354
http://www.mcgraw-hill.com.sg
mghasia@mcgraw-hill.com

SOUTH AFRICA
McGraw-Hill South Africa
TEL +27-11-622-7512
FAX +27-11-622-9045
robyn_swanepoel@mcgraw-hill.com

SPAIN
McGraw-Hill/
Interamericana de España, S.A.U.
TEL +34-91-180-3000
FAX +34-91-372-8513
http://www.mcgraw-hill.es
professional@mcgraw-hill.es

UNITED KINGDOM, NORTHERN,
EASTERN, & CENTRAL EUROPE
McGraw-Hill Education Europe
TEL +44-1-628-502500
FAX +44-1-628-770224
http://www.mcgraw-hill.co.uk
emea_queries@mcgraw-hill.com

ALL OTHER INQUIRIES Contact:
McGraw-Hill/Osborne
TEL +1-510-420-7700
FAX +1-510-420-7703
http://www.osborne.com
omg_international@mcgraw-hill.com

Sound Off!

Visit us at **www.osborne.com/bookregistration** and let us know what you thought of this book. While you're online you'll have the opportunity to register for newsletters and special offers from McGraw-Hill/Osborne.

We want to hear from you!

Sneak Peek

Visit us today at **www.betabooks.com** and see what's coming from McGraw-Hill/Osborne tomorrow!

Based on the successful software paradigm, Bet@Books™ allows computing professionals to view partial and sometimes complete text versions of selected titles online. Bet@Books™ viewing is free, invites comments and feedback, and allows you to "test drive" books in progress on the subjects that interest you the most.